EVERYMAN, I will go with thee,

and be thy guide,

In thy most need to go by thy side

JOHN FORSTER

Born in 1812 and educated at University College, London. Barrister, 1843, but devoted a large part of his life to journalism and literature. Died in 1876.

JOHN FORSTER

The Life of
Charles Dickens

IN TWO VOLUMES · VOLUME TWO

NEW EDITION

WITH NOTES AND AN INDEX BY A. J. HOPPÉ
AND ADDITIONAL AUTHOR'S FOOTNOTES

DENT: LONDON
EVERYMAN'S LIBRARY
DUTTON: NEW YORK

Made in Great Britain
at the
Aldine Press · Letchworth · Herts
for
J. M. DENT & SONS LTD
Aldine House · Bedford Street · London
First included in Everyman's Library 1927
New, augmented edition 1966
Further revised, 1969

NO. 782

SBN: 460 00782 3

CONTENTS
VOLUME TWO

BOOK SIXTH
AT THE SUMMIT
1847–52. ÆT. 35–40

BOOK SEVENTH
CONTINENT REVISITED
1852–6. ÆT. 40–44

BOOK EIGHTH
PUBLIC READER
1856–67. ÆT. 44–55

CONTENTS
BOOK NINTH
AUTHOR
1836–70. ÆT. 24–58

BOOK TENTH
AMERICA REVISITED
1867-8. ÆT. 55–6

BOOK ELEVENTH
SUMMING UP
1868–70. ÆT. 56–8

BOOK TWELFTH
THE CLOSE
1870. ÆT. 58

APPENDIX

ILLUSTRATIONS

VOLUME 2

BOOK SIXTH

AT THE SUMMIT

1847–52. ÆT. 35–40

THE LIFE OF
CHARLES DICKENS
VOLUME TWO

I

SPLENDID STROLLING

1847–52

DEVONSHIRE TERRACE remaining still in possession of Sir James Duke, a house was taken in Chester Place, Regent's Park, where, on 18 April, Dickens's fifth son, to whom he gave the name of Sydney Smith Haldimand, was born. Exactly a month * 65 before, he had attended the funeral at Highgate of his publisher Mr. William Hall, his old regard for whom had survived the recent temporary cloud, and with whom he had the association as well of his first success, as of much kindly intercourse not forgotten at this sad time. Of the summer months that followed, the greater part was passed by him at Brighton or Broadstairs; and the chief employment of his leisure, in the intervals of *Dombey*, was the management of an enterprise originating in the success of our private play, of which the design was to benefit a great man of letters.

The purpose and name had hardly been announced, when, with the statesman-like attention to literature and its followers for which Lord John Russell has been eccentric among English politicians, a civil-list pension of two hundred a year was granted to Leigh Hunt; but though this modified our plan so far as to strike out of it performances meant to be given in London, so much was still thought necessary as might clear off past liabilities, and enable a delightful writer better to enjoy the easier future that had at last been opened to him. Reserving therefore anything realised beyond a certain sum for a dramatic author of merit, Mr. John Poole, to whom help had become also important, it was proposed to give, on Leigh Hunt's behalf, two representations of Ben Jonson's comedy, one at

Manchester and the other at Liverpool, to be varied by different farces in each place; and with a prologue of Talfourd's which Dickens was to deliver in Manchester, while a similar address by Sir Edward Bulwer Lytton was to be spoken by me in Liverpool. Among the artists and writers associated in the scheme were Mr. Frank Stone, Mr. Augustus Egg, Mr. John Leech, and Mr. George Cruikshank; Mr. Douglas Jerrold, Mr. Mark Lemon, Mr. Dudley Costello, and Mr. George Henry Lewes; the general management and supreme control being given to Dickens.

Leading men in both cities contributed largely to the design, and my friend Mr. Alexander Ireland of Manchester has lately sent me some letters not more characteristic of the energy of Dickens in regard to it than of the eagerness of everyone addressed to give what help they could. Making personal mention of his fellow-sharers in the enterprise he describes the troop, in one of those letters, as "the most easily governable company of actors on earth"; and to this he had doubtless brought them, but not very easily. One or two of his managerial troubles at rehearsals remain on record in letters to myself, and may give amusement still. Comedy and farces are referred to indiscriminately, but the farces were the most recurring plague. "Good Heaven! I find that A. hasn't twelve words, and I am in hourly expectation of rebellion!"—"You were right about the green baize, that it would certainly muffle the voices; and some of our actors, by Jove, haven't too much of that commodity at the best."—"B. shocked me so much the other night by a restless, stupid movement of his hands in his first scene with you, that I took a turn of an hour with him yesterday morning, and I hope quieted his nerves a little."— "I made a desperate effort to get C. to give up his part. Yet in spite of all the trouble he gives me I am sorry for him, he is so evidently hurt by his own sense of not doing well. He clutched the part, however, tenaciously; and three weary times we dragged through it last night."—"That infernal E. forgets everything."—"I plainly see that F. when nervous, which he is sure to be, loses his memory. Moreover, his asides are inaudible, even at Miss Kelly's; and as regularly as I stop him to say them again, he exclaims (with a face of agony) that 'he'll speak loud on the night,' as if anybody ever did without doing it always!"—"G. not born for it at all, and too innately conceited, I much fear, to do anything well. I thought him better last night, but I would as soon laugh at a kitchen poker."—"Fancy

H., ten days after the casting of that farce, wanting F.'s part therein! Having himself an excellent old man in it already, and a quite admirable part in the other farce." From which it will appear that my friend's office was not a sinecure, and that he was not, as few amateur-managers have ever been, without the experiences of Peter Quince. Fewer still, I suspect, have fought through them with such perfect success, for the company turned out at last would have done credit to any enterprise. They deserved the term applied to them by Maclise, who had invented it first for Macready, on his being driven to "star" in the provinces when his managements in London closed. They were "splendid strollers." * 66

On Monday, 26 July, we played at Manchester, and on Wednesday the 28th at Liverpool; the comedy being followed on the first night by *A Good Night's Rest* and *Turning the Tables*, and on the second by *Comfortable Lodgings, or Paris in 1750*; and the receipts being, on the first night £440 12s., and on the second, £463 8s. 6d. But though the married members of the company who took their wives defrayed that part of the cost, and every one who acted paid three pounds ten to the benefit fund for his hotel charges, the expenses were necessarily so great that the profit was reduced to four hundred guineas, and, handsomely as this realised the design, expectations had been raised to five hundred. There was just that shade of disappointment, therefore, when, shortly after we came back and Dickens had returned to Broadstairs, I was startled by a letter from him. On 3 August he had written: "All well. Children" (who had been going through whooping cough) "immensely improved. Business arising out of the late blaze of triumph, worse than ever." Then came what startled me, the very next day. As if his business were not enough, it had occurred to him that he might add the much longed-for hundred pounds to the benefit fund by a little *jeu d'esprit* in form of a history of the trip, to be published with illustrations from the artists; and his notion was to write it in the character of Mrs. Gamp. It was to be, in the phraseology of that notorious woman, a new "Piljians Projiss"; and was to bear upon the title-page its description as an Account of a late Expedition into the North, for an Amateur Theatrical Benefit, written by Mrs. Gamp (who was an eyewitness), Inscribed to Mrs. Harris, Edited by Charles Dickens, and published, with illustrations on wood by so and so in aid of the benefit fund. "What do you think of this idea for it? The argument would be, that Mrs. Gamp, being on the eve of an excursion to Margate as a relief from her professional fatigues, comes to the knowledge of the intended excursion of our party; hears that several of the ladies concerned are in an interesting situation; and decides to accompany the party unbeknown, in a second-class carriage—'in case.' There, she finds a gentleman from the Strand in a checked suit, who is going down with the wigs"—the theatrical hairdresser employed on these occasions, Mr. Wilson, had eccentric points of character that were a fund of infinite mirth to Dickens—"and to his politeness Mrs. Gamp is indebted for much support and countenance during the excursion. She will describe the whole thing in her own manner: sitting, in each place of performance, in the orchestra, next the gentleman who plays the kettle-drums. She gives her critical opinion of Ben Jonson as a literary character, and refers to the different members of the party, in the course of her description of the trip: having always an invincible animosity towards Jerrold, for Caudle reasons. She addresses herself, generally, to Mrs. Harris, to whom the book is dedicated—but is discursive. Amount of matter, half a sheet of *Dombey*: may be a page or so more, but not less." Alas! it never arrived at even that small size, but perished prematurely, as I feared it would, from failure of the artists to furnish needful nourishment. Of course it could not live alone. Without suitable illustration it must have lost its point and pleasantry. "Mac will make a little garland of the ladies for the title-page. Egg and Stone will themselves originate something fanciful, and I will settle with Cruikshank and Leech. I have no doubt the little thing will be droll and attractive." So it certainly would have been, if the Thanes of art had not fallen from him; but on their desertion it had to be abandoned after the first few pages were written. They were placed at my disposal then; and, though the little jest had lost much of its flavour now, I cannot find it in my heart to omit them here. There are so many friends of Mrs. Gamp who will rejoice at this unexpected visit from her!

"I. Mrs. Gamp's Account of her Connexion with this Affair

"Which Mrs. Harris's own words to me, was these: 'Sairey Gamp,' she says, 'why not go to Margate? Srimps,' says that dear creetur, 'is to your liking, Sairey; why not go to Margate for a week, bring your constitootion up with srimps, and come back to them loving arts as knows and wallies of you, blooming? Sairey,' Mrs. Harris says, 'you are but poorly. Don't denige it, Mrs. Gamp, for books is in your looks. You must have rest. Your mind,' she says, 'is too strong for you; it gets you down and treads upon you, Sairey. It is useless to disguige the fact—the blade is a wearing out the sheets.' 'Mrs. Harris,' I says to her, 'I could not undertake to say, and I will not deceive you ma'am, that I am the woman I could wish to be. The time of worrit as I had with Mrs. Colliber, the baker's lady, which was so bad in her mind with her first, that she would not so much as look at bottled stout, and kept to gruel through the month, has agued me, Mrs. Harris. But ma'am,' I says to her, 'talk not of Margate, for if I do go anywheres, it is elsewheres and not there.' 'Sairey,' says Mrs. Harris, solemn, 'whence this mystery? If I have ever deceived the hardest-working, soberest, and best of women, which her name is well beknown is S. Gamp Midwife Kingsgate Street High Holborn, mention it. If not,' says Mrs. Harris, with the tears a standing in her eyes, 'reweal your intentions.' 'Yes, Mrs. Harris,' I says, 'I will. Well I knows you Mrs. Harris; well you knows me; well we both knows wot the characters of one another is. Mrs. Harris then,' I says, 'I *have* heard as there *is* a expedition going down to Manjestir and Liverpool, a play-acting. If I goes anywheres for change, it is along with that.' Mrs. Harris clasps her hands, and drops into a chair, as if her time was come—which I know'd it couldn't be, by rights, for six weeks odd. 'And have I lived to hear,' she says, 'of Sairey Gamp, as always kept hersef respectable, in company with play-actors!' 'Mrs. Harris,' I says to her, 'be not alarmed—not reg'lar play-actors—hammertoors.' 'Thank Evans!' says Mrs. Harris, and bustiges into a flood of tears.

"When the sweet creetur had compoged hersef (which a sip of brandy and warm water, and sugared pleasant, with a little nutmeg did it), I proceeds in these words. 'Mrs. Harris, I am told as these Hammertoors are litter'ry and artistickle.' 'Sairey,' says that best of wimmin, with a shiver and a slight relasp, 'go on, it might be worse.' 'I likewise hears,' I says to her, 'that they're agoin play-acting, for the benefit of two litter'ry men; one as has had his wrongs a long time ago, and has got his rights at last, and one as has made a many people merry in his time, but is very dull and sick and lonely his own sef, indeed.' 'Sairey,' says Mrs. Harris, 'you're an Inglish woman, and that's no business of you'rn.'

"'No, Mrs. Harris,' I says, 'that's very true; I hope I knows my dooty and my country. But,' I says, 'I am informed as there is Ladies in this party, and that half a dozen of 'em, if not more, is in various stages of a interesting state. Mrs. Harris, you and me well knows what Ingeins often does. If I accompanies this expedition, unbeknown and second cladge, may I not combine my calling, with change of air, and prove a service to my feller creeturs?' 'Sairey,' was Mrs. Harris's reply, 'you was born to be a blessing to your sex, and bring 'em through it. Good go with you! But keep your distance till called in, Lord bless you Mrs. Gamp; for people is known by the company they keeps, and litterary and artistickle society might be the ruin of you before you was aware, with your best customers, both sick and monthly, if they took a pride in themselves."

"II. Mrs. Gamp is Descriptive

"The number of the cab had a seven in it I think, and a ought I know—and if this should meet his eye (which it was a black 'un, new done, that he saw with; the other was tied up), I give him warning that he'd better take that umbreller and patten to the Hackney Coach Office before he repents it. He was a young man in a weskit with sleeves to it and strings behind, and needn't flatter himsef with a suppogition of escape, as I gave this description of him to the Police the moment I found he had drove off with my property; and if he thinks there an't laws enough he's much mistook—I tell him that.

"I do assure you, Mrs. Harris, when I stood in the railways office that morning with my bundle on my arm and one patten in my hand, you might have knocked me down with a feather, far less porkmangers which was a lumping against me, continual and sewere all round. I was drove about like a brute animal and almost worritted into fits, when a gentleman with a large shirt-collar and a hook nose, and a eye like one of Mr. Sweedlepipes's hawks, and long locks of hair, and wiskers that I wouldn't have no lady as I was engaged to meet suddenly a turning round a corner, for any sum of money you could offer me, says, laughing, 'Halloa, Mrs. Gamp, what are *you* up to!' I didn't know him from a man (except by his clothes); but I says faintly, 'If you're a Christian man, show me where to get a second-cladge ticket for Manjestir, and have me put in a carriage, or I shall drop!' Which he kindly did, in a cheerful kind of a way, skipping about in the strangest manner as ever I see, making all kinds of actions, and looking and vinking at me from under the brim of his hat (which was a good deal turned up), to that extent, that I should have thought he meant something but for being so flurried as not to have no thoughts at all until I was put into a carriage along with a individgle—the politest as ever I see—in a shepherd's plaid suit with a long gold watch-guard hanging round his neck, and his hand a trembling through nervousness worse than a aspian leaf.

"'I'm wery appy, ma'am,' he says—the politest vice as ever I heerd!—'to go down with a lady belonging to our party.'

"'Our party, sir!' I says.

"'Yes, ma'am,' he says, 'I'm Mr. Wilson. I'm going down with the wigs.'

"Mrs. Harris, wen he said he was agoing down with the wigs, such was my state of confugion and worrit that I thought he must be connected with the Government in some ways or another, but directly moment he explains himsef, for he says:

"'There's not a theatre in London worth mentioning that I don't attend punctually. There's five-and-twenty wigs in these boxes, ma'am,' he says, a pinting towards a heap of luggage, 'as was worn at the Queen's Fancy Ball. There's a black wig, ma'am,' he says, 'as was worn by Garrick; there's a red one, ma'am,' he says, 'as was worn by Kean; there's a brown one, ma'am,' he says, 'as was worn by Kemble; there's a yellow one, ma'am,' he says, 'as was made for Cooke; there's a grey one, ma'am,' he says, 'as I measured Mr. Young for, mysef; and there's a white one, ma'am, that Mr. Macready went mad in. There's a flaxen one as was got up express for Jenny Lind the night she came out at the Italian Opera. It was very much applauded was that wig, ma'am, through the evening. It had a great reception. The audience broke out the moment they see it.'

"'Are you in Mr. Sweedlepipes's line, sir?' I says.

"'Which is that, ma'am?' he says—the softest and genteelest vice I ever heerd, I do declare, Mrs. Harris!

"'Hair-dressing,' I says.

"'Yes, ma'am,' he replies, 'I have that honour. Do you see this, ma'am?' he says, holding up his right hand.

"'I never see such a trembling,' I says to him. And I never did!

"'All along of Her Majesty's Costume Ball, ma'am,' he says. 'The excitement did it. Two hundred and fifty-seven ladies of the first rank and fashion had their heads got up on that occasion by this hand, and my t'other one. I was at it eight-and-forty hours on my feet, ma'am, without rest. It was a Powder ball, ma'am. We have a Powder piece at Liverpool.

Have I not the pleasure,' he says, looking at me curious, 'of addressing Mrs. Gamp?'

"'Gamp I am, sir,' I replies. 'Both by name and natur.'

"'Would you like to see your beeograffer's moustache and wiskers, ma'am?' he says. 'I've got 'em in this box.'

"'Drat my beeograffer, sir,' I says, 'he has given me no region to wish to know anythink about him.'

"'Oh, Missus Gamp, I ask your parden'—I never see such a polite man, Mrs. Harris! 'P'raps,' he says, 'if you're not of the party, you don't know who it was that assisted you into this carriage!'

"'No, sir,' I says, 'I don't, indeed.'

"'Why, ma'am,' he says, a wisperin', 'that was George, ma'am.'

"'What George, sir? I don't know no George,' says I.

"'The great George, ma'am,' says he. 'The Crookshanks.'

"If you'll believe me, Mrs. Harris, I turns my head, and see the wery man a making pictur's of me on his thumb nail, at the winder! while another of 'em—a tall, slim, melancolly gent, with dark hair and a bage vice—looks over his shoulder, with his head o' one side as if he understood the subject, and coolly says, '*I*'ve draw'd her several times—in *Punch*,' he says too! The owdacious wretch!

"'Which I never touches, Mr. Wilson,' I remarks out loud —I couldn't have helped it, Mrs. Harris, if you had took my life for it!—'which I never touches, Mr. Wilson, on account of the lemon!'

"'Hush!' says Mr. Wilson. 'There he is!'

"I only see a fat gentleman with curly black hair and a merry face, a standing on the platform rubbing his two hands over one another, as if he was washing of 'em, and shaking his head and shoulders wery much; and I was a wondering wot Mr. Wilson meant, wen he says, 'There's Dougladge, Mrs. Gamp!' he says. 'There's him as wrote the life of Mrs. Caudle!'

"Mrs. Harris, wen I see that little willain bodily before me, it give me such a turn that I was all in a tremble. If I hadn't lost my umbreller in the cab, I must have done him a injury with it! Oh the bragian little traitor! right among the ladies, Mrs. Harris; looking his wickedest and deceitfullest of eyes while he was a talking to 'em; laughing at his own jokes as loud as you please; holding his hat in one hand to cool his-sef, and tossing back his iron-grey mop of a head of hair with the other, as if it was so much shavings—there, Mrs. Harris, I see him getting encouragement from the pretty delooded creeturs, which never know'd that sweet saint, Mrs. C., as I did, and being treated with as much confidence as if he'd never wiolated none of the domestic ties, and never showed up nothing! Oh the aggrawation of that Dougladge! Mrs. Harris, if I hadn't apologiged to Mr. Wilson, and put a little bottle to my lips which was in my pocket for the journey, and which it is very rare indeed I have about me, I could not have abared the sight of him—there, Mrs. Harris! I could not!—I must have tore him, or have give way and fainted.

"While the bell was a ringing, and the luggage of the hammer-toors in great confusion—all a litter'ry indeed—was handled up, Mr. Wilson demeens his-sef politer than ever. 'That,' he says, 'Mrs. Gamp,' a pinting to a officer-looking gentleman, that a lady with a little basket was a taking care on, 'is another of our party. He's a author too—continivally going up the walley of the Muses, Mrs. Gamp. There,' he says, alluding to a fine looking, portly gentleman, with a face like a amiable full moon, and a short mild gent, with a pleasant smile, 'is two more of our astists, Mrs. G., well beknowed at the Royal Academy, as sure as stones as stones, and eggs is eggs. This resolute gent,' he says, 'a coming along here as is aperrently going to take the railways by storm—him with the tight legs, and his weskit very much buttoned, and his mouth very much shut, and his coat a flying open, and his heels a-giving it to the platform, is a cricket and beeograffer, and our principal tragegian.' 'But who,' says I, when the bell had left off, and the train had begun to move, 'who, Mr. Wilson, is the wild gent in the prespiration, that's been a-tearing up and down all this time with a great box of papers under his arm, a-talking to everybody wery indistinct, and exciting of himself dreadful?' 'Why?' says Mr. Wilson, with a smile. 'Because, sir,' I says, 'he's being left behind.' 'Good God!' cries Mr. Wilson, turning pale and putting out his head, 'it's *your* beeograffer—the Manager—and he has got the money, Mrs. Gamp!' Hous'ever, someone chucked him into the train and we went off. At the first shreek of the whistle, Mrs. Harris, I turned white, for I had took notice of some of them dear creeturs as was the cause of my being in company, and I know'd the danger that—but Mr. Wilson, which is a married man, puts his hand on mine, and says, 'Mrs. Gamp, calm yourself; it's only the Ingein.'"

Of those of the party with whom these humorous liberties were taken, there are only two now living to complain of their

friendly caricaturist; and Mr. Cruikshank will perhaps join me
in a frank forgiveness not the less heartily for the kind words
about himself that reached me from Broadstairs not many days
after Mrs. Gamp. "At Canterbury yesterday" (2 September)
"I bought George Cruikshank's *Bottle.* I think it very powerful
indeed; the two last plates most admirable, except that the
boy and girl in the very last are too young, and the girl more
like a circus-phenomenon than that no-phenomenon she is
intended to represent. I question, however, whether anybody
else living could have done it so well. There is a woman in the
last plate but one, garrulous about the murder, with a child in
her arms, that is as good as Hogarth. Also, the man who is
stooping down, looking at the body. The philosophy of the
thing, as a great lesson, I think all wrong; because to be striking,
and original too, the drinking should have begun in sorrow, or
poverty, or ignorance—the three things in which, in its awful
aspect, it *does* begin. The design would then have been a double-
handed sword—but too 'radical' for good old George, I suppose."

The same letter made mention of other matters of interest.
His accounts for the first half-year of *Dombey* were so much in
excess of what had been expected from the new publishing
arrangements, that from this date all embarrassments connected
with money were brought to a close. His future profits varied
of course with his varying sales, but there was always enough,
and savings were now to begin. "The profits of the half-year
are brilliant. Deducting the hundred pounds a month paid six
times, I have still to receive two thousand two hundred and
twenty pounds, which I think is tidy. Don't you? . . . Stone is
still here, and I lamed his foot by walking him seventeen miles
the day before yesterday; but otherwise he flourisheth. . . .
Why don't you bring down a carpet-bag-full of books, and take
possession of the drawing-room all the morning? My opinion is
that Goldsmith would die more easy by the seaside. Charley
and Walley have been taken to school this morning in high
spirits, and at London Bridge will be folded in the arms of
Blimber. The Government is about to issue a Sanitary commission, and Lord John, I am right well pleased to say, has
appointed Henry Austin secretary." Mr. Austin, who afterwards held the same office under the Sanitary Act, had married
his youngest sister Letitia; and of his two youngest brothers
I may add that Alfred, also a civil engineer, became one of
the sanitary inspectors, and that Augustus was now placed in
a city employment by Mr. Thomas Chapman, which after a

little time he surrendered, and then found his way to America, where he died.

The next Broadstairs letter (5 September) resumed the subject of Goldsmith, whose life I was then bringing nearly to completion. "Supposing your *Goldsmith* made a general sensation, what should you think of doing a cheap edition of his works? I have an idea that we might do some things of that sort with considerable effect. There is really no edition of the great British novelists in a handy nice form, and would it not be a likely move to do it with some attractive feature that could not be given to it by the Teggs and such people? Supposing one wrote an essay on Fielding for instance, and another on Smollett, and another on Sterne, recalling how one read them as a child (no one read them younger than I, I think), and how one gradually grew up into a different knowledge of them, and so forth—would it not be interesting to many people? I should like to know if you descry anything in this. It is one of the dim notions fluctuating within me. . . . The profits, brave indeed, * 67 are four hundred pounds more than the utmost I expected. . . . The same yearnings have been mine, in reference to the Praslin business. It is pretty clear to me, for one thing, that the Duchess was one of the most uncomfortable women in the world, and that it would have been hard work for anybody to have got on with her. It is strange to see a bloody reflection of our friends Eugène Sue and Dumas in the whole melodrama. Don't you think so . . . remembering what we often said of the canker at the root of all that Paris life? I dreamed of you, in a wild manner, all last night. . . . A sea fog here, which prevents one's seeing the low-water mark. A circus on the cliff to the right, and of course I have a box to-night! Deep slowness in the Inimitable's brain. A shipwreck on the Goodwin Sands last Sunday, which WALLY, with a hawk's eye, SAW GO DOWN: for which assertion, subsequently confirmed and proved, he was horribly maltreated at the time."

Devonshire Terrace meanwhile had been quitted by his tenant; and coming up joyfully himself to take possession, he brought for completion in his old home an important chapter of *Dombey*. On the way he lost his portmanteau, but "Thank God! the MS. of the chapter wasn't in it. Whenever I travel, and have anything of that valuable article, I always carry it in my pocket." He had begun at this time to find difficulties * 68 in writing at Broadstairs, of which he told me on his return. "Vagrant music is getting to that height here, and is so impossible to be escaped from, that I fear Broadstairs and I must part company in time to come. Unless it pours of rain, I cannot write half-an-hour without the most excruciating organs, fiddles, bells, or glee-singers. There is a violin of the most torturing kind under the window now (time, ten in the morning) and an Italian box of music on the steps—both in full blast." He closed with a mention of improvements in the Margate theatre since his memorable last visit. In the past two years it had been managed by a son of the great comedian, Dowton, with whose name it is pleasant to connect this note. "We went to the manager's benefit on Wednesday" (10 September): "*As You Like It* really very well done, and a most excellent house. Mr. Dowton delivered a sensible and modest kind of speech on the occasion, setting forth his conviction that a means of instruction and entertainment possessing such a literature as the stage in England, could not pass away; and that what inspired great minds, and delighted great men, two thousand years ago, and did the same in Shakespeare's day, must have within itself a principle of life superior to the whim and fashion of the hour. And with that, and with cheers, he retired. He really seems a most respectable man, and he has cleared out this dust-hole of a theatre into something like decency."

He was to be in London at the end of the month: but I had from him meanwhile his preface for his first completed book in the popular edition (*Pickwick* being now issued in that form, with an illustration by Leslie); and sending me shortly after (12 September) the first few slips of the story of the *Haunted Man* proposed for his next Christmas book, he told me he must finish it in less than a month if it was to be done at all, *Dombey* having now become very importunate. This prepared me for his letter of a week's later date. "Have been at work all day, and am seedy in consequence. *Dombey* takes so much time, and requires to be so carefully done, that I really begin to have serious doubts whether it is wise to go on with the Christmas book. Your kind help is invoked. What do you think? Would there be any distinctly bad effect in holding this idea over for another twelvemonth? saying nothing whatever till November; and then announcing in the *Dombey* that its occupation of my entire time prevents the continuance of the Christmas series until next year, when it is proposed to be renewed. There might not be anything in that but a possibility of an extra lift for the little book when it did come—eh? On the other hand, I am very loath to lose the money. And still more so to leave any gap

<!-- marginal note: * 69 -->

at Christmas firesides which I ought to fill. In short I am (forgive the expression) BLOWED if I know what to do. I am a literary Kitely—and you ought to sympathise and help. If I had no *Dombey*, I could write and finish the story with the bloom on—— but there's the rub. . . . Which unfamiliar quotation reminds me of a Shakespearian (put an *e* before the *s*; I like it much better) speculation of mine. What do you say to 'take arms against a sea of troubles' having been originally written 'make arms,' which is the action of swimming. It would get rid of a horrible grievance in the figure, and make it plain and apt. I think of setting up a claim to live in The House at Stratford rent-free, on the strength of this suggestion. You are not to suppose that I am anything but disconcerted to-day, in the agitation of my soul concerning Christmas; but I have been brooding, like Dombey himself, over *Dombey* these two days, until I really can't afford to be depressed." To his Shakespearian suggestion I replied that it would hardly give him the claim he thought of setting up, for that swimming through your troubles would not be "opposing" them. And upon the other point I had no doubt of the wisdom of delay. The result was that the Christmas story was laid aside until the following year.

The year's closing incidents were his chairmanship at a meeting of the Leeds Mechanics' Society on 1 December, and his opening of the Glasgow Athenæum on the 28th; where, to immense assemblages in both, he contrasted the obstinacy * 70 and cruelty of the power of ignorance with the docility and gentleness of the power of knowledge; pointed the use of popular institutes in supplementing what is first learnt in life, by the later education for its employments and the equipment for its domesticities and duties, which the grown person needs from day to day as much as the child its reading and writing; and he closed at Glasgow with allusion to a bazaar set on foot by the ladies of the city, under patronage of the queen, for adding books to its Athenæum Library. "We never tire of the friendships we form with books," he said, "and here they will possess the added charm of association with their donors. Some neighbouring Glasgow widow will be mistaken for that remoter one whom Sir Roger de Coverley could not forget; Sophia's muff will be seen and loved, by another than Tom Jones, going down the High Street some winter day; and the grateful students of a library thus filled will be apt, as to the fair ones who have helped to people it, to couple them in their thoughts with

Principles of the Population and Additions to the History of Europe, by an author of older date than Sheriff Alison." At which no one laughed so loudly as the Sheriff himself, who had cordially received Dickens as his guest, and stood with him on the platform.

On the last day but one of the old year he wrote to me from Edinburgh. "We came over this afternoon, leaving Glasgow at one o'clock. Alison lives in style in a handsome country house out of Glasgow, and is a capital fellow, with an agreeable wife, nice little daughter, cheerful niece, all things pleasant in his household. I went over the prison and lunatic asylum with *71 him yesterday; at the Lord Provost's had gorgeous state-lunch with the Town Council; and was entertained at a great dinner-party at night. Unbounded hospitality and enthoozymoozy the order of the day, and I have never been more heartily received anywhere, or enjoyed myself more completely. The great chemist, Gregory, who spoke at the meeting, returned with us to Edinburgh to-day, and gave me many new lights on the road regarding the extraordinary pains Macaulay seems for years to have taken to make himself disagreeable and disliked here. No one else, on that side, would have had the remotest chance of being unseated at the last election; and, though Gregory voted for him, I thought he seemed quite as well pleased as anybody else that he didn't come in. . . . I am sorry to report the Scott Monument a failure. It is like the spire of a Gothic church taken off and stuck in the ground." On the first day of 1848, still in Edinburgh, he wrote again: " Jeffrey, who is obliged to hold a kind of morning court in his own study during the holidays, came up yesterday in great consternation, to tell me that a person had just been to make and sign a declaration of bankruptcy; and that on looking at the signature he saw it was James Sheridan Knowles. He immediately sent after, and spoke with him; and of what passed I am eager to talk with you." The talk will bring back the main subject of this chapter, from which another kind of strolling has led me away; for its results were other amateur performances, of which the object was to benefit Knowles.

This was the year when a committee had been formed for the purchase and preservation of Shakespeare's house at Stratford, and the performances in question took the form of contributions to the endowment of a curatorship to be held by the author of *Virginius* and the *Hunchback*. The endowment was abandoned upon the town and council of Stratford finally (and very properly) taking charge of the house; but the sum realised was not withdrawn from the object really desired, and one of the finest of dramatists profited yet more largely by it than Leigh Hunt did by the former enterprise. It may be proper to remark also, that, like Leigh Hunt, Knowles received soon after, through Lord John Russell, the same liberal pension; and that smaller claims to which attention had been similarly drawn were not forgotten, Mr. Poole, after much kind help from the Bounty Fund, being a little later placed on the Civil List for half the amount by the same minister and friend of letters.

Dickens threw himself into the new scheme with all his old energy; and prefatory mention may be made of our difficulty in selection of a suitable play to alternate with our old Ben Jonson. The *Alchemist* had been such a favourite with some of us, that, before finally laying it aside, we went through two or three rehearsals, in which I recollect thinking Dickens's Sir Epicure Mammon as good as anything he had done; and now * 71A the same trouble, with the same result, arising from a vain desire to please everybody, was taken successively with Beaumont and Fletcher's *Beggar's Bush*, and Goldsmith's *Good Natured Man*, with Jerrold's characteristic drama of the *Rent Day*, and Bulwer's masterly comedy of *Money*. Choice was at last made of Shakespeare's *Merry Wives*, in which Lemon played Falstaff, I took again the jealous husband as in Jonson's play, and Dickens was Justice Shallow; to which was added a farce, *Love, Law, and Physick*, in which Dickens took the part he had acted long ago, before his days of authorship; and, besides the professional actresses engaged, we had for our Dame Quickly the lady to whom the world owes incomparably the best *Concordance* to Shakespeare that has ever been published, Mrs. Cowden Clarke. The success was undoubtedly very great. At Manchester, Liverpool, and Edinburgh there were single representations; but Birmingham and Glasgow had each two nights, and two were given at the Haymarket, on one of which the queen and prince were present. The gross receipts from the nine performances, before the necessary large deductions for London and local charges, were two thousand five hundred and fifty-one pounds and eightpence.[1] The first representation was in London on 15 April, the last in Glasgow on

---

[1] I give the sums taken at the several theatres. Haymarket, £319 14s.; Manchester, £266 12s. 6d.; Liverpool, £467 6s. 6d.; Birmingham, £327 10s., and £262 18s. 6d.; Edinburgh, £325 1s. 6d.; Glasgow, £471 7s. 8d., and (at half the prices of the first night) £210 10s.

20 July, and everywhere Dickens was the leading figure. In the enjoyment as in the labour he was first. His animal spirits, unresting and supreme, were the attraction of rehearsal at morning, and of the stage at night. At the quiet early dinner, and the more jovial unrestrained supper, where all engaged were assembled daily, his was the brightest face, the lightest step, the pleasantest word. There seemed to be no need for rest to that wonderful vitality.

Of the novel begun in Switzerland, at which he had worked assiduously for twenty months, and which the April number in 1848 brought to its close, some account remains to be given.

II

"DOMBEY AND SON"

1846-8

THOUGH his proposed new "book in shilling numbers" had been mentioned to me three months before he quitted England, he knew little himself at that time or when he left excepting the fact, then also named, that it was to do with Pride what its predecessor had done with Selfishness. But this limit he soon overpassed; and the succession of independent groups of character, surprising for the variety of their forms and handling, with which he enlarged and enriched his plan, went far beyond the range of the passion of Mr. Dombey and Mr. Dombey's second wife.

Obvious causes have led to grave under-estimates of this novel. Its first five numbers forced up interest and expectation so high that the rest of necessity fell short; but it is not therefore true of the general conception that thus the wine of it had been drawn, and only the lees left. In the treatment of acknowledged masterpieces in literature it not seldom occurs that the genius and the art of the master have not pulled together to the close; but if a work of imagination is to forfeit its higher meed of praise because its pace at starting has not been uniformly kept, hard measure would have to be dealt to books of undeniable greatness. Among other critical severities it was said here, that Paul died at the beginning not for any need of the story, but only to interest its readers somewhat more; and that Mr. Dombey relented at the end for just the same reason. What is now to be told will show how little ground existed for either imputation. The so-called "violent change" in the hero has more lately been revived in the notices of Mr. Taine, who says that "*it spoils a fine novel*"; but it will be seen that in the apparent alteration no unnaturalness of change was involved, and certainly the adoption of it was not a sacrifice to "public morality." While every other portion of the tale had to submit to such varieties in development as the characters

19

themselves entailed, the design affecting Paul and his father had been planned from the opening, and was carried without real alteration to the close. Of the perfect honesty with which Dickens himself repelled such charges as those to which I have adverted, when he wrote the preface to his collected edition, remarkable proof appears in the letter to myself which accompanied the manuscript of his proposed first number. No other line of the tale had at this time been placed on paper.

When the first chapter only was done, and again when all was finished but eight slips, he had sent me letters formerly quoted. What follows came with the manuscript of the first four chapters on 25 July. "I will now go on to give you an outline of my immediate intentions in reference to *Dombey*. I design to show Mr. D. with that one idea of the Son taking firmer and firmer possession of him, and swelling and bloating his pride to a prodigious extent. As the boy begins to grow up, I shall show him quite impatient for his getting on, and urging his masters to set him great tasks, and the like. But the natural affection of the boy will turn towards the despised sister; and I purpose showing her learning all sorts of things, of her own application and determination, to assist him in his lessons: and helping him always. When the boy is about ten years old (in the fourth number), he will be taken ill, and will die; and when he is ill, and when he is dying, I mean to make him turn always for refuge to the sister still, and keep the stern affection of the father at a distance. So Mr. Dombey—for all his greatness, and for all his devotion to the child—will find himself at arms' length from him even then; and will see that his love and confidence are all bestowed upon his sister, whom Mr. Dombey has used—and so has the boy himself too, for that matter—as a mere convenience and handle to him. The death of the boy is a death-blow, of course, to all the father's schemes and cherished hopes; and 'Dombey and Son,' as Miss Tox will say at the end of the number, 'is a Daughter after all.' . . . From that time, I purpose changing his feeling of indifference and uneasiness towards his daughter into a positive hatred. For he will always remember how the boy had his arm round her neck when he was dying, and whispered to her, and would take things only from her hand, and never thought of him. . . . At the same time I shall change *her* feeling towards *him* for one of a greater desire to love him, and to be loved by him; engendered in her compassion for his loss, and her love for the dead boy whom, in his way, he loved so well too. So I mean to carry the story on, through all the branches and off-shoots and meanderings that come up; and through the decay and downfall of the house, and the bankruptcy of Dombey, and all the rest of it; when his only staff and treasure, and his unknown Good Genius always, will be this rejected daughter, who will come out better than any son at last, and whose love for him, when discovered and understood, will be his bitterest reproach. For the struggle with himself, which goes on in all such obstinate natures, will have ended then; and the sense of his injustice, which you may be sure has never quitted him, will have at last a gentler office than that of only making him more harshly unjust. . . . I rely very much on Susan Nipper grown up, and acting partly as Florence's maid, and partly as a kind of companion to her, for a strong character throughout the book. I also rely on the Toodles, and on Polly, who, like everybody else, will be found by Mr. Dombey to have gone over to his daughter and become attached to her. This is what cooks call 'the stock of the soup.' All kinds of things will be added to it, of course." Admirable is the illustration thus afforded of his way of working, and interesting the evidence it gives of the feeling for his art with which this book was begun.

The close of the letter put an important question affecting gravely a leading person in the tale. ". . . About the boy, who appears in the last chapter of the first number, I think it would be a good thing to disappoint all the expectations that chapter seems to raise of his happy connection with the story and the heroine, and to show him gradually and naturally trailing away, from that love of adventure and boyish light-heartedness, into negligence, idleness, dissipation, dishonesty, and ruin. To show, in short, that common, every-day, miserable declension of which we know so much in our ordinary life; to exhibit something of the philosophy of it, in great temptations and an easy nature; and to show how the good turns into bad, by degrees. If I kept some little notion of Florence always at the bottom of it, I think it might be made very powerful and very useful. What do you think? Do you think it may be done, without making people angry? I could bring out Solomon Gills and Captain Cuttle well, through such a history; and I descry, anyway, an opportunity for good scenes between Captain Cuttle and Miss Tox. This question of the boy is very important. . . . Let me hear all you think about it. Hear! I wish I could."

For reasons that need not be dwelt upon here, but in which Dickens ultimately acquiesced, Walter was reserved for a happier future; and the idea thrown out took modified shape, amid circumstances better suited to its excellent capabilities, in the striking character of Richard Carstone in the tale of *Bleak House*. But another point had risen meanwhile for settlement not admitting of delay. In the first enjoyment of writing after his long rest, to which a former letter has referred, he had over-written his number by nearly a fifth; and upon his proposal to transfer the fourth chapter to his second number, replacing it by another of fewer pages, I had to object that this might damage his interest at starting. Thus he wrote on 7 August: ". . . I have received your letter to-day with the greatest de-light, and am overjoyed to find that you think so well of the number. I thought well of it myself, and that it was a great plunge into a story; but I did not know how far I might be stimulated by my paternal affection. . . . What should you say, for a notion of the illustrations, to 'Miss Tox introduces the Party'? and 'Mr. Dombey and Family'? meaning Polly Toodle, the baby, Mr. Dombey, and little Florence: whom I think it would be well to have. Walter, his uncle, and Captain Cuttle, might stand over. It is a great question with me, now, whether I had not better take this last chapter bodily out, and make it the last chapter of the second number; writing some other new one to close the first number. I think it would be impossible to take out six pages without great pangs. Do you think such a proceeding as I suggest would weaken number one very much? I wish you would tell me, as soon as you can after receiving this, what your opinion is on the point. If you thought it would weaken the first number, beyond the counter-balancing advantage of strengthening the second, I would cut down some-how or other, and let it go. I shall be anxious to hear your opinion. In the meanwhile I will go on with the second, which I have just begun. I have not been quite myself since we returned from Chamonix, owing to the great heat." Two days later: "I have begun a little chapter to end the first number, and certainly think it will be well to keep the ten pages of Wally and Co. entire for number two. But this is still subject to your opinion, which I am very anxious to know. I have not been in writing cue all the week; but really the weather has rendered it next to impossible to work." Four days later: "I shall send you with this (on the chance of your being favourable to that view of the subject) a small chapter to close the first number, in lieu of the Solomon Gills one. I have been hideously idle all the week, and have done nothing but this trifling interloper;

but hope to begin again on Monday—ding dong. . . . The ink-stand is to be cleaned out to-night, and refilled, preparatory to execution. I trust I may shed a good deal of ink in the next fortnight." Then, the day following, on arrival of my letter, he submitted to a hard necessity. "I received yours to-day. A decided facer to me! I had been counting, alas! with a miser's greed, upon the gained ten pages. . . . No matter. I have no doubt you are right, and strength is everything. The addition of two lines to each page, or something less—coupled with the enclosed cuts, will bring it all to bear smoothly. In case more cutting is wanted, I must ask you to try your hand. I shall agree to whatever you propose." These cuttings, absolutely necessary as they were, were not without much disadvantage; and in the course of them he had to sacrifice a passage fore-shadowing his final intention as to Dombey. It would have shown, thus early, something of the struggle with itself that such pride must always go through; and I think it worth preserving in a note.[1]

Several letters now expressed his anxiety about the illustrations. A nervous dread of caricature in the face of his merchant-hero, had led him to indicate by a living person the type of city-gentleman he would have had the artist select; and this is all he meant by his reiterated urgent request, "I do wish he could get a glimpse of A., for he is the very Dombey." But as the glimpse of A. was not to be had, it was resolved to send for selection by himself glimpses of other letters of the alphabet,

---

[1] "He had already laid his hand upon the bell-rope to convey his usual summons to Richards, when his eye fell upon a writing-desk, belonging to his deceased wife, which had been taken, among other things, from a cabinet in her chamber. It was not the first time that his eye had lighted on it. He carried the key in his pocket; and he brought it to his table and opened it now—having previously locked the room door—with a well-accustomed hand.

"From beneath a heap of torn and cancelled scraps of paper, he took one letter that remained entire. Involuntarily holding his breath as he opened this document, and 'bating in the stealthy action something of his arrogant demeanour, he sat down, resting his head upon one hand, and read it through.

"He read it slowly and attentively, and with a nice particularity to every syllable. Otherwise than as his great deliberation seemed unnatural, and perhaps the result of an effort equally great, he allowed no sign of emotion to escape him. When he had read it through, he folded and refolded it slowly several times, and tore it carefully into fragments. Checking his hand in the act of throwing these away, he put them in his pocket, as if unwilling to trust them even to the chances of being reunited and deciphered; and instead of ringing, as usual, for little Paul, he sat solitary all the evening in his cheerless room."—From the original MS. of *Dombey and Son*.

actual heads as well as fanciful ones; and the sheetful I sent out, which he returned when the choice was made, I here reproduce in facsimile.[1] In itself amusing, it now has the important use of showing, once for all, in regard to Dickens's intercourse with his artists, that they certainly had not an easy time with him; that, even beyond what is ordinary between author and illustrator, his requirements were exacting; that he was apt, as he has said himself, to build up temples in his mind not always makable with hands; that in the results he had rarely anything but disappointment; and that of all notions to connect with him the most preposterous would be that which directly reversed these relations, and depicted him as receiving from any artist the inspiration he was always vainly striving to give. An assertion of this kind was contradicted in my first volume [2]; but it has since been repeated so explicitly, that to prevent any possible misconstruction from a silence I would fain have persisted in, the distasteful subject is again reluctantly introduced.

It originated with a literary friend of the excellent artist by whom *Oliver Twist* was illustrated from month to month, during the earlier part of its monthly issue. This gentleman stated, in a paper written and published in America, that Mr. Cruikshank, by executing the plates before opportunity was afforded him of seeing the letterpress, had suggested to the writer the finest effects in his story; and to this opposing my clear recollection of all the time the tale was in progress, it became my duty to say that within my own personal knowledge the alleged fact was not true. " Dickens," the artist is reported as saying to his admirer, " ferreted out that bundle of drawings, and when he came to the one which represents Fagin in the cell, he silently studied it for half an hour, and told me he was tempted to change the whole plot of his story. . . . I consented to let him write up to my designs; and that was the way in which Fagin, Sikes and Nancy were created." Happily I was able to add the complete refutation of this folly by producing a letter of Dickens written at the time, which proved incontestably that the closing illustrations, including the two specially named in support of the preposterous charge, Sikes and his Dog, and Fagin in his Cell, had not even been seen by Dickens until his finished book

---

[1] *See pages* 110–11.

[2] It is hardly necessary to remind the reader that this work appeared originally in three volumes, with an interval between publication of each: the first in 1871, the second in 1872, and the third in 1873.

was on the eve of appearance. As however the distinguished artist, notwithstanding the refreshment of his memory by this letter, has permitted himself again to endorse the statement of his friend, I can only again print the words with which Dickens himself repels the imputation on his memory. To some it may be more satisfactory if I print the letter in facsimile; and so leave for ever a charge in itself so incredible that nothing would have justified further allusion to it but the knowledge of my friend's old and true regard for Mr. Cruikshank, of which evidence will shortly appear, and my own respect for an original genius well able to subsist of itself without taking what belongs to others.

My dear Cruikshank.

I returned suddenly to town yesterday afternoon to look at the latter pages of Oliver Twist before it was delivered to the booksellers, when I saw the majority of the plates in the last volume for the first time.

With reference to the last one. Does Maylie and Oliver. Without entering into the question of great haste or slow or any other cause which may have led to its being what it is — I am quite sure there can be little difference of opinion between us with respect to the result — my

I ask you whether you will object to ~~closing~~ *(designing)* *this plate afresh and doing so* at once *in order that as few impressions as possible of the present one may go forth?*

I ~~ask quite frankly~~ *(feel confident)* *you know me too well to feel hurt by this enquiry, and with equal confidence in you I have lost no time in preferring it.*

* 72

Resuming the *Dombey* letters I find him on 30 August in better heart about his illustrator. "I shall gladly acquiesce in whatever more changes or omissions you propose. Browne seems to be getting on well. . . . He will have a good subject in Paul's christening. Mr. Chick is like D, if you'll mention that when you think of it. The little chapter of Miss Tox and the Major, which you alas! (but quite wisely) rejected from the first number, I have altered for the last of the second. I have not quite finished the middle chapter yet—having, I should say, three good days' work to do at it; but I hope it will be all a worthy successor to number one. I will send it as soon as finished." Then, a little later: "Browne is certainly interesting himself, and taking pains. I think the cover very good: perhaps with a little too much in it, but that is an ungrateful objection." The second week of September brought me the finished MS. of number two; and his letter of 3 October, noticing objections taken to it, gives additional touches to this picture of him while at work. The matter on which he is engaged is one of his masterpieces. There is nothing in all his writings more perfect, for what it shows of his best qualities, than the life and death of Paul Dombey. The comedy is admirable; nothing strained, everything hearty and wholesome in the laughter and fun; all who contribute to the mirth, Doctor Blimber and his pupils, Mr. Toots, the Chicks and the Toodles, Miss Tox and the Major, Paul and Mrs. Pipchin, up to his highest mark; and the serious scenes never falling short of it, from the death of Paul's mother in the first number, to that of Paul himself in the fifth, which, as the author of the *Two Old Men's Tales* with hardly exaggeration said, threw a whole nation into mourning. But see how eagerly this fine writer takes every suggestion, how little of self-esteem and self-sufficiency there is, with what a consciousness of the tendency of his humour to exuberance he surrenders what is needful to restrain it, and of what small account to him is any special piece of work in his care and his considerateness for the general design. I think of Ben Jonson's experience of the greatest of all writers. "He was indeed honest, and of an open and free nature; had an excellent phantasy, brave notions and gentle expressions; wherein he flowed with that facility, that sometimes it was necessary he should be stopped." Who it was that stopped him, and the ease of doing it, no one will doubt. Whether he, as well as the writer of later time, might not with more advantage have been left alone, is the only question.

Thus ran the letter of 3 October: "Miss Tox's colony I will smash. Walter's allusion to Carker (would you take it *all* out?) shall be dele'd. Of course, you understand the man? I turned that speech over in my mind; but I thought it natural that a boy should run on, with such a subject, under the circumstances: having the matter so presented to him. . . . I thought of the possibility of malice on christening points of faith, and put the drag on as I wrote. Where would you make the insertion, and to what effect? *That* shall be done too. I want you to think the number sufficiently good stoutly to back up the first. It occurs to me—might not your doubt about the christening be a reason for not making the ceremony the subject of an illustration? Just turn this over. Again: if I could do it (I shall have leisure to consider the possibility before I begin), do you think it would be advisable to make number three a kind of half-way house between Paul's infancy, and his being eight or nine years old?—In that case I should probably not kill him until the fifth number. Do you think the people so likely to be pleased with Florence, and Walter, as to relish

another number of them at their present age? Otherwise, Walter
will be two or three and twenty, straightway. I wish you would
think of this. . . . I am sure you are right about the christening.
It shall be artfully and easily amended. . . . Eh?"

Meanwhile, two days before this letter, his first number had
been launched with a sale that transcended his hopes, and
brought back *Nickleby* days. "The *Dombey* sale is BRILLIANT!"
he wrote to me on the 11th. "I had put before me thirty
thousand as the limit of the most extreme success, saying that
if we should reach that, I should be more than satisfied and
more than happy; you will judge how happy I am! I read the
second number here last night to the most prodigious and
uproarious delight of the circle. I never saw or heard people
laugh so. You will allow me to observe that my reading of
the Major has merit." What a valley of the shadow he had
just been passing, in his journey through his Christmas book,
has before been told; but always, and with only too much
eagerness, he sprang up under pressure. "A week of perfect
idleness," he wrote to me on the 26th, "has brought me round
again—idleness so rusting and devouring, so complete and unbroken, that I am quite glad to write the heading of the first
chapter of number three to-day. I shall be slow at first, I fear,
in consequence of that change of the plan. But I allow myself
nearly three weeks for the number; designing, at present, to
start for Paris on the 16th of November. Full particulars in
future bills. Just going to bed. I think I can make a good effect,
on the after story, of the feeling created by the additional
number before Paul's death." . . . Five more days confirmed him
in this hope. "I am at work at *Dombey* with good speed, thank
God. All well here. Country stupendously beautiful. Mountains
covered with snow. Rich, crisp weather." There was one drawback. The second number had gone out to him, and the illustrations he found to be so "dreadfully bad" that they made him
"curl his legs up." They made him also more than usually
anxious in regard to a special illustration on which he set much
store, for the part he had in hand.

The first chapter of it was sent me only four days later (nearly
half the entire part, so freely his fancy was now flowing and overflowing), with intimation for the artist: "The best subject for
Browne will be at Mrs. Pipchin's; and if he liked to do a quiet
odd thing, Paul, Mrs. Pipchin, and the Cat, by the fire, would
be very good for the story. I earnestly hope he will think it
worth a little extra care. The second subject, in case he shouldn't

take a second from that same chapter, I will shortly describe as soon as I have it clearly (to-morrow or next day), and send it to *you* by post." The result was not satisfactory; but as the artist more than redeemed it in the later course of the tale, and the present disappointment was mainly the incentive to that better success, the mention of the failure here will be excused for what it illustrates of Dickens himself. "I am really *distressed* by the illustration of Mrs. Pipchin and Paul. It is so frightfully and wildly wide of the mark. Good Heaven! in the commonest and most literal construction of the text, it is all wrong. She is described as an old lady, and Paul's 'miniature arm-chair' is mentioned more than once. He ought to be sitting in a little arm-chair down in a corner of the fireplace, staring up at her. I can't say what pain and vexation it is to be so utterly misrepresented. I would cheerfully have given a hundred pounds to have kept this illustration out of the book. He never could have got that idea of Mrs. Pipchin if he had attended to the text. Indeed I think he does better without the text; for then the notion is made easy to him in short description, and he can't help taking it in."

He felt the disappointment more keenly, because the conception of the grim old boarding-house keeper had taken back his thoughts to the miseries of his own child-life, and made her, as her prototype in verity was, a part of the terrible reality. * 73 I had forgotten, until I again read this letter, that he thus early proposed to tell me that story of his boyish sufferings which a question from myself, of some months later date, so fully elicited. He was now hastening on with the close of his third number, to be ready for departure to Paris (4 November). ". . . I hope to finish the number by next Tuesday or Wednesday. It is hard writing under these bird-of-passage circumstances, but I have no reason to complain, God knows, having come to no knot yet. . . . I hope you will like Mrs. Pipchin's establishment. It is from the life, and I was there —I don't suppose I was eight years old; but I remember it all as well, and certainly understood it as well, as I do now. We should be devilish sharp in what we do to children. I thought of that passage in my small life, at Geneva. Shall I leave you my life in MS. when I die? There are some things in it that would touch you very much, and that might go on the same shelf with the first volume of Holcroft's."

On the Monday week after that was written he left Lausanne for Paris, and my first letter to him there was to say that he had overwritten his number by three pages. "I have taken out about two pages and a half," he wrote by return from the Hôtel Brighton, "and the rest I must ask you to take out with the assurance that you will satisfy me in whatever you do. The sale, prodigious indeed! I am very thankful." Next day he wrote as to Walter. "I see it will be best as you advise, to give that idea up; and indeed I don't feel it would be reasonable to carry it out now. I am far from sure it could be wholesomely done, after the interest he has acquired. But when I have disposed of Paul (poor boy!) I will consider the subject further." The subject was never resumed. He was at the opening of his admirable fourth part, when, on 6 December, he wrote from the Rue de Courcelles: "Here am I, writing letters, and delivering opinions, politico-economical and otherwise, as if there were no undone number, and no undone Dick! Well. Così va il mondo (God bless me! Italian! I beg your pardon) —and one must keep one's spirits up, if possible, even under *Dombey* pressure. Paul, I shall slaughter at the end of number five. His school ought to be pretty good, but I haven't been able to dash at it freely, yet. However, I have avoided unnecessary dialogue so far, to avoid overwriting; and all I *have* written is point."

And so, in "point," it went to the close; the rich humour of its picture of Doctor Blimber and his pupils, alternating with the quaint pathos of its picture of little Paul; the first a good-natured exposure of the forcing-system and its fruits, as useful as the sterner revelation in *Nickleby* of the atrocities of Mr. Squeers, and the last even less attractive for the sweet sadness of its foreshadowing of a child's death, than for those images of a vague, strange thoughtfulness, of a shrewd unconscious intellect, of mysterious small philosophies and questionings, by which the young old-fashioned little creature has a glamour thrown over him as he is passing away. It was wonderfully original, this treatment of the part that thus preceded the close of Paul's little life; and of which the first conception, as I have shown, was an after-thought. It took the death itself out of the region of pathetic commonplaces, and gave it the proper relation to the sorrow of the little sister that survives it. It is a fairy vision to a piece of actual suffering; a sorrow with heaven's hues upon it, to a sorrow with all the bitterness of earth.

The number had been finished, he had made his visit to London, and was again in the Rue de Courcelles, when on Christmas Day he sent me its hearty old wishes, and a letter

of Jeffrey's on his new story of which the first and second part
had reached him. "Many merry Christmases, many happy new
years, unbroken friendship, great accumulation of cheerful recollections, affection on earth, and Heaven at last! . . . Is it not a
strange example of the hazard of writing in parts, that a man
like Jeffrey should form his notion of Dombey and Miss Tox
on three months' knowledge? I have asked him the same
question, and advised him to keep his eye on both of them as
time rolls on. I do not at heart, however, lay much real stress
on his opinion, though one is naturally proud of awakening such
sincere interest in the breast of an old man who has so long
worn the blue and yellow. . . . He certainly did some service in
his old criticisms, especially to Crabbe. And though I don't think
so highly of Crabbe as I once did (feeling a dreary want of fancy
in his poems), I think he deserved the painstaking and conscientious tracking with which Jeffrey followed him." . . . Six
days later he described himself sitting down to the performance
of one of his greatest achievements, his number five, "most
abominably dull and stupid. I have only written a slip, but
I hope to get to work in strong earnest to-morrow. It occurred
to me on special reflection, that the first chapter should be with
Paul and Florence, and that it should leave a pleasant impression of the little fellow being happy, before the reader is called
upon to see him die. I mean to have a genteel breaking-up at
Doctor Blimber's therefore, for the Midsummer vacation; and
to show him in a little quiet light (now dawning through the
chinks of my mind), which I hope will create an agreeable
impression." Then, two days later: ". . . I am working very
slowly. You will see in the first two or three lines of the enclosed
first subject, with what idea I am ploughing along. It is difficult;
but a new way of doing it, it strikes me, and likely to be pretty."
    And then, after three days more, came something of a damper
to his spirits, as he thus toiled along. He saw public allusion
made to a review that had appeared in *The Times* of his Christmas book, and it momentarily touched what he too truly called
his morbid susceptibility to exasperation. "I see that the 'good
old *Times*' are again at issue with the inimitable B. Another
touch of a blunt razor on B.'s nervous system.—Friday morning.
Inimitable very mouldy and dull. Hardly able to work. Dreamed
of *Timeses* all night. Disposed to go to New Zealand and start
a magazine." But soon he sprang up, as usual, more erect for
the moment's pressure; and after not many days I heard that
the number was as good as done. His letter was very brief, and

told me that he had worked so hard the day before (Tuesday, 12 January), and so incessantly, night as well as morning, that he had breakfasted and lain in bed till midday. "I hope I have been very successful." There was but one small chapter more to write, in which he and his little friend were to part company for ever; and the greater part of the night of the day on which it was written. Thursday, the 14th, he was wandering desolate and sad about the streets of Paris. I arrived there the following morning on my visit; and as I alighted from the malle-poste, a little before eight o'clock, I found him waiting for me at the gate of the post office bureau.

I left him on 2 February with his writing-table in readiness for number six; but on the 4th, enclosing me subjects for illustration, he told me he was "not under weigh yet. Can't begin." Then, on the 7th, his birthday, he wrote to me he should be late. "Could not begin before Thursday last, and find it very difficult indeed to fall into the new vein of the story. I see no hope of finishing before the 16th at the earliest, in which case the steam will have to be put on for this short month. But it can't be helped. Perhaps I shall get a rush of inspiration. . . . I will send the chapters as I write them, and you must not wait, of course, for me to read the end in type. To transfer to Florence, instantly, all the previous interest, is what I am aiming at. For that, all sorts of other points must be thrown aside in this number. . . . We are going to dine again at the Embassy to-day—with a very ill will on my part. All well. I hope when I write next I shall report myself in better cue . . . I have had a tremendous outpouring from Jeffrey about the last part, which he thinks the best thing past, present, or to come." Three more days and I had the MS. of the completed chapter, nearly half the number (in which as printed it stands second, the small middle chapter having been transposed to its place). "I have taken the most prodigious pains with it; the difficulty, after Paul's death being very great. May you like it! My head aches over it now (I write at one o'clock in the morning), and I am strange to it. . . . I think I shall manage Dombey's second wife (introduced by the Major), and the beginning of that business in his present state of mind, very naturally and well. . . . Paul's death has amazed Paris. All sorts of people are open-mouthed with admiration. . . . When I have done, I'll write you *such* a letter! Don't cut me short in your letters just now, because I'm working hard. . . . *I*'ll make up. . . . Snow—snow—snow— a foot thick." The day after this, came the brief chapter which was printed as the first: and then, on the 16th, which he had fixed as his limit for completion, the close reached me; but I had meanwhile sent him out so much of the proof as convinced him that he had underwritten his number by at least two pages, and determined him to come to London. The incident has been told which soon after closed his residence abroad, and what remained of his story was written in England.

I shall not further dwell upon it in any detail. It extended over the whole of the year; and the interest and passion of it, when both became centred in Florence and in Edith Dombey, took stronger hold of him than any of his previous writings, excepting only the close of the *Old Curiosity Shop*. Jeffrey compared Florence to Little Nell, but the differences from the outset are very marked, and it is rather in what disunites or separates them that we seem to find the purpose in each. If the one, amid much strange and grotesque violence surrounding her, expresses the innocent unconsciousness of childhood to such rough ways of the world, passing unscathed as Una to her home beyond it, the other is this character in action and resistance, a brave young resolute heart that will *not* be crushed, and neither sinks nor yields, but works out her own redemption from earth's roughest trials. Of Edith from the first Jeffrey judged more rightly; and, when the story was nearly half done, expressed his opinion about her, and about the book itself, in language that pleased Dickens for the special reason that at the time this part of the book had seemed to many to have fallen greatly short of the splendour of its opening. Jeffrey said however quite truly, claiming to be heard with authority as his "Critic-laureate," that of all his writings it was perhaps the most finished in diction, and that it equalled the best in the delicacy and fineness of its touches, "while it rises to higher and deeper passions, not resting, like most of the former, in sweet thoughtfulness and thrilling and attractive tenderness, but boldly wielding all the lofty and terrible elements of tragedy, and bringing before us the appalling struggles of a proud, scornful, and repentant spirit." Not that she was exactly this. Edith's worst qualities are but the perversion of what should have been her best. A false education in her, and a tyrant passion in her husband, make them other than nature meant; and both show how life may run its evil course against the higher dispensations.

As the catastrophe came in view, a nice point in the management of her character and destiny arose. I quote from a letter of 19 November, when he was busy with his fourteenth part

"Of course she hates Carker in the most deadly degree. I have not elaborated that, now, because (as I was explaining to Browne the other day) I have relied on it very much for the effect of her death. But I have no question that what you suggest will be an improvement. The strongest place to put it in, would be the close of the chapter immediately before this last one. I want to make the two first chapters as light as I can, but I will try to do it, solemnly, in that place." Then came the effect of this fourteenth number on Jeffrey; raising the question of whether the end might not come by other means than her death, and bringing with it a more bitter humiliation for her destroyer. While engaged on the fifteenth (21 December) Dickens thus wrote to me: "I am thoroughly delighted that you like what I sent. I enclose designs. Shadow-plate, poor. But I think Mr. Dombey admirable. One of the prettiest things in the book ought to be at the end of the chapter I am writing now. But in Florence's marriage, and in her subsequent return to her father, I see a brilliant opportunity. . . . Note from Jeffrey this morning, who won't believe (positively refuses) that Edith is Carker's mistress. What do you think of a kind of inverted Maid's Tragedy, and a tremendous scene of her un-deceiving Carker, and giving him to know that she never meant that?" So it was done; and when he sent me the chapter in which Edith says adieu to Florence, I had nothing but pleasure to express. "I need not say," he wrote in reply, "I can't, how delighted and overjoyed I am by what you say and feel of it. I propose to show Dombey *twice* more; and in the end, leave him exactly as you describe." The end came; and, at the last moment when correction was possible, this note arrived. "I suddenly remember that I have forgotten Diogenes. Will you put him in the last little chapter? After the word 'favourite' in reference to Miss Tox, you can add, 'except with Diogenes, who is growing old and wilful.' Or, on the last page of all, after 'and with them two children: boy and girl' (I quote from memory), you might say 'and an old dog is generally in their company,' or to that effect. Just what you think best."

That was on Saturday, 25 March, 1848, and may be my last reference to *Dombey* until the book, in its place with the rest, finds critical allusion when I close. But as the confidences revealed in this chapter have dealt wholly with the leading currents of interests, there is yet room for a word on incidental persons in the story, of whom I have seen other so-called confidences alleged which it will be only right to state

have really no authority. And first let me say what unquestionable evidence these characters give of the unimpaired freshness,
variety, and fitness of Dickens's invention at this time. Glorious
Captain Cuttle, laying his head to the wind and fighting through
everything; his friend Jack Bunsby, with a head too ponderous   * 75
to lay-to, and so falling victim to the inveterate MacStinger;
good-hearted, modest, considerate Toots, whose brains rapidly
go as his whiskers come, but who yet gets back from contact
with the world, in his shambling way, some fragments of the
sense pumped out of him by the forcing Blimbers; breathless
Susan Nipper, beaming Polly Toodle, the plaintive Wickam
and the awful Pipchin, each with her duty in the starched
Dombey household so nicely appointed as to seem born for only
that; simple thoughtful old Gills and his hearty young lad of a
nephew; Mr. Toodle and his children, with the charitable grinder's
decline and fall; Miss Tox, obsequious flatterer from nothing
but good-nature; spectacled and analytic, but not unkind Miss
Blimber; and the good droning dull benevolent Doctor himself,
withering even the fruits of his well-spread dinner-table with his
It is remarkable, Mr. Feeder, that the Romans—"at the mention
of which terrible people, their implacable enemies, every young
gentleman fastened his gaze upon the Doctor, with an assumption of the deepest interest." So vivid and life-like were all
these people, to the very youngest of the young gentlemen,
that it became natural eagerly to seek out for them actual
prototypes; but I think I can say with some confidence of them
all, that, whatever single traits may have been taken from
persons known to him (a practice with all writers, and very
specially with Dickens), only two had living originals. His own
experience of Mrs. Pipchin has been related; I had myself some
knowledge of Miss Blimber; and the Little Wooden Midshipman did actually (perhaps does still) occupy his post of observation in Leadenhall Street. The names that have been connected,
I doubt not in perfect good faith, with Sol Gills, Perch the
Messenger, and Captain Cuttle, have certainly not more foundation than the fancy a courteous correspondent favours me with,
that the redoubtable Captain must have sat for his portrait
to Charles Lamb's blustering, loud-talking, hook-handed Mr.
Mingay. As to the amiable and excellent city-merchant whose
name has been given to Mr. Dombey, he might with the
same amount of justice or probability be supposed to have
originated Coriolanus or Timon of Athens.

III

THE portion of Dickens's life over which his adventures of strolling extended was in other respects not without interest; and this chapter will deal with some of his seaside holidays before I pass to the publication in 1848 of the story of *The Haunted Man*, and to the establishment in 1850 of the Periodical which had been in his thoughts for half a dozen years before, and has had foreshadowings nearly as frequent in my pages.

Among the incidents of 1848 before the holiday season came, were the dethronement of Louis Philippe, and birth of the second French republic: on which I ventured to predict that a Gore House friend of ours, and *his* friend, would in three days be on the scene of action. The three days passed, and I had this letter. "Mardi, Février 29, 1848. MON CHER. Vous êtes homme de la plus grande pénétration! Ah, mon Dieu, que vous êtes absolument magnifique! Vous prévoyez presque toutes les choses qui vont arriver; et aux choses qui viennent d'arriver vous êtes merveilleusement au-fait. Ah, cher enfant, quelle idée sublime vous vous aviez à la tête quand vous prévîtes si claire-ment que M. le Comte Alfred d'Orsay se rendrait au pays de sa naissance! Quel magicien! Mais—c'est tout égal, mais—il n'est pas parti. Il reste à Gore House, où, avant-hier, il y avait un grand dîner à tout le monde. Mais quel homme, quel ange, néanmoins! MON AMI, je trouve que j'aime tant la République, qu'il me faut renoncer ma langue et écrire seulement le langage de la République de France—langage des Dieux et des Anges —langage, en un mot, des Français! Hier au soir je rencontrai à l'Athenæum Monsieur Mack Leese, qui me dit que MM. les Commissionnaires des Beaux Arts lui avaient écrit, par leur secrétaire, un billet de remerciements à propos de son tableau dans la Chambre des Députés, et qu'ils lui avaient prié de faire l'autre tableau en fresque, dont on y a besoin. Ce qu'il a promis. Voici des nouvelles pour les champs de Lincoln's Inn! Vive la gloire

36

de France! Vive la République! Vive le Peuple! Plus de Royauté!
Plus de Bourbons! Plus de Guizot! Mort aux traîtres! Faisons
couler le sang pour la liberté, la justice, la cause populaire!
Jusqu'à cinq heures et demie, adieu, mon brave! Recevez
l'assurance de ma considération distinguée, et croyez-moi, CON-
CITOYEN! votre tout dévoué, CITOYEN CHARLES DICKENS." I
proved to be not quite so wrong, nevertheless, as my friend
supposed.

Somewhat earlier than usual this summer, on the close of
the Shakespeare House performances, he tried Broadstairs once
more, having no important writing in hand: but in the brief
interval before leaving he saw a thing of celebrity in those
days, the Chinese junk; and I had all the details in so good a
description that I could not resist the temptation of using some
parts of it at the time. "Drive down to the Blackwall railway,"
he wrote to me, "and for a matter of eighteen-pence you are
at the Chinese Empire in no time. In half a score of minutes,
the tiles and chimney-pots, backs of squalid houses, frowsy
pieces of waste ground, narrow courts and streets, swamps,
ditches, masts of ships, gardens of duckweed, and unwholesome little bowers of scarlet beans, whirl away in a flying dream,
and nothing is left but China. How the flowery region ever
came into this latitude and longitude is the first thing one asks;
and it is not certainly the least of the marvel. As Aladdin's
palace was transported hither and thither by the rubbing of a
lamp, so the crew of Chinamen aboard the *Keying* devoutly
believed that their good ship would turn up, quite safe, at the
desired port, if they only tied red rags enough upon the mast,
rudder, and cable. Somehow they did not succeed. Perhaps they
ran short of rag; at any rate they hadn't enough on board to
keep them above water; and to the bottom they would undoubtedly have gone but for the skill and coolness of a dozen
English sailors, who brought them over the ocean in safety.
Well, if there be any one thing in the world that this extraordinary craft is not at all like, that thing is a ship of any
kind. So narrow, so long, so grotesque; so low in the middle,
so high at each end, like a China pen-tray; with no rigging,
with nowhere to go to aloft; with mats for sails, great warped
cigars for masts, gaudy dragons and sea-monsters disporting
themselves from stem to stern, and *on* the stern a gigantic cock
of impossible aspect, defying the world (as well he may) to
produce his equal—it would look more at home at the top of
a public building, or at the top of a mountain, or in an avenue

of trees, or down in a mine, than afloat on the water. As for
the Chinese lounging on the deck, the most extravagant imagination would never dare to suppose them to be mariners. Imagine
a ship's crew, without a profile among them, in gauze pinafores
and plaited hair; wearing stiff clogs a quarter of a foot thick
in the sole; and lying at night in little scented boxes, like back-
gammon men or chess-pieces, or mother-of-pearl counters! But
by Jove! even this is nothing to your surprise when you go
down into the cabin. There you get into a torture of perplexity.
As, what became of all those lanterns hanging to the roof when
the Junk was out at sea? Whether they dangled there, banging
and beating against each other, like so many jesters' baubles?
Whether the idol Chin Tee, of the eighteen arms, enshrined in
a celestial Punch's Show, in the place of honour, ever tumbled
out in heavy weather? Whether the incense and the joss-stick
still burnt before her, with a faint perfume and a little thread
of smoke, while the mighty waves were roaring all around?
Whether that preposterous tissue-paper umbrella in the corner
was always spread, as being a convenient maritime instrument
for walking about the decks with in a storm? Whether all the
cool and shiny little chairs and tables were continually sliding
about and bruising each other, and if not why not? Whether
anybody on the voyage ever read those two books printed in
characters like bird-cages and fly-traps? Whether the Mandarin
passenger, He Sing, who had never been ten miles from home
in his life before, lying sick on a bamboo couch in a private
china closet of his own (where he is now perpetually writing
autographs for inquisitive barbarians), ever began to doubt the
potency of the Goddess of the Sea, whose counterfeit presentment,
like a flowery monthly nurse, occupies the sailors' joss-house in
the second gallery? Whether it is possible that the said Mandarin,
or the artist of the ship, Sam Sing, Esquire, R.A. of Canton, *can*
ever go ashore without a walking-staff of cinnamon, agreeably
to the usage of their likenesses in British tea-shops? Above all,
whether the hoarse old ocean could ever have been seriously
in earnest with this floating toy-shop; or had merely played
with it in lightness of spirit—roughly, but meaning no harm
—as the bull did with another kind of china-shop on St.
Patrick's Day in the morning."

The reply made on this brought back comment and sequel
not less amusing. "Yes, there can be no question that this is
Finality in perfection; and it is a great advantage to have the
doctrine so beautifully worked out, and shut up in a corner of

a dock near a fashionable white-bait house for the edification of man. Thousands of years have passed away since the first junk was built on this model, and the last junk ever launched was no better for that waste and desert of time. The mimic eye painted on their prows to assist them in finding their way, has opened as wide and seen as far as any actual organ of sight in all the interval through the whole immense extent of that strange country. It has been set in the flowery head to as little purpose for thousands of years. With all their patient and ingenious but never advancing art, and with all their rich and diligent agricultural cultivation, not a new twist or curve has been given to a ball of ivory, and not a blade of experience has been grown. There is a genuine finality in that; and when one comes from behind the wooden screen that encloses the curious sight, to look again upon the river and the mighty signs on its banks of life, enterprise, and progress, the question that comes nearest is beyond doubt a home one. Whether *we* ever by any chance, in storms, trust to red rags; or burn joss-sticks before idols; or grope our way by the help of conventional eyes that have no sight in them; or sacrifice substantial facts for absurd forms? The ignorant crew of the *Keying* refused to enter on the ship's books, until 'a considerable amount of silvered-paper, tinfoil, and joss-stick' had been laid in by the owners for the purposes of their worship. And I wonder whether *our* seamen, let alone our bishops and deacons, ever stand out upon points of silvered-paper and tinfoil and joss-sticks. To be sure Christianity is not Chin-Teeism, and that I suppose is why we never lose sight of the end in contemptible and insignificant quarrels about the means. There is enough matter for reflection aboard the *Keying* at any rate to last one's voyage home to England again."

Other letters of the summer from Broadstairs will complete what he wrote from the same place last year on Mr. Cruikshank's efforts in the cause of temperance, and will enable me to say, what I know he wished to be remembered in his story, that there was no subject on which through his whole life he felt more strongly than this. No man advocated temperance, even as far as possible its legislative enforcement, with greater earnestness; but he made important reservations. Not thinking drunkenness to be a vice inborn, or incident to the poor more than to other people, he never would agree that the existence of a gin-shop was the alpha and omega of it. Believing it to be *the* "national horror," he also believed that many operative causes had to do with having made it so; and his objection to the temperance agitation was that these were left out of account altogether. He thought the gin-shop not fairly to be rendered the exclusive object of attack, until, in connection with the classes who mostly made it their resort, the temptations that led to it, physical and moral, should have been more bravely dealt with. Among the former he counted foul smells, disgusting habitations, bad workshops, and workshop-customs, scarcity of light, air, and water, in short the absence of all easy means of decency and health; and among the latter, the mental weariness and languor so induced, the desire of wholesome relaxation, the craving for *some* stimulus and excitement, not less needful than the sun itself to lives so passed, and last, and inclusive of all the rest, ignorance, and the want of rational mental training generally applied. This was consistently Dickens's "platform" throughout the years he was known to me; and holding it to be within the reach as well as the scope of legislation, which even our political magnates have been discovering lately, he thought intemperance to be but the one result that, out of all or those arising from the absence of legislation, was the most wretched. For him, drunkenness had a teeming and reproachful history anterior to the drunken stage; and he thought it the first duty of the moralist bent upon annihilating the gin-shop, to "strike deep and spare not" at those previous remediable evils. Certainly this was not the way of Mr. Cruikshank, any more than it is that of the many excellent people who take part in temperance agitations. His former tale of the *Bottle*, as told by his admirable pencil, was that of a decent working man, father of a boy and a girl, living in comfort and good esteem until near the middle age, when happening unluckily to have a goose for dinner one day in the bosom of his thriving family, he jocularly sends out for a bottle of gin, persuades his wife, until then a picture of neatness, and good housewifery, to take a little drop after the stuffing, and the whole family from that moment drink themselves to destruction. The sequel, of which Dickens now wrote to me, traced the lives of the boy and girl after the wretched deaths of their drunken parents, through gin-shop, beer-shop, and dancing-rooms, up to their trial for robbery: when the boy is convicted, dying aboard the hulks; and the girl desolate and mad after her acquittal, flings herself from London Bridge into the night-darkened river.

"I think," said Dickens, "the power of that closing scene quite extraordinary. It haunts the remembrance like an awful reality. It is full of passion and terror, and I doubt very much whether any hand but his could so have rendered it. There are other fine things too. The death-bed scene on board the hulks; the convict who is composing the face, and the other who is drawing the screen round the bed's head; seem to me master-pieces worthy of the greatest painter. The reality of the place, and the fidelity with which every minute object illustrative of it is presented, are surprising. I think myself no bad judge of this feature, and it is remarkable throughout. In the trial scene at the Old Bailey, the eye may wander round the Court, and observe everything that is a part of the place. The very light and atmos-phere are faithfully reproduced. So, in the gin-shop and the beer-shop. An inferior hand would indicate a fragment of the fact, and slur it over; but here every shred is honestly made out. The man behind the bar in the gin-shop, is as real as the convicts at the hulks, or the barristers round the table in the Old Bailey. I found it quite curious, as I closed the book, to recall the number of faces, I had seen of individual identity, and to think what a chance they have of living, as the Spanish friar said to Wilkie, when the living have passed away. But it only makes more exasper-ating to me the obstinate one-sidedness of the thing. When a man shows so forcibly the side of the medal on which the people in their faults and crimes are stamped, he is the more bound to help us to a glance at that other side on which the faults and vices of the governments placed over the people are not less gravely impressed."

This led to some remark on Hogarth's method in such matters, and I am glad to be able to preserve a masterly criticism of that great Englishman, by a writer who closely resembled him in genius; as another generation will be prob-ably more apt than our own to discover. "Hogarth avoided the Drunkard's Progress, I conceive, precisely because the causes of drunkenness among the poor were so numerous and widely spread, and lurked so sorrowfully deep and far down in all human misery, neglect, and despair, that even *his* pencil could not bring them fairly and justly into the light. It was never his plan to be content with only showing the effect. In the death of the miser-father, his shoes new-soled with the binding of his Bible, before the young Rake begins his career; in the worldly father, listless daughter, impoverished young lord, and crafty lawyer, of the first plate of Marriage-à-la-mode; in the detestable advances through the stages of Cruelty; and in the progress downward of Thomas Idle; you see the effects indeed, but also the causes. He was never disposed to spare the kind of drunkenness that was of more 'respectable' engender-ment, as one sees in his Midnight Modern Conversation, the election plates, and crowds of stupid aldermen and other guzzlers. But after one immortal journey down Gin Lane, he turned away in pity and sorrow—perhaps in hope of better things, one day, from better laws and schools and poor men's homes—and went back no more. The scene of Gin Lane, you know, is that just cleared away for the extension of Oxford Street, which we were looking at the other day; and I think it a remarkable trait of Hogarth's picture, that, while it exhibits drunkenness in the most appalling forms, it also forces on attention a most neglected wretched neighbourhood, and an unwholesome, indecent abject condition of life that might be put as frontispiece to our sanitary report of a hundred years later date. I have always myself thought the purpose of this fine piece to be not adequately stated even by Charles Lamb. 'The very houses seem absolutely reeling' it is true; but beside that wonderful picture of what follows intoxication, we have indication quite as powerful of what leads to it among the neglected classes. There is no evi-dence that any of the actors in the dreary scene have ever been much better than we see them there. The best are pawning the commonest necessaries, and tools of their trades; and the worst are homeless vagrants who give us no clue to their having been otherwise in bygone days. All are living and dying miserably. Nobody is interfering for prevention or for cure, in the genera-tion going out before us, or the generation coming in. The beadle is the only sober man in the composition except the pawn-broker, and he is mightily indifferent to the orphan-child crying beside its parent's coffin. The little charity-girls are not so well taught or looked after, but that they can take to dram-drinking already. The church indeed is very prominent and handsome; but as, quite passive in the picture, it coldly surveys these things in progress under shadow of its tower, I cannot but bethink me that it was not until this year of grace 1848 that a Bishop of London first came out respecting something wrong in poor men's social accommodations, and I am confirmed in my suspicion that Hogarth had many meanings which have not grown obsolete in a century."

Another art-criticism by Dickens should be added. Upon a separate publication by Leech of some drawings on stones called the Rising Generation, from designs done for Mr. Punch's gallery, he wrote at my request a little essay of which a few

sentences will find appropriate place with his letter on the other
great caricaturist of his time. I use that word, as he did, only
for want of a better. Dickens was of opinion that, in this particular line of illustration, while he conceded all his fame to the
elder and stronger contemporary, Mr. Leech was the very first
Englishman who had made Beauty a part of his art; and he held,
that, by striking out this course, and setting the successful
example of introducing always into his most whimsical pieces
some beautiful faces or agreeable forms, he had done more than
any other man of his generation to refine a branch of art to
which the facilities of steam-printing and wood-engraving were
giving almost unrivalled diffusion and popularity. His opinion
of Leech in a word was that he turned caricature into character;
and would leave behind him not a little of the history of his
time and its follies, sketched with inimitable grace.

"If we turn back to a collection of the works of Rowlandson
or Gilray, we shall find, in spite of the great humour displayed
in many of them, that they are rendered wearisome and unpleasant by a vast amount of personal ugliness. Now, besides
that it is a poor device to represent what is satirised as being
necessarily ugly, which is but the resource of an angry child
or a jealous woman, it serves no purpose but to produce a disagreeable result. There is no reason why the farmer's daughter
in the old caricature who is squalling at the harpsichord (to
the intense delight, by the by, of her worthy father, whom it
is her duty to please) should be squab and hideous. The satire
on the manner of her education, if there be any in the thing at
all, would be just as good, if she were pretty. Mr. Leech would
have made her so. The average of farmers' daughters in
England are not impossible lumps of fat. One is quite as likely
to find a pretty girl in a farm-house, as to find an ugly one,
and we think, with Mr. Leech, that the business of this style
of art is with the pretty one. She is not only a pleasanter object,
but we have more interest in her. We care more about what
does become her, and does not become her. Mr. Leech represented the other day certain delicate creatures with bewitching
countenances encased in several varieties of that amazing gar-
ment, the ladies' paletot. Formerly those fair creatures would
have been made as ugly and ungainly as possible, and then
the point would have been lost. The spectator, with a laugh
at the absurdity of the whole group, would not have cared how
such uncouth creatures disguised themselves, or how ridiculous
they became. . . . But to represent female beauty as Mr. Leech

represents it, an artist must have a most delicate perception of it; and the gift of being able to realise it to us with two or three slight, sure touches of his pencil. This power Mr. Leech possesses, in an extraordinary degree. . . . For this reason, we enter our protest against those of the Rising Generation who are precociously in love being made the subject of merriment by a pitiless and unsympathising world. We never saw a boy more distinctly in the right than the young gentleman kneeling on the chair to beg a lock of hair from his pretty cousin, to take back to school. Madness is in her apron, and Virgil dog's-eared and defaced is in her ringlets. Doubts may suggest themselves of the perfect disinterestedness of the other young gentleman contemplating the fair girl at the piano—doubts engendered by his worldly allusion to 'tin'; though even that may have arisen in his modest consciousness of his own inability to support an establishment—but that he should be 'deucedly inclined to go and cut that fellow out,' appears to us one of the most natural emotions of the human breast. The young gentleman with the dishevelled hair and clasped hands who loves the transcendent beauty with the bouquet, and can't be happy without her, is to us a withering and desolate spectacle. Who *could* be happy without her? . . . The growing youths are not less happily observed and agreeably depicted than the grown women. The languid little creature who 'hasn't danced since he was quite a boy,' is perfect; and the eagerness of the small dancer whom he declines to receive for a partner at the hands of the glorious old lady of the house (the little feet quite ready for the first position, the whole heart projected into the quadrille, and the glance peeping timidly at the desired one out of a flutter of hope and doubt) is quite delightful to look at. The intellectual juvenile who awakens the tremendous wrath of a Norma of private life by considering woman an inferior animal, is lecturing at the present moment, we understand, on the Concrete in connection with the Will. The legs of the young philosopher who considers Shakespeare an overrated man, were seen by us dangling over the side of an omnibus last Tuesday. We have no acquaintance with the scowling young gentleman who is clear that 'if his Governor don't like the way he goes on in, why he must have chambers and so much a week'; but if he is not by this time in Van Dieman's Land, he will certainly go to it through Newgate. We should exceedingly dislike to have personal property in a strong box, to live in the suburb of Camberwell, and to be in the relation of bachelor-uncle to that youth. . . . In all his designs, whatever Mr. Leech desires to do, he does. His drawing seems to us charming; and the expression indicated, though by the simplest means, is exactly the natural expression, and is recognised as such immediately. Some forms of our existing life will never have a better chronicler. His wit is good-natured, and always the wit of a gentleman. He has a becoming sense of responsibility and self-restraint; he delights in agreeable things; he imparts some pleasant air of his own to things not pleasant in themselves; he is suggestive and full of matter; and he is always improving. Into the tone as well as into the execution of what he does, he has brought a certain elegance which is altogether new, without involving any compromise of what is true. Popular art in England has not had so rich an acquisition." Dickens's closing allusion was to a remark made by Mr. Ford in a review of *Oliver Twist* formerly referred to. "It is eight or ten years since a writer in the *Quarterly Review*, making mention of Mr. George Cruikshank, commented on the absurdity of excluding such a man from the Royal Academy, because his works were not produced in certain materials, and did not occupy a certain space in its annual shows. Will no Associates be found upon its books one of these days, the labours of whose oil and brushes will have sunk into the profoundest obscurity, when many pencil-marks of Mr. Cruikshank and of Mr. Leech will be still fresh in half the houses in the land?"

Of what otherwise occupied him at Broadstairs in 1848 there is not much to mention until the close of his holiday. He used to say that he never went for more than a couple of days from his own home without something befalling him that never happened to anyone else, and his Broadstairs adventure of the present summer verged closer on tragedy than comedy. Returning there one day in August after bringing up his boys to school, it had been arranged that his wife should meet him at Margate; but he had walked impatiently far beyond the place for meeting when at last he caught sight of her, not in a small chaise but in a large carriage and pair followed by an excited crowd, and with the youth that should have been driving the little pony bruised and bandaged on the box behind the two prancing horses. "You may faintly imagine my amazement at encountering this carriage, and the strange people, and Kate, and the crowd, and the bandaged one, and all the rest of it." And then in a line or two I had the story. "At the top of a steep hill on the road, with a ditch on each side, the pony bolted, whereupon what does John but jump out! He says he was thrown out, but it cannot be. The reins immediately became entangled in the wheels, and away went the pony down the hill madly, with Kate inside rending the Isle of Thanet with her screams. The accident might have been a fearful one, if the pony had not, thank Heaven, on getting to the bottom, pitched over the side; breaking the shaft and cutting her hind legs, but in the most extraordinary manner smashing her own way apart. She tumbled down, a bundle of legs with her head tucked underneath, and left the chaise standing on the bank! A Captain Devaynes and his wife were passing in their carriage at the moment, saw the accident with no power of preventing it, got Kate out, laid her on the grass, and behaved with infinite kindness. All's well that ends well, and I think she's really none the worse for the fright. John is in bed a good deal bruised, but without any broken bone, and likely soon to come right; though for the present plastered all over, and, like Squeers, a brown-paper parcel chock-full of nothing but groans. The women generally have no sympathy for him whatever, and the nurse says, with indignation, How could he go and leave a unprotected female in the shay!"

Holiday incidents there were many, but none that need detain us. This was really a summer idleness: for it was the interval between two of his important undertakings, there was no periodical yet to make demands on him, and only the task of finishing his *Haunted Man* for Christmas lay ahead. But he did even his nothings in a strenuous way, and on occasion could make gallant fight against the elements themselves. He reported himself, to my horror, thrice wet through on a single day, "dressed four times," and finding all sorts of great things, brought out by the rains, among the rocks on the sea-beach. He also sketched now and then morsels of character for me, of which I will preserve one. "F. is philosophical, from sunrise to bedtime: chiefly in the French line, about French women going mad, and in that state coming to their husbands, and saying, 'Mon ami, je vous ai trompé. Voici les lettres de mon amant!' Whereupon the husbands take the letters and think them waste paper, and become extra-philosophical at finding that they really *were* the lover's effusions: though what there is of philosophy in it all, or anything but unwholesomeness, it is not easy to see." (A remark that it might not be out of place to offer to Mr. Taine's notice.) "Likewise about dark shades coming over our wedded Emmeline's face at parties; and about F. handing her to her carriage, and saying, 'May I come in,

for a lift homeward?' and she bending over him out of the
window, and saying in a low voice, I DARE NOT! And then of
the carriage driving away like lightning, leaving F. more
philosophical than ever on the pavement." Not till the close
of September I heard of work intruding itself, in a letter twitting
me for a broken promise in not joining him: "We are reasonably
jolly, but rurally so; going to bed o' nights at ten, and bathing
o' mornings at half-past seven; and not drugging ourselves with
those dirty and spoiled waters of Lethe that flow round the base
of the great pyramid." Then, after mention of the friends who
had left him, Sheriff Gordon, the Leeches, Lemon, Egg and
Stone: "reflection and pensiveness are coming. I have NOT

'—seen Fancy write
With a pencil of light
On the blotter so solid, commanding the sea!'

but I shouldn't wonder if she were to do it, one of these days.
Dim visions of divers things are floating around me; and I must
go to work, head foremost, when I get home. I am glad, after
all, that I have not been at it here, for I am all the better for
my idleness, no doubt. . . . Roche was very ill last night, and
looks like one with his face turned to the other world, this
morning. When *are* you coming? Oh what days and nights
there have been here, this week past!" My consent to a suggestion in his next letter, that I should meet him on his way
back, and join him in a walking-excursion home, got me full
absolution for broken promises; and the way we took will remind
friends of his later life, when he was lord of Gadshill, of an object
of interest which he delighted in taking them to see. "You will
come down booked for Maidstone (I will meet you at Paddock
Wood), and we will go thither in company over a most beautiful
little line of railroad. The eight miles walk from Maidstone to
Rochester, and a visit to the Druidical altar on the wayside,
are charming. This could be accomplished on the Tuesday; and
Wednesday we might look about us at Chatham, coming home
by Cobham on Thursday. . . ."

His first seaside holiday in 1849 was at Brighton, where he
passed some weeks in February; and not, I am bound to add,
without the *un*usual adventure to signalise his visit. He had
not been a week in his lodgings, where Leech and his wife
joined him, when both his landlord and the daughter of his
landlord went raving mad, and the lodgers were driven away
to the Bedford Hotel. "If you could have heard the cursing and

crying of the two; could have seen the physician and nurse quoited out into the passage by the madman at the hazard of their lives; could have seen Leech and me flying to the doctor's rescue; could have seen our wives pulling us back; could have seen the M.D. faint with fear; could have seen three other M.D.'s come to his aid; with an atmosphere of Mrs. Gamps, strait-waistcoats, struggling friends and servants, surrounding the whole; you would have said it was quite worthy of me, and quite in keeping with my usual proceedings." The letter ended with a word on what then his thoughts were full of, but for which no name had yet been found. "A sea-fog to-day, but yesterday inexpressibly delicious. My mind running, like a high sea, on names—not satisfied yet, though." When he next wrote from the seaside, in the beginning of July, he had found the name; had started his book; and was "rushing to Broadstairs" to write the fourth number of *David Copperfield*.

In this came the childish experiences which had left so deep an impression upon him, and over which he had some difficulty in throwing the needful disguises. "Fourteen miles to-day in the country," he had written to me on 21 June, "revolving number four!" Still he did not quite see his way. Three days later he wrote: "On leaving you last night, I found myself summoned on a special jury in the Queen's Bench to-day.
* 76 I have taken no notice of the document, and hourly expect to be dragged forth to a dungeon for contempt of court. I think I should rather like it. It might help me with a new notion or two in my difficulties. Meanwhile I shall take a stroll to-night in the green fields from seven to ten, if you feel inclined to join." His troubles ended when he got to Broadstairs, from which he wrote on 10 July to tell me that agreeably to the plan we had discussed he had introduced a great part of his MS. into the number. "I really think I have done it ingeniously, and with a very complicated interweaving of truth and fiction. Vous verrez. I am getting on like a house afire in point of health, and ditto ditto in point of number."

In the middle of July the number was nearly done, and he was still doubtful where to pass his longer summer holiday. Leech wished to join him in it, and both desired a change from
* 77 Broadstairs. At first he thought of Folkestone, but disappointment there led to a sudden change. "I propose" (15 July) "returning to town to-morrow by the boat from Ramsgate, and going off to Weymouth or the Isle of Wight, or both, early the next morning." A few days after, his choice was made.

He had taken a house at Bonchurch, attracted there by the friend who had made it a place of interest for him during the last few years, the Rev. James White, with whose name and its associations my mind connects inseparably many of Dickens's happiest hours. To pay him fitting tribute would not be easy, if here it were called for. In the kindly shrewd Scotch face, a keen sensitiveness to pleasure and pain was the first thing that struck any common observer. Cheerfulness and gloom coursed over it so rapidly that no one could question the tale they told. But the relish of his life had outlived its more than usual share of sorrows; and quaint sly humour, love of jest and merriment, capital knowledge of books, and sagacious quips at men, made his companionship delightful. Like his life, his genius was made up of alternations of mirth and melancholy. He would be immersed, at one time, in those darkest Scottish annals from which he drew his tragedies; and overflowing, at another, into Sir Frizzle Pumpkin's exuberant farce. The tragic histories may probably perish with the actor's perishable art; but three little abstracts of history written at a later time in prose, with a sunny clearness of narration and a glow of picturesque interest to my knowledge unequalled in books of such small pretension, will find, I hope, a lasting place in literature. They are filled with felicities of phrase, with breadth of understanding and judgment, with manful honesty, quiet sagacity, and a constant cheerful piety, valuable for all and priceless for the young. Another word I permit myself to add. With Dickens, White was popular supremely for his eager good fellowship; and few men brought him more of what he always liked to receive. But he brought nothing so good as his wife. "He is excellent, but she is better," is the pithy remark of his first Bonchurch letter; and the true affection and respect that followed is happily still borne her by his daughters.

Of course there is something strange to be recorded of the Bonchurch holiday, but it does not come till nearer the ending; and, with more attention to Mrs. Malaprop's advice to begin with a little aversion, might probably not have come at all. He began with an excess of liking. Of the Undercliff he was full of admiration. "From the top of the highest downs," he wrote in his second letter (28 July) "there are views which are only to be equalled on the Genoese shore of the Mediterranean; the variety of walks is extraordinary; things are cheap, and everybody is civil. The waterfall acts wonderfully, and the sea bathing is delicious. Best of all, the place is certainly cold rather than hot, in the summer time. The evenings have been even chilly. White very jovial, and emulous of the Inimitable in respect of gin-punch. He had made some for our arrival. Ha! ha! not bad for a beginner. . . . I have been, and am, trying to work this morning; but I can't make anything of it, and am going out to think. I am invited by a distinguished friend to dine with you on the 1st of August, but I have pleaded distance and the being resident in a cave on the seashore; my food, beans; my drink, the water from the rock. . . . I must pluck up heart of grace to write to Jeffrey, of whom I had but poor accounts from Gordon just before leaving. Talfourd delightful, and amuses me mightily. I am really quite enraptured at his success, and think of his happiness with uncommon pleasure." Our friend was now on the bench; which he adorned with qualities that are justly the pride of that profession, and with accomplishments which have become more rare in its highest places than they were in former times. His elevation only made those virtues better known. Talfourd assumed nothing with the ermine but the privilege of more frequent intercourse with the tastes and friends he loved, and he continued to be the most joyous and least affected of companions. Such small oddities or foibles as he had, made him secretly only dearer to Dickens, who had no friend he was more attached to; and the many happy nights made happier by the voice so affluent in generous words, and the face so bright with ardent sensibility, come back to me sorrowfully now. "Deaf the prais'd ear, and mute the tuneful tongue." The poet's line has a double application and sadness.

He wrote again on 1 August. "I have just begun to get into work. We are expecting the Queen to come by very soon, in grand array, and are going to let off ever so many guns. I had a letter from Jeffrey yesterday morning, just as I was going to write to him. He has evidently been very ill, and I begin to have fears for his recovery. It is a very pathetic letter as to his state of mind; but only in a tranquil contemplation of death, which I think very noble." His next letter, four days later, described himself as continuing still at work; but also taking part in dinners at Blackgang, and picnics of "tremendous success" on Shanklin Down. "Two charity sermons for the school are preached to-day, and I go to the afternoon one. The examination of said school t'other day was very funny. All the boys made Buckstone's bow in the *Rough Diamond*, and some in a very wonderful manner recited pieces of poetry, about a clock, and may we be like the clock, which is always a-going and a-doing of its duty, and always tells the truth (supposing it to be a slap-up chronometer I presume, for the American clock in the school was lying frightfully at that moment); and after being bothered to death by the multiplication table, they were refreshed with a public tea in Lady Jane Swinburne's garden." (There was a reference in one of his letters, but I have lost it, to a golden-haired lad of the Swinburnes whom his own boys used to play with, since become more widely known.) "The rain came in with the first tea-pot, and has been active ever since. On Friday we had a grand, and what is better, a very good dinner at 'parson' Fielden's, with some choice port. On Tuesday we are going on another picnic; with the materials for a fire, at my express stipulation; and a great iron pot to boil potatoes in. These things, and the eatables, go to the ground in a cart. Last night we had some very good merriment at White's, where pleasant Julian Young and his wife (who are staying about five miles off) showed some droll new games" —and roused the ambition in my friend to give a "mighty conjuring performance for all the children in Bonchurch," for which I sent him the materials and which went off in a tumult of wild delight. To the familiar names in this letter I will add one more, grieving freshly even now to connect it with suffering. "A letter from Poole has reached me since I began this letter, with tidings in it that you will be very sorry to hear. Poor Regnier has lost his only child; the pretty daughter who dined with us that nice day at your house, when we all pleased the poor mother by admiring her so much. She died of a sudden attack of malignant typhus. Poole was at the funeral, and writes that he never saw, or could have imagined, such intensity of grief as Regnier's at the grave. How one loves him for it. But is it not always true, in comedy and in tragedy, that the more real the man the more genuine the actor?"

After a few more days I heard of progress with his writing in spite of all festivities. "I have made it a rule that the Inimitable is invisible, until two every day. I shall have half the number done, please God, to-morrow. I have not worked quickly here yet, but I don't know what I *may* do. Divers cogitations have occupied my mind at intervals, respecting the dim design." The design was the weekly periodical so often in his thoughts, of which more will appear in my next chapter. His letter closed with intimations of discomfort in his health; of an obstinate cough; and of a determination he had formed to mount daily to the top of the downs. "It makes a great difference in the climate to get a blow there and come down again." Then I heard of the doctor "stethoscoping" him, of his hope that all was right in that quarter, and of rubbings "à la St. John Long" being ordered for his chest. But the mirth still went on. "There has been a Doctor Lankester at Sandown, a very good merry fellow, who has made one at the picnics, and whom I went over and dined with, along with Danby (I remember your liking for Danby, and don't wonder at it), Leech, and White." A letter towards the close of August resumed yet more of his ordinary tone. "We had games and forfeits last night at White's. Davy Roberts's pretty little daughter is there for a week, with her husband, Bicknell's son. There was a dinner first to say good-bye to Danby, who goes to other clergyman's duty, and we were very merry. Mrs. White unchanging; White comically various in his moods. Talfourd comes down next Tuesday, and we think of going over to Ryde on Monday, visiting the play, sleeping there (I don't mean at the play) and bringing the Judge back. Browne is coming down when he has done his month's work. Should you like to go to Alum Bay, while you are here? It would involve a night out, but I think would be very pleasant; and if you think so too, I will arrange it *sub rosa*, so that we may not be, like Bobadil, 'oppressed by numbers.' I mean to take a fly over from Shanklin to meet you at Ryde; so that we can walk back from Shanklin over the landslip, where the scenery is wonderfully beautiful. Stone and Egg are coming next month, and we hope to see Jerrold before we go." Such notices from his letters may be thought hardly worth preserving: but a wonderful vitality in every circumstance, as long as life under any conditions remained to the writer, is the picture they contribute to; nor would it be complete without the addition, that fond as he was, in the intervals of his work, of this abundance and variety of enjoyments, to no man were so essential also those quieter hours of thought, and talk, not obtainable when "oppressed by numbers."

My visit was due at the opening of September, but a few days earlier came the full revelation of which only a passing shadow had reached in two or three previous letters. "Before I think of beginning my next number, I perhaps cannot do better than give you an imperfect description of the results of the climate of Bonchurch after a few weeks' residence. The first salubrious effect of which the Patient becomes conscious is an almost continual feeling of sickness, accompanied with great prostration of strength, so that his legs tremble under him, and his arms quiver when he wants to take hold of any object. An extraordinary disposition to sleep (except at night, when his rest, in the event of his having any, is broken by incessant dreams) is always present at the same time; and, if he have anything to do requiring thought and attention, this overpowers him to such a degree that he can only do it in snatches: lying down on beds in the fitful intervals. Extreme depression of mind, and a disposition to shed tears from morning to night, develops itself at the same period. If the Patient happen to have been a good walker, he finds ten miles an insupportable distance; in the achievement of which his legs are so unsteady, that he goes from side to side of the road, like a drunken man. If he happen to have ever possessed any energy of any kind, he finds it quenched in a dull, stupid languor. He has no purpose, power, or object in existence whatever. When he brushes his hair in the morning, he is so weak that he is obliged to sit upon a chair to do it. He is incapable of reading, at all times. And his bilious system is so utterly overthrown, that a ball of boiling fat appears to be always behind the top of the bridge of his nose, simmering between his haggard eyes. If he should have caught a cold, he will find it impossible to get rid of it, as his system is wholly incapable of making any effort. His cough will be deep, monotonous, and constant. 'The faithful watch-dog's honest bark' will be nothing to it. He will abandon all present idea of overcoming it, and will content himself with keeping an eye upon his blood-vessels to preserve them whole and sound. *Patient's name, Inimitable B. . . .* It's a mortal mistake! —That's the plain fact. Of all the places I ever have been in, I have never been in one so difficult to exist in, pleasantly. Naples is hot and dirty, New York feverish, Washington bilious, Genoa exciting, Paris rainy—but Bonchurch, smashing. I am quite convinced that I should die here, in a year. It's not hot, it's not close, I don't know what it is, but the prostration of it is *awful*. Nobody here has the least idea what I think of it; but I find from all sorts of hints from Kate, Georgina, and the Leeches, that they are all affected more or less in the same way, and find it very difficult to make head against. I make no sign, and pretend not to know what is going on. But they are right. I believe the Leeches will go soon, and small blame to 'em!— For me, when I leave here at the end of this September, I must go down to some cold place; as Ramsgate for example, for a week or two; or I seriously believe I shall feel the effects of it for a long time. . . . What do you think of *that*? . . . The longer I live, the more I doubt the doctors. I am perfectly convinced, that, for people suffering under a wasting disease, this Undercliff is madness altogether. The doctors, with the old miserable folly of looking at one bit of a subject, take the patient's lungs and the Undercliff's air, and settle solemnly that they are fit for each other. But the whole influence of the place, never taken into consideration, is to reduce and overpower vitality. I am quite confident that I should go down under it, as if it were so much lead, slowly crushing me. An American resident in Paris many years, who brought me a letter from Olliffe, said, the day before yesterday, that he had always had a passion for the sea never to be gratified enough, but that after living here a month, he could not bear to look at it; he couldn't endure the sound of it; he didn't know how it was, but it seemed associated with the decay of his whole powers." These were grave imputations against one of the prettiest places in England; but of the generally depressing influence of that Undercliff on particular temperaments, I had already enough experience to abate something of the surprise with which I read the letter. What it too bluntly puts aside are the sufferings other than his own, protected and sheltered by what only aggravated his; but my visit gave me proof that he had really very little overstated the effect upon himself. Making allowance, which sometimes he failed to do, for special peculiarities, and for the excitability never absent when he had in hand an undertaking such as *Copperfield*, there was a nervous tendency to misgivings and apprehensions to the last degree unusual with him, which seemed to make the commonest things difficult; and though he stayed out his time, and brought away nothing that his happier associations with the place and its residents did not long survive, he never returned to Bonchurch.

In the month that remained he completed his fifth number, and with the proof there came the reply to some questions of which I hardly remember more than that they referred to doubts having reference, among other things, to the propriety of the kind of delusion he had first given to poor Mr. Dick, which appeared to be a little too farcical for that really touching delineation of character. "Your suggestion is perfectly wise and sound," he wrote back (22 August). "I have acted on it. I have also, instead of the bull and china-shop delusion, given Dick the idea, that, when the head of King Charles the First was cut off, some of the trouble was taken out of it, and put into his (Dick's)." When he next wrote, there was news very welcome to me for the pleasure to himself it involved. "Browne has sketched an uncommonly characteristic and capital Mr. Micawber for the next number. I hope the present number is a good one. I hear nothing but pleasant accounts of the general satisfaction." The same letter told me of an intention to go to Broadstairs, put aside by doubtful reports of its sanitary condition; but it will be seen presently that there was another graver interruption. With his work well off his hands, however, he had been getting on better where he was; and they had all been very merry. "Yes," he said, writing after a couple of days (23 September), "we have been sufficiently rollicking since I finished the number; and have had great games at rounders every afternoon, with all Bonchurch looking on; but I begin to long for a little peace and solitude. And now for my less pleasing piece of news. The sea has been running very high, and Leech, while bathing, was knocked over by a bad blow from a great wave on the forehead. He is in bed, and had twenty of his namesakes on his temples this morning. When I heard of him just now, he was asleep—which he had not been all night." He closed his letter hopefully, but next day (24 September) I had a less favourable report. "Leech has been very ill with congestion of the brain ever since I wrote, and being still in excessive pain has had ice to his head continuously, and been bled in the arm besides. Beard and I sat up there, all night." On the 26th he wrote. "My plans are all unsettled by Leech's illness; as of course I do not like to leave this place while I can be of any service to him and his good little wife. But all visitors are gone to-day, and Winterbourne once more left to the engaging family of the inimitable B. Ever since I wrote to you Leech has been seriously worse, and again very heavily bled. The night before last he was in such an alarming state of restlessness, which nothing could relieve, that I proposed to Mrs. Leech to try magnetism. Accordingly in the middle of the night I fell to; and, after a very fatiguing bout of it, put him to sleep for an hour and thirty-five minutes. A change came on in the sleep, and he is decidedly better. I talked to the astounded little Mrs. Leech across him, when he was asleep, as if he had been a truss of hay. . . . What do you think of my setting up in the magnetic line with a large brass plate? 'Terms, twenty-five guineas per nap.'" When he wrote on the 30th, he had completed his sixth number; and his friend was so clearly on the way to recovery that he was himself next day to leave for Broadstairs with his wife, her sister, and the two little girls. "I will merely add that I entreat to be kindly remembered to Thackeray" (who had a dangerous illness at this time); "that I think I have, without a doubt, *got* the Periodical notion; and that I am writing under the depressing and discomforting influence of paying off the tribe of bills that pour in upon an unfortunate family-young man on the eve of a residence like this. So no more at present from the disgusted, though still inimitable, and always affectionate B."

He stayed at Broadstairs till he had finished his number seven, and what else chiefly occupied him were thoughts about the Periodical of which account will presently be given. "Such a night and day of rain," ran his first letter, "I should think the oldest inhabitant never saw! and yet, in the ould formiliar Broadstairs, I somehow or other don't mind it much. The change has done Mamey a world of good, and I have begun to sleep again. As for news, you might as well ask me for dolphins. Nobody in Broadstairs—to speak of. Certainly nobody in Ballard's. We are in the part, which is the house next door to the hotel itself, that we once had for three years running, and just as quiet and snug now as it was then. I don't think I shall return before the 20th or so, when the number is done; but I *may*, in some inconstant freak, run up to you before. Preliminary despatches and advices shall be forwarded in any case to the fragrant neighbourhood of Clare Market and the Portugal Street burying-ground." Such was his polite designation of my whereabouts: for which nevertheless he had secret likings. "On the Portsmouth railway, coming here, encountered Kenyon. On the ditto ditto at Reigate, encountered young Dilke, and took him in tow to Canterbury. On the ditto ditto at ditto (meaning Reigate), encountered Fox, M.P. for Oldham, and his daughter. All within an hour. Young Dilke great about the proposed Exposition under the direction of H.R.H. Prince Albert, and evincing, very pleasantly to me, unbounded faith in our old friend his father." There was one more letter, taking a rather gloomy view of public affairs in connection with an inflated pastoral from Doctor Wiseman "given out of the Flaminian Gate," and speaking dolefully of some family matters; which was subscribed, each word forming a separate line, "Yours Despondently, And Disgustedly, Wilkins Micawber."

His visit to the little watering-place in the following year was signalised by his completion of the most famous of his novels, and his letters otherwise were occupied by elaborate managerial preparation for the private performances at Kneb-worth. But again the plague of itinerant music flung him into such fevers of irritation, that he finally resolved against any renewed attempt to carry on important work here; and the summer of 1851, when he was busy with miscellaneous writing only, was the last of his regular residences in the place. He then let his London house for the brief remainder of its term; running away at the end of May, when some grave family sorrows had befallen him, from the crowds and excitements of the Great Exhibition; and I will only add generally of these seaside residences that his reading was considerable and very various at such intervals of labour. One of them, as I remember, took in all the minor tales as well as the plays of Voltaire, several of the novels (old favourites with him) of Paul de Kock, Ruskin's *Lamps of Architecture*, and a surprising number of books of African and other travel for which he had insatiable relish: but there was never much notice of his reading in his letters. "By the by, I observe, reading that wonderful book the *French Revolution* again for the 500th time, that Carlyle, who knows everything, don't know what Mumbo Jumbo is. It is not an Idol. It is a secret preserved among the men of certain African tribes, and never revealed by any of them, for the punishment of their women. Mumbo Jumbo comes in hideous form out of the forest, or the mud, or the river, or where not, and flogs some woman who has been backbiting, or scolding, or with some other domestic mischief disturbing the general peace. Carlyle's seems to confound him with the common Fetish; but he is quite another thing. He is a disguised man; and all about him is a freemasons' secret *among the men*."—"I finished the *Scarlet Letter* yesterday. It falls off sadly after that fine opening scene. The psychological part of the story is very much overdone, and not truly done I think. Their suddenness of meeting and agreeing to go away together after all those years, is very poor. Mr. Chillingworth ditto. The child out of nature altogether. And Mr. Dimmesdale certainly never could have begotten her." In Mr. Hawthorne's earlier books he had taken especial pleasure; his *Mosses from an Old Manse* having been the first book he placed in my hands on his return from America, with reiterated injunctions to read it. I will add a word or two of what he wrote of the clever story of another popular witer, because it hits well the sort of ability that has become so common, which escapes the highest point of cleverness, but stops short only at the very verge of it. "The story extremely good indeed; but all the strongest things of which it is capable, missed. It shows just how far that kind of power can go. It is more like a note of the idea than anything else. It seems to me as if it were written by somebody who lived next door to the people, rather than inside of 'em."

IV

IT has been seen that his fancy for his Christmas book of 1848 first arose to him at Lausanne in the summer of 1846, and that, after writing its opening pages in the autumn of the following year, he laid it aside under the pressure of his *Dombey*. These lines were in the letter that closed his 1848 Broadstairs holiday. "At last I am a mentally matooring of the Christmas book— or, as poor Macrone used to write, 'booke,' 'boke,' 'buke,' etc." It was the first labour to which he applied himself at his return.

In London it soon came to maturity; was published duly as *The Haunted Man, or the Ghost's Bargain*; sold largely, beginning with a subscription of twenty thousand; and had a great success on the Adelphi stage, to which it was rather cleverly adapted by Lemon. He had placed on its title-page originally four lines from Tennyson's *Departure*.

> And o'er the hills, and far away
> Beyond their utmost purple rim,
> Beyond the night, across the day,
> Thro' all the world IT followed him;

but they were less applicable to the close than to the opening of the tale, and were dropped before publication. The hero is a great chemist, a lecturer at an old foundation, a man of studious philosophic habits, haunted with recollections of the past "o'er which his melancholy sits on brood," thinking his knowledge of the present a worthier substitute, and at last parting with that portion of himself which he thinks he can safely cast away. The recollections are of a great wrong done him in early life, and of all the sorrow consequent upon it; and the ghost he holds nightly conference with, is the darker present-ment of himself embodied in those bitter recollections. This part is finely managed. Out of heaped-up images of gloomy and wintry fancies, the supernatural takes a shape which is not forced or violent; and the dialogue which is no dialogue, but a kind of dreary dreamy echo, is a piece of ghostly imagination better than Mrs. Radcliffe. The boon desired is granted and the bargain struck. He is not only to lose his own recollection of grief and wrong, but to destroy the like memory in all whom he approaches. By this means the effect is shown in humble as well as higher minds, in the worst poverty as in competence or ease, always with the same result. The over-thinking sage loses his own affections and sympathy, sees them crushed in others, and is brought to the level of the only creature whom he cannot change or influence, an outcast of the streets, a boy whom the mere animal appetites have turned into a small fiend. Never having had his mind awakened, evil is this creature's good; avarice, irreverence, and vindictiveness, are his nature; sorrow has no place in his memory; and from his brutish propensities the philosopher can take nothing away. The juxtaposition of two people whom such opposite means have put in the same moral position is a stroke of excellent art. There are plenty of incredibilities and inconsistencies, just as in the pleasant *Cricket on the Hearth*, which we do not care about, but enjoy rather than otherwise; and, as in that charming little book, there were minor characters as delightful as anything in Dickens. The Tetterby group, in whose humble, homely, kindly, ungainly figures there is everything that could suggest itself to a clear eye, a piercing wit, and a loving heart, became enormous favourites. Tilly Slowboy and her little dot of a baby, charging folks with it as if it were an offensive instrument, or handing if about as if it were something to drink, were not more popular than poor Johnny Tetterby staggering under his Moloch of an infant, the Juggernaut that crushes all his enjoyments. The story itself consists of nothing more than the effects of the Ghost's gift upon the various groups of people introduced, and the way the end is arrived at is very specially in Dickens's manner. What the highest exercise of the intellect had missed is found in the simplest form of the affections. The wife of the custodian of the college where the chemist is professor, in whom are all the unselfish virtues that can beautify and endear the humblest condition, is the instrument of the change. Such sorrow as she has suffered had made her only zealous to relieve others' sufferings: and the discontented wise man learns from her example that the world is, after all, a much happier compromise than it seems to be, and life easier than wisdom is apt to think it; that grief gives joy its relish, purifying what it touches truly; and that "sweet are the uses of adversity" when

its clouds are not the shadow of dishonour. All this can be shown
but lightly within such space, it is true; and in the machinery
a good deal has to be taken for granted. But Dickens was quite
justified in turning aside from objections of that kind. "You
must suppose," he wrote to me (21 November), "that the
Ghost's saving clause gives him those glimpses without which
it would be impossible to carry out the idea. Of course my
point is that bad and good are inextricably linked in remembrance, and that you could not choose the enjoyment of
recollecting only the good. To have all the best of it you must
remember the worst also. My intention in the other point you
mention is, that he should not know himself how he communi-
cates the gift, whether by look or touch; and that it should
diffuse itself in its own way in each case. I can make this clearer
by a very few lines in the second part. It is not only necessary
to be so, for the variety of the story, but I think it makes the
thing wilder and stranger." Critical niceties are indeed out of
place, where wildness and strangeness of means matter less
than that there should be clearness of drift and intention.
Dickens leaves no doubt as to this. He thoroughly makes out
his fancy, that no man should so far question the mysterious
dispensations of evil in this world as to desire to lose the
recollection of such injustice or misery as he may suppose it
to have done to himself. There may have been sorrow, but
there was the kindness that assuaged it; there may have been
wrong, but there was the charity that forgave it; and with
both are connected inseparably so many thoughts that soften
and exalt whatever else is in the sense of memory, that what
is good and pleasurable in life would cease to continue so if
these were forgotten. The old proverb does not tell you to
forget that you may forgive, but to forgive that you may
forget. It is forgiveness of wrong, for forgetfulness of the evil
that was in it; such as poor old Lear begged of Cordelia.

The design for his much-thought-of new Periodical was still
"dim," as we have seen, when the first cogitation of it at Bonchurch occupied him; but the expediency of making it clearer
came soon after with a visit from Mr. Evans, who brought his
half-year's accounts of sales, and some small disappointment
for him in those of *Copperfield*. "The accounts are rather shy,
after *Dombey*, and what you said comes true after all. I am
not sorry I cannot bring myself to care much for what opinions
people may form; and I have a strong belief, that, if any of
my books are read years hence, *Dombey* will be remembered

as among the best of them: but passing influences are important for the time, and as *Chuzzlewit* with its small sale sent me up, *Dombey's* large sale has tumbled me down. Not very much, however, in real truth. These accounts only include the first three numbers, have of course been burdened with all the heavy expenses of number one, and ought not in reason to be complained of. But it is clear to me that the Periodical must be set a-going in the spring; and I have already been busy, at odd half-hours, in shadowing forth a name and an idea. Evans says they have but one opinion repeated to them of *Copperfield*, and they feel very confident about it. A steady twenty-five thousand, which it is now on the verge of, will do very well. The back numbers are always going off. Read the enclosed."

It was a letter from a Russian man of letters, dated from St. Petersburg, and signed "Trinarch Ivansvitch Wredenskii," sending him a translation of *Dombey* into Russian; and informing him that his works, which before had only been translated in the journals, and with certain omissions, had now been translated in their entire form by his correspondent, though even he had found an omission to be necessary in his version of *Pickwick*. He adds, with an exquisite courtesy to our national tongue which is yet not forgetful of the claims of his own nationality, that his difficulties (in the Sam Weller direction and others) had arisen from the "impossibility of portraying faithfully the beauties of the original in the Russian language, which, though the richest in Europe in its expressiveness, is far from being elaborate enough for literature like other civilised languages." He had however, he assured Dickens, been unremitting in his efforts to live with his thoughts; and the exalted opinion he had formed of them was attended by only one wish, that such a writer "could but have expanded under a Russian sky!" Still, his fate was an enviable one. "For the last eleven years your name has enjoyed a wide celebrity in Russia, and from the banks of the Neva to the remotest parts of Siberia you are read with avidity. Your *Dombey* continues to inspire with enthusiasm the whole of the literary Russia." Much did we delight in the good Wredenskii; and for a long time, on anything going "contrary" in the public or private direction with him, he would tell me he had ordered his portmanteau to be packed for the more sympathising and congenial climate of "the remotest parts of Siberia."

The week before he left Bonchurch I again had news of the old and often recurring fancy. "The old notion of the Periodical, which had been agitating itself in my mind for so long, I really think is at last gradually growing into form." This was on 24 September; and on 7 October, from Broadstairs, I had something of the form it had been taking. "I do great injustice to my floating ideas (pretty speedily and comfortably settling down into orderly arrangement) by saying anything about the Periodical now: but my notion is a weekly journal, price either three-halfpence or twopence, matter in part original and in part selected, and always having, if possible, a little good poetry. . . . Upon the selected matter, I have particular notions. One is, that it should always be *a subject*. For example, a history of Piracy; in connection with which there is a vast deal of extraordinary, romantic, and almost unknown matter. A history of Knight-errantry, and the wild old notion of the Sangreal. A history of Savages, showing the singular respects in which all savages are like each other; and those in which civilised men, under circumstances of difficulty, soonest become like savages. A history of remarkable characters, good and bad, *in* history; to assist the reader's judgment in his observation of men, and in his estimates of the truth of many characters in fiction. All these things, and fifty others that I have already thought of, would be compilations; through the whole of which the general intellect and purpose of the paper should run, and in which there would be scarcely less interest than in the original matter. The original matter to be essays, reviews, letters, theatrical criticisms, etc., as amusing as possible, but all distinctly and boldly going to what in one's own view ought to be the spirit of the people and the time. . . . Now to bind all this together, and to get a character established as it were which any of the writers may maintain without difficulty, I want to suppose a certain SHADOW, which may go into any place, by sunlight, moonlight, starlight, firelight, candlelight, and be in all homes, and all nooks and corners, and be supposed to be cognisant of everything, and go everywhere, without the least difficulty. Which may be in the Theatre, the Palace, the House of Commons, the Prisons, the Unions, the Churches, on the Railroad, on the Sea, abroad and at home: a kind of semi-omniscient, omnipresent, intangible creature. I don't think it would do to call the paper THE SHADOW: but I want something tacked to that title, to express the notion of its being a cheerful, useful, and always welcome Shadow. I want to open the first number with this Shadow's account of himself and his family. I want to have all the correspondence addressed to him.

I want him to issue his warnings from time to time, that he is going to fall on such and such a subject; or to expose such and such a piece of humbug; or that he may be expected shortly in such and such a place. I want the compiled part of the paper to express the idea of this Shadow's having been in libraries, and among the books referred to. I want him to loom as a fanciful thing all over London; and to get up a general notion of 'What will the Shadow say about this, I wonder? What will the Shadow say about this? Is the Shadow here?' and so forth. Do you understand? . . . I have an enormous difficulty in expressing what I mean, in this stage of the business; but I think the importance of the idea is, that once stated on paper, there is no difficulty in keeping it up. That it presents an odd, unsubstantial, whimsical, new thing: a sort of previously un-thought-of Power going about. That it will concentrate into one focus all that is done in the paper. That it sets up a creature which isn't the Spectator, and isn't Isaac Bickerstaff, and isn't anything of that kind: but in which people will be perfectly willing to believe, and which is just as mysterious and quaint enough to have a sort of charm for their imagination, while it will represent common-sense and humanity. I want to express in the title, and in the grasp of the idea to express also, that it is the Thing at everybody's elbow, and in everybody's footsteps. At the window, by the fire, in the street, in the house, from infancy to old age, everybody's inseparable companion. . . . Now do you make anything out of this? which I let off as if I were a bladder full of it, and you had punctured me. I have not breathed the idea to anyone; but I have a lively hope that it *is* an idea, and that out of it the whole scheme may be hammered."

Excellent the idea doubtless, and so described in his letter that hardly anything more characteristic survives him. But I could not make anything out of it that had a quite feasible look. The ordinary ground of miscellaneous reading, selection, and compilation out of which it was to spring, seemed to me no proper soil for the imaginative produce it was meant to bear. As his fancies grew and gathered round it, they had given it too much of the range and scope of his own exhaustless land of invention and marvel; and the very means proposed for letting in the help of others would only more heavily have weighted himself. Not to trouble the reader now with objec-tions given him in detail, my judgment was clear against his plan; less for any doubt of the effect if its parts could be brought to combine, than for my belief that it was not in that view practicable; and though he did not immediately accept my reasons, he acquiesced in them ultimately. "I do not lay much stress on your grave doubts about Periodical, but more anon." The more anon resolved itself into conversations out of which the shape given to the project was that which it finally took.

It was to be a weekly miscellany of general literature; and its stated objects were to be, to contribute to the entertainment and instruction of all classes of readers, and to help in the discussion of the more important social questions of the time. It was to comprise short stories by others as well as himself; matters of passing interest in the liveliest form that could be given to them; subjects suggested by books that might most be attracting attention; and poetry in every number if possible, but in any case something of romantic fancy. This was to be a cardinal point. There was to be no mere utilitarian spirit; with all familiar things, but especially those repellent on the surface, something was to be connected that should be fanciful or kindly; and the hardest workers were to be taught that their lot is not necessarily excluded from the sympathies and graces of imagination. This was all finally settled by the close of 1849, when a general announcement of the intended adventure was made. There remained only a title and an assistant-editor; and I am happy now to remember that for the latter important duty Mr. Wills † 13 was chosen at my suggestion. He discharged its duties with admirable patience and ability for twenty years, and Dickens's later life had no more intimate friend.

The title took some time and occupied many letters. One of the first thought-of has now the curious interest of having foreshadowed, by the motto proposed to accompany it, the title of the series of *All the Year Round* which he was led to substitute for the older series in 1859. "THE ROBIN. With this motto from Goldsmith. *The redbreast, celebrated for its affection to mankind, continues with us, the year round.*" That however was rejected. Then came: "MANKIND. This I think very good." It followed the other nevertheless. After it came: "And here a strange idea, but with decided advantages. 'CHARLES DICKENS. A weekly journal designed for the instruction and entertainment of all classes of readers. CONDUCTED BY HIMSELF.'" Still something was wanting in that also. Next day there arrived: "I really think if there *be* anything wanting in the other name, that this is very pretty, and just supplies it. THE HOUSEHOLD VOICE.

I have thought of many others, as—The Household Guest. The Household Face. The Comrade. The Microscope. The Highway of Life. The Lever. The Rolling Years. The Holly Tree (with two lines from Southey for a motto). Everything. But I rather think the Voice is it." It was near indeed; but the following day came, "Household Words. This is a very pretty name": and the choice was made.

The first number appeared on Saturday, 30 March, 1850, and contained among other things the beginning of a story by a very original writer, Mrs. Gaskell, for whose powers he had a high admiration, and with whom he had friendly intercourse during many years. Other opportunities will arise for mention of those with whom this new labour brought him into personal communication, but I may at once say that of all the writers, before unknown, whom his journal helped to make familiar to a wide world of readers, he had the strongest personal interest in Mr. Sala, and placed at once in the highest rank his capabilities of help in such an enterprise. An illustrative trait of what I have named as its cardinal point to him will fitly close my account of its establishment. Its first number, still unpublished, had not seemed to him quite to fulfil his promise, "tenderly to cherish the light of fancy inherent in all breasts"; and, as soon as he received the proof of the second, I heard from him. "Looking over the suggested contents of number two at breakfast this morning" (Brighton: 14 March, 1850) "I felt an uneasy sense of their being a want of something tender, which would apply to some universal household knowledge. Coming down in the railroad the other night (always a wonderfully suggestive place to me when I am alone) I was looking at the stars, and revolving a little idea about them. Putting now these two things together, I wrote the enclosed little paper, straightway; and should like you to read it before you send it to the printers (it will not take you five minutes), and let me have a proof by return." This was the child's "dream of a star," which opened his second number; and, though it appears among his reprinted pieces, it may justify a word or two of description. It is of a brother and sister, constant child-companions, who used to make friends of a star, watching it together until they knew when and where it would rise, and always bidding it good-night; so that when the sister dies the lonely brother still connects her with the star, which he then sees opening as a world of light, and its rays making a shining pathway from earth to heaven; and he also sees angels waiting to receive travellers up that sparkling road, his little sister among them; and he thinks ever after that he belongs less to the earth than to the star where his sister is; and he grows up to youth and through manhood and old age, consoled still under the successive domestic bereavements that fall to his earthly lot by renewal of that vision of his childhood; until at last, lying on his own bed of death, he feels that he is moving as a child to his child-sister, and he thanks his heavenly Father that the star had so often opened before to receive the dear ones who awaited him.

His sister Fanny and himself, he told me long before this paper was written, used to wander at night about a churchyard near their house, looking up at the stars; and her early death, of which I am shortly to speak, had vividly reawakened all the childish associations which made her memory dear to him.

V

IN AID OF LITERATURE AND ART

1850-2

IN the year of the establishment of *Household Words* Dickens resumed what I have called his splendid strolling on behalf of a scheme for the advantage of men of letters, to which a great brother-author had given the sanction of his genius and name. In November 1850, in the hall of Lord Lytton's old family seat in Knebworth Park, there were three private performances by the original actors in Ben Jonson's *Every Man in His Humour*, of which all the circumstances and surroundings were very brilliant; some of the gentlemen of the county played both in comedy and farces; our generous host was profuse of all noble encouragement; and amid the general pleasure and excitement hopes rose high. Recent experience had shown what the public interest in this kind of amusement might place within reach of its providers; and there came to be discussed the possibility of making permanent such help as had been afforded to fellow writers, by means of an endowment that should not be mere charity, but should combine something of both pension-list and college-lectureship, without the drawbacks of either. It was not enough considered that schemes for self-help, to be successful, require from those they are meant to benefit, not only a general assent to their desirability, but zealous co-operation. Too readily assuming what should have had more thorough investigation, the enterprise was set on foot, and the "Guild of Literature and Art" originated at Knebworth. A five-act comedy was to be written by Sir Edward Lytton; and, when a certain sum of money had been obtained by public representations of it, the details of the scheme were to be drawn up, and appeal made to those whom it addressed more especially. In a very few months everything was ready, except a farce which Dickens was to have written to follow the comedy, and which unexpected cares of management and preparation were held to absolve him from. There were other reasons. "I have written the first scene," he told me (23 March, 1851), "and it has droll points in it, 'more

68

farcical points than you commonly find in farces,' really better. Yet I am constantly striving, for my reputation's sake, to get into it a meaning that is impossible in a farce; constantly thinking of it, therefore, against the grain; and constantly impressed with a conviction that I could never act in it myself with that wild abandonment which can alone carry a farce off. Wherefore I have confessed to Bulwer Lytton and asked for absolution.' There was substituted a new farce of Lemon's, to which, however, Dickens soon contributed so many jokes and so much Gampish and other fun of his own, that it came to be in effect a joint piece of authorship; and Gabblewigg, which the manager took to himself, was one of those personation parts requiring five or six changes of face, voice, and gait in the course of it, from which, as we have seen, he derived all the early theatrical ambition that the elder Mathews had awakened in him. "You have no idea," he continued, "of the immensity of the work as the time advances, for the Duke even throws the whole of the audience on us, or he would get (he says) into all manner of scrapes."

"The Duke" was the Duke of Devonshire, of whose love of letters and interest for men of that calling I have given on a former page, one of the many instances that adorned a life which alone perhaps in England was genuinely and completely that of the Grand Seigneur. Well-read and very accomplished, he had the pleasing manners which proceed from a kind nature; and splendid in his mode of living beyond any other English noble, his magnificence, by the ease and elegance that accompanied it, was relieved from all offence of ostentation. He had offered his house in Piccadilly for the first representations, and in his princely way discharged all the expenses attending them. A movable theatre was built and set up in the great drawing-room, the library was turned into a green-room, and here Lytton's comedy was presented. While the rehearsals were in progress our friend Macready was bidding adieu to the art of which he had long been the leading ornament; and before the comedy was produced its author presided at the farewell dinner to that distinguished actor on his quitting the stage. Dickens and myself came up for it from Malvern, and a few words from his speech proposing the chairman's health will illustrate the enterprise on foot and indicate its most generous helper. "There is a popular prejudice, a kind of superstition, that authors are not a particularly united body, and I am afraid that this may contain half a grain or so of the veracious. But of our chairman I have never in my life made public mention without adding what I can never repress, that in the path we both tread I have uniformly found him to be, from the first, the most generous of men; quick to encourage, slow to disparage, and ever anxious to assert the order of which he is so great an ornament. That we men of letters are, or have been, invariably or inseparably attached to each other, it may not be possible to say, formerly or now; but there cannot now be, and there cannot ever have been, among the followers of literature, a man so entirely without the grudging little jealousies that too often over-shadow its brightness, as he who now occupies that chair. Nor was there ever a time when such reason existed for bearing testimony to his great consideration for the evils sometimes unfortunately attendant upon literature, though never on his own pursuit of it. For, in conjunction with some other gentlemen now present, I have just embarked in a design with him to smooth the rugged way of young labourers both in literature and the fine arts, and to soften, but by no eleemosynary means, the declining years of meritorious age. If it prosper, as I hope it will, and as I know it ought, there will one day in England be an honour where there is now a reproach; and a future race of men of letters will gratefully remember that it originated in the sympathies, and was made practicable by the generosity, of Sir Edward Bulwer Lytton."

The design nevertheless did not prosper, and both the great writers who had associated themselves with it are now passed away. Since it first was mentioned on this page, Lord Lytton has himself been borne to the Abbey where Dickens is laid, and which never opened to receive a more varied genius, a more gallant spirit, a man more constant to his friends, more true to any cause he represented, or whose name will hereafter be found entitled to a more honoured place in the history of his time. The Guild design failed because the support indispensable to success was not, as Dickens too sanguinely hoped, given to it by literary men themselves. But one part of his prediction may yet have fulfilment, since the failure has made it perhaps even more rather than less likely that future followers of literature will have reason to remember, how wise and well-directed was the unavailing effort to enable the most sensitive of all professions to receive assistance in its hour of distress without the loss of self-respect or dignity. How high Dickens had carried his hope in this respect, and to what depth of disappointment he fell at its collapse, will have mention on a later page.

Lytton's comedy, *Not so Bad as We Seem*, was played for the first time at Devonshire House on 16 May, 1851, before the Queen and Prince and as large an audience as places could be found for; the farce of *Mr. Nightingale's Diary* being reserved for the second performance. The success abundantly realised expectation; and, after many representations at the Hanover Square Rooms in London, strolling began in the country, and was continued at intervals for considerable portions of this and the following year. From much of it, I was myself disabled by illness and occupation, and substitutes had to be found; but to this I owe a lively and characteristic picture of Dickens amid the incidents and accidents to which his theatrical career exposed him, which may be taken from the closing performances. The company carried with them, it should be said, the theatre constructed for Devonshire House, as well as the admirable scenes which Stanfield, David Roberts, Thomas Grieve, Telbin, Absolon, and Louis Haghe had painted as their generous free-offerings to the comedy; of which the representations were thus rendered irrespective of theatres or their managers, and took place in the large halls or concert-rooms of the various towns and cities. A design for the card of membership, taken from an incident in the life of Defoe, expressed the interest felt in the undertaking by another distinguished artist, Mr. E. M. Ward.

"The comedy," Dickens wrote from Sunderland on 29 August, 1852, "is so far improved by the reductions which your absence and other causes have imposed on us, that it acts now only two hours and twenty-five minutes, all waits included, and goes 'like wildfire,' as Mr. Tonson says. We have had prodigious houses, though smaller rooms (as to their actual size) than I had hoped for. The Duke was at Derby, and no end of minor radiances. Into the room at Newcastle (where Lord Carlisle was by the by) they squeezed six hundred people, at twelve and sixpence, into a space reasonably capable of holding three hundred. Last night, in a hall built like a theatre, with pit, boxes, and gallery, we had about twelve hundred—I dare say more. They began with a round of applause when Coote's white waistcoat appeared in the orchestra, and wound up the farce with three deafening cheers. I never saw such good fellows. Stanny is their fellow-townsman; was born here; and they applauded his scene as if it were himself. But what I suffered from a dreadful anxiety that hung over me all the time, I can never describe. When we got here at noon, it appeared that the hall was a perfectly new one, and had only had the slates put upon the roof by torchlight over night. Further, that the proprietors of some opposition rooms had declared the building to be unsafe, and that there was a panic in the town about it; people having had their money back, and being undecided whether to come or not, and all kinds of such horrors. I didn't know what to do. The horrible responsibility of risking an accident of that awful nature seemed to rest only upon me; for I had only to say we wouldn't act, and there would be no chance of danger. I was afraid to take Sloman into council lest the panic should infect our men. I asked W. what *he* thought, and he consolingly observed that his digestion was so bad that death had no terrors for him! I went and looked at the place; at the rafters, walls, pillars, and so forth; and fretted myself into a belief that they really were slight! To crown all, there was an arched iron roof without any brackets or pillars, on a new principle! The only comfort I had was in stumbling at length on the builder, and finding him a plain practical north-countryman with a foot rule in his pocket. I took him aside, and asked him should we, or could we, prop up any weak part of the place: especially the dressing-rooms, which were under our stage, the weight of which must be heavy on a new floor, and dripping wet walls. He told me there wasn't a stronger building in the world; and that, to allay the apprehension, they had opened it, on Thursday night, to thousands of the working people, and induced them to sing, and beat with their feet, and make every possible trial of the vibration. Accordingly there was nothing for it but to go on. I was in such dread, however, lest a false alarm should spring up among the audience and occasion a rush, that I kept Catherine and Georgina out of the front. When the curtain went up and I saw the great sea of faces rolling up to the roof, I looked here and looked there, and thought I saw the gallery out of the perpendicular, and fancied the lights in the ceiling were not straight. Rounds of applause were perfect agony to me, I was so afraid of their effect upon the building. I was ready all night to rush on in case of an alarm—a false alarm was my main dread—and implore the people for God's sake to sit still. I had our great farce-bell rung to startle Sir Geoffrey instead of throwing down a piece of wood, which might have raised a sudden apprehension. I had a palpitation of the heart, if any of our people stumbled up or down a stair. I am sure I never acted better, but the anxiety of my mind was so intense, and the relief at last so great, that I am

half-dead to-day, and have not yet been able to eat or drink anything or to stir out of my room. I shall never forget it. As to the short time we had for getting the theatre up; as to the upsetting, by a runaway pair of horses, of one of the vans at the Newcastle railway station *with all the scenery in it, every atom of which was turned over*; as to the fatigue of our carpenters, who have now been up four nights, and who were lying dead asleep in the entrances last night; I say nothing, after the other gigantic nightmare, except that Sloman's splendid knowledge of his business, and the good temper and cheerfulness of all the workmen, are capital. I mean to give them a supper at Liverpool, and address them in a neat and appropriate speech. We dine at two to-day (it is now one) and go to Sheffield at four, arriving there at about ten. I had been as fresh as a daisy; walked from Nottingham to Derby, and from Newcastle here; but seem to have had my nerves crumpled up last night, and have an excruciating headache. That's all at present. I shall never be able to bear the smell of new deal and fresh mortar again as long as I live."

Manchester and Liverpool closed the trip with enormous success at both places; and Sir Edward Lytton was present at a public dinner which was given in the former city, Dickens's brief word about it being written as he was setting foot in the train that was to bring him to London. "Bulwer spoke brilliantly at the Manchester dinner, and his earnestness and determination about the Guild was most impressive. It carried everything before it. They are now getting up annual subscriptions, and will give us a revenue to begin with. I swear I believe that people to be the greatest in the world. At Liverpool I had a Round Robin on the stage after the play was over, a place being left for your signature, and as I am going to have it framed, I'll tell Green to send it to Lincoln's Inn Fields. You have no idea how good Tenniel, Topham, and Collins have been in what they had to do."

These names, distinguished in art and letters, represent additions to the company who had joined the enterprise; and the last of them, Mr. Wilkie Collins, became, for all the rest of the life of Dickens, one of his dearest and most valued friends.

VI

EXCEPTING always the haunts and associations of his childhood, Dickens had no particular sentiment of locality, and any special regard for houses he had lived in was not a thing noticeable in him. But he cared most for Devonshire Terrace, perhaps for the bit of ground attached to it; and it was with regret he suddenly discovered, at the close of 1847, that he should have to resign it "next Lady Day three years. I had thought the lease two years more." To that brief remaining time belong some incidents of which I have still to give account; and I connect them with the house in which he lived during the progress of what is generally thought his greatest book, and of what I think were his happiest years.

We had never had such intimate confidences as in the interval since his return from Paris; but these have been used in my narrative of the childhood and boyish experiences, and what remain are incidental only. Of the fragment of autobiography there also given, the origin has been told: but the intention of leaving such a record had been also in his mind at an earlier date; and it was the very depth of our interest in the opening of his fragment that led to the larger design in which it became absorbed. "I hardly know why I write this," was his own comment on one of his personal revelations, "but the more than friendship which has grown between us seems to force it on me in my present mood. We shall speak of it all, you and I, Heaven grant, wisely and wonderingly many and many a time in after years. In the meanwhile I am more at rest for having opened all my heart and mind to you. . . . This day eleven years, poor dear Mary died."

That was written on 7 May, 1848, but another sadness impending at the time was taking his thoughts still farther back; to when he trotted about with his little elder sister in the small garden to the house at Portsea. The faint hope for her which Elliotson had given him in Paris had since completely broken down; and I was to hear, in less than two months after the letter just quoted, how nearly the end was come. "A change

74

took place in poor Fanny," he wrote on 5 July, "about the middle of the day yesterday, which took me out there last night. Her cough suddenly ceased almost, and, strange to say, she immediately became aware of her hopeless state; to which she resigned herself, after an hour's unrest and struggle, with extraordinary sweetness and constancy. The irritability passed, and all hope faded away; though only two nights before, she had been planning for 'after Christmas.' She is greatly changed. I had a long interview with her to-day, alone; and when she had expressed some wishes about the funeral, and her being buried in unconsecrated ground" (Mr. Burnett's family were dissenters), "I asked her whether she had any care or anxiety in the world. She said No, none. It was hard to die at such a time of life, but she had no alarm whatever in the prospect of the change; felt sure we should meet again in a better world; and although they had said she might rally for a time, did not really wish it. She said she was quite calm and happy, relied upon the mediation of Christ, and had no terror at all. She had worked very hard, even when ill; but believed that was in her nature, and neither regretted nor complained of it. Burnett had been always very good to her; they had never quarrelled; she was sorry to think of his going back to such a lonely home; and was distressed about her children, but not painfully so. She showed me how thin and worn she was; spoke about an invention she had heard of that she would like to have tried, for the deformed child's back; called to my remembrance all our sister Letitia's patience and steadiness; and, though she shed tears sometimes, clearly impressed upon me that her mind was made up, and at rest. I asked her very often, if she could ever recall anything that she could leave to my doing, to put it down, or mention it to somebody if I was not there; and she said she would, but she firmly believed that there was nothing—nothing. Her husband being young, she said, and her children infants, she could not help thinking sometimes, that it would be very long in the course of nature before they were reunited; but she knew that was a mere human fancy, and could have no reality after she was dead. Such an affecting exhibition of strength and tenderness, in all that early decay, is quite indescribable. I need not tell you how it moved me. I cannot look round upon the dear children here, without some misgiving that this sad disease will not perish out of our blood with her; but I am sure I have no selfishness in the thought, and God knows how small the world looks to one who comes out of such a sick-room on a bright summer day. I don't know why I write this before going to bed. I only know that in the very pity and grief of my heart, I feel as if it were doing something." After not many weeks she died, and the little child who was her last anxiety did not long survive her.

In all the later part of the year Dickens's thoughts were turning much to the form his next book should assume. A suggestion that he should write it in the first person, by way of change, had been thrown out by me, which he took at once very gravely; and this, with other things, though as yet not dreaming of any public use of his early personal trials, conspired to bring about the resolve to use them. His determination once taken, with what a singular truthfulness he contrived to blend the fact with the fiction may be shown by a small occurrence of this time. It has been inferred, from the vividness of the boy-impressions of Yarmouth in David's earliest experiences, that the place must have been familiar to his own boyhood: but the truth was that at the close of 1848 he first saw that celebrated seaport. One of its earlier months had been signalised by an adventure in which Leech, Lemon, and myself took part with him, when, obtaining horses from Salisbury, we passed the whole of a March day in riding over every part of the Plain; visiting Stonehenge, and exploring Hazlitt's "hut" at Winterslow, birthplace of some of his finest essays; altogether with so brilliant a success that now (13 November) he proposed to "repeat the Salisbury Plain idea in a new direction in mid-winter, to wit, Blackgang Chine in the Isle of Wight, with dark winter cliffs and roaring oceans." But mid-winter brought with it too much dreariness of its own, to render these stormy accompaniments to it very palatable; and on the last day of the year he bethought him "it would be better to make an outburst to some old cathedral city we don't know, and what do you say to Norwich and Stanfield Hall?" Thither accordingly the three friends went, illness at the last disabling me; and of the result I heard (12 January, 1849) that Stanfield Hall, the scene of a recent frightful tragedy, had nothing attractive unless the term might be applied to "a murderous look that seemed to invite such a crime. We arrived," continued Dickens, "between the Hall and Potass farm, as the search was going on for the pistol in a manner so consummately stupid, that there was nothing on earth to prevent any of Rush's labourers from accepting five pounds from Rush junior to find the weapon and give it to him. Norwich, a disappointment" (one pleasant face "transformeth a city," but he was unable yet to connect it with our delightful friend Elwin); "all save its place of execution, which we found fit for a gigantic scoundrel's exit. But the success of the trip, for me, was to come. Yarmouth, sir, where we went afterwards, is the strangest place in the wide world: one hundred and forty-six miles of hill-less marsh between it and London. More when we meet. I shall certainly try my hand at it." He made it the home of his "little Em'ly."

Everything now was taking that direction with him; and soon, to give his own account of it, his mind was upon names "running like a high sea." Four days after the date of the last-quoted letter ("all over happily, thank God, by four o'clock this morning") there came the birth of his eighth child and sixth son; whom at first he meant to call by Oliver Goldsmith's name, but settled afterwards into that of Henry Fielding; and to whom that early friend Ainsworth who had first made us known to each other, welcome and pleasant companion always, was asked to be godfather. Telling me of the change in the name of the little fellow, which he had made in a kind of homage to the style of work he was now so bent on beginning, he added, "What should you think of this for a notion of a character? 'Yes, that is very true; but now, *What's his motive?*' I fancy I could make something like it into a kind of amusing and more innocent Pecksniff. 'Well now, yes—no doubt that was a fine thing to do! But now, stop a moment, let us see—*What's his motive?*'" Here again was but one of the many outward signs of fancy and fertility that accompanied the outset of all his more important books; though, as in their cases also, other moods of the mind incident to such beginnings were less favourable. "Deepest despondency, as usual, in commencing, besets me;" is the opening of the letter in which he speaks of what of course was always one of his first anxieties, the selection of a name. In this particular instance he had been undergoing doubts and misgivings to more than the usual degree. It was not until 23 February he got to anything like the shape of a feasible title. "I should like to know how the enclosed (one of those I have been thinking of) strikes you, on a first acquaintance with it. It is odd, I think, and new: but it may have A.'s difficulty of being 'too comic, my boy.' I suppose I should have to add, though, by way of motto, 'And in short it led to the very Mag's Diversions. *Old Saying.*' Or would it be better, there being equal authority for either, 'And in short they all played Mag's Diversions. *Old Saying*'?"

"*Mag's Diversions.*
Being the personal history of
MR. THOMAS MAG THE YOUNGER,
Of Blunderstone House."

This was hardly satisfactory, I thought; and it soon became apparent that he thought so too, although within the next three days I had it in three other forms. "*Mag's Diversions,* being the Personal History, Adventures, Experience, and Observation of Mr. David Mag the Younger, of Blunderstone House." The second omitted Adventures, and called his hero Mr. David Mag the Younger, of Copperfield House. The third made nearer approach to what the destinies were leading him to, and transformed Mr. David Mag into Mr. David Copperfield the Younger and his great-aunt Margaret; retaining still as his leading title, *Mag's Diversions.* It is singular that it should never have occurred to him, while the name was thus strangely as by accident bringing itself together, that the initials were but his own reversed. He was much startled when I pointed this out, and protested it was just in keeping with the fates and chances which were always befalling him. "Why else," he said, "should I so obstinately have kept to that name when once it turned up?"

It was quite true that he did so, as I had curious proof following close upon the heels of his third proposal. "I wish," he wrote on 25 February, "you would look over carefully the titles now enclosed, and tell me to which you most incline. You will see that they give up *Mag* altogether, and refer exclusively to one name—that which I last sent you. I doubt whether I could, on the whole, get a better name.

"1. *The Copperfield Disclosures.* Being the personal history, experience, and observation, of Mr. David Copperfield the Younger, of Blunderstone House.

"2. *The Copperfield Records.* Being the personal history, experience, and observation, of Mr. David Copperfield the Younger, of Copperfield Cottage.

"3. *The Last Living Speech and Confession of David Copperfield, Junior,* of Blunderstone Lodge, who was never executed at the Old Bailey. being his personal history found among his papers.

"4. *The Copperfield Survey of the World as it Rolled.* Being the personal history, experience, and observation of David Copperfield the Younger, of Blunderstone Rookery.

"5. *The Last Will and Testament of Mr. David Copperfield.* Being his personal history left as a legacy.

"6. *Copperfield, Complete.* Being the whole personal history and experience of Mr. David Copperfield of Blunderstone House, which he never meant to be published on any account.

Or, the opening words of No. 6 might be *Copperfield's Entire*; and *The Copperfield Confessions* might open Nos. 1 and 2. Now, WHAT SAY YOU?"

What I said is to be inferred from what he wrote back on the 28th. "The *Survey* has been my favourite from the first. Kate picked it out from the rest, without my saying anything about it. Georgy too. You hit upon it, on the first glance. Therefore I have no doubt that it is indisputably the best title; and I will stick to it." There was a change nevertheless. His completion of the second chapter defined to himself, more clearly than before, the character of the book; and the propriety of rejecting everything not strictly personal from the name given to it. The words proposed, therefore, became ultimately these only: "The Personal History, Adventures, Experience, and Observation of David Copperfield the Younger, of Blunderstone Rookery, which he never meant to be published on any account." And the letter which told me that with this name it was finally to be launched on 1 May, told me also (19 April) the difficulties that still beset him at the opening. "My hand is out in the matter of *Copperfield*. To-day and yesterday I have done nothing. Though I know what I want to do, I am lumbering on like a stage-waggon. I can't even dine at the Temple to-day, I feel it so important to stick at it this evening, and make some head. I am quite aground; quite a literary Benedict, as he appeared when his heels wouldn't stay upon the carpet; and the long Copperfieldian perspective looks snowy and thick, this fine morning." The allusion was to * 80 a dinner at his house the night before; when not only Rogers had to be borne out, having fallen sick at the table, but, as we rose soon after to quit the dining-room, Mr. Jules Benedict had quite suddenly followed the poet's lead, and fallen prostrate on the carpet in the midst of us. Amid the general consternation there seemed a want of proper attendance on the sick: the distinguished musician faring in this respect hardly so well as the famous bard, by whose protracted sufferings in the library, whither he had been removed, the sanitary help available on the establishment was still absorbed: and as Dickens had been eloquent during dinner on the atrocities of a pauper-farming case at Tooting which was then exciting a fury of indignation, Fonblanque now declared him to be no better himself than a second Drouet, reducing his guests to a lamentable state by the food he had given them, and aggravating their sad condition by absence of all proper nursing. The joke was well kept up by Quin and Edwin Landseer, Lord Strangford joining in with a tragic sympathy for his friend the poet; and the banquet so dolefully interrupted ended in uproarious mirth. For nothing really serious had happened. Benedict went laughing away with his wife, and I helped Rogers on with his over-shoes for his usual night-walk home. "Do you know how many waistcoats I wear?" asked the poet of me, as I was doing him this service. I professed my inability to guess. "Five" he said: "and here they are!" Upon which he opened them, in the manner of the grave-digger in *Hamlet,* and showed me every one.

That dinner was in the April of 1849, and among others present were Mrs. Procter and Mrs. Macready, dear and familiar names always in his house. No swifter or surer perception than Dickens's for what was solid and beautiful in character; he rated it higher than intellectual effort; and the same lofty place, first in his affection and respect, would have been Macready's and Procter's, if the one had not been the greatest of actors, and the other a poet as genuine as old Fletcher or Beaumont. There were present at this dinner also the American minister and Mrs. Bancroft (it was the year of that visit of Macready to America, which ended in the disastrous Forrest riots); and it had among its guests Lady Graham, the wife of Sir James Graham, and sister of Tom Sheridan's wife, than whom not even the wit and beauty of her nieces, Mrs. Norton and Lady Dufferin, did greater justice to the brilliant family of the Sheridans; so many of whose members, and these three above all, Dickens prized among his friends. The table that day will be "full" if I add the celebrated singer Miss Catherine Hayes, and her homely good-natured Irish mother, who startled us all very much by complimenting Mrs. Dickens on her having had for her father so clever a painter as Mr. Hogarth.

Others familiar to Devonshire Terrace in these years will be indicated if I name an earlier dinner (3 January), for the "christening" of the *Haunted Man,* when, besides Lemons, Evanses, Leeches, Bradburys, and Stanfields, there were present Tenniel, Topham, Stone, Robert Bell, and Thomas Beard. Next month (24 March) I met at his table, Lord and Lady Lovelace; Milner Gibson, Mowbray Morris, Horace Twiss, and their wives; Lady Molesworth and her daughter (Mrs. Ford); John Hardwick, Charles Babbage, and Doctor Locock. That distinguished physician had attended the poor girl, Miss Abercrombie, whose death by strychnine led to the exposure of Wainewright's murders; and the opinion he had formed of her chances of recovery, the external indications of that poison being then but imperfectly known, was first shaken, he told me, by the gloomy and despairing cries of the old family nurse, that her mother and her uncle had died exactly so! These, it was afterwards proved, had been among the murderer's former victims. The Lovelaces were frequent guests after the return from Italy, Sir George Crawford, so friendly in Genoa, having married Lord Lovelace's sister; and few had a greater warmth of admiration for Dickens than Lord Byron's "Ada," on whom Paul Dombey's death laid a strange fascination. They were again at a dinner got up in the following year for Scribe and the composer Halévy, who had come over to bring out the *Tempest* at Her Majesty's Theatre, then managed by Mr. Lumley, who with M. Van de Weyer, Mrs. Gore and her daughter, the Hogarths, and I think the fine French comedian, Samson, were also amongst those present. Earlier that year there were gathered at his dinner-table the John Delanes, Isambard Brunels, Thomas Longmans (friends since the earliest Broadstairs days, and special favourites always), Lord Mulgrave, and Lord Carlisle, with all of whom his intercourse was intimate and frequent, and became especially so with Delane in later years. Lord Carlisle amused us that night, I remember, by repeating what the good old Brougham had said to him of "those *Punch* people," expressing what was really his fixed belief. "They never get my face, and are obliged" (which, like Pope, he always pronounced obleeged) "to put up with my plaid trousers!" Of Lord Mulgrave, pleasantly associated with the first American experiences, let me add that he now went with us to several outlying places of amusement of which he wished to acquire some knowledge, and which Dickens knew better than any man; small theatres, saloons, and gardens in city or borough, to which the Eagle and Britannia were as palaces; and I think he was of the party one famous night in the summer of 1849 (29 June), when with Talfourd, Edwin Landseer, and Stanfield we went to the *Battle of Waterloo* at Vauxhall, and were astounded to see pass in immediately before us, in a bright white overcoat, the great Duke himself, Lady Douro on his arm, the little Ladies Ramsay by his side, and everybody cheering and clearing the way before him. That the old hero enjoyed it all, there could be no doubt, and he made no secret of his delight in "Young Hernandez"; but the "Battle" was undeniably tedious, and it was impossible not to sympathise with the repeatedly and very audibly expressed wish of Talfourd, that "the Prussians would come up!"

The preceding month was that of the start of *David Copper-field*, and to one more dinner (on the 12th) I may especially refer for those who were present at it. Carlyle and Mrs. Carlyle came, Thackeray and Rogers, Mrs. Gaskell and Kenyon, Jerrold and Hablot Browne, with Mr. and Mrs. Tagart; and it was a delight to see the enjoyment of Dickens at Carlyle's laughing reply to questions about his health, that he was, in the language of Mr. Peggotty's housekeeper, a lorn lone creature and everything went contrairy with him. Things were not likely to go better, I thought, as I saw the great writer—kindest as well as wisest of men, but not very patient under sentimental philosophies—seated next the good Mr. Tagart, who soon was heard launching at him various metaphysical questions in regard to heaven and such like; and the relief was great when Thackeray introduced, with quaint whimsicality, a story which he and I had just heard Macready relate in talking to us about his boyish days, of a country actor who had supported himself for six months on his judicious treatment of the "tag" to the *Castle Spectre*. In the original it stands that you are to do away with suspicion, banish vile mistrust, and, almost in the words we had just heard from the minister to the philosopher, " Believe there is a heaven, nor doubt that heaven is just!" in place of which Macready's friend, observing that the drop fell for the most part quite coldly, substituted one night the more telling appeal, "And give us your Applause, for *that* is ALWAYS JUST!" which brought down the house with rapture.

This chapter would far outrun its limits if I spoke of other as pleasant gatherings under Dickens's roof during the years which I am now more particularly describing; when, besides the dinners, the musical enjoyments and dancings, as his children became able to take part in them, were incessant. "Remember that for my Biography!" he said to me gravely on Twelfth-day in 1849, after telling me what he had done the night before; and as gravely I now redeem my laughing promise that I would. Little Mary and her sister Kate had taken much pains to teach their father the polka, that he might dance it with them at their brother's birthday festivity (held this year on the 7th, as the 6th was a Sunday); and in the middle of the previous night as he lay in bed, the fear had fallen on him suddenly that the step was forgotten, and then and there, in that wintry dark cold night, he got out of bed to practise it. Anything *more* characteristic could hardly be told, unless I were able to show him dancing it afterwards, and excelling the youngest performer in untiring vigour and vivacity. There was no one who approached him on these occasions excepting only our attached friend Captain Marryat, who had a frantic delight in dancing, especially with children, of whom and whose enjoyments he was as fond as it became so thoroughly good-hearted a man to be. His name would have stood first among those I have been recalling, as he was among the first in Dickens's liking; but in the autumn of 1848 he had unexpectedly passed away. Other names however still reproach me for omission as my memory goes back. With Marryat's on a former page of this book stands that of Monckton Milnes, familiar with Dickens over all the period since, and still more prominent in Tavistock House days when with Lady Houghton he brought fresh claims to my friend's admiration and regard. Of Bulwer Lytton's frequent presence in all his houses, and of Dickens's admiration for him as one of the supreme masters in his art, so unswerving and so often publicly declared, it would be needless again to speak. Nor shall I dwell upon his interchange of hospitalities with distinguished men in the two great professions so closely allied to literature and its followers; Denmans, Pollocks, Campbells, and Chittys; Watsons, Southwood Smiths, Lococks, and Elliotsons. To Alfred Tennyson, through all the friendly and familiar days I am describing, he gave full allegiance and honoured welcome. Tom Taylor was often with him; and there was a charm for him I should find it difficult to exaggerate in Lord Dudley Stuart's gentle yet noble character, his refined intelligence and generous public life, expressed so perfectly in his chivalrous face. Incomplete indeed would be the list if I did not add to it the frank and hearty Lord Nugent, who had so much of his grandfather, Goldsmith's friend, in his lettered tastes and jovial enjoyments. Nor should I forget occasional days with dear old Charles Kemble and one or other of his daughters; with Alexander Dyce; and with Harness and his sister, or his niece and her husband, Mr. and Mrs. Archdale; made especially pleasant by talk about great days of the stage. It was something to hear Kemble on his sister's Mrs. Beverley; or to see Harness and Dyce exultant in recollecting her Volumnia. The enchantment of the Mrs. Beverley, her brother would delightfully illustrate by imitation of her manner of restraining Beverley's intemperance to their only friend, "You are too busy, sir!" when she quietly came down the stage from a table at which she had seemed to be occupying herself, laid her hand softly on her husband's arm, and in a gentle half-whisper, "No, not too busy; mistaken perhaps; but——" not only stayed his temper but reminded him of obligations forgotten in the heat of it. Up to where the tragic terror began, our friend told us, there was nothing but this composed domestic sweetness, expressed even in the simplicity and neat arrangement of her dress, her cap with the strait band, and her hair gathered up underneath; but all changing when the passion *did* begin; one single disordered lock escaping at the first outbreak, and, in the final madness, all of it streaming dishevelled down her beautiful face. Kemble made no secret of his belief that his sister had the highest genius of the two; but he spoke with rapture of "John's" Macbeth and parts of his Othello; comparing his "Farewell the tranquil mind" to the running down of a clock, an image which he did not know that Hazlitt had applied to the delivery of "To-morrow and to-morrow," in the other tragedy. In all this Harness seemed to agree; and I thought a distinction was not ill put by him, on the night of which I speak, in his remark that the nature in Kemble's acting only supplemented his magnificent art, whereas, though the artist was not less supreme in his sister, it was on nature she most relied, bringing up the other power only to the aid of it. "It was in another sense like your writing," said Harness to Dickens, "the commonest natural feelings made great, even when not rendered more refined by art." Her Constance would have been fishwify, he declared, if its wonderful truth had not overborne every other feeling; and her Volumnia escaped being vulgar only by being so excessively grand. But it was just what was so called "vulgarity" that made its passionate appeal to the vulgar in a better meaning of the word. When she first entered, Harness said, swaying and surging from side to side with every movement of the Roman crowd itself, as it went out and returned in confusion, she so absorbed her son into herself as she looked at him, so swelled and amplified in her pride and glory for him, that "the people in the pit blubbered all round," and he could no more help it than the rest.

There are yet some other names that should have place in these rambling recollections, though I by no means affect to remember all. One Sunday evening Mazzini made memorable by taking us to see the school he had established in Clerkenwell for the Italian organ-boys. This was after dining with Dickens, who had been brought into personal intercourse with the great Italian by having given money to a begging impostor who made unauthorised use of his name. Edinburgh friends made

him regular visits in the spring time: not Jeffrey and his family
alone, but Sheriff Gordon and his, with whom he was not less
intimate, Lord Murray and his wife, Sir William Allan and his
niece, Lord Robertson with his wonderful Scotch mimicries,
and Peter Fraser with his enchanting Scotch songs; our excellent
friend Liston the surgeon, until his fatal illness came in December
1848, being seldom absent from those assembled to bid such
visitors welcome. Allan's name may remind me of other artists
often at his house, Eastlakes, Leslies, Friths, and Wards, besides
those who have had frequent mention, and among whom I
should have included Charles as well as Edwin Landseer, and
William Boxall. Nor should I drop from this section of his
friends, than whom none were more attractive to him, such
celebrated names in the sister arts as those of Miss Helen Faucit,
an actress worthily associated with the brightest days of our
friend Macready's managements, Mr. Sims Reeves, Mr. John
Parry, Mr. Phelps, Mr. Webster, Mr. Harley, Mr. and Mrs.
Keeley, Mr. Whitworth, and Miss Dolby. Mr. George Henry
Lewes he had an old and great regard for; among other men
of letters should not be forgotten the cordial Thomas Ingoldsby,
and many-sided true-hearted Charles Knight. Mr. R. H. Horne
and his wife were frequent visitors both in London and at seaside holidays; and I have met at his table Mr. and Mrs. S. C.
Hall. There were the Duff Gordons too, the Lyells, and, very
old friends of us both, the Emerson Tennents; there was the
good George Raymond. Mr. Frank Beard and his wife; the
Porter Smiths, valued for Macready's sake as well as their own;
Mr. and Mrs. Charles Black, near connections by marriage of
George Cattermole, with whom there was intimate intercourse
both before and during the residence in Italy; Mr. T. J. Thompson, brother of Mrs. Smithson formerly named, and his wife,
whose sister Frederick Dickens married; Mr. Mitton, his own
early companion; and Mrs. Torrens, who had played with the
amateurs in Canada. These are all in my memory so connected
with Devonshire Terrace, as friends or familiar acquaintance,
that they claim this word before leaving it; and visitors from
America, I may remark, had always a grateful reception. Of
the Bancrofts mention has been made, and with them should
be coupled the Abbot Lawrences, Prescott, Hillard, George
Curtis, and Felton's brother. Felton himself did not visit England
until the Tavistock House time. In 1847 there was a delightful
day with the Coldens and the Wilkses, relatives by marriage
of Jeffrey; in the following year, I think at my rooms because

of some accident that closed Devonshire Terrace that day
(25 April), Dickens, Carlyle, and myself, forgathered with the
admirable Emerson; and M. Van de Weyer will remember a
dinner where he took joyous part with Dickens in running down
a phrase which the learned in books, Mr. Cogswell, on a mission
here for the Astor library, had startled us by denouncing as
an uncouth Scotch barbarism—*open up*. You found it constantly
in Hume, he said, but hardly anywhere else; and he defied us
to find it more than once through the whole of the volumes of
Gibbon. Upon this, after brief wonder and doubt, we all thought
it best to take part in a general assault upon *open up*, by invention of phrases on the same plan that should show it in exaggerated burlesque, and support Mr. Cogswell's indictment.
Then came a struggle who should carry the absurdity farthest;
and the victory remained with M. Van de Weyer until Dickens
surpassed even him, and "opened up" depths of almost frenzied
absurdity that would have delighted the heart of Leigh Hunt.
It will introduce the last and not least honoured name into
my list of his acquaintance and friends, if I mention his amusing
little interruption one day to Professor Owen's description of
a telescope of huge dimensions built by an enterprising clergyman who had taken to the study of the stars; and who was
eager, said Owen, to see farther into heaven—he was going to
say, than Lord Rosse; if Dickens had not dryly interposed, "than
his professional studies had enabled him to penetrate."

Some incidents that belong specially to the three years that
closed his residence in the home thus associated with not the
least interesting part of his career, will further show what now
were his occupations and ways of life. In the summer of 1849
he came up from Broadstairs to attend a Mansion House dinner,
which the lord mayor of that day had been moved by a laudable
ambition to give to "literature and art," which he supposed
would be adequately represented by the Royal Academy, the
contributors to *Punch*, Dickens, and one or two newspaper men.
On the whole the result was not cheering; the worthy chief
magistrate, no doubt quite undesignedly, expressing too much
surprise at the unaccustomed faces around him to be altogether
complimentary. In general (this was the tone) we are in the
habit of having princes, dukes, ministers, and what not for our
guests, but what a delight, all the greater for being unusual,
to see gentlemen like you! In other words, what could possibly
be pleasanter than for people satiated with greatness to get for
a while by way of change into the butler's pantry? This in

substance was Dickens's account to me next day, and his reason for having been very careful in his acknowledgment of the toast of "The Novelists." He was nettled not a little therefore by a jesting allusion to himself in the *Daily News* in connection with the proceedings, and asked me to forward a remonstrance. Having a strong dislike to all such displays of sensitiveness, I suppressed the letter; but it is perhaps worth printing now. Its date is Broadstairs, Wednesday, 11 July, 1849. "I have no other interest in, or concern with, a most facetious article on last Saturday's dinner at the Mansion House, which appeared in your paper of yesterday, and found its way here to-day, than that it misrepresents me in what I said on the occasion. If you should not think it at all damaging to the wit of that satire to state what I did say, I shall be much obliged to you. It was this. . . . That I considered the compliment of a recognition of Literature by the citizens of London the more acceptable to us because it was unusual in that hall, and likely to be an advantage and benefit to them in proportion as it became in future less unusual. That, on behalf of the novelists, I accepted the tribute as an appropriate one; inasmuch as we had sometimes reason to hope that our imaginary worlds afforded an occasional refuge to men busily engaged in the toils of life, from which they came forth none the worse to a renewal of its strivings; and certainly that the chief magistrate of the greatest city in the world might be fitly regarded as the representative of that class of our readers."

Of an incident towards the close of the year, though it had important practical results, brief mention will here suffice. We saw the Mannings executed on the walls of Horsemonger Lane Gaol; and with the letter which Dickens wrote next day to *The Times* descriptive of what we had witnessed on that memorable morning, there began an active agitation against public executions which never ceased until the salutary change was effected which has worked so well. Shortly after this he visited Rockingham Castle, the seat of Mr. and Mrs. Watson, his Lausanne friends; and I must preface by a word or two the amusing letter in which he told me of this visit. It was written in character, and the character was that of an American visitor to England..

"I knew him, Horatio"; and a very kindly honest man he was, who had come to England authorised to make inquiry into our general agricultural condition, and who discharged his mission by publishing some reports extremely creditable to his good sense and ability, expressed in a plain nervous English that reminded one of the rural writings of Cobbett. But in an evil hour he published also a series of private letters to friends written from the various residences his introductions had opened to him; and these were filled with revelations as to the internal economy of English noblemen's country houses, of a highly startling description. As for example, how, on arrival at a house your "name is announced, and your portmanteau immediately taken into your chamber, which the servant shows you, with every convenience." How "you are asked by the servant at breakfast what you will have, or you get up and help yourself." How at dinner you don't dash at the dishes, or contend for the "fixings," but wait till "his portion is handed by servants to everyone." How all the wines, fruit, glasses, candlesticks, lamps, and plate are "taken care of" by butlers, who have under-butlers for their "adjuncts"; how ladies never wear "white satin shoes or white gloves more than once"; how dinner-napkins are "never left upon the table, but either thrown into your chair or on the floor under the table"; how no end of pains are taken to "empty slops"; and above all what a national propensity there is to brush a man's clothes and polish his boots, whensoever and wheresoever the clothes and boots can be seized without the man. This was what Dickens good-humouredly laughs at.

"Rockingham Castle: Friday, thirtieth of November, 1849. Picture to yourself, my dear F., a large old castle, approached by an ancient keep, portcullis, etc., filled with company, waited on by six-and-twenty servants; the slops (and wine-glasses) continually being emptied; and my clothes (with myself in them) always being carried off to all sorts of places; and you will have a faint idea of the mansion in which I am at present staying. I should have written to you yesterday, but for having had a very busy day. Among the guests is a Miss B., sister of the Honourable Miss B. (of Salem, Mass.), whom we once met at the house of our distinguished literary countryman Colonel Landor. This lady is renowned as an amateur actress, so last night we got up in the great hall some scenes from the *School for Scandal*; the scene with the lunatic on the wall, from the *Nicholas Nickleby* of Major-General the Hon. C. Dickens (Richmond, Va.); some conjuring; and then finished off with country dances; of which we had two admirably good ones, quite new to me, though really old. Getting the words, and making the preparations, occupied (as you may believe) the whole day; and it was three o'clock before I got to bed. It was

† 15

an excellent entertainment, and we were all uncommonly merry.
. . . I had a very polite letter from our enterprising countryman Major Bentley (of Lexington, Ky.), which I shall show * 81
you when I come home. We leave here this afternoon, and I
shall expect you according to appointment, at a quarter past
ten a.m. to-morrow. Of all the country-houses and estates I
have yet seen in England, I think this is by far the best. Everything undertaken eventuates in a most magnificent hospitality;
and you will be pleased to hear that our celebrated fellow citizen
General Boxall (Pittsburg, Penn.) is engaged in handing down
to posterity the face of the owner of the mansion and of his
youthful son and daughter. At a future time it will be my duty
to report on the turnips, mangel-wurzel, ploughs, and live stock;
and for the present I will only say that I regard it as a fortunate
circumstance for the neighbouring community that this patri-
mony should have fallen to my spirited and enlightened host.
Everyone has profited by it, and the labouring people in especial
are thoroughly well cared-for and looked after. To see all the
household, headed by an enormously fat housekeeper, occupying
the back benches last night, laughing and applauding without
any restraint; and to see a blushing sleek-headed footman
produce, for the watch-trick, a silver watch of the most portentous dimensions, amidst the rapturous delight of his brethren
and sisterhood; was a very pleasant spectacle, even to a conscientious republican like yourself or me, who cannot but contemplate the parent country with feelings of pride in our own
land, which (as was well observed by the Honourable Elias
Deeze, of Hartford, Conn.) is truly the land of the free. Best
remembrances from Columbia's daughters. Ever thine, my dear
F.,—H. C." Dickens, during the too brief time his excellent
friend was spared to him, often repeated his visits to Rockingham, always a surpassing enjoyment; and in the winter of 1850
he accomplished there, with help of the country carpenter, "a
very elegant little theatre," of which he constituted himself
manager, and had among his actors a brother of the lady
referred to in his letter, "a very good comic actor, but loose
in words"; poor Augustus Stafford, "more than passable"; and
"a son of Vernon Smith's, really a capital low comedian." It
will be one more added to the many examples I have given
of his untiring energy both in work and play, if I mention
the fact that this theatre was opened at Rockingham for
their first representation on Wednesday, 15 January; that
after the performance there was a country dance which lasted

far into the morning; and that on the next evening, after a railway journey of more than 120 miles, he dined in London with the prime minister, Lord John Russell.

A little earlier in that winter we had together taken his eldest son to Eton, and a little later he had a great sorrow. "Poor dear Jeffrey!" he wrote to me on 29 January, 1850. "I bought a *Times* at the station yesterday morning, and was so stunned by the announcement, that I felt it in that wounded part of me almost directly; and the bad symptoms (modified) returned within a few hours. I had a letter from him in extraordinary good spirits within this week or two—he was better, he said, than he had been for a long time—and I sent him proof-sheets of the number only last Wednesday. I say nothing of his wonderful abilities and great career, but he was a most affectionate and devoted friend to me; and though no man could wish to live and die more happily, so old in years and yet so young in faculties and sympathies, I am very very deeply grieved for his loss." He was justly entitled to feel pride in being able so to word his tribute of sorrowing affection. Jeffrey had completed with consummate success, if ever man did, the work appointed him in this world; and few, after a life of such activities, have left a memory so unstained and pure. But other and sharper sorrows awaited Dickens.

The chief occupation of the past and present year, *David Copperfield*, will have a section to itself, and in this may be touched but lightly. Once fairly in it, the story bore him irresistibly along; certainly with less trouble to himself in the composition, beyond that ardent sympathy with the creatures of the fancy which always made so absolutely real to him their sufferings or sorrows; and he was probably never less harassed by interruptions or breaks in his invention. His principal hesitation occurred in connection with the child-wife Dora, who had become a great favourite as he went on; and it was shortly after her fate had been decided, in the early autumn of * 82 1850, but before she breathed her last, that a third daughter was born to him, to whom he gave his dying little heroine's name. On these and other points, without forestalling what waits to be said of the composition of this fine story, a few illustrative words from his letters will properly find a place here. "*Copperfield* half done," he wrote of the second number on 6 June. "I feel, thank God, quite confident in the story. I have a move in it ready for this month; another for next; and another for the next." "I think it is necessary"

(15 November) "to decide against the special pleader. Your reasons quite suffice. I am not sure but that the banking house might do. I will consider it in a walk." "Banking business impracticable" (17 November) "on account of the confinement: which would stop the story, I foresee. I have taken, for the present at all events, the proctor. I am wonderfully in harness, and nothing galls or frets." "*Copperfield* done" (20 November) "after two days' very hard work indeed; and I think a smashing number. His first dissipation I hope will be found worthy of attention, as a piece of grotesque truth." "I feel a great hope" (23 January, 1850) "that I shall be remembered by little Em'ly, a good many years to come." "I begin to have my doubts of being able to join you" (20 February), "for *Copperfield* runs high, and must be done to-morrow. But I'll do it if possible, and strain every nerve. Some beautiful comic love, I hope, in the number." "Still undecided about Dora" (7 May), "but MUST decide to-day." "I have been" (Tuesday, 20 August) * 83 "very hard at work these three days, and have still Dora to kill. But with good luck, I may do it to-morrow. Obliged to go to Shepherd's Bush to-day, and can consequently do little this morning. Am eschewing all sorts of things that present themselves to my fancy—coming in such crowds!" "Work in a very decent state of advancement" (13 August) "domesticity notwithstanding. I hope I shall have a splendid number. I feel the story to its minutest point." "Mrs. Micawber is still" (15 August), "I regret to say, in *statu quo*. Ever yours, WILKINS MICAWBER." The little girl was born the next day, the 16th, and received the name of Dora Annie. The most part of what remained of the year was passed away from home.

The year following did not open with favourable omen, both the child and its mother having severe illness. The former rallied, however, and "little Dora is getting on bravely, thank God!" was his bulletin of the early part of February. Soon after, it was resolved to make trial of Great Malvern for Mrs. Dickens; and lodgings were taken there in March, Dickens and her sister accompanying her, and the children being left in London. "It is a most beautiful place," he wrote to me (15 March). "O Heaven, to meet the Cold Waterers (as I did this morning when I went out for a shower-bath) dashing down the hills, with severe expressions on their countenances, like men doing matches and not exactly winning! Then, a young lady in a grey polka going *up* the hills, regardless of legs; and meeting a young gentleman (a bad case, I should say) with a

light black silk cap on under his hat, and the pimples of I don't
know how many douches under that. Likewise an old man who
ran over a milk-child, rather than stop!—with no neckcloth,
on principle; and with his mouth wide open to catch the morning
air." He had to return to London after the middle of March,
for business connected with a charitable Home established at
Shepherd's Bush by Miss Coutts in the benevolent hope of res-
cuing fallen women by testing their fitness for emigration, frequently mentioned in his letters, and which largely and regularly
occupied his time for several years. On this occasion his stay was
prolonged by the illness of his father, whose health had been
failing latterly, and graver symptoms were now spoken of. "I
saw my poor father twice yesterday," he wrote to me on the
27th, "the second time between ten and eleven at night. In
the morning I thought him not so well. At night, as well as anyone in such a situation could be." Next day he was so much
better that his son went back to Malvern: but the end came
suddenly. We were expecting him at Knebworth, and I supposed
that some accident had detained him in Malvern; but at my
return this letter waited me. "Devonshire Terrace, Monday,
thirty-first of March, 1851. . . . My poor father died this morning
at five and twenty minutes to six. They had sent for me to
Malvern, but I passed John on the railway. . . . Arrived at eleven
last night, and was in Keppel Street at a quarter past eleven.
He did not know me, nor anyone. He began to sink at about
noon yesterday, and never rallied afterwards. I remained there
until he died—O so quietly. . . . I hardly know what to do. I am
going up to Highgate to get the ground. Perhaps you may like
to go, and I should like it if you do. I will not leave here before
two o'clock, but I must go down to Malvern again, at night.
. . ." Mr. John Dickens was laid in Highgate Cemetery on
5 April; and the stone placed over him by the son who has
made his name a famous one in England, bore tribute to his
"zealous, useful, cheerful spirit." What more is to be said of
him will be most becomingly said in speaking of *David Copperfield*. While the book was in course of being written, all that had
been best in him came more and more vividly back to its
author's memory; as time wore on, nothing else was remembered; and five years before his own death, after using in one
of his letters to me a phrase rather out of the common with
him, this was added: "I find this looks like my poor father,
whom I regard as a better man the longer I live."

　　He was at this time under promise to take the chair at the

General Theatrical Fund on 14 April. Great efforts were made to relieve him from the promise; but such special importance was attached to his being present, and the Fund so sorely then required help, that, no change of day being found possible for the actors who desired to attend, he yielded to the pressure put upon him; of which the result was to throw upon me a sad responsibility. The reader will understand why, even at this distance of time, my allusion to it is brief.

The train from Malvern brought him up only five minutes short of the hour appointed for the dinner, and we first met that day at the London Tavern. I never heard him to greater advantage than in the speech that followed. His liking for this Fund was the fact of its not confining its benefits to any special or exclusive body of actors, but opening them undoubtingly to all; and he gave a description of the kind of actor, going down to the infinitesimally small, not omitted from such kind help, which had a half-pathetic humour in it that makes it charming still. "In our Fund," he said, "the word exclusiveness is not known. We include every actor, whether he be Hamlet or Benedict: the ghost, the bandit, or the court physician; or, in his one person, the whole king's army. He may do the light business, or the heavy, or the comic, or the eccentric. He may be the captain who courts the young lady, whose uncle still unaccountably persists in dressing himself in a costume one hundred years older than his time. Or he may be the young lady's brother in the white gloves and inexpressibles, whose duty in the family appears to be to listen to the female members of it whenever they sing, and to shake hands with everybody between all the verses. Or he may be the baron who gives the fête, and who sits uneasily on the sofa under a canopy with the baroness while the fête is going on. Or he may be the peasant at the fête who comes on to the stage to swell the drinking chorus, and who, it may be observed, always turns his glass upside down before he begins to drink out of it. Or he may be the clown who takes away the doorstep of the house where the evening party is going on. Or he may be the gentleman who issues out of the house on the false alarm, and is precipitated into the area. Or, if an actress, she may be the fairy who resides for ever in a revolving star with an occasional visit to a bower or a palace. Or again, if an actor, he may be the armed head of the witch's cauldron; or even that extraordinary witch concerning whom I have observed in country places, that he is much less like the notion formed from the description of

Hopkins than the Malcolm or Donalbain of the previous scenes
This society, in short, says, 'Be you what you may, be you
actor or actress, be your path in your profession never so high
or never so low, never so haughty or never so humble, we
offer you the means of doing good to yourselves, and of doing
good to your brethren.'"

Half an hour before he rose to speak I had been called out
of the room. It was the servant from Devonshire Terrace to tell
me his child Dora was suddenly dead. She had not been strong
from her birth; but there was just at this time no cause for
special fear, when unexpected convulsions came, and the frail
little life passed away. My decision had to be formed at once;
and I satisfied myself that it would be best to permit his part
of the proceedings to close before the truth was told to him.
But as he went on, after the sentences I have quoted, to speak
of actors having to come from scenes and sickness, of suffering,
aye, even of death itself, to play their parts before us, my
part was very difficult. "Yet how often is it with all of us," he
proceeded to say, and I remember to this hour with what
anguish I listened to words that had for myself alone, in all
the crowded room, their full significance: "how often is it with
all of us, that in our several spheres we have to do violence to
our feelings, and to hide our hearts in carrying on this fight of
life, if we would bravely discharge in it our duties and respon-
sibilities." In the disclosure that followed when he left the
chair, Mr. Lemon, who was present, assisted me; and I left
this good friend with him next day, when I went myself to
Malvern and brought back Mrs. Dickens and her sister. The
little child lies in a grave at Highgate near that of Mr. and
Mrs. John Dickens; and on the stone which covers her is
now written also her father's name, and those of two of
her brothers.

One more public discussion he took part in, before quitting
London for the rest of the summer; and what he said (it was a
meeting, with Lord Carlisle in the chair, in aid of Sanitary
reform) very pregnantly illustrates what was remarked by me
on a former page. He declared his belief that neither education
nor religion could do anything really useful in social improvement until the way had been paved for their ministrations by
cleanliness and decency. He spoke warmly of the services of
Lord Ashley in connection with ragged schools, but he put the
case of a miserable child tempted into one of those schools out
of the noisome places in which his life was passed, and he asked

what a few hours' teaching could effect against the ever-renewed lesson of a whole existence. "But give him, and his, a glimpse of heaven through a little of its light and air; give them water; help them to be clean; lighten the heavy atmosphere in which their spirits flag, and which makes them the callous things they are; take the body of the dead relative from the room where the living live with it, and where such loathsome familiarity deprives death itself of awe; and then, but not before, they will be brought willingly to hear of Him whose thoughts were so much with the wretched, and who had compassion for all human sorrow." He closed by proposing Lord Ashley's health as having preferred the higher ambition of labouring for the poor to that of pursuing the career open to him in the service of the State; and as having also had "the courage on all occasions to face the cant which is the worst and commonest of all, the cant about the cant of philanthropy." Lord Shaftesbury first dined with him in the following year at Tavistock House.

Shortly after the Sanitary meeting, came the first Guild performances; and then Dickens left Devonshire Terrace, never to return to it. With intervals of absence, chiefly at the Guild representations, he stayed in his favourite Fort House by the sea until October, when he took possession of Tavistock House; † 16 and from his letters may be added a few notices of this last holiday at Broadstairs, which he had always afterwards a kindly word for; and to which he said pleasant adieu in the sketch of our watering-place, written shortly before he left. "It is more delightful here" (1 June) "than I can express. Corn growing, larks singing, garden full of flowers, fresh air on the sea.—O it is wonderful! Why can't you come down next Saturday (bringing work) and go back with me on Wednesday for the *Copperfield* banquet? Concerning which, of course, I say yes to Talfourd's kind proposal. Lemon by all means. And—don't you think—Browne? Whosoever, besides, pleases Talfourd will please me." Great was the success of this banquet. The scene was the Star and Garter at Richmond; Thackeray and Alfred Tennyson joined in the celebration; and the generous giver was in his best vein. I have rarely seen Dickens happier than he was amid the sunshine of that day. Jerrold and Thackeray returned to town with us; and a little argument between them about money and its uses, led to an avowal of Dickens about himself to which I may add the confirmation of all our years of intercourse. "No man," he said, "attaches less importance to the possession of money, or less disparagement to the want of it, than I do."

I joined him for the August regatta and stayed a pleasant fortnight. His paper on "Our Watering-place" appeared while I was there, and great was the local excitement. But now his own restlessness with fancies for a new book had risen beyond bounds, and for the time he was eager to open it in that prettiest quaintest bit of English landscape, Strood Valley, which reminded him always of a Swiss scene. I had not left him many days when these lines followed me. "I very nearly packed up a portmanteau and went away, the day before yesterday, into the mountains of Switzerland, alone! Still the victim of an intolerable restlessness, I shouldn't be at all surprised if I wrote to you one of these mornings from under Mont Blanc. I sit down between whiles to think of a new story, and, as it begins to grow, such a torment of a desire to be anywhere but where I am; and to be going I don't know where, I don't know why; takes hold of me, that it is like being *driven away*. If I had had a passport, I sincerely believe I should have gone to Switzerland the night before last. I should have remembered our engagement—say, at Paris, and have come back for it; but should probably have left by the next express train." It was not until the end of November, when he had settled himself in his new London abode, that the book was begun (and as generally happened with the more important incidents of his life, though always accidentally, begun on a Friday); but precedence is due, before anything more is said of *Bleak House*, to what remains to be said of *Copperfield*.

It was the last book written in Devonshire Terrace; and on the page opposite is engraved a drawing by Maclise of this house where so many of Dickens's masterpieces were composed, done on the first anniversary of the day when his daughter Kate was born.

OCTOBER

VII

"DAVID COPPERFIELD"

OCTOBER

VII

1850

DICKENS never stood so high in reputation as at the completion of *Copperfield*. From the first it had surpassed in popularity, though not in sale, all his previous books excepting *Pickwick*. "You gratify me more than I can tell you," he wrote to Lytton, "by what you say about *Copperfield*, because I hope myself that some heretofore deficient qualities are there." If the power was not greater than in *Chuzzlewit*, the subject had more attractiveness; there was more variety of incident, with a freer play of character; and there was withal a suspicion, which though general and vague had sharpened interest not a little, that underneath the fiction lay something of the author's life. How much was not known by the world until he had passed away. When engaged upon its close he had written thus (21 October, 1850): "I am within three pages of the shore; and am strangely divided, as usual in such cases, between sorrow and joy. Oh, my dear Forster, if I were to say half of what *Copperfield* makes me feel to-night, how strangely, even to you, I should be turned inside-out! I seem to be sending some part of myself into the Shadowy World."

To be acquainted with English literature is to know that into its most famous prose fiction autobiography has entered largely in disguise, and that the characters most familiar to us in the English novel had originals in actual life. Smollett never wrote a story that was not in some degree a recollection of his own adventures; and Fielding, who put something of his wife into all his heroines, had been as fortunate in finding, not Trulliber only, but Parson Adams himself, among his living experiences. To come later down, there was hardly anyone ever known to Scott of whom his memory had not treasured up something to give minuter reality to the people of his fancy; and we know exactly whom to look for in Dandie Dinmont and Jonathan Oldbuck, in the office of Alan Fairford and the sick-room of Crystal Croftangry. We are to observe also that it is never anything complete that is thus taken from life by a genuine writer, but only leading traits, or such as may give greater finish; that the fine artist will embody in his portraiture of one person his experiences of fifty; and that this would have been Fielding's answer to Trulliber if he had objected to the pigsty, and to Adams if he had sought to make a case of scandal out of the affair in Mrs. Slipslop's bedroom. Such questioning befell Dickens repeatedly in the course of his writings, where he freely followed, as we have seen, the method thus common to the masters in his art; but there was an instance of alleged wrong in the course of *Copperfield* where he felt his vindication to be hardly complete, and what he did thereupon was characteristic.

"I have had the queerest adventure this morning," he wrote (28 December, 1849) on the eve of his tenth number, "the receipt of the enclosed from Miss Moucher! It is serio-comic, but there is no doubt one is wrong in being tempted to such a use of power." Thinking a grotesque little oddity among his acquaintance to be safe from recognition, he had done what Smollett did sometimes, but never Fielding, and given way, in the first outburst of fun that had broken out around the fancy, to the temptation of copying too closely peculiarities of figure and face amounting in effect to deformity. He was shocked at discovering the pain he had given, and a copy is before me of the assurances by way of reply which he at once sent to the complainant. That he was grieved and surprised beyond measure. That he had not intended her altogether. That all his characters, being made up out of many people, were composite, and never individual. That the chair (for table) and other matters were undoubtedly from her, but that other traits were not hers at all; and that in Miss Moucher's "Ain't I volatile" his friends had quite correctly recognised the favourite utterance of a different person. That he felt nevertheless he had done wrong, and would now do anything to repair it. That he had intended to employ the character in an unpleasant way, but he would, whatever the risk or inconvenience, change it all, so that nothing but an agreeable impression should be left. The reader will remember how this was managed, and that the thirty-second chapter went far to undo what the twenty-second had done.

A much earlier instance is the only one known to me where a character in one of his books intended to be odious was copied wholly from a living original. The use of such material, never without danger, might have been justifiable here if anywhere, and he had himself a satisfaction in always admitting the identity of Mr. Fang in *Oliver Twist* with Mr. Laing of Hatton Garden. But the avowal of his purpose in that case, and his mode of setting about it, mark strongly a difference of procedure from that which, following great examples, he adopted in his later books. An allusion to a common friend in one of his letters of the present date—"A dreadful thought occurs to me! how brilliant in a book!"—expresses both the continued strength of his temptations and the dread he had brought himself to feel of immediately yielding to them; but he had no such misgivings in the days of *Oliver Twist*. Wanting an insolent and harsh police-magistrate, he bethought him of an original ready to his hand in one of the London offices; and instead of pursuing his later method of giving a personal appearance that should in some sort render difficult the identification of mental peculiarities, he was only eager to get in the whole man complete upon his page, figure and face as well as manners and mind.

He wrote accordingly (from Doughty Street on 3 June, 1837) to Mr. Haines, a gentleman who then had general supervision over the police reports for the daily papers. "In my next number of *Oliver Twist* I must have a magistrate; and, casting about for a magistrate whose harshness and insolence would render him a fit subject to be *shown up*, I have as a necessary consequence stumbled upon Mr. Laing of Hatton Garden celebrity. I know the man's character perfectly well; but as it would be necessary to describe his personal appearance also, I ought to have seen him, which (fortunately or unfortunately as the case may be) I have never done. In this dilemma it occurred to me that perhaps I might under your auspices be smuggled into the Hatton Garden office for a few moments some morning. If you can further my object I shall be really very greatly obliged to you." The opportunity was found; the magistrate was brought up before the novelist; and shortly after, on some fresh outbreak of intolerable temper, the Home-Secretary found it an easy and popular step to remove Mr. Laing from the bench.

This was a comfort to everybody, saving only the principal person; but the instance was highly exceptional, and it rarely indeed happens that to the individual objection natural in every such case some consideration should not be paid. In the book that followed *Copperfield*, characters appeared having resemblances in manner and speech to distinguished writers too vivid to be mistaken by their personal friends. To Lawrence Boythorn, under whom Landor figured, no objection was made; but

Harold Skimpole, recognisable for Leigh Hunt, led to much remark; the difference being, that ludicrous traits were employed in the first to enrich without impairing an attractive person in the tale, whereas to the last was assigned a part in the plot which no fascinating foibles or gaieties of speech could redeem from contempt. Though a want of consideration was thus shown to the friend whom the character would be likely to recall to many readers, it is nevertheless very certain that the intention of Dickens was not at first, or at any time, an unkind one. He erred from thoughtlessness only. What led him to the subject at all, he has himself stated. Hunt's philosophy of moneyed obligations, always, though loudly, half jocosely proclaimed, and his ostentatious wilfulness in the humouring of that or any other theme on which he cared for the time to expatiate, had * 83A so often seemed to Dickens to be whimsical and attractive, that, wanting an "airy quality" for the man he invented, this of Hunt occurred to him; and "partly for that reason, and partly, he has since often grieved to think, for the pleasure it afforded to find a delightful manner reproducing itself under his hand, he yielded to the temptation of too often making the character speak like his old friend." This apology was made after Hunt's death,[1] and mentioned a revision of the first sketch, so as to render it less like, at the suggestion of two other friends of Hunt. The friends were Procter (Barry Cornwall) and myself; the feeling having been mine from the first that the likeness was too like. Procter did not immediately think so, but a little reflection brought him to that opinion. "You will see from the enclosed," Dickens wrote (17 March, 1852), "that Procter is much of my mind. I will nevertheless go through the character again in the course of the afternoon, and soften down words here and there." But before the day closed Procter had again written to him, and next morning this was the result. "I have again gone over every part of it very carefully, and I think I have made it much less like. I have also changed Leonard to Harold. I have no right to give Hunt pain, and I am so bent upon not doing it that I wish you would look at all the proof once more, and indicate any particular place in which you feel it particularly like. Whereupon I will alter that place."

Upon the whole the alterations were considerable, but the radical wrong remained. The pleasant sparkling airy talk, which could not be mistaken, identified with odious qualities a friend

[1] In a paper in *All the Year Round*.

only known to the writer by attractive ones; and for this there was no excuse. Perhaps the only person acquainted with the original who failed to recognise the copy, was the original himself (a common case); but good-natured friends in time told Hunt everything, and painful explanations followed, where nothing was possible to Dickens but what amounted to a friendly evasion of the points really at issue. The time for redress had gone. I yet well remember with what eager earnestness, on one of these occasions, he strove to set Hunt up again in his own esteem. "Separate in your own mind," he said to him, "what you see of yourself from what other people tell you that they see. As it has given you so much pain, I take it at its worst, and say I am deeply sorry, and that I feel I did wrong in doing it. I should otherwise have taken it at its best, and ridden off upon what I strongly feel to be the truth, that there is nothing in it that *should* have given you pain. Everyone in writing must speak from points of his experience, and so I of mine with you: but when I have felt it was going too close I stopped myself, and the most blotted parts of my MS. are those in which I have been striving hard to make the impression I was writing from, *un*like you. The diary-writing I took from Haydon, not from you. I now first learn from yourself that you ever set anything to music, and I could not have copied *that* from you. The character is not you, for there are traits in it common to fifty thousand people besides, and I did not fancy you would ever recognise it. Under similar disguises my own father and mother are in my books, and you might as well see your likeness in Micawber." The distinction is that the foibles of Mr. Micawber and of Mrs. Nickleby, however laughable, make neither of them in speech or character less lovable; and that this is not to be said of Skimpole's. The kindly or unkindly impression makes all the difference where liberties are taken with a friend; and even this entirely favourable condition will not excuse the practice to many, where near relatives are concerned.

For what formerly was said of the Micawber resemblances, Dickens has been sharply criticised; and in like manner it was thought objectionable in Scott that for the closing scenes of Crystal Croftangry he should have found the original of his fretful patient at the death-bed of his own father. Lockhart, who tells us this, adds with a sad significance that he himself lived to see the curtain fall at Abbotsford upon even such another scene. But to no purpose will such objections still be made. All great novelists will continue to use their experiences of nature and fact, whencesoever derivable; and a remark made to Lockhart by Scott himself suggests their vindication. "If a man will paint from nature, he will be most likely to interest and amuse those who are daily looking at it."

The Micawber offence otherwise was not grave. We have seen in what way Dickens was moved or inspired by the rough lessons of his boyhood, and the groundwork of the character was then undoubtedly laid; but the rhetorical exuberance impressed itself upon him later, and from this, as it expanded and developed in a thousand amusing ways, the full-length figure took its great charm. Better illustration of it could not perhaps be given than by passages from letters of Dickens, written long before Micawber was thought of, in which this peculiarity of his father found frequent and always agreeable expression. Several such have been given in this work from time to time, and one or two more may here be added. It is proper to preface them by saying that no one could know the elder Dickens without secretly liking him the better for these flourishes of speech, which adapted themselves so readily to his gloom as well as to his cheerfulness, that it was difficult not to fancy they had helped him considerably in both, and had rendered more tolerable to him, if also more possible, the shade and sunshine of his chequered life. "If you should have an opportunity, *pendente lite*, as my father would observe—indeed did on some memorable ancient occasions when he informed me that the ban-dogs would shortly have him at bay"—Dickens wrote in December 1847. "I have a letter from my father" (May 1841) "lamenting the fine weather, invoking congenial tempests, and informing me that it will not be possible for him to stay more than another year in Devonshire, as he must then proceed to Paris to consolidate Augustus's French." "There has arrived," he writes from the Peschiere in September 1844, "a characteristic letter for Kate from my father. He dates it Manchester, and says he has reason to believe that he will be in town with the pheasants, on or about the first of October. He has been with Fanny in the Isle of Man for nearly two months: finding there, as he goes on to observe, troops of friends, and every description of continental luxury at a cheap rate." Describing in the same year the departure from Genoa of an English physician and acquaintance, he adds: "We are very sorry to lose the benefit of his advice—or, as my father would say, to be deprived, to a certain extent, of the concomitant advantages, whatever they may be, resulting from his medical skill, such as it is, and his professional attendance, in so far as it may be so considered." Thus also it delighted Dickens to remember that it was of one of his connections his father wrote a celebrated sentence; "And I must express my tendency to believe that his longevity is (to say the least of it) extremely problematical": and that it was to another, who had been insisting somewhat obtrusively on dissenting and nonconformist superiorities, he addressed words which deserve to be no less celebrated; "The Supreme Being must be an entirely different individual from what I have every reason to believe Him to be, if He would care in the least for the society of your relations." There was a laugh in the enjoyment of all this, no doubt, but with it much personal fondness; and the feeling of the creator of Micawber, as he thus humoured and remembered the foibles of his original, found its counterpart in that of his readers for the creation itself, as its part was played out in the story. Nobody likes Micawber less for his follies; and Dickens liked his father more, the more he recalled his whimsical qualities. "The longer I live, the better man I think him," he exclaimed afterwards. The fact and the fancy had united whatever was most grateful to him in both.

It is a tribute to the generally healthful and manly tone of the story of *Copperfield* that such should be the outcome of the eccentricities of this leading personage in it; and the superiority in this respect of Micawber over Skimpole is one of the many indications of the inferiority of *Bleak House* to its predecessor. With leading resemblances that make it difficult to say which character best represents the principle or no principle of impecuniosity, there cannot be any doubt which has the advantage in moral and intellectual development. It is genuine humour against personal satire. Between the worldly circumstances of the two, there is nothing to choose; but as to everything else it is the difference between shabbiness and greatness. Skimpole's sunny talk might be expected to please as much as Micawber's gorgeous speech, the design of both being to take the edge off poverty. But in the one we have no relief from attendant meanness or distress, and we drop down from the airiest fancies into sordidness and pain; whereas in the other nothing pitiful or merely selfish ever touches us. At its lowest depth of what is worst, we never doubt that something better must turn up; and of a man who sells his bedstead that he may entertain his friend, we altogether refuse to think nothing but badly. This is throughout the free and cheery style of *Copperfield*. The masterpieces of Dickens's humour are not in it; but he has nowhere given such variety of play to his invention, and the book is unapproached among his writings for its completeness of effect and uniform pleasantness of tone.

What has to be said hereafter of those writings generally, will properly restrict what is said here, as in previous instances, mainly to personal illustration. The *Copperfield* disclosures formerly made will for ever connect the book with the author's individual story; but too much has been assumed, from those revelations, of a full identity of Dickens with his hero, and of a supposed intention that his own character as well as parts of his career should be expressed in the narrative. It is right to warn the reader as to this. He can judge for himself how far the childish experiences are likely to have given the turn to Dickens's genius; whether their bitterness had so burnt into his nature, as, in the hatred of oppression, the revolt against abuse of power, and the war with injustice under every form displayed in his earliest books, to have reproduced itself only; and to what extent mere compassion for his own childhood may account for the strange fascination always exerted over him by child-suffering and sorrow. But, many as are the resemblances in Copperfield's adventures to portions of those of Dickens, and often as reflections occur to David which no one intimate with Dickens could fail to recognise as but the reproduction of his, it would be the greatest mistake to imagine anything like a complete identity of the fictitious novelist with the real one, beyond the Hungerford scenes; or to suppose that the youth, who then received his first harsh schooling in life, came out of it as little harmed or hardened as David did. The language of the fiction reflects only faintly the narrative of the actual fact; and the man whose character it helped to form was expressed not less faintly in the impulsive impressionable youth, incapable of resisting the leading of others, and only disciplined into self-control by the later griefs of his entrance into manhood. Here was but another proof how thoroughly Dickens understood his calling, and that to weave fact with fiction unskilfully would be only to make truth less true.

The character of the hero of the novel finds indeed his right place in the story he is supposed to tell, rather by unlikeness than by likeness to Dickens, even where intentional resemblance might seem to be prominent. Take autobiography as a design to show that any man's life may be as a mirror of existence to all men, and the individual career becomes altogether secondary to the variety of experiences received and rendered back in it. This particular form in imaginative literature has too often led to the indulgence of mental analysis, metaphysics, and sentiment, all in excess: but Dickens was carried safely over these allurements by a healthy judgment and sleepless creative fancy; and even the method of his narrative is more simple here than it generally is in his books. His imaginative growths have less luxuriance of underwood, and the crowds of external images always rising so vividly before him are more within control.

Consider Copperfield thus in his proper place in the story, and sequence as well as connection will be given to the varieties of its childish adventure. The first warm nest of love in which his vain fond mother, and her quaint kind servant, cherish him; the quick-following contrast of hard dependence and servile treatment; the escape from that premature and dwarfed maturity by natural relapse into a more perfect childhood; the then leisurely growth of emotions and faculties into manhood; these are component parts of a character consistently drawn. The sum of its achievement is to be a successful cultivation of letters; and often as such imaginary discipline has been the theme of fiction, there are not many happier conceptions of it. The ideal and real parts of the boy's nature receive development in the proportions which contribute best to the end desired; the readiness for impulsive attachments that had put him into the leading of others, has underneath it a base of truthfulness on which at last he rests in safety; the practical man is the outcome of the fanciful youth; and a more than equivalent for the graces of his visionary days, is found in the active sympathies that life has opened to him. Many experiences have come within its range, and his heart has had room for all. Our interest in him cannot but be increased by knowing how much he expresses of what the author had himself gone through; but David includes far less than this, and infinitely more.

That the incidents arise easily, and to the very end connect themselves naturally and unobtrusively with the characters of which they are a part, is to be said perhaps more truly of this than of any other of Dickens's novels. There is a profusion of distinct and distinguishable people, and a prodigal wealth of detail; but unity of drift or purpose is apparent always, and the tone is uniformly right. By the course of the events we learn the value of self-denial and patience, quiet endurance of unavoidable ills, strenuous effort against ills remediable; and everything in the fortunes of the actors warns us, to strengthen our generous emotions and to guard the purities of home. It is easy thus to account for the supreme popularity of *Copperfield*, without the addition that it can hardly have had a reader, man or lad, who did not discover that he was something of a Copperfield himself. Childhood and youth live again for all of us in its marvellous boy-experiences. Mr. Micawber's presence must not prevent my saying that it does not take the lead of the other novels in humorous creation; but in the use of humour to bring out prominently the ludicrous in any object or incident without excluding or weakening its most enchanting sentiment, it stands decidedly first. It is the perfection of English mirth. We are apt to resent the exhibition of too much goodness, but it is here so qualified by oddity as to become not merely palatable but attractive; and even pathos is heightened by what in other hands would only make it comical. That there are also faults in the book is certain, but none that are incompatible with the most masterly qualities; and a book becomes everlasting by the fact, not that faults are not in it, but that genius nevertheless is there.

Of its method, and its author's generally, in the delineation of character, something will have to be said on a later page. The author's own favourite people in it, I think, were the Peggotty group; and perhaps he was not far wrong. It has been their fate, as with all the leading figures of his invention, to pass their names into the language, and become types; and he has nowhere given happier embodiment to that purity of homely goodness, which, by the kindly and all-reconciling influences of humour, may exalt into comeliness and even grandeur the clumsiest forms of humanity. What has been indicated in the style of the book as its greatest charm is here felt most strongly. The ludicrous so helps the pathos, and the humour so uplifts and refines the sentiment, that mere rude affection and simple manliness in these Yarmouth boatmen, passed through the fires of unmerited suffering and heroic endurance, take forms half-chivalrous half-sublime. It is one of the cants of critical superiority to make supercilious mention of the serious passages in this great writer; but the storm and ship-wreck at the close of *Copperfield*, when the body of the seducer is flung dead upon the shore amid the ruins of the home he has wasted and by the side of the man whose heart he has broken, the one as unconscious of what he had failed to reach as the other of what he has perished to save, is a description that may compare with the most impressive in the language. And to those who, knowing Dickens best, know what realities his books were to him, the expression of his sense of suffering in composing such passages, will have in it not a grain of pretence or affectation. "I have been tremendously at work these two days" (15 September), "eight hours at a stretch yesterday, and six hours and a half to-day, with the Ham and Steerforth chapter, which has completely knocked me over—utterly defeated me."

There are other people drawn into this catastrophe who are among the failures of natural delineation in the book. But though Miss Dartle is curiously unpleasant, there are some natural traits in her (which Dickens's least lifelike people are never without); and it was from one of his lady friends, very familiar to him indeed, he copied her peculiarity of never saying anything outright, but hinting it merely, and making more of it that way. Of Mrs. Steerforth it may also be worth remembering that Thackeray had something of a fondness for her. "I knew how it would be when I began," says a pleasant letter all about himself written immediately after she appeared in the story. "My letters to my mother are like this, but then she likes 'em —like Mrs. Steerforth: don't you like Mrs. Steerforth?"

Turning to another group there is another elderly lady to be liked without a shadow of misgiving; abrupt, angular, extravagant, but the very soul of magnanimity and rectitude; a character thoroughly made out in all its parts; a gnarled and knotted piece of female timber, sound to the core; a woman Captain Shandy would have loved for her startling oddities, and who is linked to the gentlest of her sex by perfect womanhood. Dickens has done nothing better, for solidness and truth all round, than Betsy Trotwood. It is one of her oddities to have a fool for a companion; but this is one of them that has also most pertinence and wisdom. By a line thrown out in *Wilhelm Meister*, that the true way of treating the insane was, in all respects possible, to act to them as if they were sane, Goethe anticipated what it took a century to apply to the most terrible disorder of humanity; and what Mrs. Trotwood does for Mr. Dick goes a step further, by showing how often asylums might be dispensed with, and how large might be the number of deficient intellects manageable with patience in their own homes. Characters hardly less distinguishable for truth as well as oddity are the kind old nurse and her husband the carrier, whose vicissitudes alike of love and of mortality are condensed into the three words since become part of universal speech, *Barkis is willin'*. There is wholesome satire of much utility in the conversion of the brutal schoolmaster of the earlier scenes into the tender Middlesex magistrate at the close. Nor is the humour anywhere more subtle than in the country undertaker, who makes up in fulness of heart for scantness of breath, and has so little of the vampire propensity of the town undertaker in *Chuzzlewit*, that he dares not even inquire after friends who are ill for fear of unkindly misconstruction. The test of a master in creative fiction, according to Hazlitt, is less in contrasting characters that are unlike than in distinguishing those that are like; and to many examples of the art in Dickens, such as the Shepherd and Chadband, Creakle and Squeers, Charley Bates and the Dodger, the Guppys and the Wemmicks, Mr. Jaggers and Mr. Vholes, Sampson Brass and Conversation Kenge, Jack Bunsby, Captain Cuttle and Bill Barley, the Perkers and Pells, the Dodsons and Foggs, Sarah Gamp and Betsy Prig, and a host of others, is to be added the nicety of distinction between those eminent furnishers of funerals, Mr. Mould and Messrs. Omer and Joram. All the mixed mirth and sadness of the story are skilfully drawn into the handling of this portion of it; and, amid wooings and preparations for weddings and church-ringing bells for baptisms, the steadily-going rat-tat of the hammer on the coffin is heard.

Of the heroines who divide so equally between them the impulsive, easily swayed, not disloyal but sorely distracted affections of the hero, the spoilt foolishness and tenderness of the loving little child-wife, Dora, is more attractive than the too unfailing wisdom and self-sacrificing goodness of the angel-wife, Agnes. The scenes of the courtship and housekeeping are matchless; and the glimpses of Doctors' Commons, opening those views, by Mr. Spenlow, of man's vanity of expectation and inconsistency of conduct in neglecting the sacred duty of making a will, on which he largely moralises the day before he dies intestate, form a background highly appropriate to David's domesticities. This was among the reproductions of personal experience in the book; but it was a sadder knowledge that came with the conviction some years later, that David's contrasts in his earliest married life between his happiness enjoyed and his happiness once anticipated, the "vague unhappy loss or want of something" of which he so frequently complains, reflected also a personal experience which had not been supplied in fact so successfully as in fiction.

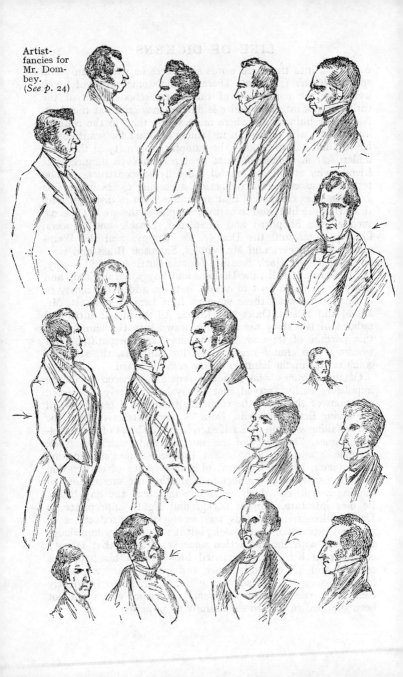

Artist-fancies for Mr. Dombey.
(See p. 24)

Artist-
fancies for
Mr. Dom-
bey.
(See p. 24)

BOOK SEVENTH

CONTINENT REVISITED

1852–6. ÆT. 40–43

I

THESE books were written between 1851 and 1854, when for a portion of the time the author was living abroad; and, reserving to another section the home life that filled the same interval, some account of both novels will be given here. *Little Dorrit,* though begun in Paris, was not finished until some time after the continental residence had closed, and belongs therefore to a later division. *David Copperfield* had been written between the opening of 1849 and October 1850, its publication covering that time; and its sale, which has since taken the lead of all his books but *Pickwick,* never then exceeding twenty-five thousand. But though it remained thus steady for the time, the popularity of the book added largely to the sale of its successor. *Bleak House* was begun in his new abode of Tavistock House at the end of November 1851; was carried on, amid the excitements of the Guild performances, through the following year; was finished at Boulogne in the August of 1853; and was dedicated to "his friends and companions in the Guild of Literature and Art." *Hard Times* was planned and begun in the winter of 1853, amid the busy preparation of Christmas theatricals for his children to be presently described; was finished at Boulogne in the summer of 1854; and was dedicated to Carlyle.

The autobiographical form of *Copperfield* was in some respect continued in *Bleak House* by means of extracts from the personal relation of its heroine. But the distinction between the narrative of David and the diary of Esther, like that between Micawber and Skimpole, marks the superiority of the first to its successor. To represent a storyteller as giving the most surprising vividness to manners, motives, and characters of which we are to believe her, all the time, as artlessly unconscious, as she is also entirely ignorant of the good qualities in herself she is naïvely revealing in the story, was a difficult enterprise, full of hazard in any case, not worth success, and certainly not successful. Ingenuity is more apparent than freshness, the invention is neither easy nor unstrained, and though the old marvellous power over the real is again abundantly manifest, there is some alloy of the artificial. Nor can this be said of Esther's relation without some general application to the book of which it forms so large a part. The novel is nevertheless, in the very important particular of construction, perhaps the best thing done by Dickens.

In his later writings he had been assiduously cultivating this essential of his art, and here he brought it very nearly to perfection. Of the tendency of composing a story piecemeal to induce greater concern for the part than for the whole, he had been always conscious; but I remember a remark also made by him to the effect that to read a story in parts had no less a tendency to prevent the reader's noticing how thoroughly a work so presented might be calculated for perusal as a whole. Look back from the last to the first page of the present novel, and not even in the highest examples of this kind of elaborate care will it be found that event leads more closely to event, or that the separate incidents have been planned with a more studied consideration of the bearing they are severally to have on the general result. Nothing is introduced at random, everything tends to the catastrophe, the various lines of the plot converge and fit to its centre, and to the larger interest all the rest is irresistibly drawn. The heart of the story is a Chancery suit. On this the plot hinges; and on incidents connected with it, trivial or important, the passion and suffering turn exclusively. Chance words, or the deeds of chance people, to appearance irrelevant, are found everywhere influencing the course taken by a train of incidents of which the issue is life or death, happiness or misery, to men and women perfectly unknown to them, and to whom they are unknown. Attorneys of all possible grades, law clerks of every conceivable kind, the copyist, the law stationer, the usurer, all sorts of money-lenders, suitors of every description, haunters of the Chancery Court and their victims, are for ever moving round about the lives of the chief persons in the tale, and drawing them on insensibly, but very certainly, to the issues that await them. Even the fits of the little law-stationer's servant help directly in the chain of small things that lead indirectly to Lady Dedlock's death. One strong chain of interest holds together Chesney Wold and its inmates,

Bleak House and the Jarndyce group, Chancery with its sorry and sordid neighbourhood. The characters multiply as the tale advances, but in each the drift is the same. "There's no great odds betwixt my noble and learned brother and myself," says the grotesque proprietor of the rag and bottle shop under the wall of Lincoln's Inn, "they call me Lord Chancellor and my shop Chancery, and we both of us grub on in a muddle." *Edax rerum* the motto of both, but with a difference. Out of the lumber of the shop emerge slowly some fragments of evidence by which the chief actors in the story are sensibly affected, and to which Chancery itself might have succumbed if its devouring capacities had been less complete. But by the time there is found among the lumber the will which puts all to rights in the Jarndyce suit, it is found to be too late to put anything to rights. The costs have swallowed up the estate, and there is an end of the matter.

What in one sense is a merit, however, may in others be a defect, and this book has suffered by the very completeness with which its Chancery moral is worked out. The didactic in Dickens's earlier novels derived its strength from being merely incidental to interest of a higher and more permanent kind, and not in a small degree from the playful sportiveness and fancy that lighted up its graver illustrations. Here it is of sterner stuff, too little relieved, and all-pervading. The fog so marvellously painted in the opening chapter has hardly cleared away when there arises, in *Jarndyce* v. *Jarndyce*, as bad an atmosphere to breathe in; and thenceforward to the end, clinging round the people of the story as they come or go, in dreary mist or in heavy cloud, it is rarely absent. Dickens has himself described his purpose to have been to dwell on the romantic side of familiar things. But it is the romance of discontent and misery, with a very restless dissatisfied moral, and is too much brought about by agencies disagreeable and sordid. The Guppys, Weevles, Snagsbys, Chadbands, Krooks, and Smallweeds, even the Kenges, Vholeses, and Tulkinghorns, are much too real to be pleasant; and the necessity becomes urgent for the reliefs and contrasts of a finer humanity. These last are not wanting; yet it must be said that we hardly escape, even with them, into the old freedom and freshness of the author's imaginative worlds, and that the too conscious unconsciousness of Esther flings something of a shade on the radiant goodness of John Jarndyce himself. Nevertheless there are very fine delineations in the story. The crazed little Chancery lunatic, Miss Flite;

the loud-voiced tender-souled Chancery victim, Gridley; the poor good-hearted youth, Richard, broken up in life and character by the suspense of the Chancery suit on whose success he is to "begin the world," believing himself to be saving money when he is stopped from squandering it, and thinking that having saved it he is entitled to fling it away; trooper George, with the Bagnets and their household, where the most ludicrous points are more forcible for the pathetic touches underlying them; the Jellyby interior, and its philanthropic strong-minded mistress, placid and smiling amid a household muddle out-muddling Chancery itself; the model of deportment, Turvey-drop the elder, whose relations to the young people, whom he so superbly patronises by being dependent on them for every-thing, touch delightfully some subtle points of truth; the inscrutable Tulkinghorn, and the immortal Bucket; all these, and especially the last, have been added by this book to the list of people more intimately and permanently known to us than the scores of actual familiar acquaintance whom we see around us living and dying.

But how do we know them? There are plenty to tell us that it is by vividness of external observation rather than by depth of imaginative insight, by tricks of manner and phrase rather than by truth of character, by manifestation outwardly rather than what lies behind. Another opportunity will present itself for some remark on this kind of criticism, which has always had a special pride in the subtlety of its differences from what the world may have shown itself prone to admire. "In my father's library," wrote Landor to Southey's daughter Edith, "was the *Critical Review* from its commencement; and it would have taught me, if I could not even at a very early age teach myself better, that Fielding, Sterne, and Goldsmith were really worth nothing." It is a style that will never be without culti-vators, and its frequent application to Dickens will be shown hereafter. But in speaking of a book in which some want of all the freshness of his genius first became apparent, it would be wrong to omit to add that his method of handling a character is as strongly impressed on the better portions of it as on the best of his writings. It is difficult to say when a peculiarity becomes too grotesque, or an extravagance too farcical, to be within the limits of art, for it is the truth of these as of graver things that they exist in the world in just the proportions and degree in which genius can discover them. But no man had ever so surprising a faculty as Dickens of becoming himself what he was representing; and of entering into mental phases and processes so absolutely, in conditions of life the most varied, as to reproduce them completely in dialogue without need of an explanatory word. (He only departed from this method once, with a result which will then be pointed out.) In speaking on a former page of the impression of reality thus to a singular degree conveyed by him, it was remarked that where characters so revealed themselves the author's part in them was done; and in the book under notice there is none, not excepting those least attractive which apparently present only prominent or salient qualities, in which it will not be found that the characteristic feature embodied, or the main idea personified, contains as certainly also some human truth universally applicable. To expound or discuss his creations, to lay them psychologically bare, to analyse their organisms, to subject to minute demonstration their fibrous and other tissues, was not at all Dickens's way. His genius was his fellow-feeling with his race; his mere personality was never the bound or limit to his perceptions, however strongly sometimes it might colour them; he never stopped to dissect or anatomise his own work; but no man could better adjust the outward and visible oddities in a delineation to its inner and unchangeable veracities. The rough estimates we form of character, if we have any truth of perception, are on the whole correct; but men touch and interfere with one another by the contact of their extremes, and it may very often become necessarily the main business of a novelist to display the salient points, the sharp angles, or the prominences merely.

The pathetic parts of *Bleak House* do not live largely in remembrance, but the deaths of Richard and of Gridley, the wandering fancies of Miss Flite, and the extremely touching way in which the gentleman-nature of the pompous old baronet, Dedlock, asserts itself under suffering, belong to a high order of writing. There is another most affecting example, taking the lead of the rest, in the poor street-sweeper Jo; which has made perhaps as deep an impression as anything in Dickens. "We have been reading *Bleak House* aloud," the good Dean Ramsay wrote to me very shortly before his death. "Surely it is one of his most powerful and successful! What a triumph is Jo! Uncultured nature is *there* indeed; the intimations of true heart-feeling, the glimmerings of higher feeling, all are there; but everything still consistent and in harmony. Wonderful is the genius that can show all this, yet keep it only and really part of the character itself, low or common as it may be, and use no morbid or fictitious colouring. To my mind, nothing in the field of fiction is to be found in English literature surpassing the death of Jo!" What occurs at and after the inquest is as worth remembering. Jo's evidence is rejected because he cannot exactly say what will be done to him after he is dead if he should tell a lie;[1] but he manages to say afterwards very exactly what the deceased while he lived did to him. That one cold winter night, when he was shivering in a doorway near his crossing, a man turned to look at him, and came back, and having questioned him and found he had not a friend in the world, said, "Neither have I. Not one!" and gave him the price of a supper and a night's lodging. That the man had often spoken to him since, and asked him if he slept of a night, and how he bore cold and hunger, or if he ever wished to die; and would say in passing "I am as poor as you to-day, Jo" when he had no money, but when he had any would always give some. "He wos werry good to me," says the boy, wiping his eyes with his wretched sleeve. "Wen I see him a-layin' so stritched out just now, I wished he could have heerd me tell him so. He wos werry good to me, he wos!" The inquest over, the body is flung into a pestiferous churchyard in the next street, houses overlooking it on every side, and a reeking little tunnel of a court giving access to its iron gate. "With the night comes a slouching figure through the tunnel-court, to the outside of the iron gate. It holds the gate with its hands, and looks in within the bars; stands looking in, for a little while. It then, with an old broom it carries, softly sweeps the step, and makes the archway clean. It does so, very busily, and trimly; looks in again, a little while; and so departs." These are among the things in Dickens that cannot be forgotten; and if *Bleak House* had many

---

[1] "O! Here's the boy, gentlemen! Here he is, very muddy, very hoarse, very ragged. Now, boy!—But stop a minute. Caution. This boy must be put through a few preliminary paces. Name, Jo. Nothing else that he knows on. Don't know that everybody has two names. Never heerd of sich a think. Don't know that Jo is short for a longer name. Thinks it long enough for *him*. *He* don't find no fault with it. Spell it? No. *He* can't spell it. No father, no mother, no friends. Never been to school. What's home? Know's a broom's a broom, and knows it's wicked to tell a lie. Don't recollect who told him about the broom, or about the lie, but knows both. Can't exactly say what'll be done to him arter he's dead if he tells a lie to the gentleman here, but believes it'll be something wery bad to punish him, and serve him right—and so he'll tell the truth. 'This won't do, gentlemen,' says the coroner, with a melancholy shake of the head. . . . '*Can't exactly say* won't do, you know. . . . It's terrible depravity. Put the boy aside.' Boy put aside; to the great edification of the audience: —especially of Little Swills, the Comic Vocalist."

more faults than have been found in it, such salt and savour as this might freshen it for some generations.

The first intention was to have made Jo more prominent in the story, and its earliest title was taken from the tumbling tenements in Chancery, "Tom-all-Alone's," where he finds his wretched habitation; but this was abandoned. On the other hand, Dickens was encouraged and strengthened in his design of assailing Chancery abuses and delays by receiving, a few days after the appearance of his first number, a striking pamphlet on the subject containing details so apposite that he took from them, without change in any material point, the memorable case related in his fifteenth chapter. Anyone who examines the tract will see how exactly true is the reference to it made by * 84 Dickens in his preface. "The case of Gridley is in no essential altered from one of actual occurrence, made public by a disinterested person who was professionally acquainted with the whole of the monstrous wrong from beginning to end." The suit, of which all particulars are given, affected a single farm, in value not more than £1200, but all that its owner possessed in the world, against which a bill had been filed for a £300 legacy left in the will bequeathing the farm. In reality there was only one defendant, but in the bill, by the rule of the Court, there were seventeen; and, after two years had been occupied over the seventeen answers, everything had to begin over again because an eighteenth had been accidentally omitted. "What a mockery of justice this is," says Mr. Challinor, "the facts speak for themselves, and I can personally vouch for their accuracy. The costs already incurred in reference to this £300 legacy are not less than from £800 to £900, and the parties are no forwarder. Already near five years have passed by, and the plaintiff would be glad to give up his chance of the legacy if he could escape from his liability to costs, while the defendants who own the little farm left by the testator, have scarce any other prospect before them than ruin."

"I wish you would look," Dickens wrote on 20 January, 1854, "at the enclosed titles for the *Household Words* story, between this and two o'clock or so, when I will call. It is my usual day, you observe, on which I have jotted them down—Friday! It seems to me that there are three very good ones among them. I should like to know whether you hit upon the same." On the paper enclosed was written: 1. According to Cocker. 2. Prove it. 3. Stubborn Things. 4. Mr. Gradgrind's

Facts. 5. The Grindstone. 6. Hard Times. 7. Two and Two are Four. 8. Something Tangible. 9. Our Hard-headed Friend. 10. Rust and Dust. 11. Simple Arithmetic. 12. A Matter of Calculation. 13. A Mere Question of Figures. 14. The Gradgrind Philosophy. The three selected by me were 2, 6, and 11; the three that were his own favourites were 6, 13, and 14; and as 6 had been chosen by both, that title was taken.

It was the first story written by him for his weekly periodical; and in the course of it the old troubles of the *Clock* came back, with the difference that the greater brevity of the weekly portions made it easier to write them up to time, but much more difficult to get sufficient interest into each. "The difficulty of the space," he wrote after a few weeks' trial, "is CRUSHING. Nobody can have an idea of it who has not had an experience of patient fiction-writing with some elbow-room always, and open places in perspective. In this form, with any kind of regard to the current number, there is absolutely no such thing." He went on, however; and, of the two designs he started with, accomplished one very perfectly and the other at least partially. He more than doubled the circulation of his journal; and he wrote a story which, though not among his best, contains things as characteristic as any he has written. I may not go as far as Mr. Ruskin in giving it a high place; but to anything falling from that writer, however one may differ from it, great respect is due, and every word here said of Dickens's intention is in ✱ 85   the most strict sense just. "The essential value and truth of Dickens's writings," he says, "have been unwisely lost sight of by many thoughtful persons, merely because he presents his truth with some colour of caricature. Unwisely, because Dickens's caricature, though often gross, is never mistaken. Allowing for his manner of telling them, the things he tells us are always true. I wish that he could think it right to limit his brilliant exaggeration to works written only for public amusement; and when he takes up a subject of high national importance, such as that which he handled in *Hard Times*, that he would use severer and more accurate analysis. The usefulness of that work (to my mind, in several respects, the greatest he has written) is with many persons seriously diminished, because Mr. Bounderby is a dramatic monster instead of a characteristic example of a worldly master; and Stephen Blackpool a dramatic perfection, instead of a characteristic example of an honest workman. But let us not lose the use of Dickens's wit and insight, because he chooses to speak in a circle of stage fire.

He is entirely right in his main drift and purpose in every book he has written; and all of them, but especially *Hard Times*, should be studied with close and earnest care by persons interested in social questions. They will find much that is partial, and, because partial, apparently unjust; but if they examine all the evidence on the other side, which Dickens seems to overlook, it will appear, after all their trouble, that his view was the finally right one, grossly and sharply told." The best points in it, out of the circle of stage fire (an expression of wider application to this part of Dickens's life than its inventor supposed it to be), were some sketches among the riding-circus people and the Bounderby household; but it is a wise hint of Mr. Ruskin's that there may be, in the drift of a story, truths of sufficient importance to set against defects of workmanship; and here they challenged wide attention. You cannot train anyone properly, unless you cultivate the fancy, and allow fair scope to the affections. You cannot govern men on a principle of averages; and to buy in the cheapest and sell in the dearest market is not the *summum bonum* of life. You cannot treat the working man fairly unless, in dealing with his wrongs and his delusions, you take equally into account the simplicity and tenacity of his nature, arising partly from limited knowledge, but more from honesty and singleness of intention. Fiction cannot prove a case, but it can express forcibly a righteous sentiment; and this is here done unsparingly upon matters of universal concern. The book was finished at Boulogne in the middle of July, and is inscribed to Carlyle.

* 86

An American admirer accounted for the vivacity of the circus-scenes by declaring that Dickens had "arranged with the master of Astley's Circus to spend many hours behind the scenes with the riders and among the horses"; a thing just as likely as that he went into training as a stroller to qualify for Mr. Crummles in *Nickleby*. Such successes belonged to the experiences of his youth; he had nothing to add to what his marvellous observation had made familiar from almost childish days; and the glimpses we get of them in the *Sketches by Boz* are in these points as perfect as anything his later experience could supply. There was one thing nevertheless which the choice of his subject made him anxious to verify while *Hard Times* was in hand; and this was a strike in a manufacturing town. He had gone to Preston to see one at the end of January, and was somewhat disappointed. "I am afraid I shall not be able to get much here. Except the crowds at the street-corners reading the placards pro and con; and the cold absence of smoke from the mill-chimneys; there is very little in the streets to make the town remarkable. I am told that the people 'sit at home and mope.' The delegates with the money from the neighbouring places come in to-day to report the amounts they bring; and to-morrow the people are paid. When I have seen both these ceremonies, I shall return. It is a nasty place (I thought it was a model town); and I am in the Bull Hotel, before which some time ago the people assembled supposing the masters to be here, and on demanding to have them out were remonstrated with by the landlady in person. I saw the account in an Italian paper, in which it was stated that 'the populace then environed the Palazzo Bull, until the padrona of the Palazzo heroically appeared at one of the upper windows and addressed them!' One can hardly conceive anything less likely to be represented to an Italian mind by this description, than the old, grubby, smoky, mean, intensely formal red brick house with a narrow gateway and a dingy yard, to which it applies. At the theatre last night I saw *Hamlet*, and should have done better to 'sit at home and mope' like the idle workmen. In the last scene, Laertes on being asked how it was with him replied (verbatim) 'Why, like a woodcock—on account of my treachery.'"

II

HOME INCIDENTS

1853-4-5

THE first number of *Bleak House* had appeared in March 1852, * 86A
and its sale was mentioned in the same letter from Tavistock
House (7 March) which told of his troubles in the tale at its
outset, and of other anxieties incident to the common lot and
inseparable equally from its joys and sorrows, through which
his life was passing at the time. "My Highgate journey yesterday was a sad one. Sad to think how all journeys tend that way.
I went up to the cemetery to look for a piece of ground. In no
hope of a Government bill, and in a foolish dislike to leaving * 87
the little child shut up in a vault there, I think of pitching a
tent under the sky. . . . Nothing has taken place here: but I
believe, every hour, that it must next hour. Wild ideas are upon
me of going to Paris—Rouen—Switzerland—somewhere—and
writing the remaining two-thirds of the next No. aloft in some
queer inn room. I have been hanging over it, and have got
restless. Want a change I think. Stupid. We were at 30,000
when I last heard. . . . I am sorry to say that after all kinds of
evasions, I am obliged to dine at Lansdowne House to-morrow.
But maybe the affair will come off to-night and give me an
excuse! I enclose proofs of No. 2. Browne has done Skimpole,
and helped to make him singularly unlike the great original.
Look it over, and say what occurs to you. . . . Don't you think
Mrs. Gaskell charming? With one ill-considered thing that looks
like a want of natural perception, I think it masterly." His last
allusion is to the story by a delightful writer then appearing
in *Household Words*; and of the others it only needs to say
that the family affair which might have excused his absence
at the Lansdowne dinner did not come off until four days
later. On 13 March his last child was born; and the boy,
his seventh son, bears his godfather's distinguished name,
Edward Bulwer Lytton.

The inability to "grind sparks out of this dull blade," as

he characterised his present labour at *Bleak House,* still fretting him, he struck out a scheme for Paris. "I could not get to Switzerland very well at this time of year. The Jura would be covered with snow. And if I went to Geneva I don't know where I might *not* go to." It ended at last in a flight to Dover; but he found time before he left, amid many occupations and some anxieties, for a good-natured journey to Walworth to see a youth rehearse who was supposed to have talents for the stage, and he was able to gladden Mr. Toole's friends by thinking favourably of his chances of success. "I remember what I once myself wanted in that way," he said, "and I should like to serve him."

At one of the last dinners in Tavistock House before his departure, Mr. Watson of Rockingham was present; and he was hardly settled in Camden Crescent, Dover, when he had news of the death of that excellent friend. "Poor dear Watson! It was this day two weeks when you rode with us and he dined with us. We all remarked after he had gone how happy he seemed to have got over his election troubles, and how cheerful he was. He was full of Christmas plans for Rockingham, and was very anxious that we should get up a little French piece I had been telling him the plot of. He went abroad next day to join Mrs. Watson and the children at Homburg, and then go to Lausanne, where they had taken a house for a month. He was seized at Homburg with violent internal inflammation, and died—without much pain—in four days. . . . I was so fond of him that I am sorry you didn't know him better. I believe he was as thoroughly good and true a man as ever lived; and I am sure I can have no greater affection for him than he felt for me. When I think of that bright house, and his fine simple honest heart, both so open to me, the blank and loss are like a dream." Other deaths followed. "Poor d'Orsay!" he wrote after only seven days (8 August). "It is a tremendous consideration that friends should fall around us in such awful numbers as we attain middle life. What a field of battle it is!" Nor had another month quite passed before he lost, in Mrs. Macready, a very dear family friend. "Ah me! ah me!" he wrote. "This tremendous sickle certainly does cut deep into the surrounding corn, when one's own small blade has ripened. But *this* is all a Dream, may be, and death will wake us."

Able at last to settle to his work, he stayed in Dover three months; and early in October, sending home his family caravan, crossed to Boulogne to try it as a resort for seaside holiday. "I never saw a better instance of our countrymen than this place. Because it is accessible it is genteel to say it is of no character, quite English, nothing continental about it, and so forth. It is as quaint, picturesque, good a place as I know; the boat-men and fishing-people quite a race apart, and some of their villages as good as the fishing-villages on the Mediterranean. The Haute Ville, with a walk all round it on the ramparts, charming. The country walks, delightful. It is the best mixture of town and country (with sea air into the bargain) I ever saw; everything cheap, everything good; and please God I shall be writing on those said ramparts next July!"

Before the year closed, the time to which his publishing arrangements with Messrs. Bradbury and Evans were limited had expired, but at his suggestion the fourth share in such books as he might write, which they had now received for eight years, was continued to them on the understanding that the publishers' percentage should no longer be charged in the partnership accounts, and with a power reserved to himself to withdraw when he pleased. In the new year his first adventure was an ovation in Birmingham, where a silver-gilt salver and a diamond ring were presented to him, as well for eloquent service specially rendered to the Institution, as in general testi-mony of "varied literary acquirements, genial philosophy, and high moral teaching." A great banquet followed on Twelfth Night, made memorable by an offer to give a couple of readings * 88 from his books at the following Christmas, in aid of the new Midland Institute. It might seem to have been drawn from him as a grateful return for the enthusiastic greeting of his enter-tainers, but it was in his mind before he left London, It was his first formal undertaking to read in public.

His eldest son had now left Eton, and the boy's wishes pointing at the time to a mercantile career, he was sent to Leipzig for completion of his education. At this date it seemed * 89 to me that the overstrain of attempting too much, brought upon him by the necessities of his weekly periodical, became first apparent in Dickens. Not unfrequently a complaint strange upon his lips fell from him. "Hypochondriacal whisperings tell me that I am rather overworked. The spring does not seem to fly back again directly, as it always did when I put my own work aside, and had nothing else to do. Yet I have everything to keep me going with a brave heart, Heaven knows!" Courage and hopefulness he might well derive from the increasing sale of *Bleak House*, which had risen to nearly forty thousand; but he could no longer bear easily what he carried so lightly of old, and enjoyments with work, were too much for him. "What with *Bleak House* and *Household Words* and *Child's History*" (he dictated from week to week the papers which formed that little book, and cannot be said to have quite hit the mark with it), "and Miss Coutts's Home, and the invitations to feasts and festivals, I really feel as if my head would split like a fired shell if I remained here." He tried Brighton first, but did not

* 90 find it answer and returned. A few days of unalloyed enjoyment were afterwards given to the visit of his excellent American friend Felton; and on 13 June he was again in Boulogne, thanking heaven for escape from a breakdown. "If I had substituted anybody's knowledge of myself for my own, and lingered in London, I never could have got through."

What befell him in Boulogne will be given, with the incidents of his second and third summer visits to the place, on a later page. He completed *Bleak House* by the third week of August, and it was resolved to celebrate the event by a two months' trip to Italy, in company with Mr. Wilkie Collins and Mr. Augustus Egg. The start was to be made from Boulogne in the middle of October, when he would send his family home; and he described the intervening weeks as a fearful "reaction and prostration of laziness" only broken by the *Child's History*. At the end of September he wrote: "I finished the little *History* yesterday, and am trying to think of something for the Christmas number. After which I shall knock off; having had quite enough to do, small as it would have seemed to me at any other time, since I finished *Bleak House*." He added, a week before his departure: "I get letters from Genoa and Lausanne as if I were going to stay in each place at least a month. If I were to measure my deserts by people's remembrance of me, I should be a prodigy of intolerability. Have recovered my Italian, which I had all but forgotten, and am one entire and perfect chrysolite of idleness."

From this trip, of which the incidents have an interest independent of my ordinary narrative, Dickens was home again in the middle of December 1853, and kept his promise to his Birmingham friends by reading in their Town Hall his *Christmas Carol* on the 27th, and his *Cricket on the Hearth* on the 29th. The enthusiasm was great, and he consented to read his *Carol* a second time, on Friday the 30th, if seats were reserved for working men at prices within their means. The result was an addition of between four and five hundred pounds to the funds

for establishment of the new Institute; and a prettily worked
flower-basket in silver, presented to Mrs. Dickens, commemorated these first public readings "to nearly six thousand people,"
and the design they had generously helped. Other applications
then followed to such extent that limits to compliance had to
be put; and a letter of 16 May, 1854, is one of many
that express both the difficulty in which he found himself, and
his much desired expedient for solving it. "The objection you
suggest to paid public lecturing does not strike me at all. It is
worth consideration, but I do not think there is anything in it.
On the contrary, if the lecturing would have any motive power
at all (like my poor father this, in the sound!) I believe it would
tend the other way. In the Colchester matter I had already
received a letter from a Colchester magnate; to whom I had
honestly replied that I stood pledged to Christmas readings at
Bradford and at Reading, and could in no kind of reason do   * 91
more in the public way." The promise to the people of Reading
was for Talfourd's sake; the other was given after the Birmingham nights, when an institute in Bradford asked similar help,
and offered a fee of fifty pounds. At first this was entertained;
but was abandoned, with some reluctance, upon the argument
that to become publicly a reader must alter without improving
his position publicly as a writer, and that it was a change to
be justified only when the higher calling should have failed of
the old success. Thus yielding for the time, he nevertheless soon
found the question rising again with the same importunity; his
own position to it being always that of a man assenting against
his will that it should rest in abeyance. But nothing further
was resolved on yet. The readings mentioned came off as
promised, in aid of public objects; and besides others two   * 92
years later for the family of a friend, he had given the like
liberal help to institutes in Folkestone, Chatham, and again in
Birmingham, Peterborough, Sheffield, Coventry, and Edinburgh,
before the question settled itself finally in the announcement
for paid public readings issued by him in 1858.

Carrying memory back to his home in the first half of 1854,
there are few things that rise more pleasantly in connection
with it than the children's theatricals. These began with the
first Twelfth Night at Tavistock House, and were renewed until
the principal actors ceased to be children. The best of the performances were *Tom Thumb* and *Fortunio*, in '54 and '55;
Dickens now joining first in the revel, and Mr. Mark Lemon
bringing into it his own clever children and a very mountain

of child-pleasing fun in himself. Dickens had become very intimate with him, and his merry genial ways had given him unbounded popularity with the "young 'uns," who had no such favourite as "Uncle Mark." In Fielding's burlesque he was the giantess Glumdalca, and Dickens was the Ghost of Gaffer Thumb; the names by which they respectively appeared being the Infant Phenomenon and the modern Garrick. But the younger actors carried off the palm. There was a Lord Grizzle, at whose ballad of Miss Villikins, introduced by desire, Thackeray rolled off his seat in a burst of laughter that became absurdly contagious. Yet even this, with hardly less fun from the Noodles, Doodles, and King Arthurs, was not so good as the pretty, fantastic, comic grace of Dollalolla, Huncamunca, and Tom. The girls wore steadily the grave airs irresistible when put on by little children; and an actor not out of his fourth year, who went through the comic songs and the tragic exploits without a wrong note or a victim unslain, represented the small helmeted hero. He was in the bills as Mr. H——, but bore in fact the name of the illustrious author whose conception he embodied; and who certainly would have hugged him for Tom's opening song, delivered in the arms of Huncamunca, if he could have forgiven the later master in his own craft for having composed it afresh to the air of a ditty then wildly popular at the "Coal Hole." The encores were frequent, and for the most part the little fellow responded to them; but the misplaced enthusiasm that took similar form at the heroic intensity with which he stabbed Dollalolla, he rebuked by going gravely on to the close. His Fortunio, the next Twelfth Night, was not so great; yet when, as a prelude to getting the better of the Dragon, he adulterated his drink (Mr. Lemon played the Dragon) with sherry, the sly relish with which he watched the demoralisation, by this means, of his formidable adversary into a helpless imbecility, was perfect. Here Dickens played the testy old Baron, and took advantage of the excitement against the Czar raging in 1855 to denounce him (in a song) as no other than own cousin to the very Bear that Fortunio had gone forth to subdue. He depicted him in his desolation of autocracy, as the Robinson Crusoe of absolute state, who had at his court many a show-day and many a high-day, but hadn't in all his dominions a Friday. The bill, which attributed these interpolations to "the Dramatic Poet of the Establishment," deserves allusion also for the fun of the six large-lettered announcements which stood at the head of it, and could not have been bettered by

Mr. Crummles himself. "Re-engagement of that irresistible comedian" (the performer of Lord Grizzle) "Mr. Ainger!" "Reappearance of Mr. H. who created so powerful an impression last year!" "Return of Mr. Charles Dickens Junior from his German engagements!" "Engagement of Miss Kate, who declined the munificent offers of the Management last season!" "Mr. Passé, Mr. Mudperiod, Mr. Measly Servile, and Mr. Wilkini Collini!" "First appearance on any stage of Mr. Plornishmaroontigoonter (who has been kept out of bed at a vast expense)." The last performer mentioned was yet at some * 93A distance from the third year of his age. Dickens was Mr. Passé.

The home incidents of the summer and autumn of 1855 may be mentioned briefly. It was a year of much unsettled discontent with him, and upon return from a short trip to Paris with Mr. Wilkie Collins, he flung himself rather hotly into agitation with the administrative reformers, and spoke at one of the great meetings in Drury Lane Theatre. "Generally I quite agree with you that they hardly know what to be at; but it is an immensely difficult subject to start, and they must have every allowance. At any rate, it is not by leaving them alone and giving them no help, that they can be urged on to success." In the following month (April) he took occasion, even from the chair of the General Theatrical Fund, to give renewed expression to political dissatisfactions. "The Government hit took immensely; but I'm afraid to look at the report, these things are so ill done." In the summer he threw open to many friends his Tavistock House Theatre, having secured for its "lessee and manager Mr. Crummles"; for its poet Mr. Wilkie Collins, in "an entirely new and original domestic melodrama"; and for its scene-painter "Mr. Stanfield, R.A." The Lighthouse, by Mr. Wilkie * 94 Collins, was then produced, its actors being Mr. Crummles the manager (Dickens in other words), the Author of the play, Mr. Lemon, and Mr. Egg, and the manager's sister-in-law and eldest daughter. It was followed by the Guild farce of Mr. Nightingale's Diary, in which, besides the performers named, and Dickens in his old personation part, the manager's youngest daughter and Mr. Frank Stone assisted. The success was wonderful; and in the three delighted audiences who crowded to what the bills described as "the smallest theatre in the world," were not a few of the notabilities of London. Mr. Carlyle compared Dickens's wild picturesqueness in the old lighthouse keeper to the famous figure in Nicholas Poussin's bacchanalian dance in the National Gallery; and at one of the joyous suppers that followed on each

night of the play, Lord Campbell told the company that he had
much rather have written *Pickwick* than be Chief Justice of
England and a peer of Parliament.

* 94A

Then came the beginning of *Nobody's Fault*, as *Little Dorrit*
continued to be called by him up to the eve of its publication;
a flight to Folkestone, to help his sluggish fancy; and his return
to London in October, to preside at a dinner to Thackeray on his
going to lecture in America. It was a muster of more than sixty
admiring entertainers, and Dickens's speech gave happy expression to the spirit that animated all, telling Thackeray not
alone how much his friendship was prized by those present, and
how proud they were of his genius, but offering him in the
name of the tens of thousands absent who had never touched
his hand or seen his face, lifelong thanks for the treasures of
mirth, wit, and wisdom within the yellow-covered numbers of
Pendennis and *Vanity Fair*. Peter Cunningham, one of the sons
of Allan, was secretary to the banquet; and for many pleasures
given to the subject of this memoir, who had a hearty regard
for him, should have a few words to his memory.

His presence was always welcome to Dickens, and indeed to
all who knew him, for his relish of social life was great, and
something of his keen enjoyment could not but be shared by
his company. His geniality would have carried with it a pleasurable glow even if it had stood alone, and it was invigorated by
very considerable acquirements. He had some knowledge of
the works of eminent authors and artists; and he had an eager
interest in their lives and haunts, which he had made the
subject of minute and novel inquiry. This store of knowledge
gave substance to his talk, yet never interrupted his buoyancy
and pleasantry, because only introduced when called for, and
not made matter of parade or display. But the happy combination of qualities that rendered him a favourite companion, and
won him many friends, proved in the end injurious to himself.
He had done much while young in certain lines of investigation
which he had made almost his own, and there was every promise
that, in the department of biographical and literary research,
he would have produced much weightier works with advancing
years. This however was not to be. The fascinations of good
fellowship encroached more and more upon literary pursuits,
until he nearly abandoned his former favourite studies, and
sacrificed all the deeper purposes of his life to the present
temptation of a festive hour. Then his health gave way, and
he became lost to friends as well as to literature. But the

impression of the bright and amiable intercourse of his better time survived, and his old associates never ceased to think of Peter Cunningham with regret and kindness.

Dickens went to Paris early in October, and at its close was brought again to London by the sudden death of a friend, much deplored by himself, and still more so by a distinguished lady who had his loyal service at all times. An incident before his return to France is worth brief relation. He had sallied out for one of his night walks, full of thoughts of his story, one wintry rainy evening (8 November), and "pulled himself up," outside the door of Whitechapel Workhouse, at a strange sight which arrested him there. Against the dreary enclosure of the house were leaning, in the midst of the down-pouring rain and storm, what seemed to be seven heaps of rags: "dumb, wet, silent horrors" he described them, "sphinxes set up against that dead wall, and no one likely to be at the pains of solving them until the General Overthrow." He sent in his card to the Master. Against him there was no ground of complaint; he gave prompt personal attention; but the casual ward was full, and there was no help. The rag-heaps were all girls, and Dickens gave each a shilling. One girl, "twenty or so," had been without food a day and night. "Look at me," she said, as she clutched the shilling, and without thanks shuffled off. So with the rest. There was not a single "thank you." A crowd meanwhile, only less poor than these objects of misery, had gathered round the scene; but though they saw the seven shillings given away they asked for no relief to themselves, they recognised in their sad wild way the other greater wretchedness, and made room in silence for Dickens to walk on.

Not more tolerant of the way in which laws meant to be most humane are too often administered in England, he left in a day or two to resume his *Little Dorrit* in Paris. But before his life there is described, some sketches from his holiday trip to Italy with Mr. Wilkie Collins and Mr. Augustus Egg, and from his three summer visits to Boulogne, claim to themselves two intervening chapters.

III

IN SWITZERLAND AND ITALY

1853

THE first news of the three travellers was from Chamonix, on 20 October; and in it there was little made of the fatigue, and much of the enjoyment, of their Swiss travel. Great attention and cleanliness at the inns, very small windows and very bleak passages, doors opening to wintry blasts, over-hanging eaves and external galleries, plenty of milk, honey, cows, and goats, much singing towards sunset on mountain sides, mountains almost too solemn to look at—that was the picture of it, with the country everywhere in one of its finest aspects, as winter began to close in. They had started from Geneva the previous morning at four, and in their day's travel Dickens had again noticed what he spoke of formerly, the ill-favoured look of the people in the valleys owing to their hard and stern climate. "All the women were like used-up men, and all the men like a sort of fagged dogs. But the good, genuine, grateful Swiss recognition of the commonest kind word—not too often thrown to them by our countrymen—made them quite radiant. I walked the greater part of the way, which was like going up the Monument." On the day the letter was written they had been up to the Mer de Glace, finding it not so beautiful in colour as in summer, but grander in its desolation; the green ice, like the greater part of the ascent, being covered with snow. "We were alarmingly near to a very dismal accident. We were a train of four mules and two guides, going along an immense height like a chimney-piece, with sheer precipice below, when there came rolling from above, with fearful velocity, a block of stone about the size of one of the fountains in Trafalgar Square, which Egg, the last of the party, had preceded by not a yard, when it swept over the ledge, breaking away a tree, and rolled and tumbled down into the valley. It had been loosened by the heavy rains, or by some woodcutters after-wards reported to be above." The only place new to Dickens was Berne: "a surprisingly picturesque old Swiss town, with a view of the Alps from the outside of it singularly beautiful in the morning light." Everything else was familiar to him: though at that winter season, when the inns were shutting up, and all who could afford it were off to Geneva, most things in the valley struck him with a new aspect. From such of his old friends as he found at Lausanne, where a day or two's rest was taken, he had the gladdest of greetings; "and the wonderful manner in which they turned out in the wettest morning ever beheld for a Godspeed down the Lake was really quite pathetic."

He had found time to see again the deaf, dumb, and blind youth at Mr. Haldimand's Institution who had aroused so deep an interest in him seven years before, but, in his brief present visit, the old associations would not reawaken. "Tremendous efforts were made by Hertzel to impress him with an idea of me, and the associations belonging to me; but it seemed in my eyes quite a failure, and I much doubt if he had the least perception of his old acquaintance. According to his custom, he went on muttering strange eager sounds like Town and Down and Mown, but nothing more. I left ten francs to be spent in cigars for my old friend. If I had taken one with me, I think I could, more successfully than his master, have established my identity." The child similarly afflicted, the little girl whom he saw at the same old time, had been after some trial discharged as an idiot.

Before October closed, the travellers had reached Genoa, having been thirty-one consecutive hours on the road from Milan. They arrived in somewhat damaged condition, and took up their lodging in the top rooms of the Croce di Malta, "overlooking the port and sea pleasantly and airily enough, but it was no joke to get so high, and the apartment is rather vast and faded." The warmth of personal greeting that here awaited Dickens was given no less to the friends who accompanied him, and though the reader may not share in such private confidences as would show the sensation created by his reappearance, and the jovial hours that were passed among old associates, he will perhaps be interested to know how far the intervening years had changed the aspect of things and places made pleasantly familiar to us in his former letters. He wrote to his sister-in-law that the old walks were pretty much the same as ever, except that there had been building behind the Peschiere up the San Bartolommeo hill, and the whole town towards San Pietro d'Arena had been quite changed. The Bisagno looked just the same, stony just then, having very little water in it; the vicoli were fragrant with the same old flavour of "very rotten cheese kept in very hot blankets"; and everywhere he saw the mezzaro as of yore. The Jesuits' College in the Strada Nuova was become, under the changed government, the Hôtel de Ville, and a splendid caffè with a terrace-garden had arisen between it and Palaviccini's old palace. "Pal himself has gone to the dogs." Another new and handsome caffè had been built in the Piazza Carlo Felice, between the old one of the Bei Arti and the Strada Carlo Felice; and the Teatro Diurno had now stone galleries and seats like an ancient amphitheatre. "The beastly gate and guardhouse in the Albaro road are still in their dear old beastly state; and the whole of that road is just as it was. The man without legs is still in the Strada Nuova; but the beggars in general are all cleared off, and our old one-arm'd Belisario made a sudden evaporation a year or two ago. I am going to the Peschiere to-day." To myself he described his former favourite abode as converted into a girls' college; all the paintings of gods and goddesses canvassed over, and the gardens gone to ruin; "but O! what a wonderful place!" He observed an extraordinary increase everywhere else, since he was last in the splendid city, of "life, growth, and enterprise"; and he declared his first conviction to be confirmed that for picturesque beauty and character there was nothing in Italy, Venice excepted, "near brilliant old Genoa."

The voyage thence to Naples, written from the latter place, is too capital a description to be lost. The steamer in which they embarked was "the new express English ship," but they found her to be already more than full of passengers from Marseilles (among them an old friend, Sir Emerson Tennent, with his family), and everything in confusion. There were no places at the captain's table, dinner had to be taken on deck, no berth or sleeping accommodation was available, and heavy first-class fares had to be paid. Thus they made their way to Leghorn, where worse awaited them. The authorities proved to be not favourable to the "crack" English-officered vessel (she had just been started for the India mail); and her papers not being examined in time, it was too late to steam away again that day, and she had to lie all night long off the lighthouse. "The scene on board beggars description. Ladies on the tables; gentlemen under the tables; bedroom appliances not usually beheld in public airing themselves in positions where soup-tureens had been lately developing themselves; and ladies and gentlemen lying indiscriminately on the open deck, arranged like spoons on a sideboard. No mattresses, no blankets, nothing. Towards midnight attempts were made, by means of awning and flags, to make this latter scene remotely approach an Australian encampment; and we three (Collins, Egg, and self) lay together on the bare planks covered with our coats. We were all gradually dozing off, when a perfectly tropical rain fell, and in a moment drowned the whole ship. The rest of the night we passed upon the stairs, with an immense jumble of men and women. When anybody came up for any purpose we all fell down, and when anybody came down we all fell up again. Still, the good-humour in the English part of the passengers was quite extraordinary. . . . There were excellent officers aboard, and, in the morning, the first mate lent me his cabin to wash in—which I afterwards lent to Egg and Collins. Then we, the Emerson Tennents, the captain, the doctor, and the second officer, went off on a jaunt together to Pisa, as the ship was to lie all day at Leghorn. The captain was a capital fellow, but I led him, facetiously, such a life the whole day, that I got most things altered at night. Emerson Tennent's son, with the greatest amiability, insisted on turning out of his state-room for me, and I got a good bed there. The store-room down by the hold was opened for Collins and Egg; and they slept with the moist sugar, the cheese in cut, the spices, the cruets, the apples and pears, in a perfect chandler's shop — in company with what a friend of ours would call a hold gent, who had been so horribly wet through overnight that his condition frightened the authorities; a cat; and the steward, who dozed in an arm-chair, and all-night-long fell head foremost, once every five minutes, on Egg, who slept on the counter or dresser. Last night, I had the steward's own cabin, opening on deck, all to myself. It had been previously occupied by some desolate lady who went ashore at Civita Vecchia. There was little or no sea, thank Heaven, all the trip; but the rain was heavier than any I have ever seen, and the lightning very constant and vivid. We were, with the crew—some 200 people—provided with boats, at the utmost stretch, for one hundred perhaps. I could not help thinking what would happen if we met with any accident: the crew being chiefly Maltese, and evidently fellows who would cut off alone in the largest boat, on the least alarm; the speed very high; and the running, thro' all the narrow rocky channels. Thank God, however, here we are."

A whimsical postscript closed the amusing narrative. "We

towed from Civita Vecchia, the entire Greek navy, I believe; consisting of a little brig-of-war with no guns, fitted as a steamer, but disabled by having burnt the bottoms of her boilers out, in her first run. She was just big enough to carry the captain and a crew of six or so: but the captain was so covered with buttons and gold that there never would have been room for him on board to put those valuables away, if he hadn't worn them—which he consequently did, all night. Whenever anything was wanted to be done, as slackening the tow-rope or anything of that sort, our officers roared at this miserable potentate, in violent English, through a speaking trumpet; of which he couldn't have understood a word in the most favourable circumstances. So he did all the wrong things first, and the right thing always last. The absence of any knowledge of anything but English on the part of the officers and stewards was most ridiculous. I met an Italian gentleman on the cabin steps yesterday morning, vainly endeavouring to explain that he wanted a cup of tea for his sick wife. And when we were coming out of the harbour at Genoa, and it was necessary to order away that boat of music you remember, the chief officer (called 'aft' for the purpose, as 'knowing something of Italian') delivered himself in this explicit and clear Italian to the principal performer—'Now Signora, if you don't sheer off you'll be run down, so you had better trice up that guitar of yours and put about.'"

At Naples some days were passed very merrily; going up Vesuvius and into the buried cities, with Layard who had joined them, and with the Tennents. Here a small adventure befell Dickens specially, in itself extremely unimportant, but told by him with delightful humour in a letter to his sister-in-law. The old idle Frenchman, to whom all things are possible, with his snuff-box and dusty umbrella and all the delicate and kindly observation, would have enchanted Leigh Hunt, and made his way to the heart of Charles Lamb. After mentioning Mr. Lowther, then English chargé d'affaires in Naples, as a very agreeable fellow who had been at the Rockingham play, he alludes to a meeting at his house. "We had an exceedingly pleasant dinner of eight, preparatory to which I was near having the ridiculous adventure of not being able to find the house and coming back dinnerless. I went in an open carriage from the hotel in all state, and the coachman to my surprise pulled up at the end of the Chiaja. 'Behold the house,' says he, 'of Il Signor Larthoor!'—at the same time pointing with his whip into the seventh heaven where the early stars were shining. 'But the Signor Larthorr,' says I, 'lives at Pausilippo.' 'It is true,' says the coachman (still pointing to the evening star), 'but he lives high up the Salita Sant' Antonio where no carriage ever yet ascended, and that is the house' (evening star as aforesaid), 'and one must go on foot. Behold the Salita Sant' Antonio!' I went up it, a mile and a half I should think. I got into the strangest places among the wildest Neapolitans; kitchens, washing-places, archways, stables, vineyards; was baited by dogs, and answered, in profoundly unintelligible language, from behind lonely locked doors in cracked female voices, quaking with fear; but could hear of no such Englishman, nor any Englishman. By and by, I came upon a polenta-shop in the clouds, where an old Frenchman with an umbrella like a faded tropical leaf (it had not rained in Naples for six weeks) was staring at nothing at all, with a snuff-box in his hand. To him I appealed, concerning the Signor Larthoor. 'Sir,' said he, with the sweetest politeness, 'can you speak French?' 'Sir,' said I, 'a little.' 'Sir,' said he, 'I presume the Signor Loothere'—you will observe that he changed the name according to the custom of his country—'is an Englishman?' I admitted that he was the victim of circumstances and had that misfortune. 'Sir,' said he, 'one word more. *Has* he a servant with a wooden leg?' 'Great heaven, sir,' said I, 'how do I know? I should think not, but it is possible.' 'It is always,' said the Frenchman, 'possible. Almost all the things of the world are always possible.' 'Sir,' said I—you may imagine my condition and dismal sense of my own absurdity by this time —'that is true.' He then took an immense pinch of snuff, wiped the dust off his umbrella, led me to an arch commanding a wonderful view of the Bay of Naples, and pointed deep into the earth from which I had mounted. 'Below there, near the lamp, one finds an Englishman with a servant with a wooden leg. It is always possible that he is the Signor Loothere.' I had been asked at six o'clock, and it was now getting on for seven. I went back in a state of perspiration and misery not to be described, and without the faintest hope of finding the spot. But as I was going farther down to the lamp, I saw the strangest staircase up a dark corner, with a man in a white waistcoat (evidently hired) standing on the top of it fuming. I dashed in at a venture, found it was the house, made the most of the whole story, and achieved much popularity. The best of it was that as nobody ever did find the place, Lowther had put a servant at the bottom of the Salita to wait 'for an English gentleman'; but the servant (as he presently pleaded), deceived by the moustache, had allowed the English gentleman to pass unchallenged."

From Naples they went to Rome, where they found Lockhart, "fearfully weak and broken, yet hopeful of himself too" (he died the following year); smoked and drank punch with David Roberts, then painting every day with Louis Haghe in St. Peter's; and took the old walks. The Coliseum, Appian Way, and Streets of Tombs, seemed desolate and grand as ever; but generally, Dickens adds, "I discovered the Roman antiquities to be *smaller* than my imagination in nine years had made them. The Electric Telegraph now goes like a sunbeam through the cruel old heart of the Coliseum—a suggestive thing to think about, I fancied. The Pantheon I thought even nobler than of yore." The amusements were of course an attraction; and nothing at the Opera amused the party of three English more, than another party of four Americans who sat behind them in the pit. "All the seats are numbered arm-chairs, and you buy your number at the pay-place, and go to it with the easiest direction on the ticket itself. We were early, and the four places of the Americans were on the next row behind us —all together. After looking about them for some time, and seeing the greater part of the seats empty (because the audience generally wait in a caffè which is part of the theatre), one of them said 'Waal I dunno—I expect we ain't no call to set so nigh to one another neither—will you scatter Kernel, will you scatter sir?'—Upon this the Kernel 'scattered' some twenty benches off; and they distributed themselves (for no earthly reason apparently but to get rid of one another) all over the pit. As soon as the overture began, in came the audience in a mass. Then the people who had got the numbers into which they had 'scattered,' had to get them out; and as they understood nothing that was said to them, and could make no reply but 'A-mericani,' you may imagine the number of cocked hats it took to dislodge them. At last they were all got back into their right places, except one. About an hour afterwards when Moses (*Moses in Egypt* was the opera) was invoking the darkness, and there was a dead silence all over the house, unwonted sounds of disturbance broke out from a distant corner of the pit, and here and there a beard got up to look. 'What is it neow, sir?' said one of the Americans to another; 'some person seems to be getting along, again streeem.' 'Waal sir' he replied 'I dunno.

But I xpect 'tis the Kernel sir, a holdin on.' So it was. The Kernel was ignominiously escorted back to his right place, not in the least disconcerted, and in perfectly good spirits and temper." The opera was excellently done, and the price of the stalls one and threepence English. At Milan, on the other hand, the Scala was fallen from its old estate, dirty, gloomy, dull, and the performance execrable.

Another theatre of the smallest pretension Dickens sought out with avidity in Rome, and eagerly enjoyed. He had heard it said in his old time in Genoa that the finest Marionetti were here; and now, after great difficulty, he discovered the company in a sort of stable attached to a decayed palace. "It was a wet night, and there was no audience but a party of French officers and ourselves. We all sat together. I never saw anything more amazing than the performance—altogether only an hour long, but managed by as many as ten people, for we saw them all go behind, at the ringing of a bell. The saving of a young lady by a good fairy from the machinations of an enchanter, coupled with the comic business of her servant Pulcinella (the Roman Punch) formed the plot of the first piece. A scolding old peasant woman, who always leaned forward to scold and put her hands in the pockets of her apron, was incredibly natural. Pulcinella, so airy, so merry, so life-like, so graceful, he was irresistible. To see him carrying an umbrella over his mistress's head in a storm, talking to a prodigious giant whom he met in the forest, and going to bed with a pony, were things never to be forgotten. And so delicate are the hands of the people who move them, that every puppet was an Italian, and did exactly what an Italian does. If he pointed at any object, if he saluted anybody, if he laughed, if he cried, he did it as never Englishman did it since Britain first at Heaven's command arose—arose—arose, etc. There was a ballet afterwards, on the same scale, and we came away really quite enchanted with the delicate drollery of the thing. French officers more than ditto."

Of the great enemy to the health of the now capital of the kingdom of Italy, Dickens remarked in the same letter. "I have been led into some curious speculations by the existence and progress of the Malaria about Rome. Isn't it very extraordinary to think of its encroaching and encroaching on the Eternal City as if it were commissioned to swallow it up? This year it has been extremely bad, and has long outstayed its usual time. Rome has been very unhealthy, and is not free now. Few people care to be out at the bad times of sunset and sunrise, and the streets are like a desert at night. There is a church, a very little way outside the walls, destroyed by fire some 16 or 18 years ago, and now restored and re-created at an enormous expense. It stands in a wilderness. For any human creature who goes near it, or can sleep near it, after nightfall, it might as well be at the bottom of the uppermost cataract of the Nile. Along the whole extent of the Pontine Marshes (which we came across the other day), no creature in Adam's likeness lives, except the sallow people at the lonely posting-stations. I walk out from the Coliseum through the Street of Tombs to the ruins of the old Appian Way—pass no human being, and see no human habitation but ruined houses from which the people have fled, and where it is death to sleep; these houses being three miles outside a gate of Rome at its farthest extent. Leaving Rome by the opposite side, we travel for many many hours over the dreary Campagna, shunned and avoided by all but the wretched shepherds. Thirteen hours' good posting brings us to Bolsena (I slept there once before), on the margin of a stagnant lake whence the workpeople fly as the sun goes down—where it is a risk to go; where from a distance we saw a mist hang on the place; where, in the inconceivably wretched inn, no window can be opened; where our dinner was a pale ghost of a fish with an oily omelette, and we slept in great mouldering rooms tainted with ruined arches and heaps of dung—and coming from which we saw no colour in the cheek of man, woman, or child for another twenty miles. Imagine this phantom knocking at the gates of Rome; passing them; creeping along the streets; haunting the aisles and pillars of the churches; year by year more encroaching, and more impossible of avoidance."

From Rome they posted to Florence, reaching it in three days and a half, on the morning of 20 November; having then been out six weeks, with only three days' rain; and in another week they were at Venice. "The fine weather has accompanied us here," Dickens wrote on 28 November, "the place of all others where it is necessary, and the city has been a blaze of sunlight and blue sky (with an extremely clear cold air) ever since we have been in it. If you could see it at this moment you would never forget it. We live in the same house that I lived in nine years ago, and have the same sitting-room—close to the Bridge of Sighs and the Palace of the Doges. The room is at the corner of the house, and there is a narrow street of water running round the side: so that we have the Grand Canal before the two front windows, and this wild little street at the corner window; into which, too, our three bedrooms look. We established a gondola as soon as we arrived, and we slide out of the hall on to the water twenty times a day. The gondoliers have queer old customs that belong to their class, and some are sufficiently disconcerting. . . . It is a point of honour with them, while they are engaged, to be always at your disposal. Hence it is no use telling them they may go home for an hour or two—for they won't go. They roll themselves in shaggy capuccins, great coats with hoods, and lie down on the stone or marble pavement until they are wanted again. So that when I come in or go out, on foot—which can be done from this house for some miles, over little bridges and by narrow ways—I usually walk over the principal of my vassals, whose custom it is to snore immediately across the doorway. Conceive the oddity of the most familiar things in this place, from one instance: Last night we go downstairs at half-past eight, step into the gondola, slide away on the black water, ripple and plash swiftly along for a mile or two, land at a broad flight of steps, and instantly walk into the most brilliant and beautiful theatre conceivable—all silver and blue, and precious little fringes made of glittering prisms of glass. There we sit until half-past eleven, come out again (gondolier asleep outside the box-door), and in a moment are on the black silent water, floating away as if there were no dry building in the world. It stops, and in a moment we are out again, upon the broad solid Piazza of St. Mark, brilliantly lighted with gas, very like the Palais Royal at Paris, only far more handsome, and shining with no end of caffès. The two old pillars and the enormous bell-tower are as gruff and solid against the exquisite starlight as if they were a thousand miles from the sea or any undermining water; and the front of the cathedral, overlaid with golden mosaics and beautiful colours, is like a thousand rainbows even in the night."

His formerly expressed notions as to art and pictures in Italy received confirmation at this visit. "I am more than ever confirmed in my conviction that one of the great uses of travelling is to encourage a man to think for himself, to be bold enough always to declare without offence that he *does* think for himself, and to overcome the villainous meanness of professing what other people have professed when he knows (if he has capacity to originate an opinion) that his profession is untrue. The intolerable nonsense against which genteel taste and subserviency are afraid to rise, in connection with art, is astounding. Egg's honest amazement and consternation when he saw some of the most trumpeted things was what the Americans call a 'caution.' In the very same hour and minute there were scores of people falling into conventional raptures with that very poor Apollo, and passing over the most beautiful little figures and heads in the whole Vatican because they were not expressly set up to be worshipped. So in this place. There are pictures by Tintoretto in Venice more delightful and masterly than it is possible sufficiently to express. His Assembly of the Blest I do believe to be, take it all in all, the most wonderful and charming picture ever painted. Your guide-book writer, representing the general swarming of humbugs, rather patronises Tintoretto as a man of some sort of merit; and (bound to follow Eustace, Forsyth, and all the rest of them) directs you, on pain of being broke for want of gentility in appreciation, to go into ecstacies with things that have neither imagination, nature, proportion, possibility, nor anything else in them. You immediately obey, and tell your son to obey. He tells his son, and he tells his, and so the world gets at three-fourths of its frauds and miseries."

The last place visited was Turin, where the travellers arrived on 5 December, finding it, with a brightly shining sun, intensely cold and freezing hard. "There are double windows to all the rooms, but the Alpine air comes down and numbs my feet as I write (in a cap and shawl) within six feet of the fire." There was yet something better than this to report of that bracing Alpine air. To Dickens's remarks on the Sardinian race, and to what he says of the exile of the noblest Italians, the momentous events of the few following years gave striking comment; nor could better proof be afforded of the judgment he brought to the observation of what passed before him. The letter had in all respects much interest and attractiveness. "This is a remarkably agreeable place. A beautiful town, prosperous, thriving, growing prodigiously, as Genoa is; crowded with busy inhabitants; full of noble streets and squares. The Alps, now covered deep with snow, are close upon it, and here and there seem almost ready to tumble into the houses. The contrast this part of Italy presents to the rest, is amazing. Beautifully made railroads, admirably managed; cheerful, active people; spirit, energy, life, progress. In Milan, in every street, the noble palace of some exile is a barrack, and dirty soldiers are lolling out of the magnificent windows—it seems as if the whole place were being gradually absorbed into soldiers. In Naples, something like a hundred thousand troops. 'I knew,' I said to a certain Neapolitan Marchese there whom I had known before, and who came to see me the night after I arrived, 'I knew a very remarkable gentleman when I was last here; who had never been out of his own country, but was perfectly acquainted with English literature, and had taught himself to speak English in that wonderful manner that no one could have known him for a foreigner; I am very anxious to see him again, but I forget his name.'—He named him, and his face fell directly. 'Dead?' said I.—'In exile.'—'O dear me!' said I, 'I had looked forward to seeing him again, more than anyone I was acquainted with in the country!'—'What would you have?' says the Marchese in a low voice. 'He was a remarkable man—full of knowledge, full of spirit, full of generosity. Where should he be but in exile! Where could he be!' We said not another word about it, but I shall always remember the short dialogue."

On the other hand there were incidents of the Austrian occupation as to which Dickens thought the ordinary style of comment unfair; and his closing remark on their police is well worth preserving. "I am strongly inclined to think that our countrymen are to blame in the matter of the Austrian vexations to travellers that have been complained of. Their manner is so very bad, they are so extraordinarily suspicious, so determined to be done by everybody, and give so much offence. Now, the Austrian police are very strict, but they really know how to do business, and they do it. And if you treat them like gentlemen, they will always respond. When we first crossed the Austrian frontier, and were ushered into the police office, I took off my hat. The officer immediately took off his, and was as polite—still doing his duty, without any compromise—as it was possible to be. When we came to Venice, the arrangements were very strict, but were so business-like that the smallest possible amount of inconvenience consistent with strictness ensued. Here is the scene. A soldier has come into the railway carriage (a saloon on the American plan) some miles off, has touched his hat, and asked for my passport. I have given it. Soldier has touched his hat again, and retired as from the presence of a superior officer. Alighted from carriage, we pass into a place like a banking-house, lighted up with gas. Nobody bullies us or drives us there, but we must go, because the road ends there. Several soldierly clerks. One very sharp chief. My passport is brought out of an inner room, certified to be *en règle*. Very sharp chief takes it, looks at it (it is rather longer, now, than *Hamlet*), calls out—'Signor Carlo Dickens!' 'Here I am sir.' 'Do you intend remaining long in Venice sir?' 'Probably four days sir!' 'Italian is known to you sir. You have been in Venice before?' 'Once before sir.' 'Perhaps you remained longer then sir?' 'No indeed; I merely came to see, and went as I came.' 'Truly sir? Do I infer that you are going by Trieste?' 'No. I am going to Parma, and Turin, and by Paris home.' 'A cold journey sir, I hope it may be a pleasant one.' 'Thank you.' —He gives me one very sharp look all over, and wishes me a very happy night. I wish *him* a very happy night and it's done. The thing being done at all, could not be better done, or more politely—though I dare say if I had been sucking a gentish cane all the time, or talking in English to my compatriots, it might not unnaturally have been different. At Turin and at Genoa there are no such stoppages at all; but in any other part of Italy, give me an Austrian in preference to a native functionary. At Naples it is done in a beggarly, shambling, bungling, tardy, vulgar way; but I am strengthened in my old impression that Naples is one of the most odious places on the face of the earth. The general degradation oppresses me like foul air."

IV

DICKENS was in Boulogne, in 1853, from the middle of June to
the end of September, and for the next three months, as we
have seen, was in Switzerland and Italy. In the following year
he went again to Boulogne in June, and stayed, after finishing
Hard Times, until far into October. In February of 1855 he was
for a fortnight in Paris with Mr. Wilkie Collins; not taking
up his more prolonged residence there until the winter. From
November 1855 to the end of April 1856 he made the French
capital his home, working at *Little Dorrit* during all those
months. Then, after a month's interval in Dover and London,
he took up his third summer residence in Boulogne, whither his
younger children had gone direct from Paris; and stayed until
September, finishing *Little Dorrit* in London in the spring of 1857.

Of the first of these visits, a few lively notes of humour and
character out of his letters will tell the story sufficiently. The
second and third had points of more attractiveness. Those were
the years of the French-English alliance, of the great exposition
of English paintings, of the return of the troops from the
Crimea, and of the visit of the Prince Consort to the Emperor;
such interest as Dickens took in these several matters appearing
in his letters with the usual vividness, and the story of his
continental life coming out with amusing distinctness in the
successive pictures they paint with so much warmth and
colour. Another chapter will be given to Paris. This deals
only with Boulogne.

For his first summer residence, in June 1853, he had taken a
house on the high ground near the Calais road; an odd French
place with the strangest little rooms and halls, but standing in
the midst of a large garden, with wood and waterfall, a conservatory opening on a great bank of roses, and paths and
gates on one side to the ramparts, on the other to the sea.
Above all there was a capital proprietor and landlord, by whom

the cost of keeping up gardens and wood (which he called a forest) was defrayed, while he gave his tenant the whole range of both and all the flowers for nothing, sold him the garden produce as it was wanted, and kept a cow on the estate to supply the family milk. "If this were but 300 miles farther off," wrote Dickens, "how the English would rave about it! I do assure you that there are picturesque people, and town, and country, about this place, that quite fill up the eye and fancy. As to the fishing people (whose dress can have changed neither in colour nor in form for many many years), and their quarter of the town cobweb-hung with great brown nets across the narrow up-hill streets, they are as good as Naples, every bit." His description both of house and landlord, of which I tested the exactness when I visited him, was in the old pleasant vein; requiring no connection with himself to give it interest, but, by the charm and ease with which everything picturesque or characteristic was disclosed, placed in the domain of art.

"O the rain here yesterday!" (26 June.) "A great sea-fog rolling in, a strong wind blowing, and the rain coming down in torrents all day long. . . . This house is on a great hill-side, backed up by woods of young trees. It faces the Haute Ville with the ramparts and the unfinished cathedral—which capital object is exactly opposite the windows. On the slope in front, going steep down to the right, all Boulogne is piled and jumbled about in a very picturesque manner. The view is charming— closed in at last by the tops of swelling hills; and the door is within ten minutes of the post office, and within quarter of an hour of the sea. The garden is made in terraces up the hill-side, like an Italian garden; the top walks being in the before-mentioned woods. The best part of it begins at the level of the house, and goes up at the back, a couple of hundred feet per-haps. There are at present thousands of roses all about the house, and no end of other flowers. There are five great summer-houses, and (I think) fifteen fountains — not one of which (according to the invariable French custom) ever plays. The house is a doll's house of many rooms. It is one story high, with eight and thirty steps up and down—tribune wise—to the front door: the noblest French demonstration I have ever seen I think. It is a double house; and as there are only four windows and a pigeon-hole to be beheld in front, you would suppose it to contain about four rooms. Being built on the hill-side, the top story of the house at the back—there are two stories there—opens on the level of another garden. On the ground floor there is a very pretty hall, almost all glass; a little dining-room opening on a beautiful conservatory, which is also looked into through a great transparent glass in a mirror-frame over the chimney-piece, just as in Paxton's room at Chatsworth; a spare bedroom, two little drawing-rooms opening into one another, the family bedrooms, a bathroom, a glass corridor, an open yard, and a kind of kitchen with a machinery of stoves and boilers. Above, there are eight tiny bedrooms all opening on one great room in the roof, originally intended for a billiard-room. In the basement there is an admirable kitchen with every conceivable requisite in it, a noble cellar, first-rate man's room and pantry; coach-house, stable, coal-store and wood-store; and in the garden is a pavilion, containing an excellent spare bedroom on the ground floor. The getting-up of these places, the looking-glasses, clocks, little stoves, all manner of fittings, must be seen to be appreciated. The conservatory is full of choice flowers and perfectly beautiful."

Then came the charm of the letter, his description of his landlord, lightly sketched by him in print as M. Loyal-Devasseur, but here filled in with the most attractive touches his loving hand could give. "But the landlord—M. Beaucourt—is wonderful. Everybody here has two surnames (I cannot conceive why), and M. Beaucourt, as he is always called, is by rights M. Beaucourt-Mutuel. He is a portly jolly fellow with a fine open face; lives on the hill behind, just outside the top of the garden; and was a linen draper in the town, where he still has a shop, but is supposed to have mortgaged his business and to be in difficulties—all along of this place, which he has planted with his own hands; which he cultivates all day; and which he never on any consideration speaks of but as "the property." He is extraordinarily popular in Boulogne (the people in the shops invariably brightening up at the mention of his name, and congratulating us on being his tenants), and really seems to deserve it. He is such a liberal fellow that I can't bear to ask him for anything, since he instantly supplies it whatever it is. The things he has done in respect of unreasonable bed-steads and washing-stands, I blush to think of. I observed the other day in one of the side gardens—there are gardens at each side of the house too—a place where I thought the Comic Countryman" (a name he was giving just then to his youngest boy) "must infallibly trip over, and make a little descent of a dozen feet. So I said 'M. Beaucourt'—who instantly pulled off his cap and stood bareheaded—'there are some spare pieces of wood lying by the cow-house, if you would have the kindness to have one laid across here I think it would be safer.' 'Ah, mon Dieu sir,' said M. Beaucourt, 'it must be iron. This is not a portion of the property where you would like to see wood.' 'But iron is so expensive,' said I, 'and it really is not worth while——' 'Sir, pardon me a thousand times,' said M. Beaucourt, 'it shall be iron. Assuredly and perfectly it shall be iron.' 'Then M. Beaucourt,' said I, 'I shall be glad to pay a moiety of the cost.' 'Sir,' said M. Beaucourt, 'Never!' Then to change the subject, he slided from his firmness and gravity into a graceful conversational tone, and said, 'In the moonlight last night, the flowers on the property appeared, O heaven, to be *bathing themselves in the sky*. You like the property?' 'M. Beaucourt,' said I, 'I am enchanted with it; I am more than satisfied with everything.' 'And I sir,' said M. Beaucourt, laying his cap upon his breast, and kissing his hand—'I equally!' Yesterday two blacksmiths came for a day's work, and put up a good solid handsome bit of iron-railing, mortised into the stone parapet. . . . If the extraordinary things in the house defy description, the amazing phenomena in the gardens never could have been dreamed of by anybody but a Frenchman bent upon one idea. Besides a portrait of the house in the dining-room, there is a plan of the property in the hall. It looks about the size of Ireland; and to every one of the extraordinary objects there is a reference with some portentous name. There are fifty-one such references, including the Cottage of Tom Thumb, the Bridge of Austerlitz, the Bridge of Jena, the Hermitage, the Bower of the Old Guard, the Labyrinth (I have no idea which is which); and there is guidance to every room in the house, as if it were a place on that stupendous scale that without such a clue you must infallibly lose your way, and perhaps perish of starvation between bedroom and bedroom."

* 95

On 3 July there came a fresh trait of the good fellow of a landlord. "Fancy what Beaucourt told me last night. When he 'conceived the inspiration' of planting the property ten years ago, he went over to England to buy the trees, took a small cottage in the market-gardens at Putney, lived there three months, held a symposium every night attended by the principal gardeners of Fulham, Putney, Kew, and Hammersmith (which he calls Hamsterdam), and wound up with a supper at which the market-gardeners rose, clinked their glasses, and exclaimed with one accord (I quote him exactly) VIVE BEAUCOURT! He was a captain in the National Guard, and Cavaignac his general. Brave Capitaine Beaucourt! said Cavaignac, you must receive a decoration. My General, said Beaucourt, No! It is enough for me that I have done my duty. I go to lay the first stone of a house upon a Property I have—that house shall be my decoration. (Regard that house!)" Addition to the picture came in a letter of 24 July; with a droll glimpse of Shakespeare at the theatre, and of the Saturday's pig-market.

"I may mention that the great Beaucourt daily changes the orthography of this place. He has now fixed it, by having painted up outside the garden gate, 'Entrée particulière de la Villa des Moulineaux.' On another gate a little higher up, he has had painted 'Entrée des Ecuries de la Villa des Moulineaux.' On another gate a little lower down (applicable to one of the innumerable buildings in the garden), 'Entrée du Tom Pouce.' On the highest gate of the lot, leading to his own house, 'Entrée du Château Napoléonienne.' All of which inscriptions you will behold in black and white when you come. I see little of him now, as, all things being 'bien arrangées,' he is delicate of appearing. His wife has been making a trip in the country during the last three weeks, but (as he mentioned to me with his hat in his hand) it was necessary that he should remain here, to be continually at the disposition of the tenant of the Property. (The better to do this, he has had roaring dinner parties of fifteen daily; and the old woman who milks the cows has been fainting up the hill under vast burdens of champagne.)

"We went to the theatre last night, to see the *Midsummer Night's Dream*—of the Opéra Comique. It is a beautiful little theatre now, with a very good company; and the nonsense of the piece was done with a sense quite confounding in that connection. Willy Am Shay Kes Peer; Sirzhon Foll Stayffe; Lor Lattimeer; and that celebrated Maid of Honour to Queen Elizabeth, Meees Oleeveeir—were the principal characters.

"Outside the old town, an army of workmen are (and have been for a week or so, already) employed upon an immense building which I supposed might be a Fort, or a Monastery, or a Barrack, or other something designed to last for ages. I find it is for the annual fair, which begins on the 5th of August and lasts a fortnight. Almost every Sunday we have a fête, where there is dancing in the open air, and where immense men with prodigious beards revolve on little wooden horses like Italian irons, in what we islanders call a roundabout, by the hour together. But really the good humour and cheerfulness are very delightful. Among the other sights of the place, there is a pig-market every Saturday, perfectly insupportable in its absurdity. An excited French peasant, male or female, with a determined young pig, is the most amazing spectacle. I saw a little Drama enacted yesterday week, the drollery of which was perfect. *Dram. Pers.* 1. A pretty young woman with short petticoats and trim blue stockings, riding a donkey with two baskets and a pig in each. 2. An ancient farmer in a blouse, driving four pigs, his four in hand, with an enormous whip—and being drawn against walls and into smoking shops by any one of the four. 3. A cart, with an old pig (manacled) looking out of it, and terrifying six hundred and fifty young pigs in the market by his terrific grunts. 4. Collector of Octroi in an immense cocked hat, with a stream of young pigs running, night and day, between his military boots and rendering accounts impossible. 5. Inimitable, confronted by a radiation of elderly pigs, fastened each by one leg to a bunch of stakes in the ground. 6. John Edmund Reade, poet, expressing eternal devotion to and admiration of Landor, unconscious of approaching pig recently escaped from barrow. 7. Priests, peasants, soldiers, etc."

He had meanwhile gathered friendly faces round him. Frank Stone went over with his family to a house taken for him on the St. Omer road by Dickens, who was joined in the château by Mr. and Mrs. Leech and Mr. Wilkie Collins. "Leech says that when he stepped from the boat after their stormy passage, he was received by the congregated spectators with a distinct round of applause as by far the most intensely and unutterably miserable looking object that had yet appeared. The laughter was tumultuous, and he wishes his friends to know that altogether he made an immense hit." So passed the summer months: excursions with these friends to Amiens and Beauvais relieving the work upon his novel, and the trip to Italy, already described, following on its completion.

In June 1854, M. Beaucourt had again received his famous tenant, but in another cottage or château (to him convertible terms) on the much cherished property, placed on the very summit of the hill with a private road leading out to the Column, a really pretty place, rooms larger than in the other house, a noble sea view, everywhere nice prospects, good garden, and plenty of sloping turf. It was called the Villa du Camp de Droite, and here Dickens stayed, as I have intimated, until the eve of his winter residence in Paris.

The formation of the Northern Camp at Boulogne began the week after he had finished *Hard Times*, and he watched its progress, as it increased and extended itself along the cliffs towards Calais, with the liveliest amusement. At first he was startled by the suddenness with which soldiers overran the roads, became billeted in every house, made the bridges red with their trousers, and "sprang up on the pier like fantastic mustard and cress when boats were expected, many of them never having seen the sea before." But the good behaviour of the men had a reconciling effect, and their ingenuity delighted him. The quickness with which they raised whole streets of mud-huts, less picturesque than the tents, but (like most un-   * 97 picturesque things) more comfortable, was like an Arabian Nights' tale. "Each little street holds 144 men, and every corner-door has the number of the street upon it as soon as it is put up; and the postmen can fall to work as easily as in the Rue de Rivoli at Paris." His patience was again a little tried when he found baggage-wagons ploughing up his favourite walks, and trumpeters in twos and threes teaching newly-recruited trumpeters in all the sylvan places, and making the echoes hideous. But this had its amusement too. "I met to-day a weazen sun-burnt youth from the south with such an immense regimental shako on, that he looked like a sort of lucifer match-box, evidently blowing his life rapidly out, under the auspices of two magnificent creatures all hair and lungs, of such breadth across the shoulders that I couldn't see their breast-buttons when I stood in front of them."

The interest culminated as the visit of the Prince Consort approached with its attendant glories of illuminations and reviews. Beaucourt's excitement became intense. The Villa du Camp de Droite was to be a blaze of triumph on the night of the arrival; Dickens, who had carried over with him the meteor flag of England and set it streaming over a haystack in his field, now hoisted the French colours over the British Jack in honour of the national alliance; the Emperor was to subside to the station of a general officer, so that all the rejoicings should be in honour of the Prince; and there was to be a review in the open country near Wimereux, when "at one stage of the maneuvres (I am too excited to spell the word, but you know what I mean)" the whole hundred thousand men in the camp of the North were to be placed before the Prince's eyes, to show what a division of the French army might be. "I believe everything I hear," said Dickens. It was the state of mind of Hood's country gentleman after the fire at the Houses of Parliament. "Beaucourt, as one of the town council, receives summonses to turn out and debate about something, or receive somebody, every five minutes. Whenever I look out of window, or go to the door, I see an immense black object at Beaucourt's porch like a boat set up on end in the air with a pair of white trowsers below it. This is the cocked hat of an official Huissier, newly arrived with a summons, whose head is thrown back as he is in the act of drinking Beaucourt's wine." The day came at last, and all Boulogne turned out for its holiday; "but I," Dickens wrote, "had by this cooled down a little, and, reserving myself for the illuminations, I abandoned the great men and set off upon my usual country walk. See my reward. Coming home by the Calais road, covered with dust, I suddenly find myself face to face with Albert and Napoleon, jogging along in the pleasantest way, a little in front, talking extremely loud about the view, and attended by a brilliant staff of some sixty or seventy horsemen, with a couple of our royal grooms with their red coats riding oddly enough in the midst of the magnates. I took off my wide-awake without stopping to stare, whereupon the Emperor pulled off his cocked hat; and Albert (seeing, I suppose, that it was an Englishman) pulled off his. Then we went our several ways. The Emperor is broader across the chest than in the old times when we used to see him so often at Gore House, and stoops more in the shoulders. Indeed his carriage * 98 thereabouts is like Fonblanque's." The town he described as "one great flag" for the rest of the visit; and to the success of the illuminations he contributed largely himself by leading off splendidly with a hundred and twenty wax candles blazing in his seventeen front windows, and visible from that great height over all the place. "On the first eruption Beaucourt *danced and screamed* on the grass before the door; and when he was more composed, set off with Madame Beaucourt to look at the house from every possible quarter, and, he said, collect the suffrages of his compatriots."

Their suffrages seem to have gone, however, mainly in another direction. "It was wonderful," Dickens wrote, "to behold about the streets the small French soldiers of the line seizing our Guards by the hand and embracing them. It was wonderful, too, to behold the English sailors in the town, shaking hands with everybody and generally patronising everything. When the people could not get hold of either a soldier or a sailor, they rejoiced in the royal grooms, and embraced *them*. I don't think the Boulogne people were surprised by anything so much, as by the three cheers the crew of the yacht gave when the

Emperor went aboard to lunch. The prodigious volume of them, and the precision, and the circumstance that no man was left straggling on his own account either before or afterwards, seemed to strike the general mind with amazement. Beaucourt said it was *like boxing*." That was written on 10 September; but in a very few days Dickens was unwillingly convinced that whatever the friendly disposition to England might be, the war with Russia was decidedly unpopular. He was present when the false report of the taking of Sebastopol reached the Emperor and Empress. "I was at the review" (8 October) "yesterday week, very near the Emperor and Empress, when the taking of Sebastopol was announced. It was a magnificent show on a magnificent day; and if any circumstance could make it special, the arrival of the telegraphic dispatch would be the culminating point one might suppose. It quite disturbed and mortified me to find how faintly, feebly, miserably, the men responded to the call of the officers to cheer, as each regiment passed by. Fifty excited Englishmen would make a greater sign and sound than a thousand of these men do. . . . The Empress was very pretty, and her slight figure sat capitally on her grey horse. When the Emperor gave her the dispatch to read, she flushed and fired up in a very pleasant way, and kissed it with as natural an impulse as one could desire to see."   * 98A

On the night of that day Dickens went up to see a play acted at a café at the camp, and found himself one of an audience composed wholly of officers and men, with only four ladies among them, officers' wives. The steady, working, sensible faces all about him told their own story; "and as to kindness and consideration towards the poor actors, it was real benevolence." Another attraction at the camp was a conjuror, who had been called to exhibit twice before the imperial party, and whom Dickens always afterwards referred to as the most consummate master of legerdemain he had seen. Nor was he a mean authority as to this, being himself, with his tools at hand, a capital conjuror; but the Frenchman scorned help, stood among the company without any sort of apparatus, and, by the mere force of sleight of hand and an astonishing memory, performed feats having no likeness to anything Dickens had ever seen done, and totally inexplicable to his most vigilant reflection. "So far as I know, a perfectly original genius, and that puts any sort of knowledge of legerdemain, such as I supposed that I possessed, at utter defiance." The account he gave dealt with two exploits only, the easiest to describe, and, not being with cards, not the most remarkable; for he would also say of this French-man that he transformed cards into very demons. He never saw a human hand touch them in the same way, fling them about so amazingly, or change them in his, one's own, or another's hand, with a skill so impossible to follow.

"You are to observe that he was *with the company*, not in the least removed from them; and that we occupied the front row. He brought in some writing paper with him when he entered, and a black-lead pencil; and he wrote some words on half-sheets of paper. One of these half-sheets he folded into two, and gave to Catherine to hold. Madame, he says aloud, will you think of any class of objects? I have done so.—Of what class, Madame? Animals.—Will you think of a particular animal, Madame? I have done so.—Of what animal? The Lion. —Will you think of another class of objects, Madame? I have done so.—Of what class? Flowers.—The particular flower? The Rose.—Will you open the paper you hold in your hand? She opened it, and there was neatly and plainly written in pencil —*The Lion. The Rose*. Nothing whatever had led up to these words, and they were the most distant conceivable from Cath-erine's thoughts when she entered the room. He had several common school-slates about a foot square. He took one of these to a field-officer from the camp, decoré and what not, who sat about six from us, with a grave saturnine friend next him. My General, says he, will you write a name on this slate, after your friend has done so? Don't show it to me. The friend wrote a name, and the General wrote a name. The conjuror took the slate rapidly from the officer, threw it violently down on the ground with its written side to the floor, and asked the officer to put his foot upon it, and keep it there: which he did. The conjuror considered for about a minute, looking devilish hard at the General.—My General, says he, your friend wrote Dago-bert, upon the slate under your foot. The friend admits it.— And you, my General, wrote Nicholas. General admits it, and everybody laughs and applauds.—My General, will you excuse me, if I change that name into a name expressive of the power of a great nation, which, in happy alliance with the gallantry and spirit of France will shake that name to its centre? Certainly I will excuse it.—My General, take up the slate and read. General reads: DAGOBERT, VICTORIA. The first in his friend's writing; the second in a new hand. I never saw anything in the least like this; or at all approaching to the absolute certainty, the familiarity, quickness, absence of all machinery, and actual face-to-face, hand-to-hand fairness between the conjuror and the audience, with which it was done. I have not the slightest idea of the secret.—One more. He was blinded with several table napkins, and then a great cloth was bodily thrown over them and his head too, so that his voice sounded as if he were under a bed. Perhaps half a dozen dates were written on a slate. He takes the slate in his hand, and throws it violently down on the floor, as before, remains silent a minute, seems to become agitated, and bursts out thus: 'What is this I see? A great city, but of narrow streets and old-fashioned houses, many of which are of wood, resolving itself into ruins! How is it falling into ruins? Hark! I hear the crackling of a great conflagration, and, looking up, I behold a vast cloud of flame and smoke. The ground is covered with hot cinders too, and people are flying into the fields and endeavouring to save their goods. This great fire, this great wind, this roaring noise! This is the great fire of London, and the first date upon the slate must be one, six, six, six—the year in which it happened!' And so on with all the other dates. There! Now, if you will take a cab and impart these mysteries to Rogers, I shall be very glad to have his opinion of them." Rogers had taxed our credulity with some wonderful clairvoyant experiences of his own in Paris, to which here was a parallel at last!

When leaving Paris for his third visit to Boulogne, at the beginning of June 1856, he had not written a word of the ninth number of his new book, and did not expect for another month to "see land from the running sea of *Little Dorrit.*" He had resumed the house he first occupied, the cottage or villa "des Moulineaux," and after dawdling about his garden for a few days with surprising industry in a French farmer garb of blue blouse, leathern belt, and military cap, which he had mounted as "the only one for complete comfort," he wrote to me that he was getting "Now to work again—to work! The story lies before me, I hope, strong and clear. Not to be easily told; but nothing of that sort is to be easily done that *I* know of." At work it became his habit to sit late, and then, putting off his usual walk until night, to lie down among the roses reading until after tea ("middle-aged Love in a blouse and belt"), when he went down to the pier. "The said pier at evening is a phase of the place we never see, and which I hardly knew. But I never did behold such specimens of the youth of my country, male and female, as pervade that place. They are really, in their vulgarity and insolence, quite disheartening. One is so fearfully ashamed of them, and they contrast so very unfavourably with the natives." Mr. Wilkie Collins was again his companion in the summer weeks, and the presence of Jerrold for the greater part of the time added much to his enjoyment.

The last of the camp was now at hand. It had only a battalion of men in it, and a few days would see them out. At first there was horrible weather, "storms of wind, rushes of rain, heavy squalls, cold airs, sea fogs, banging shutters, flapping doors, and beaten down rose-trees by the hundred"; but then came a delightful week among the corn fields and bean fields, and afterwards the end. "It looks very singular and very miserable. The soil being sand, and the grass having been trodden away these two years, the wind from the sea carries the sand into the chinks and ledges of all the doors and windows, and chokes them;—just as if they belonged to Arab huts in the desert. A number of the non-commissioned officers made turf-couches outside their huts, and there were turf orchestras for the bands to play in; all of which are fast getting sanded over in a most Egyptian manner. The Fair is on, under the walls of the haute ville over the way. At one popular show, the Malakhoff is taken every half-hour between 4 and 11. Bouncing explosions announce every triumph of the French arms (the English have nothing to do with it); and in the intervals a man outside blows a railway whistle—straight into the dining-room. Do you know that the French soldiers call their English medal 'The Salvage Medal'—meaning that they got it for saving the English army? I don't suppose there are a thousand people in all France who believe that we did anything but get rescued by the French. And I am confident that the no-result of our precious Chelsea inquiry has wonderfully strengthened this conviction. Nobody at home has yet any adequate idea, I am deplorably sure, of what the Barnacles and the Circumlocution Office have done for us. But whenever we get into war again, the people will begin to find out."

His own household had got into a small war already, of which the commander-in-chief was his man-servant "French," the bulk of the forces engaged being his children, and the invaders two cats. Business brought him to London on the hostilities breaking out, and on his return after a few days the story of the war was told. "Dick," it should be said, was a canary very dear both to Dickens and his eldest daughter, who had so tamed to her loving hand its wild little heart that it was become the most docile of companions. "The only thing new in this garden is that war is raging against two particularly tigerish and fearful cats (from the mill, I suppose), which are always glaring in dark corners, after our wonderful little Dick. Keeping the house open at all points, it is impossible to shut them out, and they hide themselves in the most terrific manner: hanging themselves up behind draperies, like bats, and tumbling out in the dead of night with frightful caterwaulings. Hereupon French borrows Beaucourt's gun, loads the same to the muzzle, discharges it twice in vain and throws himself over with the recoil, exactly like a clown. But at last (while I was in town) he aims at the more amiable cat of the two, and shoots that animal dead. Insufferably elated by this victory, he is now engaged from morning to night in hiding behind bushes to get aim at the other. He does nothing else whatever. All the boys encourage him and watch for the enemy—on whose appearance they give an alarm which immediately serves as a warning to the creature, who runs away. They are at this moment (ready dressed for church) all lying on their stomachs in various parts of the garden. Horrible whistles give notice to the gun what point it is to approach. I am afraid to go out, lest I should be shot. Mr. Plornish says his prayers at night in a whisper, lest the cat should overhear him and take offence. The tradesmen cry out as they come up the avenue, 'Me voici! C'est moi—boulanger —ne tirez pas, Monsieur Franche!' It is like living in a state of siege; and the wonderful manner in which the cat preserves the character of being the only person not much put out by the intensity of this monomania, is most ridiculous." (6 July.) ... "About four pounds of powder and half a ton of shot have been" (13 July) "fired off at the cat (and the public in general) during the week. The finest thing is that immediately after I have heard the noble sportsman blazing away at her in the garden in front, I look out of my room door into the drawing-room, and am pretty sure to see her coming in after the birds, in the calmest manner, by the back window. Intelligence has been brought to me from a source on which I can rely, that French has newly conceived the atrocious project of tempting her into the coach-house by meat and kindness, and there, from an elevated portmanteau, blowing her head off. This I mean sternly to interdict, and to do so to-day as a work of piety."

Besides the graver work which Mr. Wilkie Collins and himself were busy with, in these months, and by which *Household Words* mainly was to profit, some lighter matters occupied the leisure of both. There were to be, at Christmas, theatricals again at Tavistock House; in which the children, with the help of their father and other friends, were to follow up the success of the *Lighthouse* by again acquitting themselves as grown-up actors; and Mr. Collins was busy preparing for them a new drama to be called *The Frozen Deep*, while Dickens was sketching a farce for Mr. Lemon to fill in. But this pleasant employment had sudden and sad interruption.

An epidemic broke out in the town, affecting the children of several families known to Dickens, among them that of his friend Mr. Gilbert A'Beckett; who, upon arriving from Paris, and finding a favourite little son stricken dangerously, sank himself under an illness from which he had been suffering, and died two days after the boy. "He had for three days shown symptoms of rallying, and we had some hope of his recovery; but he sank and died, and never even knew that the child had gone before him. A sad, sad story." Dickens meanwhile had sent his own children home with his wife, and the rest soon followed. Poor M. Beaucourt was inconsolable. "The desolation of the place is wretched. When Mamey and Katey went, Beaucourt came in and wept. He really is almost broken-hearted about it He had planted all manner of flowers for next month, and had thrown down the spade and left off weeding the garden, so that it looks something like a dreary bird-cage with all manner of grasses and chickweeds sticking through the bars and lying in the sand. 'Such a loss too,' he says, 'for Monsieur Dickens!' Then he looks in at the kitchen window (which seems to be his only relief), and sighs himself up the hill home."

Another word is to be said of this excellent man. The most touching traits recorded of him by Dickens have not had mention here, because they refer to the generosity shown by him to an English family in occupation of another of his houses, in connection with whom his losses must have been considerable, but for whom he had nothing but help and sympathy. Replying to some questions about them, put by Dickens one day, he had only enlarged on their sacrifices and self-denials. "Ah, that family, unfortunate! 'And you, Monsieur Beaucourt,' I said to him, 'you are unfortunate too, God knows!' Upon which he said in the pleasantest way in the world, Ah, Monsieur Dickens, thank you, don't speak of it!—And backed himself down the avenue with his cap in his hand, as if he were going to back himself straight into the evening star, without the ceremony of dying first. I never did see such a gentle, kind heart." The interval of residence in Paris between these two last visits to Boulogne is now to be described.

RESIDENCE IN PARIS

1855-6

In Paris Dickens's life was passed among artists, and in the exercise of his own art. His associates were writers, painters, actors, or musicians, and when he wanted relief from any strain of work he found it at the theatre. The years since his last residence in the great city had made him better known, and the increased attentions pleased him. He had to help in preparing for a translation of his books into French; and this, with continued labour at the story he had in hand, occupied him as long as he remained. It will be all best told by extracts from his letters; in which the people he met, the theatres he visited, and the incidents, public or private, that seemed to him worthy of mention, reappear with the old force and liveliness.

Nor is anything better worth preserving from them than choice bits of description of an actor or a drama, for this perishable enjoyment has only so much as may survive out of such recollections to witness for itself to another generation; and an unusually high place may be challenged for the subtlety and delicacy of what is said in these letters of things theatrical, when the writer was especially attracted by a performer or a play. Frédéric Lemaître has never had a higher tribute than Dickens paid to him during his few days' earlier stay at Paris in the spring.

"Incomparably the finest acting I ever saw, I saw last night at the Ambigu. They have revived that old piece, once immensely popular in London under the name of *Thirty Years of a Gambler's Life*. Old Lemaître plays his famous character, and never did I see anything, in art, so exaltedly horrible and awful. In the earlier acts he was so well made up, and so light and active, that he really looked sufficiently young. But in the last two, when he had grown old and miserable, he did the finest things, I really believe, that are within the power of acting. Two or three times a great cry of horror went all round the house. When he met, in the inn yard, the traveller whom he murders, and first saw his money, the manner in which the crime came into his head—and eyes—was as truthful as it was terrific. This traveller, being a good fellow, gives him wine. You should see the dim remembrance of his better days that comes over him as he takes the glass, and in a strange dazed way makes as if he were going to touch the other man's, or do some airy thing with it; and then stops and flings the contents down his hot throat, as if he were pouring it into a lime-kiln. But this was nothing to what follows after he has done the murder, and comes home, with a basket of provisions, a ragged pocket full of money, and a badly-washed bloody right hand which his little girl finds out. After the child asked him if he had hurt his hand, his going aside, turning himself round, and looking over all his clothes for spots, was so inexpressibly dreadful that it really scared one. He called for wine, and the sickness that came upon him when he saw the colour, was one of the things that brought out the curious cry I have spoken of from the audience. Then he fell into a sort of bloody mist, and went on to the end groping about, with no mind for anything, except making his fortune by staking this money, and a faint dull kind of love for the child. It is quite impossible to satisfy one's-self by saying enough of this magnificent performance. I have never seen him come near its finest points in anything else. He said two things in a way that alone would put him far apart from all other actors. One to his wife, when he has exultingly shown her the money, and she has asked him how he got it—'I found it'—and the other to his old companion and tempter, when he was charged by him with having killed that traveller, and suddenly went headlong mad and took him by the throat and howled out, 'It wasn't I who murdered him —it was Misery!' And such a dress; such a face; and, above all, such an extraordinary guilty wicked thing as he made of a knotted branch of a tree which was his walking-stick, from the moment when the idea of the murder came into his head! I could write pages about him. It is an impression quite in-effaceable. He got half-boastful of that walking-staff to himself, and half-afraid of it; and didn't know whether to be grimly pleased that it had the jagged end, or to hate it and be horrified at it. He sat at a little table in the inn-yard, drinking with the traveller; and this horrible stick got between them like the Devil, while he counted on his fingers the uses he could put the money to."

That was at the close of February. In October, Dickens's

longer residence began. He betook himself with his family, after two unsuccessful attempts in the new region of the Rue Balzac and Rue Lord Byron, to an apartment in the Avenue des Champs Elysées. Over him was an English bachelor with an establishment consisting of an English groom and five English horses. "The concierge and his wife told us that his name was *Six*, which drove me nearly mad until we discovered it to be *Sykes*." The situation was a good one, very cheerful for himself and with amusement for his children. It was a quarter of a mile above Franconi's on the other side of the way, and within a door or two of the Jardin d'Hiver. The Exposition was just below; the Barrière de l'Etoile from a quarter to half a mile below; and all Paris, including Emperor and Empress, coming from and returning to St. Cloud, thronged past the windows in open carriages or on horseback, all day long. Now it was he found himself more of a celebrity than when he had wintered in the city nine years before; the feuille- * 99 ton of the *Moniteur* was filled daily with a translation of *Chuzzlewit*; and he had soon to consider the proposal I have named, to publish in French his collected novels and tales. Before he had been a week in his new abode, Ary Scheffer, "a frank and noble fellow," had made his acquaintance; introduced him to several distinguished Frenchmen; and expressed the wish to paint him. To Scheffer was also due an advantage obtained for my friend's two little daughters of which they may always keep the memory with pride. "Mamey and Katie are learning Italian, and their master is Manin of Venetian fame, the best and the noblest of those unhappy gentlemen. He came here with a wife and a beloved daughter, and they are both dead. Scheffer made him known to me, and has been, I understand, wonderfully generous and good to him." Nor may I omit to state the enjoyment afforded him, not only by the presence in Paris during the winter of Mr. Wilkie Collins and of Mr. and Mrs. White of Bonchurch, but by the many friends from England whom the Art Exposition brought over. Sir Alexander Cockburn was one of these; Edwin Landseer, Charles Robert Leslie, and William Boxall, were others. Macready left his retreat at Sherborne to make him a visit of several days. Thackeray went to and from all the time between London and his mother's house, in the Champs Elysées too, where his daughters were. Paris for the time was also the home of Robert Lytton, who belonged to the Embassy, of the Sartorises, of the Brownings, and of others whom Dickens liked and cared for.

At the first play he went to, the performance was stopped while the news of the last Crimean engagement, just issued in a supplement to the *Moniteur*, was read from the stage. "It made not the faintest effect upon the audience; and even the hired claqueurs, who had been absurdly loud during the piece, seemed to consider the war not at all within their contract, and were as stagnant as ditch-water. The theatre was full. It is quite impossible to see such apathy, and suppose the war to be popular, whatever may be asserted to the contrary." The day before, he had met the Emperor and the King of Sardinia in the streets, "and, as usual, no man touching his hat, and very very few so much as looking round."

The success of a most agreeable little piece by our old friend Regnier took him next to the Français, where Plessy's acting enchanted him. "Of course, the interest of it turns upon a flawed piece of living china (*that* seems to be positively essential), but as in most of these cases, if you will accept the position in which you find the people, you have nothing more to bother your morality about." The theatre in the Rue Richelieu, however, was not generally his favourite resort. He used to talk of it whimsically as a kind of tomb, where you went, as the Eastern people did in the stories, to think of your unsuccessful loves and dead relations. "There is a dreary classicality at that establishment calculated to freeze the marrow. Between ourselves, even one's best friends there are at times very aggravating. One tires of seeing a man, through any number of acts, remembering everything by patting his forehead with the flat of his hand, jerking out sentences by shaking himself, and piling them up in pyramids over his head with his right forefinger. And they have a generic small comedy-piece, where you see two sofas and three little tables, to which a man enters with his hat on, to talk to another man—and in respect of which you know exactly when he will get up from one sofa to sit on the other, and take his hat off one table to put it upon the other—which

* 99A strikes one quite as ludicrously as a good farce. . . . There seems to be a good piece at the Vaudeville, on the idea of the *Town and Country Mouse*. It is too respectable and inoffensive for me to-night, but I hope to see it before I leave. . . . I have a horrible idea of making friends with Franconi, and sauntering when I am at work into their sawdust green-room."

At a theatre of a yet heavier school than the Français he had a drearier experience. "On Wednesday we went to the Odéon to see a new piece, in four acts and in verse, called *Michel*

Cervantes. I suppose such an infernal dose of ditch-water never was concocted. But there were certain passages, describing the suppression of public opinion in Madrid, which were received with a shout of savage application to France that made one stare again. And once more, here again, at every pause, steady, compact, regular as military drums, the Ça Ira!" On another night, even at the Porte St. Martin, drawn there doubtless by the attraction of repulsion, he supped full with the horrors of classicality at a performance of *Orestes* versified by Alexandre Dumas. "Nothing have I ever seen so weighty and so ridiculous. If I had not already learnt to tremble at the sight of classic drapery on the human form, I should have plumbed the utmost depths of terrified boredom in this achievement. The chorus is not preserved otherwise than that bits of it are taken out for characters to speak. It is really so bad as to be almost good. Some of the Frenchified classical anguish struck me as so unspeakably ridiculous that it puts me on the broad grin as I write."

At the same theatre, in the early spring, he had a somewhat livelier entertainment. "I was at the Porte St. Martin last night, where there is a rather good melodrama called *Sang Mêlé*, in which one of the characters is an English Lord—Lord William Falkland—who is called throughout the piece Milor Williams Fack Lorn, and is a hundred times described by others and described by himself as Williams. He is admirably played; but two English travelling ladies are beyond expression ridiculous, and there is something positively vicious in their utter want of truth. One 'set,' where the action of a whole act is supposed to take place in the great wooden verandah of a Swiss hotel overhanging a mountain ravine, is the best piece of stage carpentering I have seen in France. Next week we are to have at the Ambigu *Paradise Lost*, with the murder of Abel and the Deluge. The wildest rumours are afloat as to the un-dressing of our first parents." Anticipation far outdoes a reality of this kind; and at the fever-pitch to which rumours raised it here, Dickens might vainly have attempted to get admission on the first night, if Mr. Webster, the English manager and comedian, had not obtained a ticket for him. He went with Mr. Wilkie Collins. "We were rung in (out of the café below the Ambigu) at 8, and the play was over at half-past 1: the waits between the acts being very much longer than the acts themselves. The house was crammed to excess in every part, and the galleries awful with Blouses, who again, during the whole of

the waits, beat with the regularity of military drums the revolutionary tune of famous memory—Ça Ira! The play is a compound of *Paradise Lost* and Byron's *Cain*; and some of the
controversies between the archangel and the devil, when the
celestial power argues with the infernal in conversational French,
as 'Eh bien! Satan, crois-tu donc que notre Seigneur t'aurait
exposé aux tourments que t'endures à présent, sans avoir
prévu,' etc., are very ridiculous. All the supernatural personages are alarmingly natural (as theatre nature goes), and
walk about in the stupidest way. Which has occasioned Collins
and myself to institute a perquisition whether the French ever
have shown any kind of idea of the supernatural; and to decide
this rather in the negative. The people are very well dressed,
and Eve very modestly. All Paris and the provinces had been
ransacked for a woman who had brown hair that would fall to
the calves of her legs—and she was found at last at the Odéon.
There was nothing attractive until the 4th act, when there was
a pretty good scene of the children of Cain dancing in, and
desecrating, a temple, while Abel and his family were hammering hard at the Ark, outside, in all the pauses of the revel. The
Deluge in the fifth act was up to about the mark of a drowning
scene at the Adelphi; but it had one new feature. When the
rain ceased, and the Ark drove in on the great expanse of
water, then lying waveless as the mists cleared and the sun
broke out, numbers of bodies drifted up and down. These were
all real men and boys, each separate, on a new kind of horizontal
float. They looked horrible and real. Altogether, a really dull
business; but I dare say it will go for a long while."

A piece of honest farce is a relief from these profane absurdities.
"An uncommonly droll piece with an original comic idea in it
has been in course of representation here. It is called *Les
Cheveux de ma Femme*. A man who is dotingly fond of his
wife, and who wishes to know whether she loved anybody else
before they were married, cuts off a lock of her hair by stealth,
and takes it to a great mesmeriser, who submits it to a clairvoyante who never was wrong. It is discovered that the owner
of this hair has been up to the most frightful dissipations, in-
somuch that the clairvoyante can't mention half of them. The
distracted husband goes home to reproach his wife, and she then
reveals that she wears a wig, and takes it off."

The last piece he went to see before leaving Paris was a
French version of *As You Like It*; but he found two acts of it
to be more than enough. "In *Comme il vous Plaira* nobody

has anything to do but to sit down as often as possible on as many trunks of trees as possible. When I had seen Jacques seat himself on 17 roots of trees, and 25 grey stones, which was at the end of the second act, I came away." Only one more sketch taken in a theatre, and perhaps the best, I will give from these letters. It simply tells what is necessary to understand a particular "tag" to a play, but it is related so prettily that the thing it celebrates could not have a nicer effect than is produced by this account of it. The play in question, *Mémoires du Diable,* and another piece of enchanting interest, the *Médecin des Enfants,* were his favourites among all he saw at this time. * 100

"As I have no news, I may as well tell you about the tag that I thought so pretty to the *Mémoires du Diable*; in which piece by the way, there is a most admirable part, most admirably played, in which a man says merely 'Yes' or 'No' all through the piece, until the last scene. A certain M. Robin has got hold of the papers of a deceased lawyer, concerning a certain estate which has been swindled away from its rightful owner, a Baron's widow, into other hands. They disclose so much roguery that he binds them up into a volume lettered 'Mémoires du Diable.' The knowledge he derives from these papers not only enables him to unmask the hypocrites all through the piece (in an excellent manner), but induces him to propose to the Baroness that if he restores to her her estate and good name—for even her marriage to the deceased Baron is denied—she shall give him her daughter in marriage. The daughter herself, on hearing the offer, accepts it; and a part of the plot is, her going to a masked ball, to which he goes as the Devil, to see how she likes him (when she finds, of course, that she likes him very much). The country people about the Château in dispute, suppose him to be really the Devil, because of his strange knowledge, and his strange comings and goings; and he, being with this girl in one of its old rooms, in the beginning of the 3rd act, shows her a little coffer on the table with a bell in it. 'They suppose,' he tells her, 'that whenever this bell is rung, I appear and obey the summons. Very ignorant, isn't it? But, if *you* ever want me particularly—very particularly—ring the little bell and try.' The plot proceeds to its development. The wrong-doers are exposed; the missing document, proving the marriage, is found; everything is finished; they are all on the stage; and M. Robin hands the paper to the Baroness. 'You are reinstated in your rights, Madame; you are happy; I will not hold you to a compact made when you didn't know me; I release you and your fair daughter; the pleasure of doing what I have done, is my sufficient reward; I kiss your hand and take my leave. Farewell!' He backs himself courteously out; the piece seems concluded, everybody wonders, the girl (little Mdlle. Luther) stands amazed; when she suddenly remembers the little bell. In the prettiest way possible, she runs to the coffer on the table, takes out the little bell, rings it, and he comes rushing back and folds her to his heart. I never saw a prettier thing in my life. It made me laugh in that most delightful of ways, with the tears in my eyes; so that I can never forget it, and must go and see it again."

But great as was the pleasure thus derived from the theatre, he was, in the matter of social intercourse, even more indebted to distinguish men connected with it by authorship or acting. At Scribe's he was entertained frequently; and "very handsome and pleasant" was his account of the dinners, as of all the belongings, of the prolific dramatist—a charming place in Paris, a fine estate in the country, capital carriage, handsome pair of horses, "all made, as he says, by his pen." One of the guests the first evening was Auber, "a stolid little elderly man, rather petulant in manner," who told Dickens he had once lived at "Stock Noonton" (Stoke Newington) to study English, but had forgotten it all. "Louis Philippe had invited him to meet the Queen of England, and when L. P. presented him, the Queen said, 'We are such old acquaintances through M. Auber's works, that an introduction is quite unnecessary.'" They met again a few nights later, with the author of the *History of the Girondins*, at the hospitable table of M. Pichot, to whom Lamartine had expressed a strong desire again to meet Dickens as "un des grands amis de son imagination." "He continues to be precisely as we formerly knew him, both in appearance and manner; highly prepossessing, and with a sort of calm passion about him, very taking indeed. We talked of Defoe and Richardson, and of that wonderful genius for the minutest details in a narrative which has given them so much fame in France. I found him frank and unaffected, and full of curious knowledge of the French common people. He informed the company at dinner that he had rarely met a foreigner who spoke French so easily as your inimitable correspondent, whereat your correspondent blushed modestly, and almost immediately afterwards so nearly choked himself with the bone of a fowl (which is still in his throat), that he sat in torture for ten minutes with a strong apprehension that he was going to make the good Pichot famous by dying like the little Hunchback at his table. Scribe

* 101

and his wife were of the party, but had to go away at the ice-
time because it was the first representation at the Opéra Comique
of a new opera by Auber and himself, of which very great
expectations had been formed. It was very curious to see him
—the author of 400 pieces—getting nervous as the time approached, and pulling out his watch every minute. At last
he dashed out as if he were going into what a friend of mine
calls a plunge-bath. Whereat she rose and followed. She is the
most extraordinary woman I ever beheld; for her eldest son must
be thirty, and she has the figure of five-and-twenty, and is
strikingly handsome. So graceful too, that her manner of
rising, curtseying, laughing, and going out after him, was
pleasanter than the pleasantest thing I have ever seen done on
the stage." The opera Dickens himself saw a week later, and wrote
of it as "most charming. Delightful music, an excellent story,
immense stage tact, capital scenic arrangements, and the most
delightful prima donna ever seen or heard, in the person of
Marie Cabel. It is called *Manon Lescaut*—from the old romance
—and is charming throughout. She sings a laughing song in
it which is received with madness, and which is the only real
laughing song that ever was written. Auber told me that when
it was first rehearsed, it made a great effect upon the orchestra;
and that he could not have had a better compliment upon its
freshness than the musical director paid him, in coming and
clapping him on the shoulder with 'Bravo, jeune homme!
Cela promet bien!'"

At dinner at Regnier's he met M. Legouvet, in whose tragedy
Rachel, after its acceptance, had refused to act Medea; a caprice
which had led not only to her condemnation in costs of so much
a night until she did act it, but to a quasi rivalry against her
by Ristori, who was now on her way to Paris to play it in
Italian. To this performance Dickens and Macready subsequently went together, and pronounced it to be hopelessly bad.
"In the day entertainments, and little melodrama theatres, of
Italy, I have seen the same thing fifty times, only not at once
so conventional and so exaggerated. The papers have all been
in fits respecting the sublimity of the performance, and the
genuineness of the applause—particularly of the bouquets;
which were thrown on at the most preposterous times in the
midst of agonising scenes, so that the characters had to pick
their way among them, and a certain stout gentleman who
played King Creon was obliged to keep a wary eye, all night,
on the proscenium boxes, and dodge them as they came down.

Now Scribe, who dined here next day (and who follows on the Ristori side, being offended, as everybody has been, by the insolence of Rachel), could not resist the temptation of telling us, that, going round at the end of the first act to offer his congratulations, he met all the bouquets coming back in men's arms to be thrown on again in the second act. . . . By the by, I see a fine actor lost in Scribe. In all his pieces he has everything done in his own way; and on that same night he was showing what Rachel did not do, and wouldn't do, in the last scene of *Adrienne Lecouvreur*, with extraordinary force and intensity."

* 102   At the house of another great artist, Madame Viardot, the sister of Malibran, Dickens dined to meet George Sand, that lady having appointed the day and hour for the interesting festival, which came off duly on 10 January. "I suppose it to be impossible to imagine anybody more unlike my preconceptions than the illustrious Sand. Just the kind of woman in appearance whom you might suppose to be the Queen's monthly nurse. Chubby, matronly, swarthy, black-eyed. Nothing of the blue-stocking about her, except a little final way of settling all your opinions with hers, which I take to have been acquired in the country, where she lives, and in the domination of a small circle. A singularly ordinary woman in appearance and manner. The dinner was very good and remarkably unpretending. Ourselves, Madame and her son, the Scheffers, the Sartorises, and some Lady somebody (from the Crimea last) who wore a species of paletot, and smoked. The Viardots have a house away in the new part of Paris, which looks exactly as if they had moved into it last week and were going away next. Notwithstanding which, they had lived in it eight years. The opera the very last thing on earth you would associate with the family. Piano not even opened. Her husband is an extremely good fellow, and she is as natural as it is possible to be."

Dickens was hardly the man to take fair measure of Madame Dudevant in meeting her thus. He was not familiar with her writings, and had no very special liking for such of them as he knew. But no disappointment, nothing but amazement, awaited him at a dinner that followed soon after. Emile de Girardin gave a banquet in his honour. His description of it, which he declares to be strictly prosaic, sounds a little Oriental, but not inappropriately so. "No man unacquainted with my determination never to embellish or fancify such accounts, could believe in the description I shall let off when we meet, of dining at Emile Girardin's—of the three gorgeous drawing-rooms with ten thousand wax candles in golden sconces, terminating in a dining-room of unprecedented magnificence with two enormous transparent plate-glass doors in it, looking (across an ante-chamber full of clean plates) straight into the kitchen, with the cooks in their white paper caps dishing the dinner. From his seat in the midst of the table, the host (like a Giant in a Fairy story) beholds the kitchen, and the snow-white tables, and the profound order and silence there prevailing. Forth from the plate-glass doors issues the Banquet—the most wonderful feast ever tasted by mortal: at the present price of Truffles, that article alone costing (for eight people) at least five pounds. On the table are ground glass jugs of peculiar construction, laden with the finest growth of Champagne and the coolest ice. With the third course is issued Port Wine (previously unheard of in a good state on this continent), which would fetch two guineas a bottle at any sale. The dinner done, Oriental flowers in vases of golden cobweb are placed upon the board. With the ice is issued Brandy, buried for 100 years. To that succeeds Coffee, brought by the brother of one of the convives from the remotest East, in exchange for an equal quantity of Californian gold dust. The company being returned to the drawing-room—tables roll in by unseen agency, laden with Cigarettes from the Hareem of the Sultan, and with cool drinks in which the flavour of the Lemon arrived yesterday from Algeria, struggles voluptuously with the delicate Orange arrived this morning from Lisbon. That period past, and the guests reposing on Divans worked with many-coloured blossoms, big table rolls in, heavy with massive furniture of silver, and breathing incense in the form of a little present of Tea direct from China—table and all, I believe; but cannot swear to it, and am resolved to be prosaic. All this time the host perpetually repeats 'Ce petit dîner-ci n'est que pour faire la connaissance de Monsieur Dickens; il ne compte pas; ce n'est rien.' And even now I have forgotten to set down half of it—in particular the item of a far larger plum pudding than ever was seen in England at Christmas time, served with a celestial sauce in colour like the orange blossom, and in substance like the blossom powdered and bathed in dew, and called in the carte (carte in a gold frame like a little fish-slice to be handed about) 'Hommage à l'illustre écrivain d'Angle-terre.' That illustrious man staggered out at the last drawing-room door, speechless with wonder, finally; and even at that moment his host, holding to his lips a chalice set with precious stones and containing nectar distilled from the air that blew over the fields of beans in bloom for fifteen summers, remarked 'Le dîner que nous avons eu, mon cher, n'est rien—il ne compte pas—il a été tout-à-fait en famille—il faut dîner (en vérité, dîner) bientôt. Au plaisir! Au revoir! Au dîner!'"

The second dinner came, wonderful as the first; among the company were Regnier, Jules Sandeau, and the new Director of the Français; and his host again played Lucullus in the same style, with success even more consummate. The only absolutely new incident however was that "After dinner he asked me if I would come into another room and smoke a cigar? and on my saying Yes, coolly opened a drawer, containing about 5000 inestimable cigars in prodigious bundles—just as the Captain of the Robbers in *Ali Baba* might have gone to a corner of the cave for bales of brocade. A little man dined who was blacking shoes 8 years ago, and is now enormously rich—the richest man in Paris—having ascended with rapidity up the usual ladder of the Bourse. By merely observing that perhaps he might come down again, I clouded so many faces as to render it very clear to me that *everybody present* was at the same game for some stake or other!" He returned to that subject in a letter a few days later. "If you were to see the steps of the Bourse at about 4 in the afternoon, and the crowd of blouses and patches among the speculators there assembled, all howling and haggard with speculation, you would stand aghast at the consideration of what must be going on. Concierges and people like that perpetually blow their brains out, or fly into the Seine, 'à cause des pertes sur la Bourse.' I hardly ever take up a French paper without lighting on such a paragraph. On the other hand, thoroughbred horses without end, and red velvet carriages with white kid harness on jet black horses, go by here all day long; and the pedestrians who turn to look at them, laugh, and say, 'C'est la Bourse!' Such crashes must be staved off every week as have not been seen since Law's time."

Another picture connects itself with this, and throws light on the speculation thus raging. The French loans connected with the war, so much puffed and praised in England at the time for the supposed spirit in which they were taken up, had in fact only ministered to the commonest and lowest gambling; and the war had never in the least been popular. "Emile Girardin," wrote Dickens on 23 March, "was here yesterday, and he says that Peace is to be formally announced at Paris to-morrow amid general apathy." But the French are never wholly apathetic to their own exploits; and a display with a

touch of excitement in it had been witnessed a couple of months
before on the entry of the troops from the Crimea, when the * 103
Zouaves, as they marched past, pleased Dickens most. "A remarkable body of men," he wrote, "wild, dangerous, and
picturesque. Close-cropped head, red skull cap, Greek jacket,
full red petticoat trowsers trimmed with yellow, and high white
gaiters—the most sensible things for the purpose I know, and
coming into use in the line. A man with such things on his legs
is always free there, and ready for a muddy march; and might
flounder through roads two feet deep in mud, and, simply by
changing his gaiters (he has another pair in his haversack), be
clean and comfortable and wholesome again, directly. Plenty
of beard and moustache, and the musket carried reversewise
with the stock over the shoulder, make up the sun-burnt Zouave.
He strides like Bobadil, smoking as he goes; and when he laughs
(they were under my window for half-an-hour or so), plunges
backward in the wildest way, as if he were going to throw a
summersault. They have a black dog belonging to the regiment,
and, when they now marched along with their medals, this
dog marched after the one non-commissioned officer he invariably follows with a profound conviction that he was decorated.
I couldn't see whether he had a medal, his hair being long;
but he was perfectly up to what had befallen his regiment;
and I never saw anything so capital as his way of regarding
the public. Whatever the regiment does, he is always in his
place; and it was impossible to mistake the air of modest
triumph which was now upon him. A small dog corporeally,
but of great mind." On that night there was an illumination
in honour of the army, when the "whole of Paris, by streets
and lanes and all sorts of out of the way places, was most
brilliantly illuminated. It looked in the dark like Venice and
Genoa rolled into one, and split up through the middle by the
Corso at Rome in the carnival time. The French people certainly
do know how to humour their own countrymen, in a most
marvellous way." It was the festival time of the New Year,
and Dickens was fairly lost in a mystery of amazement at
where the money could come from that everybody was spending
on the étrennes they were giving to everybody else. All the
famous shops on the Boulevards had been blockaded for more
than a week. "There is now a line of wooden stalls, three miles
long, on each side of that immense thoroughfare; and wherever
a retiring house or two admits of a double line, there it is. All
sorts of objects from shoes and sabots, through porcelain and

crystal, up to live fowls and rabbits which are played for at a sort of dwarf skittles (to their immense disturbance, as the ball rolls under them and shakes them off their shelves and perches whenever it is delivered by a vigorous hand), are on sale in this great Fair. And what you may get in the way of ornament for twopence, is astounding." Unhappily there came dark and rainy weather, and one of the improvements of the Empire ended, as

* 104 so many others did, in slush and misery.

Some sketches connected with the Art Exposition in this winter of 1855, and with the fulfilment of Ary Scheffer's design to paint the portrait of Dickens, may close these Paris pictures. He did not think that English art showed to advantage beside the French. It seemed to him small, shrunken, insignificant, "niggling." He thought the general absence of ideas horribly apparent; "and even when one comes to Mulready, and sees two old men talking over a much-too-prominent table-cloth, and reads the French explanation of their proceedings, 'La discussion sur les principes de Docteur Whiston," one is dis-satisfied. Somehow or other they don't tell. Even Leslie's Sancho wants go, and Stanny is too much like a set-scene. It is of no use disguising the fact that what we know to be wanting in the men is wanting in their works—character, fire, purpose, and the power of using the vehicle and the model as mere means to an end. There is a horrid respectability about most of the best of them—a little, finite, systematic routine in them, strangely expressive to me of the state of England itself. As a mere fact, Frith, Ward, and Egg, come out the best in such pictures as are here, and attract to the greatest extent. The first, in the picture from the *Good-natured Man*; the second, in the Royal Family in the Temple; the third, in Peter the Great first seeing Catherine—which I always thought a good picture, and in which foreigners evidently descry a sudden dramatic touch that pleases them. There are no end of bad pictures among the French, but, Lord! the goodness also!—the fearlessness of them; the bold drawing; the dashing conception; the passion and action in

* 105 them! The Belgian department is full of merit. It has the best landscape in it, the best portrait, and the best scene of homely life, to be found in the building. Don't think it a part of my despondency about public affairs, and my fear that our national glory is on the decline, when I say that mere form and con-ventionalities usurp, in English art, as in English government and social relations, the place of living force and truth. I tried to resist the impression yesterday, and went to the English

gallery first, and praised and admired with great diligence; but it was of no use. I could not make anything better of it than what I tell you. Of course this is between ourselves. Friendship is better than criticism, and I shall steadily hold my tongue. Discussion is worse than useless when you cannot agree about what you are going to discuss." French nature is all wrong, said the English artists whom Dickens talked to; but surely not because it is French, was his reply. The English point of view is not the only one to take men and women from. The French pictures are "theatrical," was the rejoinder. But the French themselves are a demonstrative and gesticulating people, was Dickens's retort; and what thus is rendered by their artists is the truth through an immense part of the world. "I never saw anything so strange. They seem to me to have got a fixed idea that there is no natural manner but the English manner (in itself so exceptional that it is a thing apart, in all countries); and that unless a Frenchman — represented as going to the guillotine for example—is as calm as Clapham, or as respectable as Richmond Hill, he cannot be right."

To the sittings at Ary Scheffer's some troubles as well as many pleasures were incident, and both had mention in his letters. "You may faintly imagine what I have suffered from sitting to Scheffer every day since I came back. He is a most noble fellow, and I have the greatest pleasure in his society, and have made all sorts of acquaintances at his house; but I can scarcely express how uneasy and unsettled it makes me to have to sit, sit, sit, with *Little Dorrit* on my mind, and the Christmas business too—though that is now happily dismissed. On Monday afternoon, *and all day on Wednesday*, I am going to sit again. And the crowning feature is, that I do not discern the slightest resemblance, either in his portrait or his brother's! They both peg away at me at the same time." The sittings were varied by a special entertainment, when Scheffer received some sixty people in his "long atelier"—"including a lot of French who *say* (but I don't believe it) that they know English"—to whom Dickens, by special entreaty, read his *Cricket on the Hearth.*

That was at the close of November. January came, and the end of the sittings was supposed to be at hand. "The nightmare portrait is nearly done; and Scheffer promises that an interminable sitting next Saturday, beginning at 10 o'clock in the morning, shall finish it. It is a fine spirited head, painted at his very best, and with a very easy and natural appearance in it. But it does not look to me at all like, nor does it strike me that if I saw it in a gallery I should suppose myself to be the original. It is always possible that I don't know my own face. It is going to be engraved here, in two sizes and ways—the mere head and the whole thing." A fortnight later the interminable sitting came. "Imagine me if you please with No. 5 on my head and hands, sitting to Scheffer yesterday four hours! At this stage of a story, no one can conceive how it distresses me." Still this was not the last. March had come before the portrait was done. "Scheffer finished yesterday; and Collins, who has a good eye for pictures, says that there is no man living who could do the painting about the eyes. As a work of art I see in it spirit combined with perfect ease, and yet I don't see myself. So I come to the conclusion that I never *do* see myself. I shall be very curious to know the effect of it upon you." March had then begun; and at its close Dickens, who had meanwhile been in England, thus wrote: "I have not seen Scheffer since I came back but he told Catherine a few days ago that he was not satisfied with the likeness after all, and thought he must do more to it. My own impression of it, you remember?" In these few words he anticipated the impression made upon myself. I was not satisfied with it. The picture had much merit, but † 17 not as a portrait. From its very resemblance in the eyes and mouth one derived the sense of a general unlikeness. But the work of the artist's brother, Henri Scheffer, painted from the same sittings, was in all ways greatly inferior.

Before Dickens left Paris in May he had completed the arrange-
* 106 ments for a published translation of all his books, and had sent over two descriptions that the reader most anxious to follow him to a new scene would perhaps be sorry to lose. A Duchess was murdered in the Champs Elysées. "The murder over the way (the third or fourth event of that nature in the Champs Elysées since we have been here) seems to disclose the strangest state of things. The Duchess who is murdered lived alone in a great house which was always shut up, and passed her time entirely in the dark. In a little lodge outside lived a coachman (the murderer), and there had been a long succession of coachmen who had been unable to stay there, and upon whom, whenever they asked for their wages, she plunged out with an immense knife, by way of an immediate settlement. The coachman never had anything to do, for the coach hadn't been driven out for years; neither would she ever allow the horses to be taken out for exercise. Between the lodge and the house, is a miserable bit of garden, all overgrown with long rank grass,

weeds, and nettles; and in this, the horses used to be taken out to swim—in a dead green vegetable sea, up to their haunches. On the day of the murder there was a great crowd, of course; and in the midst of it up comes the Duke her husband (from whom she was separated), and rings at the gate. The police open the grate. 'C'est vrai donc,' says the Duke, 'que Madame la Duchesse n'est plus?'—'C'est trop vrai, Monseigneur.'— 'Tant mieux,' says the Duke, and walks off deliberately, to the great satisfaction of the assemblage."

The second description relates an occurrence in England of only three years' previous date, belonging to that wildly improbable class of realities which Dickens always held, with Fielding, to be (properly) closed to fiction. Only, he would add, critics should not be so eager to assume that what had never happened to themselves could not, by any human possibility, ever be supposed to have happened to anybody else. "B. was with me the other day, and, among other things that he told me, described an extraordinary adventure in his life, at a place not a thousand miles from my 'property' at Gadshill, three years ago. He lived at the tavern and was sketching one day when an open carriage came by with a gentleman and lady in it. He was sitting in the same place working at the same sketch, next day, when it came by again. So, another day, when the gentleman got out and introduced himself. Fond of art; lived at the great house yonder, which perhaps he knew; was an Oxford man and a Devonshire squire, but not resident on his estate, for domestic reasons; would be glad to see him to dinner to-morrow. He went, and found among other things a very fine library. 'At your disposition,' said the Squire, to whom he had now described himself and his pursuits. 'Use it for your writing and drawing. Nobody else uses it.' He stayed in the house *six months*. The lady was a mistress, aged five-and-twenty, and very beautiful, drinking her life away. The Squire was drunken, and utterly depraved and wicked; but an excellent scholar, an admirable linguist, and a great theologian. Two other mad visitors stayed the six months. One, a man well known in Paris here, who goes about the world with a crimson silk stocking in his breast pocket, containing a tooth-brush and an immense quantity of ready money. The other, a college chum of the Squire's, now ruined; with an insatiate thirst for drink; who constantly got up in the middle of the night, crept down to the dining-room, and emptied all the decanters. . . . B. stayed on in the place, under a sort of devilish fascination to discover what might come of it. . . . Tea or coffee never seen in the house, and very seldom water. Beer, champagne, and brandy, were the three drinkables. Breakfast: leg of mutton, champagne, beer, and brandy. Lunch: shoulder of mutton, champagne, beer, and brandy. Dinner: every conceivable dish (Squire's income, £7000 a year), champagne, beer, and brandy. The Squire had married a woman of the town from whom he was now separated, but by whom he had a daughter. The mother, to spite the father, had bred the daughter in every conceivable vice. Daughter, then 13, came from school once a month. Intensely coarse in talk, and always drunk. As they drove about the country in two open carriages, the drunken mistress would be perpetually tumbling out of one, and the drunken daughter perpetually tumbling out of the other. At last the drunken mistress drank her stomach away, and began to die on the sofa. Got worse and worse, and was always raving about Somebody's where she had once been a lodger, and perpetually shrieking that she would cut somebody else's heart out. At last she died on the sofa, and, after the funeral, the party broke up. A few months ago, B. met the man with the crimson silk stocking at Brighton, who told him that the Squire was dead 'of a broken heart'; that the chum was dead of delirium tremens; and that the daughter was heiress to the fortune. He told me all this, which I fully believe to be true, without any embellishment—just in the off-hand way in which I have told it to you."

Dickens left Paris at the end of April, and, after the summer in Boulogne which has been described, passed the winter in London, giving to his theatrical enterprise nearly all the time that *Little Dorrit* did not claim from him. His book was finished in the following spring; was inscribed to Clarkson Stanfield; and now claims to have something said about it. The theatrical enterprise to be at the same time related, with what it led to, will be found to open a new phase in the life of Dickens.

BOOK EIGHTH

PUBLIC READER

1856–67. ÆT. 44–55

I

"LITTLE DORRIT," AND A LAZY TOUR

1855–7

BETWEEN *Hard Times* and *Little Dorrit*, Dickens's principal literary work had been the contribution to *Household Words* of two tales for Christmas (1854 and 1855) which his readings afterwards made widely popular, the Story of Richard Double-dick,[1] and Boots at the Holly Tree Inn. In the latter was related, with a charming naturalness and spirit, the elopement, to get married at Gretna Green, of two little children of the mature respective ages of eight and seven. At Christmas 1855 came out the first number of *Little Dorrit*, and in April 1857 the last.

The book took its origin from the notion he had of a leading man for a story who should bring about all the mischief in it, lay it all on Providence, and say at every fresh calamity, "Well, it's a mercy, however, nobody was to blame you know!" The title first chosen, out of many suggested, was *Nobody's Fault*; and four numbers had been written, of which the first was on the eve of appearing, before this was changed. When about to fall to work he excused himself from an engagement he should have kept because "the story is breaking out all round me, and I am going off down the railroad to humour it." The humouring was a little difficult, however; and such indications of a droop in his invention as presented themselves in portions of *Bleak*

---

[1] The framework for this sketch was a graphic description, also done by Dickens, of the celebrated Charity at Rochester founded in the sixteenth century by Richard Watts, "for six poor travellers, who, not being Rogues or Proctors, may receive gratis for one night, lodging, entertainment, and fourpence each." A quaint monument to Watts is the most prominent object on the wall of the south-west transept of the cathedral, and underneath it is now placed a brass thus inscribed: "CHARLES DICKENS. Born at Portsmouth, seventh of February 1812. Died at Gadshill Place by Rochester, ninth of June 1870. Buried in Westminster Abbey. To connect his memory with the scenes in which his earliest and his latest years were passed, and with the associations of Rochester Cathedral and its neighbourhood which extended over all his life, this Tablet, with the sanction of the Dean and Chapter, is placed by his Executors."

Chapter I.
" "

I am born
Both dead. Friendless infancy — vain

Poor mother — looking stronger on a sofa?
Any matter — that the corpse?
drowned the body? No
why not help my young man?

Chapter II.

" " " "

I observe.

The things I'd come out afterwards at these now
looking back — what I remember to see now
I've sketch-follow on that I should sketch now — &c

Let it be a Card-Book
Perhaps using the Margin.

W. Harden
Murdle's murder to be
murdered

Telegram of his mother's sudden-ish
Mother's of suffering
I am writing this.

No 1.

Chapter I.

35,000 of number two on new years' day." He was still in Paris on the day of the appearance of that portion of the tale by which it will always be most vividly remembered, and thus wrote on 30 January, 1856: "I have a grim pleasure upon me to-night in thinking that the Circumlocution Office sees the light, and in wondering what effect it will make. But my head really stings with the visions of the book, and I am going, as we French say, to disembarrass it by plunging out into some of the strange places I glide into of nights in these latitudes." The Circumlocution heroes led to the Society scenes, the Hampton Court dowager-sketches, and Mr. Gowan; all parts of one satire levelled against prevailing political and social vices. Aim had been taken, in the course of it, at some living originals, disguised sufficiently from recognition to enable him to make his thrust more sure; but there was one exception self-revealed. "I had the general idea," he wrote while engaged on the sixth number, "of the Society business before the Sadleir affair, but I shaped Mr. Merdle himself out of that precious rascality. Society, the Circumlocution Office, and Mr. Gowan, are of course three parts of one idea and design. Mr. Merdle's complaint, which you will find in the end to be fraud and forgery, came into my mind as the last drop in the silver cream-jug on Hampstead Heath. I shall beg, when you have read the present number, to inquire whether you consider 'Bar' an instance, in reference to K F, of a suggested likeness in not many touches?" The likeness no one could mistake; and, though that particular Bar has since been moved into a higher and happier sphere, Westminster Hall is in no danger of losing "the insinuating Jury-droop, and persuasive double eye-glass," by which this keen observer could express a type of character in half a dozen words.

Of the other portions of the book that had a strong personal interest for him I have spoken on a former page, and I will now only add an allusion of his own. "There are some things in Flora in number seven that seem to me to be extraordinarily droll, with something serious at the bottom of them after all. Ah, well! was there *not* something very serious in it once? I am glad to think of being in the country with the long summer mornings as I approach number ten, where I have finally resolved to make Dorrit rich. It should be a very fine point in the story. . . . Nothing in Flora made me laugh so much as the confusion of ideas between gout flying upwards, and its soaring with Mr. F. to another sphere" (7 April). He had himself no inconsiderable enjoyment also of Mr. F.'s Aunt; and in the old rascal of a patriarch, the smooth-surfaced Casby, and other surroundings of poor Flora, there was fun enough to float an argosy of second-rates, assuming such to have formed the staple of the tale. It would be far from fair to say they did. The defect in the book was less the absence of excellent character or keen observation, than the want of ease and coherence among the figures of the story, and of a central interest in the plan of it. The agencies that bring about its catastrophe, too, are less agreeable even than in *Bleak House*; and, most unlike that well-constructed story, some of the most deeply-considered things that occur in it have really little to do with the tale itself. The surface-painting of both Miss Wade and Tattycoram, to take an instance, is anything but attractive, yet there is under it a rare force of likeness in the unlikeness between the two which has much subtlety of intention; and they must both have had, as well as Mr. Gowan himself, a striking effect in the novel, if they had been made to contribute in a more essential way to its interest or development. The failure nevertheless had not been for want of care and study, as well of his own design as of models by masters in his art. A happier hint of apology, for example, could hardly be given for Fielding's introduction of such an episode as the Man of the Hill between the youth and manhood of Blifil and Tom Jones, than is suggested by what Dickens wrote of the least interesting part of *Little Dorrit*. In the mere form, Fielding of course was only following the lead of Cervantes and Le Sage; but Dickens rightly judged his purpose also to have been, to supply a kind of connection between the episode and the story. "I don't see the practicability of making the History of a Self-Tormentor, with which I took great pains, a written narrative. But I do see the possibility" (he saw the other practicability before the number was published) "of making it a chapter by itself, which might enable me to dispense with the necessity of the turned commas. Do you think that would be better? I have no doubt that a great part of Fielding's reason for the introduced story, and Smollett's, also, was, that it is sometimes really impossible to present, in a full book, the idea it contains (which yet it may be on all accounts desirable to present), without supposing the reader to be possessed of almost as much romantic allowance as would put him on a level with the writer. In Miss Wade I had an idea, which I thought a new one, of making the introduced story so fit into surroundings impossible

of separation from the main story, as to make the blood of the
book circulate through both. But I can only suppose, from what
you say, that I have not exactly succeeded in this."

Shortly after the date of his letter he was in London on
business connected with the purchase of Gadshill Place, and he
went over to the Borough to see what traces were left of the
prison of which his first impression was taken in his boyhood,
which had played so important a part in this latest novel, and
every brick and stone of which he had been able to rebuild
in his book by the mere vividness of his marvellous memory.
"Went to the Borough yesterday morning before going to
Gadshill, to see if I could find any ruins of the Marshalsea.
Found a great part of the original building—now 'Marshalsea
Place.' Found the rooms that have been in my mind's eye in
the story. Found, nursing a very big boy, a very small boy,
who, seeing me standing on the Marshalsea pavement, looking
about, told me how it all used to be. God knows how he learned
it (for he was a world too young to know anything about it),
but he was right enough. . . . There is a room there—still
standing, to my amazement—that I think of taking! It is the
room through which the ever-memorable signers of Captain
Porter's petition filed off in my boyhood." "The spikes are
gone, and the wall is lowered, and anybody can go out now
who likes to go, and is not bed-ridden; and I said to the
boy, 'Who lives there?' and he said, 'Jack Pithick.' 'Who is
Jack Pithick?' I asked him. And he said, 'Joe Pithick's uncle.'"

Mention was made of this visit in the preface that appeared
with the last number; and all it is necessary to add of the completed book will be, that, though in the humour and satire of
its finer parts not unworthy of him, and though it had the clear
design, worthy of him in an especial degree, of contrasting, both
in private and in public life, and in poverty equally as in wealth,
duty done and duty not done, it made no material addition to
his reputation. His public, however, showed no falling-off in its
enormous numbers; and what is said in one of his letters,
noticeable for this touch of character, illustrates his anxiety
to avoid any set-off from the disquiet that critical discourtesies
might give. "I was ludicrously foiled here the other night in a
resolution I have kept for twenty years not to know of any
attack upon myself, by stumbling, before I could pick myself
up, on a short extract in the *Globe* from *Blackwood's Magazine*,
informing me that *Little Dorrit* is 'Twaddle.' I was sufficiently
put out by it to be angry with myself for being such a fool, and

then pleased with myself for having so long been constant to a good resolution." There was a scene that made itself part of history not four months after his death, which, if he could have lived to hear of it, might have more than consoled him. It was the meeting of Bismarck and Jules Favre under the walls of Paris. The Prussian was waiting to open fire on the city; the Frenchman was engaged in the arduous task of showing the wisdom of not doing it; and "we learn," say the papers of the day, "that while the two eminent statesmen were trying to find a basis of negotiation, Von Moltke was seated in a corner reading *Little Dorrit*." Who will doubt that the chapter on How NOT TO DO IT was then absorbing the old soldier's attention?

* 107

Preparations for the private play had gone on incessantly up to Christmas, and, in turning the schoolroom into a theatre, sawing and hammering worthy of Babel continued for weeks. The priceless help of Stanfield had again been secured, and I remember finding him one day at Tavistock House in the act of upsetting some elaborate arrangements by Dickens, with a proscenium before him made up of chairs, and the scenery planned out with walking-sticks. But Dickens's art in a matter of this kind was to know how to take advice; and no suggestion came to him that he was not ready to act upon, if it presented the remotest likelihood. In one of his great difficulties of obtaining more space, for audience as well as actors, he was told that Mr. Cooke of Astley's was a man of much resource in that way; and to Mr. Cooke he applied, with the following result. "One of the finest things" (18 October, 1856) "I have ever seen in my life of that kind was the arrival of my friend Mr. Cooke one morning this week, in an open phaeton drawn by two white ponies with black spots all over them (evidently stencilled), who came in at the gate with a little jolt and a rattle, exactly as they come into the Ring when they draw anything, and went round and round the centre bed of the front court, apparently looking for the clown. A multitude of boys who felt them to be no common ponies rushed up in a breathless state—twined themselves like ivy about the railings—and were only deterred from storming the enclosure by the glare of the Inimitable's eye. Some of these boys had evidently followed from Astley's. I grieve to add that my friend, being taken to the point of diffi-culty, had no sort of suggestion in him; no gleam of an idea; and might just as well have been the popular minister from the

Tabernacle in Tottenham Court Road. All he could say was
—answering me, posed in the garden, precisely as if I were the
clown asking him a riddle at night—that two of their stable
tents would be home in November, and that they were '20 foot
square,' and I was heartily welcome to 'em. Also, he said, 'You
might have half a dozen of my trapezes, or my middle-distance
tables, but they're all 6 foot and all too low sir.' Since then,
I have arranged to do it in my own way, and with my own
carpenter. You will be surprised by the look of the place. It is
no more like the schoolroom than it is like the sign of the Saluta-
tion Inn at Ambleside in Westmorland. The sounds in the
house remind me, as to the present time, of Chatham Dockyard
—as to a remote epoch, of the building of Noah's ark. Joiners
are never out of the house, and the carpenter appears to be
unsettled (or settled) for life."

Of course time did not mend matters, and as Christmas approached the house was in a state of siege. "All day long, a
labourer heats size over the fire in a great crucible. We eat
it, drink it, breathe it, and smell it. Seventy paint-pots (which
came in a van) adorn the stage; and thereon may be beheld,
Stanny, and three Dansons (from the Surrey Zoological Gardens), all painting at once!! Meanwhile, Telbin, in a secluded
bower in Brewer Street, Golden Square, plies *his* part of the
little undertaking." How worthily it turned out in the end,
the excellence of the performances and the delight of the
audiences, became known to all London; and the pressure
for admittance at last took the form of a tragi-comedy, composed of ludicrous makeshifts and gloomy disappointments,
with which even Dickens's resources could not deal. "My
audience is now 93," he wrote one day in despair, "and at
least 10 will neither hear nor see." There was nothing for it
but to increase the number of nights; and it was not until
20 January he described "the workmen smashing the last
atoms of the theatre."

His book was finished soon after at Gadshill Place, to be
presently described, which he had purchased the previous year,
and taken possession of in February; subscribing himself, in
the letter announcing the fact, as "the Kentish Freeholder on
his native heath, his name Protection." The new abode occupied　* 108
him in various ways in the early part of the summer; and Hans
Andersen the Dane had just arrived upon a visit to him there,　† 18
when Douglas Jerrold's unexpected death befell. It was a shock
to everyone, and an especial grief to Dickens. Jerrold's wit, and

the bright shrewd intellect that had so many triumphs, need no celebration from me; but the keenest of satirists was one of the kindliest of men, and Dickens had a fondness for Jerrold as genuine as his admiration for him. "I chance to know a good deal about the poor fellow's illness, for I was with him on the last day he was out. It was ten days ago, when we dined at a dinner given by Russell at Greenwich. He was complaining much when we met, said he had been sick three days, and attributed it to the inhaling of white paint from his study window. I did not think much of it at the moment, as we were very social; but while we walked through Leicester Square he suddenly fell into a white, hot, sick perspiration, and had to lean against the railings. Then, at my urgent request, he was to let me put him in a cab and send him home; but he rallied a little after that, and, on our meeting Russell, determined to come with us. We three went down by steamboat that we might see the great ship, and then got an open fly and rode about Blackheath: poor Jerrold mightily enjoying the air, and constantly saying that it set him up. He was rather quiet at dinner —sat next Delane—but was very humorous and good, and in spirits, though he took hardly anything. We parted with references to coming down here" (Gadshill) "and I never saw him again. Next morning he was taken very ill when he tried to get up. On the Wednesday and Thursday he was very bad, but rallied on the Friday, and was quite confident of getting well. On the Sunday he was very ill again, and on the Monday forenoon died; 'at peace with all the world' he said, and asking to be remembered to friends. He had become indistinct and insensible, until for but a few minutes at the end. I knew nothing about it, except that he had been ill and was better, until, going up by railway yesterday morning, I heard a man in the carriage, unfolding his newspaper, say to another 'Douglas Jerrold is dead.' I immediately went up there, and then to Whitefriars. . . . I propose that there shall be a night at a theatre when the actors (with old Cooke) shall play the *Rent Day* and *Black-ey'd Susan*; another night elsewhere, with a lecture from Thackeray; a day reading by me; a night reading by me; a lecture by Russell; and a subscription performance of the *Frozen Deep*, as at Tavistock House. I don't mean to do it beggingly; but merely to announce the whole series, the day after the funeral, 'In memory of the late Mr. Douglas Jerrold,' or some such phrase. I have got hold of Arthur Smith as the best man of business I know, and go to work with him to-morrow morning—inquiries being made in the meantime as to the likeliest places to be had for these various purposes. My confident hope is that we shall get close upon two thousand pounds."

The friendly enterprise was carried to the close with a vigour, promptitude, and success, that well corresponded with this opening. In addition to the performances named, there were others in the country also organised by Dickens, in which he took active personal part; and the result did not fall short of his expectations. The sum was invested ultimately for our friend's unmarried daughter, who now receives, under direction of the Court of Chancery, the income of it until lately paid by myself, the last surviving trustee.

So passed the greater part of the summer, and when the country performances were over at the end of August I had this intimation. "I have arranged with Collins that he and I will start next Monday on a ten or twelve days' expedition to out-of-the-way places, to do (in inns and coast-corners) a little tour in search of an article and in avoidance of railroads. I must get a good name for it, and I propose it in five articles, one for the beginning of every number in the October part." Next day: "Our decision is for a foray upon the fells of Cumberland; I having discovered in the books some promising moors and bleak places thereabout." Into the lake-country they went accordingly; and The Lazy Tour of Two Idle Apprentices, contributed to *Household Words*, related the trip. But his letters had descriptive touches, and some whimsical experiences, not in the published account.

Looking over the *Beauties of England and Wales* before he left London, his ambition was fired by mention of Carrick Fell, "a gloomy old mountain 1500 feet high," which he secretly resolved to go up. "We came straight to it yesterday" (9 September). "Nobody goes up. Guides have forgotten it. Master of a little inn, excellent north-countryman, volunteered. Went up, in a tremendous rain. C. D. beat Mr. Porter (name of landlord) in half a mile. Mr. P. done up in no time. Three nevertheless went on. Mr. P. again leading; C. D. and C." (Mr. Wilkie Collins) "following. Rain terrific, black mists, darkness of night. Mr. P. agitated. C. D. confident. C. (a long way down in perspective) submissive. All wet through. No poles. Not so much as a walking-stick in the party. Reach the summit at about one in the day. Dead darkness as of night. Mr. P. (excellent fellow to the last) uneasy. C. D. produces compass from pocket. Mr. P. reassured. Farm-house where dog-cart was left, N.N.W. Mr. P.

* 109

complimentary. Descent commenced. C. D. with compass triumphant, until compass, with the heat and wet of C. D.'s pocket, breaks. Mr. P. (who never had a compass), inconsolable, confesses he has not been on Carrick Fell for twenty years, and he don't know the way down. Darker and darker. Nobody discernible, two yards off, by the other two. Mr. P. makes suggestions, but no way. It becomes clear to C. D. and to C. that Mr. P. is going round and round the mountain, and never coming down. Mr. P. sits on angular granite, and says he is 'just fairly doon.' C. D. revives Mr. P. with laughter, the only restorative in the company. Mr. P. again complimentary. Descent tried once more. Mr. P. worse and worse. Council of war. Proposals from C. D. to go 'slap down.' Seconded by C. Mr. P. objects, on account of precipice called The Black Arches, and terror of the countryside. More wandering. Mr. P. terror-stricken, but game. Watercourse, thundering and roaring, reached. C. D. suggests that it must run to the river, and had best be followed, subject to all gymnastic hazards. Mr. P. opposes, but gives in. Watercourse followed accordingly. Leaps, splashes, and tumbles, for two hours. C. lost. C. D. whoops. Cries for assistance from behind. C. D. returns. C. with horribly sprained ankle, lying in rivulet!"

All the danger was over when Dickens sent his description; but great had been the trouble in binding up the sufferer's ankle and getting him painfully on, shoving, shouldering, carrying alternately, till terra firma was reached. "We got down at last in the wildest place, preposterously out of the course; and, propping up C. against stones, sent Mr. P. to the other side of Cumberland for dog-cart, so got back to his inn, and changed. Shoe or stocking on the bad foot out of the question. Foot bundled up in a flannel waistcoat. C. D. carrying C. melodramatically (Wardour to the life!) everywhere; into and out of carriages; up and down stairs; to bed; every step. And so to Wigton, got doctor, and here we are!! A pretty business, we flatter ourselves!"

* 110

Wigton, Dickens described as a place of little houses all in half-mourning, yellow stone or white stone and black, with the wonderful peculiarity that though it had no population, no business, and no streets to speak of, it had five linendrapers within range of their single window, one linendraper next door, and five more linendrapers round the corner. "I ordered a night light in my bed-room. A queer little old woman brought me one of the common Child's night lights, and seeming to think that

I looked at it with interest, said, 'It's joost a vara keeyourious thing, sir, and joost new coom oop. It'll burn awt hoors a' end, and no gootther, nor no waste, nor ony sike a thing, if ye can creedit what I say, seein' the airticle.'" In these primitive quarters there befell a difficulty about letters, which Dickens solved in a fashion especially his own. "The day after Carrick there was a mess about her letters, through our not going to a place called Mayport. So, while the landlord was planning how to get them (they were only twelve miles off), I walked off, to his great astonishment, and brought them over." The night after leaving Wigton they were at the Ship Hotel in Allonby.

Allonby his letters presented as a small untidy outlandish place: rough stone houses in half mourning, a few coarse yellow-stone lodging-houses with black roofs (bills in all the windows), five bathing-machines, five girls in straw hats, five men in straw hats (wishing they had not come); very much what Broadstairs would have been if it had been born Irish, and had not inherited a cliff. "But this is a capital little homely inn, looking out upon the sea; with the coast of Scotland, mountainous and romantic, over against the windows; and though I can just stand upright in my bedroom, we are really well lodged. It is a clean nice place in a rough wild country, and we have a very obliging and comfortable landlady." He had found indeed, in the latter, an acquaintance of old date. "The landlady at the little inn at Allonby, lived at Greta-Bridge in Yorkshire when I went down there before *Nickleby*; and was smuggled into the room to see me, after I was secretly found out. She is an immensely fat woman now. 'But I could tuck my arm round her waist then, Mr. Dickens,' the landlord said when she told me the story as I was going to bed the night before last. 'And can't you do it now,' I said. 'You insensible dog! Look at me! Here's a picture!' Accordingly, I got round as much of her as I could; and this gallant action was the most successful I have ever performed, on the whole."

On their way home the friends were at Doncaster, and this was Dickens's first experience of the St. Leger and its saturnalia. His companion had by this time so far recovered as to be able, doubled-up, to walk with a thick stick; in which condition, "being exactly like the gouty admiral in a comedy I have given him that name." The impressions received from the race-week were not favourable. It was noise and turmoil all day long, and a gathering of vagabonds from all parts of the racing earth. Every bad face that had ever caught wickedness from an innocent horse had its representative in the streets; and as Dickens, like Gulliver looking down upon his fellow-men after coming from the horse-country, looked down into Doncaster High Street from his inn-window, he seemed to see everywhere a then notorious personage who had just poisoned his betting-companion. "Everywhere I see the late Mr. Palmer with his betting-book in his hand. Mr. Palmer sits next me at the theatre; Mr. Palmer goes before me down the street; Mr. Palmer follows me into the chemist's shop where I go to buy rose-water after breakfast, and says to the chemist 'Give us soom sal volatile or soom damned thing o' that soort, in wather—my head's bad!' And I look at the back of his bad head repeated in long, long lines on the race course, and in the betting-stand and outside the betting-rooms in the town, and I vow to God that I can see nothing in it but cruelty, covetousness, calculation, insensibility, and low wickedness."

Even a half-appalling kind of luck was not absent from my friend's experiences at the race course, when, what he called a "wonderful, paralysing, coincidence" befell him. He bought the card; facetiously wrote down three names for the winners of the three chief races (never in his life having heard or thought of any of the horses, except that the winner of the Derby, who proved to be nowhere, had been mentioned to him); "and, if you can believe it without your hair standing on end, those three races were won, one after another, by those three horses!!!" That was the St. Leger Day, of which he also thought it notice-able, that, though the losses were enormous, nobody had won, for there was nothing but grinding of teeth and blaspheming of ill-luck. Nor had matters mended on the Cup-day, after which celebration "a groaning phantom" lay in the doorway of his bedroom and howled all night. The landlord came up in the morning to apologise, "and said it was a gentleman who had lost £1500 or £2000; and he had drunk a deal afterwards; and then they put him to bed, and then he—took the 'orrors, and got up, and yelled till morning." Dickens might well be-lieve, as he declared at the end of his letter, that if a boy with any good in him, but with a dawning propensity to sporting and betting, were but brought to the Doncaster races soon enough, it would cure him.

* III

II

WHAT HAPPENED AT THIS TIME

1857-8

AN unsettled feeling greatly in excess of what was usual with Dickens, more or less observable since his first residence at Boulogne, became at this time almost habitual, and the satisfactions which home should have supplied, and which indeed were essential requirements of his nature, he had failed to find in his home. He had not the alternative that under this disappointment some can discover in what is called society. It did not suit him, and he set no store by it. No man was better fitted to adorn any circle he entered, but beyond that of friends and equals he rarely passed. He would take as much pains to keep out of the houses of the great as others take to get into them. Not always wisely, it may be admitted. Mere contempt for toadyism and flunkeyism was not at all times the prevailing motive with him which he supposed it to be. Beneath his horror of those vices of Englishmen in his own rank of life, there was a still stronger resentment at the social inequalities that engender them, of which he was not so conscious and to which he owned less freely. Not the less it served secretly to justify what he might otherwise have had no mind to. To say he was not a gentleman would be as true as to say he was not a writer; but if anyone should assert his occasional preference for what was even beneath his level over that which was above it, this would be difficult of disproof. It was among those defects of temperament for which his early trials and his early successes were accountable in perhaps equal measure. He was sensitive in a passionate degree to praise and blame, which yet he made it for the most part a point of pride to assume indifference to; the inequalities of rank which he secretly resented took more galling as well as glaring prominence from the contrast of the necessities he had gone through with the fame that had come to him; and when the forces he most affected to despise assumed the form of barriers he could not easily overleap, he was led to appear frequently intolerant (for he very seldom was really so) in opinions and language. His early sufferings brought with them the healing powers of energy, will, and persistence, and taught him the inexpressible value of a determined resolve to live down difficulties; but the habit, in small as in great things, of renunciation and self-sacrifice, they did not teach; and, by his sudden leap into a world-wide popularity and influence, he became master of everything that might seem to be attainable in life, before he had mastered what a man must undergo to be equal to its hardest trials.

Nothing of all this has yet presented itself to notice, except in occasional forms of restlessness and desire of change of place, which were themselves, when his books were in progress, so incident as well to the active requirements of his fancy as to call, thus far, for no other explanation. Up to the date of the completion of *Copperfield* he had felt himself to be in possession of an all-sufficient resource. Against whatever might befall he had a set-off in his imaginative creations, a compensation derived from his art that never failed him, because there he was supreme. It was the world he could bend to his will, and make subserve to all his desires. He had otherwise, underneath his exterior of a singular precision, method, and strictly orderly arrangement in all things, and notwithstanding a temperament to which home and home interests were really a necessity, something in common with those eager, impetuous, somewhat overbearing natures, that rush at existence without heeding the cost of it, and are not more ready to accept and make the most of its enjoyments than to be easily and quickly overthrown by its burdens. But the world he had called into being had thus far borne him safely through these perils. He had his own creations always by his side. They were living, speaking companions. With them only he was everywhere thoroughly identified. He laughed and wept with them; was as much elated by their fun as cast down by their grief; and brought to the consideration of them a belief in their reality as well as in the influences they were meant to exercise, which in every circumstance sustained him.

It was during the composition of *Little Dorrit* that I think he first felt a certain strain upon his invention which brought with it other misgivings. In a modified form this was present during the later portions of *Bleak House*, of which not a few of the defects might be traced to the acting excitements amid which it was written; but the succeeding book made it plainer to him; and it is remarkable that in the interval between them he resorted for the first and only time in his life to a practice, which he abandoned at the close of his next and last story published in the twenty-number form, of putting down written "Memoranda" of suggestions for characters or incidents by way of resource to him in his writing. Never before had his teeming fancy seemed to want such help; the need being less to contribute to its fulness than to check its overflowing; but it is another proof that he had been secretly bringing before himself, at least, the possibility that what had ever been his great support might some day desert him. It was strange that he should have had such doubt, and he would hardly have confessed it openly; but apart from that wonderful world of his books, the range of his thoughts was not always proportioned to the width and largeness of his nature. His ordinary circle of activity, whether in likings or thinkings, was full of such surprising animation, that one was apt to believe it more comprehensive than it really was; and again and again, when a wide horizon might seem to be ahead of him he would pull up suddenly and stop short, as though nothing lay beyond. For the time, though each had its term and change, he was very much a man of one idea, each having its turn of absolute predominance; and this was one of the secrets of the thoroughness with which everything he took in hand was done. As to the matter of his writings, the actual truth was that his creative genius never really failed him. Not a few of his inventions of character and humour, up to the very close of his life, his Marigolds, Lirripers, Gargerys, Pips, Sapseas and many others, were as fresh and fine as in his greatest day. He had however lost the free and fertile method of the earlier time. He could no longer fill a wide-spread canvas with the same facility and certainty as of old; and he had frequently a quite unfounded apprehension of some possible breakdown, of which the end might be at any moment beginning. There came accordingly, from time to time, intervals of unusual impatience and restlessness, strange to me in connection with his home; his old pursuits were too often laid aside for other excitements and occupations; he joined a public political agitation, set on foot by administrative reformers; he got up various quasi-public private theatricals, in which he took the leading place; and though it was but part of his always generous devotion in any friendly duty to organise the series of performances on his friend Jerrold's death, yet the eagerness with which he flung himself into them, so arranging them as to assume an amount of labour in acting and travelling that might have appalled an

experienced comedian, and carrying them on week after week
unceasingly in London and the provinces, expressed but the
craving which still had possession of him to get by some means
at some change that should make existence easier. What was
highest in his nature had ceased for the time to be highest in
his life, and he had put himself at the mercy of lower accidents
and conditions. The mere effect of the strolling wandering ways
into which this acting led him could not be other than unfavourable. But remonstrance as yet was unavailing.

To one very earnestly made in the early autumn of 1857, in
which opportunity was taken to compare his recent rush up
Carrick Fell to his rush into other difficulties, here was the reply.
"Too late to say, put the curb on, and don't rush at hills—the
wrong man to say it to. I have now no relief but in action. I am
become incapable of rest. I am quite confident I should rust,
break, and die, if I spared myself. Much better to die, doing.
What I am in that way, nature made me first, and my way of
life has of late, alas! confirmed. I must accept the drawback—
since it is one—with the powers I have; and I must hold upon
the tenure prescribed to me." Something of the same sad feeling,
it is right to say, had been expressed from time to time, in
connection also with home dissatisfactions and misgivings,
through the three years preceding; but I attributed it to other
causes, and gave little attention to it. During his absences
abroad for the greater part of 1854, '55, and '56, while the
elder of his children were growing out of childhood, and his
books were less easy to him than in his earlier manhood, evidences presented themselves in his letters of the old "unhappy
loss or want of something" to which he had given a pervading
prominence in *Copperfield*. In the first of those years he made
express allusion to the kind of experience which had been one
of his descriptions in that favourite book, and, mentioning the
drawbacks of his present life, had first identified it with his
own: "the so happy and yet so unhappy existence which seeks
its realities in unrealities, and finds its dangerous comfort in a
perpetual escape from the disappointment of heart around it."

Later in the same year he thus wrote from Boulogne: "I have
had dreadful thoughts of getting away somewhere altogether by
myself. If I could have managed it, I think possibly I might
have gone to the Pyreennees (you know what I mean that word
for, so I won't rewrite it) for six months! I have put the idea
into the perspective of six months, but have not abandoned it.
I have visions of living for half a year or so, in all sorts of

inaccessible places, and opening a new book therein. A floating idea of going up above the snow-line in Switzerland, and living in some astonishing convent, hovers about me. If *Household Words* could be got into a good train, in short, I don't know in what strange place, or at what remote elevation above the level of the sea, I might fall to work next. *Restlessness*, you will say. Whatever it is, it is always driving me, and I cannot help it. I have rested nine or ten weeks, and sometimes feel as if it had been a year—though I had the strangest nervous miseries before I stopped. If I couldn't walk fast and far, I should just explode and perish." Again, four months later he wrote: "You will hear of me in Paris, probably next Sunday, and I *may* go on to Bordeaux. Have general ideas of emigrating in the summer to the mountain-ground between France and Spain. Am altogether in a dishevelled state of mind—motes of new books in the dirty air, miseries of older growth threatening to close upon me. Why is it, that as with poor David, a sense comes always crushing on me now, when I fall into low spirits, as of one happiness I have missed in life, and one friend and companion I have never made?"

Early in 1856 (20 January) the notion revisited him of writing a book in solitude. "Again I am beset by my former notions of a book whereof the whole story shall be on the top of the Great St. Bernard. As I accept and reject ideas for *Little Dorrit*, it perpetually comes back to me. Two or three years hence, perhaps you'll find me living with the Monks and the Dogs a whole winter—among the blinding snows that fall about that monastery. I have a serious idea that I shall do it, if I live." He was at this date in Paris; and during the visit to him of Macready in the following April, the self-revelations were resumed. The great actor was then living in retirement at Sherborne, to which he had gone on quitting the stage; and Dickens gave favourable report of his enjoyment of the change to his little holiday at Paris. Then, after recurring to his own old notion of having some slight idea of going to settle in Australia, only he could not do it until he should have finished *Little Dorrit*, he went on to say that perhaps Macready, if he could get into harness again, would not be the worse for some such troubles as were worrying himself. "It fills me with pity to think of him away in that lonely Sherborne place. I have always felt of myself that I must, please God, die in harness, but I have never felt it more strongly than in looking at, and thinking of, him. However strange it is to be never at rest, and never satisfied, and ever trying after something that is never reached, and to be always laden with plot and plan and care and worry, how clear it is that it must be, and that one is driven by an irresistible might until the journey is worked out! It is much better to go on and fret, than to stop and fret. As to repose—for some men there's no such thing in this life. The foregoing has the appearance of a small sermon; but it is so often in my head in these days that it cannot help coming out. The old days—the old days! Shall I ever, I wonder, get the frame of mind back as it used to be then? Something of it perhaps—but never quite as it used to be. I find that the skeleton in my domestic closet is becoming a pretty big one."

It would be unjust and uncandid not to admit that these and other similar passages in the letters that extended over the years while he lived abroad, had served in some degree as a preparation for what came after his return to England in the following year. It came with a great shock nevertheless; because it told plainly what before had never been avowed, but only hinted at more or less obscurely. The opening reference is to the reply which had been made to a previous expression of his wish for some confidences as in the old time. I give only what is strictly necessary to account for what followed, and even this with deep reluctance. "Your letter of yesterday was so kind and hearty, and sounded so gently the many chords we have touched together, that I cannot leave it unanswered, though I have not much (to any purpose) to say. My reference to 'confidences' was merely to the relief of saying a word of what has long been pent up in my mind. Poor Catherine and I are not made for each other, and there is no help for it. It is not only that she makes me uneasy and unhappy, but that I make her so too—and much more so. She is exactly what you know, in the way of being amiable and complying; but we are strangely ill-assorted for the bond there is between us. God knows she would have been a thousand times happier if she had married another kind of man, and that her avoidance of this destiny would have been at least equally good for us both. I am often cut to the heart by thinking what a pity it is, for her own sake, that I ever fell in her way; and if I were sick or disabled to-morrow, I know how sorry she would be, and how deeply grieved myself, to think how we had lost each other. But exactly the same incompatibility would arise, the moment I was well again; and nothing on earth could make her understand me, or suit us to each other. Her temperament will not

go with mine. It mattered not so much when we had only ourselves to consider, but reasons have been growing since which
make it all but hopeless that we should even try to struggle on.
What is now befalling me I have seen steadily coming, ever
since the days you remember when Mary was born; and I know
too well that you cannot, and no one can, help me. Why I have
even written I hardly know; but it is a miserable sort of comfort
that you should be clearly aware how matters stand. The mere
mention of the fact, without any complaint or blame of any
sort, is a relief to my present state of spirits—and I can get this
only from you, because I can speak of it to no one else." In
the same tone was his rejoinder to my reply. "To the most
part of what you say—Amen! You are not so tolerant as perhaps
you might be of the wayward and unsettled feeling which is part
(I suppose) of the tenure on which one holds an imaginative
life, and which I have, as you ought to know well, often only
kept down by riding over it like a dragoon—but let that go by.
I make no maudlin complaint. I agree with you as to the very
possible incidents, even not less bearable than mine, that might
and must often occur to the married condition when it is entered
into very young. I am always deeply sensible of the wonderful
exercise I have of life and its highest sensations, and have said
to myself for years, and have honestly and truly felt, This is
the drawback to such a career, and is not to be complained of.
I say it and feel it now as strongly as ever I did; and, as I told
you in my last, I do not with that view put all this forward.
But the years have not made it easier to bear for either of us;
and, for her sake as well as mine, the wish will force itself upon
me that something might be done. I know too well it is impossible. There is the fact, and that is all one can say. Nor are you
to suppose that I disguise from myself what might be urged
on the other side. I claim no immunity from blame. There is
plenty of fault on my side, I dare say, in the way of a thousand
uncertainties, caprices, and difficulties of disposition; but
only one thing will alter all that, and that is, the end which
alters everything."

It will not seem to most people that there was anything here
which in happier circumstances might not have been susceptible
of considerate adjustment; but all the circumstances were unfavourable, and the moderate middle course which the admis-
sions in that letter might wisely have prompted and wholly
justified, was unfortunately not taken. Compare what before
was said of his temperament, with what is there said by himself

of its defects, and the explanation will not be difficult. Every counteracting influence against the one idea which now predominated over him had been so weakened as to be almost powerless. His elder children were no longer children; his books had lost for the time the importance they formerly had over every other consideration in his life; and he had not in himself the resource that such a man, judging him from the surface, might be expected to have had. Not his genius only, but his whole nature, was too exclusively made up of sympathy for, and with, the real in its most intense form, to be sufficiently provided against failure in the realities around him. There was for him no "city of the mind" against outward ills, for inner consolation and shelter. It was in and from the actual he still stretched forward to find the freedom and satisfactions of an ideal, and by his very attempts to escape the world he was driven back into the thick of it. But what he would have sought there, it supplies to none; and to get the infinite out of anything so finite, has broken many a stout heart.

At the close of that last letter from Gadshill (5 September) was this question—"What do you think of my paying for this place, by reviving that old idea of some readings from my books. I am strongly tempted. Think of it." The reasons against it had great force, and took, in my judgment, greater from the time at which it was again proposed. The old ground of opposition remained. It was a substitution of lower for higher aims; a change to commonplace from more elevated pursuits; and it had so much of the character of a public exhibition for money as to raise, in the question of respect for his calling as a writer, a question also of respect for himself as a gentleman. This opinion, now strongly reiterated, was referred ultimately to two distinguished ladies of his acquaintance, who decided against it. Yet not without such momentary misgiving in the direction of "the stage," as pointed strongly to the danger, which, by those who took the opposite view, was most of all thought incident to the particular time of the proposal. It might be a wild exaggeration to fear that he was in danger of being led to adopt the stage as a calling, but he was certainly about to place himself within reach of not a few of its drawbacks and disadvantages. To the full extent he perhaps did not himself know, how much his eager present wish to become a public reader was but the outcome of the restless domestic discontents of the last four years; and that to indulge it, and the unsettled habits inseparable from it, was to abandon every hope of resettling his disordered home. There is nothing, in its application to so divine a genius as Shakespeare, more affecting than his expressed dislike to a profession, which, in the jealous self-watchfulness of his noble nature, he feared might hurt his mind. The long subsequent line of actors, admirable in private as in public life, and all the gentle and generous associations of the histrionic art, have not weakened the testimony of its greatest name against its less favourable influences; against the laxity of habits it may encourage; and its public manners, bred of public means, not always compatible with home felicities and duties. But, freely open as Dickens was to counsel in regard of his books, he was, for reasons formerly stated, less accessible to it on points of personal conduct; and when he had neither self-distrust nor self-denial to hold him back, he would push persistently forward to whatever object he had in view.

An occurrence of the time hastened the decision in this case. An enterprise had been set on foot for establishment of a hospital for sick children; a large old-fashioned mansion in * 113 Great Ormond Street, with spacious garden, had been fitted up with more than thirty beds; during the four or five years of its existence, outdoor and indoor relief had been afforded by it to nearly fifty thousand children, of whom thirty thousand were under five years of age; but, want of funds having threatened to arrest the merciful work, it was resolved to try a public dinner by way of charitable appeal, and for president the happy choice was made of one who had enchanted everybody with the joys and sorrows of little children. Dickens threw himself into the service heart and soul. There was a simple pathos in his address from the chair quite startling in its effect at such a meeting; and he probably never moved any audience so much as by the strong personal feeling with which he referred to the sacrifices made for the Hospital by the very poor themselves: from whom a subscription of fifty pounds, contributed in single pennies, had come to the treasurer during almost every year it had been open. The whole speech, indeed, is the best of the kind spoken by him; and two little pictures from it, one of the misery he had witnessed, the other of the remedy he had found, should not be absent from the picture of his own life.

"Some years ago, being in Scotland, I went with one of the most humane members of the most humane of professions, on a morning tour among some of the worst lodged inhabitants of the old town of Edinburgh. In the closes and wynds of that picturesque place (I am sorry to remind you what fast friends picturesqueness and typhus often are), we saw more poverty and sickness in an hour than many people would believe in, in a life. Our way lay from one to another of the most wretched dwellings, reeking with horrible odours; shut out from the sky and from the air, mere pits and dens. In a room in one of these places, where there was an empty porridge-pot on the cold hearth, a ragged woman and some ragged children crouching on the bare ground near it—and, I remember as I speak, where the very light, refracted from a high damp-stained wall outside, came in trembling, as if the fever which had shaken everything else had shaken even it—there lay, in an old egg-box which the mother had begged from a shop, a little, feeble, wan, sick child. With his little wasted face, and his little hot worn hands folded over his breast, and his little bright attentive eyes, I can see him now, as I have seen him for several years, looking steadily at us. There he lay in his small frail box, which was not at all a bad emblem of the small body from which he was slowly parting—there he lay, quite quiet, quite patient, saying never a word. He seldom cried, the mother said; he seldom complained; 'he lay there, seemin' to woonder what it was a' aboot.' God knows, I thought, as I stood looking at him, he had his reasons for wondering. . . . Many a poor child, sick and neglected, I have seen since that time in London; many have I also seen most affectionately tended, in unwholesome houses and hard circumstances where recovery was impossible: but at all such times I have seen my little drooping friend in his egg-box, and he has always addressed his dumb wonder to me what it meant, and why, in the name of a gracious God, such things should be! . . . But, ladies and gentlemen," Dickens added, "such things need NOT be, and will not be, if this company, which is a drop of the life-blood of the great compassionate public heart, will only accept the means of rescue and prevention which it is mine to offer. Within a quarter of a mile of this place where I speak, stands a once courtly old house, where blooming children were born, and grew up to be men and women, and married, and brought their own blooming children back to patter up the old oak staircase which stood but the other day, and to wonder at the old oak carvings on the chimney-pieces. In the airy wards into which the old state drawing-rooms and family bedchambers of that house are now converted, are lodged such small patients that the attendant nurses look like reclaimed giantesses, and the kind medical practitioner like an amiable Christian ogre. Grouped about the little low tables in the centre of the rooms, are such tiny convalescents that they seem to be playing at having been ill. On the doll's beds are such diminutive creatures that each poor sufferer is supplied with its trays of toys: and, looking round, you may see how the little tired flushed cheek has toppled over half the brute creation on its way into the ark; or how one little dimpled arm has mowed down (as I saw myself) the whole tin soldiery of Europe. On the walls of these rooms are graceful, pleasant, bright, childish pictures. At the beds' heads, hang representations of the figure of Him who was once a child Himself, and a poor one. But alas! reckoning up the number of beds that are there, the visitor to this Child's Hospital will find himself perforce obliged to stop at very little over thirty; and will learn, with sorrow and surprise, that even that small number, so forlornly, so miserably diminutive compared with this vast London, cannot possibly be maintained unless the Hospital be made better known. I limit myself to saying better known, because I will not believe that in a Christian community of fathers and mothers, and brothers and sisters, it can fail, being better known, to be well and richly endowed." It was a brave and true prediction. The Child's Hospital has never since known want. That night alone added greatly more than three thousand pounds to its funds, and Dickens put the crown to his good work by reading on its behalf, shortly afterwards, his *Christmas Carol*; when the sum realised, and the urgent demand that followed for a repetition of the pleasure given by the reading, bore down further opposition to the project of his engaging publicly in such readings for himself.

The Child's Hospital night was 9 February, its reading was appointed for 15 April, and, nearly a month before renewed efforts at remonstrance had been made. "Your view of the reading matter," Dickens replied, "I still think is unconsciously taken from your own particular point. You don't seem to me to get out of yourself in considering it. A word more upon it. You are not to think I have made up my mind. If I had, why should I not say so? I find very great difficulty in doing so because of what you urge, because I know the question to be a balance of doubts, and because I most honestly feel in my innermost heart, in this matter (as in all others for years and years), the honour of the calling by which I have always stood most conscientiously. But do you quite consider that the public exhibition of oneself takes place equally, whosoever may get the money? And have you any idea that at this moment—this very time—half the public at least supposes me to be paid? My dear F., out of the twenty or five-and-twenty letters a week that I get about readings, twenty will ask at what price, or on what terms, it can be done. The only exceptions, in truth, are when the correspondent is a clergyman, or a banker, or the member for the place in question. Why, at this very time half Scotland believes that I am paid for going to Edinburgh!—Here is Greenock writes to me, and asks could it be done for a hundred pounds? There is Aberdeen writes, and states the capacity of its hall, and says, though far less profitable than the very large hall in Edinburgh, is it not enough to come on for? W. answers such letters continually. (—At this place enter Beale. He called here yesterday morning, and then wrote to ask if I would see him to-day. I replied 'Yes,' so here he came in. With long preface called to know whether it was possible to arrange anything in the way of readings for this autumn—say six months. Large capital at command. Could produce partners, in such an enterprise, also with large capital. Represented such. Returns would be enormous. Would I name a sum? a minimum sum that I required to have, in any case? Would I look at it as a Fortune, and in no other point of view? I shook my head, and said, my tongue was tied on the subject for the present; I might be more communicative at another time. Exit Beale in confusion and disappointment.)—You will be happy to hear that at one on Friday, the Lord Provost, Dean of Guild, Magistrates, and Council of the ancient city of Edinburgh will wait (in procession) on their brother freeman, at the Music Hall, to give him hospitable welcome. Their brother freeman has been cursing their stars and his own, ever since the receipt of solemn notification to this effect." But very grateful, when it came, was the enthusiasm of the greeting, and welcome the gift of the silver wassail-bowl which followed the reading of the *Carol*. "I had no opportunity of asking any-one's advice in Edinburgh," he wrote on his return. "The crowd was too enormous, and the excitement in it much too great. But my determination is all but taken. I must do *something*, or I shall wear my heart away. I can see no better thing to do that is half so hopeful in itself, or half so well suited to my restless state."

What is pointed at in those last words had been taken as a ground of objection, and thus he turned it into an argument the other way. During all these months many sorrowful misunderstandings had continued in his home, and the relief sought from the misery had but the effect of making desperate any hope of a better understanding. "It becomes necessary," he wrote at the end of March, "with a view to the arrangements that would have to be begun next month if I decided on the readings, to consider and settle the question of the Plunge. Quite dismiss from your mind any reference whatever to present circumstances at home. Nothing can put *them* right, until we are all dead and buried and risen. It is not, with me, a matter of will, or trial, or sufferance, or good humour, or making the best of it, or making the worst of it, any longer. It is all despairingly over. Have no lingering hope of, or for, me in this association. A dismal failure has to be borne, and there an end. Will you then try to think of this reading project (as I do) apart from all personal likings and dislikings, and solely with a view to its effect on that particular relation (personally affectionate and like no other man's) which subsists between me and the public? I want your most careful consideration. If you would like, when you have gone over it in your mind, to discuss the matter with me and Arthur Smith (who would manage the whole of the Business, which I should never touch); we will make an appointment. But I ought to add that Arthur Smith plainly says, 'Of the immense return in money, I have no doubt. Of the Dash into the new position, however, I am not so good a judge.' I enclose you a rough note of my project, as it stands in my mind." * 115

Mr. Arthur Smith, a man possessed of many qualities that justified the confidence Dickens placed in him, might not have been a good judge of the "Dash" into the new position, but no man knew better every disadvantage incident to it, or was less likely to be disconcerted by any. His exact fitness to manage the scheme successfully, made him an unsafe counsellor respecting it. Within a week from this time the reading for the Charity was to be given. "They have let," Dickens wrote on 9 April, "five hundred stalls for the Hospital night; and as people come every day for more, and it is out of the question to make more, they cannot be restrained at St. Martin's Hall from taking down names for other readings." This closed the attempt at further objection. Exactly a fortnight after the reading for the children's hospital, on Thursday, 29 April, came the first public reading for his own benefit; and before the next month was over, this launch into a new life had been followed by a change in his old home. Thenceforward he and his wife lived apart. The eldest son went with his mother, Dickens at once giving effect to her expressed wish in this respect; and the other children remained with himself, their intercourse with Mrs. Dickens being left entirely to themselves. It was thus far an arrangement of a strictly private nature, and no decent person could have had excuse for regarding it in any other light, if public attention had not been unexpectedly invited to it by a printed statement in *Household Words*. Dickens was stung into this by some miserable gossip at which in ordinary circumstances no man would more determinedly have been silent; but he had now publicly to show himself, at stated times, as a public entertainer, and this, with his name even so aspersed, he found to be impossible. All he would concede to my strenuous resistance against such a publication, was an offer to suppress it, if, upon reference to the opinion of a certain distinguished man (still living), that opinion should prove to be in agreement with mine. Unhappily it fell in with his own, and the publication went on. It was followed by another statement, a letter subscribed with his name, which got into print without his sanction; nothing publicly being known of it (I was not among those who had read it privately) until it appeared in the *New York Tribune*. It had been addressed and given to Mr. Arthur Smith as an authority for correction of false rumours and scandals, and Mr. Smith had given a copy of it, with like intention, to the *Tribune* correspondent in London. Its writer referred to it † 19 always afterwards as his "violated letter."

The course taken by the author of this book at the time of these occurrences, will not be departed from here. Such illustration of grave defects in Dickens's character as the passage in his life affords, I have not shrunk from placing side by side with such excuses in regard to it as he had unquestionable right to claim should be put forward also. How far what remained of his story took tone or colour from it, and especially from the altered career on which at the same time he entered, will thus be sufficiently explained; and with anything else the public have nothing to do.

III

GADSHILL PLACE

1856-70

"I was better pleased with Gadshill Place last Saturday," he wrote to me from Paris on 13 February, 1856, "on going down there, even than I had prepared myself to be. The country, against every disadvantage of season, is beautiful; and the house is so old-fashioned, cheerful, and comfortable, that it is really pleasant to look at. The good old Rector now there, has lived in it six and twenty years, so I have not the heart to turn him out. He is to remain till Lady Day next year, when I shall go in, please God; make my alterations; furnish the house; and keep it for myself that summer." Returning to England through the Kentish country with Mr. Wilkie Collins in July, other advantages occurred to him. "A railroad opened from Rochester to Maidstone, which connects Gadshill at once with the whole sea coast, is certainly an addition to the place, and an enhancement of its value. By and by we shall have the London, Chatham and Dover, too; and that will bring it within an hour of Canterbury and an hour and a half of Dover. I am glad to hear of your having been in the neighbourhood. There is no healthier (marshes avoided), and none in my eyes more beautiful. One of these days I shall show you some places up the Medway with which you will be charmed."

The association with his youthful fancy that first made the place attractive to him has been told; and it was with wonder he had heard one day, from his friend and fellow-worker at *Household Words*, Mr. W. H. Wills, that not only was the house for sale to which he had so often looked wistfully, but that the lady chiefly interested as its owner had been long known and much esteemed by himself. Such curious chances led Dickens to the saying he so frequently repeated about the smallness of the world; but the close relation often found thus existing between things and persons far apart, suggests not so much the smallness of the world as the possible importance of the least things done in it, and is better explained by the grander teaching of Carlyle, that causes and effects, connecting every man and thing with every other, extend through all space and time.

It was at the close of 1855 the negotiation for its purchase began. "They wouldn't," he wrote (25 November), "take £1700 for the Gadshill property, but 'finally' wanted £1800. I have finally offered £1750. It will require an expenditure of about £300 more before yielding £100 a year." The usual discovery of course awaited him that this first estimate would have to be increased threefold. "The changes absolutely necessary" (9 February, 1856) "will take a thousand pounds; which sum I am always resolving to squeeze out of this, grind out of that, and wring out of the other; this, that, and the other generally all three declining to come up to the scratch for the purpose."

* 116 "This day," he wrote on 14 March, "I have paid the purchase-money for Gadshill Place. After drawing the cheque (£1790) I turned round to give it to Wills, and said, 'Now isn't it an extraordinary thing—look at the Day—Friday! I have been nearly drawing it half a dozen times when the lawyers have not been ready, and here it comes round upon a Friday as a matter of course.'" He had no thought at this time of reserving the place wholly for himself, or of making it his own residence except at intervals of summer. He looked upon it as an investment only. "You will hardly know Gadshill again," he wrote in January 1858, "I am improving it so much—yet I have no interest in the place." But continued ownership brought increased liking; he took more and more interest in his own improvements, which were just the kind of occasional occupation and resource his life most wanted in its next seven or eight years; and any further idea of letting it he soon abandoned altogether. It only once passed out of his possession thus, for four months in 1859; in the following year, on the sale of Tavistock House, he transferred to it his books and pictures and choicer furniture; and thenceforward, varied only by houses taken from time to time for the London season, he made it his permanent family abode. Now and then, even during those years, he would talk of selling it; and on his final return from America, when he had sent the last of his sons out into the world, he really might have sold it if he could then have found a house in London suitable to him, and such as he could purchase. But in this he failed; secretly to his own satisfaction, as I believe; and thereupon, in that last autumn of his life, he projected and carried out his most costly addition to Gadshill. Already of course more money had been spent upon it than his first intention in buying it would have justified. He had so enlarged the accommodation, improved the grounds and offices, and added to the land, that, taking also into account this closing outlay, the reserved price placed upon the whole after his death more than quadrupled what he had given in 1856, for the house, shrubbery, and twenty years' lease of a meadow field. It was then purchased, and is now inhabited, by his eldest son.

† 20

Its position has been described, and a history of Rochester published a hundred years ago quaintly mentions the principal interest of the locality. "Near the twenty-seventh stone from London is Gadshill, supposed to have been the scene of the robbery mentioned by Shakespeare in his play of *Henry IV.*; there being reason to think also that it was Sir John Falstaff, of truly comic memory, who under the name of Oldcastle inhabited Cooling Castle, of which the ruins are in the neighbourhood. A small distance to the left appears on an eminence the Hermitage, the seat of the late Sir Francis Head, Bart.; and close to the road, on a small ascent, is a neat building lately erected by Mr. Day. In descending Strood Hill is a fine prospect of Strood, Rochester, and Chatham, which three towns form a continued street extending above two miles in length." It had been supposed that "the neat building lately erected by Mr. Day" was that which the great novelist made famous; but Gadshill Place had no existence until eight years after the date of the history. The good rector who so long lived in it told me, in 1859, that it had been built eighty years before by a well-known character in those parts, one Stevens, grandfather-in-law of Henslow the Cambridge professor of botany. Stevens, who could only with much difficulty manage to write his name, had begun life as ostler at an inn; had become husband to the landlord's widow; then a brewer; and finally, as he subscribed himself on one occasion, "mare" of Rochester. Afterwards the house was inhabited by Mr. Lynn (from some of the members of whose family Dickens made his purchase); and, before the Rev. Mr. Hindle became its tenant, it was inhabited by a Macaroni parson named Townshend, whose horses the Prince Regent bought, throwing into the bargain a box of much desired cigars. Altogether the place had notable associations even apart from those which have connected it with the masterpieces of English humour. "THIS HOUSE, GADSHILL PLACE, stands on the summit of Shakespeare's Gadshill, ever memorable for its association with Sir John Falstaff in his noble fancy. *But, my lads, my lads, to-morrow morning, by four o'clock, early at Gadshill! there are pilgrims going to Canterbury with rich offerings, and traders riding to London with fat purses: I have vizards for you all; you have horses for yourselves.*" Illuminated by Mr. Owen Jones, and placed in a frame on the first-floor landing, these words were the greeting of the new tenant to his visitors. It was his first act of ownership.

All his improvements, it should perhaps be remarked, were not exclusively matters of choice; and to illustrate by his letters what befell at the beginning of his changes, will show what attended them to the close. His earliest difficulty was very grave. There was only one spring of water for gentlefolk and villagers, and from some of the houses or cottages it was two miles away. "We are still" (6 July) "boring for water here, at the rate of two pounds per day for wages. The men seem to like it very much, and to be perfectly comfortable." Another of his earliest experiences (5 September) was thus expressed: "Hop-picking is going on, and people sleep in the garden, and breathe in at the keyhole of the house door. I have been amazed, before this year, by the number of miserable lean wretches, hardly able to crawl, who go hop-picking. I find it is a superstition that the dust of the newly picked hop, falling freshly into the throat, is a cure for consumption. So the poor creatures drag themselves along the roads, and sleep under wet hedges, and get cured soon and finally." Towards the close of the same month (24 September) he wrote: "Here are six men perpetually going up and down the well (I know that somebody will be killed), in the course of fitting a pump: which is quite a railway terminus—it is so iron and so big. The process is much more like putting Oxford Street endwise, and laying gas along it, than anything else. By the time it is finished, the cost of this water will be something absolutely frightful. But of course it proportionately increases the value of the property, and that's my only comfort. . . . The horse has gone lame from a sprain, the big dog has run a tenpenny nail into one of his hind feet, the bolts have all flown out of the basket-carriage, and the gardener says all the fruit trees want replacing with new ones." Another note came in three days. "I have discovered that the seven miles between Maidstone and Rochester is one of the most beautiful walks in England. Five men have been looking attentively at the pump for a week, and (I should hope) may begin to fit it in the course of October. . . ."

With even such varying fortune he effected other changes. * 117
The exterior remained to the last much as it was when he used
as a boy to see it first; a plain, old-fashioned, two-story, brick-
built country house, with a bell-turret on the roof, and over the
front door a quaint neat wooden porch with pillars and seats.
But, among his additions and alterations, was a new drawing-
room built out from the smaller existing one, both being thrown
together ultimately; two good bedrooms built on a third-floor
at the back; and such re-arrangement of the ground floor as,
besides its handsome drawing-room, and its dining-room which
he hung with pictures, transformed its bedroom into a study
which he lined with books and sometimes wrote in, and changed
its breakfast-parlour into a retreat fitted up for smokers into
which he put a small billiard-table. These several rooms opened
from a hall having in it a series of Hogarth prints, until, after
the artist's death, Stanfield's noble scenes were placed there,
when the Hogarths were moved to his bedroom; and in this
hall, during his last absence in America, a parquet floor was
laid down. Nor did he omit such changes as might increase the
comfort of his servants. He built entirely new offices and
stables, and replaced a very old coachhouse by a capital servants' hall, transforming the loft above into a commodious
schoolroom or study for his boys. He made at the same time
an excellent croquet-ground out of a waste piece of orchard.

Belonging to the house, but unfortunately placed on the other
side of the high road, was a shrubbery, well wooded though in
desolate condition, in which stood two magnificent cedars; and
having obtained, in 1859, the consent of the local authorities
for the necessary underground work, Dickens constructed a
passage beneath the road from his front lawn; and in the
shrubbery thus rendered accessible, and which he then laid out
very prettily, he placed afterwards a Swiss chalet presented to
him by Mr. Fechter, which arrived from Paris in ninety-four
pieces fitting like the joints of a puzzle, but which proved to
be somewhat costly in setting on its legs by means of a foundation of brickwork. "It will really be a very pretty thing," he
wrote (January 1865), "and in the summer (supposing it not
to be blown away in the spring), the upper room will make a
charming study. It is much higher than we supposed." Once
up, it did really become a great resource in the summer months,
and much of Dickens's work was done there. "I have put five
mirrors in the chalet where I write," he told an American * 118
friend, "and they reflect and refract, in all kinds of ways, the

leaves that are quivering at the windows, and the great fields of waving corn, and the sail-dotted river. My room is up among the branches of the trees; and the birds and the butterflies fly in and out, and the green branches shoot in at the open windows, and the lights and shadows of the clouds come and go with the rest of the company. The scent of the flowers, and indeed of everything that is growing for miles and miles, is most delicious." He used to make great boast, too, not only of his crowds of singing birds all day, but of his nightingales at night.

One or two more extracts from letters having reference to these changes may show something of the interest to him with which Gadshill thus grew under his hands. A sundial on his back lawn had a bit of historic interest about it. "One of the balustrades of the destroyed old Rochester Bridge," he wrote to his daughter in June 1859, "has been (very nicely) presented to me by the contractors for the works, and has been duly stone-masoned and set up on the lawn behind the house. I have ordered a sundial for the top of it, and it will be a very good object indeed." "When you come down here next month," he wrote to me, "we have an idea that we shall show you rather a neat house. What terrific adventures have been in action; how many overladen vans were knocked up at Gravesend, and had to be dragged out of Chalk Turnpike in the dead of the night by the whole equine power of this establishment; shall be revealed at another time." That was in the autumn of 1860, when, on the sale of his London house, its contents were transferred to his country home. "I shall have an alteration or two to show you at Gadshill that greatly improve the little property; and when I get the workmen out this time, I think I'll leave off." October 1861 had now come, when the new bedrooms were built; but in the same month of 1863 he announced his transformation of the old coach-house. "I shall have a small new improvement to show you at Gads, which I think you will accept as the crowning ingenuity of the Inimitable." But of course it was not over yet. "My small work and planting," he wrote in the spring of 1866, "really, truly, and positively the last, are nearly at an end in these regions, and the result will await summer inspection." No, nor even yet. He afterwards obtained, by exchange of some land with the trustees of Watts's Charity, the much coveted meadow at the back of the house of which heretofore he had the lease only; and he was then able to plant a number of young limes and chestnuts and other quick-growing trees. He had already planted a row of limes in front.

He had no idea, he would say, of planting only for the benefit of posterity, but would put into the ground what he might himself enjoy the sight and shade of. He put them in two or three clumps in the meadow, and in a belt all round.

Still there were "more last words," for the limit was only to be set by his last year of life. On abandoning his notion, after the American readings, of exchanging Gadshill for London, a new staircase was put up from the hill; a parquet floor laid on the first landing; and a conservatory built, opening into both drawing-room and dining-room, "glass and iron," as he described it, "brilliant but expensive, with foundations as of an ancient Roman work of horrible solidity." This last addition had long been an object of desire with him; though he would hardly even now have given himself the indulgence but for the golden shower from America. He saw it first in a completed state on the Sunday before his death, when his younger daughter was on a visit to him. "Well, Katey," he said to her, "now you see POSITIVELY the last improvement at Gadshill"; and everyone laughed at the joke against himself. The success of the new conservatory was unquestionable. It was the remark of all around him that he was certainly, from this last of his improvements, drawing more enjoyment than from any of its predecessors, when the scene for ever closed.

Of the course of his daily life in the country there is not much to be said. Perhaps there was never a man who changed places so much and habits so little. He was always methodical and regular; and passed his life from day to day, divided for the most part between working and walking, the same wherever he was. The only exception was when special or infrequent visitors were with him. When such friends as Longfellow and his daughters, or Charles Eliot Norton and his wife, came, or when Mr. Fields brought his wife and Professor Lowell's daughter, or when he received other Americans to whom he owed special courtesy, he would compress into infinitely few days an enormous amount of sight-seeing and country enjoyment, castles, cathedrals, and fortified lines, lunches and picnics among cherry orchards and hop-gardens, excursions to Canterbury or Maidstone and their beautiful neighbourhoods, Druid Stone and Blue Bell Hill. "All the neighbouring country that could be shown in so short a time," he wrote of the Longfellow visit, "they saw. I turned out a couple of postilions in the old red jackets of the old red royal Dover road for our ride, and it was like a holiday ride in England fifty years ago." For Lord

Lytton he did the same, for the Emerson Tennents, for Mr Layard and Mr. Helps, for Lady Molesworth and the Higginses (Jacob Omnium), and such other less frequent visitors.

Excepting on such particular occasions however, and not always even then, his mornings were reserved wholly to himself; and he would generally preface his morning work (such was his love of order in everything around him) by seeing that all was in its place in the several rooms, visiting also the dogs, stables, and kitchen garden, and closing, unless the weather was very bad indeed, with a turn or two round the meadow before settling to his desk. His dogs were a great enjoyment to him; and, with his high road traversed as frequently as any in England by tramps and wayfarers of a singularly undesirable description, they were also a necessity. There were always two, of the mastiff kind, but latterly the number increased. His own favourite was Turk, a noble animal, full of affection and intelligence, whose death by a railway accident, shortly after the Staplehurst catastrophe, caused him great grief. Turk's sole companion up to that date was Linda, puppy of a great St. Bernard brought over by Mr. Albert Smith, and grown into a superbly beautiful creature. After Turk there was an interval of an Irish dog, Sultan, given by Mr. Percy Fitzgerald; a cross between a St. Bernard and a bloodhound, built and coloured like a lioness and of splendid proportions, but of such indomitably aggressive propensities, that, after breaking his kennel-chain and nearly devouring a luckless little sister of one of the servants, he had to be killed. Dickens always protested that Sultan was a Fenian, for that no dog, not a secretly sworn member of that body, would ever have made such a point, muzzled as he was, of rushing at and bearing down with fury anything in scarlet with the remotest resemblance to a British uniform. Sultan's successor was Don, presented by Mr. Frederick Lehmann, a grand Newfoundland brought over very young, who with Linda became parent to a couple of Newfoundlands, that were still gambolling about their master, huge, though hardly out of puppydom, when they lost him. He had given to one of them the name of Bumble, from having observed, as he described it, "a peculiarly pompous and overbearing manner he had of appearing to mount guard over the yard when he was an absolute infant." Bumble was often in scrapes. Describing to Mr. Fields a drought in the summer of 1868, when their poor supply of ponds and surface wells had become waterless, he wrote: "I do not let the great dogs swim in the canal, because the people have to drink of it. But when they get into the Medway, it is hard to get them out again. The other day Bumble (the son, Newfoundland dog) got into difficulties among some floating timber, and became frightened. Don (the father) was standing by me, shaking off the wet and looking on carelessly, when all of a sudden he perceived something amiss, and went in with a bound and brought Bumble out by the ear. The scientific way in which he towed him along was charming." The description of his own reception, on his reappearance after America, by Bumble and his brother, by the big and beautiful Linda, and by his daughter Mary's handsome little Pomeranian, may be added from his letters to the same correspondent. "The two Newfoundland dogs coming to meet me, with the usual carriage and the usual driver, and beholding me coming in my usual dress out at the usual door, it struck me that their recollection of my having been absent for any unusual time was at once cancelled. They behaved (they are both young dogs) exactly in their usual manner; coming behind the basket phaeton as we trotted along, and lifting their heads to have their ears pulled, a special attention which they receive from no one else. But when I drove into the stable-yard, Linda (the St. Bernard) was greatly excited; weeping profusely, and throwing herself on her back that she might caress my foot with her great fore-paws. Mary's little dog too, Mrs. Bouncer, barked in the greatest agitation on being called down and asked by Mary, 'Who is this?' and tore round and round me like the dog in the Faust outlines." The father and mother and their two sons, four formidable-looking companions, were with him generally in his later walks.

Round Cobham, skirting the park and village, and passing the Leather Bottle famous in the page of *Pickwick*, was a favourite walk with Dickens. By Rochester and the Medway, to the Chatham Lines, was another. He would turn out of Rochester High Street through The Vines (where some old buildings, from one of which called Restoration House he took Satis House for *Great Expectations*, had a curious attraction for him), would pass round by Fort Pitt, and coming back by Frindsbury would bring himself by some cross fields again into the high road. Or, taking the other side, he would walk through the marshes to Gravesend, return by Chalk church, and stop always to have greeting with a comical old monk who for some incomprehensible reason sits carved in stone, cross-legged with a jovial pot, over the porch of that sacred edifice. To another drearier churchyard, itself forming part of the marshes beyond the Medway, he often took friends to show them the dozen small tombstones of various sizes adapted to the respective ages of a dozen small children of one family which he made part of his story of *Great Expectations*, though, with the reserves always necessary in copying nature not to overstep her modesty by copying too closely, he makes the number that appalled little Pip not more than half the reality. About the whole of this Cooling churchyard, indeed, and the neighbouring castle ruins, there was a weird strangeness that made it one of his attractive walks in the late year or winter, when from Higham he could get to it across country over the stubble fields; and, for a shorter summer walk, he was not less fond of going round the village of Shorn and sitting on a hot afternoon in its pretty shaded churchyard. But, on the whole, though Maidstone had also much that attracted him to its neighbourhood, the Cobham neighbourhood was certainly that which he had greatest pleasure in; and he would have taken oftener than he did the walk through Cobham park and woods, which was the last he enjoyed before life suddenly closed upon him, but that here he did not like his dogs to follow.

Don now has his home there with Lord Darnley, and Linda lies under one of the cedars at Gadshill.

IV

FIRST PAID READINGS

1858-9

DICKENS gave his paid public readings successively, with not long intervals, at four several dates; in 1858-9, in 1861-3, in 1866-7, and in 1868-70; the first series under Mr. Arthur Smith's management, the second under Mr. Headland's, and the third and fourth, in America as well as before and after it, under that of Mr. George Dolby, who, excepting in America, acted for the Messrs. Chappell. The references in the present chapter are to the first series only.

It began with sixteen nights at St. Martin's Hall, the first on 29 April, the last on 22 July, 1858; and there was afterwards a provincial tour of eighty-seven readings, beginning at Clifton on 2 August, ending at Brighton on 13 November, and taking in Ireland and Scotland as well as the principal English cities: to which were added, in London, three Christmas readings, three in January, with two in the following month; and, in the provinces in the month of October, fourteen, beginning at Ipswich and Norwich, taking in Cambridge and Oxford, and closing with Birmingham and Cheltenham. The series had comprised altogether 125 readings when it ended on 27 October, 1859; and without the touches of character and interest afforded by his letters written while thus employed, the picture of the man would not be complete.

Here was one day's work at the opening which will show something of the fatigue they involved even at their outset. "On Friday we came from Shrewsbury to Chester; saw all right for the evening; and then went to Liverpool. Came back from Liverpool and read at Chester. Left Chester at 11 at night, after the reading, and went to London. Got to Tavistock House at 5 a.m. on Saturday, left it at a quarter past 10 that morning, and came down here" (Gadshill: 15 August, 1858).

The "greatest personal affection and respect" had greeted

him everywhere. Nothing could have been "more strongly marked or warmly expressed"; and the readings had "gone" quite wonderfully. What in this respect had most impressed him, at the outset of his adventures, was Exeter. "I think they were the finest audience I ever read to; I don't think I ever read in some respects so well: and I never beheld anything like the personal affection which they poured out upon me at the end. I shall always look back upon it with pleasure." He often lost his voice in these early days, having still to acquire the art of husbanding it; and in the trial to recover it would again waste its power. "I think I sang half the Irish melodies to myself as I walked about, to test it."

An audience of two thousand three hundred people (the largest he had had) greeted him at Liverpool on his way to Dublin, and, besides the tickets sold, more than two hundred pounds in money was taken at the doors. This taxed his business staff a little. "They turned away hundreds, sold all the books, rolled on the ground of my room knee-deep in checks, and made a perfect pantomime of the whole thing." (20 August.) He had to repeat the reading thrice.

It was the first time he had seen Ireland, and Dublin greatly surprised him by appearing to be so much larger and more populous than he had supposed. He found it to have altogether an unexpectedly thriving look, being pretty nigh as big, he first thought, as Paris; of which some places in it, such as the quays on the river, reminded him. Half the first day he was there, he took to explore it; walking till tired, and then hiring a car. "Power, dressed for the character of Tedy the Tiler, drove me: in a suit of patches, and with his hat unbrushed for twenty years. Wonderfully pleasant, light, intelligent, and careless." A letter to his eldest daughter makes humorous addition. "The man who drove our jaunting car yesterday hadn't a piece in his coat as big as a penny roll . . . but he was remarkably intelligent and agreeable, with something to say about everything. When we got into the Phœnix Park, he looked round him as if it were his own, and said 'THAT's a Park sir, av ye plase!' I complimented it, and he said 'Gintlemen tills me as they iv bin, sir, over Europe and never see a Park aqualling ov it. Yander's the Vice-regal Lodge, sir; in thim two corners lives the two Sicretaries, wishing I was thim sir. There's air here, sir, av yer plase! There's scenery here sir! There's mountains thim sir!'" The number of common people he saw in his drive, also "riding about in cars as hard as they could split," brought to his recollection a more distant scene, and but for the dresses he could have thought himself on the Toledo at Naples.

In respect of the number of his audience, and their reception of him, Dublin was one of his marked successes. He came to have some doubt of their capacity of receiving the pathetic, but of their quickness as to the humorous there could be no question, any more than of their heartiness. He got on wonderfully well with the Dublin people; and the Irish girls outdid the American in one particular. He wrote to his sister-in-law: "Every night since I have been in Ireland, they have beguiled my dresser out of the bouquet from my coat; and yesterday morning, as I had showered the leaves from my geranium in reading *Little Dombey*, they mounted the platform after I was gone, and picked them all up as a keepsake." The Boots at Morrison's expressed the general feeling in a patriotic point of view. "He was waiting for me at the hotel door last night. 'Whaat sart of a hoose sur?' he asked me 'Capital.' 'The Lard be praised fur the 'onor o' Dooblin!'" Within the hotel, on getting up next morning, he had a dialogue with a smaller resident, landlord's son he supposed, a little boy of the ripe age of six, which he presented, in his letter to his sister-in-law, as a colloquy between Old England and Young Ireland inadequately reported for want of the "imitation" it required for its full effect. "I am sitting on the sofa, writing, and find him sitting beside me.

"*Old England*. Holloa old chap.

"*Young Ireland*. Hal—loo!

"*Old England* (in his delightful way). What a nice old fellow you are. I am very fond of little boys.

"*Young Ireland*. Air yes? Ye'r right.

"*Old England*. What do you learn, old fellow?

"*Young Ireland* (very intent on Old England, and always childish except in his brogue). I lairn wureds of three sillibils—and wureds of two sillibils—and wureds of one sillibil.

"*Old England* (cheerfully). Get out, you humbug! You learn only words of one syllable.

"*Young Ireland* (laughs heartily). You may say that it is mostly wureds of one sillibil.

"*Old England*. Can you write?

"*Young Ireland*. Not yet, Things comes by deegrays.

"*Old England*. Can you cipher?

"*Young Ireland* (very quickly). Whaat's that?

"*Old England*. Can you make figures?

"*Young Ireland.* I can make a nought, which is not asy, being roond.

"*Old England.* I say, old boy! Wasn't it you I saw on Sunday morning in the hall, in a soldier's cap? You know!—In a soldier's cap?

"*Young Ireland* (cogitating deeply). Was it a very good cap?

"*Old England.* Yes.

"*Young Ireland.* Did it fit ankommon?

"*Old England.* Yes.

"*Young Ireland.* Dat was me!"

The last night in Dublin was an extraordinary scene. "You can hardly imagine it. All the way from the hotel to the Rotunda (a mile), I had to contend against the stream of people who were turned away. When I got there, they had broken the glass in the pay-boxes, and were offering £5 freely for a stall. Half of my platform had to be taken down, and people heaped in among the ruins. You never saw such a scene." "Ladies stood all night with their chins against my platform," he wrote to his daughter. "Other ladies sat all night upon my steps. We turned away people enough to make immense houses for a week." But he would not return after his other Irish engagements. "I have positively said No. The work is too hard. It is not like doing it in one easy room, and always the same room. With a different place every night, and a different audience with its own peculiarity every night, it is a tremendous strain . . . I seem to be always either in a railway carriage or reading, or going to bed; and I get so knocked up whenever I have a minute to remember it, that then I go to bed as a matter of course."

Belfast he liked quite as much as Dublin in another way. "A fine place with a rough people; everything looking prosperous; the railway ride from Dublin quite amazing in the order, neatness, and cleanness of all you see; every cottage looking as if it had been whitewashed the day before; and many with charming gardens, prettily kept with bright flowers." The success, too, was quite as great. "Enormous audiences. We turn away half the town. I think them a better audience on the whole than Dublin; and the personal affection is something overwhelming. I wish you and the dear girls" (he is writing to his sister-in-law) "could have seen the people look at me in the street; or heard them ask me, as I hurried to the hotel after the reading last night, to 'do me the honour to shake hands Misther Dickens and God bless you sir; not ounly for the light you've been to me this night, but for the light you've been in mee house sir (and God love your face!) this many a year!'" He had never seen men "go in to cry so undisguisedly," as they did at the Belfast *Dombey* reading; "and as to the *Boots* and *Mrs. Gamp* it was just one roar with me and them. For they made me laugh so, that sometimes I *could not* compose my face to go on." His greatest trial in this way however was a little later at Harrogate—"the queerest place, with the strangest people in it, leading the oddest lives of dancing, newspaper-reading, and tables d'hôte"—where he noticed, at the same reading, embodiments respectively of the tears and laughter to which he has moved his fellow-creatures so largely. "There was one gentleman at the *Little Dombey* yesterday morning" (he is still writing to his sister-in-law) "who exhibited—or rather concealed—the profoundest grief. After crying a good deal without hiding it, he covered his face with both his hands and laid it down on the back of the seat before him, and really shook with emotion. He was not in mourning, but I supposed him to have lost some child in old time. . . . There was a remarkably good fellow too, of thirty or so, who found something so very ludicrous in Toots that he *could not* compose himself at all, but laughed until he sat wiping his eyes with his handkerchief; and whenever he felt Toots coming again, he began to laugh and wipe his eyes afresh; and when Toots came once more, he gave a kind of cry, as if it were too much for him. It was uncommonly droll, and made me laugh heartily."

At Harrogate he read twice on one day (a Saturday), and had to engage a special engine to take him back that night to York, which, having reached at one o'clock in the morning, he had to leave, because of Sunday restrictions on travel, the same morning at half-past four, to enable him to fulfil a Monday's reading at Scarborough. Such fatigues became matters of course; but their effect, not noted at the time, was grave. Here again he was greatly touched by the personal greeting. "I was brought very near to what I sometimes dream may be my Fame," he wrote to me in October from York, "when a lady whose face I had never seen stopped me yesterday in the street, and said to me, *Mr. Dickens, will you let me touch the hand that has filled my house with many friends.*" Of the reading he adds, "I had a most magnificent assemblage, and might have filled the place for a week. . . . I think the audience possessed of a better knowledge of character than any I have seen. But I recollect Doctor Belcombe to have told me long ago that they first found out

Charles Mathews's father, and to the last understood him (he used to say) better than any other people. . . . The let is enormous for next Saturday at Manchester, stalls alone four hundred! I shall soon be able to send you the list of places to the 15th of November, the end. I shall be, O most heartily glad, when that time comes! But I must say that the intelligence and warmth of the audiences are an immense sustainment, and one that always sets me up. Sometimes before I go down to read (especially when it is in the day), I am so oppressed by having to do it that I feel perfectly unequal to the task. But the people lift me out of this directly; and I find that I have quite forgotten everything but them and the book, in a quarter of an hour."

The reception that awaited him at Manchester had very special warmth in it, occasioned by an adverse tone taken in the comment of one of the Manchester daily papers on the letter which by a breach of confidence had been then recently printed. "My violated letter" Dickens always called it (*ante*, 206). "When I came to Manchester on Saturday I found seven hundred stalls taken! When I went into the room at night 2500 people had paid, and more were being turned away from every door. The welcome they gave me was astounding in its affectionate recognition of the late trouble, and fairly for once unmanned me. I never saw such a sight or heard such a sound. When they had thoroughly done it, they settled down to enjoy themselves; and certainly did enjoy themselves most heartily to the last minute." Nor, for the rest of his English tour, in any of the towns that remained, had he reason to complain of any want of hearty greeting. At Sheffield great crowds in excess of the places came. At Leeds the hall overflowed in half an hour. At Hull the vast concourse had to be addressed by Mr. Smith on the gallery stairs, and additional readings had to be given, day and night, "for the people out of town and for the people in town."

The net profit to himself, thus far, had been upwards of three
* 120A hundred pounds a week; but this was nothing to the success in Scotland, where his profit in a week, with all expenses paid, was five hundred pounds. The pleasure was enhanced, too, by the presence of his two daughters, who had joined him over the Border. At first the look of Edinburgh was not promising. "We began with, for us, a poor room. . . . But the effect of that reading (it was the *Chimes*) was immense; and on the next night, for *Little Dombey*, we had a full room. It is our greatest triumph everywhere. Next night (*Poor Traveller, Boots,* and

Gamp) we turned away hundreds upon hundreds of people; and last night, for the *Carol*, in spite of advertisements in the morning that the tickets were gone, the people had to be got in through such a crowd as rendered it a work of the utmost difficulty to keep an alley into the room. They were seated about me on the platform, put into the doorway of the waiting-room, squeezed into every conceivable place, and a multitude turned away once more. I think I am better pleased with what was done in Edinburgh than with what has been done anywhere, almost. It was so completely taken by storm, and carried in spite of itself. Mary and Katey have been infinitely pleased and inter-ested with Edinburgh. We are just going to sit down to dinner and therefore I cut my missive short. Travelling, dinner, reading, and everything else, come crowding together into this strange life."

Then came Dundee: "An odd place," he wrote, "like Wapping, with high rugged hills behind it. We had the strangest journey here—bits of sea, and bits of railroad, alternately; which carried my mind back to travelling in America. The room is an immense new one, belonging to Lord Kinnaird, and Lord Panmure, and some others of that sort. It looks something between the Crystal Palace and Westminster Hall (I can't imagine who wants it in this place), and has never been tried yet for speaking in. Quite disinterestedly of course, I hope it will succeed." The people he thought, in respect of taste and intelligence, below any other of his Scotch audiences; but they woke up surprisingly, and the rest of his Caledonian tour was a succession of triumphs. "At Aberdeen we were crammed to the street, twice in one day. At Perth (where I thought when I arrived, there literally could be nobody to come) the gentlefolk came posting in from thirty miles round, and the whole town came besides, and filled an immense hall. They were as full of perception, fire, and en-thusiasm as any people I have seen. At Glasgow, where I read three evenings and one morning, we took the prodigiously large sum of six hundred pounds! And this at the Manchester prices, which are lower than St. Martin's Hall. As to the effect—I wish you could have seen them after Lilian died in the *Chimes*, or when Scrooge woke in the *Carol* and talked to the boy outside the window. And at the end of *Dombey* yesterday afternoon, in the cold light of day, they all got up, after a short pause, gentle and simple, and thundered and waved their hats with such astonishing heartiness and fondness that, for the first time in all my public career, they took me completely off my legs, and I saw the whole eighteen hundred of them reel to one side as if a shock from without had shaken the hall. Notwithstanding which, I must confess to you, I am very anxious to get to the end of my readings, and to be at home again, and able to sit down and think in my own study. There has been only one thing quite without alloy. The dear girls have enjoyed themselves immensely, and their trip with me has been a great success."

The subjects of his readings during this first circuit were the *Carol*, the *Chimes*, the *Trial in Pickwick*, the chapters containing *Paul Dombey*, *Boots at the Holly Tree Inn*, the *Poor Traveller* (Captain Doubledick), and *Mrs. Gamp*: to which he continued to restrict himself through the supplementary nights that closed in the autumn of 1859. Of these the most successful in their uniform effect upon his audiences were undoubtedly the *Carol*, the *Pickwick* scene, *Mrs. Gamp*, and the *Dombey*—the quickness, variety, and completeness of his assumption of character, having greatest scope in these. Here, I think, more than in the pathos or graver level passages, his strength lay; but this is entitled to no weight other than as an individual opinion, and his audiences gave him many reasons for thinking differently.

The incidents of the period covered by this chapter that had any general interest in them, claim to be mentioned briefly. At the close of 1857 he presided at the fourth anniversary of the Warehousemen and Clerks' Schools, describing and discriminating, with keenest wit and kindliest fun, the sort of schools he liked and he disliked. To the spring and summer of 1858 belongs the first collection of his writings into a succinct library form, each of the larger novels occupying two volumes. In March he paid warm public tribute to Thackeray (who had been induced to take the chair at the General Theatrical Fund) as one for whose genius he entertained the warmest admiration, who did honour to literature, and in whom literature was honoured. In May he presided at the Artists' Benevolent Fund dinner, and made striking appeal for that excellent charity. In July he took earnest part in the opening efforts on behalf of the Royal Dramatic College, which he supplemented later by a speech for the establishment of schools for actors' children; in which he took occasion to declare his belief that there were no institutions in England so socially liberal as its public schools, and that there was nowhere in the country so complete an absence of servility to mere rank, position, or riches. "A boy there, is always what his abilities or his personal qualities make him. We may differ about the curriculum and other matters, but of the frank, free, manly, independent spirit preserved in our public schools, I apprehend there can be no kind of question."

In December he was entertained at a public dinner in Coventry ✱ 123 on the occasion of receiving, by way of thanks for help rendered to their Institute, a gold repeater of special construction by the watchmakers of the town: as to which he kept faithfully his pledge to the givers, that it should be thenceforward the inseparable companion of his workings and wanderings, and reckon off the future labours of his days until he should have done with the measurement of time. Within a day from this celebration he presided at the Institutional Association of Lancashire and Cheshire in Manchester Free Trade Hall; gave prizes to candidates from a hundred and fourteen local mechanics' institutes affiliated to the Association; described in his most attractive language the gallant toiling fellows by whom the prizes had been won; and ended with the monition he never failed to couple with his eulogies of Knowledge, that it should follow the teaching of the Saviour, and not satisfy the understanding merely. "Knowledge has a very limited power when it informs the head only; but when it informs the heart as well, it has a power over life and death, the body and the soul, and dominates the universe."

This too was the year when Mr. Frith completed Dickens's portrait for me, and it was upon the walls of the Academy in † 21 the following spring. "I wish," said Edwin Landseer as he stood before it, "he looked less eager and busy, and not so much out of himself, or beyond himself. I should like to catch him asleep and quiet now and then." There is something in the objection, and he also would be envious at times of what he too surely knew could never be his lot. On the other hand who would willingly have lost the fruits of an activity on the whole so healthy and beneficent?

V

"ALL THE YEAR ROUND" AND "UNCOMMERCIAL TRAVELLER"

1859-61

IN the interval before the close of the first circuit of readings,
painful personal disputes arising out of the occurrences of the
previous year were settled by the discontinuance of *Household
Words*, and the establishment in its place of *All the Year Round*.
The disputes turned upon matters of feeling exclusively, and
involved no charge on either side that would render any detailed
reference here other than gravely out of place. The question
into which the difference ultimately resolved itself was that of
the respective rights of the parties as proprietors of *Household
Words*; and this, upon a bill filed in Chancery, was settled by
a winding-up order, under which the property was sold. It was
bought by Dickens, who, even before the sale, exactly ful-
filling a previous announcement of the proposed discontinuance
of the existing periodical and establishment of another in its
place, precisely similar but under a different title, had started
All the Year Round. It was to be regretted perhaps that he
should have thought it necessary to move at all, but he moved
† 22 strictly within his rights.

To the publishers first associated with his great success in
literature, Messrs. Chapman and Hall, he now returned for the
issue of the remainder of his books; of which he always in
future reserved the copyrights, making each the subject of such
arrangement as for the time might seem to him desirable. In
this he was met by no difficulty; and indeed it will be only proper
to add, that, in any points affecting his relations with those concerned in the production of his books, though his resentments
were easily and quickly roused, they were never very lasting.
The only fair rule therefore was, in a memoir of his life, to confine the mention of such things to what was strictly necessary
to explain its narrative. This accordingly has been done; and,
in the several disagreements it has been necessary to advert to,
I cannot charge myself with having in a single instance over-

stepped the rule. Objection has been made to my revival of the early differences with Mr. Bentley. But silence respecting them was incompatible with what absolutely required to be said, if the picture of Dickens in his most interesting time, at the outset of his career in letters, was not to be omitted altogether; and, suppressing everything of mere temper that gathered round the dispute, use was made of those letters only containing the young writer's urgent appeal to be absolved, rightly or wrongly, from engagements he had too precipitately entered into. Wrongly, some might say, because the law was undoubtedly on Mr. Bentley's side; but all subsequent reflection has confirmed the view I was led strongly to take at the time, that in the facts there had come to be involved what the law could not afford to overlook, and that the sale of brain-work can never be adjusted by agreement with the same exactness and certainty as that of ordinary goods and chattels. Quitting the subject once for all with this remark, it is not less incumbent on me to say that there was no stage of the dispute in which Mr. Bentley, holding as strongly the other view, might not think it to have sufficient justification; and certainly in later years there was no absence of friendly feeling on the part of Dickens to his old publisher. This already has been mentioned; and on the occasion of Hans Andersen's recent visit to Gadshill, Mr. Bentley was invited to meet the celebrated Dane. Nor should I omit to say, that, in the year to which this narrative has now arrived, his prompt compliance with an intercession made to him for a common friend pleased Dickens greatly.

At the opening of 1859, bent upon such a successor to *Household Words* as should carry on the associations connected with its name, Dickens was deep in search of a title to give expression to them. "My determination to settle the title arises out of my knowledge that I shall never be able to do anything for the work until it has a fixed name; also out of my observation that the same odd feeling affects everybody else." He had proposed to himself a title that, as in *Household Words*, might be capable of illustration by a line from Shakespeare; and alighting upon that wherein poor Henry the Sixth is fain to solace his captivity by the fancy, that, like birds encaged he might soothe himself for loss of liberty "at last by notes of household harmony," he for the time forgot that this might hardly be accepted as a happy comment on the occurrences out of which the supposed necessity had arisen of replacing the old by a new household friend. "Don't you think," he wrote on 24 January, "this is a good name and quotation? I have been quite delighted to get hold of it for our title.

"HOUSEHOLD HARMONY.

'At last by notes of Household Harmony.'—*Shakespeare*."

He was at first reluctant even to admit the objection when stated to him. "I am afraid we must not be too particular about the possibility of personal references and applications: otherwise it is manifest that I never can write another book. I could not invent a story of any sort, it is quite plain, incapable of being twisted into some such nonsensical shape. It would be wholly impossible to turn one through half a dozen chapters." Of course he yielded, nevertheless; and much consideration followed over sundry other titles submitted. Reviving none of those formerly rejected, here were a few of these now rejected in their turn. THE HEARTH. THE FORGE. THE CRUCIBLE. THE ANVIL OF THE TIME. CHARLES DICKENS'S OWN. SEASONABLE LEAVES. EVERGREEN LEAVES. HOME. HOME-MUSIC. CHANGE. TIME AND TIDE. TWOPENCE. ENGLISH BELLS. WEEKLY BELLS. THE ROCKET. GOOD HUMOUR. Still the great want was the line adaptable from Shakespeare, which at last exultingly he sent on 28 January. "I am dining early, before reading, and write literally with my mouth full. But I have just hit upon a name that I think really an admirable one—especially with the quotation *before* it, in the place where our present *H. W.* quotation stands.

"'The story of our lives, from year to year.'—*Shakespeare*.

ALL THE YEAR ROUND.

A weekly journal conducted by Charles Dickens."

With the same resolution and energy other things necessary to the adventure were as promptly done. "I have taken the new office," he wrote from Tavistock House on 21 February; "have got workmen in; have ordered the paper; settled with the printer; and am getting an immense system of advertising ready. Blow to be struck on the 12th of March. . . . Meantime I cannot please myself with the opening of my story" (the *Tale of Two Cities*, which *All the Year Round* was to start with), "and cannot in the least settle at it or take to it. . . . I wish you would come and look at what I flatter myself is a rather ingenious account to which I have turned the Stanfield scenery here." He had placed the *Lighthouse* scene in a single frame; had divided the scene of the *Frozen Deep* into two subjects, a British man-of-war and an Arctic sea, which he had also framed; and the schoolroom that had been the theatre was now hung with sea-pieces by a great painter of the sea. To believe them to have been but the amusement of a few mornings was difficult indeed. Seen from the due distance there was nothing wanting to the most masterly and elaborate art.

The first number of *All the Year Round* appeared on 30 April, and the result of the first quarter's accounts of the sale will tell everything that needs to be said of a success that went on without intermission to the close. "A word before I go back to Gadshill," he wrote from Tavistock House in July, "which I know you will be glad to receive. So well has *All the Year Round* gone that it was yesterday able to repay me, with five per cent. interest, all the money I advanced for its establishment (paper, print etc. all paid, down to the last number), and yet to leave a good £500 balance at the banker's!" Beside the opening of his *Tale of Two Cities* its first number had contained another piece of his writing, the "Poor Man and his Beer"; as to which an interesting note has been sent me. The Rev. T. B. Lawes, of Rothamsted, St. Albans, had been associated upon a sanitary commission with Mr. Henry Austin, Dickens's brother-in-law and counsellor in regard to all such matters in his own houses, or in the houses of the poor; and this connection led to Dickens's knowledge of a club that Mr. Lawes had established at Rothamsted, which he became eager to recommend as an example to other country neighbourhoods. The club had been set on foot to enable the agricultural labourers of the parish to have their beer and pipes independent of the public-house; and the description of it, says Mr. Lawes, "was the occupation of a drive between this place (Rothamsted) and London, twenty-five miles, Mr. Dickens refusing the offer of a bed, and saying that he could arrange his ideas on the journey. In the course of our conversation I mentioned that the labourers were very jealous of the small tradesmen, blacksmiths and others, holding allotment-gardens; but that the latter did so indirectly by paying higher rents to the labourers for a share. This circumstance is not forgotten in the verses on the Blacksmith in the same number, composed by Mr. Dickens and repeated to me while he was walking about, and which close the mention of his gains with allusion to

A share (concealed) in the poor man's field,
Which adds to the poor man's store.

It is pleasant to be able to add that the club was still flourishing when I received Mr. Lawes's letter, on 18 December, 1871.

The periodical thus established was in all respects, save one, so exactly the counterpart of what it replaced, that a mention of this point of difference is the only description of it called for. Besides his own three-volume stories of the *Tale of Two Cities* and *Great Expectations*, Dickens admitted into it other stories of the same length by writers of character and name, of which the authorship was avowed. It published tales of varied merit and success by Mr. Edmund Yates, Mr. Percy Fitzgerald, and Mr. Charles Lever. Mr. Wilkie Collins contributed to it his *Woman in White*, *No Name*, and *Moonstone*, the first of which had a pre-eminent success; Mr. Reade his *Hard Cash*; and Lord Lytton his *Strange Story*. Conferring about the latter Dickens passed a week at Knebworth, accompanied by his daughter and sister-in-law, in the summer of 1861, as soon as he had closed *Great Expectations*; and there met Mr. Arthur Helps, with whom and Lord Orford he visited the so-called "Hermit" near Stevenage, whom he described as Mr. Mopes in *Tom Tiddler's Ground*. With his great brother-artist he thoroughly enjoyed himself, as he invariably did; and reported him as "in better health and spirits than I have seen him in, in all these years—a little weird occasionally regarding magic and spirits, but always fair and frank under opposition. He was brilliantly talkative, anecdotical, and droll; looked young and well; laughed heartily; and enjoyed with great zest some games we played. In his artist-character and talk, he was full of interest and matter, saying the subtlest and finest things—but that he never fails in. I enjoyed myself immensely, as we all did."

* 124

In *All the Year Round*, as in its predecessor, the tales for Christmas were of course continued, but with a surprisingly increased popularity; and Dickens never had such sale for any of his writings as for his Christmas pieces in the latter periodical. It had reached before he died, to nearly three hundred thousand. The first was called the *Haunted House*, and had a small mention of a true occurrence in his boyhood which is not included in the bitter record on a former page. "I was taken home, and there was debt at home as well as death, and we had a sale there. My own little bed was so superciliously looked upon by a power unknown to me hazily called The Trade, that a brass coal-scuttle, a roasting-jack, and a bird-cage were obliged to be put into it to make a lot of it, and then it went for a song.

So I heard mentioned, and I wondered what song, and thought what a dismal song it must have been to sing!" The other subjects will have mention in another chapter.

His tales were not his only important work in *All the Year Round*. The detached papers written by him there had a character and completeness derived from their plan, and from the personal tone, as well as frequent individual confessions, by which their interest is enhanced, and which will always make them specially attractive. Their title expressed a personal liking. Of all the societies, charitable or self-assisting, which his tact and eloquence in the "chair" so often helped, none had interested him by the character of its service to its members, and the perfection of its management, so much as that of the Commercial Travellers. His admiration of their schools introduced him to one who then acted as their treasurer, and whom, of all the men he had known, I think he rated highest for the union of business qualities in an incomparable measure to a nature comprehensive enough to deal with masses of men, however differing in creed or opinion, humanely and justly. He never afterwards wanted support for any good work that he did not think first of Mr. George Moore, and appeal was never made to * 125 him in vain. "Integrity, enterprise, public spirit, and benevolence," he told the Commercial Travellers on one occasion, "had their synonym in Mr. Moore's name"; and it was another form of the same liking when he took to himself the character and title of a Traveller *Un*commercial. "I am both a town traveller and a country traveller, and am always on the road. Figuratively speaking, I travel for the great house of Human-interestBrothers, and have rather a large connection in the fancy goods way. Literally speaking, I am always wandering here and there from my rooms in Covent Garden, London: now about the city streets, now about the country by-roads: seeing many little things, and some great things, which, because they interest me, I think may interest others." In a few words, that was the plan and drift of the papers which he began in 1860, and continued to write from time to time until the last autumn of his life.

Many of them, such as "Travelling Abroad," "City Churches," "Dullborough," "Nurses' Stories" and "Birthday Celebrations," have supplied traits, chiefly of his younger days, to portions of this memoir; and parts of his later life receive illustration from others, such as "Tramps," "Night Walks," "Shy Neighbourhoods," "The Italian Prisoner," and "Chatham Dockyard." Indeed hardly any is without its personal interest or illustration.

One may learn from them, among other things, what kind of treatment he resorted to for the disorder of sleeplessness from which he had often suffered amid his late anxieties. Experimenting upon it in bed, he found to be too slow and doubtful a process for him; but he very soon defeated his enemy by the brisker treatment, of getting up directly after lying down, going out, and coming home tired at sunrise. "My last special feat was turning out of bed at two, after a hard day pedestrian and otherwise, and walking thirty miles into the country to breakfast." One description he did not give in his paper, but I recollect his saying that he had seldom seen anything so striking as the way in which the wonders of an equinoctial dawn (it was 15 October, 1857) presented themselves during that walk. He had never before happened to see night so completely at odds with morning, "which was which." Another experience of his night ramblings used to be given in vivid sketches of the restlessness of a great city, and the manner in which *it* also tumbles and tosses before it can get to sleep. Nor should anyone curious about his habits and ways omit to accompany him with his "Tramps" into Gadshill lanes; or to follow him into his "Shy Neighbourhoods" of the Hackney Road, Waterloo Road, Spitalfields, or Bethnal Green. For delightful observation both of country and town, for the wit that finds analogies between remote and familiar things, and for humorous personal sketches and experience, these are perfect of their kind.

"I have my eye upon a piece of Kentish road, bordered on either side by a wood, and having on one hand, between the road-dust and the trees, a skirting patch of grass. Wild flowers grow in abundance on this spot, and it lies high and airy, with a distant river stealing steadily away to the ocean, like a man's life. To gain the milestone here, which the moss, primroses, violets, blue-bells, and wild roses, would soon render illegible but for peering travellers pushing them aside with their sticks, you must come up a steep hill, come which way you may. So, all the tramps with carts or caravans—the Gipsy-tramp, the Show-tramp, the Cheap Jack—find it impossible to resist the temptations of the place; and all turn the horse loose when they come to it, and boil the pot. Bless the place, I love the ashes of the vagabond fires that have scorched its grass!" It was there he found Dr. Marigold, and Chops the Dwarf, and the White-haired Lady with the pink eyes eating meat-pie with the Giant. So, too, in his "Shy Neighbourhoods," when he relates his experiences of the bad company that birds are fond of, and of the effect upon domestic fowls of living in low districts, his method of handling the subject has all the charm of a discovery. "That anything born of an egg and invested with wings should have got to the pass that it hops contentedly down a ladder into a cellar, and calls *that* going home, is a circumstance so amazing as to leave one nothing more in this connection to wonder at." One of his illustrations is a reduced bantam family in the Hackney Road deriving their sole enjoyment from crowding together in a pawnbroker's side-entry; but seeming as if only newly come down in the world, and always in a feeble flutter of fear that they may be found out. He contrasts them with others. "I know a low fellow, originally of a good family from Dorking, who takes his whole establishment of wives, in single file, in at the door of the Jug Department of a disorderly tavern near the Haymarket, manœuvres them among the company's legs, emerges with them at the Bottle Entrance, and so passes his life: seldom, in the season, going to bed before two in the morning. . . . But the family I am best acquainted with reside in the densest part of Bethnal Green. Their abstraction from the objects among which they live, or rather their conviction that those objects have all come into existence in express subservience to fowls, has so enchanted me that I have made them the subject of many journeys at divers hours. After careful observation of the two lords and the ten ladies of whom this family consists, I have come to the conclusion that their opinions are represented by the leading lord and leading lady: the latter, as I judge, an aged personage, afflicted with a paucity of feather and visibility of quill that gives her the appearance of a bundle of office pens. When a railway goods-van that would crush an elephant comes round the corner, tearing over these fowls, they emerge unharmed from under the horses, perfectly satisfied that the whole rush was a passing property in the air, which may have left something to eat behind it. They look upon old shoes, wrecks of kettles and saucepans, and fragments of bonnets, as a kind of meteoric discharge, for fowls to peck at. . . . Gaslight comes quite as natural to them as any other light; and I have more than a suspicion that, in the minds of the two lords, the early public-house at the corner has superseded the sun. They always begin to crow when the public-house shutters begin to be taken down, and they salute the Potboy, the instant he appears to perform that duty, as if he were Phœbus in person." For the truth of the personal adventure in the same essay, which he tells in proof of a propensity to bad company in more refined members of the feathered race, I am myself in a position to vouch. Walking by a dirty court in Spitalfields one day, the quick little busy intelligence of a goldfinch, drawing water for himself in his cage, so attracted him that he bought the bird, which had other accomplishments; but not one of them would the little creature show off in his new abode in Doughty Street, and he drew no water but by stealth or under the cloak of night. "After an interval of futile and at length hopeless expectation, the merchant who had educated him was appealed to. The merchant was a bow-legged character, with a flat and cushiony nose, like the last new strawberry. He wore a fur cap, and shorts, and was of the velveteen race, velveteeny. He sent word that he would 'look round.' He looked round, appeared in the doorway of the room, and slightly cocked up his evil eye at the goldfinch. Instantly a raging thirst beset that bird; and when it was appeased, he still drew several unnecessary buckets of water, leaping about his perch and sharpening his bill with irrepressible satisfaction."

The *Uncommercial Traveller* papers, his two serial stories, and his Christmas tales, were all the contributions of any importance made by Dickens to *All the Year Round*; but he reprinted in it, on the completion of his first story, a short tale called *Hunted Down*, written for a newspaper in America called the *New York Ledger*. Its subject had been taken from the life of a notorious criminal already named, and its prin-
125A cipal claim to notice was the price paid for it. For a story not longer than half of one of the numbers of *Chuzzlewit* or *Copperfield*, he had received a thousand pounds. It was one of the indications of the eager desire which his entry on the career of a public reader had aroused in America to induce him again to visit that continent; and at the very time he had this magnificent offer from the New York journal, Mr. Fields of Boston, who was then on a visit to Europe, was pressing him so much to go that his resolution was almost shaken. "I am now," he wrote to me from Gadshill on 9 July, 1859, "getting the *Tale of Two Cities* into that state that IF I should decide to go to America late in September, I could turn to at any time, and write on with great vigour. Mr. Fields has been down here for a day, and with the strongest intensity urges that there is no drawback, no commercial excitement or crisis, no political agitation; and that so favourable an opportunity, in all respects, might not occur again for years and years. I should be one of the most unhappy of men if I were to go, and yet I cannot help

being much stirred and influenced by the golden prospect held before me."

He yielded nevertheless to other persuasion, and for that time the visit was not to be. In six months more the Civil War began, and America was closed to any such enterprise for nearly five years.

VI

At the end of the first year of residence at Gadshill it was the remark of Dickens that nothing had gratified him so much as the confidence with which his poorer neighbours treated him. He had tested generally their worth and good conduct, and they had been encouraged in any illness or trouble to resort to him for help. There was pleasant indication of the feeling thus awakened, when, in the summer of 1860, his younger daughter Kate was married to Charles Alston Collins, brother of the novelist, and younger son of the painter and academician, who might have found, if spared to witness that summer-morning scene, subjects not unworthy of his delightful pencil in many a rustic group near Gadshill. All the villagers had turned out in honour of Dickens, and the carriages could hardly get to and from the little church for the succession of triumphal arches they had to pass through. It was quite unexpected by him; and when the *feu de joie* of the blacksmith in the lane, whose enthusiasm had smuggled a couple of small cannon into his forge, exploded upon him at the return, I doubt if the shyest of men was ever so taken aback at an ovation.

To name the principal persons present that day will indicate the faces that (with addition of Miss Mary Boyle, Miss Marguerite Power, Mr. Fechter, Mr. Charles Kent, Mr. Edmund Yates, Mr. Percy Fitzgerald, and members of the family of Mr. Frank Stone, whose sudden death in the preceding year had been a great grief to Dickens) were most familiar at Gadshill in these later years. Mr. Frederic Lehmann was there with his wife, whose sister, Miss Chambers, was one of the bridesmaids; Mr. and Mrs. Wills were there, and Dickens's old fast friend Mr. Thomas Beard; the two nearest country neighbours with whom the family had become very intimate, Mr. Hulkes and Mr. Malleson, with their wives, joined the party; among the others were Henry Chorley, Chauncy Hare Townshend, and Wilkie

Collins; and, for friends special to the occasion, the bridegroom had brought his old fellow-student in art, Mr. Holman Hunt. Mr. Charles Collins had himself been bred as a painter, for success in which line he had some rare gifts; but inclination and capacity led him also to literature, and, after much indecision between the two callings, he took finally to letters. His contributions to *All the Year Round* were among the most charming of its detached papers, and two stories published independently showed strength of wing for higher flights. But his health broke down, and his taste was too fastidious for his failing power. It is possible however that he may live by two small books of description, the *New Sentimental Journey* and the *Cruise on Wheels*, which have in them unusual delicacy and refinement of humour; and if those volumes should make any readers in another generation curious about the writer, they will learn, if correct reply is given to their inquiries, that no man disappointed so many reasonable hopes with so little fault or failure of his own, that his difficulty always was to please himself, and that an inferior mind would have been more successful in both the arts he followed. He died in 1873 in his forty-fifth year; and until then it was not known, even by those nearest to him, how great must have been the suffering which he had borne, through many trying years, with uncomplaining patience.

His daughter's marriage was the chief event that crossed the even tenor of Dickens's life since his first paid readings closed; and it was followed by the sale of Tavistock House, with the resolve to make his future home at Gadshill. In the brief interval (29 July) he wrote to me of his brother Alfred's death. "I was telegraphed for to Manchester on Friday night. Arrived there at a quarter past ten, but he had been dead three hours, poor fellow! He is to be buried at Highgate on Wednesday. I brought the poor young widow back with me yesterday." All that this death involved, the troubles of his change of * 127 home, and some difficulties in working out his story, gave him more than sufficient occupation till the following spring; and as the time arrived for the new readings, the change was a not unwelcome one.

The first portion of this second series was planned by Mr. Arthur Smith, but he only superintended the six readings in London which opened it. These were the first at St. James's Hall (St. Martin's Hall having been burnt since the last readings there), and were given in March and April 1861. "We are all

well here and flourishing," he wrote to me from Gadshill
on 28 April. "On the 18th I finished the readings as I pur-
posed. We had between seventy and eighty pounds *in the
stalls*, which, at four shillings apiece, is something quite unprecedented in these times. . . . The result of the six was, that,
after paying a large staff of men and all other charges, and
Arthur Smith's ten per cent. on the receipts, and replacing
everything destroyed in the fire at St. Martin's Hall (including
all our tickets, country baggage, check-boxes, books, and a
quantity of gas-fittings and what not), I got upwards of £500.
A very great result. We certainly might have gone on through the
season, but I am heartily glad to be concentrated on my story."

It had been part of his plan that the provincial readings
should not begin until a certain interval after the close of his
story of *Great Expectations*. They were delayed accordingly
until 28 October, from which date, when they opened at
Norwich, they went on with the Christmas intervals to be
presently named to 30 January, 1862, when they closed at
Chester. Kept within England and Scotland, they took in the
border town of Berwick, and, besides the Scotch cities, comprised
the contrasts and varieties of Norwich and Lancaster, Bury St.
Edmunds and Cheltenham, Carlisle and Hastings, Plymouth and
Birmingham, Canterbury and Torquay, Preston and Ipswich,
Manchester and Brighton, Colchester and Dover, Newcastle
and Chester. They were followed by ten readings at the St.
James's Hall, between 13 March and 27 June, 1862; and by
four at Paris in January 1863, given at the Embassy in aid
of the British Charitable Fund. The second series had thus in
the number of the readings nearly equalled the first, when it
closed at London in June 1863 with thirteen readings in the
Hanover Square Rooms; and it is exclusively the subject of
such illustrations or references as this chapter will supply.

On *Great Expectations* closing in June 1861, Bulwer Lytton,
at Dickens's earnest wish, took his place in *All the Year Round*
with the *Strange Story*; and he then indulged himself in
idleness for a little while. "The subsidence of those distressing
pains in my face the moment I had done my work, made me
resolve to do nothing in that way for some time if I could help
it." But his "doing nothing" was seldom more than a figure of
speech, and what it meant in this case was soon told. "Every day
for two or three hours, I practise my new readings, and (except
in my office work) do nothing else. With great pains I have made
a continuous narrative out of *Copperfield*, that I think will

128

reward the exertion it is likely to cost me. Unless I am much mistaken, it will be very valuable in London. I have also done Nicholas Nickleby at the Yorkshire school, and hope I have got got something droll out of Squeers, John Browdie, & Co. Also, the Bastille prisoner from the *Tale of Two Cities*. Also, the Dwarf from one of our Christmas numbers." Only the first two were added to the list for the present circuit.

It was in the midst of these active preparations that painful news reached him. An illness under which Mr. Arthur Smith had been some time suffering took unexpectedly a dangerous turn, and there came to be but small chance of his recovery. A distressing interview on 28 September gave Dickens little hope. "And yet his wakings and wanderings so perpetually turn on his arrangements for the readings, and he is so desperately unwilling to relinquish the idea of 'going on with the business' to-morrow and to-morrow and to-morrow, that I had not the heart to press him for the papers. He told me that he believed he had by him '70 or 80 letters unanswered.' You may imagine how anxious it makes me, and at what a dead-stop I stand." Another week passed, and with it the time fixed at the places where his work was to have opened; but he could not bring himself to act as if all hope had gone. "With a sick man who has been so zealous and faithful, I feel bound to be very tender and patient. When I told him the other day about my having engaged Headland—'to do all the personally bustling and fatiguing part of your work,' I said—he nodded his heavy head with great satisfaction, and faintly got out of himself the words, 'Of course I pay him, and not you.'" The poor fellow died in October; and on the day after attending the funeral, * 129 Dickens heard of the death of his brother-in-law and friend, Mr. Henry Austin, whose abilities and character he respected as much as he liked the man. He lost much in losing the judicious and safe counsel which had guided him on many public questions in which he took lively interest, and it was with a heavy heart he set out at last upon his second circuit. "With what difficulty I get myself back to the readings after all this loss and trouble, or with what unwillingness I work myself up to the mark of looking them in the face, I can hardly say. As for poor Arthur Smith at this time, it is as if my right arm were gone. It is only just now that I am able to open one of the books, and screw the text out of myself in a flat dull way. Enclosed is the list of what I have to do. You will see that I have left ten days in November for the Christmas number, and also a good

Christmas margin for our meeting at Gadshill. I shall be very glad to have the money that I expect to get; but it will be earned." That November interval was also the date of the marriage of his eldest son to the daughter of Mr. Evans, so long, in connection with Mr. Bradbury, his publisher and printer.

The start of the readings at Norwich was not good, so many changes of vexation having been incident to the opening announcements as to leave some doubt of their fulfilment. But the second night, when trial was made of the *Nickleby* scenes, "we had a splendid hall, and I think *Nickleby* will top all the readings. Somehow it seems to have got in it, by accident, exactly the qualities best suited to the purpose; and it went last night, not only with roars, but with a general hilarity and pleasure that I have never seen surpassed." From this night onward, the success was uninterrupted, and here was his report to me from Brighton on 8 November. "We turned away half Dover and half Hastings and half Colchester; and, if you can believe such a thing, I may tell you that in round numbers we find 1000 stalls already taken here in Brighton! I left Colchester in a heavy snowstorm. To-day it is so warm here that I can hardly bear the fire, and am writing with the window open down to the ground. Last night I had a most charming audience for *Copperfield*, with a delicacy of perception that really made the work delightful. It is very pretty to see the girls and women generally, in the matter of Dora; and everywhere I have found that peculiar personal relation between my audience and myself on which I counted most when I entered on this enterprise. *Nickleby* continues to go in the wildest manner."

A storm was at this time sweeping round the coast, and while at Dover he had written of it to his sister-in-law (7 November): "The bad weather has not in the least touched us, and the storm was most magnificent at Dover. All the great side of the Lord Warden next to the sea had to be emptied, the break of the waves was so prodigious, and the noise so utterly confounding. The sea came in like a great sky of immense clouds, for ever breaking suddenly into furious rain; all kinds of wreck were washed in, among other things a very pretty brass-bound chest being thrown about like a feather. . . . The unhappy Ostend packet, unable to get in or go back, beat about the Channel all Tuesday night, and until noon yesterday, when I saw her come in, with five men at the wheel, a picture of misery inconceivable. . . . The effect of the readings at Hastings and Dover really seems to have outdone the best usual impression; and at Dover they wouldn't go, but sat applauding like mad. The most delicate audience I have seen in any provincial place, is Canterbury" ("an intelligent and delightful response in them," he wrote to his daughter, "like the touch of a beautiful instrument"); "but the audience with the greatest sense of humour, certainly is Dover. The people in the stalls set the example of laughing, in the most curiously unreserved way; and they laughed with such really cordial enjoyment, when Squeers read the boys' letters, that the contagion extended to me. For, one couldn't hear them without laughing too. . . . So, I am thankful to say, all goes well, and the recompense for the trouble is in every way Great."

From the opposite quarter of Berwick-on-Tweed he wrote again in the midst of storm. But first his mention of Newcastle, which he had also taken on his way to Edinburgh, reading two nights there, should be given. "At Newcastle, against the very heavy expenses, I made more than a hundred guineas profit. A finer audience there is not in England, and I suppose them to be a specially earnest people; for, while they can laugh till they shake the roof, they have a very unusual sympathy with what is pathetic or passionate. An extraordinary thing occurred on the second night. The room was tremendously crowded and my gas-apparatus fell down. There was a terrible wave among the people for an instant, and God knows what destruction of life a rush to the stairs would have caused. Fortunately a lady in the front of the stalls ran out towards me, exactly in a place where I knew that the whole hall could see her. So I addressed her, laughing, and half-asked and half-ordered her to sit down again; and, in a moment, it was all over. But the men in attendance had such a fearful sense of what might have happened (besides the real danger of Fire) that they positively shook the boards I stood on, with their trembling, when they came up to put things right. I am proud to record that the gasman's sentiment, as delivered afterwards, was, 'The more you want of the master, the more you'll find in him.' With which complimentary homage, and with the wind blowing so that I can hardly hear myself write, I conclude."

* 131

It was still blowing, in shape of a gale from the sea, when, an hour before the reading, he wrote from the King's Arms at Berwick-on-Tweed. "As odd and out of the way a place to be at, it appears to me, as ever was seen! And such a ridiculous room designed for me to read in! An immense Corn Exchange, made of glass and iron, round, dome-topp'd, lofty, utterly absurd for any such purpose, and full of thundering echoes; with a little lofty crow's nest of a stone gallery, breast high, deep in the wall, into which it was designed to put——me! I instantly struck, of course; and said I would either read in a room attached to this house (a very snug one, capable of holding 500 people), or not at all. Terrified local agents glowered, but fell prostrate, and my men took the primitive accommodation in hand. Ever since, I am alarmed to add, the people (who besought the honour of the visit) have been coming in numbers quite irreconcilable with the appearance of the place, and what is to be the end I do not know. It was poor Arthur Smith's principle that a town on the way paid the expenses of a long through-journey, and therefore I came." The reading paid more than those expenses.

Enthusiastic greeting awaited him in Edinburgh. "We had in the hall exactly double what we had on the first night last time. The success of *Copperfield* was perfectly unexampled. Four great rounds of applause with a burst of cheering at the end, and every point taken in the finest manner." But this was nothing to what befell on the second night, when, by some mistake of the local agents, the tickets issued were out of proportion to the space available. Writing from Glasgow next day (3 December) he described the scene. "Such a pouring of hundreds into a place already full to the throat, such indescribable confusion, such a rending and tearing of dresses, and yet such a scene of good humour on the whole, I never saw the faintest approach to. While I addressed the crowd in the room G. addressed the crowd in the street. Fifty frantic men got up in all parts of the hall and addressed me all at once. Other frantic men made speeches to the walls. The whole B. family were borne in on the top of a wave, and landed with their faces against the front of the platform. I read with the platform crammed with people. I got them to lie down upon it, and it was like some impossible tableau or gigantic picnic—one pretty girl in full dress, lying on her side all night, holding on to one of the legs of my table! It was the most extraordinary sight. And yet, from the moment I began to the moment of my leaving off, they never missed a point, and they ended with a burst of cheers. . . . The expenditure of lungs and spirits was (as you may suppose) rather great; and to sleep well was out of the question. I am therefore rather fagged to-day; and as the hall in which I read to-night is a large one, I must make my letter a short one. . . . My people were torn to ribbons last night. They have not a hat among them—and scarcely a coat." He came home for his Christmas rest by way of Manchester, and thus spoke of the reading there on 14 December. "*Copperfield* in the Free Trade Hall last Saturday was really a grand scene."

He was in southern latitudes after Christmas, and on 8 January wrote from Torquay: "We are now in the region of small rooms, and therefore this trip will not be as profitable as the long one. I imagine the room here to be very small. Exeter I know, and that is small too. I am very much used up on the whole, for I cannot bear this moist warm climate. It would kill me very soon. And I have now got to the point of taking so much out of myself with *Copperfield* that I might as well do Richard Wardour. . . . This is a very pretty place—a compound of Hastings, Tunbridge Wells, and little bits of the hills about Naples; but I met four respirators as I came up from the station, and three pale curates without them who seemed in a bad way." They had been not bad omens, however. The success was good, at both Torquay and Exeter; and he closed the month and this series of the country readings, at the great towns of Liverpool and Chester. "The beautiful St. George's Hall crowded to excess last night" (28 January, 1862) "and numbers turned away. Brilliant to see when lighted up, and for a reading simply perfect. You remember that a Liverpool audience is usually dull; but they put me on my mettle last night, for I never saw such an audience—no, not even in Edinburgh! The agents (alone, and of course without any reference to ready money at the doors) had taken for the two readings two hundred pounds." But as the end approached the fatigues had told severely on him. He described himself sleeping horribly, and with head dazed and worn by gas and heat. Rest, before he could resume at the St. James's Hall in March, was become an absolute necessity.

Two brief extracts from letters of the dates respectively of 8 April and 28 June will sufficiently describe the London readings. "The money returns have been quite astounding. Think of £190 a night! The effect of *Copperfield* exceeds all the expectations which its success in the country led me to form. It seems to take people entirely by surprise. If this is not new to you, I have not a word of news. The rain that raineth every day seems to have washed news away or got it under water." That was in April. In June he wrote: "I finished

* 132

my readings on Friday night to an enormous hall—nearly £200. The success has been throughout complete. It seems almost suicidal to leave off with the town so full, but I don't like to depart from my public pledge. A man from Australia is in London ready to pay £10,000 for eight months there. If——" It was an If that troubled him for some time, and led to agitating discussion. The civil war having closed America, an increase made upon the just-named offer tempted him to Australia. He tried to familiarise himself with the fancy that he should thus also get new material for observation, and he went so far as to plan an Uncommercial Traveller Upside Down. It is however very doubtful if such a scheme would have been entertained for a moment, but for the unwonted difficulties of invention that were now found to beset a twenty-number story. Such a story had lately been in his mind, and he had just chosen the title for it (*Our Mutual Friend*); but still he halted and hesitated sorely. "If it was not" (he wrote on 5 October, 1862) "for the hope of a gain that would make me more independent of the worst, I could not look the travel and absence and exertion in the face. I know perfectly well beforehand how unspeakably wretched I should be. But these renewed and larger offers tempt me. I can force myself to go aboard a ship, and I can force myself to do at that reading-desk what I have done a hundred times; but whether, with all this unsettled fluctuating distress in my mind, I could force an original book out of it, is another question." On the 22nd, still striving hard to find reasons to cope with the all but irresistible arguments against any such adventure, which indeed, with everything that then surrounded him, would have been little short of madness, he thus stated his experience of his two circuits of public reading. "Remember that at home here, the thing has never missed fire, but invariably does more the second time than it did the first; and also that I have got so used to it, and have worked so hard at it, as to get out of it more than I ever thought was in it for that purpose. I think all the probabilities for such a country as Australia are immense." The terrible difficulty was that the home argument struck both ways. "If I were to go it would be a penance and a misery, and I dread the thought more than I can possibly express. The domestic life of the readings is all but intolerable to me when I am away for a few weeks at a time merely, and what would it be——" On the other hand it was also a thought of home, far beyond the mere personal loss or gain of it, that made him willing still to risk even so much misery and penance; and he had a fancy that it might be possible to take his eldest daughter with him. "It is useless and needless for me to say what the conflict in my own mind is. How painfully unwilling I am to go, and yet how painfully sensible that perhaps I ought to go —with all the hands upon my skirts that I cannot fail to feel and see there, whenever I look round. It is a struggle of no common sort, as you will suppose, you who know the circumstances of the struggler." It closed at once when he clearly saw that to take any of his family with him, and make satisfactory arrangement for the rest during such an absence, would be impossible. By this time also he began to find his way to the new story, and better hopes and spirits had returned.

In January 1863 he had taken his daughter and his sister-in-law to Paris, and he read twice at the Embassy in behalf of the British Charitable Fund, the success being such that he consented to read twice again. He passed his birthday of that year (the 7th of the following month) at Arras. "You will remember me to-day, I know. Thanks for it. An odd birthday, but I am as little out of heart as you would have me be— floored now and then, but coming up again at the call of Time. I wanted to see this town, birthplace of our amiable Sea Green" (Robespierre); "and I find a Grande Place so very remarkable and picturesque that it is astonishing how people miss it. Here too I found, in a by-country place just near, a Fair going on, with a Religious Richardson's in it—Théâtre Religieux—'donnant six fois par jour, l'histoire de la Croix en tableaux vivants, depuis la naissance de notre Seigneur jusqu'à son sépulture. Aussi l'immolation d'Isaac, par son père Abraham.' It was just before nightfall when I came upon it; and one of the three wise men was up to his eyes in lamp oil, hanging the moderators. A woman in blue and fleshings (whether an angel or Joseph's wife I don't know) was addressing the crowd through an enormous speaking-trumpet; and a very small boy with a property lamb (I leave you to judge who *he* was) was standing on his head on a barrel-organ." Returning to England by Boulogne in the same year, as he stepped into the Folkestone boat he encountered a friend, Mr. Charles Manby (in recording a trait of character so pleasing and honourable it is not necessary that I should suppress the name), also passing over to England. "Taking leave of Manby was a shabby man of whom I had some remembrance, but whom I could not get into his place in my mind. Noticing when we stood out of the harbour that he was on the brink of the pier, waving his hat in a desolate manner, I said to Manby, 'Surely I know that man.'—'I should think you did,' said he; 'Hudson!' He is living—just living—at Paris, and Manby had brought him on. He said to Manby at parting, 'I shall not have a good dinner again, till you come back.' I asked Manby why he stuck to him. He said, Because he (Hudson) had so many people in his power, and had held his peace, and because he (Manby) saw so many Notabilities grand with him now, who were always grovelling for 'shares' in the days of his grandeur."

Upon arrival in London the second series of the readings was brought to a close.

VII

THIRD SERIES OF READINGS
1864-7

THE sudden death of Thackeray on the Christmas eve of 1863 was a painful shock to Dickens. It would not become me to speak, when he has himself spoken, of his relations with so great a writer and so old a friend.   † 23

"I saw him first, nearly twenty-eight years ago, when he proposed to become the illustrator of my earliest book. I saw * 134 him last, shortly before Christmas, at the Athenæum Club, when he told me that he had been in bed three days . . . and that he had it in his mind to try a new remedy which he laughingly described. He was cheerful, and looked very bright. In the night of that day week, he died. The long interval between these two periods is marked in my remembrance of him by many occasions when he was extremely humorous, when he was irresistibly extravagant, when he was softened and serious, when he was charming with children. . . . No one can be surer than I, of the greatness and goodness of his heart. . . . In no place should I take it upon myself at this time to discourse of his books, of his refined knowledge of character, of his subtle acquaintance with the weaknesses of human nature, of his delightful playfulness as an essayist, of his quaint and touching ballads, of his mastery over the English language. . . . But before me lies all that he had written of his latest story . . . and the pain I have felt in perusing it has not been deeper than the conviction that he was in the healthiest vigour of his powers when he worked on this last labour. . . . The last words he corrected in print were 'And my heart throbbed with an exquisite bliss.' God grant that on that Christmas Eve when he laid his head back on his pillow and threw up his arms as he had been wont to do when very weary, some consciousness of duty done, and of Christian hope throughout life humbly cherished, may have caused his own heart so to throb, when he passed away to his Redeemer's rest. He was found peacefully lying as above described, composed, undisturbed, and to all appearance asleep." [1]

Other griefs were with Dickens at this time, and close upon them came the too certain evidence that his own health was yielding to the overstrain which had been placed upon it by the occurrences and anxieties of the few preceding years. His mother, whose infirm health had been tending for more than two years to the close, died in September 1863; and on his own birthday in the following February he had tidings of the death of his second son Walter, on the last day of the old year, in the officers' hospital at Calcutta; to which he had been sent up invalided from his station, on his way home. He was a lieutenant in the 26th Native Infantry regiment, and had been doing duty with the 42nd Highlanders. In 1853 his father had thus written to the youth's godfather, Walter Savage Landor: "Walter is a very good boy, and comes home from school with honourable commendation and a prize into the bargain. He never gets into trouble, for he is a great favourite with the whole house and one of the most amiable boys in the boy-world. He comes out on birthdays in a blaze of shirt pin." The pin was a present from Landor; to whom, three years later, when the boy had obtained his cadetship through the kindness of Miss Coutts, Dickens wrote again. "Walter has done extremely well at school; has brought home a prize in triumph; and will be eligible to 'go up' for his India examination soon after next Easter. Having a direct appointment he will probably be sent out soon after he has passed, and so will fall into that strange life 'up the country' before he well knows he is alive, or what life is—which indeed seems to be rather an advanced state of knowledge." If he had lived another month he would have reached his twenty-third year, and perhaps not then the advanced state of knowledge his father speaks of. But, never forfeiting his claim to those kindly paternal words, he had the goodness and simplicity of boyhood to the close.

Dickens had at this time begun his last story in twenty numbers, and my next chapter will show through what unwonted troubles, in this and the following year, he had to fight his way. What otherwise during its progress chiefly interested him, was the enterprise of Mr. Fechter at the Lyceum, of which he had become the lessee; and Dickens was moved to this quite as much by generous sympathy with the difficulties of such a position to an artist who was not an Englishman, as by

[1] From the *Cornhill Magazine* for February 1864.

genuine admiration of Mr. Fechter's acting. He became his
helper in disputes, adviser on literary points, referee in matters
of management; and for some years no face was more familiar
than the French comedian's at Gadshill or in the office of his
journal. But theatres and their affairs are things of a season,
and even Dickens's whim and humour will not revive for us
any interest in these. No bad example, however, of the difficulties in which a French actor may find himself with English
playwrights, will appear in a few amusing words from one of
his letters about a piece played at the Princess's before the
Lyceum management was taken in hand.

"I have been cautioning Fechter about the play whereof he
gave the plot and scenes to B.; and out of which I have struck
some enormities, my account of which will (I think) amuse you.
It has one of the best first acts I ever saw; but if he can do
much with the last two, not to say three, there are resources
in his art that *I* know nothing about. When I went over the
play this day week, he was at least 20 minutes, *in a boat, in
the last scene,* discussing with another gentleman (also in the
boat) whether he should kill him or not; after which the gentleman dived overboard and swam for it. Also, in the most important and dangerous parts of the play, there was a young
person of the name of Pickles who was constantly being mentioned by name, in conjunction with the powers of light or
darkness; as, 'Great Heaven! Pickles?'—'By Hell, 'tis Pickles!'
—'Pickles? a thousand Devils!'—'Distraction! Pickles?'"   * 134A

The old year ended and the new one opened sadly enough.
The death of Leech in November affected Dickens very much,
and a severe attack of illness in February put a broad mark
between his past life and what remained to him of the future.
The lameness now began in his left foot which never afterwards
wholly left him, which was attended by great suffering, and
which baffled experienced physicians. He had persisted in his
ordinary exercise during heavy snowstorms, and to the last
he had the fancy that the illness was merely local. But that
this was an error is now certain; and it is more than probable
that if the nervous danger and disturbance it implied had been
correctly appreciated at the time, its warning might have been
of priceless value to Dickens. Unhappily he never thought of
husbanding his strength except for the purpose of making fresh
demands upon it, and it was for this he took a brief holiday in
France during the summer. "Before I went away," he wrote to
his daughter, "I had certainly worked myself into a damaged

state. But the moment I got away, I began, thank God, to get well. I hope to profit by this experience, and to make future dashes from my desk before I want them." At his return he was in the terrible railway accident at Staplehurst, on a day which proved afterwards more fatal to him; and it was with shaken nerves but unsubdued energy he resumed the labour to be presently described. He was beset by nervous apprehensions which the accident had caused to himself, not lessened by his generous anxiety to assuage the severer sufferings inflicted by it on others; his foot also troubled him more or less throughout the autumn; and that he should nevertheless have determined, on the close of his book, to undertake a series of readings involving greater strain and fatigue than any hitherto, was a startling circumstance. He had perhaps become conscious, without owning it even to himself, that for exertion of this kind the time left him was short; but, whatever pressed him on, his task of the next three years, self-imposed, was to make the most money in the shortest time without any regard to the physical labour to be undergone. The very letter announcing his new engagement shows how entirely unfit he was to enter upon it.

"For some time," he wrote at the end of February 1866, "I have been very unwell. F. B. wrote me word that with such a pulse as I described, an examination of the heart was absolutely necessary. 'Want of muscular power in the heart,' B. said. 'Only remarkable irritability of the heart,' said Doctor Brinton of Brook Street, who had been called into consultation. I was not disconcerted; for I knew well beforehand that the effect could not possibly be without the one cause at the bottom of it, of some degeneration of some function of the heart. Of course I am not so foolish as to suppose that all my work can have been achieved without *some* penalty, and I have noticed for some time a decided change in my buoyancy and hopefulness —in other words, in my usual 'tone.' But tonics have already brought me round. So I have accepted an offer, from Chappells of Bond Street, of £50 a night for thirty nights to read 'in England, Ireland, Scotland, or Paris'; they undertaking all the business, paying all personal expenses, travelling and otherwise, of myself, John" (his office servant) "and my gasman; and making what they can of it. I begin, I believe, in Liverpool on the Thursday in Easter week, and then come to London. I am going to read at Cheltenham (on my own account) on the 23rd and 24th of this month, staying with Macready of course."

The arrangement of this series of readings differed from those of its predecessors in relieving Dickens from every anxiety except of the reading itself; but, by such rapid and repeated change of nights at distant places as kept him almost wholly in a railway carriage when not at the reading desk or in bed, it added enormously to the physical fatigue. He would read at St. James's Hall in London one night, and at Bradford the next. He would read in Edinburgh, go on to Glasgow and to Aberdeen, then come back to Glasgow, read again in Edinburgh, strike off to Manchester, come back to St. James's Hall once more, and begin the same round again. It was labour that must in time have broken down the strongest man, and what Dickens was when he assumed it we have seen.

He did not himself admit a shadow of misgiving. "As to the readings" (11 March), "all I have to do is, to take in my book and read, at the appointed place and hour, and come out again. All the business of every kind, is done by Chappells. They take John and my other man, merely for my convenience. I have no more to do with any detail whatever, than you have. They transact all the business at their own cost, and on their own responsibility. I think they are disposed to do it in a very good spirit, because, whereas the original proposition was for thirty readings 'in England, Ireland, Scotland, or Paris,' they wrote out their agreement 'in London, the Provinces, or elsewhere *as you and we may agree.*' For this they pay £1500 in three sums: £500 on beginning, £500 on the fifteenth reading, £500 at the close. Every charge of every kind, they pay besides. I rely for mere curiosity on *Doctor Marigold* (I am going to begin with him in Liverpool, and at St. James's Hall). I have got him up with immense pains, and should like to give you a notion what I am going to do with him."

The success everywhere went far beyond even the former successes. A single night at Manchester, when eight hundred stalls were let, two thousand five hundred and sixty-five people admitted, and the receipts amounted to more than three hundred pounds, was followed in nearly the same proportion by all the greater towns; and on 20 April the outlay for the entire venture was paid, leaving all that remained, to the middle of the month of June, sheer profit. "I came back last Sunday," he wrote on 30 May, "with my last country piece of work for this time done. Everywhere the success has been the same. St. James's Hall last night was quite a splendid spectacle. Two more Tuesdays there, and I shall retire into private life. I have only been able to get to Gadshill once since I left it, and that was the day before yesterday."

One memorable evening he had passed at my house in the interval, when he saw Mrs. Carlyle for the last time. Her sudden death followed shortly after, and near the close of April he had thus written to me from Liverpool. "It was a terrible shock to me, and poor dear Carlyle has been in my mind ever since. How often I have thought of the unfinished novel. No one now to finish it. None of the writing women come near her at all." This was an allusion to what had passed at their meeting. It was on 2 April, the day when Mr. Carlyle had delivered his inaugural address as Lord Rector of Edinburgh University, and a couple of ardent words from Professor Tyndall had told her of the triumph just before dinner. She came to us flourishing the telegram in her hand, and the radiance of her enjoyment of it was upon her all the night. Among other things she gave Dickens the subject for a novel, from what she had herself observed at the outside of a house in her street; of which the various incidents were drawn from the condition of its blinds and curtains, the costumes visible at its windows, the cabs at its door, its visitors admitted or rejected, its articles of furniture delivered or carried away; and the subtle serious humour of it all, the truth in trifling bits of character, and the gradual progress into a half-romantic interest, had enchanted the skilled novelist. She was well into the second volume of her small romance before she left, being as far as her observation then had taken her; but in a few days exciting incidents were expected, the denouement could not be far off, and Dickens was to have it when they met again. Yet it was to something far other than this amusing little fancy his thoughts had carried him, when he wrote of no one being capable to finish what she might have begun. In greater things this was still more true. None could doubt it who had come within the fascinating influence of that sweet and noble nature. With some of the highest gifts of intellect, and the charm of a most varied knowledge of books and things, there was something "beyond, beyond." No one who knew Mrs. Carlyle could replace her loss when she had passed away.

The same letter which told of his uninterrupted success to the last, told me also that he had a heavy cold upon him, and was "very tired and depressed." Some weeks before the first batch of readings closed, Messrs. Chappell had already tempted him with an offer for fifty more nights to begin at Christmas, for which he meant, as he then said, to ask them seventy pounds a night. "It would be unreasonable to ask anything now on the ground of the extent of the late success, but I am bound to look to myself for the future. The Chappells are speculators, though of the worthiest and most honourable kind. They make some bad speculations, and have made a very good one in this case, and will set this against those. I told them when we agreed: 'I offer these thirty readings to you at fifty pounds a night, because I know perfectly well beforehand that no one in your business has the least idea of their real worth, and I wish to prove it.' The sum taken is £4720." The result of the fresh negotiation, though not completed until the beginning of August, may be at once described. "Chappell instantly accepts my proposal of forty nights at sixty pounds a night, and every conceivable and inconceivable expense paid. To make an even sum, I have made it forty-two nights for £2500. So I shall now try to discover a Christmas number (he means the subject for one), and shall, please Heaven, be quit of the whole series of readings so as to get to work on a new story for our proposed new series of *All the Year Round* early in the spring. The readings begin probably with the New Year." These were fair designs, but the fairest are the sport of circumstance, and though the subject for Christmas was found, the new series of *All the Year Round* never had a new story from its founder. With whatever consequence to himself the strong tide of the readings was to sweep on to its full. The American war had ceased, and the first renewed offers from the States had been made and rejected. Hovering over all, too, were other sterner dispositions. "I think," he wrote in September, "there is some strange influence in the atmosphere. Twice last week I was seized in a most distressing manner—apparently in the heart; but, I am persuaded, only in the nervous system."

In the midst of his ovations such checks had not been wanting. "The police reported officially," he wrote to his daughter from Liverpool on 14 April, "that three thousand people were turned away from the hall last night. . . . Except that I can *not* sleep, I really think myself in very much better training than I had anticipated. A dozen oysters and a little champagne between the parts every night, seem to constitute the best restorative I have ever yet tried." "Such a prodigious demonstration last night at Manchester," he wrote to the same correspondent twelve days later, "that I was obliged (contrary to my principle in such cases) to go back. I am very tired to-day;

for it would be of itself very hard work in that immense place, if there were not to be added eighty miles of railway and late hours to boot." "It has been very heavy work," he wrote to his sister-in-law on 11 May from Clifton, "getting up at 6.30 each morning after a heavy night, and I am not at all well to-day. We had a tremendous hall at Birmingham last night, £230 odd, 2,100 people; and I made a most ridiculous mistake. Had *Nickleby* on my list to finish with, instead of *Trial*. Read *Nickleby* with great go, *and the people remained*. Went back again at 10 o'clock, and explained the accident: but said if they liked I would give them the *Trial*. They *did* like;—and I had another half-hour of it, in that enormous place. . . . I have so severe a pain in the ball of my left eye that it makes it hard for me to do anything after 100 miles' shaking since breakfast. My cold is no better, nor my hand either." It was his left eye, it will be noted, as it was his left foot and hand; the irritability or faintness of heart was also of course on the left side; and it was on the same left side he felt most of the effect of the railway accident.

Everything was done to make easier the labour of travel, but nothing could materially abate either the absolute physical exhaustion, or the nervous strain. "We arrived here," he wrote from Aberdeen (16 May), "safe and sound between 3 and 4 this morning. There was a compartment for the men, and a charming room for ourselves furnished with sofas and easy chairs. We had also a pantry and washing-stand. This carriage is to go about with us." Two days later he wrote from Glasgow. "We halted at Perth yesterday, and got a lovely walk there. Until then I had been in a condition the reverse of flourishing; half strangled with my cold, and dyspeptically gloomy and dull; but, as I feel much more like myself this morning, we are going to get some fresh air aboard a steamer on the Clyde." The last letter during his country travel was from Portsmouth on 24 May, and contained these words: "You need have no fear about America." The readings closed in June.

The readings of the new year began with even increased enthusiasm, but not otherwise with happier omen. Here was his first outline of plan: "I start on Wednesday afternoon (15th of January) for Liverpool, and then go on to Chester, Derby, Leicester and Wolverhampton. On Tuesday the 29th I read in London again, and in February I read at Manchester and then go on into Scotland." From Liverpool he wrote on the 21st: "The enthusiasm has been unbounded. On Friday night I quite astonished myself; but I was taken so faint afterwards that they laid me on a sofa at the hall for half an hour. I attribute it to my distressing inability to sleep at night, and to nothing worse. Everything is made as easy to me as it possibly can be. Dolby would do anything to lighten the work, and *does* everything." The weather was sorely against him. "At Chester," he wrote on the 24th from Birmingham, "we read in a snowstorm and a fall of ice. I think it was the worst weather I ever saw. . . . At Wolverhampton last night the thaw had thoroughly set in, and it rained furiously, and I was again heavily beaten. We came on here after the reading (it is only a ride of forty miles), and it was as much as I could do to hold out the journey. But I was not faint, as at Liverpool. I was only exhausted." Five days later he had returned for his reading in London, and thus replied to a summons to dine with Macready at my house: "I am very tired; cannot sleep; have been severely shaken on an atrocious railway; read to-night and have to read at Leeds on Thursday. But I have settled with Dolby to put off our going to Leeds on Wednesday, in the hope of coming to dine with you, and seeing our dear old friend. I say, 'in the hope,' because if I should be a little more used up to-morrow than I am to-day, I should be constrained, in spite of myself, to take to the sofa and stick there."

On 15 February he wrote to his sister-in-law from Liverpool that they had had "an enormous turn-away" the previous night. "The day has been very fine, and I have turned it to the wholesomest account by walking on the sands at New Brighton all the morning. I am not quite right within, but believe it to be an effect of the railway shaking. There is no doubt of the fact that, after the Staplehurst experience, it tells more and more (railway shaking, that is) instead of, as one might have expected, less and less." The last remark is a strange one, from a man of his sagacity; but it was part of the too-willing self-deception which he practised, to justify him in his professed belief that these continued excesses of labour and excitement were really doing him no harm. The day after that last letter he pushed on to Scotland, and on the 17th wrote to his daughter from Glasgow. The closing night at Manchester had been enormous. "They cheered to that extent after it was over that I was obliged to huddle on my clothes (for I was undressing to prepare for the journey) and go back again. After so heavy a week, it *was* rather stiff to start on this long journey at a quarter to two in the morning; but I got more sleep than I ever got in a railway carriage before. . . . I have, as I had in the last series of readings, a curious feeling of soreness all round the body—which I suppose to arise from the great exertion of voice. . . ." Two days later he wrote to his sister-in-law from the Bridge of Allan, which he had reached from Glasgow that morning. "Yesterday I was so unwell with an internal malady that occasionally at long intervals troubles me a little, and it was attended with the sudden loss of so much blood, that I wrote to F. B. from whom I shall doubtless hear to-morrow. . . . I felt it a little more exertion to read, afterwards, and I passed a sleepless night after that again; but otherwise I am in good force and spirits to-day: I may say, in the best force. . . . The quiet of this little place is sure to do me good." He rallied again from this attack, and though he still complained of sleeplessness, wrote cheerfully from Glasgow on the 21st, describing himself indeed as confined to his room, but only because "in close hiding from a local poet who has christened his infant son in my name, and consequently haunts the building." On getting back to Edinburgh he wrote to me, with intimation that many troubles had beset him; but that the pleasure of his audiences, and the providence and forethought of Messrs. Chappell, had borne him through. "Everything is done for me with the utmost liberality and consideration. Every want I can have on these journeys is anticipated, and not the faintest spark of the tradesman spirit ever peeps out. I have three men in constant attendance on me; besides Dolby, who is an agreeable companion, an excellent manager, and a good fellow."

On 4 March he wrote from Newcastle: "The readings have made an immense effect in this place, and it is remarkable that although the people are individually rough, collectively they are an unusually tender and sympathetic audience; while their comic perception is quite up to the high London standard. The atmosphere is so very heavy that yesterday we escaped to Tynemouth for a two hours' sea walk. There was a high north wind blowing, and a magnificent sea running. Large vessels were being towed in and out over the stormy bar, with prodigious waves breaking on it; and, spanning the restless uproar of the waters, was a quiet rainbow of transcendent beauty. The scene was quite wonderful. We were in the full enjoyment of it when a heavy sea caught us, knocked us over, and in a moment drenched us and filled even our pockets. We had nothing for it but to shake ourselves together (like Doctor Marigold), and dry ourselves as well as we could by hard walking in the wind and sunshine. But we were wet through for all that, when we came back here to dinner after half an hour's railway drive. I am wonderfully well, and quite fresh and strong." Three days later he was at Leeds; from which he was to work himself round through the most important neighbouring places to another reading in London, before again visiting Ireland.

This was the time of the Fenian excitements; it was with great reluctance he consented to go; and he told us all at his first arrival that he should have a complete breakdown. More than 300 stalls were gone at Belfast two days before the reading, but on the afternoon of the reading in Dublin not fifty were taken. Strange to say however a great crowd pressed in at night, he had a tumultuous greeting, and on 22 March I had this announcement from him: "You will be surprised to be told that we have done WONDERS! Enthusiastic crowds have filled the halls to the roof each night, and hundreds have been turned away. At Belfast the night before last we had £246 5s. In Dublin to-night everything is sold out, and people are besieging Dolby to put chairs anywhere, in doorways, on my platform, in any sort of hole or corner. In short the readings are a perfect rage at a time when everything else is beaten down." He took the Eastern Counties at his return, and this brought the series to a close. "The reception at Cambridge was something to be proud of in such a place. The colleges mustered in full force, from the biggest guns to the smallest; and went beyond even Manchester in the roars of welcome and rounds of cheers. The place was crammed, and all through the reading everything was taken with the utmost heartiness of enjoyment." The temptation of offers from America had meanwhile again been presented to him so strongly, and in such unlucky connection with immediate family claims threatening excess of expenditure even beyond the income he was making, that he was fain to write to his sister-in-law: "I begin to feel myself drawn towards America as Darnay in the *Tale of Two Cities* was attracted to Paris. It is my Loadstone Rock." Too surely it was to be so; and Dickens was not to be saved from the consequence of yielding to the temptation, by any such sacrifice as had rescued Darnay.

The letter which told me of the close of his English readings had in it no word of the further enterprise, yet it seemed to be in some sort a preparation for it. "Last Monday evening" (14 May) "I finished the 50 readings with great success. You have no idea how I have worked at them. Finding it necessary,

* 136

as their reputation widened, that they should be better than at first, I have *learnt them all*, so as to have no mechanical drawback in looking after the words. I have tested all the serious passion in them by everything I know; made the humorous points much more humorous; corrected my utterance of certain words; cultivated a self-possession not to be disturbed; and made myself master of the situation. Finishing with *Dombey* (which I had not read for a long time), I learnt that, like the rest; and did it to myself, often twice a day, with exactly the same pains as at night, over and over and over again. . . ."
Six days later brought his reply to a remark, that no degree of excellence to which he might have brought his readings could reconcile me to what there was little doubt would soon be pressed upon him. "It is curious" (20 May) "that you should touch the American subject, because I must confess that my mind is in a most disturbed state about it. That the people there have set themselves on having the readings, there is no question. Every mail brings me proposals, and the number of Americans at St. James's Hall has been surprising. A certain Mr. Grau, who took Ristori out, and is highly responsible, wrote to me by the last mail (for the second time) saying that if I would give him a word of encouragement he would come over immediately and arrange on the boldest terms for any number I chose, and would deposit a large sum of money at Coutts's. Mr. Fields writes to me on behalf of a committee of private gentlemen at Boston who wished for the credit of getting me out, who desired to hear the readings and did not want profit, and would put down as a guarantee £10,000— also to be banked here. Every American speculator who comes to London repairs straight to Dolby, with similar proposals. And, thus excited, Chappells, the moment this last series was over, proposed to treat for America!" Upon the mere question of these various offers he had little difficulty in making up his mind. If he went at all, he would go on his own account, making no compact with anyone. Whether he should go at all, was what he had to determine.

One thing with his usual sagacity he saw clearly enough. He must make up his mind quickly. "The Presidential election would be in the autumn of next year. They are a people whom a fancy does not hold long. They are bent upon my reading there, and they believe (on no foundation whatever) that I am going to read there. If I ever go, the time would be when the Christmas number goes to press. Early in this next November."

Every sort of inquiry he accordingly set on foot; and so far came to the immediate decision, that, if the answers left him no room to doubt that a certain sum might be realised, he would go. "Have no fear that anything will induce me to make the experiment, if I do not see the most forcible reasons for believing that what I could get by it, added to what I have got, would leave me with a sufficient fortune. I should be wretched beyond expression there. My small powers of description cannot describe the state of mind in which I should drag on from day to day." At the end of May he wrote: "Poor dear Stanfield!" (our excellent friend had passed away the week before). "I cannot think even of him, and of our great loss, for this spectre of doubt and indecision that sits at the board with me and stands at the bedside. I am in a tempest-tossed condition, and can hardly believe that I stand at bay at last on the American question. The difficulty of determining amid the variety of statements made to me is enormous, and you have no idea how heavily the anxiety of it sits upon my soul. But the prize looks so large!" One way at last seemed to open by which it was possible to get at some settled opinion. "Dolby sails for America" (2 July) "on Saturday the 3rd of August. It is impossible to come to any reasonable conclusion, without sending eyes and ears on the actual ground. He will take out my MS. for the *Children's Magazine*. I hope it is droll, and very child-like; though the joke is a grown-up one besides. You must try to like the pirate story, for I am very fond of it." The allusion is to his pleasant *Holiday Romance* which he had written for Mr. Fields.

Hardly had Mr. Dolby gone when there came that which should have availed to dissuade, far more than any of the arguments which continued to express my objection to the enterprise. "I am laid up," he wrote on 6 August, "with another attack in my foot, and was on the sofa all last night in tortures. I cannot bear to have the fomentations taken off for a moment. I was so ill with it on Sunday, and it looked so fierce, that I came up to Henry Thompson. He has gone into the case heartily, and says that there is no doubt the complaint originates in the action of the shoe, in walking, on an enlargement in the nature of a bunion. Erysipelas has supervened upon the injury; and the object is to avoid a gathering, and to stay the erysipelas where it is. Meantime I am on my back and chafing. . . . I didn't improve my foot by going down to Liverpool to see Dolby off, but I have little doubt of its yielding to treatment, and repose." A few days later he was chafing still; the accomplished surgeon he consulted having dropped other hints that somewhat troubled him. "I could not walk a quarter of a mile to-night for £500. I make out so many reasons against supposing it to be gouty that I really do not think it is."

So momentous in my judgment were the consequences of the American journey to him that it seemed right to preface thus much of the inducements and temptations that led to it. My own part in the discussion was that of steady dissuasion throughout: though this might perhaps have been less persistent if I could have reconciled myself to the belief, which I never at any time did, that public readings were a worthy employment for a man of his genius. But it had by this time become clear to me that nothing could stay the enterprise. The result of Mr. Dolby's visit to America—drawn up by Dickens himself in a paper possessing still the interest of having given to the readings when he crossed the Atlantic much of the form they then 136A assumed   reached me when I was staying at Ross; and upon it was founded my last argument against the scheme. This he received in London on 28 September, on which day he thus wrote to his eldest daughter: "As I telegraphed after I saw you, I am off to Ross to consult with Mr. Forster and Dolby together. You shall hear, either on Monday, or by Monday's post from London, how I decide finally." The result he wrote to her three days later: "You will have had my telegram that I go to America. After a long discussion with Forster, and consideration of what is to be said on both sides, I have decided to go through with it. We have telegraphed 'Yes' to Boston." Seven days later he wrote to me: "The *Scotia* being full, I do not sail until Lord Mayor's Day; for which glorious anniversary I have engaged an officer's cabin on deck in the *Cuba*. I am not in very brilliant spirits at the prospect before me, and am deeply sensible of your motive and reasons for the line you have taken; but I am not in the least shaken in the conviction that I could never quite have given up the idea."

The remaining time was given to preparations; on 2 November there was a Farewell Banquet in the Freemasons' Hall over which Lord Lytton presided; and on the 9th Dickens sailed for Boston. Before he left he had contributed his part to the last of his Christmas Numbers; all the writings he was able to complete were done; and the interval of his voyage may be occupied by a general review of the literary labour of his life.

BOOK NINTH

AUTHOR

1836–70. ÆT. 24–58

DICKENS AS A NOVELIST

1836–70

WHAT I have to say generally of Dickens's genius as a writer may introduce the notices, which still remain to be given, of his books from the *Tale of Two Cities* to the time at which we have arrived, leaving *Edwin Drood* for mention in its place; and these will be accompanied, as in former notices of individual stories, by illustrations drawn from his letters and life. His literary work was so intensely one with his nature that he is not separable from it, and the man and the method throw a singular light on each other. But some allusion to what has been said of these books, by writers assuming to speak with authority, will properly precede what has to be offered by me; and I shall preface this part of my task with the hint of Carlyle, that in looking at a man out of the common it is good for common men to make sure that they "see" before they attempt to "oversee" him.

Of the French writer, M. Henri Taine, it has before been remarked that his inability to appreciate humour is fatal to his pretensions as a critic of the English novel. But there is much that is noteworthy in his criticism notwithstanding, as well as remarkable in his knowledge of our language; his position entitles him to be heard without a suspicion of partisanship or intentional unfairness; whatever the value of his opinion, the elaboration of its form and expression is itself no common tribute; and what is said in it of Dickens's handling in regard to style and character, embodies temperately objections which have since been taken by some English critics without his impartiality and with less than his ability. As to style M. Taine does not find that the natural or simple prevails sufficiently. The tone is too passionate. The imaginative or poetic side of allusion is so uniformly dwelt on, that the descriptions cease to be subsidiary, and the minute details of pain or pleasure wrought out by them become active agencies in the tale. So vivid and eager is the display of fancy that everything is borne along with it; imaginary objects take the precision of real ones; living thoughts are controlled by inanimate things; the chimes console the poor old ticket-porter; the cricket steadies the rough carrier's doubts; the sea waves soothe the dying boy; clouds, flowers, leaves, play their several parts; hardly a form of matter without a living quality; no silent thing without its voice. Fondling and exaggerating thus what is occasional in the subject of his criticism, into what he has evidently at last persuaded himself is a fixed and universal practice with Dickens, M. Taine proceeds to explain the exuberance by comparing such imagination in its vividness to that of a monomaniac. He fails altogether to apprehend that property in Humour which involves the feeling of the subtlest and most effective analogies, and from which is drawn the rare insight into sympathies between the nature of things and their attributes or opposites, in which Dickens's fancy revelled with such delight. Taking the famous lines which express the lunatic, the lover, and the poet as "of Imagination all compact," in a sense that would have startled not a little the great poet who wrote them, M. Taine places on the same level of creative fancy the phantoms of the lunatic and the personages of the artist. He exhibits Dickens as from time to time, in the several stages of his successive works of fiction, given up to one idea, possessed by it, seeing nothing else, treating it in a hundred forms, exaggerating it, and so dazzling and overpowering his readers with it that escape is impossible. This he maintains to be equally the effect as Mr. Mell the usher plays the flute, as Tom Pinch enjoys or exposes his Pecksniff, as the guard blows his bugle while Tom rides to London, as Ruth Pinch crosses Fountain Court or makes the beefsteak pudding, as Jonas Chuzzlewit commits and returns from the murder, and as the storm which is Steerforth's death-knell beats on the Yarmouth shore. To the same kind of power he attributes the extraordinary clearness with which the commonest objects in all his books, the most ordinary interiors, any old house, a parlour, a boat, a school, fifty things that in the ordinary tale-teller would pass unmarked, are made vividly present and indelible; are brought out with a strength of relief, precision, and force, unapproached in any other writer of prose fiction; with everything minute yet nothing cold, "with all the passion and the patience of the painters of his country." And while excitement in the reader is thus maintained to an extent incompatible with a natural style or simple narrative, M. Taine yet thinks he has discovered, in this very power of awakening a feverish sensibility and moving laughter or tears at the commonest things, the source of Dickens's astonishing popularity. Ordinary people, he says, are so tired of what is always around them, and take in so little of the detail that makes up their lives, that when, all of a sudden, there comes a man to make these things interesting, and turn them into objects of admiration, tenderness, or terror, the effect is enchantment. Without leaving their arm-chairs or their firesides, they find themselves trembling with emotion, their eyes are filled with tears, their cheeks are broad with laughter, and, in the discovery they have thus made that they too can suffer, love, and feel, their very existence seems doubled to them. It had not occurred to M. Taine that to effect so much might seem to leave little not achieved.

So far from it, the critic had satisfied himself that such a power of style must be adverse to a just delineation of character. Dickens is not calm enough, he says, to penetrate to the bottom of what he is dealing with. He takes sides with it as friend or enemy, laughs or cries over it, makes it odious or touching, repulsive or attractive, and is too vehement and not enough inquisitive to paint a likeness. His imagination is at once too vivid and not sufficiently large. Its tenacious quality, and the force and concentration with which his thoughts penetrate into the details he desires to apprehend, form limits to his knowledge, confine him to single traits, and prevent his sounding all the depths of a soul. He seizes on one attitude, trick, expression, or grimace; sees nothing else; and keeps it always unchanged. Mercy Pecksniff laughs at every word, Mark Tapley is nothing but jolly, Mrs. Gamp talks incessantly of Mrs. Harris, Mr. Chillip is invariably timid, and Mr. Micawber is never tired of emphasising his phrases or passing with ludicrous brusqueness from joy to grief. Each is the incarnation of some one vice, virtue, or absurdity; whereof the display is frequent, invariable, and exclusive. The language I am using condenses with strict accuracy what is said by M. Taine, and has been repeated *ad nauseam* by others, professing admirers as well as open detractors. Mrs. Gamp and Mr. Micawber, who belong to the first rank of humorous creation, are thus without another word dismissed by the French critic; and he shows no consciousness whatever in doing it, of that very fault in himself for which Dickens is condemned, of mistaking lively observation for real insight.

He has however much concession in reserve, being satisfied, by his observation of England, that it is to the people for whom Dickens wrote his deficiencies in art are mainly due. The taste of his nation had prohibited him from representing character in a grand style. The English require too much morality and religion for genuine art. They made him treat love, not as holy and sublime in itself, but as subordinate to marriage; forced him to uphold society and the laws, against nature and enthusiasm; and compelled him to display, in painting such a seduction as in *Copperfield*, not the progress, ardour, and intoxication of passion, but only the misery, remorse, and despair. The result of such surface religion and morality, combined with the trading spirit, M. Taine continues, leads to so many national forms of hypocrisy, and of greed as well as worship for money, as to justify this great writer of the nation in his frequent choice of those vices for illustration in his tales. But his defect of method again comes into play. He does not deal with vices in the manner of a physiologist, feeling a sort of love for them, and delighting in their finer traits as if they were virtues. He gets angry over them. (I do not interrupt M. Taine, but surely, to take one instance illustrative of many, Dickens's enjoyment in dealing with Pecksniff is as manifest as that he never ceases all the time to make him very hateful.) He cannot, like Balzac, leave morality out of account, and treat a passion, however loathsome, as that great tale-teller did, from the only safe ground of belief, that it is a force, and that force of whatever kind is good. It is essential to an artist of that superior grade, M. Taine holds, no matter how vile his subject, to show its education and temptations, the form of brain or habits of mind that have reinforced the natural tendency, to deduce it from its cause, to place its circumstances around it, and to develop its effects to their extremes. In handling such and such a capital miser, hypocrite, debauchee, or what not, he should never trouble himself about the evil consequences of the vices. He should be too much of a philosopher and artist to remember that he is a respectable citizen. But this is what Dickens never forgets, and he renounces all beauties requiring so corrupt a soil. M. Taine's conclusion upon the whole nevertheless is, that though those triumphs of art which become the property of all the earth have not been his, much has yet been achieved by him. Out of his unequalled observation, his satire, and his sensibility, has proceeded a series of original characters existing nowhere but in England, which will exhibit to future generations not the record of his own genius only, but that of his country and his times.

Between the judgment thus passed by the distinguished French lecturer, and the later comment to be now given from an English critic, certainly not in arrest of that judgment, may fitly come a passage from one of Dickens's letters saying something of the limitations placed upon the artist in England. It may read like a quasi-confession of one of M. Taine's charges, though it was not written with reference to his own but to one of Scott's later novels. "Similarly" (15 August, 1856) "I have always a fine feeling of the honest state into which we have got, when some smooth gentleman says to me or to someone else when I am by, how odd it is that the hero of an English book is always uninteresting—too good—not natural, etc. I am continually hearing this of Scott from English people here, who pass their lives with Balzac and Sand. But O my smooth friend, what a shining impostor you must think yourself and what an ass you must think me, when you suppose that by putting a brazen face upon it you can blot out of my knowledge the fact that this same unnatural young gentleman (if to be decent is to be necessarily unnatural), whom you meet in those other books and in mine, *must* be presented to you in that unnatural aspect by reason of your morality, and is not to have, I will not say any of the indecencies you like, but not even any of the experiences, trials, perplexities, and confusions inseparable from the making or unmaking of all men!"

M. Taine's criticism was written three or four years before Dickens's death, and to the same date belong some notices in England which adopted more or less the tone of depreciation; conceding the great effects achieved by the writer, but disputing the quality and value of his art. For it is incident to all such criticism of Dickens to be of necessity accompanied by the admission, that no writer has so completely impressed himself on the time in which he lived, that he has made his characters a part of literature, and that his readers are the world.

But, a little more than a year after his death, a paper was published of which the object was to reconcile such seeming inconsistency, to expound the inner meanings of "Dickens in relation to Criticism," and to show that, though he had a splendid genius and a wonderful imagination, yet the objectors were to be excused who called him only a stagy sentimentalist and a clever caricaturist. This critical essay appeared in the *Fortnightly Review* for February 1872, with the signature of Mr. George Henry Lewes; and the pretentious airs of the performance, with its prodigious professions of candour, force upon me the painful task of stating what it really is. During Dickens's life, especially when any fresh novelist could be found available for strained comparison with him, there were plenty of attempts to write him down: but the trick of studied depreciation was never carried so far or made so odious as in this case, by intolerable assumptions of an indulgent superiority; and to repel it in such a form once for all is due to Dickens's memory.

The paper begins by the usual concessions—that he was a writer of vast popularity, that he delighted no end of people, that his admirers were in all classes and all countries, that he stirred the sympathy of masses not easily reached through literature and always to healthy emotion, that he impressed a new direction on popular writing, and modified the literature of his age in its spirit no less than its form. The very splendour of these successes, on the other hand, so deepened the shadow of his failures, that to many there was nothing but darkness. Was it unnatural? Could greatness be properly ascribed, by the fastidious, to a writer whose defects were so glaring, exaggerated, untrue, fantastic, and melodramatic? Might they not fairly insist on such defects as outweighing all positive qualities, and speak of him with condescending patronage or sneering irritation? Why, very often such men, though their talk would be seasoned with quotations from, and allusions to, his writings, and though they would lay aside their most favourite books to bury themselves in his new "number," had been observed by this critic to be as niggardly in their praise of him as they were lavish in their scorn. He actually heard "*a very distinguished man*," on one occasion, express measureless contempt for Dickens, and a few minutes afterwards admit that Dickens had "entered into his life." And so the critic betook himself to the task of reconciling this immense popularity and this critical contempt, which he does after the following manner.

He says that Dickens was so great in "fun" (humour he does not concede to him anywhere) that Fielding and Smollett are small in comparison, but that this would only have been a passing amusement for the world if he had not been "gifted with an imagination of marvellous vividness, and an emotional sympathetic nature capable of furnishing that imagination with elements of universal power." To people who think that words should carry some meaning it might seem, that, if only a man could be "gifted" with all this, nothing more need be said. With marvellous imagination, and a nature to endow it with elements of universal power, what secrets of creative art could possibly be closed to him? But this is a reckoning without your philosophical critic. The vividness of Dickens's imagination M. Taine found to be simply monomaniacal, and his follower finds it to be merely hallucinative. Not the less he heaps upon it epithet after epithet. He talks of its irradiating splendour; calls it glorious as well as imperial and marvellous; and, to make us quite sure he is not with these fine phrases puffing-off an inferior article, he interposes that such imagination is "common to all great writers." Luckily for great writers in general, however, their creations are of the old, immortal, commonplace sort; whereas Dickens in his creative processes, according to this philosophy of criticism, is tied up hard and fast within hallucinative limits.

"He was," we are told, "a seer of visions." Amid silence and darkness, we are assured, he heard voices and saw objects; of which the revived impressions to him had the vividness of sensations, and the images his mind created in explanation of them had the coercive force of realities; so that what he brought into existence in this way, no matter how fantastic and unreal, was (whatever this may mean) universally intelligible. "His types established themselves in the public mind like personal experiences. Their falsity was unnoticed in the blaze of their illumination. Every humbug seemed a Pecksniff, every jovial improvident a Micawber, every stinted serving-wench a Marchioness." The critic, indeed, saw through it all, but he gave his warnings in vain. "In vain critical reflection showed these figures to be merely masks; not characters, but personified characteristics; caricatures and distortions of human nature. The vividness of their presentation triumphed over reflection; their creator managed to communicate to the public his own unhesitating belief." What, however, is the public? Mr. Lewes goes on to relate. "Give a child a wooden horse, with hair for mane and tail, and wafer-spots for colouring, he will never be disturbed by the fact that this horse does not move its legs but runs on wheels; and this wooden horse, which he can handle and draw, is believed in more than a pictured horse by a Wouvermanns or an Ansdell (!!). It may be said of Dickens's human figures that they too are wooden, and run on wheels; but these are details which scarcely disturb the belief of admirers. Just as the wooden horse is brought within the range of the child's emotions, and dramatising tendencies, when he can handle and draw it, so Dickens's figures are brought within the range of the reader's interests, and receive from these interests a sudden illumination, when they are the puppets of a drama every incident of whieh appeals to the sympathies."

Risum teneatis ? But the smile is grim that rises to the face of one to whom the relations of the writer and his critic, while both writer and critic lived, are known; and who sees the drift of now scattering such rubbish as this over an established fame. As it fares with the imagination that is imperial, so with the drama every incident of which appeals to the sympathies. The one being explained by hallucination, and the other by the wooden horse, plenty of fine words are to spare by which contempt may receive the show of candour. When the characters in a play are puppets, and the audiences of the theatre fools or children, no wise man forfeits his wisdom by proceeding to admit that the successful playwright, "with a fine felicity of instinct," seized upon situations, for his wooden figures, having "irresistible hold over the domestic affections"; that, through his puppets, he spoke "in the mother-tongue of the heart"; that, with his spotted horses and so forth, he "painted the life he knew and everyone knew"; that he painted, of course, nothing ideal or heroic, and that the world of thought and passion lay beyond his horizon; but that, with his artificial performers and his feeble-witted audiences, "all the resources of the bourgeois epic were in his grasp; the joys and pains of childhood, the petty tyrannies of ignoble natures, the genial pleasantries of happy natures, the life of the poor, the struggles of the street and back parlour, the insolence of office, the sharp social contrasts, east wind and Christmas jollity, hunger, misery, and hot punch"—"so that even critical spectators who complained that these broadly painted pictures were artistic daubs could not wholly resist their effective suggestiveness." Since Trinculo and Caliban were under one cloak, there has surely been no such delicate monster with two voices. "His forward voice, now, is to speak well of his friend; his backward voice is to utter foul speeches and to detract." One other of the foul speeches I may not overlook, since it contains what is alleged to be a personal revelation of Dickens made to the critic himself.

"When one thinks of Micawber always presenting himself in the same situation, moved with the same springs and uttering the same sounds, always confident of something turning up, always crushed and rebounding, always making punch—and his wife always declaring she will never part from him, always referring to his talents and her family—when one thinks of the 'catchwords' personified as characters, one is reminded of the frogs whose brains have been taken out for physiological purposes, and whose actions henceforth want the distinctive peculiarity of organic action, that of fluctuating spontaneity." Such was that sheer inability of Dickens, indeed, to comprehend this complexity of the organism, that it quite accounted, in the view of this philosopher, for all his unnaturalness, for the whole of his fantastic people, and for the strained dialogues of which his books are made up, painfully resembling in their incongruity "the absurd and eager expositions which insane patients pour into the listener's ear when detailing their wrongs, or their schemes. Dickens once declared to me," Mr. Lewes continues, "that every word said by his characters was distinctly *heard* by him; I was at first not a little puzzled to account for the fact that he could hear language so utterly unlike the language of real feeling, and not be aware of its preposterousness; but the surprise vanished when I thought of the phenomena of hallucination." Wonderful sagacity! to unravel easily such a bewildering "puzzle"! And so to the close. Between the uncultivated whom Dickens moved, and the cultivated he failed to move; between the power that so worked in delf as to stir the universal heart, and the commonness that could not meddle with porcelain or aspire to any noble clay; the pitiful see-saw is continued up to the final sentence, where, in the impartial critic's eagerness to discredit even the value of the emotion awakened in such men as Jeffrey by such creations as Little Nell, he reverses all he has been saying about the cultivated and uncultivated, and presents to us a cultivated philosopher, in his ignorance of the stage, applauding an actor whom every uncultivated playgoing apprentice despises as stagey. But the bold stroke just exhibited, of bringing forward Dickens himself in the actual crisis of one of his fits of hallucination, requires an additional word.

To establish the hallucinative theory, he is said on one occasion to have declared to the critic that every word uttered by his characters was distinctly *heard* by him before it was written down. Such an averment, not credible for a moment as thus made, indeed simply not true to the extent described, may yet be accepted in the limited and quite different sense which a passage in one of Dickens's letters gives to it. All writers of genius to whom their art has become as a second nature, will be found capable of doing upon occasion what the vulgar may think to be "hallucination," but hallucination will never account for. After Scott began the *Bride of Lammermoor* he had one of his terrible seizures of cramp, yet during his torment he dictated that fine novel; and when he rose from his bed, and the published book was placed in his hands, "he did not," James Ballantyne explicitly assured Lockhart, "recollect one single incident, character, or conversation it contained." When Dickens was under the greatest trial of his life, and illness and sorrow were contending for the mastery over him, he thus wrote to me: "Of my distress I will say no more than that it has borne a terrible, frightful, horrible proportion to the quickness of the gifts you remind me of. But may I not be forgiven for thinking it a wonderful testimony to my being made for my art, that when, in the midst of this trouble and pain, I sit down to my book, some beneficent power shows it all to me, and tempts me to be interested, and I don't invent it—really do not— *but see it*, and write it down. . . . It is only when it all fades away and is gone, that I begin to suspect that its momentary relief has cost me something."

Whatever view may be taken of the man who wrote those words, he had the claim to be judged by reference to the highest models in the art which he studied. In the literature of his time, from 1836 to 1870, he held the most conspicuous place, and his claim to the most popular one in the literature of fiction was by common consent admitted. He obtained this rank by the sheer force of his genius, unhelped in any way, and he held it without dispute. As he began he closed. After he had written for only four months, and after he had written incessantly for four and thirty years, he was of all living writers the most widely read. It is of course quite possible that such popularity might imply rather littleness in his contemporaries than greatness in him: but his books are the test to judge by. Each thus far, as it appeared, has had notice in these pages for its illustration of his life, or of his method of work or of the variety and versatility in the manifestations of his power. But his latest books remain still for notice, and will properly suggest what is further to be said of his general place in literature.

His leading quality was Humour. It has no mention in either of the criticisms cited, but it was his highest faculty; and it accounts for his magnificent successes, as well as for his not infrequent failures, in characteristic delineation. He was conscious of this himself. Five years before he died, a great and generous brother-artist, Lord Lytton, amid much ungrudging praise of a work he was then publishing, asked him to consider, as to one part of it, if the modesties of art were not a little overpassed. "I cannot tell you," he replied, "how highly I prize your letter, or with what pride and pleasure it inspires me. Nor do I for a moment question its criticism (if objection so generous and easy may be called by that hard name) otherwise than on this ground—that I work slowly and with great care, and never give way to my invention recklessly, but constantly restrain it; and that I think it is my infirmity to fancy or perceive relations in things which are not apparent generally. Also, I have such an inexpressible enjoyment of what I see in a droll light, that I dare say I pet it as if it were a spoilt child. This is all I have to offer in arrest of judgment." To perceive relations in things which are not apparent generally, is one of those exquisite properties of humour by which are discovered the affinities between the high and the low, the attractive and the repulsive, the rarest things and things of every day, which bring us all upon the level of a common humanity. It is this which gives humour an immortal touch that does not belong of necessity to pictures, even the most exquisite, of mere character or manners; the property which in its highest aspects Carlyle so subtly described as a sort of inverse sublimity, exalting into our affections what is below us as the other draws down into our affections what is above us. But it has a danger which Dickens also hints at, and into which he often fell. All humour has in it, is indeed identical with, what ordinary people are apt to call exaggeration; but there is an excess beyond the allowable even here, and to "pet" or magnify out of proper bounds its sense of what is droll, is to put the merely grotesque in its place. What might have been overlooked in a writer with no uncommon faculty of invention, was thrown into overpowering prominence by Dickens's wealth of fancy; and a splendid excess of his genius came to be objected to as its integral and essential quality.

It cannot be said to have had any place in his earlier books. His powers were not at their highest and the humour was less fine and subtle, but there was no such objection to be taken. No misgiving interrupted the enjoyment of the wonderful freshness of animal spirits in *Pickwick*; but beneath its fun, laughter, and light-heartedness were indications of ability of the first rank in the delineation of character. Some caricature was in the plan; but as the circle of people widened beyond the cockney club, and the delightful oddity of Mr. Pickwick took more of an independent existence, a different method revealed itself, nothing appeared beyond the exaggerations permissible to humorous comedy, and the art was seen which can combine traits vividly true to particular men or women with propensities common to all mankind. This has its highest expression in Fielding: but even the first of Dickens's books showed the same kind of mastery; and, by the side of its lifelike middle-class people universally familiar, there was one figure before seen by none but at once knowable by all, delightful for the surprise it gave by its singularity and the pleasure it gave by its truth; and, though short of the highest in this form of art, taking rank with the class in which live everlastingly the dozen unique inventions that have immortalised the English novel. The groups in *Oliver Twist*, Fagin and his pupils, Sikes and Nancy, Mr. Bumble and his parish-boy, belong to the same period; when Dickens also began those pathetic delineations that opened to the neglected, the poor, and the fallen, a world of compassion and tenderness. Yet I think it was not until the third book, *Nickleby*, that he began to have his place as a writer conceded to him; and that he ceased to be regarded as a mere phenomenon or marvel of fortune, who had achieved success by any other means than that of deserving it, and who challenged no criticism better worth the name than such as he has received from the *Fortnightly* reviewer. It is to be added to what before was said of *Nickleby*, that it established beyond dispute his mastery of dialogue, or that power of making characters real existences, not by describing them but by letting them describe themselves, which belongs only to story-tellers of the first rank. Dickens never excelled the easy handling of the subordinate groups in this novel, and he never repeated its mistakes in the direction of aristocratic or merely polite and dissipated life. It displayed more than before of his humour on the tragic side; and, in close connection with its affecting scenes of starved and deserted childhood, were placed those contrasts of miser and spendthrift, of greed and generosity, of hypocrisy and simple-heartedness, which he handled in later books with greater force and fulness, but of which the first formal expression was here. It was his first general picture, so to speak, of the character and manners of his time, which it was the design more or less of all his books to exhibit; and it suffers by comparison with his later productions, because the humour is not to the same degree enriched by imagination; but it is free from the not infrequent excess into which that supreme gift also tempted its possessor. None of the tales is more attractive throughout, and on the whole it was a step in advance even of the stride previously taken. Nor was the gain lost in the succeeding story of the *Old Curiosity Shop*. The humorous traits of Mrs. Nickleby could hardly be surpassed; but, in Dick Swiveller and the Marchioness, there was a subtlety and lightness of touch that led to finer issues; and around Little Nell and her fortunes, surpassingly   * 137 touching and beautiful, let criticism object what it will, were gathered some small characters that had a deeper intention and more imaginative insight, than anything yet done. Strokes of this kind were also observable in the hunted life of the murderer in *Barnaby Rudge*; and his next book, *Chuzzlewit*, was, as it still remains, one of his greatest achievements. Even so brief a retrospect of the six opening years of Dickens's literary labour will help to a clearer judgment of the work of the twenty-eight more years that remained to him.

To the special observations already made on the series of stories which followed the return from America, *Chuzzlewit*, *Dombey*, *Copperfield*, and *Bleak House*, in which attention has been directed to the higher purpose and more imaginative treatment that distinguished them, a general remark is to be added.   * 138 Though the range of character they traverse is not wide, it is surrounded by a fertility of invention and illustration without example in any previous novelist; and it is represented in these books, so to speak, by a number and variety of existences sufficiently real to have taken places as among the actual people of the world. Could half as many known and universally recognisable men and women be selected out of one story, by any other prose writer of the first rank, as at once rise to the mind from one of the masterpieces of Dickens? So difficult of dispute is this, that as much perhaps will be admitted; but then it will be added, if the reply is by a critic of the school burlesqued by Mr. Lewes, that after all they are not individual or special men and women so much as general impersonations of men and women, abstract types made up of telling catchwords or surface traits, though with such accumulation upon them of a wonderful wealth of humorous illustration, itself filled with minute and accurate knowledge of life, that the real nakedness of the land of character is hidden. Well, what can be rejoined to this, but that the poverty or richness of any territory worth survey will for the most part lie in the kind of observation brought to it. There was no finer observer than Johnson of the manners of his time, and he protested of their greatest delineator that he knew only the shell of life. Another

of his remarks, after a fashion followed by the criticisers of
Dickens, places Fielding below one of his famous contemporaries;
but who will not now be eager to reverse such a comparison, as
that Fielding tells you correctly enough what o'clock it is by
looking at the face of the dial, but that Richardson shows you
how the watch is made? There never was a subtler or a more
sagacious observer than Fielding, or who better deserved what
is generously said of him by Smollett, that he painted the
characters and ridiculed the follies of life with equal strength,
humour, and propriety. But might it not be said of him, as of
Dickens, that his range of character was limited; and that his
method of proceeding from a central idea in all his leading
people, exposed him equally to the charge of now and then
putting human nature itself in place of the individual who
should only be a small section of it? This is in fact but another
shape of what I have expressed on a former page, that what
a character, drawn by a master, will roughly present upon its
surface, is frequently such as also to satisfy its more subtle
requirements; and that when only the salient points or sharper
prominences are thus displayed, the great novelist is using his
undoubted privilege of showing the large degree to which human
intercourse is carried on, not by men's habits or ways at their
commonest, but by the touching of their extremes. A definition of
Fielding's genius has been made with some accuracy in the saying, that he shows common propensities in connection with the
identical unvarnished adjuncts which are peculiar to the individual, nor could a more exquisite felicity of handling than this
be any man's aim or desire; but it would be just as easy, by
employment of the critical rules applied to Dickens, to trans-
form it into matter of censure. Partridge, Adams, Trulliber,
Squire Western, and the rest, present themselves often enough
under the same aspects, and use with sufficient uniformity the
same catchwords, to be brought within the charge of mannerism;
and though M. Taine cannot fairly say of Fielding as of Dickens,
that he suffers from too much morality, he brings against him
precisely the charge so strongly put against the later novelist
of "looking upon the passions not as simple forces but as
objects of approbation or blame." We must keep in mind all
this to understand the worth of the starved fancy, that can find
in such a delineation as that of Micawber only the man described
by Mr. Lewes as always in the same situation, moved with the
same springs and uttering the same sounds, always confident of
something turning up, always crushed and rebounding, always

making punch, and his wife always declaring she will never part from him. It is not thus that such creations are to be viewed; but by the light which enables us to see why the country squires, village schoolmasters, and hedge parsons of Fielding became immortal. The later ones will live, as the earlier do, by the subtle quality of genius that makes their doings and sayings part of those general incentives which pervade mankind. Who has not had occasion, however priding himself on his unlikeness to Micawber, to think of Micawber as he reviewed his own experiences? Who has not himself waited, like Micawber, for something to turn up? Who has not at times discovered, in one or other acquaintance or friend, some one or other of that cluster of sagacious hints and fragments of human life and conduct which the kindly fancy of Dickens embodied in this delightful form? If the irrepressible New Zealander ever comes over to achieve his long promised sketch of St. Paul's, who can doubt that it will be no other than our undying Micawber, who had taken to colonisation the last time we saw him, and who will thus again have turned up? There are not many conditions of life or society to which his and his wife's experiences are not applicable; and when, the year after the immortal couple made their first appearance on earth, Protection was in one of its then frequent difficulties, declaring it could not live without something widely different from existing circumstances shortly turning up, and imploring its friends to throw down the gauntlet and boldly challenge society to turn up a majority and rescue it from its embarrassments, a distinguished wit seized upon the likeness to Micawber, showed how closely it was borne out by the jollity and gin-punch of the banquets at which the bewailings were heard, and asked whether Dickens had stolen from the farmer's friends or the farmer's friends had stolen from Dickens. "Corn," said Mr. Micawber, "may be gentlemanly, but it is not remunerative. . . . I ask myself this question: if corn is not to be relied on, what is? We must live. . . ." Loud as the general laughter was, I think the laughter of Dickens himself was loudest, at this discovery of so exact and unexpected a likeness.

A readiness in all forms thus to enjoy his own pleasantry was indeed always observable (it is common to great humorists, nor would it be easier to carry it further than Sterne did), and his own confession on the point may receive additional illustration before proceeding to the later books. He accounted by it, as we have seen, for occasional even grotesque extravagances.

In another of his letters there is this passage: "I can report that I have finished the job I set myself, and that it has in it something—to me at all events—so extraordinarily droll, that though I have been reading it some hundred times in the course of the working, I have never been able to look at it with the least composure, but have always roared in the most unblushing manner. I leave you to find out what it was." It was the encounter of the major and the tax-collector in the second *Mrs. Lirriper*. Writing previously of the papers in *Household Words* called "The Lazy Tour of Two Idle Apprentices," after saying that he and Mr. Wilkie Collins had written together a story in the second part, "in which I think you would find it very difficult to say where I leave off and he comes in," he had said of the preceding descriptions: "Some of my own tickle me very much; but that may be in great part because I know the originals, and delight in their fantastic fidelity." "I have been at work with such a will," he writes later of a piece of humour for the holidays, "that I have done the opening and conclusion of the Christmas number. They are done in the character of a waiter, and I think are exceedingly droll. The thread on which the stories are to hang, is spun by this waiter, and is, purposely, very slight; but has, I fancy, a ridiculously comical and unexpected end. The waiter's account of himself includes (I hope) everything you know about waiters, presented humorously." In this last we have a hint of the "fantastic fidelity" with which, when a fancy "tickled" him, he would bring out what Corporal Nym calls the humour of it under so astonishing a variety of conceivable and inconceivable aspects of subtle exaggeration, that nothing was left to the subject but that special individual illustration of it. In this, however, humour was not his servant but his master: because it reproduced too readily, and carried too far, the grotesque imaginings to which great humorists are prone; which lie indeed deep in their nature; and from which they derive their genial sympathy with eccentric characters that enables them to find motives for what to other men is hopelessly obscure, to exalt into types of humanity what the world turns impatiently aside at, and to enshrine in a form for eternal homage and love such whimsical absurdity as Captain Toby Shandy's. But Dickens was too conscious of these excesses from time to time, not zealously to endeavour to keep the leading characters in his more important stories under some strictness of discipline. To confine exaggeration within legitimate limits was an art he laboriously studied; and, in whatever proportions of failure or success, during the vicissitudes of both that attended his later years, he continued to endeavour to practise it. In regard to mere description, it is true, he let himself loose more frequently, and would sometimes defend it even on the ground of art; nor would it be fair to omit his reply, on one occasion, to some such remonstrance as M. Taine has embodied in his adverse criticism, against the too great imaginative wealth thrown by him into mere narrative. "It does not seem to me to be enough to say of any description that it is the exact truth. The exact truth must be there; but the merit or art in the narrator, is the manner of stating the truth. As to which thing in literature, it always seems to me that there is a world to be done. And in these times, when the tendency is to be frightfully literal and catalogue-like—to make the thing, in short, a sort of sum in reduction that any miserable creature can do in that way—I have an idea (really founded on the love of what I profess), that the very holding of popular literature through a kind of popular dark age, may depend on such fanciful treatment."

II

THE "TALE OF TWO CITIES"

DICKENS'S next story to *Little Dorrit* was the *Tale of Two Cities*, of which the first notion occurred to him while acting with his friends and his children in the summer of 1857 in Mr. Wilkie Collins's drama of *The Frozen Deep*. But it was only a vague fancy, and the sadness and trouble of the winter of that year were not favourable to it. Towards the close (27) of January 1858, talking of improvements at Gadshill in which he took little interest, it was again in his thoughts. "Growing inclinations of a fitful and undefined sort are upon me sometimes to fall to work on a new book. Then I think I had better not worry my worried mind yet awhile. Then I think it would be of no use if I did, for I couldn't settle to one occupation.—And that's all!" "If I can discipline my thoughts," he wrote three days later, "into the channel of a story, I have made up my mind to get to work on one: always supposing that I find myself, on the trial, able to do well. Nothing whatever will do me the least 'good' in the way of shaking the one strong possession of change impending over us that every day makes stronger; but if I could work on with some approach to steadiness, through the summer, the anxious toil of a new book would have its neck well broken before beginning to publish, next October or November. Sometimes, I think I may continue to work; sometimes, I think not. What do you say to the title, ONE OF THESE DAYS?" That title held its ground very briefly. "What do you think," he wrote after six weeks, "of *this* name for my story—BURIED ALIVE? Does it seem too grim? Or, THE THREAD OF GOLD? Or, THE DOCTOR OF BEAUVAIS?" But not until twelve months later did he fairly buckle himself to the task he had contemplated so long. *All the Year Round* had taken the place of *Household Words* in the interval; and the tale was then started to give strength to the new weekly periodical, in which it was resolved to publish it.

"This is merely to certify," he wrote on 11 March, 1859, "that I have got exactly the name for the story that is wanted; exactly what will fit the opening to a T. A TALE OF TWO CITIES. Also, that I have struck out a rather original and bold idea. That is, at the end of each month to publish the monthly part in the green cover, with the two illustrations, at the old shilling. This will give *All the Year Round* always the interest and precedence of a fresh weekly portion during the month; and will give me my old standing with my old public, and the advantage (very necessary in this story) of having numbers of people who read it in no portions smaller than a monthly part. . . . My American ambassador pays a thousand pounds for the first year, for the privilege of republishing in America one day after we publish here. Not bad? . . ." He had to struggle at the opening through a sharp attack of illness, and on 9 July progress was thus reported. "I have been getting on in health very slowly and through irksome botheration enough. But I think I am round the corner. This cause—and the heat—has tended to my doing no more than hold my ground, my old month's advance, with the *Tale of Two Cities*. The small portions thereof, drive me frantic; but I think the tale must have taken a strong hold. The run upon our monthly parts is surprising, and last month we sold 35,000 back numbers. A note I have had from Carlyle about it has given me especial pleasure." A letter of the following month expresses the intention he had when he began the story, and in what respect it differs as to method from all his other books. Sending in proof four numbers ahead of the current publication, he adds: "I hope you will like them. Nothing but the interest of the subject, and the pleasure of striving with the difficulty of the form of treatment —nothing in the way of mere money, I mean—could else repay the time and trouble of the incessant condensation. But I set myself the little task of making *a picturesque story*, rising in every chapter, with characters true to nature, but whom the story should express more than they should express themselves by dialogue. I mean in other words, that I fancied a story of incident might be written (in place of the odious stuff that *is* written under that pretence), pounding the characters in its own mortar, and beating their interest out of them. If you could have read the story all at once, I hope you wouldn't have stopped halfway." Another of his letters supplies the last * 139 illustration I need to give of the design and meanings in regard to this tale expressed by himself. It was a reply to some objections of which the principal were, a doubt if the feudal cruelties came sufficiently within the date of the action to justify his use of them, and some question as to the manner of disposing of the chief revolutionary agent in the plot. "I had of course full knowledge of the formal surrender of the feudal privileges, but these had been bitterly felt quite as near to the time of the Revolution as the Doctor's narrative, which you will remember dates long before the Terror. With the slang of the new philosophy on the one side, it was surely not unreasonable or unallowable, on the other, to suppose a nobleman wedded to the old cruel ideas, and representing the time going out as his nephew represents the time coming in. If there be anything certain on earth, I take it that the condition of the French peasant generally at that day was intolerable. No later inquiries or provings by figures will hold water against the tremendous testimony of men living at the time. There is a curious book printed at Amsterdam, written to make out no case whatever, and tiresome enough in its literal dictionary-like minuteness; scattered up and down the pages of which is full authority for my marquis. This is Mercier's *Tableau de Paris*. Rousseau is the authority for the peasant's shutting up his house when he had a bit of meat. The tax-tables are the authority for the wretched creature's impoverishment. . . . I am not clear, and I never have been clear, respecting the canon of fiction which forbids the interposition of accident in such a case as Madame Defarge's death. Where the accident is inseparable from the passion and action of the character; where it is strictly consistent with the entire design, and arises out of some culminating proceeding on the part of the individual which the whole story has led up to; it seems to me to become, as it were, an act of divine justice. And when I use Miss Pross (though this is quite another question) to bring about such a catastrophe, I have the positive intention of making that half-comic intervention a part of the desperate woman's failure; and of opposing that mean death, instead of a desperate one in the streets which she wouldn't have minded, to the dignity of Carton's. Wrong or right, this was all design, and seemed to me to be in the fitness of things."

These are interesting intimations of the care with which Dickens worked; and there is no instance in his novels, excepting this, of a deliberate and planned departure from the method of treatment which had been pre-eminently the source of his popularity as a novelist. To rely less upon character than upon incident, and to resolve that his actors should be expressed by the story more than they should express themselves by dialogue, was for him a hazardous, and can hardly be called an entirely successful, experiment. With singular dramatic vivacity, much constructive art, and with descriptive passages of a high order everywhere (the dawn of the terrible outbreak in the journey of the marquis from Paris to his country seat, and the London crowd at the funeral of the spy, may be instanced for their power), there was probably never a book by a great humorist, and an artist so prolific in the conception of character, with so little humour and so few rememberable figures. Its merits lie elsewhere. Though there are excellent traits and touches all through the revolutionary scenes, the only full-length that stands out prominently is the picture of the wasted life saved at last by heroic sacrifice. Dickens speaks of his design to make impressive the dignity of Carton's death, and in this he succeeded perhaps even beyond his expectation. Carton suffers himself to be mistaken for another, and gives his life that the girl he loves may be happy with that other; the secret being known only to a poor little girl in the tumbril that takes them to the scaffold, who at the moment has discovered it, and whom it strengthens also to die. The incident is beautifully told; and it is at least only fair to set against verdicts not very favourable as to this effort of his invention, what was said of the particular character and scene, and of the book generally, by an American critic whose literary studies had most familiarised him with the rarest forms of imaginative writing. "Its portrayal of the noble-natured castaway makes it   * 140 almost a peerless book in modern literature, and gives it a place among the highest examples of literary art. . . . The conception of this character shows in its author an ideal of magnanimity and of charity unsurpassed. There is not a grander, lovelier figure than the self-wrecked, self-devoted Sydney Carton, in literature or history; and the story itself is so noble in its spirit, so grand and graphic in its style, and filled with a pathos so profound and simple, that it deserves and will surely take a place among the great serious works of imagination." I should myself prefer to say that its distinctive merit is less in any of its conceptions of character, even Carton's, than as a specimen of Dickens's power in imaginative story-telling. There is no piece of fiction known to me, in which the domestic life of a few simple private people is in such a manner knitted and interwoven with the outbreak of a terrible public event, that the one seems but part of the other. When made conscious of the first sultry drops of a thunderstorm that fall upon a little group sitting in an obscure English lodging, we are witness to the actual beginning of a tempest which is preparing to sweep away everything in France. And, to the end, the book in this respect is really remarkable.

"GREAT EXPECTATIONS"

THE *Tale of Two Cities* was published in 1859; the series of papers collected as the *Uncommercial Traveller* were occupying Dickens in 1860; and it was while engaged in these, and throwing off in the course of them capital "samples" of fun and enjoyment, he thus replied to a suggestion that he should let himself loose upon some single humorous conception, in the vein of his youthful achievements in that way. "For a little piece I have been writing—or am writing; for I hope to finish it to-day—such a very fine, new, and grotesque idea has opened upon me, that I begin to doubt whether I had not better cancel the little paper, and reserve the notion for a new book. You shall judge as soon as I get it printed. But it so opens out before *me* that I can see the whole of a serial revolving on it, in a most singular and comic manner." This was the germ of Pip and Magwitch, which at first he intended to make the groundwork of a tale in the old twenty-number form, but for reasons perhaps fortunate brought afterwards within the limits of a less elaborate novel. "Last week," he wrote on 4 October, 1860, "I got to work on the new story. I had previously very carefully considered the state and prospects of *All the Year Round*, and, the more I considered them, the less hope I saw of being able to get back, *now*, to the profit of a separate publication in the old 20 numbers." (A tale, which at the time was appearing in his serial, had disappointed expectation.) "However, I worked on, knowing that what I was doing would run into another groove; and I called a council of war at the office on Tuesday. It was perfectly clear that the one thing to be done was, for me to strike in. I have therefore decided to begin the story as of the length of the *Tale of Two Cities* on the first of December—begin publishing, that is. I must make the most I can out of the book. You shall have the first two or three weekly parts to-morrow. The name is GREAT EXPECTATIONS. I think a good name?" Two days later he wrote: "The sacrifice of *Great Expectations* is really and truly made for myself. The property of *All the Year Round* is far too valuable, in every way, to be much endangered. Our fall is not large, but we have a considerable advance in hand of the story we are now publishing, and there is no vitality in it, and no chance whatever of stopping the fall; which on the contrary would be certain to increase. Now, if I went into a twenty-number serial, I should cut off my power of doing anything serial here for two good years—and that would be a most perilous thing. On the other hand, by dashing in now, I come in when most wanted; and if Reade and Wilkie follow me, our course will be shaped out handsomely and hopefully for between two and three years. A thousand pounds are to be paid for early proofs of the story to America." A few more days brought the first instalment of the tale, and explanatory mention of it. "The book will be written in the first person throughout, and during these first three weekly numbers you will find the hero to be a boy-child, like David. Then he will be an apprentice. You will not have to complain of the want of humour as in the *Tale of Two Cities*. I have made the opening, I hope, in its general effect exceedingly droll. I have put a child and a good-natured foolish man, in relations that seem to me very funny. Of course I have got in the pivot on which the story will turn too—and which indeed, as you remember, was the grotesque tragi-comic conception that first encouraged me. To be quite sure I had fallen into no unconscious repetitions, I read *David Copperfield* again the other day, and was affected by it to a degree you would hardly believe."

It may be doubted if Dickens could better have established his right to the front rank among novelists claimed for him, than by the ease and mastery with which, in these two books of *Copperfield* and *Great Expectations*, he kept perfectly distinct the two stories of a boy's childhood, both told in the form of autobiography. A subtle penetration into character marks the unlikeness in the likeness; there is enough at once of resemblance and of difference in the position and surroundings of each to account for the divergences of character that arise; both children are good-hearted, and both have the advantage of association with models of tender simplicity and oddity, perfect in their truth and quite distinct from each other; but a sudden tumble into distress steadies Peggotty's little friend, and as unexpected a stroke of good fortune turns the head of the small protégé of Joe Gargery. What a deal of spoiling nevertheless, a nature that is really good at the bottom of it will stand without permanent damage, is nicely shown in Pip; and the way he reconciles his determination to act very shabbily to his early friends, with a conceited notion that he is setting them a moral example, is part of the shading of a character drawn with extraordinary skill. His greatest trial comes out of his good luck; and the foundations of both are laid at the opening of the tale, in a churchyard down by the Thames, as it winds past desolate marshes twenty miles to the sea, of which a masterly picture in half a dozen lines will give only average example of the descriptive writing that is everywhere one of the charms of the book. It is strange, as I transcribe the words, with what wonderful vividness they bring back the very spot on which we stood when he said he meant to make it the scene of the opening of his story—Cooling Castle ruins and the desolate church, lying out among the marshes seven miles from Gadshill! "My first most vivid and broad impression . . . on a memorable raw afternoon towards evening . . . was . . . that this bleak place, overgrown with nettles, was the churchyard, and that the dark flat wilderness beyond the churchyard, intersected with dykes and mounds and gates, with scattered cattle feeding on it, was the marshes; and that the low leaden line beyond, was the river; and that the distant savage lair from which the wind was rushing, was the sea. . . . On the edge of the river . . . only two black things in all the prospect seemed to be standing upright . . . one, the beacon by which the sailors steered, like an unhooped cask upon a pole, an ugly thing when you were near it; the other, a gibbet with some chains hanging to it which had once held a pirate." Here Magwitch, an escaped convict from Chatham, terrifies the child Pip into stealing for him food and a file; and though recaptured and transported, he carries with him to Australia such a grateful heart for the small creature's service, that on making a fortune there he resolves to make his little friend a gentleman. This requires circumspection; and is so done, through the Old Bailey attorney who has defended Magwitch at his trial (a character of surprising novelty and truth), that Pip imagines his present gifts and "great expectations" to have come from the supposed rich lady of the story (whose eccentricities are the unattractive part of it, and have yet a weird character that somehow fits in with the kind of wrong she has suffered). When therefore the closing scenes bring back Magwitch himself, who risks his life to gratify his longing to see the gentleman he has made, it is an unspeakable horror to the youth to discover his benefactor in the convicted felon. If anyone doubts Dickens's power of so drawing a character as to get to the heart of it, seeing beyond surface peculiarities into the moving springs of the human being himself, let him narrowly examine those scenes. There is not a grain of sub-stitution of mere sentiment, or circumstance, for the inner and absolute reality of the position in which these two creatures find themselves. Pip's loathing of what had built up his fortune, and his horror of the uncouth architect, are apparent in even his most generous efforts to protect him from exposure and sentence. Magwitch's convict habits strangely blend themselves with his wild pride in, and love for, the youth whom his money has turned into a gentleman. He has a craving for his good opinion; dreads to offend him by his "heavy grubbing," or by the oaths he lets fall now and then; and pathetically hopes his Pip, his dear boy, won't think him "low"; but, upon a chum of Pip's appearing unexpectedly while they are together, he pulls out a jack-knife by way of hint he can defend himself, and produces afterwards a greasy little clasped black Testa-ment on which the startled new-comer, being found to have no hostile intention, is sworn to secrecy. At the opening of the story there had been an exciting scene of the wretched man's chase and recapture among the marshes, and this has its parallel at the close in his chase and recapture on the river while poor Pip is helping to get him off. To make himself sure of the actual course of a boat in such circumstances, and what possible incidents the adventure might have, Dickens hired a steamer for the day from Blackwall to Southend. Eight or nine friends and three or four members of his family were on board, and he seemed to have no care, the whole of that summer day (22 May, 1861), except to enjoy their enjoyment and entertain them with his own in shape of a thousand whims and fancies; but his sleepless observation was at work all the time, and nothing had escaped his keen vision on either side of the river. The fifteenth chapter of the third volume is a masterpiece.

The characters generally afford the same evidence as those two that Dickens's humour, not less than his creative power, was at its best in this book. The Old Bailey attorney Jaggers, and his clerk Wemmick (both excellent, and the last one of the oddities that live in everybody's liking for the goodheartedness of its comic surprises), are as good as his earliest efforts in that line; the Pumblechooks and Wopsles are as perfect as bits of *Nickleby* fresh from the mint; and the scene in which Pip, and Pip's chum Herbert, make up their accounts and schedule their debts and obligations, is original and delightful as Micawber himself. It is the art of living upon nothing and making the best of it, in its most pleasing form. Herbert's intentions to trade east and west, and get himself into business transactions of a magnificent extent and variety, are as perfectly warranted to us, in his way of putting them, by merely "being in a counting-house and looking about you," as Pip's means of paying his debts are lightened and made easy by his method of simply adding them up with a margin. "The time comes," says Herbert, "when you see your opening. And you go in, and you swoop upon it, and you make your capital, and then there you are! When you have once made your capital you have nothing to do but employ it." In like manner Pip tells us, "Suppose your debts to be one hundred and sixty-four pounds four and two-pence, I would say, leave a margin and put them down at two hundred; or suppose them to be four times as much, leave a margin and put them down at seven hundred." He is sufficiently candid to add, that, while he has the highest opinion of the wisdom and prudence of the margin, its dangers are that in the sense of freedom and solvency it imparts there is a tendency to run into new debt. But the satire that thus enforces the old warning against living upon vague hopes, and paying ancient debts by contracting new ones, never presented itself in more amusing or kindly shape. A word should be added of the father of the girl that Herbert marries, Bill Barley, ex-ship's-purser, a gouty, bed-ridden, drunken old rascal, who lies on his back in an upper floor on Mill Pond Bank, by Chinks's Basin, where he keeps, weighs, and serves out the family stores or provisions, according to old professional practice, with one eye at a telescope which is fitted on his bed for the convenience of sweeping the river. This is one of those sketches, slight in itself but made rich with a wealth of comic observation, in which Dickens's humour took especial delight; and to all this part of the story there is a quaint riverside flavour that gives it amusing reality and relish.

Sending the chapters that contain it, which open the third division of the tale, he wrote thus: "It is a pity that the third portion cannot be read all at once, because its purpose would be much more apparent; and the pity is the greater, because the general turn and tone of the working out and winding up, will be away from all such things as they conventionally go. But what must be, must be. As to the planning out from week to week, nobody can imagine what the difficulty is, without trying. But, as in all such cases, when it is overcome the pleasure is proportionate. Two months more will see me through it, I trust. All the iron is in the fire, and I have 'only' to beat it out." One other letter throws light upon an objection taken not unfairly to the too great speed with which the heroine, after being married, reclaimed, and widowed, is in a page or two again made love to, and remarried by the hero. This summary proceeding was not originally intended. But, over and above its popular acceptance, the book had interested some whose opinions Dickens specially valued (Carlyle among them, I remember); and upon Bulwer Lytton objecting to a close that should leave Pip a solitary man, Dickens substituted what now stands. "You will be surprised," he wrote, "to hear that I have changed the end of *Great Expectations* from and after Pip's return to Joe's, and finding his little likeness there. Bulwer, who has been, as I think you know, extraordinarily taken by the book, so strongly urged it upon me, after reading the proofs, and supported his view with such good reasons, that I resolved to make the change. You shall have it when you come back to town. I have put in as pretty a little piece of writing as I could, and I have no doubt the story will be more acceptable through the alteration." This turned out to be the case; but the first ending nevertheless seems to be more consistent with the drift, as well as natural working out, of the tale.

* 141

IV

CHRISTMAS SKETCHES

BETWEEN that fine novel, which was issued in three volumes in the autumn of 1861, and the completion of his next serial story, were interposed three sketches in his happiest vein at which everyone laughed and cried in the Christmas times of 1862, '3, and '4. Of the waiter in *Somebody's Luggage* Dickens has himself spoken; and if any theme is well treated, when, from the point of view taken, nothing more is left to say about it, that bit of fun is perfect. Call it exaggeration, grotesqueness, or by what hard name you will, laughter will always intercept any graver criticism. Writing from Paris of what he was himself responsible for in the articles left by Somebody with his wonderful Waiter, he said that in one of them he had made the story a camera obscura of certain French places and styles of people; having founded it on something he had noticed in a French soldier. This was the tale of Little Bebelle, which had a small French corporal for its hero, and became highly popular. But the triumph of the Christmas achievements in these days was Mrs. Lirriper. She took her place at once among people known to everybody; and all the world talked of Major Jemmy Jackman, and his friend the poor elderly lodging-house keeper of the Strand, with her miserable cares and rivalries and worries, as if they had both been as long in London and as well known as Norfolk Street itself. A dozen volumes could not have told more than those dozen pages did. The *Legacy* followed the *Lodgings* in 1864, and there was no falling off in the fun and laughter.

V

"OUR MUTUAL FRIEND"

THE publication of *Our Mutual Friend*, in the form of the earliest stories, extended from May 1864 to November 1865. Four years earlier he had chosen this title as a good one, and he held to it through much objection. Between that time and his actual commencement there is mention, in his letters, of the three leading notions on which he founded the story. In his waterside wanderings during his last book, the many handbills he saw posted up, with dreary description of persons drowned in the river, suggested the long-shore-men and their ghastly calling whom he sketched in Hexam and Riderhood. "I think," he had written, "a man, young and perhaps eccentric, feigning to be dead, and *being* dead to all intents and purposes external to himself, and for years retaining the singular view of life and character so imparted, would be a good leading incident for a story"; and this he partly did in Rokesmith. For other actors in the tale, he had thought of "a poor impostor of a man marrying a woman for her money; she marrying *him* for *his* money; after marriage both finding out their mistake, and entering into a league and covenant against folks in general": with whom he had proposed to connect some Perfectly New people. "Everything new about them. If they presented a father and mother, it seemed as if THEY must be bran new, like the furniture and the carriages—shining with varnish, and just home from the manufacturers." These groups took shape in the Lammles and the Veneerings. "I must use somehow," is the remark of another letter, "the uneducated father in fustian and the educated boy in spectacles whom Leech and I saw at Chatham"; of which a hint is in Charley Hexam and his father. The benevolent old Jew whom he makes the unconscious agent of a rascal, was meant to wipe out a reproach against his Jew in *Oliver Twist* as bringing dislike upon the religion of the race he belonged to.

Having got his title in 1861 it was his hope to have begun

* 142

in '62. "Alas!" he wrote in the April of that year, "I have hit upon nothing for a story. Again and again I have tried. But this odious little house" (he had at this time for a few weeks exchanged Gadshill for a friend's house near Kensington) "seems to have stifled and darkened my invention." It was not until the autumn of the following year he saw his way to a beginning. "The Christmas number has come round again" (30 August, 1863)—"it seems only yesterday that I did the last —but I am full of notions besides for the new twenty numbers. When I can clear the Christmas stone out of the road, I think I can dash into it on the grander journey." He persevered through much difficulty; which he described six weeks later, with characteristic glance at his own ways when writing, in a letter from the office of his journal. "I came here last night, to evade my usual day in the week—in fact to shirk it—and get back to Gads for five or six consecutive days. My reason is, that I am exceedingly anxious to begin my book. I am bent upon getting to work at it. I want to prepare it for the spring; but I am determined not to begin to publish with less than five numbers done. I see my opening perfectly, with the one main line on which the story is to turn; and if I don't strike while the iron (meaning myself) is hot, I shall drift off again, and have to go through all this uneasiness once more."

He had written, after four months, very nearly three numbers, when upon a necessary rearrangement of his chapters he had to hit upon a new subject for one of them. "While I was considering" (25 February) "what it should be, Marcus, who has done an excellent cover, came to tell me of an extraordinary trade he had found out, through one of his painting requirements. I immediately went with him to Saint Giles's to look at the place, and found—what you will see." It was the establishment of Mr. Venus, preserver of animals and birds, and articulator of human bones; and it took the place of the last chapter of No. 2, which was then transferred to the end of No. 3. But a start with three full numbers done, though more than enough to satisfy the hardest self-conditions formerly, did not satisfy him now. With his previous thought given to the story, with his Memoranda to help him, with the people he had in hand to work it with, and ready as he still was to turn his untiring observation to instant use on its behalf, he now moved, with the old large canvas before him, somewhat slowly and painfully. "If I were to lose" (29 March) "a page of the five numbers I have proposed to myself to be ready by the publication day, I should

* 143

feel that I had fallen short. I have grown hard to satisfy, and write very slowly. And I have so much—not fiction—that *will* be thought of, when I don't want to think of it, that I am forced to take more care than I once took."

The first number was launched at last, on the first of May; and after two days he wrote: "Nothing can be better than *Our Friend*, now in his thirtieth thousand, and orders flowing in fast." Yet between the first and second number there was a drop of five thousand, strange to say, for the larger number was again reached, and much exceeded, before the book closed. "This leaves me" (10 June) "going round and round like a carrier pigeon before swooping on number seven." Thus far he had held his ground; but illness came, with some other anxieties, and on 29 July he wrote sadly enough. "Although I have not been wanting in industry, I have been wanting in invention, and have fallen back with the book. Looming large before me is the Christmas work, and I can hardly hope to do it without losing a number of *Our Friend*. I have very nearly lost one already, and two would take one half of my whole advance. This week I have been very unwell; am still out of sorts; and, as I know from two days' slow experience, have a very mountain to climb before I shall see the open country of my work." The three following months brought hardly more favourable report. "I have not done my number. This death of poor Leech (I suppose) has put me out woefully. Yesterday and the day before I could do nothing; seemed for the time to have quite lost the power; and am only by slow degrees getting back into the track to-day." He rallied after this, and satisfied himself for a while; but in February 1865 that formidable illness in his foot broke out which, at certain times for the rest of his life, deprived him more or less of his inestimable solace of bodily exercise. In April and May he suffered severely; and after trying the sea went abroad for more complete change. "Work and worry, without exercise, would soon make an end of me. If I were not going away now, I should break down. No one knows as I know to-day how near to it I have been."

That was the day of his leaving for France, and the day of his return brought these few hurried words: "Saturday, tenth of June 1865. I was in the terrific Staplehurst accident yester- † 24 day, and worked for hours among the dying and dead. I was in the carriage that did not go over, but went off the line, and hung over the bridge in an inexplicable manner. No words can describe the scene.[1] I am away to Gads." Though with characteristic energy he resisted the effects upon himself of that terrible ninth of June, they were for some time evident; and, up to the day of his death on its fatal fifth anniversary, were perhaps never wholly absent. But very few complaints fell from him. "I am curiously weak—weak as if I were recovering from a long illness." "I begin to feel it more in my head. I sleep well and eat well; but I write half a dozen notes, and turn faint and sick." "I am getting right, though still low in pulse and very nervous. Driving into Rochester yesterday I felt more shaken than I have since the accident." "I cannot bear railway travelling yet. A perfect conviction, against the senses, that the carriage is down on one side (and generally that is the left, and *not* the side on which the carriage in the accident really went over), comes upon me with anything like speed, and is inexpressibly distressing." These are passages from his letters up to the close of June. Upon his book the immediate result was that another lost number was added to the losses of the preceding months, and "alas!" he wrote at the opening of July, "for the two numbers you write of! There is only one in existence. I have but just begun the other." "Fancy!" he added next day, "fancy my having under-written number sixteen by two and a half pages—a thing I have not done since *Pickwick*!" He did it once with *Dombey*, and was to do it yet again.

The book thus begun and continued under adverse influences, though with fancy in it, descriptive power, and characters well designed, will never rank with his higher efforts. It has some pictures of a rare veracity of soul amid the lowest forms of social degradation, placed beside others of sheer falsehood and pretence amid unimpeachable social correctness, which lifted the writer to his old place; but the judgment of it on the whole must be, that it wants freshness and natural development.

[1] He thus spoke of it in his "Postscript in lieu of Preface" (dated 2 September, 1865), which accompanied the last number of the story under notice. "On Friday the ninth of June in the present year Mr. and Mrs. Boffin (in their manuscript dress of receiving Mr. and Mrs. Lammle at breakfast) were on the South Eastern Railway with me, in a terribly destructive accident. When I had done what I could to help others, I climbed back into my carriage—nearly turned over a viaduct, and caught aslant upon the turn—to extricate the worthy couple. They were much soiled, but otherwise unhurt. The same happy result attended Miss Bella Wilfer on her wedding-day, and Mr. Riderhood inspecting Bradley Headstone's red neckerchief as he lay asleep. I remember with devout thankfulness that I can never be much nearer parting company with my readers for ever, than I was then, until there shall be written against my life the two words with which I have this day closed this book—THE END."

This indeed will be most freely admitted by those who feel most strongly that all the old cunning of the master hand is yet in the wayward loving Bella Wilfer, in the vulgar canting Podsnap, and in the dolls' dressmaker Jenny Wren, whose keen little quaint weird ways, and precocious wit sharpened by trouble, are fitted into a character as original and delightfully conceived as it is vividly carried through to the last. A dull coarse web her small life seems made of; but even from its taskwork, which is undertaken for childhood itself, there are glittering threads cast across its woof and warp of care. The unconscious philosophy of her tricks and manners has in it more of the subtler vein of the satire aimed at in the book, than even the voices of society which the tale begins and ends with. In her very kindliness there is the touch of malice that shows a childish playfulness familiar with unnatural privations; this gives a depth as well as tenderness to her humours which entitles them to rank with the writer's happiest things; and though the odd little creature's talk is incessant when she is on the scene, it has the individuality that so seldom tires. It is veritably her own small "trick" and "manner," and is never mistakable for anyone else's. "I have been reading," Dickens wrote to me from France while he was writing the book, "a capital little story by Edmond About—*The Notary's Nose*. I have been trying other books; but so infernally conversational, that I forget who the people are before they have done talking, and don't in the least remember what they talked about before when they begin talking again!" The extreme contrast to his own art could not be defined more exactly; and other examples from this tale will be found in the differing members of the Wilfer family, in the riverside people at the Fellowship Porters, in such marvellous serio-comic scenes as that of Rogue Riderhood's restoration from drowning, and in those short and simple annals of Betty Higden's life and death which might have given saving virtue to a book more likely than this to perish prematurely. It has not the creative power which crowded his earlier page, and transformed into popular realities the shadows of his fancy; but the observation and humour he excelled in are not wanting to it, nor had there been, in his first completed work, more eloquent or generous pleading for the poor and neglected, than this last completed work contains. Betty Higden finishes what Oliver Twist began.

VI

"DR. MARIGOLD'S PRESCRIPTIONS"

HE had scarcely closed that book in September, wearied somewhat with a labour of invention which had not been so free or self-sustaining as in the old facile and fertile days, when his customary contribution to Christmas became due from him; and his fancy, let loose in a narrower field, resumed its old luxury of enjoyment. Here are notices of it from his letters. "If people at large understand a Cheap Jack, my part of the Christmas number will do well. It is wonderfully like the real thing, of course a little refined and humoured." "I do hope that in the beginning and end of this Christmas number you will find something that will strike you as being fresh, forcible, and full of spirits." He described its mode of composition afterwards. "Tired with *Our Mutual*, I sat down to cast about for an idea, with a depressing notion that I was, for the moment, overworked. Suddenly, the little character that you will see, and all belonging to it, came flashing up in the most cheerful manner, and I had only to look on and leisurely describe it." This was *Dr. Marigold's Prescriptions*, one of the most popular of all the pieces selected for his readings, and a splendid example of his humour, pathos, and character. "I received your letter in praise of Dr. Marigold," he writes to Lord Lytton (31 December), "and read and re-read all your generous words, fifty times over, with inexpressible delight. I cannot tell you how they gratified and affected me." The piece was worthy of the praise. It expressed, as perfectly as anything he has ever done, that which constitutes in itself very much of the genius of all his writing, the wonderful neighbourhood in this life of ours, of serious and humorous things; the laughter close to the pathos, but never touching it with ridicule. There were two more Christmas pieces before he made his last visit to America: *Barbox Brothers* with *The Boy at Mugby Station*, and *No Thoroughfare*: the last a joint piece of work with Mr. Wilkie Collins, who during Dickens's absence in the States transformed it into a play for Mr. Fechter, with a view to which it had been planned originally. There were also two papers written for first publication in America, *George Silverman's Explanation*, and *Holiday Romance*, containing about the quantity of half a shilling number of his ordinary serials, and paid for at a rate unexampled in literature. They occupied him not many days in the writing, and he received a thousand pounds for them. The same had before been paid for *Hunted Down*. Reserving for mention in its place what was written after his return, it will be proper here to interpose, before the closing word of my criticism, some account of the manuscript volume found among his papers containing memoranda for use in his writings; and covering the period from the opening of *Little Dorrit* to the close of *Our Mutual Friend*.

VII

HINTS FOR BOOKS WRITTEN AND UNWRITTEN

1855–65

DICKENS began the Book of Memoranda for possible use in his work, to which occasional reference has been made, in January 1855, six months before the first page of *Little Dorrit* was written; and I find no allusion leading me to suppose, except in one very doubtful instance, that he had made addition to its entries, or been in the habit of resorting to them, after the date of *Our Mutual Friend*. It seems to comprise that interval of ten years in his life.

In it were put down any hints or suggestions that occurred to him. A mere piece of imagery or fancy, it might be at one time; at another the outline of a subject or a character; then a bit of description or dialogue; no order or sequence being observed in any. Titles for stories were set down too, and groups of names for the actors in them; not the least curious of the memoranda belonging to this class. More rarely, entry is made of some oddity of speech; and he has thus preserved in it, *verbatim et literatim*, what he declared to have been as startling a message as he ever received. A confidential servant at Tavistock House, having conferred on some proposed changes in his bedroom with the party that was to do the work, delivered this ultimatum to her master. "The gas-fitter says, sir, that he can't alter the fitting of your gas in your bedroom without taking up almost the ole of your bedroom floor, and pulling your room to pieces. He says, of course you can have it done if you wish, and he'll do it for you and make a good job of it, but he would have to destroy your room first, and go entirely under the jistes."

It is very interesting in this book, last legacy as it is of the literary remains of such a writer, to compare the way in which fancies were worked out with their beginnings entered in its pages. Those therefore will first be taken that in some form or other appeared afterwards in his writings, with such reference to the latter as may enable the reader to make comparison for himself.

"Our House. Whatever it is, it is in a first-rate situation, and a fashionable neighbourhood. (Auctioneer called it 'a gentlemanly residence.') A series of little closets squeezed up into the corner of a dark street—but a Duke's Mansion round the corner. The whole house just large enough to hold a vile smell. The air breathed in it, at the best of times, a kind of Distillation of Mews." He made it the home of the Barnacles in *Little Dorrit*.

What originally he meant to express by Mrs. Clennam in the same story has narrower limits, and a character less repellent, in the Memoranda than it assumed in the book. "Bed-ridden (or room-ridden) twenty—five-and-twenty—years; any length of time. As to most things, kept at a standstill all the while. Thinking of altered streets as the old streets—changed things as the unchanged things—the youth or girl I quarrelled with all those years ago, as the same youth or girl now. Brought out of doors by an unexpected exercise of my latent strength of character, and then how strange!"

One of the people of the same story who becomes a prominent actor in it, Henry Gowan, a creation on which he prided himself as forcible and new, seems to have risen to his mind in this way. "I affect to believe that I would do anything myself for a ten-pound note, and that anybody else would. I affect to be always book-keeping in every man's case, and posting up a little account of good and evil with everyone. Thus the greatest rascal becomes the 'dearest old fellow,' and there is much less difference than you would be inclined to suppose between an honest man and a scoundrel. While I affect to be finding good in most men, I am in reality decrying it where it really is, and setting it up where it is not. Might not a presentation of this far from uncommon class of character, if I could put it strongly enough, be likely to lead some men to reflect, and change a little? I think it has never been done."

In *Little Dorrit* also will be found a picture which seems to live with a more touching effect in his first pleasing fancy of it. "The ferryman on a peaceful river, who has been there from youth, who lives, who grows old, who does well, who does ill, who changes, who dies—the river runs six hours up and six hours down, the current sets off that point, the same allowance must be made for the drifting of the boat, the same tune is always played by the rippling water against the prow."

Here was an entry made when the thought occurred to him of the close of old Dorrit's life. "First sign of the father failing and breaking down. Cancels long interval. Begins to talk about the turnkey who first called him the Father of the Marshalsea —as if he were still living. 'Tell Bob I want to speak to him. See if he is on the Lock, my dear.'" And here was the first notion of Clennam's reverse of fortune. "His falling into difficulty, and himself imprisoned in the Marshalsea. Then she, out of all her wealth and changed station, comes back in her old dress, and devotes herself in the old way."

He seems to have designed, for the sketches of society in the same tale, a "Full-length portrait of his lordship, surrounded by worshippers"; of which, beside that brief memorandum, only his first draft of the general outline was worked at. "Sensible men enough, agreeable men enough, independent men enough in a certain way;—but the moment they begin to circle round my lord, and to shine with a borrowed light from his lordship, heaven and earth how mean and subservient! What a competition and outbidding of each other in servility."

The last of the Memoranda hints used in the story whose difficulties at its opening seem first to have suggested them, ran thus: "The unwieldy ship taken in tow by the snorting little steam tug"—by which was prefigured the patriarch Casby and his agent Panks.

In a few lines is the germ of the tale called *Hunted Down*: "Devoted to the Destruction of a man. Revenge built up on love. The secretary in the Wainewright case, who had fallen in love (or supposed he had) with the murdered girl."—The hint on which he worked in his description of the villain of that story, is also in the Memoranda. "The man with his hair parted straight up the front of his head, like an aggravating gravel-walk. Always presenting it to you. 'Up here, if you please. Neither to the right nor left. Take me exactly in this direction. Straight up here. Come off the grass——'"

His first intention as to the *Tale of Two Cities* was to write it upon a plan proposed in this manuscript book. "How as to a story in two periods—with a lapse of time between, like a French Drama? Titles for such a notion. TIME! THE LEAVES OF THE FOREST. SCATTERED LEAVES. THE GREAT WHEEL. ROUND AND ROUND. OLD LEAVES. LONG AGO. FAR APART. FALLEN LEAVES. FIVE AND TWENTY YEARS. YEARS AND YEARS. ROLLING YEARS. DAY AFTER DAY. FELLED TREES. MEMORY CARTON. ROLLING STONES. TWO GENERATIONS." That special title of *Memory Carton* shows that what led to the greatest success of the book as written was always in his mind; and another of the memoranda is this rough hint of the character itself. "The drunken?—dissipated?—What?—LION—and his JACKAL and Primer, stealing down to him at unwonted hours."

In connection with the same book, another fancy may be copied from which the domesticities of Mr. and Mrs. Cruncher were taken. "A man, and his wife—or daughter—or niece. The man, a reprobate and ruffian; the woman (or girl) with good in her, and with compunctions. He believes nothing, and defies everything; yet has suspicions always, that she is 'praying against' his evil schemes, and making them go wrong. He is very much opposed to this, and is always angrily harping on it. 'If she *must* pray, why can't she pray in their favour, instead of going against 'em? She's always ruining me—she always is—and calls that, Duty! There's a religious person! Calls it Duty to fly in my face! Calls it Duty to go sneaking against me!'"

The studies of Silas Wegg and his patron as they exist in *Our Mutual Friend*, are hardly such good comedy as in the form which the first notion seems to have intended. "Gibbon's Decline and Fall. The two characters. One reporting to the other as he reads. Both getting confused as to whether it is not all going on now." In the same story may be traced, more or less clearly, other fancies which had found their first expression in the Memoranda. A touch for Bella Wilfer is here. "Buying poor shabby—FATHER?—a new hat. So incongruous that it makes him like African King Boy, or King George; who is usually full dressed when he has nothing upon him but a cocked hat or a waistcoat." Here undoubtedly is the voice of Podsnap. "I stand by my friends and acquaintances;—not for their sakes, but because they are *my* friends and acquaintances. *I* know them, *I* have licensed them, they have taken out *my* certificate. Ergo, I champion them as myself." To the same redoubtable person another trait clearly belongs. "And by denying a thing, supposes that he altogether puts it out of existence." A third very perfectly expresses the boy, ready for mischief, who does all the work there is to be done in Eugene Wrayburn's place of business. "The office boy for ever looking out of window, who never has anything to do."

The poor wayward purposeless good-hearted master of the boy, Eugene himself, is as evidently in this: "If they were great things, I, the untrustworthy man in little things, would do them earnestly—But O No, I wouldn't!" What follows has a more direct reference; being indeed almost literally copied in the story. "As to the question whether I, Eugene, lying ill and sick even unto death, may be consoled by the representation that coming through this illness, I shall begin a new life, and have energy and purpose and all I have yet wanted: '*I hope* I should, but *I know* I shouldn't. Let me die, my dear.'"

Other fancies preserved in his Memoranda were left wholly unemployed, receiving from him no more permanent form of any kind than that which they have in this touching record; and what most people would probably think the most attractive and original of all the thoughts he had thus set down for future use, are those that were never used.

Here were his first rough notes for the opening of a story. "Beginning with the breaking up of a large party of guests at a country house: house left lonely with the shrunken family in it: guests spoken of, and introduced to the reader that way. —Or, beginning with a house abandoned by a family fallen into reduced circumstances. Their old furniture there, and number-less tokens of their old comforts. Inscriptions under the bells downstairs—'Mr. John's Room,' 'Miss Caroline's Room.' Great gardens trimly kept to attract a tenant: but no one in them. A landscape without figures. Billiard room: table covered up, like a body. Great stables without horses, and great coach-houses without carriages. Grass growing in the chinks of the stone-paving, this bright cold winter day. *Downhills.*" Another opening had also suggested itself to him. "Open a story by bringing two strongly contrasted places and strongly contrasted sets of people, into the connection necessary for the story, by means of an electric message. Describe the message—*be* the message—flashing along through space, over the earth, and under the sea." Connected with which in some way would seem to be this other notion, following it in the Memoranda. "Representing London—or Paris, or any other great place— in the new light of being actually unknown to all the people in the story, and only taking the colour of their fears and fancies and opinions. So getting a new aspect, and being unlike itself. An *odd* unlikeness of itself."

The subjects for stories are various, and some are striking. There was one he clung to much, and thought of frequently as in a special degree available for a series of papers in his periodical; but when he came to close quarters with it the difficulties were found to be too great. "English landscape. The beautiful pros-pect, trim fields, clipped hedges, everything so neat and orderly

—gardens, houses, roads. Where are the people who do all this? There must be a great many of them, to do it. Where are they all? And are *they*, too, so well kept and so fair to see? Suppose the foregoing to be wrought out by an Englishman: say from China: who knows nothing about his native country." To which may be added a fancy that savours of the same mood of discontent, political and social. "How do I know that I, a man, am to learn from insects—unless it is to learn how little my littlenesses are? All that botheration in the hive about the queen bee, may be, in little, me and the court circular."

A domestic story he met with in the State Trials struck him greatly by its capabilities, and I may preface it by mentioning another subject, not entered in the Memoranda, which for a long time impressed him as capable of attractive treatment. It was after reading one of the witch-trials that this occurred to him; and the heroine was to be a girl who for a special purpose had taken a witch's disguise, and whose trick was not discovered until she was actually at the stake. Here is the State Trials story as told by Dickens. "There is a case in the State Trials, where a certain officer made love to a (supposed) miser's daughter, and ultimately induced her to give her father slow poison, while nursing him in sickness. Her father discovered it, told her so, forgave her, and said 'Be patient my dear—I shall not live long, even if I recover: and then you shall have all my wealth.' Though penitent then, she afterwards poisoned him again (under the same influence), and successfully. Whereupon it appeared that the old man had no money at all, and had lived on a small annuity which died with him, though always feigning to be rich. He had loved this daughter with great affection."

A theme verging closely on ground that some might think dangerous, is sketched in the following fancy. "The father (married young) who, in perfect innocence, venerates his son's young wife, as the realisation of his ideal of woman. (He not happy in his own choice.) The son slights her, and knows nothing of her worth. The father watches her, protects her, labours for her, endures for her—is for ever divided between his strong natural affection for his son as his son, and his resentment against him as this young creature's husband." Here is another, less dangerous, which he took from an actual occurrence made known to him when he was at Bonchurch. "The idea of my being brought up by my mother (me the narrator), my father being dead; and growing up in this belief until I find that my father is the gentleman I have sometimes seen, and oftener heard of, who has the handsome young wife, and the dog I once took notice of when I was a little child, and who lives in the great house and drives about."

Very admirable is this. "The girl separating herself from the lover who has shown himself unworthy—loving him still—living single for his sake—but never more renewing their old relations. Coming to him when they are both grown old, and nursing him in his last illness." Nor is the following less so. "Two girls *mis-marrying* two men. The man who has evil in him, dragging the superior woman down. The man who has good in him, raising the inferior woman up." Dickens would have been at his best in working out both fancies.

In some of the most amusing of his sketches of character, women also take the lead. "The lady *un peu passée*, who is determined to be interesting. No matter how much I love that person—nay, the more so for that very reason—I MUST flatter, and bother, and be weak and apprehensive and nervous, and what not. If I were well and strong, agreeable and self-denying, my friend might forget me." Another not remotely belonging to the same family is as neatly hit off. "The sentimental woman feels that the comic, undesigning, unconscious man, is 'Her Fate.'—I her fate? God bless my soul, it puts me into a cold perspiration to think of it. *I* her fate? How can *I* be her fate? I don't mean to be. I don't want to have anything to do with her.—Sentimental woman perceives nevertheless that Destiny must be accomplished."

Other portions of a female group are as humorously sketched and hardly less entertaining. "The enthusiastically complimentary person, who forgets you in her own flowery prosiness: as—'I have no need to say to a person of your genius and feeling, and wide range of experience'—and then, being short-sighted, puts up her glass to remember who you are."—"Two sisters" (these were real people known to him). "One going in for being generally beloved (which she is not by any means); and the other for being generally hated (which she needn't be)." —"The bequeathed maid-servant, or friend. Left as a legacy. And a devil of a legacy too."—"The woman who is never on any account to hear of anything shocking. For whom the world is to be of barley-sugar."—"The lady who lives on her enthusiasm; and hasn't a jot."—"Bright-eyed creature selling jewels. The stones and the eyes." Much significance is in the last few words. One may see to what uses Dickens would have turned them.

A more troubled note is sounded in another of these female characters. "I am a common woman—fallen. Is it devilry in me—is it a wicked comfort—what is it—that induces me to be always tempting other women down, while I hate myself!" This next, with as much truth in it, goes deeper than the last. "The prostitute who will not let one certain youth approach her. 'O let there be someone in the world, who having an inclination towards me has not gratified it, and has not known me in my degradation!' She almost loving him.—Suppose, too, this touch in her could not be believed in by his mother or mistress: by some handsome and proudly virtuous woman, always revolting from her." A more agreeable sketch than either follows, though it would not please M. Taine so well. "The little baby-like married woman—so strange in her new dignity, and talking with tears in her eyes, of her sisters 'and all of them' at home. Never from home before, and never going back again." Another from the same manuscript volume not less attractive, which was sketched from his sister-in-law in his own home, I gave upon a former page.

The female character in its relations with the opposite sex has lively illustration in the Memoranda. "The man who is governed by his wife, and is heartily despised in consequence by all other wives; who still want to govern *their* husbands, notwithstanding." An alarming family pair follows that. "The playful—and scratching—family. Father and daughter." And here is another. "The agreeable (and wicked) young-mature man, and his devoted sister." What next was set down he had himself partly seen; and, by inquiry at the hospital named, had ascertained the truth of the rest. "The two people in the Incurable Hospital.—The poor incurable girl lying on a water-bed, and the incurable man who has a strange flirtation with her; comes and makes confidences to her; snips and arranges her plants; and rehearses to her the comic songs (!) by writing which he materially helps out his living."

Two lighter figures are very pleasantly touched. "Set of circumstances which suddenly bring an easy, airy fellow into near relations with people he knows nothing about, and has never even seen. This, through his being thrown in the way of the innocent young personage of the story. 'Then there is Uncle Sam to be considered,' says she. 'Aye to be sure,' says he, 'so there is! By Jupiter, I forgot Uncle Sam. He's a rock ahead, is Uncle Sam. He must be considered, of course; he must be smoothed down; he must be cleared out of the way.

To be sure. I never thought of Uncle Sam.—By the by, Who *is* Uncle Sam?'"

There are several such sketches as that, to set against the groups of women; and some have Dickens's favourite vein of satire in them. "The man whose vista is always stopped up by the image of Himself. Looks down a long walk, and can't see round himself, or over himself, or beyond himself. Is always blocking up his own way. Would be such a good thing for him if he could knock himself down." Another picture of selfishness is touched with great delicacy. "'Too good' to be grateful to, or dutiful to, or anything else that ought to be. 'I won't thank you: you are too good.'—'Don't ask me to marry you: you are too good.'—In short, I don't particularly mind ill-using you, and being selfish with you: for you are *so* good. Virtue its own reward!" A third, which seems to reverse the dial, is but another face of it; frankly avowing faults, which are virtues. "In effect—I admit I am generous, amiable, gentle, magnanimous. Reproach me—I deserve it—I know my faults—I have striven in vain to get the better of them." Dickens would have made much, too, of the working out of the next. "The knowing man in distress, who borrows a round sum of a generous friend. Comes, in depression and tears, dines, gets the money, and gradually cheers up over his wine, as he obviously entertains himself with the reflection that his friend is an egregious fool to have lent it to him, and that *he* would have known better." And so of this other. "The man who invariably says apposite things (in the way of reproof or sarcasm) THAT HE DON'T MEAN. Astonished when they are explained to him."

Here is a fancy that I remember him to have been more than once bent upon making use of: but the opportunity never came. "The two men to be guarded against, as to their revenge. One, whom I openly hold in some serious animosity, whom I am at the pains to wound and defy, and whom I estimate as worth wounding and defying;—the other, whom I treat as a sort of insect, and contemptuously and pleasantly flick aside with my glove. But, it turns out to be the latter who is the really dangerous man; and, when I expect the blow from the other, it comes from *him*."

We have the master hand in the following bit of dialogue, which takes wider application than that for which it appears to have been intended.

"'There is some virtue in him too.'

"'Virtue! Yes. So there is in any grain of seed in a seedsman's shop—but you must put it in the ground, before you can get any good out of it.'

"'Do you mean that *he* must be put in the ground before any good comes of *him*?'

"'Indeed I do. You may call it burying him, or you may call it sowing him, as you like. You must set him in the earth, before you get any good of him.'"

One of the entries is a list of persons and places meant to have been made subjects for special description, and it will awaken regret that only as to one of them (the Mugby Refreshments) his intention was fulfilled. "A Vestryman. A Briber. A Station Waiting-Room. Refreshments at Mugby. A Physician's Waiting-Room. The Royal Academy. An Antiquary's House. A Sale Room. A Picture Gallery (for sale). A Waste-paper Shop. A Post-Office. A Theatre."

All will have been given that have particular interest or value, from this remarkable volume, when the thoughts and fancies I proceed to transcribe have been put before the reader.

"The man who is incapable of his own happiness. Or who is always in pursuit of happiness. Result, Where is happiness to be found then? Surely not Everywhere? Can that be so, after all? Is *this* my experience?"

"The people who persist in defining and analysing their (and everybody else's) moral qualities, motives and what not, at once in the narrowest spirit and the most lumbering manner; —as if one should put up an enormous scaffolding for the building of a pigsty."

"The house-full of Toadies and Humbugs. They all know and despise one another; but—partly to keep their hands in, and partly to make out their own individual cases—pretend not to detect one another."

"People realising immense sums of money, imaginatively —speculatively—counting their chickens before hatched. Inflaming each other's imaginations about great gains of money, and entering into a sort of intangible, impossible, competition as to who is the richer."

"The advertising sage, philosopher, and friend: who educates 'for the bar, the pulpit, or the stage.'"

"The character of the real refugee—not the conventional; the real."

"The mysterious character, or characters, interchanging confidences. 'Necessary to be very careful in that direction.'—'In what direction?'—'B.'—'You don't say so. What, do you mean that C.——?'—'Is aware of D. Exactly.'"

"The father and boy, as I dramatically see them. Opening with the wild dance I have in my mind."

"The old child. That is to say, born of parents advanced in life, and observing the parents of other children to be young. Taking an old tone accordingly."

"A thoroughly sulky character—perverting everything. Making the good, bad—and the bad, good."

"The people who lay all their sins, negligences and ignorances on Providence."

"The man who marries his cook at last, after being so desperately knowing about the sex."

"The swell establishment, frightfully mean and miserable in all but the 'reception rooms.' Those very showy."

"B. tells M. what my opinion is of his work, etc. Quoting the man you have once spoken to, as if he had talked a life's talk in two minutes."

"A misplaced and mis-married man; always, as it were, playing hide and seek with the world; and never finding what Fortune seems to have hidden when he was born."

"Certain women in Africa who have lost children, carry little wooden images of children on their heads, and always put their food to the lips of those images, before tasting it themselves. This is in a part of Africa where the mortality among children (judging from the number of these little memorials) is very great."

Two more entries are the last which he made. "AVAILABLE

NAMES" introduces a wonderful list in the exact following classes and order; as to which the reader may be left to his own memory for selection of such as found their way into the several stories from *Little Dorrit* to the end. The rest, not lifted into that higher notice by such favour of their creator, must remain like any other undistinguished crowd. But among them may perhaps be detected, by those who have special insight for the physiognomy of a name, some few with so great promise in them of fun and character as will make the "mute inglorious" fate which has befallen them a subject for special regret; and much ingenious speculation will probably wait upon all. Dickens has generally been thought, by the curious, to display not a few of his most characteristic traits in this particular field of invention.

First there are titles for books; and from the list subjoined were taken two for Christmas numbers and two for stories, though *Nobody's Fault* had ultimately to give way to *Little Dorrit*.

THE LUMBER ROOM.	TWO GENERATIONS.
SOMEBODY'S LUGGAGE.	BROKEN CROCKERY.
TO BE LEFT TILL CALLED FOR.	DUST.
SOMETHING WANTED.	THE HOME DEPARTMENT.
EXTREMES MEET.	THE YOUNG PERSON.
NOBODY'S FAULT.	NOW OR NEVER.
THE GRINDSTONE.	MY NEIGHBOURS.
ROKESMITH'S FORGE.	THE CHILDREN OF THE FATHERS.
OUR MUTUAL FRIEND.	NO THOROUGHFARE.
THE CINDER HEAP.	

Then comes a batch of "Christian names": Girls and Boys: which stand thus, with mention of the source from which he obtained them. These therefore can hardly be called pure invention. Some would have been reckoned too extravagant for anything but reality.

Girls from Privy Council Education lists

LELIA.	ETTY.	DORIS.
MENELLA.	REBINAH.	BALZINA.
RUBINA.	SEBA.	PLEASANT.
IRIS.	PERSIA.	GENTILLA.
REBECCA.	ARAMANDA.	

Boys from Privy Council Education lists

DOCTOR.	ZERUBBABEL.	PICKLES.
HOMER.	MAXIMILIAN.	ORANGE.
ODEN.	URBIN.	FEATHER.
BRADLEY.	SAMILIAS.	

Girls and Boys from Ditto

AMANDA, ETHLYNIDA; BOETIUS, BOLTIUS.

To which he adds supplementary lists that appear to be his own.

More Boys

ROBERT LADLE.
JOLY STICK.
BILL MARIGOLD.
STEPHEN MARQUICK.
JONATHAN KNOTWELL.
PHILIP BROWNDRESS.
HENRY GHOST.

GEORGE MUZZLE.
WALTER ASHES.
ZEPHANIAH FERRY (or FURY).
WILLIAM WHY.
ROBERT GOSPEL.
THOMAS FATHERLY.
ROBIN SCRUBBAM.

More Girls

SARAH GOLDSACKS.
ROSETTA DUST.
SUSAN GOLDRING.
CATHERINE TWO.
MATILDA RAINBIRD.
MIRIAM DENIAL.
SOPHIA DOOMSDAY.

ALICE THORNEYWORK.
SALLY GIMBLET.
VERITY HAWKYARD.
BIRDIE NASH.
AMBROSINA EVENTS.
APAULINA VERNON.
NELTIE ASHFORD.

And then come the mass of his "available names," which stand thus, without other introduction or comment:

TOWNDLING.
MOOD.
GUFF.
TREBLE.
CHILBY.
SPESSIFER.
SITTERN.
DOSTONE.
CAY-LON.
SNOWELL.
LOTTRUM.
LAMMLE.
FROSER.
SLYANT.
QUEEDY.
BESSELTHUR.
MUSTY.
GROUT.
TERTIUS JOBBER.
AMON HEADSTON.
STRAYSHOTT.
HIGDEN.
MORFIT.
GOLDSTRAW.

WODDER.
WHELPFORD.
FENNERCK.
GANNERSON.
CHINKERBLE.
BINTREY.
WOZENHAM.
STILTWALK.
STILTINGSTALK.
STILTSTALKING.
RAVENDER.
HOLBLACK.
MULLEY.
REDWORTH.
REDFOOT.
TARBOX (B).
TINKLING.
DUDDLE.
JEBUS.
POWDERHILL.
GRIMMER.
SKUSE.
TITCOOMBE.
CRABBLE.

FLEDSON.
HIRLL.
BRAYLE.
MULLENDER.
TRESLINGHAM.
BRANKLE.
MAG.
CHELLYSON.
BLENHAM—CL.
BARDOCK.
SNIGSWORTH.
SWENTON.
CASBY—BEACH.
LOWLEIGH—LOWELY.
PIGRIN.
YERBURY.
PLORNISH.
MAROON.
BANDY-NANDY.
STONEBURY.
MAGWITCH.
MEAGLES.
PANCKS.
HAGGAGE.

BARREL.
INGE.
JUMP.
JIGGINS.
BONES.
COY.
DAWN.
TATKIN.
DROWVEY.
PUDSEY.
WARBLER.
PEEX—SPEEX.
GANNAWAY.
MRS. FLINKS.
PEDSEY.
DUNCALF.
TRICKLEBANK.
SAPSEA.
READYHUFF.
DUFTY.
FOGGY.
TWINN.
BROWNSWORD.
PEARTREE.
SUDDS.
SILVERMAN.
KIMBER.
LAUGHLEY.
LESSOCK.
TIPPINS.
MINNITT.
RADLOWE.
PRATCHETT.
MAWDETT.

SWANNOCK.
TUZZEN.
TWEMLOW.
SQUAB.
JACKMAN.
SUGG.
BREMMILGE.
SILAS BLODGET.
MELVIN BEAL.
BUTTRICK.
EDSON.
SANLORN.
LIGHTWORD.
TITBULL.
BANGHAM.
KYLE—NYLE.
PEMBLE.
MAXEY.
ROKESMITH.
CHIVERY.
FLINKS.
JEE.
HARDEN.
MERDLE.
MURDEN.
TOPWASH.
PORDAGE.
DORRET—DORRIT.
CARTON.
MINIFIE.
SLINGO.
JOAD.
KINCH.

PROVIS.
STILTINGTON.
PODSNAP.
CLARRIKER.
COMPERY.
STRIVER—STRYVER.
PUMBLECHOOK.
WANGLER.
BOFFIN.
BANTINCK.
DIBTON.
WILFER.
GLIBBERY.
MULVEY.
HORLICK.
DOOLGE.
GANNERY.
GARGERY.
WILLSHARD.
RIDERHOOD.
PRATTERSTONE.
CHINKIBLE.
WOPSELL.
WOPSLE.
WHELPINGTON.
GAYVERY.
WEGG.
HUBBLE.
URRY.
KIBBLE.
SKIFFINS.
ETSER.
AKERSHEM.

The last of the Memoranda, and the last words written by Dickens in the blank paper book containing them, are these. "'Then I'll give up snuff.' Brobity.—An alarming sacrifice. Mr. Brobity's snuff-box. The Pawnbroker's account of it?" What was proposed by this must be left to conjecture; but "Brobity" is the name of one of the people in his unfinished story, and the suggestion may have been meant for some incident in it. If so, it is the only passage in the volume which can be in any way connected with the piece of writing on which he was last engaged. Some names were taken for it from the lists, but there is otherwise nothing to recall *Edwin Drood*.

VIII

CLOSING WORD

THE year after America, as the reader knows, saw the commencement of the work which death interrupted. The fragment
will hereafter be described; and here meanwhile may close my
criticism—itself a fragment left for worthier completion by a
stronger hand than mine. It suffices for the present to have
attempted to clear the ground from those distinctions and com-
parisons never safely to be applied to an original writer, and
which always more or less intercept his fair appreciation.

It was long the fashion, with critics of authority, to set up
wide divergences between novels of incident and manners, and
novels of character; the narrower range being left to Fielding
and Smollett, and the larger to Richardson; yet there are not
many now who will accept such classification. Nor is there more
truth in other like distinctions alleged between novelists who
are assumed to be real, or ideal, in their methods of treatment.
To any original novelist of the higher grade there is no meaning
in these contrasted phrases. Neither mode can exist at all perfectly without the other. No matter how sensitive the mind to
external impressions, or how keen the observation to whatever
can be seen, without the rarer seeing of imagination nothing
will be arrived at that is real in any genuine artist-sense. Reverse
the proposition, and the result is expressed in an excellent
remark of Lord Lytton's, that the happiest effort of imagination, however lofty it may be, is that which enables it to be
cheerfully at home with the real. I have said that Dickens felt
criticism, of whatever kind, with too sharp a relish for the
indifference he assumed to it; but the secret was that he believed
himself to be entitled to higher tribute than he was always in
the habit of receiving. It was the feeling which suggested a
memorable saying of Wordsworth. "I am not at all desirous
that anyone should write a critique on my poems. If they be
from above, they will do their own work in course of time; if
not, they will perish as they ought."

The something "from above" never seems to me absent from Dickens, even at his worst. When the strain upon his invention became apparent, and he could only work freely in a more confined space than of old, it was still able to assert itself triumphantly; and his influence over his readers was continued by it to the last day of his life. Looking back over the series of his writings, the first reflection that rises to the mind of any thoughtful person, is one of thankfulness that the most popular of writers, who had carried into the lowest scenes and conditions an amount of observation, fun, and humour not approached by any of his contemporaries, should never have sullied that world-wide influence by a hint of impurity or a possibility of harm. Nor is there anything more surprising than the freshness and variety of character which those writings include within the range of the not numerous types of character that were the limit of their author's genius. For, this also appears, upon any review of them collectively, that the teeming life which is in them is that of the time in which his own life was passed; and that with the purpose of showing vividly its form and pressure, was joined the hope and design to leave it better than he found it. It has been objected that humanity receives from him no addition to its best types; that the burlesque humourist is always stronger in him than the reflective moralist; that the light thrown by his genius into out-of-the-way corners of life never steadily shines in its higher beaten ways; and that beside his pictures of what man is or does, there is no attempt to show, by delineation of an exalted purpose or a great career, what man is able to be or to do. In the charge abstractedly there is truth; but the fair remark upon it is that whatever can be regarded as essential in the want implied by it will be found in other forms in his writings, that the perfect innocence of their laughter and tears has been itself a prodigious blessing, and that it is otherwise incident to so great a humorist to work after the fashion most natural to the genius of humour. What kind of work it has been in his case, the attempt is made in preceding pages to show; and on the whole it can be said with some certainty that the best ideals in this sense are obtained, not by presenting with added comeliness or grace the figures which life is ever eager to present as of its best, but by connecting the singularities and eccentricities which ordinary life is apt to reject or overlook, with the appreciation that is deepest and the laws of insight that are most universal. It is thus that everything human is happily brought within human sympathy.

It was at the heart of whatever Dickens wrote, making him the intimate of every English household, and a familiar friend where ever the language is spoken whose stores of harmless pleasure he has so largely increased. Above all it was the secret of the hope he had that his books might help to make people better; and it so guarded them from evil, that there is scarcely a page of the thousands he has written which might not be put into the hands of a little child.

I borrow that expression from the Bishop of Manchester, who, on the third day after Dickens's death, in the Abbey where he was so soon to be laid, closed a plea for the toleration of differences of opinion where the foundations of religious truth are accepted, with these words. "It will not be out of harmony with the line of thought we have been pursuing—certainly it will be in keeping with the associations of this place, dear to Englishmen, not only as one of the proudest Christian temples, but as containing the memorials of so many who by their genius in arts, or arms, or statesmanship, or literature, have made England what she is—if in the simplest and briefest words I allude to that sad and unexpected death which has robbed English literature of one of its highest living ornaments, and the news of which, two mornings ago, must have made every household in England feel as though they had lost a personal fr'end. He has been called in one notice an apostle of the people. I suppose it is meant that he had a mission, but in a style and fashion of his own; a gospel, a cheery, joyous, gladsome message, which the people understood, and by which they could hardly help being bettered; for it was the gospel of kindliness, of brotherly love, of sympathy in the widest sense of the word. I am sure I have felt in myself the healthful spirit of his teaching. Possibly we might not have been able to subscribe to the same creed in relation to God, but I think we should have subscribed to the same creed in relation to man. He who has taught us our duty to our fellow-men better than we knew it before, who knew so well to weep with them that wept, and to rejoice with them that rejoiced, who has shown forth in all his knowledge of the dark corners of the earth how much sunshine may rest upon the lowliest lot, who had such evident sympathy with suffering, and such a natural instinct of purity that there is scarcely a page of the thousands he has written which might not be put into the hands of a little child, must be regarded by those who recognise the diversity of the gifts of the spirit as a teacher sent from God. He would have been welcomed as a fellow-labourer in the common interests of humanity by Him who asked the question 'If a man love not his brother whom he hath seen, how can he love God whom he hath not seen?'"

"The loss of no single man during the present generation, if we except Abraham Lincoln alone," said Mr. Horace Greeley, describing the profound and universal grief of America at his death, "has carried mourning into so many families, and been so unaffectedly lamented through all the ranks of society." "The terrible news from England," wrote Longfellow to me (Cambridge, Mass., 12 June, 1870), "fills us all with inexpressible sadness. Dickens was so full of life that it did not seem possible he could die, and yet he has gone before us, and we are sorrowing for him. . . . I never knew an author's death cause such general mourning. It is no exaggeration to say that this whole country is stricken with grief. . . ." Nor was evidence then wanting, that far beyond the limits of society on that vast continent the English writer's influence had penetrated. Of this, very touching illustration was given on a former page; and proof even more striking has since been afforded to me, that not merely in wild or rude communities, but in life the most savage and solitary, his genius had helped to while time away.

"Like all Americans who read," writes an American gentleman, "and that takes in nearly all our people, I am an admirer and student of Dickens. . . . Its perusal" (that of my second volume) "has recalled an incident which may interest you. Twelve or thirteen years ago I crossed the Sierra Nevada mountains as a government surveyor under a famous frontiersman and civil engineer—Colonel Lander. We were too early by a month, and became snow-bound just on the very summit. Under these circumstances it was necessary to abandon the wagons for a time, and drive the stock (mules) down the mountains to the valleys where there was pasturage and running water. This was a long and difficult task, occupying several days. On the second day, in a spot where we expected to find nothing more human than a grizzly bear or an elk, we found a little hut, built of pine boughs and a few rough boards clumsily hewn out of small trees with an axe. The hut was covered with snow many feet deep, excepting only the hole in the roof which served for a chimney, and a small pit-like place in front to permit egress. The occupant came forth to hail us and solicit whisky and tobacco. He was dressed in a suit made entirely of flour-sacks, and was curiously labelled on various parts of his person *Best Family Flour. Extra.* His head was covered by a wolf's skin drawn from the brute's head—with the ears standing erect in a fierce alert manner. He was a most extraordinary object, and told us he had not seen a human being in four months. He lived on bear and elk meat and flour, laid in during his short summer. Emigrants in the season paid him a kind of ferry-toll. I asked him how he passed his time, and he went to a barrel and produced *Nicholas Nickleby* and *Pickwick*. I found he knew them almost by heart. He did not know, or seem to care, about the author; but he gloried in Sam Weller, despised Squeers, and would probably have taken the latter's scalp with great skill and cheerfulness. For Mr. Winkle he had no feeling but contempt, and in fact regarded a fowling-piece as only a toy for a squaw. He had no Bible; and perhaps if he practised in his rude savage way all Dickens taught, he might less have felt the want even of that companion."

BOOK TENTH

AMERICA REVISITED
1867–8. ÆT. 55–6

I. November and December, 1867.
II. January to April, 1868.

I

AMERICA: NOVEMBER AND DECEMBER

1867

It is the intention of this and the following chapter to narrate the incidents of the visit to America in Dickens's own language, and in that only. They will consist almost exclusively of extracts from his letters written home, to members of his family and to myself.

† 25

On the night of Tuesday, 19 November, he arrived at Boston, where he took up his residence at the Parker House Hotel; and his first letter (21st) stated that the tickets for the first four readings, all to that time issued, had been sold immediately on their becoming saleable. "An immense train of people waited in the freezing street for twelve hours, and passed into the office in their turns, as at a French theatre. The receipts already taken for these nights exceed our calculation by more than £250." Up to the last moment, he had not been able to clear off wholly a shade of misgiving that some of the old grudges might make themselves felt; but from the instant of his setting foot in Boston not a vestige of such fear remained. The greeting was to the full as extraordinary as that of twenty-five years before, and was given now, as then, to the man who had made himself the most popular writer in the country. His novels and tales were crowding the shelves of all the dealers in books in all the cities of the Union. In every house, in every car, on every steamboat, in every theatre of America, the characters, the fancies, the phraseology of Dickens were become familiar beyond those of any other writer of books. "Even in England," said one of the New York journals, "Dickens is less known than here; and of the millions here who treasure every word he has written, there are tens of thousands who would make a large sacrifice to see and hear the man who has made happy so many hours. Whatever sensitiveness there once was to adverse or sneering criticism, the lapse of a quarter of a century, and the profound significance of a great war, have modified or removed." The point was more pithily, and as truly, put by Mr. Horace Greeley in the *Tribune*. "The fame as a novelist which Mr. Dickens had already created in America, and which, at the best, has never yielded him anything particularly munificent or substantial, is become his capital stock in the present enterprise."

The first reading was appointed for 2 December, and in the interval he saw some old friends and made some new ones. Boston he was fond of comparing to Edinburgh as Edinburgh was in the days when several dear friends of his own still lived there. Twenty-five years had changed much in the American city; some genial faces were gone, and on ground which he had left a swamp he found now the most princely streets; but there was no abatement of the old warmth of kindness, and, with every attention and consideration shown to him, there was no intrusion. He was not at first completely conscious of the change in this respect, or of the prodigious increase in the size of Boston. But the latter grew upon him from day to day, and then there was impressed along with it a contrast to which it was difficult to reconcile himself. Nothing enchanted him so much as what he again saw of the delightful domestic life of Cambridge, simple, self-respectful, cordial, and affectionate; and it seemed impossible to believe that within half an hour's distance of it should be found what might at any time be witnessed in such hotels as that which he was staying at: crowds of swaggerers, loafers, bar-loungers, and dram-drinkers, that seemed to be making up, from day to day, not the least important part of the human life of the city. But no great mercantile resort in the States, such as Boston had now become, could be without that drawback; and fortunate should we account any place to be, though ever so plague-afflicted, that has yet so near it the healthier influence of the other life which our older world has well-nigh lost altogether.

"The city has increased prodigiously in twenty-five years," he wrote to his daughter Mary. "It has grown more mercantile. It is like Leeds mixed with Preston, and flavoured with New Brighton. Only, instead of smoke and fog, there is an exquisitely bright light air." "Cambridge is exactly as I left it," he wrote to me. "Boston more mercantile, and much larger. The hotel I formerly stayed at, and thought a very big one, is now regarded as a very small affair. I do not yet notice—but a day, you know, is not a long time for observation!—any marked change in character or habits. In this immense hotel I live very high up, and have a hot and cold bath in my bedroom, with other comforts not in existence in my former day. The cost of living is enormous." "Two of the staff are at New York," he wrote to his sister-in-law on 25 November, "where we are at our wits' end how to keep tickets out of the hands of speculators. We have communications from all parts of the country, but we take no offer whatever. The young undergraduates of Cambridge have made a representation to Longfellow that they are 500 strong and cannot get one ticket. I don't know what is to be done, but I suppose I must read there, somehow. We are all in the clouds until I shall have broken ground in New York." The sale of tickets, there, had begun two days before the first reading in Boston. "At the New York barriers," he wrote to his daughter on the first of December, "where the tickets were on sale and the people ranged as at the Paris theatres, speculators went up and down offering twenty dollars for anybody's place. The money was in no case accepted. But one man sold two tickets for the second, third, and fourth nights; his payment in exchange being one ticket for the first night, fifty dollars (about £7 10s.), and a 'brandy cocktail.'"

On Monday, 2 December, he read for the first time in Boston, his subjects being the *Carol* and the *Trial from Pickwick*; and his reception, from an audience than which perhaps none more remarkable could have been brought together, went beyond all expectations formed. "It is really impossible," he wrote to me next morning, "to exaggerate the magnificence of the reception or the effect of the reading. The whole city will talk of nothing else and hear of nothing else to-day. Every ticket for those announced here, and in New York, is sold. All are sold at the highest price, for which in our calculation we made no allowance; and it is impossible to keep out speculators who immediately sell at a premium. At the decreased rate of money even, we had above £450 English in the house last night; and the New York hall holds 500 people more. Everything looks brilliant beyond the most sanguine hopes, and I was quite as cool last night as though I were reading at Chatham." The next night he read again; and also on Thursday and Friday; on Wednesday he had rested; and on Saturday he travelled to New York.

He had written, the day before he left, that he was making a clear profit of thirteen hundred pounds English a week, even allowing seven dollars to the pound; but words were added having no good omen in them, that the weather was taking a turn of even unusual severity, and that he found the climate, in the suddenness of its changes, "and the wide leaps they take," excessively trying. "The work is of course rather trying too; but the sound position that everything must be subservient to it enables me to keep aloof from invitations. To-morrow," ran the close of the letter, "we move to New York. We cannot beat the speculators in our tickets. We sell no more than six to any one person for the course of four readings; but these speculators, who sell at greatly increased prices and make large profits, will employ any number of men to buy. One of the chief of them— now living in this house, in order that he may move as we move! —can put on 50 people in any place we go to; and thus he gets 300 tickets into his own hands." Almost while Dickens was writing these words an eyewitness was describing to a Phila-delphia paper the sale of the New York tickets. The pay-place was to open at nine on a Wednesday morning, and at midnight of Tuesday a long line of speculators were assembled in queue; at two in the morning a few honest buyers had begun to arrive; at five there were, of all classes, two lines of not less than 800 each; at eight there were at least 5000 persons in the two lines; at nine each line was more than three-quarters of a mile in length, and neither became sensibly shorter during the whole morning. "The tickets for the course were all sold before noon. Members of families relieved each other in the queues; waiters flew across the streets and squares from the neighbouring restaurant, to serve parties who were taking their breakfast in the open December air; while excited men offered five and ten dollars for the mere permission to exchange places with other persons standing nearer the head of the line!"

The effect of the reading in New York corresponded with this marvellous preparation, and Dickens characterised his audience as an unexpected support to him; in its appreciation quick and unfailing, and highly demonstrative in its satisfactions. On 11 December he wrote to his daughter: "Amazing success. A very fine audience, far better than at Boston. *Carol* and *Trial* on first night, great; still greater, *Copperfield* and *Bob Sawyer* on second. For the tickets of the four readings of next week there were, at nine o'clock this morning, 3000 people in waiting, and they had begun to assemble in the bitter cold as early as two o'clock in the morning." To myself he wrote on the 15th, adding touches to the curious picture. "Dolby has got into trouble about the manner of issuing the tickets for next week's series. He cannot get four thousand people into a room holding only two thousand, he cannot induce people to pay at the ordinary price for themselves instead of giving thrice as much to speculators, and he is attacked in all directions. . . . I don't much like my hall, for it has two large balconies far removed from the platform; but no one ever waylays me as I go into it or come out of it, and it is kept as rigidly quiet as the Français at a rehearsal. We have not yet had in it less than £430 per night, allowing for the depreciated currency! I send £3000 to England by this packet. From all parts of the States, applications and offers continually come in. We go to Boston next Saturday for two more readings, and come back here on Christmas Day for four more. I am not yet bound to go elsewhere, except three times, each time for two nights, to Philadelphia; thinking it wisest to keep free for the largest placcs. I have had an action brought against me by a man who considered himself injured (and really may have been) in the matter of his tickets. Personal service being necessary, I was politely waited on by a marshal for that purpose; whom I received with the greatest courtesy, apparently very much to his amazement. The action was handsomely withdrawn next day, and the plaintiff paid his own costs. . . . Dolby hopes you are satisfied with the figures so far; the profit each night exceeding the estimated profit by £130 odd. He is anxious I should also tell you that he is the most unpopular and best-abused man in America." Next day a letter to his sister-in-law related an incident too common in American cities to disconcert any but strangers. He had lodged himself, I should have said, at the Westminster Hotel in Irving Place. "Last night I was getting into bed just at 12 o'clock, when Dolby came to my door to inform me that the house was on fire. I got Scott up directly; told him first to pack the books and clothes for the readings; dressed, and pocketed my jewels and papers; while the manager stuffed himself out with money. Meanwhile the police and firemen were in the house tracing the mischief to its source in a certain fire-grate. By this time the hose was laid all through from a great tank on the roof, and everybody turned out to help. It was the oddest sight, and people had put the strangest things on! After chopping and cutting with axes through stairs, and much handing about of water, the fire was confined to a dining-room in which it had originated; and then everybody talked to everybody else, the ladies being particularly loquacious and cheerful. I may remark that the second landlord (from both, but especially the first, I have had untiring attention) no sooner saw me on this agitating occasion, than, with his property blazing, he insisted on taking me down into a room full of hot smoke, to drink brandy and water with him! And so we got to bed again about two."

Dickens had been a week in New York before he was able to identify the great city which a lapse of twenty-five years had so prodigiously increased. "The only portion that has even now come back to me," he wrote, "is the part of Broadway in which the Carlton Hotel (long since destroyed) used to stand. There is a very fine new park in the outskirts, and the number of grand houses and splendid equipages is quite surprising. There are hotels close here with 500 bedrooms and I don't know how many boarders; but this hotel is quite as quiet as, and not much larger than, Mivart's in Brook Street. My rooms are all *en suite*, and I come and go by a private door and private staircase communicating with my bedroom. The waiters are French, and one might be living in Paris. One of the two proprietors is also proprietor of Niblo's Theatre, and the greatest care is taken of me. Niblo's great attraction, the *Black Crook*, has now been played every night for 16 months (!), and is the most preposterous peg to hang ballets on that was ever seen. The people who act in it have not the slightest idea of what it is about, and never had; but, after taxing my intellectual powers to the utmost, I fancy that I have discovered Black Crook to be a malignant hunchback leagued with the Powers of Darkness to separate two lovers; and that the Powers of Lightness coming (in no skirts whatever) to the rescue, he is defeated. I am quite serious in saying that I do not suppose there are two pages of *All the Year Round* in the whole piece (which acts all night); the whole of the rest of it being ballets of all sorts, perfectly unaccountable processions, and the Donkey out of last year's Covent Garden pantomime! At the other theatres, comic operas, melodramas, and domestic dramas prevail all over the city, and my stories play no inconsiderable part in them. I go nowhere, having laid down the rule that to combine visiting with my work would be absolutely impossible. . . . The Fenian explosion at Clerkenwell was telegraphed here in a few hours. I do not think there is any sympathy whatever with the Fenians on the part of the American people, though political adventurers may make capital out of a show of it. But no doubt large sections of the Irish population of this State are themselves Fenian; and the local politics of the place are in a most depraved condition, if half of what is said to me be true. I prefer not to talk of these things, but at odd intervals I look round for myself. Great social improvements in respect of manners and forbearance have come to pass since I was here before, but in public life I see as yet but little change."

He had got through half of his first New York readings when a winter storm came on, and from this time until very near his return the severity of the weather was exceptional even for America. When the first snow fell, the railways were closed for some days; and he described New York crowded with sleighs, and the snow piled up in enormous walls the whole length of the streets. "I turned out in a rather gorgeous sleigh yesterday with any quantity of buffalo robes, and made an imposing appearance." "If you were to behold me driving out," he wrote to his daughter, "furred up to the moustache, with an immense white red-and-yellow-striped rug for a covering, you would suppose me to be of Hungarian or Polish nationality." These protections nevertheless availed him little; and when the time came for getting back to Boston, he found himself at the close of his journey with a cold and cough that never again left him until he had quitted the country, and of which the effects became more and more disastrous. For the present there was little allusion to this, his belief at the first being strong that he should overmaster it; but it soon forced itself into all his letters.

His railway journey otherwise had not been agreeable. "The railways are truly alarming. Much worse (because more worn I suppose) than when I was here before. We were beaten about yesterday, as if we had been aboard the *Cuba*. Two rivers have to be crossed, and each time the whole train is banged aboard a big steamer. The steamer rises and falls with the river, which the railroad don't do; and the train is either banged up hill or banged down hill. In coming off the steamer at one of these crossings yesterday, we we were banged up such a height that the rope broke, and one carriage rushed back with a run down-hill into the boat again. I whisked out in a moment, and two or three others after me; but nobody else seemed to care about it. The treatment of the luggage is perfectly outrageous. Nearly every case I have is already broken. When we started from Boston yesterday, I beheld, to my unspeakable amazement, Scott, my dresser, leaning a flushed countenance against the wall of the car, and *weeping bitterly*. It was over my smashed writing-desk. Yet the arrangements for luggage are excellent, if the porters would not be beyond description reckless." The same excellence of provision, and flinging away of its advantages, are observed in connection with another subject in the same letter. "The halls are excellent. Imagine one holding two thousand people, seated with exact equality for every one of them, and every one seated separately. I have nowhere, at home or abroad, seen so fine a police as the police of New York; and their bearing in the streets is above all praise. On the other hand, the laws for regulation of public vehicles, clearing of streets, and removal of obstructions, are wildly outraged by the people for whose benefit they are intended. Yet there is undoubtedly improvement in every direction, and I am taking time to make up my mind on things in general. Let me add that I have been tempted out at three in the morning to visit one of the large police station-houses, and was so fascinated by the study of a horrible photograph-book of thieves' portraits that I couldn't shut it up."

A letter of the same date (22nd) to his sister-in-law told of personal attentions awaiting him on his return to Boston by which he was greatly touched. He found his rooms garnished with flowers and holly, with real red berries, and with festoons of moss; and the homely Christmas look of the place quite affected him. "There is a certain Captain Dolliver belonging to the Boston custom-house, who came off in the little steamer that brought me ashore from the *Cuba*; and he took it into his head that he would have a piece of English mistletoe brought out in this week's Cunard, which should be laid upon my breakfast table. And there it was this morning. In such affec-t'onate touches as this, these New England people are especially amiable. . . . As a general rule you may lay it down that whatever you see about me in the papers is not true; but you may generally lend a more believing ear to the Philadelphia correspondent of *The Times*, a well-informed gentle-man. Our hotel in New York was on fire again the other night. But fires in this country are quite matters of course. There was a large one in Boston at four this morning; and I don't think a single night has passed, since I have been under the protection of the Eagle, that I have not heard the Fire Bells dolefully clanging all over both cities." The violent abuse of his manager by portions of the press is the subject of the rest of the letter, and receives further illustration in one of the same date to me. "A good specimen of the sort of newspaper you and I know something of, came out in Boston here this morning. The editor had applied for our advertisements, saying that 'it was at Mr.

D.'s disposal for paragraphs.' The advertisements were not sent; Dolby did not enrich its columns paragraphically; and among its news to-day is the item that 'this chap calling himself Dolby got drunk down town last night, and was taken to the police station for fighting an Irishman'! I am sorry to say that I don't find anybody to be much shocked by this liveliness." It is right to add what was said to me a few days later. "The *Tribune* is an excellent paper. Horace Greeley is editor in chief, and a considerable shareholder too. All the people connected with it whom I have seen are of the best class. It is also a very fine property--but here the *New York Herald* beats it hollow, hollow, hollow! Another able and well-edited paper is the *New York Times*. A most respectable journal too is Bryant's *Evening Post*, excellently written. There is generally a much more responsible and respectable tone than prevailed formerly, however small may be the literary merit, among papers pointed out to me as of large circulation. In much of the writing there is certainly improvement, but it might be more widely spread."

The time had now come when the course his readings were to take independently of the two leading cities must be settled, and the general tour made out. His agent's original plan was that they should be in New York every week. "But I say No. By the 10th of January I shall have read to 35,000 people in that city alone. Put the readings out of the reach of all the people behind them, for the time. It is that one of the popular peculiarities which I most particularly notice, that they must not have a thing too easily. Nothing in the country lasts long; and a thing is prized the more, the less easy it is made. Reflecting therefore that I shall want to close. in April, with farewell readings here and in New York, I am convinced that the crush and pressure upon these necessary to their adequate success is only to be got by absence; and that the best thing I can do is not to give either city as much reading as it wants now, but to be independent of both while both are most enthusiastic. I have therefore resolved presently to announce in New York so many readings (I mean a certain number) as the last that can be given there, before I travel to promised places; and that we select the best places, with the largest halls, on our list. This will include, East here—the two or three best New England towns; South—Baltimore and Washington; West—Cincinnati, Pittsburgh, Chicago, and St. Louis; and towards Niagara—Cleveland and Buffalo. Philadelphia we are already pledged to, for six nights; and the scheme will pretty easily bring us here again twice before the farewells. I feel convinced that this is the sound policy." (It was afterwards a little modified, as will be seen, by public occurrences and his own condition of health; the West, as well as a promise to Canada, having to be abandoned; but otherwise it was carried out.) "I read here to-morrow and Tuesday; all tickets being sold to the end of the series, even for subjects not announced. I have not read a single time at a lower clear profit per night (all deductions made) than £315. But rely upon it I shall take great care not to read oftener than four times a week—after this next week, when I stand committed to five. The inevitable tendency of the staff, when these great houses excite them, is, in the words of an old friend of ours, to 'hurge the hartist hon'; and a night or two ago I had to cut away five readings from *their* list."

An incident at Boston should have mention before he resumes his readings in New York. In the interval since he was first in America, the Harvard professor of chemistry, Dr. Webster, whom he had at that visit met among the honoured men who held chairs in their Cambridge University, had been hanged for the murder, committed in his laboratory in the college, of a friend who had lent him money, portions of whose body lay concealed under the lid of the lecture-room table where the murderer continued to meet his students. "Being in Cambridge," Dickens wrote to Lord Lytton, "I thought I would go over the Medical School, and see the exact localities where Professor Webster did that amazing murder, and worked so hard to rid himself of the body of the murdered man. (I find there is of course no rational doubt that the Professor was always a secretly cruel man.) They were horribly grim, private, cold, and quiet; the identical furnace smelling fearfully (some anatomical broth in it I suppose) as if the body were still there; jars of pieces of sour mortality standing about, like the forty robbers in *Ali Baba* after being scalded to death; and bodies near us ready to be carried in to next morning's lecture. At the house where I afterwards dined I heard an amazing and fearful story; told by one who had been at a dinner-party of ten or a dozen, at Webster's, less than a year before the murder. They began rather uncomfortably, in consequence of one of the guests (the victim of an instinctive antipathy) starting up with the sweat pouring down his face, and crying out, 'O Heaven! There's a cat somewhere in the room!' The cat was found and ejected, but they didn't get on very well. Left with their wine, they were getting on a little better; when Webster suddenly told the servants to turn the gas off and bring in that bowl of burning minerals which he had prepared, in order that the company might see how ghastly they looked by its weird light. All this was done, and every man was looking, horror-stricken, at his neighbour; when Webster was seen bending over the bowl with a rope round his neck, holding up the end of the rope, with his head on one side and his tongue lolled out, to represent a hanged man!"

Dickens read at Boston on 23 and 24 December, and on Christmas Day travelled back to New York where he was to read on the 26th. The last words written before he left were of illness. "The low action of the heart, or whatever it is, has inconvenienced me greatly this last week. On Monday night, after the reading, I was laid upon a bed, in a very faint and shady state; and on the Tuesday I did not get up till the afternoon." But what in reality was less grave took outwardly the form of a greater distress; and the effects of the cold which had struck him in travelling to Boston, as yet not known to his English friends, appear most to have alarmed those about him. I depart from my rule in this narrative, otherwise strictly observed, in singling out one of those friends for mention by name; but a business connection with the readings, as well as untiring offices of personal kindness and sympathy, threw Mr. Fields into closer relations with Dickens from arrival to de- † 26 parture, than any other person had; and his description of the condition of health in which Dickens now quitted Boston and went through the rest of the labour he had undertaken, will be a sad though fit prelude to what the following chapter has to tell. "He went from Boston to New York carrying with him a severe catarrh contracted in our climate. He was quite ill from the effects of the disease; but he fought courageously against them. . . . His spirit was wonderful, and, although he lost all appetite and could partake of very little food, he was always cheerful and ready for his work when the evening came round. A dinner was tendered to him by some of his literary friends in Boston; but he was so ill the day before that the banquet had to be given up. The strain upon his strength and nerves was very great during all the months he remained, and only a man of iron will could have accomplished what he did. He was accustomed to talk and write a good deal about eating and drinking, but I have rarely seen a man eat and drink less. He liked to dilate in imagination over the brewing of a bowl of punch, but when the punch was ready he drank less of it than anyone who might be present. It was the sentiment of the thing and not the thing itself that engaged his attention. I scarcely saw him eat a hearty meal during his whole stay. Both at Parker's hotel in Boston, and at the Westminster in New York, everything was arranged by the proprietors for his comfort, and tempting dishes to pique his invalid appetite were sent up at different hours of the day; but the influenza had seized him with masterful power, and held the strong man down till he left the country."

When he arrived in New York on the evening of Christmas Day he found a letter from his daughter. Answering her next day he told her: "I wanted it much, for I had a frightful cold (English colds are nothing to those of this country) and was very miserable. . . . It is a bad country to be unwell and travelling in. You are one of, say, a hundred people in a heated car with a great stove in it, all the little windows being closed; and the bumping and banging about are indescribable, the atmosphere detestable, the ordinary motion all but intolerable." The following day this addition was made to the letter. "I managed to read last night, but it was as much as I could do. To-day I am so very unwell that I have sent for a doctor. He has just been, and is in doubt whether I shall not have to stop reading for a while."

His stronger will prevailed, and he went on without stopping. On the last day of the year he announced to us that though he had been very low he was getting right again; that in a couple of days he should have accomplished a fourth of the entire readings; and that the first month of the new year would see him through Philadelphia and Baltimore, as well as through two more nights in Boston. He also prepared his English friends for the startling intelligence they might shortly expect, of four readings coming off in a church, before an audience of two thousand people accommodated in pews, and with himself emerging from a vestry.

II

THE reading on 3 January closed a fourth of the entire
series, and on that day Dickens wrote of the trouble brought
on them by the "speculators," which to some extent had
affected unfavourably the three previous nights in New York.
When adventurers bought up the best places, the public resented
it by refusing the worst; to prevent it by first helping themselves, being the last thing they ever thought of doing. "We try
to withhold the best seats from the speculators, but the unaccountable thing is that the great mass of the public buy of
them (prefer it), and the rest of the public are injured if we
have not got those very seats to sell them. We have now a
travelling staff of six men, in spite of which Dolby, who is
leaving me to-day to sell tickets in Philadelphia to-morrow
morning, will no doubt get into a tempest of difficulties. Of
course also, in such a matter, as many obstacles as possible
are thrown in an Englishman's way; and he may himself be
a little injudicious into the bargain. Last night, for instance,
he met one of the 'ushers' (who show people to their seats)
coming in with one of our men. It is against orders that anyone
employed in front should go out during the reading, and he
took this man to task in the British manner. Instantly, the
free and independent usher put on his hat and walked off.
Seeing which, all the other free and independent ushers (some
twenty in number) put on *their* hats and walked off; leaving
us absolutely devoid and destitute of a staff for to-night. One
has since been improvised: but it was a small matter to raise
a stir and ill-will about, especially as one of our men was equally
in fault; and really there is little to be done at night. American
people are so accustomed to take care of themselves, that one
of these immense audiences will fall into their places with an
ease amazing to a frequenter of St. James's Hall; and the
certainty with which they are all in, before I go on, is a very

331

acceptable mark of respect. Our great labour is outside; and we have been obliged to bring our staff up to six, besides a boy or two, by employment of a regular additional clerk, a Bostonian. The speculators buying the front seats (we have found instances of this being done by merchants in good position) the public won't have the back seats; return their tickets; write and print volumes on the subject; and deter others from coming. You are not to suppose that this prevails to any great extent, as our lowest house here has been £300; but it does hit us. There is no doubt about it. Fortunately I saw the danger when the trouble began, and changed the list at the right time. . . . You may get an idea of the staff's work, by what is in hand now. They are preparing, numbering, and stamping, 6000 tickets for Philadelphia, and 8000 tickets for Brooklyn. The moment those are done, another 8000 tickets will be wanted for Baltimore, and probably another 6000 for Washington; and all this in addition to the correspondence, advertisements, accounts, travelling, and the nightly business of the readings four times a week.

. . I cannot get rid of this intolerable cold! My landlord invented for me a drink of brandy, rum, and snow, called it a 'Rocky Mountain Sneezer,' and said it was to put down all less effectual sneezing; but it has not yet had the effect. Did I tell you that the favourite drink before you get up is an Eye-opener? There has been another fall of snow, succeeded by a heavy thaw."

The day after (the 4th) he went back to Boston, and next day wrote to me: "I am to read here on Monday and Tuesday, return to New York on Wednesday, and finish there (except the farewells in April) on Thursday and Friday. The New York reading of *Doctor Marigold* made really a tremendous hit. The people doubted at first, having evidently not the least idea what could be done with it, and broke out at last into a perfect chorus of delight. At the end they made a great shout, and gave a rush towards the platform as if they were going to carry me off. It puts a strong additional arrow into my quiver. Another extraordinary success has been *Nickleby* and *Boots at the Holly Tree* (appreciated here in Boston, by the by, even more than *Copperfield*); and think of our last New York night bringing £500 English into the house, after making more than the necessary deduction for the present price of gold! The manager is always going about with an immense bundle that looks like a sofa-cushion, but is in reality paper-money, and it had risen to the proportions of a sofa on the morning he left for Philadelphia. Well, the work is hard, the climate is hard, the life is hard:

but so far the gain is enormous. My cold steadily refuses to stir an inch. It distresses me greatly at times, though it is always good enough to leave me for the needful two hours. I have tried allopathy, homœopathy, cold things, warm things, sweet things, bitter things, stimulants, narcotics, all with the same result. Nothing will touch it."

In the same letter, light was thrown on the ecclesiastical mystery. "At Brooklyn I am going to read in Mr. Ward Beecher's chapel: the only building there available for the purpose. You must understand that Brooklyn is a kind of sleeping-place for New York, and is supposed to be a great place in the money way. We let the seats pew by pew! the pulpit is taken down for my screen and gas! and I appear out of the vestry in canonical form! These ecclesiastical entertainments come off on the evenings of the 16th, 17th, 20th, and 21st of the present month." His first letter after returning to New York (9 January) made additions to the Brooklyn picture. "Each evening an enormous ferry-boat will convey me and my state-carriage (not to mention half a dozen wagons and any number of people and a few score of horses) across the river to Brooklyn, and will bring me back again. The sale of tickets there was an amazing scene. The noble army of speculators are now furnished (this is literally true, and I am quite serious) each man with a straw mattress, a little bag of bread and meat, two blankets, and a bottle of whisky. With this outfit, *they lie down in line on the pavement* the whole of the night before the tickets are sold: generally taking up their position at about 10. It being severely cold at Brooklyn, they made an immense bonfire in the street—a narrow street of wooden houses—which the police turned out to extinguish. A general fight then took place; from which the people farthest off in the line rushed bleeding when they saw any chance of ousting others nearer the door, put their mattresses in the spots so gained, and held on by the iron rails. At 8 in the morning Dolby appeared with the tickets in a portmanteau. He was immediately saluted with a roar of Halloa! Dolby! Dolby! So Charley has let you have the carriage, has he, Dolby? How is he, Dolby? Don't drop the tickets, Dolby! Look alive, Dolby, etc., in the midst of which he proceeded to business, and concluded (as usual) by giving universal dissatisfaction. He is now going off upon a little journey to look over the ground and cut back again. This little journey (to Chicago) is twelve hundred miles on end, by railway, besides the back again!" It might tax the Englishman, but was nothing to the native American. It was part of his New York landlord's ordinary life in a week, Dickens told me, to go to Chicago and look at his theatre there on a Monday; to pelt back to Boston and look at his theatre there on a Thursday; and to come rushing to New York on a Friday, to apostrophise his enormous ballet.

Three days later, still at New York, he wrote to his sister-in-law. "I am off to Philadelphia this evening for the first of three visits of two nights each, tickets for all being sold. My cold steadily refuses to leave me, but otherwise I am as well as I can hope to be under this heavy work. My New York readings are over (except the farewell nights), and I look forward to the relief of being out of my hardest hall. On Friday I was again dead beat at the end, and was once more laid upon a sofa. But the faintness went off after a little while. We have now cold bright frosty weather, without snow; the best weather for me." Next day from Philadelphia he wrote to his daughter that he was lodged in The Continental, one of the most immense of American hotels, but that he found himself just as quiet as elsewhere. "Everything is very good, my waiter is German, and the greater part of the servants seem to be coloured people. The town is very clean, and the day as blue and bright as a fine Italian day. But it freezes very very hard, and my cold is not improved; for the cars were so intolerably hot that I was often obliged to stand upon the brake outside, and then the frosty air bit me indeed. I find it necessary (so oppressed am I with this American catarrh as they call it) to dine at three o'clock instead of four, that I may have more time to get voice; so that the days are cut short and letter-writing not easy."

He nevertheless found time in this city to write to me (14 January) the most interesting mention he had yet made of such opinions as he had been able to form during his present visit, apart from the pursuit that absorbed him. Of such of those opinions as were given on a former page, it is only necessary to repeat that while the tone of party politics still impressed him unfavourably, he had thus far seen everywhere great changes for the better socially. I will add other points from the same letter. That he was unfortunate in his time of visiting New York, as far as its politics were concerned, what has since happened conclusively shows. "The Irish element is acquiring such enormous influence in New York city, that when I think of it, and see the large Roman Catholic cathedral rising there, it seems unfair to stigmatise as 'American' other monstrous things that one also sees. But the general corruption in respect of the local funds appears to be stupendous, and there is an alarming thing as to some of the courts of law which I am afraid is native-born. A case came under my notice the other day in which it was perfectly plain, from what was said to me by a person interested in resisting an injunction, that his first proceeding had been to 'look up the Judge.'" Of such occasional provincial oddity, harmless in itself but strange in large cities, as he noticed in the sort of half-disappointment at the small fuss made by himself about the readings, and in the newspaper references to "Mr. Dickens's extraordinary composure" on the platform, he gives an illustration. "Last night here in Phila-delphia (my first night), a very impressible and responsive audience were so astounded by my simply walking in and opening my book that I wondered what was the matter. They evidently thought that there ought to have been a flourish, and Dolby sent in to prepare for me. With them it is the simplicity of the operation that raises wonder. With the newspapers 'Mr. Dickens's extraordinary composure' is not reasoned out as being necessary to the art of the thing, but is sensitively watched with a lurking doubt whether it may not imply disparage-ment of the audience. Both these things strike me as drolly expressive. . . ."

His testimony as to improved social habits and ways was expressed very decidedly. "I think it reasonable to expect that as I go westward, I shall find the old manners going on before me, and may tread upon their skirts mayhap. But so far, I have had no more intrusion or boredom than I have when I lead the same life in England. I write this is an immense hotel, but I am as much at peace in my own rooms, and am left as wholly un-disturbed, as if I were at the Station Hotel in York. I have now read in New York city to 40,000 people, and am quite as well known in the streets there as I am in London. People will turn back, turn again and face me, and have a look at me, or will say to one another, 'Look here! Dickens coming!' But no one ever stops me or addresses me. Sitting reading in the carriage outside the New York post office while one of the staff was stamping the letters inside, I became conscious that a few people who had been looking at the turn-out had discovered me within. On my peeping out good-humouredly, one of them (I should say a merchant's book-keeper) stepped up to the door, took off his hat, and said in a frank way: 'Mr. Dickens, I should very much like to have the honour of shaking hands with you' —and, that done, presented two others. Nothing could be more quiet or less intrusive. In the railways cars, if I see anybody who clearly wants to speak to me, I usually anticipate the wish by speaking myself. If I am standing on the brake outside (to avoid the intolerable stove), people getting down will say with a smile: 'As I am taking my departure, Mr. Dickens, and can't trouble you for more than a moment, I should like to take you by the hand, sir.' And so we shake hands and go our ways. . . . Of course many of my impressions come through the readings. Thus I find the people lighter and more humorous than formerly; and there must be a great deal of innocent imagination among every class, or they never could pet with such extraordinary pleasure as they do, the Boots's story of the elopement of the two little children. They seem to see the children; and the women set up a shrill undercurrent of half-pity and half-pleasure that is quite affecting. To-night's reading is my 26th; but as all the Philadelphia tickets for four more are sold, as well as four at Brooklyn, you must assume that I am at—say—my 35th reading. I have remitted to Coutts's in English gold £10,000 odd; and I roughly calculate that on this number Dolby will have another thousand pounds profit to pay me. These figures are of course between ourselves, at present; but are they not magnificent? The expenses, always recollect, are enormous. On the other hand we never have occasion to print a bill of any sort (bill-printing and posting are great charges at home); and have just now sold off £90 worth of bill-paper, provided beforehand, as a wholly useless incumbrance."

Then came, as ever, the constant shadow that still attended him, the slave in the chariot of his triumph. "The work is very severe. There is now no chance of my being rid of this American catarrh until I embark for England. It is very distressing. It likewise happens, not seldom, that I am so dead beat when I come off that they lay me down on a sofa after I have been washed and dressed, and I lie there, extremely faint, for a quarter of an hour. In that time I rally and come right." One week later from New York, where he had become due on the 16th for the first of his four Brooklyn readings, he wrote to his sister-in-law. "My cold sticks to me, and I can scarcely exaggerate what I undergo from sleeplessness. I rarely take any breakfast but an egg and a cup of tea—not even toast or bread and butter. My small dinner at 3, and a little quail or some such light thing when I come home at night, is my daily fare; and at the hall I have established the custom of taking an egg beaten up in sherry before going in, and another between the parts, which I think pulls me up. . . . It is snowing hard now, and I begin to move to-morrow. There is so much floating ice in the river, that we are obliged to have a pretty wide margin of time for getting over the ferry to read." The last of the readings over the ferry was on the day when this letter was written. "I finished at my church to-night. It is Mrs. Stowe's brother's, and a most wonderful place to speak in. We had it enormously full last night (*Marigold* and *Trial*), but it scarcely required an effort. Mr. Ward Beecher being present in his pew, I sent to invite him to come round before he left. I found him to be an unostentatious, evidently able, straight-forward, and agreeable man; extremely well-informed, and with a good knowledge of art."

Baltimore and Washington were the cities in which he was now, on quitting New York, to read for the first time; and as to the latter some doubts arose. The exceptional course had been taken in regard to it, of selecting a hall with space for not more than 700 and charging everybody five dollars; to which Dickens, at first greatly opposed, had yielded upon use of the argument, "you have more people at New York, thanks to the speculators, paying more than five dollars every night." But now other suggestions came. "Horace Greeley dined with me last Saturday," he wrote on the 20th, "and didn't like my going to Washington, now full of the greatest rowdies and worst kind of people in the States. Last night at eleven came B. expressing like doubts; and though they may be absurd I thought them worth attention, B. coming so close on Greeley." Mr. Dolby was in consequence sent express to Washington with power to with-draw or go on, as inquiry on the spot might dictate; and Dickens took the additional resolve so far to modify the last arrange-ments of his tour as to avoid the distances of Chicago, St. Louis, and Cincinnati, to content himself with smaller places and profits, and thereby to get home nearly a month earlier. He was at Philadelphia on 23 January, when he announced this intention. "The worst of it is, that everybody one advises with has a monomania respecting Chicago. 'Good heavens, sir,' the great Philadelphia authority said to me this morning, 'if you don't read in Chicago the people will go into fits!' Well, I answered, I would rather they went into fits than I did. But he didn't seem to see it at all."

From Baltimore he wrote to his sister-in-law on the 29th, in the hour's interval he had to spare before going back to Phila-delphia. "It has been snowing hard for four and twenty hours

—though this place is as far south as Valencia in Spain, and my manager, being on his way to New York, has a good chance of being snowed up somewhere. This is one of the places where Butler carried it with a high hand during the war, and where the ladies used to spit when they passed a Northern soldier. They are very handsome women, with an Eastern touch in them, and dress brilliantly. I have rarely seen so many fine faces in an audience. They are a bright responsive people likewise, and very pleasant to read to. My hall is a charming little opera house built by a society of Germans: quite a delightful place for the purpose. I stand on the stage, with the drop curtain down, and my screen before it. The whole scene is very pretty and complete, and the audience have a 'ring' in them that sounds deeper than the ear. I go from here to Philadelphia, to read to-morrow night and Friday; come through here again on Saturday on my way back to Washington; come back here on Saturday week for two finishing nights; then go to Philadelphia for two farewells—and so turn my back on the southern part of the country. Our new plan will give 82 readings in all." (The real number was seventy-six, six having been dropped on subsequent political excitements.) "Of course I afterwards discovered that we had finally settled the list on a Friday. I shall be halfway through it at Washington; of course on a Friday also, and my birthday." To myself he wrote on the following day from Philadelphia, beginning with a thank Heaven that he had struck off Canada and the West, for he found the wear and tear "enormous." "Dolby decided that the croakers were wrong about Washington, and went on: the rather as his raised prices, which he put finally at three dollars each, gave satisfaction. Fields is so confident about Boston, that my remaining list includes, in all, 14 more readings there. I don't know how many more we might not have had here (where I have had attentions otherwise that have been very grateful to me), if we had chosen. Tickets are now being resold at ten dollars each. At Baltimore I had a charming little theatre, and a very apprehensive impulsive audience. It is remarkable to see how the Ghost of Slavery haunts the town; and how the shambling, untidy, evasive, and postponing Irrepressible proceeds about his free work, going round and round it, instead of at it. The melancholy absurdity of giving these people votes, at any rate at present, would glare at one out of every roll of their eyes, chuckle in their mouths, and bump in their heads, if one did not see (as one cannot help seeing in the country) that their enfranchisement is a mere party trick to get votes. Being at the Penitentiary the other day (this, while we mention votes), and looking over the books, I noticed that almost every man had been 'pardoned' a day or two before his time was up. Why? Because if he had served his time out, he would have been *ipso facto* disfranchised. So, this form of pardon is gone through to save his vote; and as every officer of the prison holds his place only in right of his party, of course his hopeful clients vote for the party that has let them out! When I read in Mr. Beecher's church at Brooklyn, we found the trustees had suppressed the fact that a certain upper gallery holding 150 was 'the Coloured Gallery.' On the first night not a soul could be induced to enter it; and it was not until it became known next day that I was certainly not going to read there more than four times, that we managed to fill it. One night at New York, on our second or third row, there were two well-dressed women with a tinge of colour—I should say, not even quadroons. But the holder of one ticket who found his seat to be next them, demanded of Dolby 'What he meant by fixing him next to those two Gord darmed cusses of niggers?' and insisted on being supplied with another good place. Dolby firmly replied that he was perfectly certain Mr. Dickens would not recognise such an objection on any account, but he could have his money back if he chose. Which, after some squabbling, he had. In a comic scene in the New York Circus one night, when I was looking on, four white people sat down upon a form in a barber's shop to be shaved. A coloured man came as the fifth customer, and the four immediately ran away. This was much laughed at and applauded. In the Baltimore Penitentiary, the white prisoners dine on one side of the room, the coloured prisoners on the other; and no one has the slightest idea of mixing them. But it is indubitably the fact that exhalations not the most agreeable arise from a number of coloured people got together, and I was obliged to beat a quick retreat from their dormitory. I strongly believe that they will die out of this country fast. It seems, looking at them, so manifestly absurd to suppose it possible that they can ever hold their own against a restless, shifty, striving, stronger race."

On 4 February he wrote from Washington. "You may like to have a line to let you know that it is all right here, and that the croakers were simply ridiculous. I began last night. A charming audience, no dissatisfaction whatever at the raised prices, nothing missed or lost, cheers at the end of the *Carol*, and rounds upon rounds of applause all through. All the foremost men and their families had taken tickets for the series of four. A small place to read in. £300 in it." It will be no violation of the rule of avoiding private detail if the very interesting close of this letter is given. Its anecdote of President Lincoln was repeatedly told by Dickens after his return, and I am under no necessity to withhold from it the authority of Mr. Sumner's name. "I am going to-morrow to see the President, who has sent to me twice. I dined with Charles Sumner last Sunday, against my rule; and as I had stipulated for no party, Mr. Secretary Stanton was the only other guest, besides his own secretary. Stanton is a man with a very remarkable memory, and extraordinarily familiar with my books. . . . He and Sumner having been the first two public men at the dying President's bedside, and having remained with him until he breathed his last, we fell into a very interesting conversation after dinner, when, each of them giving his own narrative separately, the usual discrepancies about details of time were observable. Then Mr. Stanton told me a curious little story which will form the remainder of this short letter.

"On the afternoon of the day on which the President was shot, there was a cabinet council at which he presided. Mr. Stanton, being at the time commander-in-chief of the Northern troops that were concentrated about here, arrived rather late. Indeed they were waiting for him, and on his entering the room, the President broke off in something he was saying, and remarked: 'Let us proceed to business, gentlemen.' Mr. Stanton then noticed, with great surprise, that the President sat with an air of dignity in his chair instead of lolling about it in the most ungainly attitudes, as his invariable custom was; and that instead of telling irrelevant or questionable stories, he was grave and calm, and quite a different man. Mr. Stanton, on leaving the council with the Attorney-General, said to him, 'That is the most satisfactory cabinet meeting I have attended for many a long day! What an extraordinary change in Mr. Lincoln!' The Attorney-General replied, 'We all saw it, before you came in. While we were waiting for you, he said, with his chin down on his breast, "Gentlemen, something very extraordinary is going to happen, and that very soon."' To which the Attorney-General had observed, 'Something good, sir, I hope?' when the President answered very gravely: 'I don't know; I don't know. But it will happen, and shortly too!' As they were all impressed by his manner, the Attorney-General took him up again: 'Have you received any information, sir, not yet disclosed to us?'

'No,' answered the President: 'but I have had a dream. And I have now had the same dream three times. Once, on the night preceding the Battle of Bull Run. Once, on the night preceding' such another (naming a battle also not favourable to the North). His chin sank on his breast again, and he sat reflecting. 'Might one ask the nature of this dream, sir?' said the Attorney-General. 'Well,' replied the President, without lifting his head or changing his attitude, 'I am on a great broad rolling river—and I am in a boat—and I drift—and I drift!—but this is not business'—suddenly raising his face and looking round the table as Mr. Stanton entered, 'let us proceed to business, gentlemen.' Mr. Stanton and the Attorney-General said, as they walked on together, it would be curious to notice whether anything ensued on this; and they agreed to notice. He was shot that night."

On his birthday, 7 February, Dickens had his interview with President Andrew Johnson. "This scrambling scribblement is resumed this morning, because I have just seen the President: who had sent to me very courteously asking me to make my own appointment. He is a man with a remarkable face, indicating courage, watchfulness, and certainly strength of purpose. It is a face of the Webster type, but without the 'bounce' of Webster's face. I would have picked him out anywhere as a character of mark. Figure, rather stoutish for an American; a trifle under the middle size; hands clasped in front of him; manner, suppressed, guarded, anxious. Each of us looked at the other very hard. . . . It was in his own cabinet that I saw him. As I came away, Thornton drove up in a sleigh —turned out for a state occasion—to deliver his credentials. There was to be a cabinet council at 12. The room was very like a London club's ante-drawing room. On the walls, two engravings only: one, of his own portrait; one, of Lincoln's. . . . In the outer room was sitting a certain sunburnt General Blair, with many evidences of the war upon him. He got up to shake hands with me, and then I found that he had been out on the Prairie with me five-and-twenty years ago. . . . The papers having referred to my birthday's falling to-day, my room is filled with most exquisite flowers. They came pouring in from all sorts of people at breakfast time. The audiences here are really very fine. So ready to laugh or cry, and doing both so freely, that you would suppose them to be Manchester shillings rather than Washington half-sovereigns. Alas! alas! my cold worse than ever." So he had written too at the opening of his letter.

* 146

The first reading had been four days earlier, and was described to his daughter in a letter on the 4th, with a comical incident that occurred in the course of it. "The gas was very defective indeed last night, and I began with a small speech to the effect that I must trust to the brightness of their faces for the illumination of mine. This was taken greatly. In the *Carol* a most ridiculous incident occurred. All of a sudden, I saw a dog leap out from among the seats in the centre aisle, and look very intently at me. The general attention being fixed on me, I don't think anybody saw this dog; but I felt so sure of his turning up again and barking, that I kept my eye wandering about in search of him. He was a very comic dog, and it was well for me that I was reading a comic part of the book. But when he bounced out into the centre aisle again, in an entirely new place, and (still looking intently at me) tried the effect of a bark upon my proceedings, I was seized with such a paroxysm of laughter that it communicated itself to the audience, and we roared at one another, loud and long." Three days later the sequel came, in a letter to his sister-in-law. "I mentioned the dog on the first night here? Next night, I thought I heard (in *Copperfield*) a suddenly-suppressed bark. It happened in this wise: One of our people standing just within the door, felt his leg touched, and looking down beheld the dog, staring intently at me, and evidently just about to bark. In a transport of presence of mind and fury, he instantly caught him up in both hands, and threw him over his own head out into the entry, where the check-takers received him like a game at ball. Last night he came again, *with another dog*; but our people were so sharply on the look-out for him that he didn't get in. He had evidently promised to pass the other dog, free."

What is expressed in these letters, of a still active, hopeful, enjoying, energetic spirit, able to assert itself against illness of the body and in some sort to over-master it, was also so strongly impressed upon those who were with him, that, seeing his sufferings as they did, they yet found it difficult to understand the extent of them. The sadness thus ever underlying his triumph makes it all very tragical. "That afternoon of my birthday," he wrote from Baltimore on the 11th, "my catarrh was in such a state that Charles Sumner, coming in at five o'clock, and finding me covered with mustard poultice, and apparently voiceless, turned to Dolby and said: 'Surely, Mr. Dolby, it is impossible that he can read to-night!' Says Dolby: 'Sir, I have told Mr. Dickens so, four times to-day, and I have been very anxious.

last Tuesday in a very curious state. Perhaps you know that
Great Falls of the Genessee River (really very fine, even so n
Niagara) are at that place. In the height of a sudden thaw,
immense bank of ice above the rapids refused to yield; so t
the town was threatened (for the second time in four ye
with submersion. Boats were ready in the streets, all the ped
were up all night, and none but the children slept. In the d
of the night a thundering noise was heard, the ice gave w
the swollen river came raging and roaring down the Falls, a
the town was safe. Very picturesque! but 'not very good
business,' as the manager says. Especially as the hall sta
in the centre of danger, and had ten feet of water in it on
last occasion of flood. But I think we had above £200 Engl
On the previous night at Syracuse—a most out of the way a
unintelligible-looking place, with apparently no people in i
we had £375 odd. Here we had, last night, and shall h
to-night, whatever we can cram into the hall.

"This Buffalo has become a large and important town, w
numbers of German and Irish in it. But it is very curious
notice, as we touch the frontier, that the American female bea
dies out; and a woman's face clumsily compounded of Germ
Irish, Western America, and Canadian, not yet fused togeth
and not yet moulded, obtains instead. Our show of Beauty
ight is, generally, remarkable; but we had not a dozen pre
women in the whole throng last night, and the faces were
blunt. I have just been walking about, and observing the sa
hing in the streets. . . . The winter has been so severe, t
he hotel on the English side at Niagara (which has the b
iew of the Falls, and is for that reason very preferable) is
et open. So we go, perforce, to the American: which telegra
ack to our telegram: 'all Mr. Dickens's requirements perfec
nderstood.' I have not yet been in more than two very
ns. I have been in some, where a good deal of what is po
rly called 'slopping round' has prevailed; but have been a
get on very well. 'Slopping round,' so used, means unti
ss and disorder. It is a comically expressive phrase, and l
any meanings. Fields was asking the price of a quarter-ca
sherry the other day. 'Wa'al Mussr Fields,' the mercha
plies, 'that varies according to quality, as is but nay'tral.
r wa'ant a sherry just to slop round with it, I can fix y
me at a very low figger.'"
His letter was resumed at Rochester on the 18th. "After t
ost brilliant days at the Falls of Niagara, we got back h

But you have no idea how he will change, when he gets to the
little table.' After five minutes of the little table I was not (for
the time) even hoarse. The frequent experience of this return
of force when it is wanted, saves me a vast amount of anxiety;
but I am not at times without the nervous dread that I may
some day sink altogether." To the same effect in another letter
he adds: "Dolby and Osgood," the latter represented the publishing firm of Mr. Fields and was one of the travelling staff.
"who do the most ridiculous things to keep me in spirits (I am
often very heavy, and rarely sleep much), are determined to
have a walking match at Boston on the last day of February
to celebrate the arrival of the day when I can say '*next* month!'
for home." The match ended in the Englishman's defeat; which
Dickens doubly commemorated, by a narrative of the American
victory in sporting-newspaper style, and by a dinner in Boston
to a party of dear friends there.

After Baltimore he was reading again at Philadelphia, from
which he wrote to his sister-in-law on the 13th as to a characteristic trait observed in both places. "Nothing will induce the
people to believe in the farewells. At Baltimore on Tuesday
night (a very brilliant night indeed), they asked as they came
out: 'When will Mr. Dickens read here again?' 'Never.' 'Nonsense! Not come back, after such houses as these?' 'Come. Say
when he'll read again.' Just the same here. We could as soon
persuade them that I am the President, as that to-morrow night
I am going to read here for the last time. . . . There is a child in
this house—a little girl—to whom I presented a black doll when
I was here last; and as I have just seen her eye at the keyhole
since I began writing this, I think she and the doll must be
outside still. 'When you sent it up to me by the coloured boy,'
she said after receiving it (coloured boy is the term for black
waiter), 'I gave such a cream that Ma come running in and
creamed too, 'cos she fort I'd hurt myself. But I creamed a
cream of joy.' She had a friend to play with her that day, and
brought the friend with her—to my infinite confusion. A friend
all stockings and much too tall, who sat on the sofa very far
back with her stocking sticking stiffly out in front of her, and
glared at me, and never spake a word. Dolby found us confronted
in a sort of fascination, like serpent and bird."

On the 15th he was again at New York, in the thick of more
troubles with the speculators. They involved even charges of
fraud in ticket-sales at Newhaven and Providence; indignation
meetings having been held by the mayors, and unavailing

attempts made by his manager to turn the wrath aside. "I expect him back here presently half bereft of his senses, and I should be wholly bereft of mine if the situation were not comical as well as disagreeable. We can sell at our own box-office to any extent; but we cannot buy back of the speculators, because we have informed the public that all the tickets are gone; and even if we made the sacrifice of buying at their price and selling at ours, we should be accused of treating with them and of making money by it." It ended in Providence by his going himself to the place and making a speech; and in New-haven it ended by his sending back the money taken, with intimation that he would not read until there had been a new distribution of the tickets approved by all the town. Fresh disturbance broke out upon this; but he stuck to his determination to delay the reading until the heats had cooled down, and what should have been given in the middle of February he did not give until the close of March.

The readings he had promised at the smaller outlying places by the Canadian frontier and Niagara district, including Syracuse, Rochester, and Buffalo, were appointed for that same March month which was to be the interval between the close of the ordinary readings and the farewells in the two leading cities. All that had been promised in New York were closed when he returned to Boston on 23 February, ready for the increase he had promised there; but the check of a sudden political excitement came. It was the month when the vote was taken for impeachment of President Johnson. "It is well" (25 February) "that the money has flowed in hitherto so fast, for I have a misgiving that the great excitement about the President's impeachment will damage our receipts. . . . The vote was taken at 5 last night. At 7 the three large theatres here, all in a rush of good business, were stricken with paralysis. At 8 our long line of outsiders waiting for unoccupied places, was nowhere. To-day you hear all the people in the streets talking of only one thing. I shall suppress my next week's promised readings (by good fortune, not yet announced), and watch the course of events. Nothing in this country, as I before said, lasts long; and I think it likely that the public may be heartily tired of the President's name by the 9th of March, when I read at a considerable distance from here. So behold me with a whole week's holiday in view!" Two days later he wrote pleasantly to his sister-in-law of his audiences. "They have come to regard the readings and the reader as their peculiar

---

property; and you would be both amused and pleased if could see the curious way in which they show this incre interest in both. Whenever they laugh or cry, they have t to applauding as well; and the result is very inspiriting. I remain here until Saturday the 7th; but after to-morrow shall not read here until the 1st of April, when I begi farewells—six in number." On the 28th he wrote: "To-m fortnight we purpose being at the Falls of Niagara, and th shall come back and really begin to wind up. I have got to the *Carol* so well that I can't remember it, and occasiona dodging about in the wildest manner, to pick up lost They took it so tremendously last night that I was s every five minutes. One poor young girl in mourning bur a passion of grief about Tiny Tim, and was taken out. a fine house, and, in the interval while I was out, they the little table with flowers. The cough has taken a fre as if it were a novelty, and is even worse than ever There is a lull in the excitement about the President: articles of impeachment are to be produced this afternoon then it may set in again. Osgood came into camp la from selling in remote places, and reports that at R and Buffalo (both places near the frontier), tickets wer by Canada people, who had struggled across the frozen clambered over all sorts of obstructions to get them. those distant halls turn out to be smaller than represe I have no doubt—to use an American expression—tha 'get along.' The second half of the receipts cannot r be expected to come up to the first; political circu and all other surroundings, considered."

His old ill luck in travel pursued him. On the day was written a snow-storm began, with a heavy gal and "after all the hard weather gone through," he 2 March, "this is the worst day we have seen. graphed that the storm prevails over an immense country, and is just the same at Chicago as here. I l prove a wind up. We are getting sick of the ver sleigh-bells even." The roads were so bad and th. much out of time, that he had to start a and on 6 March his tour north-west began, wi still blowing and the snow falling heavily. On wrote to me from Buffalo:

"We go to the Falls of Niagara to-morrow pleasure; and I take all the men, as a treat. We fou

last night. To-morrow morning we turn out at 6 for a long railway journey back to Albany. But it is nearly all 'back' now, thank God! I don't know how long, though, before turning, we might have gone on at Buffalo. . . . We went everywhere at the Falls, and saw them in every aspect. There is a suspension bridge across, now, some two miles or more from the Horse Shoe; and another, half a mile nearer, is to be opened in July. They are very fine but very ticklish, hanging aloft there, in the continual vibration of the thundering water: nor is one greatly reassured by the printed notice that troops must not cross them at step, that bands of music must not play in crossing, and the like. I shall never forget the last aspect in which we saw Niagara yesterday. We had been everywhere, when I thought of struggling (in an open carriage) up some very difficult ground for a good distance, and getting where we could stand above the river, and see it, as it rushes forward to its tremendous leap, coming for miles and miles. All away to the horizon on our right was a wonderful confusion of bright green and white water. As we stood watching it with our faces to the top of the Falls, our backs were towards the sun. The majestic valley below the Falls, so seen through the vast cloud of spray, was made of rainbow. The high banks, the riven rocks, the forests, the bridge, the buildings, the air, the sky, were all made of rainbow. Nothing in Turner's finest water-colour drawings, done in his greatest day, is so ethereal, so imaginative, so gorgeous in colour, as what I then beheld. I seemed to be lifted from the earth and to be looking into Heaven. What I once said to you, as I witnessed the scene five and twenty years ago, all came back at this most affecting and sublime sight. The 'muddy vesture of our clay' falls from us as we look. . . . I chartered a separate carriage for our men, so that they might see all in their own way, and at their own time.

"There is a great deal of water out between Rochester and New York, and travelling is very uncertain, as I fear we may find to-morrow. There is again some little alarm here on account of the river rising too fast. But our to-night's house is far ahead of the first. Most charming halls in these places; excellent for sight and sound. Almost invariably built as theatres, with stage, scenery, and good dressing-rooms. Audience seated to perfection (every seat always separate), excellent doorways and passages, and brilliant light. My screen and gas are set up in front of the drop-curtain, and the most delicate touches will tell anywhere. No creature but my own men ever near me." His anticipation of the uncertainty that might beset his travel back had dismal fulfilment. It is described in a letter written on the 21st from Springfield to his valued friend, Mr. Frederic Ouvry, having much interest of its own, and making lively addition to the picture which these chapters give. The unflagging spirit that bears up under all disadvantages is again marvellously shown. "You can hardly imagine what my life is with its present condition—how hard the work is, and how little time I seem to have at my disposal. It is necessary to the daily recovery of my voice that I should dine at 3 when not travelling; I begin to prepare for the evening at 6; and I get back to my hotel, pretty well knocked up, at half-past 10. Add to all this, perpetual railway travelling in one of the severest winters ever known; and you will descry a reason or two for my being an indifferent correspondent. Last Sunday evening I left the Falls of Niagara for this and two intervening places. As there was a great thaw, and the melted snow was swelling all the rivers, the whole country for three hundred miles was flooded. On the Tuesday afternoon (I had read on the Monday) the train gave in, as under circumstances utterly hopeless, and stopped at a place called Utica; the greater part of which was under water, while the high and dry part could produce nothing particular to eat. Here, some of the wretched passengers passed the night in the train, while others stormed the hotel. I was fortunate enough to get a bedroom, and garnished it with an enormous jug of gin-punch; over which I and the manager played a double-dummy rubber. At six in the morning we were knocked up: 'to come aboard and try it.' At half-past six we were knocked up again with the tidings 'that it was of no use coming aboard or trying it.' At eight all the bells in the town were set a-going, to summon us to 'come aboard' instantly. And so we started, through the water, at four or five miles an hour; seeing nothing but drowned farms, barns adrift like Noah's arks, deserted villages, broken bridges, and all manner of ruin. I was to read at Albany that night, and all the tickets were sold. A very active superintendent of works assured me that if I could be 'got along,' he was the man to get me along: and that if I couldn't be got along, I might conclude that it couldn't possibly be fixed. He then turned on a hundred men in seven-league boots, who went ahead of the train, each armed with a long pole and pushing the blocks of ice away. Following this cavalcade, we got to land at last, and arrived in time for me to read the *Carol* and *Trial* triumphantly. My people (I had five of the staff with me) turned to at their work with a will, and did a day's labour in a couple of hours. If we had not come in as we did, I should have lost £350, and Albany would have gone distracted. You may conceive what the flood was, when I hint at the two most notable incidents of our journey:—1. We took the passengers out of two trains, who had been in the water, immovable all night and all the previous day. 2. We released a large quantity of sheep and cattle from trucks that had been in the water I don't know how long, but so long that the creatures in them had begun to eat each other, and presented a most horrible spectacle."   * 148

Beside Springfield, he had engagements at Portland, New Bedford, and other places in Massachusetts, before the Boston farewells began; and there wanted but two days to bring him to that time, when he thus described to his daughter the labour which was to occupy them. His letter was from Portland on 29 March, and it will be observed that he no longer compromises or glozes over what he was and had been suffering During his terrible travel to Albany his cough had somewhat spared him, but the old illness had broken out in his foot; and, though he persisted in ascribing it to the former supposed origin ("having been lately again wet, from walking in melted snow, which I suppose to be the occasion of its swelling in the old way"), it troubled him sorely, extended now at intervals to the right foot also, and lamed him for all the time he remained in the States. "I should have written to you by the last mail, but I really was too unwell to do it. The writing day was last Friday, when I ought to have left Boston for New Bedford (55 miles) before eleven in the morning. But I was so exhausted that I could not be got up, and had to take my chance of an evening train's producing me in time to read—which it just did. With the return of snow, nine days ago, my cough became as bad as ever. I have coughed every morning from two or three till five or six, and have been absolutely sleepless. I have had no appetite besides, and no taste. Last night here, I took some laudanum;   * 149 and it is the only thing that has done me good, though it made me sick this morning. But the life, in this climate, is so very hard! When I did manage to get to New Bedford, I read with my utmost force and vigour. Next morning, well or ill, I must turn out at seven, to get back to Boston on my way here. I dined at Boston at three, and at five had to come on here (a hundred and thirty miles or so) for to-morrow night: there being no Sunday train. To-morrow night I read here in a very large place; and Tuesday morning at six I must again start, to get back to Boston once more. But after to-morrow night I have only the farewells, thank God! Even as it is, however, I have had to write to Dolby (who is in New York) to see my doctor there, and ask him to send me some composing medicine that I can take at night, inasmuch as without sleep I cannot get through. However sympathetic and devoted the people are about one, they CAN NOT be got to comprehend, seeing me able to do the two hours when the time comes round, that it may also involve much misery." To myself on the 30th he wrote from the same place, making like confession. No comment could deepen the sadness of the story of suffering, revealed in his own simple language. "I write in a town three parts of which were burnt down in a tremendous fire three years ago. The people lived in tents while their city was rebuilding. The charred trunks of the trees with which the streets of the old city were planted, yet stand here and there in the new thoroughfares like black spectres. The rebuilding is still in progress everywhere. Yet such is the astonishing energy of the people that the large hall in which I am to read to-night (its predecessor was burnt) would compare very favourably with the Free Trade Hall at Manchester! . . . I am nearly used up. Climate, distance, catarrh, travelling, and hard work, have begun (I may say so, now they are nearly all over) to tell heavily upon me. Sleeplessness besets me; and if I had engaged to go on into May, I think I must have broken down. It was well that I cut off the Far West and Canada when I did. There would else have been a sad complication. It is impossible to make the people about one understand, how-ever zealous and devoted (it is impossible even to make Dolby understand until the pinch comes), that the power of coming up to the mark every night, with spirits and spirit, may coexist with the nearest approach to sinking under it. When I got back to Boston on Thursday, after a very hard three weeks, I saw that Fields was very grave about my going on to New Bedford (55 miles) next day, and then coming on here (180 miles) *next* day. But the stress is over, and so I can afford to look back upon it, and think about it, and write about it." On the 31st he closed his letter at Boston, and he was at home when I heard of him again. "The latest intelligence, my dear old fellow, is, that I have arrived here safely, and that I am certainly better. I consider my work virtually over, now. My impression is, that the political crisis will damage the farewells by about one half. I cannot yet speak by the card; but my predictions here, as to our proceedings, have thus far been invariably right. We took last night at Portland, £360 English; where a costly Italian troupe, using the same hall to-night, had not booked £14! It is the same all over the country, and the worst is not seen yet. Everything is becoming absorbed in the Presidential impeachment, helped by the next Presidential election. Connecticut is particularly excited. The night after I read at Hartford this last week, there were two political meetings in the town; meetings of two parties; and the hotel was full of speakers coming in from outlying places. So at Newhaven: the moment I had finished, carpenters came in to prepare for next night's politics. So at Buffalo. So everywhere very soon."

In the same tone he wrote his last letter to his sister-in-law from Boston. "My notion of the farewells is pretty certain now to turn out right. We had £300 English here last night. To-day is a Fast Day, and to-night we shall probably take much less. Then it is likely that we shall pull up again, and strike a good reasonable average; but it is not at all probable that we shall do anything enormous. Every pulpit in Massachusetts will resound with violent politics to-day and to-night." That was on the second of April, and a postcript was added. "Friday afternoon the 3rd. Catarrh worse than ever! and we don't know (at four o'clock) whether I can read to-night or must stop. Otherwise, all well."

Dickens's last letter from America was written to his daughter Mary from Boston on 9 April, the day before his sixth and last farewell night. "I not only read last Friday when I was doubtful of being able to do so, but read as I never did before, and astonished the audience quite as much as myself. You never saw or heard such a scene of excitement. Longfellow and all the Cambridge men have urged me to give in. I have been very near doing so, but feel stronger to-day. I cannot tell whether the catarrh may have done me any lasting injury in the lungs or other breathing organs, until I shall have rested and got home. I hope and believe not. Consider the weather! There have been two snowstorms since I wrote last, and to-day the town is blotted out in a ceaseless whirl of snow and wind. Dolby is as tender as a woman, and as watchful as a doctor. He never leaves me during the reading, now, but sits at the side of the platform, and keeps his eye upon me all the time. Ditto George the gasman, steadiest and most reliable man I ever employed. I have *Dombey* to do to-night, and must go through it carefully; so here ends my report. The personal affection of the people in this place is charming to the last. Did I tell you that the New York Press are going to give me a public dinner on Saturday the 18th?"

In New York, where there were five farewell nights, three thousand two hundred and ninety-eight dollars were the receipts of the last, on 20 April; those of the last at Boston, on the 8th, having been three thousand four hundred and fifty-six dollars. But, on earlier nights in the same cities respectively, these sums also had been reached; and indeed, making allowance for an exceptional night here and there, the receipts varied so wonderfully little, that a mention of the highest average returns from other places will give no exaggerated impression of the ordinary receipts throughout, excluding fractions of dollars, the lowest were New Bedford ($1640), Rochester ($1906), Springfield ($1970), and Providence ($2140). Albany and Worcester averaged something less than $2400; while Hartford, Buffalo, Baltimore, Syracuse, Newhaven, and Portland rose to $2600. Washington's last night was $2610, no night there having less than $2500. Philadelphia exceeded Washington by $300, and Brooklyn went ahead of Philadelphia by $200. The amount taken at the four Brooklyn readings was 11,128 dollars.

The New York public dinner was given at Delmonico's, the hosts were more than two hundred, and the chair was taken by Mr. Horace Greeley. Dickens attended with great difficulty, and spoke in pain. But he used the occasion to bear his testimony to the changes of twenty-five years; the rise of vast new cities; growth in the graces and amenities of life; much improvement in the press, essential to every other advance; and changes in himself leading to opinions more deliberately formed. He promised his kindly entertainers that no copy of his *Notes*, or his *Chuzzlewit*, should in future be issued by him without accompanying mention of the changes to which he had referred that night; of the politeness, delicacy, sweet temper, hospitality, and consideration in all ways for which he had to thank them; and of his gratitude for the respect shown, during all his visit, to the privacy enforced upon him by the nature of his work and the condition of his health.

He had to leave the room before the proceedings were over. On the following Monday he read to his last American audience, telling them at the close that he hoped often to recall them, equally by his winter fire and in the green summer weather, and never as a mere public audience but as a host of personal friends. He sailed two days later in the *Russia*, and reached England in the first week of May 1868.

BOOK ELEVENTH

SUMMING UP

1868–70. ÆT. 56–8

I

LAST READINGS
1868–70

FAVOURABLE weather helped Dickens pleasantly home. He had profited greatly by the sea voyage, perhaps more greatly by its repose; and on 25 May he described himself to his Boston friends as brown beyond belief, and causing the greatest disappointment in all quarters by looking so well. "My doctor was quite broken down in spirits on seeing me for the first time last Saturday. *Good lord! seven years younger!* said the doctor, recoiling." That he gave all the credit to "those fine days at sea," and none to the rest from such labours as he had passed through, the close of the letter too sadly showed. "We are already settling—think of this! the details of my farewell course of readings."

Even on his way out to America that enterprise was in hand. From Halifax he had written to me: "I told the Chappells that when I got back to England, I would have a series of farewell readings in town and country; and then read No More. They at once offer in writing to pay all expenses whatever, to pay the ten per cent. for management, and to pay me, for a series of 75, six thousand pounds." The terms were raised and settled before the first Boston readings closed. The number was to be a hundred: and the payment, over and above expenses and percentage, eight thousand pounds. Such a temptation undoubtedly was great; and though it was a fatal mistake which Dickens committed in yielding to it, it was not an ignoble one. He did it under no excitement from the American gains, of which he knew nothing when he pledged himself to the enterprise. No man could care essentially less for mere money than he did. But the necessary provision for many sons was a constant anxiety; he was proud of what the readings had done to abridge this care; and the very strain of them under which it seems that his health had first given way, and which he always steadily refused to connect especially with them, had also broken the old confidence of being at all times available for his

355

higher pursuit. What affected his health only he would not regard as part of the question either way. That was to be borne as the lot more or less of all men; and the more thorough he could make his feeling of independence, and of ability to rest, by what was now in hand, the better his final chances of a perfect recovery would be. That was the spirit in which he entered on this last engagement. It was an opportunity offered for making a particular work really complete before he should abandon it for ever. Something of it will not be indiscernible even in the summary of his past acquisitions, which with a pardonable exultation he now sent me.

"We had great difficulty in getting our American accounts squared to the point of ascertaining what Dolby's commission amounted to in English money. After all, we were obliged to call in the aid of a money-changer, to determine what he should pay as his share of the average loss of conversion into gold. With this deduction made, I think his commission (I have not the figures at hand) was £2888; Ticknor and Fields had a commission of £1000, besides 5 per cent. on all Boston receipts. The expenses in America to the day of our sailing were 38,948 dollars;—roughly 39,000 dollars, or £13,000. The preliminary expenses were £614. The average price of gold was nearly 40 per cent. and yet my profit was within a hundred or so of £20,000. Supposing me to have got through the present engagement in good health, I shall have made by the readings, *in two years*, £33,000 that is to say: £13,000 received from the Chappells, and £20,000 from America. What I had made by them before, I could only ascertain by a long examination of Coutts's books. I should say, certainly not less than £10,000: for I remember that I made half that money in the first town and country campaign with poor Arthur Smith. These figures are of course between ourselves; but don't you think them rather remarkable? The Chappell bargain began with £50 a night and everything paid; then became £60; and now rises to £80."

The last readings were appointed to begin with October; and at the request of an old friend, Chauncy Hare Townshend, who died during his absence in the States, he had accepted the trust, which occupied him some part of the summer, of examining and selecting for publication a bequest of some papers on matters of religious belief, which were issued in a small volume the following year. There came also in June a visit from Longfellow and his daughters, with later summer visits from the Eliot Nortons; and at the arrival of friends whom he loved and honoured as he did these, from the great country to which he owed so much, infinite were the rejoicings of Gadshill. Nothing could quench his old spirit in this way. But, in the intervals of my official work, I saw him frequently that summer, and never without the impression that America had told heavily upon him. There was manifest abatement of his natural force, the elasticity of bearing was impaired, and the wonderful brightness of eye was dimmed at times. One day, too, as he walked from his office with Miss Hogarth to dine at our house, he could read only the halves of the letters over the shop doors that were on his right as he looked. He attributed it to medicine. It was an additional unfavourable symptom that his right foot had become affected as well as the left, though not to anything like the same extent, during the journey from the Canada frontier to Boston. But all this disappeared upon any special cause for exertion; and he was never unprepared to lavish freely for others the reserved strength that should have been kept for himself. This indeed was the great danger, for it dulled the apprehension of us all to the fact that absolute and pressing danger did positively exist.

He had scarcely begun these last readings than he was beset by a misgiving, that, for a success large enough to repay Messrs. Chappell's liberality, the enterprise would require a new excitement to carry him over the old ground; and it was while engaged in Manchester and Liverpool at the outset of October that this announcement came. "I have made a short reading of the murder in *Oliver Twist*. I cannot make up my mind, however, whether to do it or not. I have no doubt that I could perfectly petrify an audience by carrying out the notion I have of the way of rendering it. But whether the impression would not be so horrible as to keep them away another time, is what I cannot satisfy myself upon. What do you think? It is in three short parts: 1. Where Fagin sets Noah Claypole on to watch Nancy. 2. The scene on London Bridge. 3. Where Fagin rouses Claypole from his sleep to tell his perverted story to Sikes: and the Murder, and the Murderer's sense of being haunted. I have adapted and cut about the text with great care, and it is very powerful. I have to-day referred the book and the question to the Chappells as so largely interested." I had a strong dislike to this proposal, less perhaps on the ground which ought to have been taken of the physical exertion it would involve, than because such a subject seemed to be altogether out of the province of reading; and it was resolved, that, before doing it, trial should be made to a limited private audience in St. James's Hall. The note announcing this, from Liverpool on 25 October, is for other reasons worth printing. "I give you earliest notice that the Chappells suggest to me the 18th of November" (the 14th was chosen) "for trial of the *Oliver Twist* murder, when everything in use for the previous day's reading can be made available. I hope this may suit you? We have been doing well here; and how it was arranged, nobody knows, but we had £410 at St. James's Hall last Tuesday, having advanced from our previous £360. The expenses are such, however, on the princely scale of the Chappells, that we never begin at a smaller, often at a larger, cost than £180. . . . I have not been well, and have been heavily tired. However, I have little to complain of —nothing, nothing; though, like Mariana, I am aweary. But, think of this. If all go well and (like Mr. Dennis) I 'work off' this series triumphantly, I shall have made of these readings £28,000 in a year and a half." This did not better reconcile me to what had been too clearly forced upon him by the supposed necessity of some new excitement to ensure a triumphant result; and even the private rehearsal only led to a painful correspondence between us, of which a few words are all that need now be preserved. "We might have agreed," he wrote, "to differ about it very well, because we only wanted to find out the truth if we could, and because it was quite understood that I wanted to leave behind me the recollection of something very passionate and dramatic, done with simple means, if the art would justify the theme." Apart from mere personal considerations, the whole question lay in these last words. It was impossible for me to admit that the effect to be produced was legitimate, or such as it was desirable to associate with the recollection of his readings.

Mention should not be omitted of two sorrows which affected him at this time. At the close of the month before the readings began, his youngest son went forth from home to join an elder brother in Australia. "These partings are hard hard things" (26 September), "but they are the lot of us all, and might have to be done without means or influence, and then would be far harder. God bless him!" Hardly a month later, the last of his surviving brothers, Frederick, the next to himself, died at Darlington. "He had been tended" (24 October), "with the greatest care and affection by some local friends. It was a wasted life, but God forbid that one should be hard upon it, or upon anything in this world that is not deliberately and coldly wrong."

Before October closed the renewal of his labour had begun to tell upon him. He wrote to his sister-in-law on the 29th of sickness and sleepless nights, and of its having become necessary, when he had to read, that he should lie on the sofa all day. After arrival at Edinburgh in December, he had been making a calculation that the railway travelling over such a distance involved something more than thirty thousand shocks to the nerves; but he went on to Christmas, alternating these far-off places with nights regularly intervening in London, without much more complaint than of an inability to sleep. Trade reverses at Glasgow had checked the success there, but Edinburgh made compensation. "The affectionate regard of the people exceeds all bounds and is shown in every way. The audiences do everything but embrace me, and take as much pains with the readings as I do. . . . The keeper of the Edinburgh hall, a fine old soldier, presented me on Friday night with the most superb red camellia for my button-hole that ever was seen. Nobody can imagine how he came by it, as the florists had had a considerable demand for that colour, from ladies in the stalls, and could get no such thing."

* 151

The second portion of the enterprise opened with the New Year; and the *Sikes and Nancy* scenes, everywhere his prominent subject, exacted the most terrible physical exertion from him. In January he was at Clifton, where he had given, he told his sister-in-law, "by far the best Murder yet done"; while at the same date he wrote to his daughter: "At Clifton on Monday night we had a contagion of fainting; and yet the place was not hot. I should think we had from a dozen to twenty ladies taken out stiff and rigid, at various times! It became quite ridiculous." He was afterwards at Cheltenham. "Macready is of opinion that the Murder is two Macbeths. He declares that he heard every word of the reading, but I doubt it. Alas! he is sadly infirm." On the 27th he wrote to his daughter from Torquay that the place into which they had put him to read, and where a pantomime had been played the night before, was something between a Methodist chapel, a theatre, a circus, a riding-school, and a cow-house. That day he wrote to me from Bath: "Landor's ghost goes along the silent streets here before me. . . . The place looks to me like a cemetery which the Dead have succeeded in rising and taking. Having built streets of their old gravestones, they wander about scantly trying to 'look alive.' A dead failure."

In the second week of February he was in London, under

engagement to return to Scotland (which he had just left) after
the usual weekly reading at St. James's Hall, when there was
a sudden interruption. "My foot has turned lame again!" was
his announcement to me on the 15th, followed next day by
this letter. "Henry Thompson will not let me read to-night, and
will not let me go to Scotland to-morrow. Tremendous house
here, and also in Edinburgh. Here is the certificate he drew up
for himself and Beard to sign. 'We the undersigned hereby
certify that Mr. C. D. is suffering from inflammation of the
foot (caused by over-exertion), and that we have forbidden his
appearance on the platform this evening, as he must keep his
room for a day or two.' I have sent up to the Great Western
Hotel for apartments, and, if I can get them, shall move there
this evening. Heaven knows what engagements this may
involve in April! It throws us all back, and will cost me some
five hundred pounds."

A few days' rest again brought so much relief, that, against
the urgent entreaties of members of his family as well as other
friends, he was in the railway carriage bound for Edinburgh
on the morning of 20 February, accompanied by Mr. Chappell
himself. "I came down lazily on a sofa," he wrote to me from
Edinburgh next day, "hardly changing my position the whole
way. The railway authorities had done all sorts of things, and
I was more comfortable than on the sofa at the hotel. The foot
gave me no uneasiness, and has been quiet and steady all night."
He was nevertheless under the necessity, two days later, of
consulting Mr. Syme; and he told his daughter that this great
authority had warned him against over-fatigue in the readings,
and given him some slight remedies, but otherwise reported him
in "just perfectly splendid condition." With care he thought
the pain might be got rid of. "What made Thompson think it
was gout? he said often, and seemed to take that opinion
extremely ill." Again before leaving Scotland he saw Mr. Syme,
and wrote to me on the second of March of the indignation
with which he again treated the gout diagnosis, declaring the
disorder to be an affection of the delicate nerves and muscles
originating in cold. "I told him that it had shown itself in
America in the other foot as well. 'Now I'll just swear,' said he,
'that beyond the fatigue of the readings you'd been tramping
in the snow within two or three days.' I certainly had. 'Well,'
said he triumphantly, 'and how did it first begin? In the snow.
Gout? Bah!—Thompson knew no other name for it, and just
called it gout. Bah!'" Yet the famous pupil, Sir Henry Thomp-

* 152

son, went certainly nearer the mark than the distinguished master, Mr. Syme, in giving to this distressing trouble a more than local character.

The whole of that March month he went on with the scenes from *Oliver Twist*. "The foot goes famously," he wrote to his daughter. "I feel the fatigue in it (four Murders in one week) but not overmuch. It merely aches at night; and so does the other, sympathetically, I suppose." At Hull on the 8th he heard of the death of the old and dear friend, Emerson Tennent, to whom he had inscribed his last book; and on the morning of the 12th I met him at the funeral. He had read the *Oliver Twist* scenes the night before at York; had just been able to get to the express train, after shortening the pauses in the reading, by a violent rush when it was over; and had travelled through the night. He appeared to me "dazed" and worn. No man could well look more so than he did, that sorrowful morning.

The end was near. A public dinner, which will have mention on a later page, had been given him in Liverpool on 10 April, with Lord Dufferin in the chair, and a reading was due from him in Preston on the 22nd of that month. But on Sunday the 18th we had ill report of him from Chester, and on the 21st he wrote from Blackpool to his sister-in-law: "I have come to this Sea-Beach Hotel (charming) for a day's rest. I am much better than I was on Sunday; but shall want careful looking to, to get through the readings. My weakness and deadness are all on the left side; and if I don't look at anything I try to touch with my left hand, I don't know where it is. I am in (secret) consultation with Frank Beard, who says that I have given him indisputable evidences of overwork which he could wish to treat immediately; and so I have telegraphed for him. I have had a delicious walk by the sea to-day, and I sleep soundly, and have picked up amazingly in appetite. My foot is greatly better too, and I wear my own boot." Next day was appointed for the reading at Preston; and from that place he wrote to me, while waiting the arrival of Mr. Beard: "Don't say anything about it, but the tremendously severe nature of this work is a little shaking me. At Chester last Sunday I found myself extremely giddy, and extremely uncertain of my sense of touch, both in the left leg and the left hand and arms. I had been taking some slight medicine of Beard's; and immediately wrote to him describing exactly what I felt, and asking him whether those feelings *could be* referable to the medicine? He promptly replied: 'There can be no mistaking them from your exact account. The medicine cannot possibly have caused them. I recognise indisputable symptoms of overwork, and I wish to take you in hand without any loss of time.' They have greatly modified since, but he is coming down here this afternoon. To-morrow night at Warrington I shall have but 25 more nights to work through. If he can coach me up for them, I do not doubt that I shall get all right again —as I did when I became free in America. The foot has given me very little trouble. Yet it is remarkable that it is *the left foot too*; and that I told Henry Thompson (before I saw his old master Syme) that I had an inward conviction that whatever it was, it was not gout. I also told Beard, a year after the Staplehurst accident, that I was certain that my heart had been fluttered, and wanted a little helping. This the stethoscope confirmed; and considering the immense exertion I am undergoing, and the constant jarring of express trains, the case seems to me quite intelligible. Don't say anything in the Gad's direction about my being a little out of sorts. I have broached the matter of course; but very lightly. Indeed there is no reason for broaching it otherwise."

Even to the close of that letter he had buoyed himself up with the hope that he might yet be "coached" and that the readings need not be discontinued. But Mr. Beard stopped them at once, and brought his patient to London. On Friday morning the 23rd, the same envelope brought me a note from himself to say that he was well enough, but tired; in perfectly good spirits, not at all uneasy, and writing this himself that I should have it under his own hand; with a note from his eldest son to say that his father appeared to him to be very ill, and that a consultation had been appointed with Sir Thomas Watson. The statement of that distinguished physician, sent to myself in June 1872, completes for the present the sorrowful narrative.

"It was, I think, on the 23rd of April, 1869, that I was asked to see Charles Dickens, in consultation with Mr. Carr Beard. After I got home I jotted down, from their joint account, what follows.

"After unusual irritability, C. D. found himself, last Saturday or Sunday, giddy, with a tendency to go backwards, and to turn round. Afterwards, desiring to put something on a small table, he pushed it and the table forwards, undesignedly. He had some odd feeling of insecurity about his left leg, as if there was something unnatural about his heel; but he could lift, and he did not drag, his leg. Also he spoke of some strangeness of his left hand and arm; missed the spot on which he wished to lay that hand, unless he carefully looked at it; felt an unreadiness to lift his hands towards his head, especially his left hand —when, for instance, he was brushing his hair.

"He had written thus to Mr. Carr Beard.

"'Is it possible that anything in my medicine can have made me extremely giddy, extremely uncertain of my footing, especially on the left side, and extremely indisposed to raise my hands to my head. These symptoms made me very uncomfortable on Saturday (qy. Sunday?) night, and all yesterday, etc.'

"The state thus described showed plainly that C. D. had been on the brink of an attack of paralysis of his left side, and possibly of apoplexy. It was, no doubt, the result of extreme hurry, overwork, and excitement, incidental to his readings.

"On hearing from him Mr. Carr Beard had gone at once to Preston, or Blackburn (I am not sure which), had forbidden his reading that same evening, and had brought him to London.

"When I saw him he *appeared* to be well. His mind was unclouded, his pulse quiet. His heart was beating with some slight excess of the natural impulse. He told me he had of late sometimes, but rarely, lost or misused a word; that he forgot names, and numbers, but had always done that; and he promised implicit obedience to our injunctions.

"We gave him the following certificate.

"'The undersigned certify that Mr. Charles Dickens has been seriously unwell, through great exhaustion and fatigue of body and mind consequent upon his public readings and long and frequent railway journeys. In our judgment Mr. Dickens will not be able with safety to himself to resume his readings for several months to come.

"'THOS. WATSON, M.D.
"'F. CARR BEARD.'

"However, after some weeks, he expressed a wish for my sanction to his endeavours to redeem, in a careful and moderate way, some of the reading engagements to which he had been pledged before those threatenings of brain-mischief in the North of England.

"As he had continued uniformly to seem and to feel perfectly well, I did not think myself warranted to refuse that sanction: and in writing to enforce great caution in the trials, I expressed some apprehension that he might fancy we had been too peremptory in our injunctions of mental and bodily repose in April; and I quoted the following remark, which occurs somewhere in one of Captain Cook's Voyages. 'Preventive measures are always invidious, for when most successful, the necessity for them is the least apparent.'

153   "I mention this to explain the letter which I send herewith, and which I must beg you to return to me, as a precious remembrance of the writer with whom I had long enjoyed very friendly and much valued relations.

"I scarcely need say that if what I have now written, can, *in any way*, be of use to you, it is entirely at your service and disposal—nor need I say with how much interest I have read the first volume of your late friend's Life. I cannot help regretting that a great pressure of professional work at the time, prevented my making a fuller record of a case so interesting."

The twelve readings to which Sir Thomas Watson consented, with the condition that railway travel was not to accompany them, were further to be delayed until the opening months of 1870. They were an offering from Dickens by way of small compensation to Messrs. Chappell for the breakdown of the enterprise on which they had staked so much. But here practically he finished his career as a public reader, and what remains will come with the sad winding-up of the story. One effort only intervened, by which he hoped to get happily back to his old pursuits; but to this, as to that which preceded it, sterner Fate said also No, and his Last Book, like his Last Readings, prematurely closed.

II

1869–70

THE last book undertaken by Dickens was to be published in illustrated monthly numbers, of the old form, but to close with the twelfth.[1] It closed, unfinished, with the sixth number, which was itself underwritten by two pages.

His first fancy for the tale was expressed in a letter in the middle of July. "What should you think of the idea of a story beginning in this way?—Two people, boy and girl, or very young, going apart from one another, pledged to be married after many years—at the end of the book. The interest to arise out of the tracing of their separate ways, and the impossibility of telling what will be done with that impending fate." This was laid aside; but it left a marked trace on the story as afterwards designed, in the position of Edwin Drood and his betrothed.

[1] In drawing the agreement for the publication, Mr. Ouvry had, by Dickens's wish, inserted a clause thought to be altogether needless, but found to be sadly pertinent. It was the first time such a clause had been inserted in one of his agreements. "That if the said Charles Dickens shall die during the composition of the said work of the *Mystery of Edwin Drood*, or shall otherwise become incapable of completing the said work for publication in twelve monthly numbers as agreed, it shall be referred to John Forster, Esq., one of Her Majesty's Commissioners in Lunacy, or in the case of his death, incapacity, or refusal to act, then to such person as shall be named by Her Majesty's Attorney-General for the time being, to determine the amount which shall be repaid by the said Charles Dickens, his executors or administrators, to the said Frederic Chapman as a fair compensation for so much of the said work as shall not have been completed for publication." The sum to be paid at once for 25,000 copies was £7500; publisher and author sharing equally in the profit of all sales beyond that impression; and the number reached, while the author yet lived, was 50,000. The sum paid for early sheets to America was £1000; and Baron Tauchnitz paid liberally, as he always did, for his Leipzig reprint. "All Mr. Dickens's works," M. Tauchnitz writes to me, "have been published under agreement by me. My intercourse with him lasted nearly twenty-seven years. The first of his letters is in October 1843, and his last at the close of March, 1870. Our long relations were not only never troubled by the least disagreement, but were the occasion of most hearty personal feeling; and I shall never lose the sense of his kind and friendly nature. On my asking him his terms for *Edwin Drood*, he replied, 'Your terms shall be mine.'"

I first heard of the later design in a letter dated "Friday the 6th of August 1869," in which after speaking, with the usual unstinted praise he bestowed always on what moved him in others, of a little tale he had received for his journal, he spoke of the change that had occurred to him for the new tale by himself. "I laid aside the fancy I told you of, and have a very curious and new idea for my new story. Not a communicable idea (or the interest of the book would be gone), but a very strong one, though difficult to work." The story, I learnt immediately afterward, was to be that of the murder of a nephew by his uncle; the originality of which was to consist in the review of the murderer's career by himself at the close, when its temptations were to be dwelt upon as if, not he the culprit, but some other man, were the tempted. The last chapters were to be written in the condemned cell, to which his wickedness, all elaborately elicited from him as if told of another, had brought him. Discovery by the murderer of the utter needlessness of the murder for its object, was to follow hard upon commission of the deed; but all discovery of the murderer was to be baffled till towards the close, when, by means of a gold ring which had resisted the corrosive effects of the lime into which he had thrown the body, not only the person murdered was to be identified but the locality of the crime and the man who committed it. So much was told to me before any of the book was written; and it will be recollected that the ring, taken by Drood to be given to his betrothed only if their engagement went on, was brought away with him from their last interview. Rosa was to marry Tartar, and Crisparkle the sister of Landless, who was himself, I think, to have perished in assisting Tartar finally to unmask and seize the murderer.

Nothing had been written, however, of the main parts of the design excepting what is found in the published numbers; there was no hint or preparation for the sequel in any notes of chapters in advance; and there remained not even what he had himself so sadly written of the book by Thackeray also interrupted by death. The evidence of matured designs never to be accomplished, intentions planned never to be executed, roads of thought marked out never to be traversed, goals shining in the distance never to be reached, was wanting here. It was all a blank. Enough had been completed nevertheless to give promise of a much greater book than its immediate predecessor. "I hope his book is finished," wrote Longfellow when the news of his death was flashed to America. "It is certainly one of his most beautiful works, if not the most beautiful of all. It would be too sad to think the pen had fallen from his hand, and left it incomplete." Some of its characters are touched with subtlety, and in its descriptions his imaginative power was at its best. Not a line was wanting to the reality, in the most minute local detail, of places the most widely contrasted; and we saw with equal vividness the lazy cathedral town and the lurid opium-eater's den. * 15: Something like the old lightness and buoyancy of animal spirits gave a new freshness to the humour; the scenes of the child-heroine and her luckless betrothed had both novelty and nicety of character in them; and Mr. Grewgious in chambers with his clerk and the two waiters, the conceited fool Sapsea, and the blustering philanthropist Honeythunder, were first-rate comedy. Miss Twinkleton was of the family of Miss La Creevy; and the lodging-house keeper, Miss Billickin, though she gave Miss Twinkleton but a sorry account of her blood, had that of Mrs. Todgers in her veins. "I was put in early life to a very genteel boarding-school, the mistress being no less a lady than yourself, of about your own age, or it may be some years younger, and a poorness of blood flowed from the table which has run through my life." Was ever anything better said of a school-fare of starved gentility?

The last page of *Edwin Drood* was written in the Chalet in the afternoon of his last day of consciousness; and I have thought there might be some interest in a facsimile of the greater part of this final page of manuscript that ever came from his hand, at which he had worked unusually late in order to finish the chapter. It has very much the character, in its excessive care of correction and interlineation, of all his later manuscripts; and in order that comparison may be made with his earlier and easier method, I place beside it a portion of a page of the original of *Oliver Twist*. His greater pains and elaboration of writing, it may be mentioned, become first very obvious in the later parts of *Martin Chuzzlewit*; but not the least remarkable feature in all his manuscripts, is the accuracy with which the portions of each representing the several numbers are exactly adjusted to the space the printer has to fill. Whether without erasure or so interlined as to be illegible, nothing is wanting, and there is nothing in excess. So assured had the habit become, that we have seen him remarking upon an instance the other way, in *Our Mutual Friend*, as not having happened to him for thirty years. Certainly the exceptions had been few and unimportant; but *Edwin Drood* more startlingly showed him how unsettled

"No" — replied the Dodger "not here, for this
ain't the shop for justice, besides which my
attorney is a-breakfasting this morning with
the Wice President of the House of Commons, but
I shall have something to say with he and so with
a wery numerous and 'spectable circle of acquaintance as'll make
them beaks wish they'd never been born, or
that they'd got their own footman to
hit 'em up to their own hat-pegs afore they
let 'em come out this morning to try it on
upon me. See —

"There; he's fully committed:" interposed the
clerk "take him away:"

the habit he most prized had become, in the clashing of old and new pursuits. "When I had written" (22 December, 1869) "and, as I thought, disposed of the first two Numbers of my story, Clowes informed me to my horror that they were, together, *twelve printed pages too short ! ! !* Consequently I had to transpose a chapter from number two to number one, and remodel number two altogether! This was the more unlucky, that it came upon me at the time when I was obliged to leave the book, in order to get up the readings" (the additional twelve for which Sir Thomas Watson's consent had been obtained); "quite gone out of my mind since I left them off. However, I turned to it and got it done, and both numbers are now in type. Charles Collins has designed an excellent cover." It was his wish that his son-in-law should have illustrated the story; but this not being practicable, upon an opinion expressed by Mr. Millais which the result thoroughly justified, choice was made of Mr. S. L. Fildes.

This reference to the last effort of Dickens's genius had been written as it thus stands, when a discovery of some interest was made by the writer. Within the leaves of one of Dickens's other manuscripts were found some detached slips of his writing, on paper only half the size of that used for the tale, so cramped, interlined, and blotted as to be nearly illegible, which on close inspection proved to be a scene in which Sapsea the auctioneer is introduced as the principal figure, among a group of characters new to the story. The explanation of it perhaps is, that, having become a little nervous about the course of the tale, from a fear that he might have plunged too soon into the incidents leading on to the catastrophe, such as the Datchery assumption in the fifth number (a misgiving he had certainly expressed to his sister-in-law), it had occurred to him to open some fresh veins of character incidental to the interest, though not directly part of it, and so to handle them in connection with Sapsea as a little to suspend the final development even while assisting to strengthen it. Before beginning any number of a serial, he used, as we have seen in former instances, to plan briefly what he intended to put into it chapter by chapter; and his first number-plan of *Drood* had the following: "Mr. Sapsea. Old Tory jackass. Connect Jasper with him. (He will want a solemn donkey by and by)": which was effected by bringing together both Durdles and Jasper, for connection with Sapsea, in the matter of the epitaph for Mrs. Sapsea's tomb. The scene now discovered might in this view have been designed to strengthen and carry forward that element in the tale; and otherwise it very sufficiently expresses itself. It would supply an answer, if such were needed, to those who have asserted that the hopeless decadence of Dickens as a writer had set in before his death. Among the lines last written by him, these are the very last we can ever hope to receive; and they seem to me a delightful specimen of the power possessed by him in his prime, and the rarest which any novelist can have, of revealing a character by a touch. Here are a couple of people, Kimber and Peartree, not known to us before, whom we read off thoroughly in a dozen words; and as to Sapsea himself, auctioneer and Mayor of Cloisterham, we are face to face with what before we only dimly realised, and we see the solemn jackass, in his business pulpit, playing off the airs of Mr. Dean in his Cathedral pulpit, with Cloisterham laughing at the impostor.

How Mr. Sapsea Ceased to be a Member of the Eight Club

Told by himself

"Wishing to take the air, I proceeded by a circuitous route to the club, it being our weekly night of meeting. I found that we mustered our full strength. We were enrolled under the denomination of the Eight Club. We were eight in number; we met at eight o'clock during eight months of the year; we played eight games of four-handed cribbage, at eightpence the game; our frugal supper was composed of eight rolls, eight mutton chops, eight pork sausages, eight baked potatoes, eight marrow-bones, with eight toasts, and eight bottles of ale. There may, or may not, be a certain harmony of colour in the ruling idea of this (to adopt a phrase of our lively neighbours) reunion. It was a little idea of mine.

"A somewhat popular member of the Eight Club, was a member by the name of Kimber. By profession, a dancing-master. A commonplace, hopeful sort of man, wholly destitute of dignity or knowledge of the world.

"As I entered the Club-room, Kimber was making the remark: 'And he still half-believes him to be very high in the Church.'

"In the act of hanging up my hat on the eighth peg by the door, I caught Kimber's visual ray. He lowered it, and passed

a remark on the next change of the moon. I did not take particular notice of this at the moment, because the world was
often pleased to be a little shy of ecclesiastical topics in my
presence. For I felt that I was picked out (though perhaps only
through a coincidence) to a certain extent to represent what
I call our glorious constitution in Church and State. The phrase
may be objected to by captious minds; but I own to it as mine.
I threw it off in argument some little time back. I said; 'OUR
GLORIOUS CONSTITUTION in CHURCH and STATE.'

"Another member of the Eight Club was Peartree; also
member of the Royal College of Surgeons. Mr. Peartree is not
accountable to me for his opinions, and I say no more of them
here than that he attends the poor gratis whenever they want
him, and is not the parish doctor. Mr. Peartree may justify it
to the grasp of *his* mind thus to do his republican utmost to
bring an appointed officer into contempt. Suffice it that Mr.
Peartree can never justify it to the grasp of *mine*.

"Between Peartree and Kimber there was a sickly sort of
feeble-minded alliance. It came under my particular notice
when I sold off Kimber by auction. (Goods taken in execution.)
He was a widower in a white under-waistcoat, and slight shoes
with bows, and had two daughters not ill-looking. Indeed the
reverse. Both daughters taught dancing in scholastic establishments for Young Ladies—had done so at Mrs. Sapsea's; nay,
Twinkleton's—and both, in giving lessons, presented the un-
womanly spectacle of having little fiddles tucked under their
chins. In spite of which, the younger one might, if I am correctly
informed—I will raise the veil so far as to say I KNOW she might
—have soared for life from this degrading taint, but for having
the class of mind allotted to what I call the common herd,
and being so incredibly devoid of veneration as to become
painfully ludicrous.

"When I sold off Kimber without reserve, Peartree (as poor
as he can hold together) had several prime household lots
knocked down to him. I am not to be blinded; and of course
it was as plain to me what he was going to do with them, as
it was that he was a brown hulking sort of revolutionary subject who had been in India with the soldiers, and ought (for
the sake of society) to have his neck broke. I saw the lots shortly
afterwards in Kimber's lodgings—through the window—and I
easily made out that there had been a sneaking pretence of
lending them till better times. A man with a smaller knowledge
of the world than myself might have been led to suspect that

Kimber had held back money from his creditors, and fraudulently bought the goods. But, besides that I knew for certain he had no money, I knew that this would involve a species of forethought not to be made compatible with the frivolity of a caperer, inoculating other people with capering, for his bread.

"As it was the first time I had seen either of those two since the sale, I kept myself in what I call Abeyance. When selling him up, I had delivered a few remarks—shall I say a little homily?—concerning Kimber, which the world did regard as more than usually worth notice. I had come up into my pulpit, it was said, uncommonly like—and a murmur of recognition had repeated his (I will not name whose) title, before I spoke. I had then gone on to say that all present would find, in the first page of the catalogue that was lying before them, in the last paragraph before the first lot, the following words: 'Sold in pursuance of a writ of execution issued by a creditor.' I had then proceeded to remind my friends, that however frivolous, not to say contemptible, the business by which a man got his goods together, still his goods were as dear to him, and as cheap to society (if sold without reserve), as though his pursuits had been of a character that would bear serious contemplation. I had then divided my text (if I may be allowed so to call it) into three heads: firstly, Sold; secondly, In pursuance of a writ of execution; thirdly, Issued by a creditor; with a few moral reflections on each, and winding up with, 'Now to the first lot' in a manner that was complimented when I afterwards mingled with my hearers.

"So, not being certain on what terms I and Kimber stood, I was grave, I was chilling. Kimber, however, moving to me, I moved to Kimber. (I was the creditor who had issued the writ. Not that it matters.)

"'I was alluding, Mr. Sapsea,' said Kimber, 'to a stranger who entered into conversation with me in the street as I came to the Club. He had been speaking to you just before, it seemed, by the churchyard; and though you had told him who you were, I could hardly persuade him that you were not high in the Church.'

"'Idiot!' said Peartree.

"'Ass!' said Kimber.

"'Idiot and Ass!' said the other five members.

"'Idiot and Ass, gentlemen,' I remonstrated, looking around me, 'are strong expressions to apply to a young man of good appearance and address.' My generosity was roused; I own it.

"'You'll admit that he must be a Fool,' said Peartree.

"'You can't deny that he must be a Blockhead,' said Kimber.

"Their tone of disgust amounted to being offensive. Why should the young man be so calumniated? What had he done? He had only made an innocent and natural mistake. I controlled my generous indignation, and said so.

"'Natural?' repeated Kimber. '*He's* a Natural!'

"The remaining six members of the Eight Club laughed unanimously. It stung me. It was a scornful laugh. My anger was roused in behalf of an absent, friendless stranger. I rose (for I had been sitting down).

"'Gentlemen,' I said with dignity, 'I will not remain one of this Club allowing opprobrium to be cast on an unoffending person in his absence. I will not so violate what I call the sacred rites of hospitality. Gentlemen, until you know how to behave yourselves better, I leave you. Gentlemen, until then I withdraw, from this place of meeting, whatever personal qualifications I may have brought into it. Gentlemen, until then you cease to be the Eight Club, and must make the best you can of becoming the Seven.'

"I put on my hat and retired. As I went downstairs I distinctly heard them give a suppressed cheer. Such is the power of demeanour and knowledge of mankind. I had forced it out of them.

"II

"Whom should I meet in the street, within a few yards of the door of the inn where the Club was held, but the selfsame young man whose cause I had felt it my duty so warmly—and I will add so disinterestedly—to take up.

"'Is it Mr. Sapsea,' he said doubtfully, 'or is it——'

"'It is Mr. Sapsea,' I replied.

"'Pardon me, Mr. Sapsea; you appear warm, sir.'

"'I have been warm,' I said, 'and on your account.' Having stated the circumstances at some length (my generosity almost overpowered him), I asked him his name.

"'Mr. Sapsea,' he answered, looking down, 'your penetration is so acute, your glance into the souls of your fellow men is so penetrating, that if I was hardy enough to deny that my name is Poker, what would it avail me?'

"I don't know that I had quite exactly made out to a fraction that his name *was* Poker, but I daresay I had been pretty near doing it.

"'Well, well,' said I, trying to put him at his ease by nodding my head in a soothing way. 'Your name is Poker, and there is no harm in being named Poker.'

"'Oh Mr. Sapsea!' cried the young man, in a very well-behaved manner. 'Bless you for those words!' He then, as if ashamed of having given way to his feelings, looked down again.

"'Come, Poker,' said I, 'let me hear more about you. Tell me. Where are you going to, Poker? and where do you come from?'

"'Ah Mr. Sapsea!' exclaimed the young man. 'Disguise from you is impossible. You know already that I come from somewhere, and am going somewhere else, If I was to deny it, what would it avail me?'

"'Then don't deny it,' was my remark.

"'Or,' pursued Poker, in a kind of despondent rapture, 'or if I was to deny that I came to this town to see and hear you, sir, what would it avail me? Or if I was to deny——'"

The fragment ends there, and the hand that could alone have completed it is at rest for ever.

Some personal characteristics remain for illustration before the end is briefly told.

III

1836–70

OBJECTION has been taken to this biography as likely to disappoint its readers in not making them "talk to Dickens as
Boswell makes them talk to Johnson." But where will the blame
lie if a man takes up *Pickwick* and is disappointed to find that
he is not reading *Rasselas*? A book must be judged for what it
aims to be, and not for what it cannot by possibility be. I suppose so remarkable an author as Dickens hardly ever lived who
carried so little of authorship into ordinary social intercourse.
Potent as the sway of his writings was over him, it expressed
itself in other ways. Traces or triumphs of literary labour,
displays of conversational or other personal predominance, were
no part of the influence he exerted over friends. To them he was
only the pleasantest of companions, with whom they forgot that
he had ever written anything, and felt only the charm which a
nature of such capacity for supreme enjoyment causes everyone around it to enjoy. His talk was unaffected and natural,
never bookish in the smallest degree. He was quite up to the
average of well-read men; but as there was no ostentation of it
in his writing, so neither was there in his conversation. This
was so attractive because so keenly observant, and lighted up
with so many touches of humorous fancy; but, with every
possible thing to give relish to it, there were not many things
to bring away.

Of course a book must stand or fall by its contents. Macaulay
said very truly that the place of books in the public estimation
is fixed, not by what is written about them, but by what is
written in them. I offer no complaint of any remark made upon
these volumes, but there have been some misapprehensions.
Though Dickens bore outwardly so little of the impress of his
writings, they formed the whole of that inner life which essentially constituted the man; and as in this respect he was actually,
I have thought that his biography should endeavour to present

him. The story of his books, therefore, at all stages of their progress, and of the hopes or designs connected with them, was my first care. With that view, and to give also to the memoir what was attainable of the value of autobiography, letters to myself, such as were never addressed to any other of his correspondents, and covering all the important incidents in the life to be retraced, were used with few exceptions exclusively; and † 28 though the exceptions are much more numerous in the later sections, this general plan has guided me to the end. Such were my limits indeed, that half even of those letters had to be put aside; and to have added all such others as were opened to me would have doubled the size of my book, not contributed to it a new fact of life or character, and altered materially its design. It would have been so much lively illustration added to the subject, but out of place here. The purpose here was to make Dickens the sole central figure in the scenes revived, narrator as well as principal actor; and only by the means employed could consistency or unity be given to the self-revelation, and the picture made definite and clear. It is the peculiarity of few men to be to their most intimate friend neither more nor less than they are to themselves, but this was true of Dickens; and what kind or quality of nature such intercourse expressed in him, of what strength, tenderness, and delicacy susceptible, of what steady level warmth, of what daily unresting activity of intellect, of what unbroken continuity of kindly impulse through the change and vicissitude of three-and-thirty years, the letters to myself given in these volumes could alone express. Gathered from various and differing sources, their interest could not have been as the interest of these; in which everything comprised in the successive stages of a most attractive career is written with unexampled care and truthfulness, and set forth in definite pictures of what he saw and stood in the midst of, unblurred by vagueness or reserve. Of the charge of obtruding myself to which their publication has exposed me, I can only say that I studied nothing so hard as to suppress my own personality, and have to regret my ill success where I supposed I had even too perfectly succeeded. But we have all of us frequent occasion to say, parodying Mrs. Peachum's remark, that we are bitter bad judges of ourselves.

The other properties of these letters are quite subordinate to this main fact that the man who wrote them is thus perfectly seen in them. But they do not lessen the estimate of his genius. Admiration rises higher at the writer's mental forces, who, putting so much of himself into his work for the public, had still so much overflowing for such private intercourse. The sunny health of nature in them is manifest; its largeness, spontaneity, and manliness; but they have also that which highest intellects appreciate best. "I have read them," Lord Russell wrote to me, "with delight and pain. His heart, his imagination, his qualities of painting what is noble, and finding diamonds hidden far away, are greater here than even his works convey to me. How I lament he was not spared to us longer. I shall have a fresh grief when he dies in your volumes." Shallower people are more apt to find other things. If the bonhommie of a man's genius is obvious to all the world, there are plenty of knowing ones ready to take the shine out of the genius, to discover that after all it is not so wonderful, that what is grave in it wants depth, and the humour has something mechanical. But it will be difficult even for these to look over letters so marvellous in the art of reproducing to the sight what has once been seen, so natural and unstudied in their wit and fun, and with such a constant well-spring of sprightly runnings of speech in them, point of epigram, ingenuity of quaint expression, absolute freedom from every touch of affectation, and to believe that the source of this man's humour, or of whatever gave wealth to his genius, was other than habitual, unbounded, and resistless.

There is another consideration of some importance. Sterne did not more incessantly fall back from his works upon himself than Dickens did, and undoubtedly one of the impressions left by the letters is that of the intensity and tenacity with which he recognised, realised, contemplated, cultivated, and thoroughly enjoyed, his own individuality in even its most trivial manifestations. But if anyone is led to ascribe this to self-esteem, to a narrow exclusiveness, or to any other invidious form of egotism, let him correct the impression by observing how Dickens bore himself amid the universal blazing-up of America, at the beginning and at the end of his career. Of his hearty, undisguised, and unmistakable enjoyment of his astonishing and indeed quite bewildering popularity, there can be as little doubt as that there is not a particle of vanity in it, any more than of false modesty or grimace. While realising fully the fact of it, and the worth of the fact, there is not in his whole being a fibre that answers falsely to the charmer's voice. Few men in the world, one fancies, could have gone through such grand displays of fireworks, not merely with so marvellous an absence

* 156

of what the French call *pose*, but unsoiled by the smoke of a cracker. No man's strong individuality was ever so free from conceit.

Other personal incidents and habits, and especially some matters of opinion of grave importance, will help to make his character better known. Much questioning followed a brief former reference to his religion, but, inconsistent or illogical as the conduct described may be, there is nothing to correct in my statement of it; and to any doubt there still may be in regard to the essentials of his faith, answer will be afforded by a letter written on the occasion of his youngest boy leaving home in September 1868 to join his brother in Australia, than which none worthier appears in his story. "I write this note to-day because your going away is much upon my mind, and because I want you to have a few parting words from me, to think of now and then at quiet times. I need not tell you that I love you dearly, and am very, very sorry in my heart to part with you. But this life is half made up of partings, and these pains must be borne. It is my comfort and my sincere conviction that you are going to try the life for which you are best fitted. I think its freedom and wildness more suited to you than any experiment in a study or office would have been; and without that training, you could have followed no other suitable occupation. What you have always wanted until now, has been a set, steady, constant purpose. I therefore exhort you to persevere in a thorough determination to do whatever you have to do as well as you can do it. I was not so old as you are now, when I first had to win my food, and to do it out of this determination; and I have never slackened in it since. Never take a mean advantage of anyone in any transaction, and never be hard upon people who are in your power. Try to do to others as you would have them do to you, and do not be discouraged if they fail sometimes. It is much better for you that they should fail in obeying the greatest rule laid down by Our Saviour than that you should. I put a New Testament among your books for the very same reasons, and with the very same hopes, that made me write an easy account of it for you, when you were a little child. Because it is the best book that ever was, or will be, known in the world; and because it teaches you the best lessons by which any human creature, who tries to be truthful and faithful to duty, can possibly be guided. As your brothers have gone away, one by one, I have written to each such words as I am now writing to you, and have entreated them all to

* 157

guide themselves by this Book, putting aside the interpretations and inventions of Man. You will remember that you have never at home been harassed about religious observances, or mere formalities. I have always been anxious not to weary my children with such things, before they are old enough to form opinions respecting them. You will therefore understand the better that I now most solemnly impress upon you the truth and beauty of the Christian Religion, as it came from Christ Himself, and the impossibility of your going far wrong if you humbly but heartily respect it. Only one thing more on this head. The more we are in earnest as to feeling it, the less we are disposed to hold forth about it. Never abandon the wholesome practice of saying your own private prayers, night and morning. I have never abandoned it myself, and I know the comfort of it. I hope you will always be able to say in after life, that you had a kind father. You cannot show your affection for him so well, or make him so happy, as by doing your duty." They who most intimately knew Dickens will know best that every word there is written from his heart, and is radiant with the truth of his nature.

To the same effect, in the leading matter, he expressed himself twelve years before, and again the day before his death; replying in both cases to correspondents who had addressed him as a public writer. A clergyman, the Rev. R. H. Davies, had been struck by the hymn in the Christmas tale of the "Wreck of the *Golden Mary*" (*Household Words*, 1856). "I beg to thank you," Dickens answered (Christmas Eve, 1856), "for your very acceptable letter—not the less gratifying to me because I am myself the writer you refer to. . . . There cannot be many men, I believe, who have a more humble veneration for the New Testament, or a more profound conviction of its all-sufficiency, than I have. If I am ever (as you tell me I am) mistaken on this subject, it is because I discountenance all obtrusive professions of and tradings in religion, as one of the main causes why real Christianity has been retarded in this world; and because my observation of life induces me to hold in unspeakable dread and horror, those unseemly squabbles about the letter which drive the spirit out of hundreds of thousands." In precisely similar tone, to a reader of *Edwin Drood* (Mr. J. M. Makeham), who had pointed out to him that his employment as a figure of speech of a line from Holy Writ in his tenth chapter might be subject to misconstruction, he wrote from Gadshill on Wednesday the eighth of June, 1870. "It would be quite inconceivable to me, but for your letter, that any reasonable reader could possibly attach a scriptural reference to that passage. . . . I am truly shocked to find that any reader can make the mistake. I have always striven in my writings to express veneration for the life and lessons of our Saviour; because I feel it; and because I re-wrote that history for my children—every one of whom knew it, from having it repeated to them, long before they could read, and almost as soon as they could speak. But I have never made proclamation of this from the housetops."

A dislike of all display was rooted in him; and his objection to posthumous honours, illustrated by the instructions in his will, was very strikingly expressed two years before his death, when Mr. Thomas Fairbairn asked his help to a proposed recognition of Rajah Brooke's services by a memorial in Westminster Abbey. "I am very strongly impelled" (24 June, 1868) "to comply with any request of yours. But these posthumous honours of committee, subscriptions, and Westminster Abbey are so profoundly unsatisfactory in my eyes that—plainly— I would rather have nothing to do with them in any case. My daughter and her aunt unite with me in kindest regards to Mrs. Fairbairn, and I hope you will believe in the possession of mine until I am quietly buried without any memorial but such as I have set up in my lifetime." Asked a year later (August 1869) to say something on the inauguration of Leigh Hunt's bust at his grave in Kensal Green, he told the committee that he had a very strong objection to speech-making beside graves. "I do not expect or wish my feelings in this wise to guide other men; still, it is so serious with me, and the idea of ever being the subject of such a ceremony myself is so repugnant to my soul, that I must decline to officiate."

His aversion to every form of what is called patronage of literature was part of the same feeling. A few months earlier ✱ 158 he had received an application for support to such a scheme from a person assuming a title to which he had no pretension, but which appeared to sanction the request. "I beg to be excused," was his reply, "from complying with the request you do me the honour to prefer, simply because I hold the opinion that there is a great deal too much patronage in England. The better the design, the less (as I think) should it seek such adventitious aid, and the more composedly should it rest on its own merits." This was the belief Southey held; it extended to the support by way of patronage given by such societies as the Literary Fund, which Southey also strongly resisted; and it

survived the failure of the Guild whereby it was hoped to
establish a system of self-help, under which men engaged in
literary pursuits might be as proud to receive as to give. Though
there was no project of his life into which he flung himself with
† 29 greater eagerness than the Guild, it was not taken up by the
class it was meant to benefit, and every renewed exertion more
largely added to the failure. There is no room in these pages
for the story, which will add its chapter some day to the vanity
of human wishes; but a passage from a letter to Bulwer Lytton
at its outset will be some measure of the height from which the
writer fell, when all hope for what he had so set his heart upon
ceased. "I do devoutly believe that this plan carried by the
support which I trust will be given to it, will change the status
of the literary man in England, and make a revolution in his
position which no government, no power on earth but his own,
could ever effect. I have implicit confidence in the scheme—so
splendidly begun—if we carry it out with a steadfast energy.
I have a strong conviction that we hold in our hands the peace
and honour of men of letters for centuries to come, and that
you are destined to be their best and most enduring benefactor.
. . . Oh what a procession of new years may walk out of all this
for the class we belong to, after we are dust."

These views about patronage did not make him more indulgent to the clamour with which it is so often invoked for the
ridiculously small. "You read that life of Clare?" he wrote
(15 August, 1865). "Did you ever see such preposterous exaggeration of small claims? And isn't it expressive, the perpetual
prating of him in the book as *the Poet*? So another Incompetent
used to write to the Literary Fund when I was on the committee:
'This leaves the Poet at his divine mission in a corner of the
single room. The Poet's father is wiping his spectacles. The
Poet's mother is weaving.'—Yah!" He was equally intolerant
of every magnificent proposal that should render the literary
man independent of the bookseller, and he sharply criticised
even a compromise to replace the half-profit system by one of
royalties on copies sold. "What does it come to?" he remarked
of an ably written pamphlet in which this was urged (10 November, 1866): "what is the worth of the remedy after all? You
and I know very well that in nine cases out of ten the author
is at a disadvantage with the publisher because the publisher
has capital and the author has not. We know perfectly well that
in nine cases out of ten money is advanced by the publisher
before the book is producible—often, long before. No young or

unsuccessful author (unless he were an amateur and an independent gentleman) would make a bargain for having that royalty, to-morrow, if he could have a certain sum of money, or an advance of money. The author who could command that bargain, could command it to-morrow, or command anything else. For the less fortunate or the less able, I make bold to say —with some knowledge of the subject, as a writer who made a publisher's fortune long before he began to share in the real profits of his books—that if the publishers met next week, and resolved henceforth to make this royalty bargain and no other, it would be an enormous hardship and misfortune because the authors could not live while they wrote. The pamphlet seems to me just another example of the old philosophical chess-playing, with human beings for pieces. 'Don't want money.' 'Be careful to be born with means, and have a banker's account.' 'Your publisher will settle with you, at such and such long periods according to the custom of his trade, and you will settle with your butcher and baker weekly, in the meantime, by drawing cheques as I do.' 'You must be sure not to want money, and then I have worked it out for you splendidly.'"

Less has been said in this work than might perhaps have been wished, of the way in which his editorship of *Household Words* and of *All the Year Round* was discharged. It was distinguished above all by liberality; and a scrupulous consideration and delicacy, evinced by him to all his contributors, was part of the esteem in which he held literature itself. It was said in a newspaper after his death, evidently by one of his contributors, that he always brought the best out of a man by encouragement and appreciation; that he liked his writers to feel unfettered; and that his last reply to a proposition for a series of articles had been: "Whatever you see your way to, I will see mine to, and we know and understand each other well enough to make the best of these conditions." Yet the strong feeling of personal responsibility was always present in his conduct of both journals; and varied as the contents of a number might be, and widely apart the writers, a certain individuality of his own was never absent. He took immense pains (as indeed was his habit about everything) with numbers in which he had written nothing; would often accept a paper from a young or unhandy contributor, because of some single notion in it which he thought it worth rewriting for; and in this way, or by helping generally to give strength and attractiveness to the work of others, he grudged no trouble. "I have had a story," he wrote * 158A

(22 June, 1856), "to hack and hew into some form for *Household Words* this morning, which has taken me four hours of close attention. And I am perfectly addled by its horrible want of continuity after all, and the dreadful spectacle I have made of the proofs—which look like an inky fishing-net." A few lines from another letter will show the difficulties in which he was often involved by the plan he adopted for Christmas numbers, of putting within a framework by himself a number of stories by separate writers to whom the leading notion had before been severally sent. "As yet" (25 November, 1859), "not a story has come to me in the least belonging to the idea (the simplest in the world; which I myself described in writing, in the most elaborate manner); and every one of them turns, by a strange fatality, on a criminal trial!" It had all to be set right by him, and editorship on such terms was not a sinecure.

It had its pleasures as well as pains, however, and the greatest was when he fancied he could descry unusual merit in any writer. A letter will give one instance for illustration of many; the lady to whom it was addressed, admired under her assumed name of Holme Lee, having placed it at my disposal. (Folkestone: 14 August, 1855.) "I read your tale with the strongest emotion, and with a very exalted admiration of the great power displayed in it. Both in severity and tenderness I thought it masterly. It moved me more than I can express to you. I wrote to Mr. Wills that it had completely unsettled me for the day, and that by whomsoever it was written, I felt the highest respect for the mind that had produced it. It so happened that I had been for some days at work upon a character externally like the Aunt. And it was very strange to me indeed to observe how the two people seemed to be near to one another at first, and then turned off on their own ways so wide asunder. I told Mr. Wills that I was not sure whether I could have prevailed upon myself to present to a large audience the terrible consideration of hereditary madness, when it was reasonably probable that there must be many—or some—among them whom it would awfully, because personally, address. But I was not obliged to ask myself the question, inasmuch as the length of the story rendered it unavailable for *Household Words*. I speak of its length in reference to that publication only; relatively to what is told in it, I would not spare a page of your manuscript. Experience shows me that a story in four portions is best suited to the peculiar requirements of such a journal, and I assure you it will be an uncommon satisfaction to me if this correspondence should lead to your enrolment among its contributors. But my strong and sincere conviction of the vigour and pathos of this beautiful tale, is quite apart from, and not to be influenced by, any ulterior results. You had no existence to me when I read it. The actions and sufferings of the characters affected me by their own force and truth, and left a profound impression on me." The experience there mentioned did not prevent him from ∗ 159 admitting into his later periodical, *All the Year Round*, longer serial stories, published with the names of known writers; and to his own interference with these he properly placed limits. "When one of my literary brothers does me the honour to undertake such a task, I hold that he executes it on his own personal responsibility, and for the sustainment of his own reputation; and I do not consider myself at liberty to exercise that control over his text which I claim as to other contributions." Nor had he any greater pleasure, even in these cases, than to help younger novelists to popularity. "You asked me about new writers last night. If you will read *Kissing the Rod*, a book I have read to-day, you will not find it hard to take an interest in the author of such a book." That was Mr. Edmund Yates, in whose literary successes he took the greatest interest himself, and with whom he continued to the last an intimate personal intercourse which had dated from kindness shown at a very trying time. "I think," he wrote of another of his contributors, Mr. Percy Fitzgerald, for whom he had also much personal liking, and of whose powers he thought highly, "you will find *Fatal Zero* a very curious bit of mental development, deepening as the story goes on into a picture not more startling than true." My mention of these pleasures of editorship shall close with what I think to him was the greatest. He gave to the world, while yet the name of the writer was unknown to him, the pure and pathetic verse of Adelaide Procter. "In the spring of the year 1853 I observed a short poem among the proffered contributions, very different, as I thought, from the shoal of verses perpetually setting through the office of such a periodical." The contributions had been large and frequent ∗ 160 under an assumed name, when at Christmas 1854 he discovered that Miss Mary Berwick was the daughter of his old and dear friend, Barry Cornwall.

But periodical writing is not without its drawbacks, and its effect on Dickens, who engaged in it largely from time to time, was observable in the increased impatience of allusion to national institutions and conventional distinctions to be found in his later books. Party divisions he cared for less and less as life moved on; but the decisive, peremptory, dogmatic style into which a habit of rapid remark on topics of the day will betray the most candid and considerate commentator, displayed its influence, perhaps not always consciously to himself, in the underlying tone of bitterness that runs through the books which followed *Copperfield*. The resentment against remediable wrongs is as praiseworthy in them as in the earlier tales; but the exposure of Chancery abuses, administrative incompetence, politico-economic shortcomings, and social flunkeyism, in *Bleak House*, *Little Dorrit*, *Hard Times*, and *Our Mutual Friend*, would not have been made less odious by the cheerier tone that had struck with much sharper effect at prison abuses, parish wrongs, Yorkshire schools, and hypocritical humbug, in *Pickwick*, *Oliver Twist*, *Nickleby*, and *Chuzzlewit*. It will be remembered of him always that he desired to set right what was wrong, that he held no abuse to be unimprovable, that he left none of the evils named exactly as he found them, and that to influences drawn from his writings were due not a few of the salutary changes which marked the age in which he lived; but anger does not improve satire, and it gave latterly, from the causes named, too aggressive a form to what, after all, was but a very wholesome hatred of the cant that everything English is perfect, and that to call a thing *un*-English is to doom it to abhorred extinction.

"I have got an idea for occasional papers in *Household Words* called the Member for Nowhere. They will contain an account of his views, votes, and speeches; and I think of starting with his speeches on the Sunday question. He is a member of the Government of course. The moment they found such a member in the House, they felt that he must be dragged (by force, if necessary) into the Cabinet." "I give it up reluctantly," he wrote afterwards, "and with it my hope to have made every man in England feel something of the contempt for the House of Commons that I have. We shall never begin to do anything until the sentiment is universal." That was in August 1854; and the breakdown in the Crimea that winter much embittered his radicalism. "I am hourly strengthened in my old belief," he wrote (3 February, 1855), "that our political aristocracy and our tuft-hunting are the death of England. In all this business I don't see a gleam of hope. As to the popular spirit, it has come to be so entirely separated from the Parliament and Government, and so perfectly apathetic about them both, that I seriously think it a most portentous sign." A couple of months later: "I have rather a bright idea, I think, for *Household Words* this morning: a fine little bit of satire: an account of an Arabic MS. lately discovered very like the *Arabian Nights*—called the Thousand and One Humbugs. With new versions of the best known stories." This also had to be given up, and is only mentioned as another illustration of his political discontents and of their connection with his journal-work. The influence from his early life which unconsciously strengthened them in certain social directions has been hinted at, and of his absolute sincerity in the matter there can be no doubt. The mistakes of Dickens were never such as to cast a shade on his integrity. What he said with too much bitterness, in his heart he believed; and had, alas! too much ground for believing. "A country," he wrote (27 April, 1855), "which is discovered to be in this tremendous condition as to its war affairs; with an enormous black cloud of poverty in every town which is spreading and deepening every hour, and not one man in two thousand knowing anything about, or even believing in, its existence; with a non-working aristocracy, and a silent parliament, and everybody for himself and nobody for the rest; this is the prospect, and I think it a very deplorable one." Admirably did he say, of a notorious inquiry at that time: "O what a fine aspect of political economy it is, that the noble professors of the science on the adulteration committee should have tried to make Adulteration a question of Supply and Demand! We shall never get to the Millennium, sir, by the rounds of that ladder; and I, for one, won't hold by the skirts of that Great Mogul of impostors, Master M'Culloch!" Again he wrote (30 September, 1855): "I really am serious in thinking—and I have given as painful consideration to the subject as a man with children to live and suffer after him can honestly give to it—that representative government is become altogether a failure with us, that the English gentilities and subserviences render the people unfit for it, and that the whole thing has broken down since that great seventeenth-century time, and has no hope in it."

With the good sense that still overruled all his farthest extremes of opinion he yet never thought of parliament for himself. He could not mend matters, and for him it would have been a false position. The people of the town of Reading and others applied to him during the first half of his life, and in the last half some of the Metropolitan constituencies. To one of the latter a reply is before me in which he says: "I declare that as to all matters on the face of this teeming earth, it appears to me that the House of Commons and Parliament altogether is become just the dreariest failure and nuisance that ever bothered this much-bothered world." To a private inquiry of apparently about the same date he replied: "I have thoroughly satisfied myself, having often had occasion to consider the question, that I can be far more usefully and independently employed in my chosen sphere of action than I could hope to be in the House of Commons; and I believe that no consideration would induce me to become a member of that extraordinary assembly." Finally, upon a reported discussion in Finsbury whether or not he should be invited to sit for that borough, he promptly wrote (November 1861): "It may save some trouble if you will kindly confirm a sensible gentleman who doubted at that meeting whether I was quite the man for Finsbury. I am not at all the sort of man; for I believe nothing would induce me to offer myself as a parliamentary representative of that place, or of any other under the sun." The only direct attempt to join a political agitation was his speech at Drury Lane for administrative reform, and he never repeated it. But every movement for practical social reforms, to obtain more efficient sanitary legislation, to get the best compulsory education practicable for the poor, and to better the condition of labouring people, he assisted earnestly to his last hour; and the readiness with which he took the chair at meetings having such objects in view, the help he gave to important societies working in beneficent ways for themselves or the community, and the power and attractiveness of his oratory, made him one of the forces of the time. His speeches derived singular charm from the buoyancy of his perfect self-possession, and to this he added the advantages of a person and manner which had become as familiar and as popular as his books. The most miscellaneous assemblages listened to him as to a personal friend.

Two incidents at the close of his life will show what upon these matters his latest opinions were. At the great Liverpool dinner after his country readings in 1869, over which Lord Dufferin eloquently presided, he replied to a remonstrance from Lord Houghton against his objection to entering public life, that when he took literature for his profession he intended it to be his sole profession; that at that time it did not appear to him to be so well understood in England, as in some other countries, that literature was a dignified calling by which any man might stand or fall; and he resolved that in his person at least it should

* 161

stand "by itself, of itself, and for itself"; a bargain which "no consideration on earth would now induce him to break." Here however he probably failed to see the entire meaning of Lord Houghton's regret, which would seem to have been meant to say, in more polite form, that to have taken some part in public affairs might have shown him the difficulty in a free state of providing remedies very swiftly for evils of long growth. A half reproach from the same quarter for alleged unkindly sentiments to the House of Lords, he repelled with vehement warmth; insisting on his great regard for individual members, and declaring that there was no man in England he respected more in his public capacity, loved more in his private capacity, or from whom he had received more remarkable proofs of his honour and love of literature, than Lord Russell. In Birmingham shortly after, discoursing on education to the members of the Midland Institute, he told them they should value self-improvement, not because it led to fortune but because it was good and right in itself; counselled them in regard to it that Genius was not worth half so much as Attention, or the art of taking an immense deal of pains, which he declared to be, in every study and pursuit, the one sole, safe, certain, remunerative quality; and summed up briefly his political belief. "My faith in the people governing is, on the whole, infinitesimal; my faith in the People governed is, on the whole, illimitable." This he afterwards (January 1870) explained to mean that he had very little confidence in the people who govern us ("with a small p"), and very great confidence in the People whom they govern ("with a large P"). "My confession being shortly and elliptically stated, was, with no evil intention I am absolutely sure, in some quarters inversely explained." He added that his political opinions had already been not obscurely stated in an "idle book or two"; and he reminded his hearers that he was the inventor "of a certain fiction called the Circumlocution Office, said to be very extravagant, but which I *do* see rather frequently quoted as if there were grains of truth at the bottom of it." It may nevertheless be suspected, with some confidence, that the construction of his real meaning was not far wrong which assumed it as the condition precedent to his illimitable faith, that the people, even with the big P, should be "governed." It was his constant complaint that, being much in want of government, they had only sham governors; and he had returned from his second American visit, as he came back from his first, indisposed to believe that the political problem had been solved in the land of the free. From the pages of his last book, the bitterness of allusion so frequent in the books just named was absent altogether; and his old unaltered wish to better what was bad in English institutions, carried with it no desire to replace them by new ones.

In a memoir published shortly after his death there appeared this statement. "For many years past Her Majesty the Queen has taken the liveliest interest in Mr. Dickens's literary labours, and has frequently expressed a desire for an interview with him. . . . This interview took place on the 9th of April, when he received her commands to attend her at Buckingham Palace, and was introduced by his friend Mr. Arthur Helps, the clerk of the Privy Council. . . . Since our author's decease the journal with which he was formerly connected has said: 'The Queen was ready to confer any distinction which Mr. Dickens's known views and tastes would permit him to accept, and after more than one title of honour had been declined Her Majesty desired that he would, at least, accept a place in her Privy Council.'" As nothing is too absurd for belief, it will not be superfluous to say that Dickens knew of no such desire on her Majesty's part; and though all the probabilities are on the side of his unwillingness to accept any title or place of honour, certainly none was offered to him.

It had been hoped to obtain her Majesty's name for the Jerrold performances in 1857, but, being a public effort in behalf of an individual, assent would have involved "either perpetual compliance or the giving of perpetual offence." Her Majesty however then sent, through Colonel Phipps, a request to Dickens that he would select a room in the palace, do what he would with it, and let her see the play there. "I said to Col. Phipps thereupon" (21 June, 1857) "that the idea was not quite new to me; that I did not feel easy as to the social position of my daughters, etc., at a Court under those circumstances; and that I would beg her Majesty to excuse me, if any other way of her seeing the play could be devised. To this Phipps said he had not thought of the objection, but had not the slightest doubt I was right. I then proposed that the Queen should come to the Gallery of Illustration a week before the subscription night, and should have the room entirely at her own disposal, and should invite her own company. This, with the good sense that seems to accompany her good nature on all occasions, she resolved within a few hours to do." The effect of the performance was a great gratification. "My gracious sovereign" (5 July, 1857)

"was so pleased that she sent round begging me to go and see her and accept her thanks. I replied that I was in my Farce dress, and must beg to be excused. Whereupon she sent again, saying that the dress 'could not be so ridiculous as that,' and repeating the request. I sent my duty in reply, but again hoped her Majesty would have the kindness to excuse my presenting myself in a costume and appearance that were not my own. I was mighty glad to think, when I woke this morning, that I had carried the point."

The opportunity of presenting himself in his own costume did not arrive till the year of his death, another effort meanwhile made having proved also unsuccessful. "I was put into a state of much perplexity on Sunday" (30 March, 1858). "I don't know who had spoken to my informant, but it seems that the Queen is bent upon hearing the *Carol* read, and has expressed her desire to bring it about without offence; hesitating about the manner of it, in consequence of my having begged to be excused from going to her when she sent for me after the *Frozen Deep*. I parried the thing as well as I could; but being asked to be prepared with a considerate and obliging answer, as it was known the request would be preferred, I said, 'Well! I supposed Col. Phipps would speak to me about it, and if it were he who did so, I should assure him of my desire to meet any wish of her Majesty's, and should express my hope that she would indulge me by making one of some audience or other—for I thought an audience necessary to the effect.' Thus it stands; but it bothers me." The difficulty remained, but her Majesty's continued interest in the *Carol* was alleged to have been shown by her purchase of it with Dickens's autograph at Thackeray's sale; and at last there came, in the year of his death, the interview with the author whose popularity dated from her accession, whose books had entertained larger numbers of her subjects than those of any other contemporary writer, and whose genius will be counted among the glories of her reign. Accident led to it. Dickens had brought with him from America some large and striking photographs of the Battle Fields of the Civil War, which the Queen, having heard of them through Mr. Helps, expressed a wish to look at. Dickens sent them at once; and went afterwards to Buckingham Palace with Mr. Helps, at her Majesty's request, that she might see and thank him in person.

It was in the middle of March, not April. "Come now, sir, this is an interesting matter; do favour us with it," was the cry of Johnson's friends after his conversation with George the

* 162

Third; and again and again the story was told to listeners ready to make marvels of its commonplaces. But the romance even of the eighteenth century in such a matter is clean gone out of the nineteenth. Suffice it that the Queen's kindness left a strong impression on Dickens. Upon her Majesty's regret not to have heard his readings, Dickens intimated that they were become now a thing of the past, while he acknowledged gratefully her Majesty's compliment in regard to them. She spoke to him of the impression made upon her by his acting in the *Frozen Deep*; and on his stating, in reply to her inquiry, that the little play had not been very successful on the public stage, said this did not surprise her, since it no longer had the advantage of his performance in it. Then arose a mention of some alleged discourtesy shown to Prince Arthur in New York, and he begged her Majesty not to confound the true Americans of that city with the Fenian portion of its Irish population; on which she made the quiet comment that she was convinced the people about the Prince had made too much of the affair. He related to her the story of President Lincoln's dream on the night before his murder. She asked him to give her his writings, and could she have them that afternoon? but he begged to be allowed to send a bound copy. Her Majesty then took from a table her own book upon the Highlands, with an autograph inscription "to Charles Dickens"; and, saying that the "humblest" of writers would be ashamed to offer it to "one of the greatest" but that Mr. Helps, being asked to give it, had remarked that it would be valued most from herself, closed the interview by placing it in his hands. "Sir," said Johnson, "they may say what they like of the young King, but Louis the Fourteenth could not have shown a more refined courtliness"; and Dickens was not disposed to say less of the young king's granddaughter. That the grateful impression sufficed to carry him into new ways, I had immediate proof, coupled with intimation of the still surviving strength of old memories. "As my sovereign desires" (26 March, 1870) "that I should attend the next levee, don't faint with amazement if you see my name in that unwonted connection. I have scrupulously kept myself free for the second of April, in case you should be accessible." The name appeared at the levee accordingly, his daughter was at the drawing-room that followed, and Lady Houghton writes to me: "I never saw Mr. Dickens more agreeable than at a dinner at our house about a fortnight before his death, when he met the King of the Belgians and the Prince of Wales at the special desire of the latter." Up to nearly the hour of dinner, it was doubtful if he could go. He was suffering from the distress in his foot; and on arrival at the house, being unable to ascend the stairs, had to be assisted at once into the dining-room.

The friend who had accompanied Dickens to Buckingham Palace, writing of him after his death, briefly but with admirable knowledge and taste, said that he ardently desired, and confidently looked forward to, a time when there would be a more intimate union than exists at present between the different classes in the state, a union that should embrace alike the highest and the lowest. This perhaps expresses, as well as a few words could, what certainly was always at his heart; and he might have come to think it, when his life was closing, more possible of realisation some day than he ever thought it before. The hope of it was on his friend Talfourd's lips when he died, and his own most jarring opinions might at last have joined in the effort to bring about such reconcilement. More on this head it needs not to say. Whatever may be the objection to special views held by him, he would, wanting even the most objectionable, have been less himself. It was by something of the despot seldom separable from genius, joined to a truthfulness of nature belonging to the highest characters, that men themselves of a rare faculty were attracted to find in Dickens what Sir Arthur Helps has described, "a man to confide in, and look up to as a leader, in the midst of any great peril."

Mr. Layard also held that opinion of him. He was at Gadshill during the Christmas before Dickens went for the last time to America, and witnessed one of those scenes, not infrequent there, in which the master of the house was pre-eminently at home. They took generally the form of cricket matches; but this was, to use the phrase of his friend Bobadil, more popular and diffused; and of course he rose with the occasion. "The more you want of the master, the more you'll find in him," said the gasman employed about his readings. "Footraces for the villagers," he wrote on Christmas Day, "come off in my field to-morrow. We have been all hard at work all day, building a course, making countless flags, and I don't know what else. Layard is chief commissioner of the domestic police. The country police predict an immense crowd." There were between two and three thousand people; and somehow, by a magical kind of influence, said Layard, Dickens seemed to have bound every creature present, upon what honour the creature had, to keep order. What was the special means used or the art employed, it might have been difficult to say; but this was the result. Writing on New Year's Day, Dickens himself described it to me. "We had made a very pretty course, and taken great pains. Encouraged by the cricket matches experience, I allowed the landlord of the Falstaff to have a drinking-booth on the ground. Not to seem to dictate or distrust, I gave all the prizes (about ten pounds in the aggregate) in money. The great mass of the crowd were labouring men of all kinds, soldiers, sailors, and navvies. They did not, between half-past ten, when we began, and sunset, displace a rope or a stake; and they left every barrier and flag as neat as they found it. There was not a dispute, and there was no drunkenness whatever. I made them a little speech from the lawn, at the end of the games, saying that please God we would do it again next year. They cheered most lustily and dispersed. The road between this and Chatham was like a Fair all day; and surely it is a fine thing to get such perfect behaviour out of a reckless seaport town. Among other oddities we had A Hurdle Race for Strangers. One man (he came in second) ran 120 yards and leaped over ten hurdles, in twenty seconds, *with a pipe in his mouth, and smoking it all the time.* 'If it hadn't been for your pipe,' I said to him at the winning-post, 'you would have been first.' 'I beg your pardon, sir,' he answered, 'but if it hadn't been for my pipe, I should have been nowhere.'" The close of the letter had this rather memorable announcement. "The sale of the Christmas number was, yesterday evening, 255,380." Would it be absurd to say that there is something in such a vast popularity in itself electrical, and, though founded on books, felt where books never reach?

It is also very noticeable that what would have constituted the strength of Dickens if he had entered public life, the attractive as well as the commanding side of his nature, was that which kept him most within the circle of home pursuits and enjoyments. This "better part" of him had now long survived that sorrowful period of 1857–8, when, for reasons which I have not thought myself free to suppress, a vaguely disturbed feeling for the time took possession of him, and occurrences led to his adoption of other pursuits than those to which till then he had given himself exclusively. It was a sad interval in his life; but, though changes incident to the new occupation then taken up remained, and with them many adverse influences which brought his life prematurely to a close, it was, with any reference to that feeling, an interval only, and the dominant impression of the later years, as of the earlier, takes the marvellously domestic home-loving shape in which also the strength of his genius is found. It will not do to draw round any part of such a man too hard a line, and the writer must not be charged with inconsistency who says that Dickens's childish sufferings, and the sense they burnt into him of the misery of loneliness and a craving for joys of home, though they led to what was weakest in him, led also to what was greatest. It was his defect as well as his merit in maturer life not to be able to live alone. When the fancies of his novels were upon him and he was under their restless influence, though he often talked of shutting himself up in out of the way solitary places, he never went anywhere unaccompanied by members of his family. His habits of daily living he carried with him wherever he went. In Albaro and Genoa, at Lausanne and Geneva, in Paris and Boulogne, his ways were as entirely those of home as in London and Broadstairs. If it is the property of a domestic nature to be personally interested in every detail, the smallest as the greatest, of the four walls within which one lives, then no man had it so essentially as Dickens. No man was so inclined naturally to derive his happiness from home concerns. Even the kind of interest in a house which is commonly confined to women, he was full of. Not to speak of changes of importance, there was not an additional hook put up wherever he inhabited, without his knowledge, or otherwise than as part of some small ingenuity of his own. Nothing was too minute for his personal superintendence. Whatever might be in hand, theatricals for the little children, entertainments for those of larger growth, cricket matches, dinners, field sports, from the first New Year's Eve dance in Doughty Street to the last musical party in Hyde Park Place, he was the centre and soul of it. He did not care to take measure of its greater or less importance. It was enough that a thing was to do, to be worth his while to do it as if there was nothing else to be done in the world. The cry of Laud and Wentworth was his, alike in small and great things; and to no man was more applicable the German "Echt," which expresses reality as well as thoroughness. The usual result followed, in all his homes, of an absolute reliance on him for everything. Under every difficulty, and in every emergency, his was the encouraging influence, the bright and ready help. In illness, whether of the children or any of the servants, he was better than a doctor. He was so full of resource, for which everyone eagerly turned to him, that his mere presence in the sick-room was a healing influence, as if nothing could fail if he

* 16:

were only there. So that at last, when, all through the awful
night which preceded his departure, he lay senseless in the room
where he had fallen, the stricken and bewildered ones who
tended him found it impossible to believe that what they saw
before them alone was left, or to shut out wholly the strange
wild hope that he might again be suddenly among them *like*
himself, and revive what they could not connect, even then,
with death's despairing helplessness.

It was not a feeling confined to the relatives whom he had thus
taught to have such exclusive dependence on him. Among the
consolations addressed to those mourners came words from one
whom in life he had most honoured, and who also found it difficult to connect him with death, or to think that he should
never see that blithe face any more. "It is almost thirty years,"
Mr. Carlyle wrote, "since my acquaintance with him began;
and on my side, I may say, every new meeting ripened it into
more and more clear discernment of his rare and great worth
as a brother man; a most cordial, sincere, clear-sighted, quietly
decisive, just and loving man: till at length he had grown to
such a recognition with me as I have rarely had for any man
of my time. This I can tell you three, for it is true and will be
welcome to you: to others less concerned I had as soon *not* speak
on such a subject." "I am profoundly sorry for *you*," Mr. Carlyle at the same time wrote to me; "and indeed for myself and
for us all. It is an event world-wide; a *unique* of talents suddenly
extinct; and has 'eclipsed,' we too may say, 'the harmless
gaiety of nations.' No death since 1866 has fallen on me with
such a stroke. No literary man's hitherto ever did. The good,
the gentle, high-gifted, ever-friendly, noble Dickens—every inch
of him an Honest Man."

Of his ordinary habits of activity I have spoken, and they
were doubtless carried too far. In youth it was all well, but he
did not make allowance for years. This has had abundant
illustration, but will admit of a few words more. To all men
who do much, rule and order are essential; method in everything was Dickens's peculiarity; and between breakfast and
luncheon, with rare exceptions, was his time of work. But his
daily walks were less of rule than of enjoyment and necessity.
In the midst of his writing they were indispensable, and especially, as it has often been shown, at night. Mr. Sala is an authority
on London streets, and, in the eloquent and generous tribute
he was among the first to offer to his memory, has described
himself encountering Dickens in the oddest places and most

inclement weather, in Ratcliffe Highway, on Haverstock Hill, on Camberwell Green, in Gray's Inn Lane, in the Wandsworth Road, at Hammersmith Broadway, in Norton Folgate, and at Kensal New Town. "A hansom whirled you by the Bell and Horns at Brompton, and there he was striding, as with seven-league boots, seemingly in the direction of North End, Fulham. The Metropolitan Railway sent you forth at Lisson Grove, and you met him plodding speedily towards the Yorkshire Stingo. He was to be met rapidly skirting the grim brick wall of the prison in Coldbath Fields, or trudging along the Seven Sisters Road at Holloway, or bearing, under a steady press of sail, underneath Highgate Archway, or pursuing the even tenor of his way up the Vauxhall Bridge Road." But he was equally at home in the intricate byways of narrow streets as in the lengthy thoroughfares. Wherever there was "matter to be heard and learned," in back streets behind Holborn, in Borough courts and passages, in City wharfs or alleys, about the poorer lodging-houses, in prisons, workhouses, ragged-schools, police-courts, rag-shops, chandlers' shops, and all sorts of markets for the poor he carried his keen observation and untiring study. "I was among the Italian Boys from 12 to 2 this morning," says one of his letters. "I am going out to-night in their boat with the Thames Police," says another. It was the same when he was in Italy or Switzerland, as we have seen; and when, in later life, he was in French provincial places. "I walk miles away into the country, and you can scarcely imagine by what deserted ramparts and silent little cathedral closes, or how I pass over rusty drawbridges and stagnant ditches out of and into the decaying town." For several consecutive years I accompanied him every Christmas Eve to see the marketings for Christmas down the road from Aldgate to Bow; and he had a surprising fondness for wandering about in poor neighbourhoods on Christmas Day, past the areas of shabby genteel houses in Somers or Kentish Towns, and watching the dinners preparing or coming in. But the temptations of his country life led him on to excesses in walking. "Coming in just now," he wrote in his third year at Gadshill, "after twelve miles in the rain, I was so wet that I have had to change and get my feet into warm water before I could do anything." Again, two years later: "A south-easter blowing enough to cut one's throat. I am keeping the house for my cold, as I did yesterday. But the remedy is so new to me, that I doubt if it does me half the good of a dozen miles in the snow. So, if this mode of treatment fails to-day, I shall try that to-morrow." He tried it perhaps too often. In the winter of 1865 he first had the attack in his left foot which materially disabled his walking-power for the rest of his life. He supposed its cause to be overwalking in the snow, and that this had aggravated the suffering is very likely; but, read by the light of what followed, it may now be presumed to have had more serious origin. It recurred at intervals, before America, without any such provocation; in America it came back, not when he had most been walking in the snow, but when nervous exhaustion was at its worst with him; after America, it became prominent on the eve of the occurrence at Preston which first revealed the progress that disease had been making in the vessels of the brain; and in the last year of his life, as will immediately be seen, it was a constant trouble and most intense suffering, extending then gravely to his left hand also, which had before been only slightly affected.

It was from a letter of 21 February, 1865, I first learnt that he was suffering tortures from a "frost-bitten" foot, and ten days later brought more detailed account. "I got frost-bitten by walking continually in the snow, and getting wet in the feet daily. My boots hardened and softened, hardened and softened, my left foot swelled, and I still forced the boot on; sat in it to write, half the day; walked in it through the snow, the other half; forced the boot on again next morning; sat and walked again; and being accustomed to all sorts of changes in my feet, took no heed. At length, going out as usual, I fell lame on the walk, and had to limp home dead lame, through the snow, for the last three miles—to the remarkable terror, by the by, of the two big dogs." The dogs were Turk and Linda. Boisterous companions as they always were, the sudden change in him brought them to a standstill; and for the rest of the journey they crept by the side of their master as slowly as he did, never turning from him. He was greatly moved by the circumstance, and often referred to it. Turk's look upward to his face was one of sympathy as well as fear, he said; but Linda was wholly struck down.

The saying in his letter to his youngest son that he was to do to others what he would that they should do to him, without being discouraged if they did not do it, and his saying to the Birmingham people that they were to attend to self-improvement not because it led to fortune, but because it was right; express a principle that at all times guided himself. Capable of strong attachments, he was not what is called an effusive man;

but he had no half-heartedness in any of his likings. The one thing entirely hateful to him, was indifference. "I give my heart to very few people; but I would sooner love the most implacable man in the world than a careless one, who, if my place were empty to-morrow, would rub on and never miss me." There was nothing he more repeatedly told his children than that they were not to let indifference in others appear to justify it in themselves. "All kind things," he wrote, "must be done on their own account, and for their own sake, and without the least reference to any gratitude." Again he laid it down, while he was making some exertion for the sake of a dead friend that did not seem likely to win proper appreciation from those it was to serve. "As to gratitude from the family—as I have often remarked to you, one does a generous thing because it is right and pleasant, and not for any response it is to awaken in others." The rule in another form frequently appears in his letters; and it was enforced in many ways upon all who were dear to him. It is worth while to add his comment on a regret of a member of his family at an act of self-devotion supposed to have been thrown away: "Nothing of what is nobly done can ever be lost." It is also to be noted as in the same spirit, that it was not the loud but the silent heroisms he most admired. Of Sir John Richardson, one of the few who have lived in our days entitled to the name of a hero, he wrote from Paris in 1856. "Lady Franklin sent me the whole of that Richardson memoir; and I think Richardson's manly friendship, and love of Franklin, one of the noblest things I ever knew in my life. It makes one's heart beat high, with a sort of sacred joy." (It is the feeling as strongly awakened by the earlier exploits of the same gallant man to be found at the end of Franklin's first voyage, and never to be read without the most exalted emotion.) It was for something higher than mere literature he valued the most original writer and powerful teacher of the age. "I would go at all times farther to see Carlyle than any man alive."

Of his attractive points in society and conversation I have particularised little, because in truth they were himself. Such as they were, they were never absent from him. His acute sense of enjoyment gave such relish to his social qualities that probably no man, not a great wit or a professed talker, ever left, in leaving any social gathering, a blank so impossible to fill up. In quick and varied sympathy, in ready adaptation to every whim or humour, in help to any mirth or game, he stood for a dozen men. If one may say such a thing, he seemed to be always the more himself for being somebody else, for continually putting off his personality. His versatility made him unique. What he said once of his own love of acting, applied to him equally when at his happiest among friends he loved; sketching a character, telling a story, acting a charade, taking part in a game; turning into comedy an incident of the day, describing the last good or bad thing he had seen, reproducing in quaint, tragical, or humorous form and figure, some part of the passionate life with which all his being overflowed. "Assumption has charms for me so delightful—I hardly know for how many wild reasons—that I feel a loss of Oh I can't say what exquisite foolery, when I lose a chance of being someone not in the remotest degree like myself." How it was, that from one of such boundless resource in contributing to the pleasure of his friends, there was yet, as I have said, so comparatively little to bring away, may be thus explained. But it has been also seen that no one at times said better things, and to happy examples formerly given I will add one or two of a kind he more rarely indulged. "He is below par on the Exchange," a friend remarked of a notorious puffing actor; "he doesn't stand well at Lloyd's." "Yet no one stands so well with the underwriters," said Dickens; a pun that Swift would have envied. "I call him an incubus!" said a non-literary friend, at a loss to express the boredom inflicted on him by a popular author. "Pen-and-ink-ubus, you mean," interposed Dickens. So, when Stanfield said of his midshipman son, then absent on his first cruise, "your boy has got his sea-legs on by this time!" "I don't know," remarked Dickens, "about his getting his sea-legs on; but if I may judge from his writing, he certainly has not got his A B C legs on."

Other agreeable pleasantries might be largely cited from his letters. "An old priest" (he wrote from France in 1862), "the express image of Frédéric Lemaître got up for the part, and very cross with the toothache, told me in a railway carriage the other day, that we had no antiquities in heretical England. 'None at all,' I said. 'You have some ships, however?' 'Yes; a few.' 'Are they strong?' 'Well,' said I, 'your trade is spiritual, my father: ask the ghost of Nelson.' A French captain who was in the carriage was immensely delighted with this small joke. I met him at Calais yesterday going somewhere with a detachment; and he said—Pardon! But he had been so limited as to suppose an Englishman incapable of that bonhommie!" In humouring a joke he was excellent, both in letters and talk; and for this kind of enjoyment his least important little notes

are often worth preserving. Take one small instance. So freely
had he admired a tale told by his friend and solicitor Mr.
Frederic Ouvry, that he had to reply to a humorous proposal
for publication of it, in his own manner, in his own periodical.
"Your modesty is equal to your merit. . . . I think your way
of describing that rustic courtship in middle life, quite matchless. . . . A cheque for £1000 is lying with the publisher. We
would willingly make it more, but that we find our law charges
so exceedingly heavy." His letters have also examples now and
then of what he called his conversational triumphs. "I have
distinguished myself" (28 April, 1861) "in two respects lately.
I took a young lady, unknown, down to dinner, and, talking
to her about the Bishop of Durham's Nepotism in the matter
of Mr. Cheese, I found she was Mrs. Cheese. And I expatiated
to the member for Marylebone, Lord Fermoy, generally con-
ceiving him to be an Irish member, on the contemptible
character of the Marylebone constituency and Marylebone
representation."

Among his good things should not be omitted his telling of
a ghost story. He had something of a hankering after them, as
the readers of his briefer pieces will know; and such was his
interest generally in things supernatural, that, but for the strong
restraining power of his common sense, he might have fallen
into the follies of spiritualism. As it was, no man was readier
to apply sharp tests to such a ghost narrative as will be found,
for example, in the 125th number of *All the Year Round*, which
before its publication both Mr. Layard and myself saw at Gadshill, and identified as one related by Lord Lytton. It was published in September, and a day or two afterwards Dickens
wrote to Lytton: "The artist himself who is the hero of that
story has sent me in black and white his own account of the
whole experience, so very original, so very extraordinary, so
very far beyond the version I have published, that all other
like stories turn pale before it." The ghost thus reinforced came
out in the number published on 5 October; and the reader
who cares to turn to it, and compare what Dickens in the
interval (17 September) wrote to myself, will have some measure
of his readiness to believe in such things. "Upon the publication of the ghost story, up has started the portrait-painter
who saw the phantoms! He had been, it seems, engaged to
write his adventure elsewhere as a story for Christmas, and
not unnaturally supposed, when he saw himself anticipated by
us, that there had been treachery at his printers'. 'In particular,'

says he, 'how else was it possible that the date, the 13th of September, could have been got at? For I never told the date, until I wrote it.' Now, *my* story had NO DATE; but seeing, when I looked over the proof, the great importance of having *a* date, I (C. D.) wrote in, unconsciously, the exact date on the margin of the proof!" The reader will remember the Doncaster race story; and to other like illustrations of the subject already given, may be added this dream. "Here is a curious case at first-hand" (30 May, 1863). "On Thursday night in last week, being at the office here, I dreamed that I saw a lady in a red shawl with her back towards me (whom I supposed to be E.). On her turning round I found that I didn't know her, and she said 'I am Miss Napier.' All the time I was dressing next morning, I thought—What a preposterous thing to have so very distinct a dream about nothing! and why Miss Napier? for I never heard of any Miss Napier. That same Friday night, I read. After the reading, came into my retiring-room, Mary Boyle and her brother, and *the* Lady in the red shawl whom they present as 'Miss Napier'! These are all the circumstances, exactly told."

Another kind of dream has had previous record, with no superstition to build itself upon but the loving devotion to one tender memory. With longer or shorter intervals this was with him all his days. Never from his waking thoughts was the recollection altogether absent; and though the dream would leave him for a time, it unfailingly came back. It was the feeling of his life that always had a mastery over him. What he said on the sixth anniversary of the death of his sister-in-law, that friend of his youth whom he had made his ideal of all moral excellence, he might have said as truly after twenty-six years more; for in the very year before he died, the influence was potently upon him. "She is so much in my thoughts at all times, especially when I am successful, and have greatly prospered in anything, that the recollection of her is an essential part of my being, and is as inseparable from my existence as the beating of my heart is." Through later troubled years, whatever was worthiest in him found in this an ark of safety; and it was the nobler part of his being which had thus become also the essential. It gave to success what success by itself had no power to give; and nothing could consist with it, for any length of time, that was not of good report and pure. What more could I say that was not better said from the pulpit of the Abbey where he rests?

"He whom we mourn was the friend of mankind, a philanthropist in the true sense; the friend of youth, the friend of the poor, the enemy of every form of meanness and oppression. I am not going to attempt to draw a portrait of him. Men of genius are different from what we suppose them to be. They have greater pleasures and greater pains, greater affections and greater temptations, than the generality of mankind, and they can never be altogether understood by their fellow-men. . . . But we feel that a light has gone out, that the world is darker to us, when they depart. There are so very few of them that we cannot afford to lose them one by one, and we look vainly round for others who may supply their places. He whose loss we now mourn occupied a greater space than any other writer in the minds of Englishmen during the last thirty-three years. We read him, talked about him, acted him; we laughed with him; we were roused by him to a consciousness of the misery of others, and to a pathetic interest in human life. Works of fiction, indirectly, are great instructors of this world; and we can hardly exaggerate the debt of gratitude which is due to a writer who has led us to sympathise with these good, true, sincere, honest English characters of ordinary life, and to laugh at the egotism, the hypocrisy, the false respectability of religious professors and others. To another great humorist who lies in this church the words have been applied that his death eclipsed the gaiety of nations. But of him who has been recently taken I would rather say, in humbler language, that no one was ever so much beloved or so much mourned."

BOOK TWELFTH

THE CLOSE

1870.   ÆT. 58

BOOK TWELFTH

THE CLOSE

1870 — 79

I. Last Days
II. Westminster Abbey

I

LAST DAYS

1869–70

THE summer and autumn of 1869 were passed quietly at Gadshill. He received there, in June, the American friends to whom
he had been most indebted for unwearying domestic kindness
at his most trying time in the States. In August, he was at the
dinner of the International boat race; and, in a speech that
might have gone far to reconcile the victors to changing places
with the vanquished, gave the healths of the Harvard and the
Oxford crews. He went to Birmingham, in September, to fulfil
a promise that he would open the session of the Institute; and
there, after telling his audience that his invention, such as it
was, never would have served him as it had done, but for the
habit of commonplace, patient, drudging attention, he declared
his political creed to be infinitesimal faith in the people governing and illimitable faith in the People governed. In such engagements as these, with nothing of the kind of strain he had most
to dread, there was hardly more movement or change than was
necessary to his enjoyment of rest.

He had been able to show Mr. Fields something of the interest
of London as well as of his Kentish home. He went over its
General Post Office with him, took him among its cheap theatres
and poor lodging-houses, and piloted him by night through its
most notorious thieves' quarter. Its localities that are pleasantest
to a lover of books, such as Johnson's Bolt Court and Goldsmith's Temple Chambers, he explored with him; and, at his
visitor's special request, mounted a staircase he had not ascended
for more than thirty years, to show the chamber in Furnival's Inn
where the first page of *Pickwick* was written. One more book,
unfinished, was to close what that famous book began; and the
original of the scene of its opening chapter, the opium-eater's
den, was the last place visited. "In a miserable court at night,"
says Mr. Fields, "we found a haggard old woman blowing at

a kind of pipe made of an old ink-bottle; and the words that Dickens puts into the mouth of this wretched creature in *Edwin Drood*, we heard her croon as we leaned over the tattered bed in which she was lying."

Before beginning his novel he had written his last paper for his weekly publication. It was a notice of my *Life of Landor*, and contained some interesting recollections of that remarkable man. His memory at this time dwelt much, as was only natural, with past pleasant time, as he saw familiar faces leaving us or likely to leave; and, on the death of one of the comedians associated with the old bright days of Covent Garden, I had intimation of a fancy that had never quitted him since the Cheltenham reading. "I see in the paper to-day that Meadows is dead. I had a talk with him at Coutts's a week or two ago, when he said he was seventy-five, and very weak. Except for having a tearful eye, he looked just the same as ever. My mind still constantly misgives me concerning Macready. Curiously, I don't think he has been ever, for ten minutes together, out of my thoughts since I talked with Meadows last. Well, the year that brings trouble brings comfort too; I have a great success in the boy-line to announce to you. Harry has won the second scholarship at Trinity Hall, which gives him £50 a year as long as he stays there; and I begin to hope that he will get a fellowship."

† 30   I doubt if anything ever more truly pleased him than this little success of his son Henry at Cambridge. Henry missed the fellowship, but was twenty-ninth wrangler in a fair year, when the wranglers were over forty.

He finished his first number of *Edwin Drood* in the third week of October. And on the 26th read it at my house with great spirit. A few nights before we had seen together at the Olympic a little drama taken from his *Copperfield*, which he sat out with more than patience, even with something of enjoyment; and another pleasure was given him that night by its author, Mr. Halliday, who brought into the box another dramatist, Mr. Robertson, to whom Dickens, who then first saw him, said that to himself the charm of his little comedies was "their unassuming form," which had so happily shown that "real wit could afford to put off any airs of pretension to it." He was at Gadshill till the close of the year; coming up for a few special occasions, such as Procter's eighty-second birthday; and at my house on New Year's Eve he read to us a fresh number of his *Edwin Drood*. Yet these very last days of December had not been without a reminder of the grave warnings of April. The pains in somewhat modified form had returned in both his left hand and his left foot a few days before we met; and they were troubling him still on that day. But he made so light of them himself; so little thought of connecting them with the uncertainties of touch and tread of which they were really part; and read with such an overflow of humour Mr. Honeythunder's boisterous phil-anthropy; that there was no room, then, for anything but enjoy-ment. His only allusion to an effect from his illness was his mention of a now invincible dislike which he had to railway travel. This had decided him to take a London house for the twelve last readings in the early months of 1870, and he had become Mr. Milner Gibson's tenant at 5 Hyde Park Place.

St. James's Hall was to be the scene of these readings, and they were to occupy the interval from 11 January to 15 March; two being given in each week to the close of January, and the remaining eight on each of the eight Tuesdays following. Nothing was said of any kind of apprehension as the time approached; but, with a curious absence of the sense of danger, there was certainly both distrust and fear. Sufficient precaution was sup-posed to have been taken by arrangement for the presence, at * 164 each reading, of his friend and medical attendant, Mr. F. C. Beard; but this resolved itself, not into any measure of safety, the case admitting of none short of stopping the reading alto-gether, but simply into ascertainment of the exact amount of strain and pressure, which, with every fresh exertion, he was placing on those vessels of the brain where the Preston trouble too surely had revealed that danger lay. No supposed force in reserve, no dominant strength of will, can turn aside the penalties sternly exacted for disregard of such laws of life as were here plainly overlooked; and though no one may say that it was not already too late for any but the fatal issue, there will be no presumption in believing that life might yet have been for some time prolonged if these readings could have been stopped.

"I am a little shaken," he wrote on 9 January, "by my journey to Birmingham to give away the Institution's prizes on Twelfth Night, but I am in good heart; and, notwithstanding Lowe's worrying scheme for collecting a year's taxes in a lump, which they tell me is damaging books, pictures, music, and theatres beyond precedent, our 'let' at St. James's Hall is enormous." He opened with *Copperfield* and the *Pickwick Trial*; and I may briefly mention, from the notes taken by Mr. Beard and placed at my disposal, at what cost of exertion to himself he gratified the crowded audiences that then and to the close made these evenings memorable. His ordinary pulse on the first night was at 72; but never on any subsequent night was lower than 82, and had risen on the later nights to more than 100. After *Copperfield* on the first night it went up to 96, and after *Marigold* on the second to 99; but on the first night of the *Sikes and Nancy* scenes (Friday, 21 January) it went from 80 to 112, and on the second night (1 February) to 118. From this, through the six remaining nights, it never was lower than 110 after the first piece read; and after the third and fourth readings of the *Oliver Twist* scenes it rose, from 90 to 124 on 15 February, and from 94 to 120 on 8 March; on the former occasion, after twenty minutes' rest, falling to 98, and on the latter, after fifteen minutes' rest, falling to 82. His ordinary pulse on entering the room, during these last six nights, was more than once over 100, and never lower than 84; from which it rose, after *Nickleby* on 22 February, to 112. On 8 February, when he read *Dombey*, it had risen from 91 to 114; on 1 March, after *Copperfield*, it rose from 100 to 124; and when he entered the room on the last night it was at 108, having risen only two beats more when the reading was done. The pieces on this occasion were the *Christmas Carol*, followed by the *Pickwick Trial*; and probably in all his life he never read so well. On his return from the States, where he had to address his effects to audiences composed of immense numbers of people, a certain loss of refinement had been observable; but the old delicacy was now again delightfully manifest, and a subdued tone, as well in the humorous as the serious portions, gave something to all the reading as of a quiet sadness of farewell. The charm of this was at its height when he shut the volume of *Pickwick* and spoke in his own person. He said that for fifteen years he had been reading his own books to audiences whose sensitive and kindly recognition of them had given him instruction and enjoyment in his art such as few men could have had; but that he nevertheless thought it well now to retire upon older associations, and in future to devote himself exclusively to the calling which had first made him known. "In but two short weeks from this time I hope that you may enter, in your own homes, on a new series of readings at which my assistance will be indispensable; but from these garish lights I vanish now for evermore, with a heartfelt, grateful, respectful, affectionate farewell." The brief hush of silence as he moved from the platform; and the prolonged tumult of sound that followed suddenly, stayed him, and again for another moment brought him back; will not be forgotten by any present.

Little remains to be told that has not in it almost unmixed pain and sorrow. Hardly a day passed, while the readings went on or after they closed, unvisited by some effect or other of the disastrous excitement shown by the notes of Mr. Beard. On 23 January, when for the last time he met Carlyle, he came to us with his left hand in a sling; on 7 February, when he passed with us his last birthday, and on the 25th, when he read the third number of his novel, the hand was still swollen and painful; and on 21 March, when he read admirably his fourth number, he told us that as he came along, walking up the length of Oxford Street, the same incident had recurred as on the day of a former dinner with us, and he had not been able to read, all the way, more than the right-hand half of the names over the shops. Yet he had the old fixed persuasion that this was rather the effect of a medicine he had been taking than of any grave cause, and he still strongly believed his other troubles to be exclusively local. Eight days later he wrote: "My uneasiness and hemorrhage, after having quite left me, as I supposed, has come back with an aggravated irritability that it has not yet displayed. You have no idea what a state I am in to-day from a sudden violent rush of it; and yet it has not the slightest effect on my general health that I know of." This was a disorder which troubled him in his earlier life; and during the last five years, in his intervals of suffering from other causes, it had from time to time taken aggravated form.

His last public appearances were in April. On the 5th he took the chair for the newsvendors, whom he helped with a genial address in which even his apology for little speaking overflowed with irrepressible humour. He would try, he said, like Falstaff, "but with a modification almost as large as himself," less to speak himself than to be the cause of speaking in others. "Much in this manner they exhibit at the door of a snuff-shop the effigy of a Highlander with an empty mull in his hand, who, apparently having taken all the snuff he can carry, and discharged all the sneezes of which he is capable, politely invites his friends and patrons to step in and try what they can do in the same line." On the 30th of the same month he returned thanks for "Literature" at the Royal Academy dinner, and I may preface my allusion to what he then said with what he had written to me the day before. Three days earlier Daniel Maclise had passed away. "Like you at Ely, so I at Higham, had the shock of first reading at a railway station of the death of our old dear friend and companion. What the shock would be, you know too well. It has been only after great difficulty, and after hardening and steeling myself to the subject by at once thinking of it and avoiding it in a strange way, that I have been able to get any command over it or over myself. If I feel at the time that I can be sure of the necessary composure, I shall make a little reference to it at the Academy to-morrow. I suppose you *165 won't be there." The reference made was most touching and manly. He told those who listened that since he first entered the public lists, a very young man indeed, it had been his constant fortune to number among his nearest and dearest friends members of that Academy who had been its pride; and who had now, one by one, so dropped from his side that he was grown to believe, with the Spanish monk of whom Wilkie spoke, that the only realities around him were the pictures which he loved, and all the moving life but a shadow and a dream. "For many years I was one of the two most intimate friends and most constant companions of Mr. Maclise, to whose death the Prince of Wales has made allusion, and the President has referred with the eloquence of genuine feeling. Of his genius in his chosen art, I will venture to say nothing here; but of his fertility of mind and wealth of intellect I may confidently assert that they would have made him, if he had been so minded, at least as great a writer as he was a painter. The gentlest and most modest of men, the freshest as to his generous appreciation of young aspirants and the frankest and largest-hearted as to his peers, incapable of a sordid or ignoble thought, gallantly sustaining the true dignity of his vocation, without one grain of self-ambition, wholesomely natural at the last as at the first, 'in wit a man, simplicity a child,'—no artist of whatsoever denomination, I make bold to say, ever went to his rest leaving a golden memory more pure from dross, or having devoted himself with a truer chivalry to the art-goddess whom he worshipped." These were the last public words of Dickens, and he could not have spoken any worthier of himself, or better deserved than by him of whom they were spoken.

Upon his appearance at the dinner of the Academy had followed some invitations he was led to accept; greatly to his own regret, he told me on the night (7 May) when he read to us the fifth number of *Edwin Drood*; for he was now very eager to get back to the quiet of Gadshill. He dined with Mr. Motley, then American minister; had met Mr. Disraeli at a dinner at

Lord Stanhope's; had breakfasted with Mr. Gladstone; and on the 17th was to attend the Queen's ball with his daughter. But she had to go there without him; for on the 16th I had intimation of a sudden disablement. "I am sorry to report, that, in the old preposterous endeavour to dine at preposterous hours and preposterous places, I have been pulled up by a sharp attack in my foot. And serve me right. I hope to get the better of it soon, but I fear I must not think of dining with you on Friday. I have cancelled everything in the dining way for this week, and that is a very small precaution after the horrible pain I have had and the remedies I have taken." He had to excuse himself also from the General Theatrical Fund dinner, where the Prince of Wales was to preside; but at another dinner a week later, where the King of the Belgians and the Prince were to be present, so much pressure was put upon him that he went, still suffering as he was, to dine with Lord Houghton.

We met for the last time on Sunday, 22 May, when I dined with him in Hyde Park Place. The death of Mr. Lemon, of which he heard that day, had led his thoughts to the crowd of friendly companions in letters and art who had so fallen from the ranks since we played Ben Jonson together that we were left almost alone. "And none beyond his sixtieth year," he said, "very few even fifty." It is no good to talk of it, I suggested. "We shall not think of it the less" was his reply; and an illustration much to the point was before us, afforded by an incident deserving remembrance in this story. Not many weeks before, a correspondent had written to him from Liverpool describing himself as a self-raised man, attributing his prosperous career to what Dickens's writings had taught him at its outset of the wisdom of kindness, and sympathy for others; and asking pardon for the liberty he took in hoping that he might be permitted to offer some acknowledgment of what not only had cheered and stimulated him through all his life, but had contributed so much to the success of it. The letter enclosed £500. Dickens was greatly touched by this; and told the writer, in sending back his cheque, that he would certainly have taken it if he had not been, though not a man of fortune, a prosperous man himself; but that the letter, and the spirit of its offer, had so gratified him, that if the writer pleased to send him any small memorial of it in another form he would gladly receive it. The memorial soon came. A richly worked basket of silver, inscribed "from one who has been cheered and stimulated by Mr. Dickens's writings, and held the author among his first remembrances when he became prosperous," was accompanied by an extremely handsome silver centrepiece for the table, of which the design was four figures representing the Seasons. But the kindly donor shrank from sending Winter to one whom he would fain connect with none save the brighter and milder days, and he had struck the fourth figure from the design. "I never look at it," said Dickens, "that I don't think most of the Winter." The gift had yet too surely foreshadowed the truth, for the winter was never to come to him.

A matter discussed that day with Mr. Ouvry was briefly resumed in a note of 29 May, the last I ever received from him; which followed me to Exeter, and closed thus. "You and I can speak of it at Gads by and by. Foot no worse. But no better." The old trouble was upon him when we parted, and this must have been nearly the last note written before he quitted London. He was at Gadshill on 30 May; and I heard no more until the telegram reached me at Launceston on the night of 9 June, which told me that the "by and by" was not to come in this world.

The few days at Gadshill had been given wholly to work on his novel. He had been easier in his foot and hand; and though he was suffering severely from the local hemorrhage before named, he made no complaint of illness. But there was observed in him a very unusual appearance of fatigue. "He seemed very weary." He was out with his dogs for the last time on Monday, 6 June, when he walked with his letters into Rochester. On Tuesday the 7th, after his daughter Mary had left on a visit to her sister Kate, not finding himself equal to much fatigue, he drove to Cobham Wood with his sister-in-law, there dismissed the carriage, and walked round the park and back. He returned in time to put up in his new conservatory some Chinese lanterns sent from London that afternoon; and the whole of the evening, he sat with Miss Hogarth in the dining-room that he might see their effect when lighted. More than once he then expressed his satisfaction at having finally abandoned all intention of exchanging Gadshill for London; and this he had done more impressively some days before. While he lived, he said, he should wish his name to be more and more associated with the place; and he had a notion that when he died he should like to lie in the little graveyard belonging to the Cathedral at the foot of the Castle wall.

On 8 June he passed all the day writing in the Chalet. He came over for luncheon; and, much against his usual custom, returned to his desk. Of the sentences he was then writing, the last of his long life of literature, a portion has been given in facsimile on a previous page; and the reader will observe with a painful interest, not alone its evidence of minute labour at this fast-closing hour of time with him, but the direction his thoughts had taken. He imagines such a brilliant morning as had risen with that 8 June shining on the old city of Rochester. He sees in surpassing beauty, with the lusty ivy gleaming in the sun, and the rich trees waving in the balmy air, its antiquities and its ruins; its Cathedral and Castle. But his fancy, then, is not with the stern dead forms of either; but with that which makes warm the cold stone tombs of centuries, and lights them up with flecks of brightness, "fluttering there like wings." To him, on that sunny summer morning, the changes of glorious light from moving boughs, the songs of birds, the scents from garden, woods, and fields, have penetrated into the Cathedral, have subdued its earthy odour, and are preaching the Resurrection and the Life.

He was late in leaving the Chalet; but before dinner, which was ordered at six o'clock with the intention of walking afterwards in the lanes, he wrote some letters, among them one to his friend Mr. Charles Kent appointing to see him in London next day; and dinner was begun before Miss Hogarth saw, with alarm, a singular expression of trouble and pain in his face. "For an hour," he then told her, "he had been very ill"; but he wished dinner to go on. These were the only really coherent words uttered by him. They were followed by some, that fell from him disconnectedly, of quite other matters; of an approaching sale at a neighbour's house, of whether Macready's son was with his father at Cheltenham, and of his own intention to go immediately to London; but at these latter he had risen, and his sister-in-law's help alone prevented him from falling where he stood. Her effort then was to get him on the sofa, but after a slight struggle he sank heavily on his left side. "On the ground" were the last words he spoke. It was now a little over ten minutes past six o'clock. His two daughters came that night with Mr. F. Beard, who had also been telegraphed for, and whom they met at the station. His eldest son arrived early next morning, and was joined in the evening (too late) by his younger son from Cambridge. All possible medical aid had been summoned. The surgeon of the neighbourhood was there from the first, and a physician from London was in attendance as well as Mr. Beard. But human help was unavailing. There was effusion on the brain; and though stertorous breathing continued all night, and until ten minutes past six o'clock on the evening of Thursday, 9 June, there had never been a gleam of hope during the twenty-four hours. He had lived four months beyond his 58th year.

II

WESTMINSTER ABBEY

1870

THE excitement and sorrow at his death are within the memory of all. Before the news of it even reached the remoter parts of England, it had been flashed across Europe; was known in the distant continents of India, Australia, and America; and not in English-speaking communities only, but in every country of the civilised earth, had awakened grief and sympathy. In his own land it was as if a personal bereavement had befallen everyone. Her Majesty the Queen telegraphed from Balmoral "her deepest regret at the sad news of Charles Dickens's death"; and this was the sentiment alike of all classes of her people. There was not an English journal that did not give it touching and noble utterance; and *The Times* took the lead in suggesting that the only fit resting-place for the remains of a man so dear to England was the Abbey in which the most illustrious Englishmen are laid.

With the expression thus given to a general wish, the Dean of Westminster lost no time in showing ready compliance; and on the morning of the day when it appeared was in communication with the family and the executors. The public homage of a burial in the Abbey had to be reconciled with his own instructions to be privately buried without previous announcement of time or place, and without monument or memorial. He would himself have preferred to lie in the small graveyard under Rochester Castle wall, or in the little churches of Cobham or Shorne; but all these were found to be closed; and the desire of the Dean and Chapter of Rochester to lay him in their Cathedral had been entertained, when the Dean of Westminster's request, and the considerate kindness of his generous assurance that there should be only such ceremonial as would strictly obey all injunctions of privacy, made it a grateful duty to accept that offer. The spot already had been chosen by the Dean; and before midday on the following morning, Tuesday, 14 June, with knowledge of those only who took part in the burial, all was done. The solemnity had not lost by the simplicity. Nothing so grand or so touching could have accompanied it, as the stillness and the silence of the vast cathedral. Then, later in the day and all the following day, came unbidden mourners in such crowds, that the Dean had to request permission to keep open the grave until Thursday; but after it was closed they did not cease to come, and "all day long," Doctor Stanley wrote on the 17th, "there was a constant pressure to the spot, and many flowers were strewn upon it by unknown hands, many tears shed from unknown eyes." He alluded to this in the impressive funeral discourse delivered by him in the Abbey on the morning of Sunday the 19th, pointing to the fresh flowers that then had been newly thrown (as they still are thrown, in this fourth year after the death), and saying that "the spot would thenceforward be a sacred one with both the New World and the Old, as that of the representative of the literature, not of this island only, but of all who speak our English tongue." The stone placed upon it is inscribed

CHARLES DICKENS
BORN FEBRUARY THE SEVENTH, 1812
DIED JUNE THE NINTH, 1870

The highest associations of both the arts he loved surround him where he lies. Next to him is RICHARD CUMBERLAND. Mrs. PRITCHARD'S monument looks down upon him, and immediately behind is DAVID GARRICK'S. Nor is the actor's delightful art more worthily represented than the nobler genius of the author. Facing the grave, and on its left and right, are the monuments of CHAUCER, SHAKESPEARE, and DRYDEN, the three immortals who did most to create and settle the language to which CHARLES DICKENS has given another undying name.

APPENDIX

THE WILL OF CHARLES DICKENS

"I, CHARLES DICKENS, of Gadshill Place, Higham in the county
of Kent, hereby revoke all my former Wills and Codicils and
declare this to be my last Will and Testament. I give the sum
of £1000 free of legacy duty to Miss Ellen Lawless Ternan, late
of Houghton Place, Ampthill Square, in the county of Middle--
sex. I GIVE the sum of £19 19 0 to my faithful servant Mrs.
Anne Cornelius. I GIVE the sum of £19 19 0 to the daughter and
only child of the said Mrs. Anne Cornelius. I GIVE the sum of
£19 19 0 to each and every domestic servant, male and female,
who shall be in my employment at the time of my decease, and
shall have been in my employment for a not less period of time
than one year. I GIVE the sum of £1000 free of legacy duty to
my daughter Mary Dickens. I also give to my said daughter
an annuity of £300 a year, during her life, if she shall so long
continue unmarried; such annuity to be considered as accruing
from day to day, but to be payable half-yearly, the first of such
half-yearly payments to be made at the expiration of six months
next after my decease. If my said daughter Mary shall marry,
such annuity shall cease; and in that case, but in that case only,
my said daughter shall share with my other children in the
provision hereinafter made for them. I GIVE to my dear sister-
in-law Georgina Hogarth the sum of £8000 free of legacy duty.
I also give to the said Georgina Hogarth all my personal jewellery
not hereinafter mentioned, and all the little familiar objects
from my writing-table and my room, and she will know what to
do with those things. I ALSO GIVE to the said Georgina Hogarth
all my private papers whatsoever and wheresoever, and I leave
her my grateful blessing as the best and truest friend man ever
had. I GIVE to my eldest son Charles my library of printed books,
and my engravings and prints; and I also give to my son Charles
the silver salver presented to me at Birmingham, and the silver
cup presented to me at Edinburgh, and my shirt studs, shirt

pins, and sleeve buttons. AND I BEQUEATH unto my said son Charles and my son Henry Fielding Dickens, the sum of £8000 upon trust to invest the same, and from time to time to vary the investments thereof, and to pay the annual income thereof to my wife during her life, and after her decease the said sum of £8000 and the investments thereof shall be in trust for my children (but subject as to my daughter Mary to the proviso hereinbefore contained) who being a son or sons shall have attained or shall attain the age of twenty-one years, or being a daughter or daughters shall have attained or shall attain that age or be previously married, in equal shares if more than one. I GIVE my watch (the gold repeater presented to me at Coventry), and I give the chains and seals and all appendages I have worn with it, to my dear and trusty friend John Forster, of Palace Gate House, Kensington, in the county of Middlesex aforesaid; and I also give to the said John Forster such manuscripts of my published works as may be in my possession at the time of my decease. AND I DEVISE AND BEQUEATH all my real and personal estate (except such as is vested in me as a trustee or mortgagee) unto the said Georgina Hogarth and the said John Forster, their heirs, executors, administrators, and assigns respectively, upon trust that they the said Georgina Hogarth and John Forster, or the survivor of them or the executors or administrators of such survivor, do and shall, at their, his, or her uncontrolled and irresponsible direction, either proceed to an immediate sale or conversion into money of the said real and personal estate (including my copyrights), or defer and postpone any sale or conversion into money, till such time or times as they, he, or she shall think fit, and in the meantime may manage and let the said real and personal estate (including my copyrights), in such manner in all respects as I myself could do, if I were living and acting therein; it being my intention that the trustees or trustee for the time being of this my Will shall have the fullest power over the said real and personal estate which I can give to them, him, or her. AND I DECLARE that, until the said real and personal estate shall be sold and converted into money, the rents and annual income thereof respectively shall be paid and applied to the person or persons in the manner and for the purposes to whom and for which the annual income of the monies to arise from the sale or conversion thereof into money would be payable or applicable under this my Will in case the same were sold or converted into money. AND I DECLARE that my real estate shall for the purposes of this my Will be considered as converted into personalty upon my decease. AND I DECLARE that the said trustees or trustee for the time being, do and shall, with and out of the monies which shall come to their, his, or her hands, under or by virtue of this my Will and the trusts thereof pay my just debts, funeral and testamentary expenses, and legacies. AND I DECLARE that the said trust funds or so much thereof as shall remain after answering the purposes aforesaid, and the annual income thereof, shall be in trust for all my children (but subject as to my daughter Mary to the proviso hereinbefore contained), who being a son or sons shall have attained or shall attain the age of twenty-one years, and being a daughter or daughters shall have attained or shall attain that age or be previously married, in equal shares if more than one. PROVIDED ALWAYS, that, as regards my copyrights and the produce and profits thereof, my said daughter Mary, notwithstanding the proviso hereinbefore contained with reference to her, shall share with my other children therein whether she be married or not. AND I DEVISE the estates vested in me at my decease as a trustee or mortgagee unto the use of the said Georgina Hogarth and John Forster, their heirs and assigns, upon the trusts and subject to the equities affecting the same respectively. AND I APPOINT the said GEORGINA HOGARTH and JOHN FORSTER executrix and executor of this my Will, and GUARDIANS of the persons of my children during their respective minorities. AND LASTLY, as I have now set down the form of words which my legal advisers assure me are necessary to the plain objects of this my Will, I solemnly enjoin my dear children always to remember how much they owe to the said Georgina Hogarth, and never to be wanting in a grateful and affectionate attachment to her, for they know well that she has been, through all the stages of their growth and progress, their ever useful self-denying and devoted friend. AND I DESIRE here simply to record the fact that my wife, since our separation by consent, has been in the receipt from me of an annual income of £600, while all the great charges of a numerous and expensive family have devolved wholly upon myself. I emphatically direct that I be buried in an inexpensive, unostentatious, and strictly private manner; that no public announcement be made of the time or place of my burial; that at the utmost not more than three plain mourning coaches be employed; and that those who attend my funeral wear no scarf, cloak, black bow, long hat-band, or other such revolting absurdity. I DIRECT that my name be inscribed in plain English letters on my tomb, without the addition of

'Mr.' or 'Esquire.' I conjure my friends on no account to make me the subject of any monument, memorial, or testimonial whatever. I rest my claims to the remembrance of my country upon my published works, and to the remembrance of my friends upon their experience of me in addition thereto. I commit my soul to the mercy of God through our Lord and Saviour Jesus Christ, and I exhort my dear children humbly to try to guide themselves by the teaching of the New Testament in its broad spirit, and to put no faith in any man's narrow construction of its letter here or there. IN WITNESS whereof I the said Charles Dickens, the testator, have to this my last Will and Testament set my hand this 12th day of May in the year of our Lord 1869.

"CHARLES DICKENS.

"Signed published and declared by the above-named Charles Dickens the testator as and for his last Will and Testament in the presence of us (present together at the same time) who in his presence at his request and in the presence of each other have hereunto subscribed our names as witnesses.

"G. HOLSWORTH,
    "26 Wellington Street, Strand.

"HENRY WALKER,
    "26 Wellington Street, Strand.

"I, CHARLES DICKENS of Gadshill Place near Rochester in the county of Kent Esquire declare this to be a Codicil to my last Will and Testament which Will bears date the 12th day of May 1869. I GIVE to my son Charles Dickens the younger all my share and interest in the weekly journal called *All the Year Round*, which is now conducted under Articles of Partnership made between me and William Henry Wills and the said Charles Dickens the younger, and all my share and interest in the stereotypes stock and other effects belonging to the said partnership, he defraying my share of all debts and liabilities of the said partnership which may be outstanding at the time of my decease, and in all other respects I confirm my said Will. IN WITNESS whereof I have hereunto set my hand the 2nd day of June in the year of our Lord 1870.

"CHARLES DICKENS.

"Signed and declared by the said CHARLES
DICKENS, the testator as and for a Codicil to
his Will in the presence of us present at the
same time who at his request in his presence
and in the presence of each other hereunto
subscribe our names as witnesses.

    "G. HOLSWORTH,
        "26 Wellington Street, Strand.

    "H. WALKER,
        "26 Wellington Street, Strand."

The real and personal estate—taking the property bequeathed
by the last codicil at a valuation of something less than two
years' purchase; and of course before payment of the legacies,
the (inconsiderable) debts, and the testamentary and other
expenses,—amounted as nearly as may be calculated, to
£93,000.

AUTHOR'S ADDITIONAL FOOTNOTES

VOLUME II

* 65 (p. 3). He [Sydney] entered the Royal Navy, and survived his father only a year and eleven months. He was a lieutenant at the time of his death, from a sharp attack of bronchitis; being then on board the P. & O. steamer *Malta*, invalided from his ship the *Topaze*, and on his way home. He was buried at sea on 2nd May 1872. Poor fellow! He was the smallest in size of all the children, in his manhood reaching only to a little over five feet; and throughout his childhood was never called by any other name than the 'Ocean Spectre', from a strange little weird yet most attractive look in his large wondering eyes, very happily caught in a sketch in oils by the good Frank Stone, done at Bonchurch in September 1849 and remaining in his aunt's possession. 'Stone has painted', Dickens then wrote to me, 'the Ocean Spectre, and made a very pretty little picture of him.' It was a strange chance that led his father to invent this playful name for one whom the ocean did indeed take to itself at last.

* 66 (p. 5). I think it right to place on record here Leigh Hunt's own allusion to the incident (*Autobiography*, p. 432), though it will be thought to have too favourable a tone, and I could have wished that other names had also found mention in it. But I have already stated quite unaffectedly my own opinion of the very modest pretensions of the whole affair, and these kind words of Hunt may stand *valeant quantum*. 'Simultaneous with the latest movement about the pension was one of the part of my admirable friend Dickens and other distinguished men, Forsters and Jerrolds, who, combining kindly purpose with an amateur inclination for the stage, had condescended to show to the public what excellent actors, indeed, some of them were. . . . They proposed . . . a benefit for myself . . . and the piece performed on the occasion was Ben Jonson's *Every Man in his Humour*. . . . If anything had been needed to show how men of letters include actors, on the common principle of the greater including the less, these gentlemen would have furnished it. Mr Dickens's Bobadil had a spirit in it of intellectual apprehension beyond anything the existing stage has shown . . . and Mr Forster delivered the verses of Ben Jonson with a musical flow and a sense to their grace and beauty unknown, I believe, to the recitation of actors at present. At least I have never heard anything like it since Edmund Kean's.'

* 67 (p. 13). Another, which for many reasons we may regret went also into the limbo of unrealized designs, is sketched in the subjoined (7th January 1848). 'Mac and I think of going to Ireland for six weeks on the spring, and seeing whether anything is to be done there, in the way of a book? I fancy it might turn out well.' The Mac of course is Maclise.

* 68 (p. 13). 'Here we are' (23rd August) 'in the noble old premises; and very nice they look, all things considered. . . . Trifles happen to me which occur to nobody else. My portmanteau "fell off" a cab last night somewhere between London-bridge and here. It contained on a moderate calculation £70 worth of clothes. I have no shirt to put on, and am obliged to send out to a barber to come and shave me.'

*69 (p. 14). 'Do you see anything to object to in it? I have never had so much difficulty, I think, in setting about any slight thing; for I really didn't know that I had a word to say, and nothing seems to live 'twixt what *I have*

425

said and silence. The advantage of it is, that the latter part opens an idea for future prefaces all through the series, and may serve perhaps to make a feature of them.' (7th September 1847.)

* 70 (p. 15). From his notes on these matters I may quote. 'The Leeds appears to be a very important institution, and I am glad to see that George Stephenson will be there, besides the local lights, inclusive of all the Baineses. They talk at Glasgow of 6,000 people.' (26th November.) 'You have got Southey's *Holly Tree*. I have not. Put it in your pocket today. It occurs to me (up to the eyes in a mass of Glasgow Athenaeum papers) that I could quote it with good effect in the North.' (24th December.) 'A most brilliant demonstration last night, and I think I never did better. Newspaper reports bad.' (29th December.)

* 71 (p. 16). 'Tremendous distress at Glasgow, and a truly damnable jail, exhibiting the separate system in a most absurd and hideous form. Governor practical and intelligent; very anxious for the associated silent system; and much comforted by my fault-finding.' (30th December.)

* 71A (p. 17). It would amuse the reader, but occupy too much space, to add to my former illustrations of his managerial troubles; but from an elaborate paper of rules for rehearsals, which I have found in his handwriting, I quote the opening and the close: 'Remembering the very imperfect condition of all our plays at present, the general expectation in reference to them, the kind of audience before which they will be presented, and the near approach of the nights of performance, I hope everybody concerned will abide by the following regulations, and will aid in strictly carrying them out.' Elaborate are the regulations set forth, but I take only the three last: 'Silence, on the stage and in the theatre, to be faithfully observed; the lobbies, etc., being always available for conversation. No book to be referred to on the stage; but those who are imperfect to take their words from the prompter. Everyone to act, as nearly as possible, as on the night of performance; everyone to speak out, so as to be audible through the house. And every mistake of exit, entrance, or situation, to be corrected *three times* successively. 'He closes thus: 'All who were concerned in the first getting up of *Every Man in his Humour*, and remember how carefully the stage was always kept then, and who have been engaged in the late rehearsals of the *Merry Wives*, and have experienced the difficulty of getting on, or off: of being heard, or of hearing anybody else: will, I am sure, acknowledge the indispensable necessity of these regulations.'

* 72 (p. 26). 'I will now explain that *Oliver Twist*, the ——, the ——, etc.' (naming books by another writer) 'were produced in an entirely different manner from what would be considered as the usual course; for *I, the Artist, suggested to the Authors of those works the original idea, or subject*, for them to write out—furnishing, at the same time, the *principal characters and the scenes*. And then, as the tale had to be produced in monthly parts, the *Writer*, or *Author*, and the Artist, had every month to arrange and settle what scenes, or subjects, and characters were to be introduced, and the Author had to *weave in* such scenes as I wished to represent.' *The Artist and the Author*, by George Cruikshank, p. 15. (Bell & Daldy, 1872.) The italics are Mr Cruikshank's own.

* 73 (p. 29). I take, from his paper of notes for the number, the various names, beginning with that of her real prototype, out of which the name selected came to him at last. 'Mrs Roylance . . . House at the sea-side. Mrs Wrychin. Mrs Tipchin. Mrs Alchin. Mrs Somching. Mrs Pipchin.'

* 74 (p. 32). 'Edinburgh, 31st *January* 1847. [From Lord Jeffery.] Oh, my dear, dear Dickens! what a No. 5 you have now given us! I have so cried and

sobbed over it last night, and again this morning; and felt my heart purified by those tears, and blessed and loved you for making me shed them; and I never can bless and love you enough. Since the divine Nelly was found dead on her humble couch, beneath the snow and the ivy, there has been nothing like the actual dying of that sweet Paul, in the summer sunshine of that lofty room. And the long vista that leads us so gently and sadly, and yet so gracefully and winningly, to the plain consummation! Every trait so true, and so touching—and yet lightened by the fearless innocence which goes *playfully* to the brink of the grave, and that pure affection which bears the unstained spirit, on its soft and lambent flash, at once to its source in eternity. . . .' In the same letter he told him of his having been reading the *Battle of Life* again, charmed with its sweet writing and generous sentiments.

* 75 (p. 35). 'Isn't Bunsby good?' I heard Lord Denman call out, with unmistakable glee and enjoyment, over Talfourd's table—I think to Sir Edward Ryan; one of the few survivors of that pleasant dinner party of May 1847.

* 76 (p. 48). My friend Mr Shirley Brooks sends me a 'characteristic' cutting from an autograph catalogue in which these few lines are given from an early letter in the Doughty-street days. 'I always pay my taxes when they won't call any longer, in order to get a dab name in the parish and so escape all honours.' It is a touch of character, certainly; but though his motives in later life was the same, his method was not. He attended to the tax-collector, but of any other parochial or political application took no notice whatever.

* 77 (p. 48). Even in the modest retirement of a note I fear that I shall offend the dignity of history, and of biography, by printing the lines in which this intention was announced to me. They were written 'in character'; and the character was that of the 'waterman' at the Charing-cross cabstand, first discovered by George Cattermole, whose imitations of him were a delight to Dickens at this time, and adapted themselves in the exuberance of his admiration to every conceivable variety of subject. The painter of the Derby Day will have a fullness of satisfaction in remembering this. 'Sloppy', the hero in question, had a friend 'Jack', in whom he was supposed to typify his own early and hard experiences before he became a convert to temperance; and Dickens used to point to 'Jack' as the justification of himself and Mrs Gamp for their portentous invention of Mrs Harris. It is amazing nonsense to repeat; but the hear Cattermole, in the gruff, hoarse accents of what seemed to be the remains of a deep bass voice wrapped up in wet straw, repeat the wild proceedings of Jack, was not to be forgotten. ' Yes sir, Jack went mad sir, just afore he 'stablished hisself by Sir Robert Peel's-s-s, sir. He was allis a callin' for a pint o' beer sir, and they brings him water sir. Yes sir. And so sir, I sees him dodgin' about one day sir, yes sir, and at last he gits a hopportunity sir and claps a pitch-plaster on the mouth o' th' pump sir, and says he's done for his wust henemy sir. Yes sir. And then they finds him a-sittin' on the top o' the corn-chest sir, yes sir, a crammin' a old pistol with wisps o' hay and horse-beans sir, and swearin' he's goin' to blow hisself to hattoms, yes sir, but he doesn't, no sir. For I sees him arterwards a lying on the straw a manifacktrin' Bengal cheroots out o' corn-chaff sir and swearin' he'd make 'em smoke sir, but they hulloxed him off round by the corner of Drummins's-s-s-s-s-s sir, just afore I come here sir, yes sir. And so you never see'd us together sir, no sir.' This was the remarkable dialect in which Dickens wrote from Broadstairs on the 13th July. 'About Saturday sir?—Why sir, I'm a-going to Folkestone a Saturday sir!—not on accounts of the manifacktring of Bengal cheroots as there is there but for the survayin' o' the coast sir. 'Cos you see sir, bein' here sir, and not a finishin' my work sir till tomorrow sir, I couldn't go

afore! And if I wos to come home, and not go, and come back agin sir, wy it would be nat'rally a hulloxing of myself sir. Yes sir. Wy sir, I b'lieve that the gent as is a goin' to 'stablish hisself sir, in the autumn, along with me round the corner sir (by Drummins's-s-s-s-s bank) is a comin' down to Folkestone Saturday arternoon—Leech by name sir—yes sir—another Jack sir—and if you wos to come down along with him sir by the train as gits to Folkestone twenty minutes arter five, you'd find me a smoking a Bengal cheroot (made of clover-chaff and horse-beans sir) on the platform. You couldn't spend your arternoon better sir. Dover, Sandgate, Herne Bay —they're all to be wisited sir, most probable, till sich times as a 'ouse is found sir. Yes sir. Then decide to come sir, and say you will, and do it. I shall be here till arter post time Saturday mornin' sir. Come on then!

SLOPPY
'His X mark.'

* 78 (p. 54). It stood originally thus: '"Do you recollect the date", said Mr Dick, looking earnestly at me, and taking up his pen to note it down, "when that bull got into the china warehouse and did so much mischief?" I was very much surprised by the inquiry; but remembering a song about such an occurrence that was popular at Salem House, and thinking he might want to quote it, replied that I believed it was on St Patrick's Day. "Yes, I know," said Mr Dick—"in the morning; but what year?" I could give no information on this point.' Original MS. of *Copperfield*.

* 79 (p. 66). Mr Sala's first paper appeared in September 1851, and in the same month of the following year I had an allusion in a letter from Dickens which I shall hope to have Mr Sala's forgiveness for printing. 'That was very good indeed of Sala's' (some essay he had written). 'He was twenty guineas in advance, by the bye, and I told Wills delicately to make him a present of it. I find him a very conscientious fellow. When he gets money ahead, he is not like the imbecile youth who so often do the like in Wellington-street (the office of *Household Words*) and walk off, but only works more industriously. I think he improves with everything he does. He looks sharply at the alterations in his articles, I observe; and takes the hint next time.'

* 80 (p. 79). From letters of nearly the same date here is another characteristic word: 'Pen and ink before me! Am I not at work on *Copperfield*! Nothing else would have kept me here until half-past two on such a day . . . Indian news bad indeed. Sad things come of bloody war. If it were not for Elihu, I should be a peace and arbitration man.'

* 81 (p. 89). From this time to his death there was always friendly intercourse with his old publisher Mr Bentley.

* 82 (p. 90). It may be proper to record the fact that he had made a short run to Paris, with Maclise, at the end of June, of which sufficient further note will have been taken if I print the subjoined passages from a letter to me dated 24th June 1850, Hotel Windsor, Rue de Rivoli. 'There being no room in the Hotel Brighton, we are lodged (in a very good apartment) here. The heat is absolutely frightful. I never felt anything like it in Italy. Sleep is next to impossible, except in the day, when the room is dark, and the patient exhausted. We purpose leaving here on Saturday morning and going to Rouen, whence we shall proceed either to Havre or Dieppe, and so arrange our proceedings as to be home, please God, on Tuesday evening. We are going to some of the little theatres tonight and on Wednesday to the Français, for Rachel's last performance before she goes to London. There does not seem to be anything remarkable in progress, in the theatrical

way. Nor do I observe that out of doors the place is much changed, except in respect of the carriages which are certainly less numerous. I also think the Sunday is even much more a day of business than it used to be. As we are going into the country with Regnier tomorrow, I write this after letter time and before going out to dine at the Trois Frères, that it may come to you by tomorrow's post. The twelve hours' journey here is astounding—marvellously done, except in respect of the means of refreshment, which are absolutely none. Mac is very well (extremely loose as to his waistcoat, and otherwise careless in regard of buttons) and sends his love. De Fresne proposes a dinner with all the notabilities of Paris present, but I won't stand it! I really have undergone so much fatigue from work, that I am resolved not even to see him, but to please myself. I find, my child (as Horace Walpole would say), that I have written you nothing here, but you will take the will for the deed.'

* 83 (p. 91). The rest of the letter may be allowed to fill the corner of a note. The allusions to Rogers and Landor are by way of reply to an invitation I had sent him. ' I am extremely sorry to hear about Fox. Shall call to enquire, as I come by to the Temple. And will call on you (taking the chance of finding you) on my way to that Seat of Boredom. I wrote my paper for *H. W.* yesterday, and have begun *Copperfield* this morning. Still undecided about Dora, but must decide today. La difficulté d'écrire l'Anglais m'est extrêmement ennuyeuse. Ah, mon Dieu! si l'on pourrait toujours écrire cette belle langue de France! Monsieur Rogere! Ah! qu'il est homme d'esprit, homme de génie, homme des lettres! Monsieur Landore! Ah qu'il parle Français—pas parfaitement comme un ange—un peu (peut-être) comme un diable! Mais il est bon garçon—sérieusement, il est un de la vraie noblesse de la nature. Votre tout dévoué, Charles. À Monsieur Monsieur Fos-tere.'

* 83a (p. 101). Here are two passages taken from Hunt's writing in the *Tatler* (a charming little paper which it was one of the first ventures of the young firm of Chapman and Hall to attempt to establish for Hunt in 1830), to which accident had unluckily attracted Dickens's notice: 'Supposing us to be in want of patronage, and in possession of talent enough to make it an honour to notice us, we would much rather have some great and comparatively private friend, rich enough to assist us, and amiable enough to render obligation delightful, than become the public property of any man, or of any government. . . . If a divinity had given us our choice we should have said—make us La Fontaine, who goes and lives twenty years with some rich friend, as innocent of any harm in it as a child, and who writes what he thinks charming verses, sitting all day under a tree.' Such sayings will not bear to be deliberately read and thought over, but any kind of extravagance or oddity came from Hunt's lips with a curious fascination. There was surely never a man of so sunny a nature, who could draw so much pleasure from common things, or to whom books were a world so real, so exhaustless, so delightful. I was only seventeen when I derived from him the tastes which have been the solace of all subsequent years, and I well remember the last time I saw him at Hammersmith, not long before his death in 1859, when, with his delicate, worn, but keenly intellectual face, his large luminous eyes, his thick shock of wiry grey hair, and a little cape of faded black silk over his shoulders, he looked like an old French abbé. He was buoyant and pleasant as ever; and was busy upon a vindication of Chaucer and Spenser from Cardinal Wiseman, who had attacked them for alleged sensuous and voluptuous qualities.

* 84 (p. 119). By W. Challinor, Esq. of Leek in Staffordshire, by whom it has been obligingly sent to me, with a copy of Dickens's letter acknowledging the receipt of it from the author on 11th March 1852. On the first of

that month the first number of *Bleak House* had appeared, but two numbers of it were then already written.

* 85 (p. 120). It is well to remember too what he wrote about the story [*Hard Times*] to Charles Knight. It had no design, he said, to damage the really useful truths of Political Economy, but was wholly directed against 'those who see figures and averages, and nothing else; who would take the average of cold in the Crimea during twelve months as a reason for clothing a soldier in nankeen on a night when he would be frozen to death in fur; and who would comfort the labourer in travelling twelve miles a day to and from his work, by telling him that the average distance of one inhabited place from another, on the whole area of England, is not more than four miles'.

* 86 (p. 121). Here is a note at the close. 'Tavistock House. Look at that! Boulogne, of course. Friday, 14th of July, 1854. I am three parts mad, and the fourth delirious, with perpetual rushing at *Hard Times*. I have done what I hope is a good thing with Stephen, taking his story as a whole; and hope to be over in town with the end of the book on Wednesday night. . . . I have been looking forward through so many weeks and sides of paper to this Stephen business, that now—as usual—it being over, I feel as if nothing in the world, in the way of intense and violent rushing hither and thither, could quite restore my balance.'

* 86A (p. 123). I subjoin the dozen titles successively proposed for *Bleak House*. 1. 'Tom-all-Alone's. The Ruined House'; 2. 'Tom-all-Alone's. The Solitary House that was always shut up'; 3. 'Bleak House Academy'; 4. 'The East Wind'; 5. 'Tom-all-Alone's. The Ruined [House, Building, Factory, Mill] that got into Chancery and never got out'; 6. 'Tom-all-Alone's. The Solitary House where the Grass grew'; 7. 'Tom-all-Alone's. The Solitary House that was always shut up and never Lighted'; 8. 'Tom-all-Alone's. The Ruined Mill, that got into Chancery and never got out'; 9. 'Tom-all-Alone's. The Solitary House where the Wind howled'; 10. 'Tom-all-Alone's. The Ruined House that got into Chancery and never got out'; 11. 'Bleak House and the East Wind. How they both got into Chancery and never got out'; 12. 'Bleak House.'

* 87 (p. 123). He was greatly interested in the movement for closing town and city graves (see the close of the eleventh chapter of *Bleak House*), and providing places of burial under State supervision.

* 88 (p. 125). The promise was formally conveyed next morning in a letter to one who took the lead then and since in all good work for Birmingham, Mr Arthur Ryland. The reading would, he said in his letter (7th January 1853), 'take about two hours, with a pause of ten minutes half way through. There would be some novelty in the thing, as I have never done it in public, though I have in private, and (if I may say so) with a great effect on the hearers.'

* 89 (p. 125). Baron Tauchnitz, describing to me his long and uninterrupted friendly intercourse with Dickens, has this remark: 'I give also a passage from one of his letters written at the time when he sent his son Charles, through my mediation, to Leipzig. He says in it what he desires for his son. "I want him to have all interest in, and to acquire a knowledge of, the life around him, and to be treated like a gentleman though pampered in nothing. By punctuality in all things, great or small, I set great store."'

*90 (p. 126). From one of his letters while there I take a passage of observation full of character. 'Great excitement here about a wretched woman who has murdered her child. Apropos of which I observed a curious thing last night. The newspaper offices (local journals) had placards like this outside:

CHILD MURDER IN BRIGHTON.

INQUEST. COMMITTAL OF THE MURDERESS.

I saw so many common people stand profoundly staring at these lines for half-an-hour together—and even go back to stare again—that I feel quite certain they had not the power of thinking about the thing at all connectedly or continuously, without having something about it before their sense of sight. Having got that, they were considering the case, wondering how the devil they had come into that power. I saw one man in a smock frock lose the said power the moment he turned away, and bring his hobnails back again.'

* 91 (p. 127). 'After correspondence with all parts of England, and every kind of refusal and evasion on my part, I am now obliged to decide this question—whether I shall read two nights at Bradford for a hundred pounds. If I do, I may take as many hundred pounds as I choose.' 27th January 1854.

* 92 (p. 127). On 28th December 1854 he wrote from Bradford: 'The hall is enormous, and they expect to seat 3,700 people tonight! Notwithstanding which, it seems to me a tolerably easy place—except that the width of the platform is so very great to the eye at first.' From Folkestone, on his way to Paris, he wrote in the autumn of 1855: '16th Sept. I am going to read for them here, on the 5th of next month, and have answered in the last fortnight thirty applications to do the like all over England, Ireland and Scotland. Fancy my having to come from Paris in December, to do this, at Peterborough, Birmingham and Sheffield—old promises.' Again: '23rd Sept. I am going to read here, next Friday week. There are (as there are everywhere) a Literary Institution and a Working Men's Institution, which have not the slightest sympathy or connexion. The stalls are five shillings, but I have made them fix the working men's admission at three-pence, and I hope it may bring them together. The event comes off in a carpenter's shop, as the biggest place that can be got.' In 1157, at Paxton's request, he read his *Carol* at Coventry for the Institute.

* 93 (p. 128).

My name it is Tom Thumb,	I have kill'd the giants tall;
Small my size,	And now I'm paid for all,
Small my size,	Small my size,
My name it is Tom Thumb,	Small my size;
Small my size.	And now I'm paid for all,
Yet though I am so small,	Small my size.

* 93A (p. 129). He went with the rest to Boulogne in the summer, and an anecdote transmitted in one of his father's letters will show that he maintained the reputation as a comedian which his early debut had awakened. 'ORIGINAL ANECDOTE OF THE PLORNISHGHENTER. This distinguished wit, being at Boulogne with his family, made a close acquaintance with his landlady, whose name was M. Beaucourt—the only French word with which he was at that time acquainted. It happened that one day he was left unusually long in a bathing-machine when the tide was making, accompanied by his two young brothers and little English nurse, without being drawn to land. The little nurse, being frightened, cried "M'soo! M'soo!" The two young brothers being frightened, cried "Ici! Ici!" Our wit, at once perceiving that his English was of no use to him under the foreign circumstances, immediately fell to bawling "Beau-court!" which he continued to shout at the utmost pitch of his voice and with great gravity, until rescued.—*New Boulogne Jest Book*, page 578.'

* 94 (p. 129). For the scene of the Eddystone Lighthouse at this little play, afterwards placed in a frame in the hall at Gadshill, a thousand guineas was given at the Dickens sale. It occupied the great painter only one or two mornings, and Dickens will tell how it originated. Walking on Hampstead Heath to think over his Theatrical Fund speech, he met Mr Lemon, and they went together to Stanfield. 'He has been very ill, and he told us that large pictures are too much for him, and he must confine himself to small ones. But I would not have this, I declared he must paint bigger ones than ever, and what would he think of beginning upon an act-drop for a proposed vast theatre at Tavistock House? He laughed and caught at this, we cheered him up very much, and he said he was quite a man again.' April 1855.

* 94A (p. 130). Sitting at Nisi Prius not long before, the Chief Justice, with the same eccentric liking for literature, had committed what was called at the time a breach of judicial decorum. (Such indecorums were less uncommon in the great days of the Bench.) 'The name,' he said, 'of the illustrious Charles Dickens has been called on the jury, but he has not answered. If his great Chancery suit had been still going on, I certainly would have excused him, but, as that is over, he might have done us the honour of attending here that he might have seen how we went on at common law.'

* 95 (p. 148). Prices are reported in one of the letters; and, considering what they have been since, the touch of disappointment hinted at may raise a smile. 'Provisions are scarcely as cheap as I expected, though very different from London: besides which, a pound weight here, is a pound and a quarter English. So that meat at 7d. a pound, is actually a fourth less. A capital dish of asparagus costs us about fivepence; a fowl, one and threepence; a duck, a few halfpence more; a dish of fish, about a shilling. The very best wine at tenpence that I ever drank—I used to get it very good for the same money in Genoa, but not so good. The common people very engaging and obliging.'

* 96 (p. 150). Besides the old friends before named, Thackeray and his family were here in the early weeks, living 'in a melancholy but very good château on the Paris road, where their landlord (a Baron) has supplied them, T. tells me, with one milk-jug as the entire crockery of the establishment.' Our friend soon tired of this, going off to Spa, and on his return, after ascending the hill to smoke a farewell cigar with Dickens, left for London and Scotland in October.

* 97 (p. 151). Another of his letters questioned even the picturesqueness a little, for he discovered that on a sunny day the white tents, seen from a distance, looked exactly like an immense washing establishment with all the linen put out to dry.

* 98 (p. 152). The picture had changed drearily in less than a year and a half, when (17th February 1856) Dickens thus wrote from Paris. 'I suppose mortal man out of bed never looked so ill and worn as the Emperor does just now. He passed close by me on horseback, as I was coming in at the door on Friday, and I never saw so haggard a face. Some English saluted him, and he lifted his hat as slowly, painfully, and laboriously, as if his arm were made of lead. I think he *must* be in pain.'

* 98A (p. 153). I permit myself to quote from the bill of one of his entertainments in the old merry days of Bonchurch, of course drawn up by himself, whom it describes as 'The Unparalleled Necromancer RHIA RHAMA RHOOS, educated cabalistically in the Orange Groves of Salamanca and the

Ocean Caves of Alum Bay,' some of whose proposed wonders it thus prefigures:

THE LEAPING CARD WONDER
Two Cards being drawn from the Pack by two of the company, and placed, with the Pack, in the Necromancer's box, will leap forth at the command of any lady of not less than eight, or more than eighty, years of age.
* *This wonder is the result of nine years' seclusion in the mines of Russia.*

THE PYRAMID WONDER
A shilling being lent to the Necromancer by any gentleman of not less than twelve months, or more than one hundred years, of age, and carefully marked by the said gentleman, will disappear from within a brazen box at the word of command, and pass through the hearts of an infinity of boxes, which will afterwards build themselves into pyramids and sink into a small mahogany box, at the necromancer's bidding.
* *Five thousand guineas were paid for the acquisition of this wonder, to a Chinese Mandarin, who died of grief immediately after parting with the secret.*

THE CONFLAGRATION WONDER
A Card being drawn from the Pack by any lady, not under a direct and positive promise of marriage, will be immediately named by the Necromancer, destroyed by fire, and reproduced from its own ashes.
* *An annuity of one thousand pounds has been offered to the Necromancer by the Directors of the Sun Fire Office for the Secret of this wonder—and refused ! ! !*

THE LOAF OF BREAD WONDER
The watch of any truly prepossessing Lady, of any age, single or married, being locked by the Necromancer in a strong box, will fly at the word of command from within that box into the heart of an ordinary half-quartern loaf, whence it shall be cut out in the presence of the whole company, whose cries of astonishment will be audible at a distance of some miles.
* *Ten years in the Plains of Tartary were devoted to the study of this wonder.*

THE TRAVELLING DOLL WONDER
The travelling doll is composed of solid wood throughout, but, by putting on a travelling dress of the simplest construction, becomes invisible, performs enormous journeys in half a minute, and passes from visibility to invisibility with an expedition so astonishing that no eye can follow its transformations.
* *The Necromancer's attendant usually faints on beholding this wonder, and is only revived by the administration of brandy and water.*

THE PUDDING WONDER
The company having agreed among themselves to offer to the Necromancer, by way of loan, the hat of any gentleman whose head has arrived at maturity of size, the Necromancer, without removing that hat for an instant from before the eyes of the delighted company, will light a fire in it, make a plum-pudding in his magic saucepan, boil it over the said fire, produce it in two minutes, thoroughly done, cut it, and dispense it in portions to the whole company, for their consumption then and there; returning the hat at last, wholly uninjured by fire, to its lawful owner.
* *The extreme liberality of this wonder awakening the jealousy of the beneficent Austrian Government, when exhibited in Milan, the Necromancer had the honour to be seized, and confined for five years in the fortress of that city.*

* 99 (p. 161). 'It is surprising what a change nine years have made in my notoriety here. So many of the rising French generation now read English (and *Chuzzlewit* is now being translated daily in the *Moniteur*), that I can't

go into a shop and give my card without being acknowledged in the pleasantest way possible. A curiosity-dealer brought home some little knick-knacks I had bought, the other night, and knew all about my books from beginning to end of 'em. There is much of the personal friendliness in my readers, here, that is so delightful at home; and I have been greatly surprised and pleased by the unexpected discovery.' To this I may add a line from one of his letters six years later. 'I see my books in French at every railway station great and small.' 13th October 1862.

* 99A (p. 162). He wrote a short and very comical account of one of these stock performances at the Français in which he brought out into strong relief all their conventionalities and formal habits, their regular surprises surprising nobody, and their mysterious disclosures of immense secrets known to everybody beforehand, which he meant for *Household Words;* but it occurred to him that it might give pain to Regnier, and he destroyed it.

* 100 (p. 165). Before he saw this he wrote: 'That piece you spoke of (the *Médecin des Enfants*) is one of the very best melodramas I have ever read. Situations, admirable. I will send it to you by Landseer. I am very curious indeed to go and see it; and it is an instance to me of the powerful emotions from which art is shut out in England by the conventionalities.' After seeing it he writes: 'The low cry of excitement and expectation that goes round the house when any one of the great situations is felt to be coming, is very remarkable indeed. I suppose there has not been so great a success of the genuine and worthy kind (for the authors have really taken the French dramatic bull by the horns, and put the adulterous wife in the right position), for many years. When you come over and see it, you will say you never saw anything so admirably done. There is one actor, Bignon (M. Delormel), who has a good deal of Macready in him; sometimes looks very like him; and who seems to me the perfection of manly good sense.' 17th April 1856.

* 101 (p. 166). I subjoin from another of these French letters of later date a remark on *Robinson Crusoe.* 'You remember my saying to you some time ago how curious I thought it that *Robinson Crusoe* should be the only instance of an universally popular book that could make no one laugh and could make no one cry. I have been reading it again just now, in the course of my numerous refreshings at those English wells, and I will venture to say that there is not in literature a more surprising instance of an utter want of tenderness and sentiment, than the death of Friday. It is as heartless as *Gil Blas,* in a very different and far more serious way. But the second part altogether will not bear enquiry. In the second part of *Don Quixote* are some of the finest things. But the second part of *Robinson Crusoe* is perfectly contemptible, in the glaring defect that it exhibits the man who was 30 years on that desert island with no visible effect made on his character by that experience. De Foe's women too—Robinson Crusoe's wife for instance —are terrible dull commonplace fellows without breeches; and I have no doubt he was a precious dry and disagreeable article himself—I mean De Foe: not Robinson. Poor dear Goldsmith (I remember as I write) derived the same impression.'

* 102 (p. 168). When in Paris six years later Dickens saw this fine singer in an opera by Gluck, and the reader will not be sorry to have his description of it, 'Last night I saw Madame Viardot do Gluck's *Orphée.* It is a most extraordinary performance—pathetic in the highest degree, and full of quite sublime acting. Though it is unapproachably fine from first to last, the beginning of it, at the tomb of Eurydice, is a thing that I cannot remember at this moment of writing, without emotion. It is the finest presentation of

grief that I can imagine. And when she has received hope from the Gods, and encouragement to go into the other world and seek Eurydice, Viardot's manner of taking the relinquished lyre from the tomb and becoming radiant again, is most noble. Also she recognizes Eurydice's touch, when at length the hand is put in hers from behind, like a most transcendent genius. And when, yielding to Eurydice's entreaties she had turned round and slain her with a look, her despair over the body is grand in the extreme. It is worth a journey to Paris to see, for there is no such Art to be otherwise looked upon. Her husband stumbled over me by mere chance, and took me to her dressing-room. Nothing could have happened better as a genuine homage to the performance, for I was disfigured with crying.' 30th November 1862.

* 103 (p. 171). Here is another picture of regiments in the streets of which the date is the 30th January. 'It was cold this afternoon, as bright as Italy, and these Elysian Fields crowded with carriages, riders and foot passengers. All the fountains were playing, all the Heavens shining. Just as I went out at 4 o'clock, several regiments that had passed out at the Barrière in the morning to exercise in the country, came marching back in the straggling French manner, which is far more picturesque and real than anything you can imagine in that way. Alternately great storms of drums played, and then the most delicious and skilful bands, "Trovatore" music, "Barber of Seville" music, all sorts of music with well-marked melody and time. All bloused Paris (led by the Inimitable, and a poor cripple who works himself up and down all day in a big-wheeled car) went at quick march down the avenue, in a sort of hilarious dance. If the colours with the golden eagle on the top had only been unfurled, we should have followed them anywhere, in any cause—much as the children follow Punches in the better cause of Comedy. Napoleon on the top of the Column seemed up to the whole thing, I thought.'

* 104 (p. 172). 'We have wet weather here—and dark too for these latitudes —and oceans of mud. Although numbers of men are perpetually scooping and sweeping it away in this thoroughfare, it accumulates under the windows so fast, and in such sludgy masses, that to get across the road is to get half over one's shoes in the first outset of a walk.' . . . 'It is difficult,' he added (20th January) to picture the change made in this place by the removal of the paving stones (too ready for barricades), and macadamization. It suits neither the climate nor the soil. We are again in a sea of mud. One cannot cross the road of the Champs Elysées here, without being half over one's boots.' A few more days brought a welcome change. 'Three days ago the weather changed here in an hour, and we have had bright weather and hard frost ever since. All the mud disappeared with marvellous rapidity, and the sky became Italian. Taking advantage of such a happy change, I started off yesterday morning (for exercise and meditation) on a scheme I have taken into my head, to walk round the walls of Paris. It is a very odd walk, and will make a good description. Yesterday I turned to the right when I got outside the Barrière de l'Etoile, walked round the wall till I came to the river, and then entered Paris beyond the site of the Bastille. Today I mean to turn to the left when I get outside the Barrière, and see what comes of that.'

* 105 (p. 172). This was much the tone of Edwin Landseer also, whose praise of Horace Vernet was nothing short of rapture; and how well I remember the humour of his description of the Emperor on the day when the prizes were given, and, as his old friend the great painter came up, the comical expression in his face that said plainly 'What a devilish odd thing this is altogether, isn't it?' composing itself to gravity as he took Edwin by the hand, and said in cordial English 'I am very glad to see you'. He stood,

Landseer told us, in a recess so arranged as to produce a clear echo of every word he said, and this had a startling effect. In the evening of that day Dickens, Landseer, Boxall, Leslie 'and three others' dined together in the Palais Royal.

* 106 (p. 174). 'I forget whether' (6th January 1856) 'I have already told you that I have received a proposal from a responsible bookselling house here, for a complete edition, authorized by myself, of a French translation of all my books. The terms involve questions of space and amount of matter; but I should say, at a rough calculation, that I shall get about £300 by it —perhaps £50 more.' 'I have arranged' (30th January) 'with the French bookselling house to receive, by monthly payments of £40, the sum of £440 for the right to translate all my books; that is, what they call my Romances, and what I call my Stories. This does not include the Christmas Books, *American Notes, Pictures from Italy*, or the *Sketches*; but they are to have the right to translate them for extra payments if they choose. In consideration of this venture as to the unprotected property, I cede them the right of translating all future Romances at a thousand francs (£40) each. Considering that I get so much for what is otherwise worth nothing, and get my books before so clever and important a people, I think this is not a bad move?' The first friend with whom he advised about it, I should mention, was the famous Leipzig publisher, M. Tauchnitz, in whose judgment, as well as in his honour and good faith, he had implicit reliance, and who thought the offer fair. On 17th April he wrote: 'On Monday I am going to dine with all my translators at Hachette's, the bookseller who has made the bargain for the complete edition, and who began this week to pay his monthly £40 for a year. I don't mean to go out any more. Please to imagine me in the midst of my French dressers.' He wrote an address for the edition in which he praised the liberality of his publishers and expressed his pride in being so presented to the French people whom he sincerely loved and honoured. Another word may be added. 'It is rather appropriate that the French translation edition will pay my rent for the whole year, and travelling charges to boot.' 24th February 1856.

* 107 (p. 186). *Pall Mall Gazette* of 3rd October, Paris letter of 25th September 1870.

* 108 (p. 187). In the same letter was an illustration of the ruling passion in death, which, even in so undignified a subject, might have interested Pope. 'You remember little Wieland who did grotesque demons so well. Did you ever hear how he died? He lay very still in bed with the life fading out of him—suddenly sprang out of it, threw what is professionally called a flip-flap, and fell dead on the floor.'

* 109 (p. 189). One of its incidents made such an impression on him that it will be worth while to preserve his description of it. 'I have been (by mere accident) seeing the serpents fed today, with the live birds, rabbits and guinea pigs—a sight so very horrible that I cannot get rid of the impression, and am, at this present, imagining serpents coming up the legs of the table with their infernal flat heads, and their tongues like the Devil's tail (evidently taken from that model, in the magic lanterns and other such popular representations), elongated for dinner. I saw one small serpent, whose father was asleep, go up to a guinea pig (white and yellow, and with a gentle eye—every hair upon him erect with horror); corkscrew himself on the tip of his tail; open a mouth which couldn't have swallowed the guinea pig's nose; dilate a throat which wouldn't have made him a stocking; and show him what his father meant to do with him when he came out of that

ill-looking Hookah into which he had resolved himself. The guinea-pig backed against the side of the cage—said "I know it, I know it!"—and his eye glared and his coat turned wiry, as he made the remark. Five small sparrows crouching together in a little trench at the back of the cage, peeped over the brim of it, all the time; and when they saw the guinea pig give it up, and the young serpent go away looking at him over about two yards and a quarter of shoulder, struggled which should get into the innermost angle and be seized last. Everyone of them then hid his eyes in another's breast, and then they all shook together like dry leaves—as I daresay they may be doing now, for old Hookah was as dull as laudanum. . . . Please to imagine two small serpents, one beginning on the tail of a white mouse, and one on the head, and each pulling his own way, and the mouse very much alive all the time, with the middle of him madly writhing.'

* 110 (p. 190). There was a situation in the *Frozen Deep* where Richard Wardour played by Dickens, had thus to carry about Frank Aldersley in the person of Wilkie Collins.

* 111 (p. 192). The mention of a performance of Lord Lytton's *Money* at the theatre will supply the farce to this tragedy. 'I have rarely seen anything finer than Lord Glossmore, a chorus-singer in bluchers, drab trowsers, and a brown sack; and Dudley Smooth, in somebody else's wig, hindside before. Stout also, in anything he could lay hold of. The waiter at the club had an immense moustache, white trowsers and a striped jacket; and he brought everybody who came in, a vinegar-cruet. The man who read the will began thus: "I so-and-so, being of unsound mind but firm in body . . ." In spite of all this, however, the real character, humour, wit and good writing of the comedy, made themselves apparent; and the applause was loud and repeated, and really seemed genuine. Its capital things were not lost altogether. It was succeeded by a Jockey Dance by five ladies, who put their whips in their mouths and worked imaginary winners up to the float —an immense success.'

* 111A (p. 194). Anything more completely opposed to the Micawber type could hardly be conceived, and yet there were moments (really and truly only moments) when the fancy would arise that if the conditions of his life had been reversed, something of a vagabond existence (using the word in Goldsmith's meaning) might have supervened. It would have been an unspeakable misery to him, but it might have come nevertheless. The question of hereditary transmission had a curious attraction for him. and considerations connected with it were frequently present to his mind. Of a youth who had fallen into a father's weakness without the possibility of having himself observed them for imitation, he thus wrote on one occasion: 'It suggests the strangest consideration as to which of our own failings we are really responsible for, and as to which of them we cannot quite reasonably hold ourselves to be so. What A. evidently derived from his father cannot in his case be derived from observation and observation, but must be in the very principles of his individuality as a living creature.'

* 112 (p. 200). 'You may as well know' (20th March 1858) 'that I went on' (I designate the ladies by A and B respectively) 'and propounded the matter [the suggested Readings] to A, without any preparation. Result.— "I am surprised, and I should have been surprised if I had seen it in the newspaper without previous confidence from you. But nothing more. N-no. Certainly not. Nothing more. I don't see that there is anything derogatory in it, even now when you ask me that question. I think upon the whole that most people would be glad you should have the money, rather than other people. It might be misunderstood here and there, at first; but I think the

thing would very soon express itself, and that your own power of making it express itself would be very great." As she wished me to ask B, who was in another room, I did so. She was for a moment tremendously disconcerted, *"under the mpression that it was to lead to the stage"* (!!). Then, withouts knowing anything of A's opinion, closely followed it. That absurd association had never entered my head or yours; but it might enter some other heads for all that. Take these two opinions for whatever they are worth. A (being very much interested and very anxious to help to a right conclusion) proposed to ask a few people of various degrees who know what the Readings are, what *they* think—not compromising me, but suggesting the project afar-off, as an idea in somebody else's mind. I thanked her, and said "Yes", of course.'

* 113 (p. 201). The Board of Health returns, showing that out of every annual thousand of deaths in London, the immense proportion of four hundred were those of children under four years old, had established the necessity for such a scheme. Of course the stress of this mortality fell on the children of the poor, 'dragged up rather than brought up', as Charles Lamb expressed it, and perishing unhelped by the way.

* 114 (p. 203). See Chapter ix of *Our Mutual Friend.*

* 115 (p. 205). Here is the rough note, in which the reader will be interested to observe the limits originally placed to the proposal. The first Readings were to comprise only the *Carol*, and for others a new story was to be written. He had not yet the full confidence in his power or versatility as an actor which subsequent experience gave him. 'I propose to announce in a short and plain advertisement (what is quite true) that I cannot so much as answer the numerous applications that are made to me to read, and that compliance with ever so few of them is, in any reason, impossible. That I have therefore resolved upon a course of readings of the *Christmas Carol* both in town and country, and that those in London will take place at St Martin's Hall on certain evenings. Those evenings will be either four or six Thursdays, in May and the beginning of June . . . I propose an Autumn Tour, for the country, extending through August, September and October. It would comprise the Eastern Counties, the West, Lancashire, Yorkshire and Scotland. I should read from 35 to 40 times in this tour, at the least. At each place where there was a great success, I would myself announce that I should come back, on the turn of Christmas, to read a new Christmas story written for that purpose. This story I should first read a certain number of times in London. I have the strongest belief that by April in next year, a very large sum of money indeed would be gained by these means. Ireland would be still untouched, and I conceive America alone (if I could resolve to go there) to be worth Ten Thousand Pounds. In all these proceedings, the Business would be wholly detached from me, and I should never appear in it. I would have an office, belonging to the Readings and to nothing else, opened in London; I would have the advertisements emanating from it, and also signed by some one belonging to it; and they should always mention me as a third person—just as the Child's Hospital, for instance, in addressing the public, mention me.'

* 116 (p. 208). On New Year's Day he had written from Paris. 'When in London Coutts's advised me not to sell out the money for Gadshill Place (the title of my estate sir, my place down in Kent) until the conveyance was settled and ready.'

* 117 (p. 211). 'As to the carpenters,' he wrote to his daughter in September 1860, 'they are absolutely maddening. They are always at work yet never

seem to do anything. L. was down on Friday, and said (with his eye fixed on Maidstone and rubbing his hands to conciliate his moody employer) that "he didn't think there would be very much left to do after Saturday the 29th". I didn't throw him out of window.'

* 118 (p. 211). As surely, however, as he did any work there, so surely his indispensable little accompaniments of work were carried along with him; and of these I will quote what was written shortly after his death by his son-in-law, Mr Charles Collins, to illustrate a very touching sketch by Mr Fildes of his writing-desk and vacant chair. 'Ranged in front of, and round about him, were always a variety of objects for his eye to rest on in the intervals of actual writing, and any one of which he would have instantly missed had it been removed. There was a French bronze group representing a duel with swords, fought by a couple of very fat toads, one of them (characterized by that particular buoyancy which belongs to corpulence) in the act of making a prodigious lunge forward, which the other receives in the very middle of his digestive apparatus, and under the influence of which it seems likely that he will satisfy the wounded honour of his opponent by promptly expiring. There was another bronze figure which always stood near the toads, also of French manufacture, and also full of comic suggestion. It was a statuette of a dog-fancier, such a one as you used to see on the bridges or quays of Paris with a profusion of little dogs stuck under his arms and into his pockets, and everywhere where little dogs could possibly be insinuated, all for sale, and all, as even a casual glance at the vendor's exterior would convince the most unsuspicious person, with some screw loose in their physical constitutions or moral natures, to be discovered immediately after purchase. There was the long gilt leaf with the rabbit sitting erect upon its haunches, the huge paper-knife often held in his hand during his public readings, and the little fresh green cup ornamented with the leaves and blossoms of the cowslip, in which a few fresh flowers were always placed every morning—for Dickens invariably worked with flowers on his writing-table. There was also the register of the day of the week and of the month, which stood always before him; and when the room in the chalet in which he wrote his last paragraphed was opened, some time after his death, the first thing to be noticed by those who entered was this register, set at "Wednesday, June 8"—the day of his seizure.' It remains to this day as it was found.

* 119 (p. 214). Dickens's interest in dogs (as in the habits and ways of all animals) was inexhaustible, and he welcomed with delight any new trait. The subjoined, told him by a lady friend, was a great acquisition. 'I must close' (14th May 1867) 'with an odd story of a Newfoundland dog. An immense black good-humoured Newfoundland dog. He came from Oxford and had lived all his life at a brewery. Instructions were given him that if he were let out every morning alone, he would immediately find out the river; regularly take a swim; and gravely come home again. This he did with the greatest punctuality, but after a little while was observed to smell of beer. She was so sure that he smelt of beer that she resolved to watch him. Accordingly, he was seen to come back from his swim, round the usual corner, and to go up a flight of steps into a beer-shop. Being instantly followed, the beer-shopkeeper is seen to take down a pot (pewter pot), and is heard to say: "Well, old chap! Come for your beer as usual have you?", Upon which he draws a pint and puts it down, and the dog drinks it. Being required to explain how this comes to pass, the man says, "Yes ma'am. I know he's your dog ma'am, but I didn't when he first come. He looked in ma'am—as a Brickmaker might—and then he comes in—as a Brickmaker might—and he wagged his tail at the pots, and he giv' a sniff round, and conveyed to me as he was used to beer. So I draw'd him a drop, and he

drunk it up. Next morning he come agen by the clock and I drawed him a pint, and ever since he has took his pint reglar."'

* 120 (p. 218). This was the *Carol* and *Pickwick*. 'We are reduced some-times', he adds, 'to a ludicrous state of distress by the quantity of silver we have to carry about. Arthur Smith is always accompanied by an immense black leather-bag full.' Mr Smith had an illness a couple of days later, and Dickens whimsically describes his rapid recovery on discovering the state of their balances. 'He is now sitting opposite to me on a bag of £40 of silver. It must be dreadfully hard.'

* 120A (p. 222). 'That is no doubt immense, our expenses being necessarily large, and the travelling party being always five.' Another source of profit was the sale of the copies of the several Readings prepared by himself. 'Our people alone sell eight, ten, and twelve dozen a night.' A later letter says: 'The men with the reading books were sold out, for about the twentieth time, at Manchester. Eleven dozen of the *Poor Traveller, Boots*, and *Gamp* being sold in about ten minutes, they had no more left; and Manchester became green with the little tracts, in every bookshop, outside every omni-bus, and passing along ever street. The sale of them, apart from us, must be very great.' 'Did I tell you,' he writes in another letter, 'that the agents for our tickets who are also booksellers, say very generally that the readings decidedly increase the sale of the books they are taken from? We were first told of this by a Mr. Parke, a wealthy old gentleman in a very large way at Wolverhampton, who did all the business for love, and would not take a farthing. Since then, we have constantly come upon it; and M'Glashin and Gill at Dublin were very strong about it indeed.'

* 121 (p. 224). The last of them were given immediately after his completion of the *Tale of Two Cities*: 'I am a little tired; but as little, I suspect, as any man could be with the work of the last four days, and perhaps the change of work was better than subsiding into rest and rust. The Norwich people were a noble audience. There, and at Ipswich and Bury, we had the demon-strativeness of the great working-towns, and a much finer perception.' 14th October 1859.

* 122 (p. 224). Two pleasing little volumes may here be named as devoted to special descriptions of the several Readings; by his friends Mr Charles Kent in England (*Charles Dickens as a Reader*), and by Miss Kate Field in America (*Pen Photographs*).

* 123 (p. 225). Let me subjoin his own note of a less important incident of that month which will show his quick and sure eye for any bit of acting out of the common. The lady has since justified its closing prediction. Describing an early dinner with Chauncy Townshend, he adds (17th December 1858): 'I escaped at half-past seven, and went to the Strand Theatre: having taken a stall beforehand, for it is always crammed. I really wish you would go, between this and next Thursday, to see the *Maid and the Magpie* burlesque there. There is the strangest thing in it that ever I have seen on the stage. The boy, Pippo, by Miss Wilton. While it is astonishingly impudent (must be, or it couldn't be done at all), it is so stupendously like a boy, and unlike a woman, that it is perfectly free from offence. I never have seen such a thing. Priscilla Horton, as a boy, not to be thought of beside it. She does an imitation of the dancing of the Christy Minstrels—wonderfully clever—which, in the audacity of its thorough-going, is surprising. A thing that you *can not* imagine a woman's doing at all; and yet the manner, the appearance, the levity, impulse, and spirits of it, are so exactly like a boy that you cannot think of anything like her son in association with it. It begins at 8,

and is over by a quarter past 9. I never have seen such a curious thing, and the girl's talent is unchallengeable. I call her the cleverest girl I have ever seen on the stage in my time, and the most singularly original.'

* 124 (p. 230). From the same letter, dated 1st July 1861, I take what follows. 'Poor Lord Campbell's seems to me as easy and good a death as one could desire. There must be a sweep of these men very soon, and one feels as if it must fall out like the breaking of an arch—one stone goes from a prominent place, and then the rest begin to drop. So, one looks, not without satisfaction (in our sadness) at lives so rounded and complete, towards Brougham, and Lyndhurst, and Pollock . . .' Yet, of Dickens's own death, Pollock lived to write to me as the death of 'one of the most distinguished and honoured men England has ever produced; in whose loss every man among us feels that he has lost a friend and an instructor.' Temple-Hatton, 10th June 1870.

* 125 (p. 231). If space were available here, his letters would supply many proofs of his interest in Mr George Moore's admirable projects; but I can only make exception for his characteristic allusion to an incident that tickled his fancy very much at the time. 'I hope' (20th August 1863) 'you have been as much amused as I am by the account of the Bishop of Carlisle at (my very particular friend's) Mr George Moore's schools? It strikes me as the funniest piece of weakness I ever saw, his addressing those unfortunate children concerning Colenso. I cannot get over the ridiculous image I have erected in my mind, of the shovel-hat and apron holding forth, at the safe distance, to that safe audience. There is nothing so extravagant in Rabelais, or so satirically humorous in Swift or Voltaire.'

* 125A (p. 234). Eight years later he wrote 'Holiday Romance' for a child's magazine published by Mr Fields, and 'George Silverman's Explanation' — of the same length, and for the same price. There are no other such instances I suppose, in the history of literature.

*126 (p. 236). 'You will be grieved', he wrote (Saturday, 19th November 8159) 'to hear of poor [Frank] Stone. On Sunday he was not well. On Monday, went to Dr Todd, who told him he had aneurism of the heart. On Tuesday, went to Dr Walsh, who told him he hadn't. On Wednesday I met him in a cab in the Square here, and he got out to talk to me. I walked about with him a little while at a snail's pace, cheering him up; but when I came home, I told them that I thought him much changed, and in danger. Yesterday at 2 o'clock he died of spasm of the heart. I am going up to Highgate to look for a grave for him.

* 127 (p. 237). He was now hard at work on his story; and a note written from Gadshill after the funeral [of his brother Alfred] shows, what so frequently was incident to his pursuits, the hard conditions under which sorrow, and its claim on his exertion, often came to him. 'Tomorrow I have to work against time and tide and everything else to fill up a No. keeping open for me, and the stereotype plates of which must go to America on Friday. But indeed the enquiry into poor Alfred's affairs; the necessity of putting the widow and children somewhere; the difficulty of knowing what to do for the best; and the need I feel under of being as composed and deliberate as I can be, and yet of not shirking or putting off the occasion that there is for doing a duty; would have brought me back here to be quiet, under any circumstances.'

* 128 (p. 238). The same letter adds: 'The fourth edition of *Great Expectations* is now going to press; the third being nearly out. Bulwer's story keeps us up bravely. As well as we can make out, we have risen fifteen hundred.'

* 129 (p. 239). 'There was a very touching thing in the Chapel' (at Brompton). 'When the body [of Arthur Smith] was to be taken up and carried to the grave, there stepped out, instead of the undertaker's men with their hideous paraphernalia, the men who had always been with the two brothers at the Egyptian Hall; and they, in their plain, decent own mourning clothes, carried the poor fellow away. Also, standing about among the gravestones, dressed in black, I noticed every kind of person who had ever had to do with him—from our own gas man and doorkeepers and bill-stickers, up to Johnson the printer and that class of man. The father and Albert and he now lie together, and the grave, I suppose, will be no more disturbed. I wrote a little inscription for the stone, and it is quite full.'

* 130 (p. 240). Of his former manager he writes in the same letter: 'I miss him dreadfully. The sense I used to have of compactness and comfort about me while I was reading, is quite gone; and on my coming out for the ten minutes, when I used to find him always ready for me with something cheerful to say, it is forlorn . . . Besides which, H. and all the rest of them are always somewhere, and he was always everywhere.'

* 131 (p. 241). The more detailed account of the scene which he wrote to his daughter is also well worth giving. 'A most tremendous hall here last night. Something almost terrible in the cram. A fearful thing might have happened. Suddenly, when they were all very still over Smike, my gas batten came down, and it looked as if the room were falling. There were three great galleries crammed to the roof, and a high steep flight of stairs; and a panic must have destroyed numbers of people. A lady in the front row of stalls screamed, and ran out wildly towards me, and for one instant there was a terrible wave in the crowd. I addressed that lady, laughing (for I knew she was in sight of everybody there), and called out as if it happened every night—"There's nothing the matter I assure you; don't be alarmed; pray sit down——" and she sat down directly, and there was a thunder of applause. It took some five minutes to mend, and I looked on with my hands in my pockets; for I think if I had turned my back for a moment, there might still have been a move. My people were dreadfully alarmed—Boycott' (the gas-man) 'in particular, who I suppose had some notion that the whole place might have taken fire—"but there stood the master", he did me the honour to say afterwards, in addressing the rest, "as cool as ever I see him a lounging at a railway station".'

* 132 (p. 243). The letter referred also to the death of his American friend Professor Felton. 'Your mention of poor Felton's death is a shock of surprise as well as grief to me, for I had not heard a word about it. Mr Fields told me when he was here that the effect of that hotel disaster of bad drinking water had not passed away; so I suppose, as you do, that he sank under it. Poor dear Felton! It is 20 years since I told you of the delight my first knowledge of him gave me, and it is as strongly upon me to this hour. I wish our ways had crossed a little oftener, but that would not have made it better for us now. Alas! alas! all ways have the same finger-post at the head of them, and at every turning in them.'

* 133 (p. 244). I give the letter in which he puts the scheme formally before me, after the renewed and larger offers had been submitted. 'If there were reasonable hope and promise, I could make up my mind to go to Australia and get money. I would not accept the Australian people's offer. I would take no money from them; would bind myself to nothing with them; but would merely make them my agents at such and such a per centage, and go and read there. I would take some man of literary pretensions as a secretary (Charles Collins? What think you?) and with his aid' (he afterwards made the proposal to his old friend Mr Thomas Beard) 'would do, for *All the Year*

Round while I was away, The Uncommercial Traveller Upside Down. If the notion of these speculators be anything like accurate, I should come back rich. I should have seen a great deal of novelty to book. I should have been very miserable too . . . Of course one cannot possibly count upon the money to be realized by a six months' absence, but £12,000 is supposed to be a low estimate. Mr S. brought me letters from members of the legislature, newspaper editors, and the like, exhorting me to come, saying how much the people talk of me, and dwelling on the kind of reception that would await me. No doubt this is so, and of course a great deal of curious experience for after use would be gained over and above the money. Being my own master too, I could "work" myself more delicately than if I bound myself for money beforehand. A few years hence, if all other circumstances were the same, I might not be so well fitted for the excessive wear and tear. This is about the whole case. But pray do not suppose that I am in my own mind favourable to going, or that I have any fancy for going.' That was late in October. From Paris in November (1862), he wrote: 'I mentioned the question to Bulwer when he dined with us last Sunday, and he was all for going. He said that not only did he think the whole population would go to the Readings, but that the country would strike me in some quite new aspect for a Book; and that wonders might be done with such book in the way of profit, over there as well as here.'

* 134 (p. 247). There had been some estrangement between them since the autumn of 1858, hardly now worth mention even in a note. Thackeray, justly indignant at a published description of himself by the member of a club to which both he and Dickens belonged, referred it to the Committee, who decided to expel the writer. Dickens, thinking expulsion too harsh a penalty for an offence thoughtlessly given, and, as far as might be, manfully atoned for by withdrawal and regret, interposed to avert that extremity. Thackeray resented the interference, and Dickens was justly hurt by the manner in which he did so. Neither was wholly right, nor was either altogether in the wrong.

* 134A (p. 249). As I have thus fallen on theatrical subjects, I may add one or two practical experiences which befell Dickens at theatres in the autumn of 1864, when he sallied forth from his office upon these night wanderings to 'cool' a boiling head. 'I went the other night (8th October) to see the *Streets of London* at the Princess's. A piece that is really drawing all the town, and filling the house with nightly overflows. It is the most depressing instance, without exception, of an utterly degraded and debased theatrical taste that has ever come under my writhing notice. For not only do the audiences—of all classes—go, but they are unquestionably delighted. At Astley's there has been much puffing at great cost of a certain Miss Ada Isaacs Menkin [*sic*], who is to be seen bound on the horse in Mazeppa "ascending the fearful precipices not as hitherto done by a dummy." Last night, having a boiling head, I went out from here to cool myself on Waterloo Bridge, and I thought I would go and see this heroine. Applied at the box-door for a stall. "None left sir." For a box-ticket. "Only standing-room sir." Then the man (busy in counting great heaps of veritable checks) recognizes me and says—"Mr. Smith will be very much concerned when he hears that you went away sir" —"Never mind, I'll come again." "You never go behind I think sir, or—?" "No thank you, I never go behind." "Mr. Smith's box, sir—" "No thank you, I'll come again." Now who do you think the lady is? If you don't already know, ask that question of the highest Irish mountains that look eternal, and they'll never tell you—Mrs. Heenan!' This lady, who turned out to be one of Dickens's greatest admirers, addressed him at great length on hearing of this occurrence, and afterwards dedicated a volume of poems to him! There was a pleasanter close to his letter. 'Contrariwise I assisted

another night at the Adelphi (where I couldn't, with careful calculation, get the house up to Nine Pounds), and saw quite an admirable performance of Mr. Toole and Mrs. Mellon—she, an old servant, wonderfully like Anne— he, showing a power of passion very unusual indeed in a comic actor, as such things go, and of a quite remarkable kind.'

* 135 (p. 250). Here are allusions to his foot at that time. 'I have got a boot on today—made on an Otranto scale, but really not very discernible from its ordinary sized companion.' After a few days' holiday: 'I began to feel my foot stronger the moment I breathed the sea air. Still, during the ten days I have been away, I have never been able to wear a boot after four or five in the afternoon, but have passed all the evening with the foot up, and nothing on it. I am burnt brown and have walked by the sea perpetually, yet I feel certain that if I wore a boot this evening, I should be taken with those torments again before the night was out.' This last letter ended thus: 'As a relief to my late dismal letters, I send you the newest American story. Backwoods Doctor is called in to the little boy of a woman-settler. Stares at the child some time through a pair of spectacles. Ultimately takes them off, and says to the mother: 'We'al Marm, this is small-pox. 'Tis Marm, small-pox. But I am not posted up in Pustuls, and I do not know as I could bring him along slick through it. But I'll tell you wa'at I can do Marm:—I can send him a draft as will certainly put him into a most eternal Fit, and I am almighty smart at Fits, and we might git round Old Grisly that way.'''

* 136 (p. 257). He wrote to me on 15th March from Dublin: 'So profoundly discouraging were the accounts from here in London last Tuesday that I held several councils with Chappell about coming at all; had actually drawn up a bill announcing (indefinitely) the postponement of the readings; and had meant to give him a reading to cover the charges incurred—but yielded at last to his representation the other way. We ran through a snow storm nearly the whole way, and in Wales got snowed up, came to a stoppage, and had to dig the engine out ... We got to Dublin at last, found it snowing and raining, and heard that it had been snowing and raining since the first day of the year. . . . As to outward signs of trouble or preparation, they are very few. At Kingstown our boat was waited for by four armed policemen, and some stragglers in various dresses who were clearly detectives. But there was no sign of soldiery. My people carry a long heavy box containing gas-fittings. This was immediately laid hold of; but one of the stragglers instantly interposed on seeing my name, and came to me in the carriage and apologized. . . . The worst looking young fellow I ever saw, turned up at Holyhead before we went to bed there, and sat glooming and glowering by the coffee-room fire while we warmed ourselves. He said he had been snowed up with us (which we didn't believe), and was horribly disconcerted by some box of his having gone to Dublin without him. We said to one another "Fenian": and certainly he disappeared in the morning, and let his box go where it would.' What Dickens heard and saw in Dublin, during this visit, convinced him that Fenianism and disaffection had found their way into several regiments.

* 136A (p. 260). This renders it worth preservation in a note. He called it

'THE CASE IN A NUTSHELL.'

'1. I think it may be taken as proved, that general enthusiasm and excitement are awakened in America on the subject of the Readings, and that the people are prepared to give me a great reception. *The New York Herald*, indeed, is of opinion that "Dickens must apologise first"; and where a *New York Herald* is possible, anything is possible. But the prevailing tone, both of the press and of people of all conditions, is highly favourable. I have an opinion myself that the Irish element in New York is dangerous; for the reason that the Fenians would be glad to damage a conspicuous Englishman. This is merely an opinion of my own.

2. All our original calculations were based on 100 Readings. But an unexpected result of careful enquiry on the sopt, is the discovery that the month of May is generally considered (in the large cities) bad for such a purpose. Admitting that what governs an ordinary case in this wise, governs mine, this reduces the Readings to 80, and consequently at a blow makes a reduction of 20 per cent. in the means of making money within the half year—unless the objection should not apply in my exceptional instance.

3. I dismiss the consideration that the great towns of America could not possibly be exhausted—or even visited—within 6 months, and that a large harvest would be left unreaped. Because I hold a second series of Readings in America is to be set down as out of the question: whether regarded as involving two more voyages across the Atlantic, or a vacation of five months in Canada.

4. The narrowed calculation we have made, is this: What is the largest amount of clear profit derivable, under the most advantageous circumstances possible, as to their public reception, from 80 Readings and no more? In making this calculation, the expenses have been throughout taken on the New York scale—which is the dearest; as much as 20 per cent. has been deducted for management, including Mr. Dolby's commission; and no credit has been taken for any extra payment on reserved seats, though a good deal of money is confidently expected from this source. But on the other hand it is to be observed that four Readings (and a fraction over) are supposed to take place every week, and that the estimate of receipts is based on the assumption that the audiences are, on all occasions, as large as the rooms will reasonably hold.

5. So considering 80 Readings, we bring out the nett profit of that number; remaining to me after payment of all charges whatever, as £15,500.

6. But it yet remains to be noted that the calculation assumes New York City, and the State of New York, to be good for a very large proportion of the 80 Readings; and that the calculation also assumes the necessary travelling not to extend beyond Boston and adjacent places, New York City and adjacent places, Philadelphia, Washington, and Baltimore. But, if the calculation should prove too sanguine on this head, and if these places should *not* be good for so many Readings, then it may prove impracticable to get through 80 within the time: by reason of other places that would come into the list, lying wide asunder, and necessitating long and fatiguing journeys.

7. The loss consequent on the conversion of paper money into gold (with gold at the present ruling premium) is allowed for in the calculation. It counts seven dollars to the pound.'

* 137 (p. 275). 'Do you know *Master Humphrey's Clock*? I admire Nell in the *Old Curiosity Shop* exceedingly. The whole thing is a good deal borrowed from *Wilhelm Meister*. But Little Nell is a far purer, lovelier, more *English* conception than Mignon, treasonable as the saying would seem to some. No doubt it was suggested by Mignon.' Sara Coleridge to Aubrey de Vere (*Memoirs and Letters*). Expressing no opinion on this comparison, I may state it as within my knowledge that the book referred to was not then known to Dickens.

* 138 (p. 275). The distinction I then pointed out was remarked by Sara Coleridge (*Memoirs and Letters*) in writing of her children. 'They like to talk

to me . . . above all about the productions of Dickens, the never-to-be-exhausted fun of *Pickwick*, and the capital new strokes of *Martin Chuzzlewit*. This last work contains, besides all the fun, some very marked and available morals. I scarce know any book in which the evil and odiousness of selfishness are more forcibly brought out, or in a greater variety of exhibitions. In the midst of the merry quotations, or at least on any fair opportunity, I draw the boys' attention to these points.'

* 139 (p. 281). The opening of this letter (25th August 1859), referring to a conviction for murder, afterwards reversed by a Home Office pardon against the continued and steadily expressed opinion of the judge who tried the case, is much too characteristic of the writer to be lost. 'I cannot easily tell you how much interested I am by what you tell me of our brave and excellent friend. . . . I have often had more than half a mind to write and thank that upright judge. I declare to heaven that I believe such a service one of the greatest that a man of intellect and courage can render to society. . . . Of course I have been driving the girls out of their wits here, by incessantly proclaiming that there needed no medical evidence either way, and that the case was plain without it. . . . Lastly of course, though a merciful man (because a merciful man, I mean), I would hang any Home Secretary, Whig, Tory, Radical or otherwise, who should step in between so black a scoundrel and the gallows. . . . I am reminded of Tennyson by thinking that King Arthur would have made short work of the amiable man! How fine the Idylls are! Lord! what a blessed thing it is to read a man who really can write. I thought nothing could be finer than the first poem, till I came to the third; but when I had read the last, it seemed to me to be absolutely unapproachable.' Other literary likings rose and fell with him, but he never faltered in his allegiance to Tennyson.

* 140 (p. 283). Mr Grant White, whose edition of Shakespeare has been received with much respect in England.

* 141 (p. 289) [First ending of *Great Expectations*.] There was no Chapter xx as now; but the sentence which opens it ('For eleven years' in the original, altered to 'eight years') followed the paragraph about his business partnership with Herbert, and led to Biddy's question whether he is sure he does not fret for Estella ('I am sure and certain, Biddy' as originally written, altered to 'O no—I think not, Biddy'): from which point here was the close. 'It was two years more, before I saw herself. I had heard of her as leading a most unhappy life, and as being separated from her husband who had used her with great cruelty, and who had become quite renowned as a compound of pride, brutality and meanness. I had heard of the death of her husband (from an accident consequent on ill-treating a horse), and of her being married again to a Shropshire doctor, who, against his interest, had once very manfully interposed, on an occasion when he was in professional attendance on Mr Drummle, and had witnessed some outrageous treatment of her. I had heard that the Shropshire doctor was not rich, and that they lived on her own personal fortune. I was in England again—in London, and walking along Piccadilly with little Pip—when a servant came running after me to ask would I step back to a lady in a carriage who wished to speak to me. It was a little pony carriage, which the lady was driving; and the lady and I looked sadly enough on one another. "I am greatly changed, I know; but I thought you would like to shake hands with Estella too, Pip. Lift up that pretty child and let me kiss it!" (She supposed the child, I think, to be my child.) I was very glad afterwards to have had the interview; for in her face and in her voice, and in her touch, she gave me the assurance, that suffering had been stronger than Miss Havisham's teaching, and had given her a heart to understand what my heart used to be.'

*142 (p. 291). On this reproach, from a Jewish lady whom he esteemed, he had written two years before. 'Fagin, in *Oliver Twist*, is a Jew, because it unfortunately was true, of the time to which that story refers, that that class of criminal almost invariably *was* a Jew. But surely no sensible man or woman of your persuasion can fail to observe—firstly, that all the rest of the wicked *dramatis personae* are Christians; and, secondly, that he is called "The Jew", not because of his religion, but because of his race.'

* 143 (p. 292). Mr Marcus Stone had, after the separate issue of the *Tale of Two Cities*, taken the place of Mr Hablot Browne as his illustrator. *Hard Times* and the first edition of *Great Expectations* were not illustrated; but when Pip's story appeared in one volume, Mr Stone contributed designs for it.

* 144 (p. 302). The date when this fancy dropped into his Memoranda is fixed by the following passage in a letter to me of the 25th August 1862. 'I am trying to coerce my thoughts into hammering out the Christmas number. And I have an idea of opening a book (not the Christmas number —a book) by bringing together two strongly contrasted places and two strongly contrasted sets of people, with which and with whom the story is to rest, through the agency of an electric message. I think a fine thing might be made of the message itself shooting over the land and under the sea, and it would be a curious way of sounding the key note.'

* 145 (p. 320). Among these I think he was most delighted with the great naturalist and philosopher [Jean Louis Rodolph] Agassiz, whose death is unhappily announced while I write, and as to whom it will no longer be unbecoming to quote his allusion. 'Agassiz, who married the last Mrs Felton's sister, is not only one of the most accomplished but the most natural and jovial of men.' Again he says: 'I cannot tell you how pleased I was by Agassiz, a most charming fellow, or how I have regretted his seclusion for a while by reason of his mother's death.' A valued corrospondent, Mr Grant Wilson, sends me a list of famous Americans who greeted Dickens at his first visit, and in the interval had passed away. 'It is melancholy to contemplate the large number of American authors who had, between the first and second visits of Mr Dickens, "gone hence, to be no more seen". The sturdy Cooper, the gentle Irving, his friend and kinsman Paulding, Prescott the historian and Percival the poet, the eloquent Everett, Nathaniel Hawthorne, Edgar A. Poe, N. P. Willis, the genial Halleck, and many lesser lights, including Prof. Felton and Geo. P. Morris, had died during the quarter of a century that elapsed between Dickens's visits to this country, leaving a new generation of writers to extend the hand of friendship to him on his second coming.' Let me add to this that Dickens was pleased, at the second visit, to see his old secretary who had travelled so agreeably through his first tour of triumph. 'He would have known him anywhere.'

* 146 (p. 341). A few days later he described it to his daughter, 'I couldn't help laughing at myself on my birthday at Washington; it was observed so much as though I were a little boy. Flowers and garlands of the most exquisite kind, arranged in all manner of green baskets, bloomed over the room; letters radiant with good wishes poured in; a shirt pin, a handsome silver travelling bottle, a set of gold shirt studs and a set of gold sleeve links were on the dinner table. Also, by hands unknown, the hall at night was decorated; and after 'Boots at the Holly Tree', the whole audience rose and remained, great people and all, standing and cheering, until I went back to the table and made them a little speech.'

* 147 (p. 343). Mr Dolby unconsciously contributed at this time to the same happy result by sending out some advertisements in these exact words: 'The Reading will be comprised within *two minutes*, and the audience are earnestly entreated to be seated *ten hours* before its commencement.' He had transposed the minutes and the hours.

* 148 (p. 349). What follows is from the close of the letter. 'On my return I have arranged with Chappell to take my leave of reading for good and all, in a hundred autumnal and winter Farewells *for ever*. I return by the Cunard steam-ship *Russia*. I had the second officer's cabin on deck, when I came out; and I am to have the chief steward's going home. Cunard was so considerate as to remember that it will be on the sunny side of the vessel.'

* 149 (p. 349). Here was his account of his mode of living for his last ten weeks in America. 'I cannot eat (to anything like the necessary extent) and have established this system. At 7 in the morning, in bed, a tumbler of new cream and two tablespoonsful of rum. At 12, a sherry cobbler and a biscuit. At 3 (dinner time) a pint of champagne. At five minutes to 8, an egg beaten up with a glass of sherry. Between the parts, the strongest beef tea that can be made, drunk hot. At a quarter past 10, soup, and any little thing to drink that I can fancy. I do not eat more than half a pound of solid food in the whole four-and-twenty hours, if so much.'

* 150 (p. 352). Here is the newspaper account [of the New York public dinner]: 'At about five o'clock on Saturday the hosts began to assemble, but at 5.30 news was received that the expected guest had succumbed to a painful affection of the foot. In a short time, however, another bulletin announced Mr Dickens's intention to attend the dinner at all hazards. At a little after six, having been assisted up the stairs, he was joined by Mr Greeley, and the hosts forming in two lines silently permitted the distinguished gentlemen to pass through. Mr Dickens limped perceptibly; his right foot was swathed, and he leaned heavily on the arm of Mr Greeley. He evidently suffered great pain.'

* 151 (p. 359). 'I think I shall be pretty correct in both places as to the run being on the Final readings. We had an immense house here' (Edinburgh, 12th December) 'last night, and a very large turnaway. But Glasgow being shady and the charges very great, it will be the most we can do, I fancy, on these first Scotch reading, to bring the Chappells safely home (as to them) without loss.'

* 152 (p. 360). The close of the letter has an amusing picture which I may be excused for printing in a note. 'The only news that will interest you is that the good-natured Reverdy Johnson, being at an Art Dinner in Glasgow the other night, and falling asleep over the post-prandial speeches (only too naturally), woke suddenly on hearing the name of "Johnson" in a list of Scotch painters which one of the orators was enumerating; at once plunged up, under the impression that somebody was drinking his health; and immediately, and with overflowing amiability, began returning thanks. The spectacle was then presented to the astonished company, of the American Eagle being restrained by the coat tails from swooping at the moon, while the small birds endeavoured to explain to it how the case stood, and the cock robin in possession of the chairman's eye twittered away as hard as he could split. I am told that it was wonderfully droll.'

* 153 (p. 364). In this letter [to Sir Thomas Watson] Dickens wrote: 'I thank you heartily' (23rd June 1869) 'for your great kindness and interest. It would really pain me if I thought you could seriously doubt my implicit reliance on your professional skill and advice. I feel as certain now as I felt when you came to see me on my breaking down through over fatigue, that the injunction you laid upon me to stop in my course of Readings was necessary and wise. And to its firmness I refer (humanly speaking) my

speedy recovery from that moment. I would on no account have resumed, even on the turn of this year, without your sanction. Your friendly aid will never be forgotten by me; and again I thank you for it with all my heart.'

* 154 (p. 366). 'I have a very remarkable story indeed for you to read. It is in only two chapters. A thing never to melt into other stories in the mind, but always to keep itself apart.' The story was published in the 37th number of the new series of *All the Year Round*, with the title of 'An Experience'. The 'new series' had been started to break up the too great length of volumes in sequence, and the only change it announced was the discontinuance of Christmas Numbers. He had tired of them himself; and, observing the extent to which they were now copied in all directions (as usual with other examples set by him), he supposed them likely to become tiresome to the public.

* 155 (p. 367). I subjoin what has been written to me by an American correspondent. 'I went lately with the same inspector who accompanied Dickens to see the room of the opium-smokers, old Eliza and her Lascar or Bengalee friend. There a fancy seized me to buy the bedstead which figures so accurately in *Edwin Drood*, in narrative and picture. I gave the old woman a pound for it, and have it now packed and ready for shipment to New York. Another American bought a pipe. So you see we have heartily forgiven the novelist his pleasantries at our expense. Many military men who came to England from America refuse to register their titles, especially if they be Colonels; all the result of the basting we got on that score in *Martin Chuzzlewit*.'

* 156 (p. 378). Mr Grant Wilson has sent me an extract from a letter by Fitz-Greene Halleck (author of one of the most delightful poems ever written about Burns) which exactly expresses Dickens as he was, not only in 1842, but, as far as the sense of authorship went, all his life. It was addressed to Mrs Rush of Philadelphia, and is dated 8th March 1842. 'You ask me about Mr Boz. I am quite delighted with him. He is a thorough good fellow, with nothing of the author about him but the reputation, and goes through his task as Lion with exemplary grace, patience and good nature. He has the brilliant face of a man of genius. . . . His writings you know. I wish you had listened to his eloquence at the dinner here. It was the only real specimen of eloquence I have ever witnessed. Its charm was not in its words, but in the manner of saying them.'

* 157 (p. 379). In a volume called *Home and Abroad*, by David Macrae, is printed a correspondence with Dickens on matters alluded to in the text, held in 1861, which will be found to confirm all that is here said.

* 158 (p. 381). I may quote here from a letter (Newcastle-on-Tyne, 5th September 1858) sent me by the editor of the *Northern Express*. 'The view you take of the literary character in the abstract, or of what it might and ought to be, expresses what I have striven for all through my literary life— never to allow it to be patronized, or tolerated, or treated like a good or a bad child. I am always animated by the hope of leaving it a little better understood by the thoughtless than I found it.' To James B. Manson, Esq.

* 158A (p. 383). By way of instance I subjoin an amusing insertion made by him in an otherwise indifferently written paper descriptive of the typical Englishman on the foreign stage, which gives in more comic detail experiences of his own already partly submitted to the reader. 'In a pretty piece at the Gymnase in Paris, where the prime minister of England unfortunately ruined himself by speculating in railway shares, a thorough-going English servant appeared under that thorough-going English name Tom Bob—the honest fellow having been christened Tom, and born the lawful son of Mr. and Mrs Bob. In an Italian adaptation of Dumas' pre-posterous play of KEAN, which we once saw at the great theatre of Genoa, the curtain rose upon that celebrated tragedian, drunk and fast asleep in a chair, attired in a dark blue blouse fastened round the waist with a broad belt and a most prodigious buckle, and wearing a dark red hat of the sugar-loaf shape, nearly three feet high. He bore in his hand a champagne-bottle, with the label RHUM, in large capital letters, carefully turned towards the audience; and two or three dozen of the same popular liquor, which we are nationally accustomed to drink neat as imported, by the half gallon, ornamented the floor of the apartment. Every frequenter of the Coal Hole tavern in the Strand, on that occasion, wore a sword and a beard. Every English lady, presented on the stage in Italy, wears a green veil; and almost every such specimen of our fair countrywomen carries a bright red reticule, made in the form of a monstrous heart. We do not remember to have ever seen an Englishman on the Italian stage, or in the Italian circus, without a stomach like Daniel Lambert, an immense shirt-frill, and a bunch of watch-seals each several times larger than his watch, though the watch itself was an impossible engine. And we have rarely beheld this mimic Englishman, without seeing present, then and there, a score of real Englishmen sufficiently characteristic and unlike the rest of the audience, to whom he bore no shadow of resemblance.' These views as to English people and society, of which Count d'Orsay used always to say that an average Frenchman knew about as much as he knew of the inhabitants of the moon, may receive amusing addition from one of Dickens's letters during his last visit to France; which enclosed a cleverly written Paris journal containing essays on English manners. In one of these the writer remarked that he had heard of the venality of English politicians, but could not have supposed it to be so shameless as it is, for, when he went to the House of Commons, he heard them call out ' Places! Places!' ' Give us Places!' when the Minister entered!

* 159 (p. 385). The letter is addressed to Miss Harriet Parr, whose book called *Gilbert Massenger* is the tale referred to.

* 160 (p. 385). See the introductory memoir from his pen now prefixed to every edition of the popular and delightful *Legends and Lyrics*.

* 161 (p. 388). On this remonstrance and Dickens's reply *The Times* had a leading article of which the closing sentences find fitting place in his biography. ' If there be anything in Lord Russell's theory that Life Peerages are wanted specially to represent those forms of national eminence which cannot otherwise find fitting representation, it might be urged, for the reasons we have before mentioned, that a Life Peerage is due to the most truly national representative of one important department of modern English literature. Something may no doubt be said in favour of this view, but we are inclined to doubt if Mr Dickens himself would gain anything by a Life Peerage. Mr Dickens is pre-eminently a writer of the people and for the people. To our thinking, he is far better suited for the part of the "Great Commoner" of English fiction than for even a Life Peerage. To turn Charles Dickens into Lord Dickens would be much the same mistake in literature that it was in politics to turn William Pitt into Lord Chatham.'

* 162 (p. 391). The book was entered in the catalogue as inscribed 'W. M. Thackeray, from Charles Dickens (whom he made very happy once a long way from home).' Some pleasant verses by his friend had affected him much while abroad. I quote the *Life of Dickens* published by Mr Hotten. 'Her Majesty expressed the strongest desire to possess this presentation copy.

AUTHOR'S FOOTNOTES 451

The original published price was 5s. It became Her Majesty's property for £25 10s., and was at once taken to the palace.' (Mr Bumpus the bookseller corrects Mr Hotten's statement. 'Commissioned by a private gentleman,' he brought the book for the sum named, and it is now in America.)

* 163 (p. 395). An entry, under the date of July 1833, from a printed but unpublished Diary by Mr Payne Collier, appeared lately in the *Athenaeum*, having reference to Dickens at the time when he first obtained employment as a reporter, and connecting itself with what my opening volume had related of those childish sufferings. 'Soon afterwards I observed a great difference in C. D.'s dress, for he had bought a new hat and a very handsome blue cloak, which he threw over his shoulder *à l'Espagnole*. . . . We walked together through Hungerford Market, where we followed a coal-heaver, who carried his little rosy but grimy child looking over his shoulder; and C. D. bought a half-penny-worth of cherries, and as we went along he gave them one by one to the little fellow without the knowledge of the father. . . . He informed me as he walked through it that he knew *Hunger*ford Market well. . . . He did not affect to conceal the difficulties he and his family had had to contend against.'

* 164 (p. 409). I desire to guard myself against any possible supposition that I think these Readings might have been stopped by the exercise of medical authority. I am convinced of the contrary. Dickens had pledged himself to them; and the fact that others' interests were engaged rather than his own supplied him with an overpowering motive for being determinedly set on going through with them. At the sorrowful time in the preceding year, when, yielding to the stern sentence passed by Sir Thomas Watson, he had dismissed finally the staff employed on his country readings, he had thus written to me. 'I do believe' (3rd May 1869) 'that such people as the Chappells are very rarely to be found in human affairs. To say nothing of their noble and munificent manner of sweeping away into space all the charges incurred uselessly, and all the immense inconvenience and profitless work thrown upon their establishment, comes a note this morning from the senior partner, to the effect that they feel that my overwork had been "indirectly caused by them, and by my great and kind exertions to make their venture successful to the extreme". There is something so delicate and fine in this, that I feel it deeply.' That feeling led to his resolve to make the additional exertion of these twelve last readings, and nothing would have turned him from it as long as he could stand at the desk.

* 165 (p. 412). I preserve also the closing words of the letter. 'It is very strange—you remember I suppose?—that the last time we spoke of him [Maclise] together, you said that we should one day hear that the wayward life into which he had fallen was over, and there an end of our knowledge of it.' The waywardness, which was merely the having latterly withdrawn himself too much from old friendly intercourse, had its real origin in disappointments connected with the public work in which he was engaged in those later years, and to which he sacrificed every private interest of his own. His was only the common fate of Englishmen, so engaged, who do this; and when the real story of the 'Fresco-painting for the Houses of Parliament' comes to be written, it will be another chapter added to our national misadventures and reproaches in everything connected with art and its hapless cultivators.

* 166 (p. 417). It is a duty to quote these eloquent words [from *The Times*]. 'Statesmen, men of science, philanthropists, the acknowledged benefactors of their race, might pass away, and yet not leave the void which will be caused by the death of Dickens. They may have earned the esteem of mankind; their days may have been passed in power, honour and prosperity;

they may have been surrounded by troops of friends; but, however preeminent in station, ability or public services, they will not have been, like our great and genial novelist, the intimate of every household. Indeed, such a position is attained not even by one man in an age. It needs an extraordinary combination of intellectual and moral qualities . . . before the world will thus consent to enthrone a man as their unassailable and enduring favourite. This is the position which Mr Dickens has occupied with the English and also with the American public for the third of a century. . . . Westminster Abbey is the peculiar resting-place of English literary genius; and among those whose sacred dust lies there, or whose names are recorded on the walls, very few are more worthy than Charles Dickens of such a home. Fewer still, we believe, will be regarded with more honour as time passes and his greatness grows upon us.'

EDITOR'S NOTES

(Quotations from Dickens's letters are, unless otherwise stated, from the three-volume edition edited by
Walter Dexter, 1938, and are given, as are all quotations from other Dickens copyright material, by kind
permission of Mr Henry Charles Dickens, the author's
grandson.)

VOLUME II

† 13 (p. 65). W. H. Wills had been Dickens's secretary and administrative assistant during his editorship of the *Daily News* and continued in that capacity when Forster took over the paper. (It is on
record that Dickens accepted a contribution from Wills for *Bentley's
Magazine* as far back as 1837.) J. W. T. Ley notes that, after Dickens
left the *Daily News*, Wills 'continued to act as the novelist's
almoner'; certainly from the foundation of *Household Words*, with
Wills as assistant editor, he took an increasing part in Dickens's
editorial and business affairs, especially when *Household Words* was
superseded by *All the Year Round* (1859), from which time he also
became concerned with some of Dickens's private affairs. (See also
Notes † 19 and 20).

† 14 (p. 74). Dickens lived at No. 1 Devonshire Terrace from 1839 to
1851, and wrote there some of his greatest works, including *The Old
Curiosity Shop*, *Barnaby Rudge*, *Martin Chuzzlewit*, *A Christmas
Carol*, *Dombey and Son* and *David Copperfield*. A few yards away
stood, and still stands, Marylebone Church, in which Paul Dombey
was christened and Mr Dombey married Edith Grainger. Forster
refers (i. 107) to the 'handsome house with a garden of considerable
size, shut out from the New Road [Marylebone Road], by a high
brick-wall facing the York gate into Regent's Park'; Maclise's well-
known sketch of the house is reproduced, ii. 97. A modern block of
offices now occupies the whole site; on the side wall of this building is
a plaque giving the dates of Dickens's residence, and on the front
entrance porch is engraved: 'While living in a house on this site
CHARLES DICKENS wrote six of his principal works, characters from
which appear in this sculptured panel.' The large bas-relief panel
incorporates also Dickens's head.

† 15 (p. 88). Mary Boyle, here mentioned as 'Miss B.' on the occasion
when Dickens first met her in amateur theatricals at the Watsons of
Rockingham Castle, became a great admirer and friend of Dickens.
She was a welcome guest at Tavistock House and Gadshill Place, and
she arranged for buttonhole flowers to be sent to him for his public
readings everywhere: 'Flowers have fallen in my path wherever I
have trod, and when they rained upon me in Cork I was more amazed

453

than you ever saw me' he wrote to her on 10th September 1858, and from Boston, U.S.A., on 4th December 1867, he wrote her: 'You can have no idea of the glow of pleasure and amazement with which I saw your remembrance of me lying on my dressing-table here last night . . . Ten thousand loving thanks.' Her friendship with Dickens is recorded in *Mary Boyle, her Book*, 1902. She was one of the few at Gadshill Place when Dickens died: 'Mary Boyle also came', writes Una Pope-Hennessy, 'and sat outside in a hired fly till Charley came into the porch and led her to the syringa-scented study in which lay the body of her adored friend.'

† 16 (p. 95). Tavistock House, facing Tavistock Square, was the residence of Dickens from 1851 to 1860, the period during which *Bleak House, Hard Times, Little Dorrit* and *A Tale of Two Cities* were written, and *All the Year Round* was begun. A more spacious house than No. 1 Devonshire Terrace (with a room large enough for children's theatricals), Dickens on entering it, writes Una Pope-Hennessy, 'saw to all the furnishing himself, ordering curtains and carpets, arranging for glass mirrors and console tables on the landing and planning bookcases between study and dining room, complete with dummy book-backs bearing titles that it had amused him to invent'. The house was demolished many years ago, and on the site there now stands the headquarters building of the British Medical Association.

† 17 (p. 174). Ary Scheffer's portrait of Dickens is in the National Portrait Gallery, London.

† 18 (p. 187). Forster makes only brief reference to Hans Andersen's long visit to Gadshill Place, and there is evidence that 'the Dane' outstayed his welcome. In a letter to Miss Coutts on 10th July 1857 Dickens mentioned that they were 'suffering a good deal from Andersen', and according to Miss Storey's *Dickens and Daughter*, when he had gone Dickens put up a card 'Hans Christian Andersen slept in this room for five weeks—which seemed to the family ages!'

† 19 (p. 206). At this point where Forster's narrative makes brief and, at the time it was written, necessarily discreet references to the separation of Dickens and his wife, a long note seems to be called for. It will endeavour to outline the evidence provided by latter-day researches into the matter and into the identity, and subsequent association with Dickens, of the unnamed 'young lady' referred to in the 'violated letter'—now generally agreed to be Ellen Lawless Ternan, to whom Dickens left £1,000 in his will, which Forster printed as an appendix to the *Life*.

First, here are abridged versions of Dickens's two public statements at the time of the separation, with notes of the time and circumstance of publication. The statement in *Household Words* appeared on 12th June 1858, and, after three introductory paragraphs, ran as follows:

For the first time in my life, and I believe for the last, I now deviate from the principle I have so long observed, by presenting myself in my

own journal in my own private character, and entreating all my brethren
. . . to lend their aid to the dissemination of my present words.

Some domestic trouble of mine, of long-standing, on which I will make
no further remark than that it claims to be respected, as being of a
sacredly private nature, has lately been brought to an arrangement which
involves no anger or ill-will of any kind, and the whole origin, progress,
and surrounding circumstances of which have been throughout, within
the knowledge of my children. It is amicably composed, and its details
have now but to be forgotten by those concerned in it.

By some means . . . this trouble has been made the occasion of mis-
representations, most grossly false, most monstrous and most cruel—
involving, not only me, but innocent persons dear to my heart, and
innocent persons of whom I have no knowledge, if, indeed, thay have any
existence—and so widely spread that I doubt if one reader in a thousand
will peruse these lines, by whom some touch of the breath of these
slanders will not have passed, like an unwholesome air.

Those who know me and my nature, need no assurance under any hand
that such calumnies are as irreconcilable with me as they are, in their
frantic incoherence, with one another . . .

I most solemnly declare, then—and this I do, both in my own name
and in my wife's—that all the lately whispered rumours touching the
trouble at which I have glanced are abominably false. And that whosoever repeats one of them, after this denial, will lie as wilfully and as foully
as it is possible for any false witness to lie, before heaven and earth.

                                                    Charles Dickens.

It is known that the 'distinguished man', mentioned by Forster, as
favouring publication of the above statement was J. T. Delane,
editor of *The Times*. Mr and Mrs Dickens had separated early in May,
and on 4th June 1858 Charles wrote to his wife: 'Dear Catherine—I
will not write a word as to any *causes* that have made it necessary for
me to publish the enclosed in *Household Words*. Whoever there may
be among the living, whom I will never forgive alive or dead, I
earnestly hope that all unkindness is over between you and me. But
as you are referred to in the article, I think you ought to see it. You
have only to say to Wills (who kindly brings it to you) that you do
not object to the allusion. Charles Dickens.' This letter is followed in
Mr and Mrs Charles Dickens, His Letters to Her (1935) by a copy,
endorsed by Kate Perugini, Dickens's younger daughter, as in Mrs
Dickens's handwriting, of a letter dated 5th September 1858, which
Dickens wrote to his solicitor, Frederick Ouvry; this letter expresses
his pain at finding his letter to Arthur Smith had been published in
newspapers, and indicates that he wishes Mrs Dickens to know 'that
I am no consenting party to this publication'. There was certainly
some misunderstanding between Dickens and Arthur Smith (manager
of the public readings) about the purposes of the letter, since he wrote
in a covering note to Smith: 'You have not only my full permission to
show this, but I beg you to show it to anyone who wishes to do me
right. . . .' This 'violated letter' (as Dickens called it) is dated 29th
May, one week before his letter to his wife about the *Household
Words* statement; it appeared in the *New York Tribune* on 16th
August, and was copied in some English newspapers. It ran:

Mrs Dickens and I lived unhappily together for many years. Hardly
anyone who has known us intimately can fail to have known that we are
in all respects of character and temperament wonderfully unsuited to

each other. I suppose that no two people, not vicious in themselves, ever were joined together who had a greater difficulty in understanding one another, or who had less in common. . . .

Nothing has, on many occasions, stood between us and a separation but Mrs Dickens's sister, Georgina Hogarth. From the age of fifteen she has devoted herself to our house and our children. She has been their playmate, nurse, instructress, friend, protectress, adviser and companion. . . . Mrs Dickens has often expressed to her her sense of her affectionate care and devotion in the house—never more strongly than within the last twelve months.

For some years past, Mrs Dickens has been in the habit of representing to me that it would be better for her to go away and live apart; that her always increasing estrangement made a mental disorder under which she sometimes labours—more, that she felt herself unfit for the life she had to lead as my wife, and that she would be better far away. I have uniformly replied that we must bear our misfortune, and fight the fight out to the end; that the children were the first consideration, and that I feared they must bind us together 'in appearance'.

At length, within these three weeks, it was suggested to me by Forster that, even for their sakes, it would surely be better to reconstruct and rearrange their unhappy home. I empowered him to treat with Mrs Dickens, as the friend of both of us for one-and-twenty years. Mrs Dickens wished to add, on her part, Mark Lemon, and did so. On Saturday last, Lemon wrote to Forster that Mrs Dickens 'gratefully and thankfully accepted' the terms I proposed to her. Of the pecuniary part of them, I will only say that I believe they are as generous as if Mrs Dickens were a lady of distinction and I a man of fortune. The remaining parts of them are easily described—my eldest boy to live with Mrs Dickens and take care of her; my eldest girl to keep my house; both my girls, and all my children but the eldest son, to live with me, in the continued companionship of their aunt Georgina. . . .

Two wicked persons, who should have spoken very differently of me in consideration of earned respect and gratitude, have (as I am told, and indeed to my personal knowledge) coupled with this separation the name of a young lady for whom I have great attachment and regard. I will not repeat her name—I honour it too much. Upon my soul and honour, there is not on this earth a more virtuous and spotless creature than that young lady. I know her to be innocent and pure, and as good as my own dear daughters. Further, I am quite sure that Mrs Dickens having received this assurance from me, must now believe it, in the respect I know her to have for me, and in the perfect confidence I know her in her better moments to repose in my truthfulness.

On this head, again, there is not a shadow of doubt or concealment between my children and me. All is open and plain among us, as though we were brothers and sisters. They are perfectly certain that I would not deceive them, and the confidence among us is without a fear.

                                        c.d. 29th May 1858.

[Then follows this postscript, signed by Mrs Hogarth and her youngest daughter, Helen.]

It having been stated to us that, in reference to the differences which have resulted in the separation of Mr and Mrs Charles Dickens, certain statements have been circulated that such differences are occasioned by circumstances deeply affecting the moral character of Mr Dickens and compromising the reputation and good name of others, we solemnly declare that we now disbelieve such statements. We know that they are not believed by Mrs Dickens, and we pledge ourselves, on all occasions, to contradict them, as entirely destitute of foundation.

It seems, then, that the family sources of the rumours were Dickens's mother-in-law and youngest sister-in-law; they incurred his anger to the last degree of unforgivability. Among the contemporary references to the rumours are those by Thackeray, printed in his collected *Letters* (edited by Gordon M. Ray, 1945). In a letter of May 1858 to a friend and neighbour, James Wilson, Thackeray wrote: 'You may remember some conversations which occurred at table where we met on Tuesday. I have a note from Mr Dickens on the subject of a common report derogatory to the honour of a young lady whose name has been mentioned in connection with his. He authorizes me to contradict the rumour on his solemn word and his wife's authority'; while to his mother, Mrs Carmichael-Smyth, Thackeray wrote: 'Here is sad news in the literary world—no less than a separation between Mr and Mrs Dickens—with all sorts of horrible stories buzzing about. The worst is that I'm in a manner dragged in for one. Last week going into the Garrick I heard that D. is separated from his wife on account of an intrigue with his sister-in-law. No says I no such thing—it's with an actress—and the other story has not got to Dickens's ears but this has—and he fancies that I am going about abusing him! We shall never be allowed to be friends that's clear. I had mine from a man at Epsom the first I ever heard of the matter, and should have said nothing about it but that I heard the other much worse story whereupon I told mine to counteract it. There is some row about an actress in the case, and he denies with the utmost infuriation any charge against her or himself. . . .' Another reference also in print is particularly interesting (although a little later in date and not a first-hand story) because it mentions the young lady's name. Under 10th March 1860 the diary of the American diplomat and journalist John Bigelow (*Retrospections of an Active Life*, published 1909) tells of a dinner party at Thackeray's, when Mrs Dickens was among the company, also Mrs Caulfield, 'whom I was permitted to take down to dinner'; it goes on: 'Mrs Caulfield told me that a Miss Teman [*sic*]—I think that is the name—was the source of the difficulty between Mrs Dickens and her husband. She played in private theatricals with Dickens, and he sent her a portrait in a brooch, which met with an accident requiring it to be sent to the jeweller's to be mended. The jeweller, noticing Mr Dickens's initials, sent it to his house. Mrs Dickens's sister, who had always been in love with him, and was jealous of Miss Teman, told Mrs Dickens of the brooch, and she mounted her husband with comb and brush. This, no doubt, was Mrs Dickens's version in the main.'

The public appearance together, in his theatrical productions, of Dickens and Ellen Ternan was at the Manchester Free Hall on 21st and 22nd August 1857, the chief play being Wilkie Collins's *The Frozen Deep*; they had met earlier in rehearsals at Tavistock House, where the play had first been staged some months before (as Forster, ii. 188–9, states, for the Douglas Jerrold Memorial fund), with Dickens's two daughters and Georgina Hogarth in the cast. When the Manchester productions were proposed Dickens wrote to Collins on 2nd August: 'It is an *immense* place and we shall be obliged to have actresses . . . (I am already trying to get the best who *have been* on the stage)'; on professional recommendation an established actress, Mrs

Ternan, and her daughters, Maria and Ellen, were engaged to take the places of the 'Tavistock girls'. The heroine of *The Frozen Deep*, a melodrama of Arctic exploration with Dickens and Collins in the chief male parts, was played by Maria Ternan, Ellen having a minor part; but in the farce *Uncle John*, which followed the drama, Ellen was cast as a young girl educated by an old gentleman, 'Uncle John' (played by Dickens), who falls in love with her. According to Una Pope Hennesy's biography: 'After a few rehearsals Dickens's emotional equilibrium was upset. In the play Uncle John had to load his bride with "wonderful presents—a pearl necklace and diamond ear-rings", and his impersonator found it irresistible to give his sweet little friend some real jewellery. Kate Dickens, who knew the plot and the words only too well, realized what must be going on when a bracelet ordered for Ellen was delivered to her by mistake.'

Dickens's state of mind between the time of meeting Ellen Ternan and separating from his wife may be indicated by these words in his letter to Wilkie Collins of 21st March 1858: 'I have never known a moment's peace or content, since the last night of *The Frozen Deep*. I do suppose that there never was a man so seized and rendered by one spirit.' Nearer to the time of that 'last night' is the letter to Mr De la Rue of 23rd October 1857, in which he is critical of his wife (see note † 11). On 11th October he wrote to Anne Cornelius, his trusted servant: 'I want some little changes made in the arrangement of my dressing room and the bathroom. And as I would rather not have them talked about by comparative strangers, I shall be much obliged, my old friend, if you will see them completed before you leave Tavistock House . . . I want the recess of the doorway between the Dressing Room and Mrs Dickens's room, fitted with plain white deal shelves and closed in with a plain light deal door.' He asked for a bedstead in his dressing room. Dickens is shown by Forster in letters (ii. 197–200) to have been generally restless and dissatisfied as well as unhappy about his wife; all this at a time of ceaseless activities in writing, in readings, in theatricals and speeches for charities, and in buying and altering Gadshill Place. It is pertinent also to quote here from Forster's closing pages (ii. 394) where, recalling Dickens's early 'home pursuits and enjoyments', he writes: 'This "better part" of him had now long survived that sorrowful period of 1857–8, when, for reasons which I have not thought myself free to suppress, a vaguely disturbed feeling took possession of him, and occurences led to his adoption of other pursuits than those to which till then he had given himself exclusively.'

Mr and Mrs Charles Dickens, His Letters to Her included in its appendices: the two published statements by Dickens about the separation; five short letters to Forster from Mark Lemon, who acted for Mrs Dickens in the matter (one of these letters shows that Dickens objected to F. M. Evans, his publisher, being a trustee); and a letter of 13th July 1858, from Charles Dickens, junior, to his mother, in which he quotes his father's statement to him about altering a clause in the Deed of Separation so that she should have full access to the children, '. . . but he places these restrictions on their visits . . . [portion erased, but reference no doubt to Mrs Hogarth and her youngest daughter] I positively forbid the children ever to utter one word if they are ever brought into the presence of either of the two, I charge them immediately to leave your mother's house and come back to me,"—and further in reference to Mr . . . [name erased, but probably Evans—*later editors say the name here is Mark Lemon*] "I positively forbid the children ever to see him or to speak to him, and for the same reason I absolutely prohibit them ever to be taken to Mr Evans' house."' (See note † 22 *re* Evans, and his firm Bradbury and Evans, and the unhappy outcome of their relations with Dickens.) *Mr and Mrs Charles Dickens, His Letters to Her* was edited by Walter Dexter, who states that when the letters came into the hands of Dickens's second daughter, Kate, in 1896, she deposited them with the British Museum authorities; printed as a Foreword in the book, is a note by Kate Perugini (who died in 1929 at the age of eighty-nine) which states: 'Shortly before my mother's death in 1879, she placed in my hands the letters written to her by my father . . . They would show the world, she said, that my father had once loved her; and would make it apparent that the separation which took place between them in 1858 was not owing to any fault on her side . . . I take the present opportunity of entirely exonerating my aunt [Georgina Hogarth] from any blame in the matter. . . . The cause of the parting of my father and mother is not unknown to me; but . . . I consider it to be a subject with which the public has no concern.'

This book of Dickens's letters to his wife was published in 1935, the year which saw the publication of Thomas Wright's 'revelations' about Ellen Ternan in his *Life of Charles Dickens*, a story first adumbrated by Wright in the *Daily Express* of 3rd April 1934. The story was amplified in his posthumously published autobiography, *Thomas Wright of Olney*, 1936. The next affront to the views of orthodox Dickensians came with the publication in 1939 of *Dickens and Daughter*, in which the author, Gladys Storey, set out Kate Perugini's account, as told by Kate in her old age to Miss Storey, of the break-up of Dickens's marriage and the Ellen Ternan affair. Miss Storey states that Kate informed her that she had written a life of her father but 'I told only half the truth about my father,' she said, 'and a half-truth is worse than a lie, for this reason I destroyed what I had written. But the truth *must be told* when the time comes—after my death.' The following is an often-quoted passage from this book: 'More tragic and far reaching in its effect was the association of Charles Dickens and Ellen Ternan and their resultant son (who died in infancy) than that of Nelson and Lady Hamilton and their daughter. "My father was like a madman when my mother left home," said Mrs Perugini. "He did not care a damn what happened to any of us."' It must here be stressed that no evidence whatever has been found in support of this or any other statement alleging that there was a child of the Dickens-Ellen Ternan alliance, in spite of the most thorough searches along every line of inquiry whether obvious or speculative. Indeed it is now felt by many that the friendship may have been platonic only, and certainly was so for some time after Dickens separated from his wife.

If Gladys Storey's *Dickens and Daughter* gives a second-hand account, printed ten years after Kate's death, Thomas Wright's is third-hand: 'Most of the facts relative to Miss E. L. Ternan', says Wright, 'were supplied by my friend Canon Benham who received them from Miss Ternan herself.' Canon Benham was Vicar of Margate, where Ellen's husband, the Rev. George Wharton Robinson, whom she married in 1876, was headmaster-proprietor of a school. Ellen died in 1914, and Canon Benham was also dead before Wright's story was printed. Wright's thesis is that from some time after the separation Ellen was Dickens's mistress, occupying establishments he set up for her, and Wright records from Canon Benham that Ellen was remorseful about her earlier life with Dickens. Wright's chief item about joint establishments of Dickens and Ellen is contained not in his *Life of Dickens* but in the last chapter of his *Thomas Wright of Olney*, and came, not from Canon Benham, but from a correspondent named Mrs M. R. Mackie, whose mother had had in her employ a woman '"who in her younger days had worked for Mr Charles Dickens when he lived sub-rosa at Linden Grove, Nunhead, S.E. As a child more than fifty years ago I was familiar with the house . . . [the house was No. 31, formerly No. 16 Linden Grove, called in Dickens's time Windsor Lodge] . . . our informant, Mrs Maria Goldring, always spoke most highly of her employer. . . . The name by which he was known was Tringham—or something very like it."' Inspection by Wright of the rate books of Nunhead, kept at Peckham Town Hall, showed that from January 1868 to July 1870 No. 16 Linden Grove was in the name of a Mr Tringham. Wright adds: 'The date of the disappearance of Mr Tringham's name from the rate book coincides practically with the date of Dickens's death.' Miss Storey in *Dickens and Daughter* stated that, after the separation, 'a settlement was made on Ellen Ternan, who subsequently lived in an establishment of her own at Peckham'. Una Pope-Hennessy wrote in her biography of 1945: 'I have relied not on Wright but on the information supplied by Dickens's own daughter, Mrs Perugini.'

In 1952 came Ada Nisbet's small but exhaustive monograph, *Charles Dickens and Ellen Ternan*, and at about the same time Edgar Johnson's full-scale, closely documented biography, *Charles Dickens, his Tragedy and Triumph*, the preface to which states: 'I have accepted as largely true the information about his relation with Ellen Lawless Ternan given in Thomas Wright's *Life of Charles Dickens* and Gladys Storey's *Dickens and Daughter*. I have done so because, unsatisfactory though some of their revelations may be as legal evidence, every additional fact bearing on the point that I have uncovered totally supports them.' Miss Nisbet also accepted in general the accounts of Wright and Storey; but Mr Johnson's biography and Miss Nisbet's monograph contained some impressive evidence from unpublished Dickens's letters and memoranda, and from other sources. I here gratefully acknowledge that much of the data in this note derives from one or both of these works.

The first direct evidence is in a letter dated 25th October 1858 (five months after the separation) from Dickens to W. H. Wills, his sub-editor and general factotum. This letter, now in the Huntington Collection of manuscripts, San Marino, U.S.A., was first published by Professor Franklin P. Rolfe in *Nineteenth Century Fiction* (December 1949). Written from Tavistock House, it runs:

'My dear Wills—Since I left you tonight, I have heard of a case of such extraordinary, and (apparently) dangerous and unwarrantable conduct in a Policeman, that I shall take it as a great kindness if you will go to Yardley in Scotland Yard when you know the facts for yourself, and ask him to inquire what it means. I am quite sure that if the circumstances as they stand were stated in *The Times*, there would be a most prodigious public uproar. Before you wait upon Yardley, saying that you know the young ladies and can answer for them and for their being in all things most irreproachable in themselves and most respectably connected in all ways, and that you want to know what the Devil the mystery means—see the young ladies and get the particulars from them.

'No. 31 Berners Street Oxford Street, is the address of the young ladies, and the young ladies are Miss Maria and Miss Ellen Ternan, both of whom you know. You are to understand, between you and me, that I have sent the eldest sister [Frances Eleanor] to Italy, to complete a musical education—that Mrs Ternan is gone with her, to see her comfortably established at Florence; and that our two little friends are left together, in the meanwhile, in the family lodgings. Observe that they don't live about in furnished lodgings, but have their own furniture. They have not been many weeks in their present address, and I strongly advised Mrs Ternan to move from their last one, which I thought unwholesome.

'Can you call and see them between 3 and 5 tomorrow (Tuesday)? They will expect you, unless you write to the contrary. If you can't go, will you write and make another appointment.

'(N.B. Maria is a good deal looked after. And my suspicion is, that the Policeman in question has been suborned to find out all about their domesticity by some "Swell". If so, there can be no doubt that the man ought to be dismissed.)

'They will tell you his No. They don't seem so clear about his letter, but that is no matter. The division on duty in Berners Street, is of course ascertainable by Scotland Yard authorities.

Ever faithfully, C. D.'

Here it should be interpolated that Dickens, who as seen in the letter sent Frances and her mother to Italy, continued to take a helpful interest in Ellen's two sisters. He recommended Maria for stage parts: his letter to theatrical manager, Benjamin Webster (9th September 1861) describes her as 'accomplished and attractive, well used to the stage, sings prettily, and is favourably known to London audiences'. Frances Eleanor gave up the stage early; she met in Italy, possibly on Dickens's introduction, Anthony Trollope's brother, Thomas A. Trollope and, T. A.'s wife having died in 1865, she went out to his villa in Florence as companion to his young daughter in 1866, marrying him later in that year. In July–August 1866, Dickens published Frances's short novel, *Aunt Margaret's Trouble* ('affectionately dedicated to E. L. T.' in book form) in *All the Year Round*, and her second, longer novel appeared later in the magazine. (See also last paragraph in this note.)

Ellen had moved from Berners Street by 1st July 1859, the date on an unpublished letter (also now in the Huntington Collection) by

Dickens to W. H. Wills, which, to quote Ada Nisbet, 'asks Wills to "send round" to the printer for the revises of some of his current manuscript, and then goes on to request that he "post them to Miss Ellen Ternan, 2 Houghton Place, Ampthill Square, N.W."'. This of course is the address given for Ellen Ternan (as 'late of') in Dickens's will. The letter to Benjamin Webster of September 1861, already mentioned, also gives this address for the Ternans.

Except for the very likely possibility that Ellen was with Dickens in the Staplehurst railway accident in June 1865 (see note † 24), we jump to 5th July 1866, on which date Dickens wrote a letter to an old friend of Ellen, Mrs Frances Elliot, who, when Miss Dickenson, had a small part in the 1857 Manchester production of *The Frozen Deep*. This letter is printed in the 1938 edition of the *Letters*; there are rather cryptic references in it to Frances Eleanor and her husband, T. A. Trollope, and there is this significant passage about 'N' (Nelly): 'I feel your affectionate letter truly and deeply, but it would be inexpressibly painful to N to think that you knew her history. She has no suspicion that your assertion of your friend against the opposite powers, ever brought you to the knowledge of it. She would not believe that you could see her with my eyes, or know her with my mind. Such a presentation is impossible. It would distress her for the rest of her life. I thank you none the less, but it is quite out of the question. If she could hear that, she could not have the pride and self-reliance which (mingled with the gentlest nature) has borne her, alone, through so much.'

The next item is among the several pages of memoranda which Dickens left for W. H. Wills when he went to America in 1867; this particular piece of manuscript was first brought to light in 1943 by John D. Gordan, curator of the Berg Collection in the New York Public Library, in an article in *Bookman's Holiday*. Ada Nisbet, in *Dickens and Ellen Ternan* writes: 'One paragraph of these memoranda was heavily inked out on the manuscript, either by Wills himself or perhaps by Georgina when she borrowed the Wills correspondence for use in her edition of the letters. In the R. C. Lehmann edition of the [Dickens-W. H. Wills] correspondence the memoranda are given, but this paragraph is omitted. Dr Gordan, through the aid of infra-red photography, was able to read the obliterated portion, and reported his findings in the article. . . . He did not, however, reproduce the original manuscript in its exact wording, so it is published here for the first time:

'NELLY. If she needs any help will come to you, or if she changes her address, you will immediately let me know if she changes. Until then it will be Villa Trollope, a Ricorboli, Firenze, Italy. (Here it is again more plainly written: VILLA TROLLOPE a RICORBOLI FIRENZE ITALY.)

'On the day after my arrival out I will send you a short Telegram at the office. Please copy its exact words (as they will have a special meaning for her), and post them to her as above by the very next post after receiving my telegram. And also let Gad's Hill know—and let Forster know—what the telegram is.'

A later note in the manuscript memoranda runs: 'Forster has an ample power of attorney from me, in case you should want any legal authority to act in my name. He knows Nelly as you do, and will do anything for her if you want anything done.'

In the published Dickens-Wills correspondence (*Charles Dickens as Editor*, edited by R. C. Lehmann, 1912) is to be found Dickens's promised telegram to Wills upon his arrival in America: 'Safe and well expect good letter full of hope.' But the special meaning of this for Nelly only became clear when, in Dickens's small pocket diary for 1867 (also in the Berg Collection), this 'code' was found:

'Tel: all well means *you come*
Tel: safe and well, means *you don't come*
To Wills. Who send the Te. on to Villa Trollope . . .'

From this it may be inferred that Dickens had thought that he might ask Ellen to come out to him in America after he had arrived there. As it was she remained, at least for a while, in Florence with her sister and brother-in-law. There are letters to Wills from Dickens while on his American tour (originals now in the Huntington Library), in which, writes Ada Nisbet, 'passages referring to Ellen have been obliterated with the same pen that inked out the memorandum. Most of these occur at the beginnings of the letters and indicate that Dickens was enclosing letters to Nelly, to be forwarded by Wills. Again, transcriptions made [by Professor Franklin P. Rolfe] with the aid of infra-red photography are published here for the first time.' Of thirteen passages given, the first runs: '(21st November 1867.) Will you specially observe, my dear fellow, what I am going to add. After this present mail, I shall address Nelly's letters to your care, for I do not quite know where she will be. But she will write to you, and instruct you where to forward them. In any interval between your receipt of one or more, and my Dear Girl's so writing to you, keep them by you.'

Not one of these letters from Dickens to Ellen Ternan, or of any other communication from him to her, or from her to him, has come to light. It can only be assumed that they were destroyed as part of the process of keeping secret, and eliminating any trace of, the association. There is evidence of course of destruction or mutilation of letters of all kinds by Dickens himself or by the family. In a letter to Wills of 4th September 1860, Dickens wrote: 'Yesterday I burnt, in the field at Gad's Hill, the accumulated letters and papers of twenty years. They sent up a smoke like the Genie when he got out of the casket on the sea-shore; and as it was an exquisite day when I began, and rained very heavily when I finished, I suspect my corrrespondence of having overcast the face of the Heavens.' Miss Nisbet states 'Numerous passages in the letters from Dickens to Georgina, now in the Huntington Library, have been cut out with scissors . . . Georgina herself in an unpublished letter to Frederick Ouvry dated May 5, 1879, speaks of having destroyed letters of a kind too personal for publication.'

Reverting to Dickens's pocket diary for 1867, Sir Felix Aylmer in his *Dickens Incognito* (1959) demonstrated for the first time that several short, abbreviated entries in it, like 'to Sl.' and 'At Sl:', with other related entries, pointed to Slough as a place having special significance for Dickens. A search of the local rate-books for Dickens's name was unsuccessful, but Sir Felix found, under January–April 1866, the name of John Tringham, and under May 1866–June 1867, Charles Tringham, the name used by Dickens, according to Wright, when sharing house with Ellen Ternan at Nunhead, Peckham. No precise address at Slough for Tringham was given in the rate-books, but it appeared that his successor was a Mr Butler, and Butler, later, had a shop in the High Street. Slough's local historian then brought to Sir Felix's attention the following item in *Notes on Slough and Upton*: 'In a fire in the High Street in May 1889, Elizabeth Cottage, in which Charles Dickens lodged for a time, and an adjoining building . . . were burnt down.' The author of this pamphlet on Slough, published in 1892, was Richard Bentley, grandson of Dickens's publisher of that name. ('The family lived at Upton Park, Slough. . . . The quarrel which caused the rupture between Dickens and Bentley had long been made up [by 1866–7] . . . in 1857 Bentley joined a party at Gad's Hill.') The *Windsor Express*, 11th May 1889, reported the fire which 'took place at Butler and Bowden's drapery store . . . [including] the remains of Elizabeth Cottage in which Charles Dickens lodged for some time'.

In the pocket diary, up to 24th June, the initial N (Nelly) appears more often than any other, and Sir Felix quotes entries pointing to Peckham, including: 'March 25. At Sl: Office. Houses. March 27. Meet for houses at 12½. To Peckm . . . June 22. At P. Long wait for N at house. June 26. at P. (tem:). Finish Silverman, in Linden.' Linden Grove is of course part of the Peckham address given by Wright.

The above bald summary of the first part of Sir Felix Aylmer's book shows that it contains, through the Slough evidence, some corroboration of Wright's story of the Nunhead, Peckham establishment. In an allusion to *Dickens Incognito* in his later book, *The Drood Case*, Sir Felix says that 'the argument which occupied the second part of that book was discredited by the discovery that I had allowed myself, through inadequate care in checking my material, to be led into a gross misstatement of fact. My error, however, did not affect the earlier part of the book, which was concerned with identifying Elizabeth Cottage, Slough, as a house occupied by Dickens from January 1866 to June 1867, when he paid the rates in the name of Tringham. Nothing has been forthcoming to throw doubt on this conclusion.'

For news of Ellen and Dickens at later dates there is only Miss Storey's book, *Dickens and Daughter*. The following belongs apparently to the middle of June 1869: '. . . he returned to Gad's Hill, going backwards and forwards to the office of *All the Year Round*. Ellen Ternan came to stay, followed by Katie, who, when she heard of the visit of Nelly (as her father called Miss Ternan—pronounced Ter*nan*) and that she had taken a hand at cricket, observed: "I am afraid she did not play the game!"' Then, a year later, on the day after the death of Dickens: 'That morning, Mrs Perugini (whose last letter to her father was the only one found in the pocket of the coat which had been cut from off him) went up to London to break the news to her mother. In the afternoon, Miss Ellen Ternan came to Gad's Hill. The following day Millais arrived and made a tender pencil sketch of Dickens, which he gave to Mrs Perugini. . . .'

A brief postscript to the story of Ellen Ternan is to be found in the January 1965 number of *The Dickensian*, wherein the editor, Mr Leslie C. Staples, prints six letters from her, signed 'Nelly Ternan' (one letter is reproduced in facsimile), to George Smith of the publishing firm of Smith Elder and Company, with two replies by him to Miss Ternan. The letters, now in Mr Staples's collection, are dated between November and December 1872, and concern the offer of a poem to be published anonymously (a poem later revealed by Ellen to Mr Smith as by Alfred Austin). In the letters Ellen sends to Mr Smith the kind regards of Mrs Trollope (her sister, Frances Eleanor); it may be noted that in his *Autobiography* (published 1911) Alfred Austin writes: 'With the close of May 1866 we left Perugia for Florence to be Mr [Tom] Trollope's guests for the whole summer ... our days passed very happily. The household had been most agreeably added to by the advent of Miss Frances Ternan ... who came to be companion to Trollope's only child . . . [and] became later the second wife of our host.' Mr Staples writes of Ellen's letters: 'There is nothing sensational about them. They do nothing to support the theories of either the detractors or defenders of the reputations of Ellen Ternan and her celebrated friend. But . . . they do present a picture, however slight, of Ellen's personality.'

† 20 (p. 209). The lady from whom Dickens bought Gadshill Place was Mrs Lynn Linton, a contributor to *Household Words* and *All the Year Round*. The property had belonged to her father, and soon after his death she met W. H. Wills at a dinner party and told him it would shortly be offered for sale.

J. W. T. Ley in his edition of Forster's *Life* (1928), said in a note on Gadshill: 'Today it is utilized as a school for girls. Its associations with Dickens are still well respected, and his library is preserved as he left it.' This is still the case in 1965—Mr Leslie Staples writes to me: 'The girls' school still flourishes there. A large school building has been erected alongside it at the rear but the house is left intact. The library especially, with Dickens's book-shelves, dummy book-backs, etc., is exactly as he left it.'

† 21 (p. 225). W. P. Frith's portrait of Dickens, painted for Forster, is in the Forster Collection in the Victoria and Albert Museum, South Kensington.

† 22 (p. 226). The 'painful personal disputes' which led to the cessation of *Household Words* concerned of course the separation of Mr and Mrs Dickens and the publication of Dickens's 'Personal Statement'. Bradbury and Evans, the publishers of *Household Words*, gave their version of the dispute in a statement which was published, in June 1859, in the front of Part 20 of Thackeray's *The Virginians*. (The closure of Thackeray's battle with Dickens over Edmund Yates was less than six months old: see note † 23.) Bradbury and Evans's statement put the facts, forcibly, from their point of view, as will be seen from this slightly abridged version:

Their connection with *Household Words* ceased against their will, under circumstances of which the following are material:

So far back as 1836, Bradbury and Evans had business relations with Mr Dickens, and, in 1844, an agreement was entered into, by which they acquired an interest in all the works he might write, or in any periodical he might originate, during a term of seven years. Under this agreement Bradbury and Evans became possessed of a joint, though unequal, interest with Mr Dickens in *Household Words* commenced in 1850. Friendly relations had simultaneously sprung up between them, and they were on terms of close intimacy in 1858, when circumstances led to Mr Dickens's publication of a statement on the subject of his conjugal differences, in various newspapers, including *Household Words* of 12th June.

The public disclosure of these differences took most persons by surprise, and was notoriously the subject of comments, by no means complimentary to Mr Dickens himself, as regarded the taste of this proceeding. On 17th June, however, Bradbury and Evans learned, from a common friend, that Mr Dickens had resolved to break off his connection with them, because this statement was not printed in the number of *Punch* published the day preceding—in other words, because it did not occur to Bradbury and Evans to exceed their legitimate functions as proprietors and publishers, and to require the insertion of statements on a domestic and painful subject, in the inappropriate columns of a comic miscellany. No previous request for the insertion of this statement had been made either to Bradbury and Evans, or to the editor of *Punch*. . . .

Mr Dickens, with ample time for reflection, persisted in the attitude he had taken up, and in the following November, summoned a meeting of the proprietors of *Household Words*. He did not himself attend this meeting; but a literary friend of Mr Dickens came to it as his representative, and announced there, officially, that Mr Dickens, in consequence of the non-appearance, in *Punch*, of his statement, considered that Bradbury and Evans had shown such disrespect and want of good faith towards him, as to determine him, in so far as he had the power, to disconnect himself from them in business transactions; and the friend above mentioned, on the part of Mr Dickens, accordingly moved a resolution dissolving the partnership, and discontinuing the work on 28th May. Bradbury and Evans replied that they did not and could not believe that this was the sole cause of Mr Dickens's altered feeling towards them; but they were assured that it was the sole cause. . . .

Thus, on this ground alone, Mr Dickens puts an end to personal and business relations of long standing; and by an unauthorized and premature public announcement of the cessation of *Household Words*, he forced Bradbury and Evans to an unwilling recourse to the Court of Chancery to restrain him from such proceedings, thereby injuring a valuable property in which others beside himself were interested. . . . By publicly announcing (so far as the Court of Chancery permitted) his intention to discontinue the publication of *Household Words*; by advertising a second work of a similar class under his management, by producing it, and by making it as close an imitation as was legally safe of *Household Words*, while that publication was actually still issuing, and still conducted by him; he took a course calculated to reduce the circulation and impair the prospects of a common property. . . .

Household Words having been sold on the 16th inst., under a decree in Chancery, Bradbury and Evans have no further interest in its continuance, and are now free to make this personal statement, and to associate themselves in the establishment of *Once a Week*.

Dickens completely cut off all personal friendship with F. M. Evans and sternly forbad his children to have anything to do with him. However, his eldest son, Charley, living with Mrs Dickens, courted Evans's daughter, Bessie, and married her in November 1861;

Dickens did not go to the wedding, but he relented a year later when a baby daughter was born to Bessie and Charley, and all three were at Gadshill Place for Christmas.

† 23 (p. 247). Forster's note on the quarrel between Dickens and Thackeray (a note not included in the first Everyman edition, but now given—* 134, ii.) supplies a bare reference to a literary quarrel which has become so renowned that a few details should be recorded here. It began with Edmund Yates's 'gossip column' sketch of Thackeray in a weekly paper, *Town Talk*, on 12th June 1858 (the very day that Dickens's marriage separation statement appeared in *Household Words*— to which statement Yates referred, with warm sympathy for Dickens, in the following week's issue of *Town Talk*).

Thackeray's reaction to the undoubtedly offensive sketch was to send Yates a letter (13th June) saying: 'We meet at a Club where, before you were born I believe, I and other gentlemen have been in the habit of talking, without any idea that our conversation would supply paragraphs for professional vendors of "Literary Talk". . . . Allow me to inform you that the talk which you have heard there is not intended for newspaper remark; and to beg, as I have a right to do, that you will refrain from printing comments on my private conversations; that you will forego discussions however blundering, upon my private affairs. . . .' Yates consulted Dickens, who although he disliked and disapproved of the sketch, thought that Thackeray's attitude made apology by Yates impossible; Yates therefore wrote to Thackeray concluding: 'If your letter to me were not both "slanderous and untrue", I should readily have discussed its subject with you, and avowed my earnest and frank desire to set right anything I have left wrong. Your letter being what it is, I have nothing to add to my present reply.'

Thackeray thereupon appealed to the committee of the club (the Garrick) to consider his case against Yates and to decide 'whether the practice of publishing such articles . . . will not be fatal to the comfort of the Club, and is not intolerable in a Society of Gentlemen'. The committee told Yates they would deal with the complaint at a special meeting, and Yates replied to them that his article did not mention the club, referred to no conversations there, and even if incorrect in details and in bad taste, the committee was 'not a committee of taste'. Dickens supported Yates in this, telling the committee it had no right to intervene in a private quarrel, but the committee ordered Yates 'to make ample apology to Mr Thackeray, or to retire from the Club'. At this Dickens resigned from the committee, and Yates refused to retire from the club, asking for the matter to be considered by a general meeting of club members. In a letter to W. H. Russell (7th July 1858) Dickens wrote: 'The Garrick is in convulsions . . . E. Y. can't apologize (Thackeray having written him a letter which renders it impossible) and won't retire. Committee thereupon call a General Meeting, yet pending. Thackeray *thereupon*, by way of showing what an ill thing it is for writers to attack one another in print, denounces E. Y. (in *Virginians*) as young Grub Street. Frightful mess, muddle, complication, and botheration, ensue—which witch's broth is now in full boil.' At the general meeting on 10th July a letter from Yates was read offering to apologize to the club but not to Thackeray, and Dickens spoke for Yates while regretting to oppose Thackeray, but the committee's view was adopted. Yates was given further time to apologize to Thackeray or be expelled. He refused to apologize, and his name was erased from the membership.

On 24th November, Dickens wrote to Thackeray a confidential letter asking: 'Can any conference be held between me, as representing Mr Yates, and an appointed friend of yours, as representing you, with the hope and purpose of some quiet accommodation of this deplorable matter, which will satisfy the feelings of all concerned?'; but Thackeray was not to be mollified, indeed he wrote: 'I grieve to gather from your letter that you were Mr Yates's adviser in the dispute between him and me.' Since Thackeray had submitted the case to the club, he considered it was out of his hands. So, after a few further moves, Yates gave up the struggle and the matter was closed.

From then on Dickens and Thackeray, friends for a quarter of a century, were estranged. They met by chance in Drury Lane theatre stalls in May 1861, and shook hands but did not speak (according to a Thackeray letter); their next and last encounter, when they spoke together briefly in friendly reconciliation, was, again unexpectedly, at the Athenaeum Club a week or so before Thackeray died, which was on Christmas Eve, 1863. This of course is the meeting referred to by Dickens in his obituary tribute to Thackeray in the *Cornhill*, which Forster quotes (ii. 247).

† 24 (p. 293). Dickens's own experience in the disaster to the boat-train at Staplehurst, Kent, on 9th June 1865, is described in his letter (a short passage from which is given here) to Thomas Mitton of 13th June: 'Two ladies were my fellow-passengers, an old one and a young one. This is exactly what passed. You may judge from it the precise length of the suspense: Suddenly we were off the rail, and beating the ground as the car of a half-emptied balloon might. The old lady cried out "My God!" and the young one screamed. I caught hold of them both (the old lady sat opposite and the young one on my left) and said: "We can't help oursleves, but we can be quiet and composed. Pray don't cry out." The old lady immediately answered: "Thank you. Rely upon me. Upon my soul I will be quiet." We were then all tilted down together in a corner of the carriage and stopped. I said to them thereupon: "You may be sure nothing worse can happen. Our danger *must* be over. Will you remain here without stirring, while I get out of the window?" They both answered quite collectedly "Yes" and I got out without the least notion what had happened.'

Edgar Johnson in his biography asserts as a certainty, as indeed did Una Pope-Hennessy in her earlier biography, that Ellen Ternan was the young lady in the compartment, travelling with Dickens, who had been on holiday in France. As well as the Mitton letter, there is in the 1938 edition of the *Letters*, among several others about the accident, an extract from one of 12th June to the Head Station-master, Charing Cross, asking about jewellery [given in square brackets and italics as *a gold watch, chain, charm and other trinkets*] lost by a lady who was in the same carriage with him: 'I promised the lady to make her loss known at headquarters.' Obviously this is the same letter, to the Station-master at Charing Cross, that Edgar Johnson quotes from the original manuscript (dated 12th June), then in possession of Dr A. S. W. Rosenbach of New York: 'A lady who was in the carriage with me in the terrible accident on Friday, lost, in the struggle of being got out of the carriage, a gold watch-chain with a smaller gold watch-chain attached, a bundle of charms, a gold watch-key, and a gold seal engraved "Ellen". I promised to make her loss known at headquarters, in case these trinkets should be found. . . . I would have spoken to you instead of writing, but that I am shaken; not by the beating of the carriage, but by the work afterwards of getting out the dying and the dead.' The 'gold seal engraved "Ellen"' appears to be convincing evidence. This is probably one of the puzzles on which the last word may be said in the definitive twelve-volume edition of Dickens's letters now in course of publication.

In *Mr and Mrs Charles Dickens, His Letters to Her*, there are only three letters written years after the separation; one of them, dated 11th June 1865, refers to the railway accident: 'I thank you for your letter,' he wrote. 'I was in the carriage that did not go over the bridge, but which caught on one side and hung suspended over the ruined parapet. I am shaken but not by that shock. Two or three hours' work afterwards among the dead and dying surrounded by terrific sights, render my hand unsteady.'

† 25 (p. 319). The story of the American reading tour is told in *Charles Dickens as I knew him* by George Dolby, the business manager of the readings there.

† 26 (p. 329). The Boston publisher, James T. Fields, and his wife, gave Dickens much personal care and help on the American tour. *See* Fields's *Yesterdays with Authors*, 1900, and *In and Out of Doors with Charles Dickens*, 1876.

† 27 (p. 366). In the Everyman edition of Forster's *Dickens*, G. K. Chesterton devoted part of his introduction to Forster's statements about the intended plot of *The Mystery of Edwin Drood*. J. W. T. Ley in his 1928 edition of Forster mustered to that date twenty titles as 'the principal contributions' to the much-debated subject, starting with *The Mystery of Mr E. Drood*, by Orpheus C. Kerr, 1870, and including *The Puzzle of Dickens's Last Plot*, by Andrew Lang, 1905; *The Problem of Edwin Drood*, by W. Robertson Nicoll, 1912; *The Complete Mystery of Edwin Drood*, by J. Cuming Walters, 1912; and *A New Solution of the Murder of Edwin Drood*, by Mary Kavanagh, 1923. Subsequent publications include *The Drood Murder Case*, by Richard M. Baker, 1951 and *The Mystery of Edwin Drood, Afterword*, by James Wright, 1961. The latest addition to the ever-growing number of writings about Dickens's unfinished novel is Sir Felix Aylmer's very comprehensive and intriguing work *The Drood Case*, 1964.

It has often been pointed out that the name of Helena Landless, if not the character herself, bears resemblance to Ellen Lawless Ternan.

† 28 (p. 377). When Forster died in 1876, his collection of paintings, drawings, manuscripts, and over eighteen thousand printed books, came by bequest to the South Kensington Museum, now the Victoria and Albert Museum. The three printed catalogues (*see* i. x) of the collection are out of print, but Mr John P. Harthan, keeper of the Library, Victoria and Albert Museum, has kindly sent me a photographic copy of the pages from the 1893 catalogue containing the entries of the Dickens MSS., which show under 'manuscripts of works (in whole or in part)' *Oliver Twist, The Old Curiosity Shop, Barnaby Rudge, Martin Chuzzlewit, Dombey and Son, David Copperfield, Bleak House, Hard Times, Little Dorrit, A Tale of Two Cities* and *The Mystery of Edwin Drood*, among others. Under *Letters* the first entry reads '137 to Mr Forster, 1836–1864, and some not dated'.

Shortly after these notes were completed, the first volume was published (February 1965) of the projected twelve-volume Pilgrim edition of Dickens's *Letters*, edited by Madeline House and Graham Storey with associate editors and an editorial committee of other Dickens authorities. A part of the editors' preface deals with Forster's *Life* and Dickens's letters to him used in it; this is the most convenient place in which to include a few extracts from the highly relevant part of the preface:

'. . . Out of nearly a thousand letters to himself', the editors write, 'from which Forster quoted, only fifty-five have survived (*footnote*: These are in the Victoria and Albert Museum, where there are also 126 letters to Forster from which he did not quote . . .)—all but two of them early letters, used in his Volume I (covering 1812–42). Many of Dickens's most important letters are among the hundreds of which the only available text is that given in the *Life*, and the question of Forster's editorial integrity must therefore be discussed here at some length.

'When Forster started work on the *Life* he was already a sick man, and his health became worse during the writing of the second volume (covering 1842–52). It was perhaps then, because he found the labour of transcription too heavy, that he decided to cut up the letters and paste them in his manuscript (*footnote*: As Mrs Forster told Percy Fitzgerald he did—*John Forster* by One of his Friends [Percy Fitzgerald], 1903). Altogether, of the letters which survive in the Forster Collection, only six (the two mentioned above and four others) were written in the years covered by Forster's second and third volumes. . . . The other letters must have gone the way of Forster's manuscript.'

The editors then give details of a dozen or more examples of 'the kinds of liberty Forster took', which they have found by collating the originals of the fifty-five surviving letters with the quotations from them in the *Life*; it is right to say here that sometimes their statements of correction are qualified. The following paragraphs contain fair samples of the discrepancies the editors have discovered:

'With the aim of proving his importance in the life of Dickens, he made alterations which emphasized Dickens's reliance on him. Into the letter of 11 Dec. 37 he introduced "the deed", clearly to prepare the way for the statement that it was thanks to him that Dickens obtained a share in the copyright of *Pickwick* [*see* i. 81–2]; in the

letter of 17 Jan 41 he italicized the words "on your valued suggestion" to stress his responsibility for Little Nell's death in *The Old
Curiosity Shop*, adding that the underlining was Dickens's, though it
was not [*see* i. 123]. But on each occasion, though the text was
falsified, the general picture was probably not.

'Forster also misdated a number of letters—sometimes no doubt
through failure of memory, at other times deliberately for the sake of
his story. He gave, for example, the letter of 2 July 37 as written in
late May and as referring not to his own notice of *Pickwick* in that
day's *Examiner* but to "something . . . [Forster] had remarked
publicly" about *Oliver Twist*. The reason for this change was
apparently that he wished to make Dickens say that Forster's
"sense of poor Oliver's reality" had been to him "the highest of all
praise" [*see* i. 70]. But though these words do not occur in the letter
of 2 July, it is possible that they were not invented by Forster, but
were brought in from another letter as yet untraced and probably
destroyed.'

The editors proceed later to point out that 'the longer letters which
Forster pasted into his manuscript—that is to say, a large number of
letters in his second and third volumes—are to be presumed more
authentic than the shorter extracts which he copied out by hand, no
doubt often "improving" them as he did so'. Two specific emenda-
tions among those referring to later parts of the *Life* are:

'. . . Into later chapters he introduced, once more as if quoting
from letters to himself, early ideas for *Our Mutual Friend* and *Edwin
Drood* which Dickens had noted down in his "Book of Memoranda"
[ii. 298–311].

'Even when writing his second volume, for which he had no lack
of letters addressed to himself, Forster yielded to the temptation to
print as to himself a letter to someone else. Dickens's exuberant and
immensely long letter to Maclise from Albaro, 22 July 44, which
Maclise presumably passed on to Forster who kept it, was printed in
the *Life* as Dickens's "second letter from Albaro" (to Forster understood) containing "an outbreak of whimsical enthusiasm . . ., meant
especially for Maclise" [*see* i. 316–17]. Here, as when drawing on the
"Book of Memoranda" Forster disingenuously chose his words so
that nothing he said was actually untrue.'

No praise can be too high for the work of the editors of the Pilgrim
edition of the *Letters*, as seen in the first volume. Here in this note
only that part of the work related to Forster's *Life* can be considered;
but it must be said that there can be no work of its kind (when completed it is expected to hold nearly 12,000 letters to about 1,800
correspondents) more minutely comprehensive not only in the letters
themselves but also in the elucidation and annotation of them. The
examples I have quoted do not exhaust the criticisms of Forster's
presentation of some of the letters, but they certainly enable us to
judge how important and authentic as a whole this biography is; the
opening words of the Forster section of the Pilgrim editors' preface
run: 'John Forster, although he wrote his three-volume *Life of
Dickens* within a few years of Dickens's death, had his subject
remarkably in perspective. He was, moreover, concerned not simply
with the public image, as Georgina and Mamie were [in their editions

of the letters], but with the truth, as he conceived it. The *Life* contains numerous small distortions of fact, but paradoxically these distortions were in the interest of a larger, or ideal, truth.'

† 29 (p. 382). The Guild of Literature and Art, which owed its inception to Dickens, was wound up in 1897, and, under power of an Act of Parliament, its assets were transferred to the Royal Literary Fund and the Artists' Benevolent Fund.

† 30 (p. 408). The success at Cambridge of Dickens's sixth son, Henry Fielding Dickens, was precursory to a distinguished career in law. He became a well-known Q.C. and was knighted. He died in 1933.

† 31 (p. 420). Mrs Charles Dickens died on 22nd November 1879, aged sixty-four. Her sister, Georgina Hogarth, increasingly important member of Dickens's household from 1843 until his death, and joint trustee with Forster of his estate, died on 19th April 1917, aged ninety; she edited and published three selections of Dickens's Letters, in 1882, 1893 and 1908, the first two selections in collaboration with Dickens's daughter, Mary, who died in 1896.

A few words should be added here about Mrs Charles Dickens and the separation. Mr Henry C. Dickens, the novelist's grandson, has read the proofs of these notes, and it is a pleasure to record here his rebuttal of Somerset Maugham's 'vicious slander on my grandmother's name', which was made in the chapter on Dickens in Maugham's *Ten Great Novelists*, published in 1954 and serialized in the *Sunday Times*. Maugham suggested that 'Kate allowed herself to be driven from her own house' because she 'drank', and he enlarged on this, after only an 'if' or a 'maybe', with phrases like 'driven to the bottle' and 'confirmed alcoholic'. All this, Mr H. C. Dickens rightly says, 'was a complete fabrication'. There is no evidence for it and no one even suggested it before.

INDEX

(The Works of Dickens, including miscellaneous writings referred to in the *Life*, are indexed together at the end of the DICKENS, CHARLES, entry. Subjects in the notes, * n. or † n., are indexed under the page number on which the note containing the reference appears. Authors and titles of modern books on Dickens referred to in the editor's notes are not indexed, but a list of such books is given on pages xv and xvi, vol. i.)